SELECTED

Jack Kerouac

LETTERS

1957–1969

BY JACK KEROUAC

THE LEGEND OF DULUOZ:

Visions of Gerard
Doctor Sax
Maggie Cassidy
Vanity of Duluoz
On the Road
Visions of Cody
The Subterraneans
Tristessa
Lonesome Traveller
Desolation Angels
The Dharma Bums
Book of Dreams
Big Sur
Satori in Paris

POETRY:

Mexico City Blues
Scattered Poems
Pomes All Sizes
Heaven and Other Poems
Book of Blues

OTHER WORK:

The Town and the City
The Scripture of the Golden Eternity
Some of the Dharma
Old Angel Midnight
Good Blonde and Others
Pull My Daisy
Trip Trap
Pic
The Portable Jack Kerouac
Selected Letters: 1940–1956
Atop an Underwood: Early Stories and Other Writings

SELECTED

Jack Kerouac

LETTERS

1957-1969

EDITED WITH AN INTRODUCTION
AND COMMENTARY BY

Ann Charters

VIKING

VIKING

Published by the Penguin Group
Penguin Putnam Inc., 375 Hudson Street,
New York, New York 10014, U.S.A.
Penguin Books Ltd, 27 Wrights Lane, London W8 5TZ, England
Penguin Books Australia Ltd, Ringwood, Victoria, Australia
Penguin Books Canada Ltd, 10 Alcorn Avenue,
Toronto, Ontario, Canada M4V 3B2
Penguin Books (N.Z.) Ltd, 182–190 Wairau Road,
Auckland 10, New Zealand

Penguin Books Ltd, Registered Offices:
Harmondsworth, Middlesex, England

First published in 1999 by Viking Penguin,
a member of Penguin Putnam Inc.

1 3 5 7 9 10 8 6 4 2

LIBRARY OF CONGRESS CATALOGING-IN-PUBLICATION DATA
Kerouac, Jack, 1922–1969.
[Correspondence. Selections]
Selected letters, 1957–1969 / Jack Kerouac : edited with an introduction and
commentary by Ann Charters.
p. cm.
Includes index.
ISBN 0-670-86190-1
1. Kerouac, Jack, 1922–1969–Correspondence. 2. Authors, American–20th century–
Correspondence. 3. Beat generation. I. Charters, Ann. II. Title.
PS3521.E735 Z48 1999
813'.54–dc21
[B]   99-17374

This book is printed on acid-free paper. ∞

Printed in the United States of America
Set in Bodoni Old Face
Designed by Kathryn Parise

THIS BOOK IS DEDICATED TO THE
MEMORY OF STELLA SAMPAS KEROUAC

"Stella,
Star, great sister of my friend, hello.
Jack"

—Jack Kerouac to Stella Sampas,
April 16, 1958

ACKNOWLEDGMENTS

The first person whose help I gratefully acknowledge in the preparation of this volume is Jack Kerouac himself. When he invited me to Hyannis to work together on his bibliography in the summer of 1966, he assured me, "I've kept the neatest records you ever saw." He was right. In his study was a meticulously preserved literary archive, as carefully organized as the archives I used a few years later while researching his biography in the Rare Book and Manuscript Room of the Butler Library at Columbia University, the Bancroft Library at the University of California, Berkeley, and the Humanities Research Center at the University of Texas at Austin. During our two days together in Hyannis, Kerouac showed me everything I asked to see. I listed his publications, and he answered my questions about the circumstances under which he had written his books.

In Hyannis we never had any reason to look at the folders of letters that Kerouac had filed carefully away in his room, but if he had showed me his correspondence, I would have seen his letters and those from his friends systematically gathered and put away in manila folders. At some later point, Kerouac went through the carbons he had kept of his own typed letters to his friends, as well as the original letters he had written and never sent, and annotated a good number of them, supplying dates or comments. His work organizing his letters made mine much easier when I was asked to edit this volume.

Also of key importance in the preparation of this volume is John Sampas, Kerouac's youngest brother-in-law and executor of the Kerouac literary estate. Sampas initiated the project and was extremely helpful. He allowed me access to Kerouac's letters in the archive. He also supplied information about the family background of his sister Stella Kerouac, Jack's widow, and of his brother Sebastian Sampas, Kerouac's boyhood friend in Lowell, Massachusetts. Jim Sampas was also helpful.

Sterling Lord, Kerouac's literary agent, was kind enough to let me include Kerouac's letters to him in this volume. They add an important new dimension to our knowledge of the development of Kerouac's literary career. Another significant source of new information was Kerouac's file at

Viking Penguin, which my editor David Stanford made accessible to me. Adam Gussow, who has researched and written about the relationship between Kerouac and his editors Malcolm Cowley and Keith Jennison at the Viking Press, also filled in more of the story with Xeroxes of Cowley's correspondence with Kerouac and Allen Ginsberg.

I offer special thanks to the writers who were close friends of Kerouac and gave me permission to include their letters in this volume to help give a sense of the reciprocity of their correspondence with Kerouac: Gary Snyder, Carolyn Cassady, and Philip Whalen. Lawrence Ferlinghetti generously gave me permission to include his letter to *Time* magazine defending Kerouac's *Big Sur*.

I thank the professional staff at several research libraries who helped me gather Kerouac letters: Kenneth A. Lohf at Columbia University (Kerouac's letters to Allen Ginsberg, W. S. Burroughs, Neal Cassady, James Laughlin, Lucien Carr, and Peter Orlovsky), John Skarstad at UC Davis (Kerouac's letters to Gary Snyder), Marilyn Kierstead at Reed College (Kerouac's letters to Philip Whalen), Cathy Henderson at the Humanities Research Center of the University of Texas (Kerouac's letters to Carolyn and Neal Cassady), and Francis O. Mattson, Curator of the Berg Collection at the New York Public Library (Kerouac's letters to his sister, Caroline Kerouac Blake, and Robert Giroux). Martha Mayo at the University of Massachusetts Lowell, Center for Lowell History, kindly took the time to answer my queries about material residing there.

Many other people have also been helpful, especially the Kerouac scholar Dave Moore, who supplied information, corrected errors in my commentaries and footnotes, and checked many of my transcriptions of the letters. Michael Schumacher generously shared his Xeroxes of the entire Kerouac/Ginsberg correspondence after he finished using the letters in his biography of Ginsberg. Allen Ginsberg let me read the unpublished manuscript of his annotated correspondence with Kerouac, which he compiled with the help of his student Jason Shinder at the Naropa Institute in Boulder, Colorado. I am particularly grateful to Professors Ellie DalMolin and Marie Naudin, at the University of Connecticut, who looked over my transcriptions of Kerouac's Québécois.

Kerouac's first wife, Edith Parker, her friend Jim Perrizo, and many of the people with whom Kerouac later corresponded have also been extremely generous, including John Clellon Holmes, Robert Giroux, Elbert Lenrow, Gary Snyder, Philip Whalen, Lawrence Ferlinghetti, and Carolyn Cassady, who made available to me their letters from Kerouac. Donald Allen, Rod Anstee, Andreas Brown, Neelie Cherkovski, Maureen Croteau, Faith Evans, Russell Freedman, Mark Gisbourne, James Grauerholz, James Laughlin, Charlotte Mann, Barry Miles, Malcolm Reid, Kevin Ring, Mel Smith, and Jeff Steblea also shared material and helped with the project in various ways. For volume two I am grateful to Helen Weaver, Joyce Johnson, Robert Creeley, Lois Sorrells, Stan Isaacs, Roberto Muggiati, Granville H. Jones, Bill Michell, Carroll Brown, Calvin Hall, Bernice Lemire, Jacqueline Stephens, Stanley Twardowicz, Andreas Brown, David Amram, Dan De Sole, and Albert J. Gelpi for sharing their letters from Kerouac.

Finally, I wish to acknowledge the advice of my husband, Samuel Charters, who read my early transcriptions of these Kerouac letters and told me that from a reader's point of view, they would be more accessible if they were linked by brief commentary. Later in London my editor Tony Lacey of Penguin Books Ltd. also encouraged me to add commentary. Throughout the duration of the project my editors, David Stanford and Paul Slovak, and my copy editor, Toni Dorfman, at Viking Penguin have extended steady and helpful hands. Kerouac was such a voluminous correspondent that the total number of his letters is unknown. I have included about half of the letters from 1957 through 1969 that were made available to me. Kerouac's spelling in the letters has occasionally been corrected, as indicated in the Notes at the end of this volume. Some deletions in the letters have been made to protect the privacy of living people.

Storrs, Connecticut

CONTENTS

1958

1960

1965

1966

1969

INTRODUCTION

This second and final volume of the selected letters of Jack Kerouac begins in January 1957, the year of the publication of *On the Road*, his best-selling autobiographical novel. It was destined to become an American classic in its depiction of what the novelist Robert Stone called the search for "American authenticity [which] was forever somewhere else." The letters end in October 1969, one day before Kerouac's death. As in the first volume, I have been guided in my choice of letters and commentary by my desire to create a life in letters in which Kerouac has the opportunity to tell the story of his life as eloquently as he did in what he called his "true-story novels." His letters fill in the gaps in the chronology he dramatized in his novels, most notably the three hectic years after the publication of *On the Road* and the last difficult years in Massachusetts and Florida after his mother's stroke.

What I have emphasized in my selection of letters in both volumes is Kerouac's development as a writer. The first volume documented his discovery of his literary style of spontaneous prose and his creation of eleven books written in a fever of inspiration between 1951 and 1956. The second volume demonstrates that the publication of his books and the attendant publicity and hostile critical response to his work literally destroyed him. His editor Malcolm Cowley at the Viking Press did not understand the larger design of what he tried to do as an experimental writer and failed to support him. Reviewers attacked him personally as if he were as great a threat to American society as the menace of a Communist victory during the Cold War. Saddest of all, with his alcoholism out of control, Kerouac was his own worst enemy. Characterizing himself to his friend Gary Snyder as "the great quitter," he died of severe abdominal hemorrhaging at the age of forty-seven.

For Kerouac, writing letters was a crucial middle stage in the development of his literary materials as he practiced his craft of spontaneous prose. He usually composed his letters describing the events that he dramatized in his books after he jotted down his initial notations about his raw experience in his pocket notebooks and before he sat down to write his novels.

The critic William J. Savage, Jr., at Northwestern University has suggested that "for Kerouac, the performance of writing spontaneously mattered most. His notebooks, journals, outlines, and other preparatory material should be understood as a form of rehearsal—like a jazz musician practicing improvisation—building up to the performance of composition, preparing mentally for the textual re-creation of the subject matter being written about."

My husband, Samuel Charters, adds that Kerouac's letters can also be understood in the light of Savage's theory as the first drafts of several of Kerouac's novels and other published work. Writing as a jazz musician, Kerouac composed the entries in his notebooks and journals as his private practice exercises or warm-ups, the initial stage in the process of writing spontaneous prose to re-create the events of his life, the writing "in" of his experience when he was improvising for himself. His letters are the next stage of the improvisational process, the writing "out" for a reader in a public "dress rehearsal" to prepare himself mentally for the final stage, the "textual re-creation" in spontaneous prose of his experiences in a novel. As Kerouac concluded in "Essentials of Spontaneous Prose," "*Come* from within, out—to relaxed and said."

The reader can follow Kerouac's preliminary prose drafts of Part Two of *Desolation Angels*, for example, in his 1957 letters about his travels in Tangier, France, and England to Gary Snyder, Neal Cassady, Ed White, and Allen Ginsberg in this volume. Also included is Kerouac's rehearsal for the writing of *Big Sur* in the descriptions of his experiences at Bixby Canyon in 1960 when he composed a series of letters to Ginsberg, Cassady, Lawrence Ferlinghetti, Philip Whalen, and Lew Welch. In June 1965, Kerouac's letter to his agent, Sterling Lord, about his adventures in Paris helped prepare him for his performance a month later writing *Satori in Paris* in seven consecutive nights.

In my selection of Kerouac's letters for both volumes I have chosen to emphasize his correspondence with his closest friends and professional associates, especially Ginsberg, Whalen, Snyder, Ferlinghetti, Lord, John Clellon Holmes, and Joyce Glassman, because Kerouac wrote most fully and directly about his experiences to them. As in Volume One, I have included a few letters from Kerouac's friends that contribute to themes I saw in the larger narrative of his life. By including Snyder's letter to Kerouac on October 12, 1958, after Snyder had read the portrait of himself as Japhy Ryder in *The Dharma Bums*, I suggested how one of Kerouac's friends felt about being portrayed as a fictional character in his novels. Whalen's letter to Kerouac in February 1961 showed how a loyal friend tried to practice Kerouac's writing method of spontaneous prose with surprising results. Carolyn Cassady's letter to Kerouac on October 22, 1961 described her life with Neal after his release from prison, and expressed her concern for Kerouac as a long-standing friend. Ferlinghetti's letter to *Time* magazine on September 15, 1962 revealed his anger at the media's harsh treatment of Kerouac's books and their vicious attack on his lifestyle.

Kerouac occasionally answered queries about his work from fans and academics, and I have included several of his illuminating responses in this volume. The letters written by Kerouac's mother, Gabrielle, and his third wife, Stella, give a sense of their importance in his life and his dependence upon them.

In my commentary and footnotes to the letters I have quoted at length from book reviews in magazines and newspapers if Kerouac referred to them in his correspondence. These reviews suggest the different cultural climate in the United States nearly a half century ago, when Kerouac started publishing. They also help us understand the contribution Kerouac's books made to facilitate the thaw that we take for granted today.

The novelist Thomas Pynchon described the constraints on writers like Kerouac in his introduction to *Slow Learner*. The late 1950s was "the era of *Howl, Lolita, Tropic of Cancer,* and all the excesses of law enforcement that such works provoked.... In its literary version it shaped up as traditional vs. Beat fiction." Pyncheon felt that the effect of Kerouac's books on the young writers in his generation was "exciting, liberating, strongly positive," but Pynchon wrote this tribute in 1984, too late for Kerouac to read.

Kerouac wanted his letters published. In 1959 he proposed to Lawrence Ferlinghetti at City Lights Press a book of his letters from Neal Cassady, but this project never was completed. Nor were the books of correspondence Kerouac proposed to John Clellon Holmes in 1962 and 1964, and to Andy Brown, the dealer in literary manuscripts who arranged the sale of Kerouac's letters to the University of Texas, in 1968. I regard these two volumes that I have compiled as only the beginning of our access to Kerouac's complete correspondence, which I am sure future scholars will continue to edit and publish as interest grows in his work.

I have frequently interlaced Kerouac's letters with my own commentary to give the biographical background of what was currently happening in his life if relevant to the letters. I based my selection on my attempt to have Kerouac comment as much as possible on his own writing and on what he considered the most important events in his life. Usually these events were the writing and publication of his books, and his friends' responses to his work, but his letters also document the emotional and financial costs of the frequent moves he made with his mother from one house to another, back and forth across the United States in the last twelve years of his life, in their attempt to find a place they both considered home.

Cyril Connolly, the English critic, is said to have enjoyed his own conundrum, "What is the book that takes a lifetime to write and which the author will never read? His collected letters." Through Kerouac's letters, readers get to know him better and have a greater appreciation for his commitment to writing. Since everything he wrote was based on his direct experience, his letters bring us closer to the life he actually lived before he turned it into literature.

CHRONOLOGY

1922 March 12, Jean Louis Lebris de Kerouac born in Lowell, Massachusetts, third child of Gabrielle and Leo Kerouac, French-Canadian immigrants to New England

1939 Graduates from Lowell High School

1939–40 Attends Horace Mann Preparatory School, New York City

1940–41 Attends Columbia College

1942–43 Serves in U.S. Navy and Merchant Marine

1944 Meets Lucien Carr, William Burroughs, and Allen Ginsberg; marries first wife, Edith Parker

1946–48 Writes *The Town and the City;* meets Neal Cassady in New York City

1948 Meets John Clellon Holmes and invents the term "beat generation"

1948–50 Makes early attempts to write *On the Road;* first cross-country trips with Cassady

1950 Publishes *The Town and the City;* marries second wife, Joan Haverty

1951 February/March—reads manuscripts of Burroughs's *Junkie* and Holmes's *Go;* April—writes roll manuscript of *On the Road* in three weeks in New York City; October—discovers his compositional method of "sketching" or "spontaneous prose" and begins to rewrite *On the Road* as the experimental book *Visions of Cody*

1951–52 Writes *Visions of Cody* in New York City and San Francisco

1952 Writes *Doctor Sax* in Mexico City; works as a student brakeman and writes "The Railroad Earth" in San Francisco; daughter Jan Kerouac born in Albany, New York

1953 Writes *Maggie Cassidy* and *The Subterraneans* in New York City

1954 Begins study of Buddhism in New York and California; writes "San Francisco Blues" in San Francisco, "Some of the Dharma" in New York and North Carolina

1955 Writes *Mexico City Blues,* begins *Tristessa* in Mexico City; attends "Six Poets at the Six Gallery" reading in San Francisco

1956 Finishes *Tristessa* in Mexico City and writes *Visions of Gerard* in North Carolina; writes first part of *Desolation Angels* in Washington State and Mexico City; Ginsberg's *Howl and Other Poems* published by City Lights in San Francisco

1957 *On the Road* published by the Viking Press in New York; writes *The Dharma Bums* in Florida

1958–60	Writes sketches in *Lonesome Traveler*
1959	Narrates film *Pull My Daisy* in New York City
1961	Writes second half of *Desolation Angels* in Mexico City; writes *Big Sur* in Florida
1965	Writes *Satori in Paris* in Florida
1966	Marries Stella Sampas and moves from Hyannis to Lowell, Massachusetts
1967	Writes *Vanity of Duluoz* in Lowell
1968	February 4, Neal Cassady dies in Mexico
1969	October 21, Jack Kerouac dies in Saint Petersburg, Florida

SELECTED

Jack Kerouac

LETTERS

1957–1969

1957

By the first week of January 1957, while living at his sister Caroline's new house in Orlando, Florida, Kerouac had put what he considered the finishing touches on On the Road for his editors Malcolm Cowley and Keith Jennison at the Viking Press. Concerned about the possibility of obscenity and libel suits, they had insisted that Kerouac revise the book before they signed a contract. Working on the porch where his sister had set up his typewriter on his old rolltop desk, Jack also retyped pages of The Subterraneans and completed the typescript of a new novel, Desolation Angels.

In a creative fever Kerouac had completed eleven books of prose and poetry in the last six years, chapters of what he called "the endless Duluoz Legend," the written record of his life. When Howl and Other Poems was published in May 1956, Allen Ginsberg listed the titles in his dedication of the book to Neal Cassady, William S. Burroughs, and Jack Kerouac, "new Buddha of American prose, who spit forth intelligence into eleven books written in half the number of years (1951–1956)—On the Road, Visions of Neal, Dr Sax, Springtime Mary, The Subterraneans, San Francisco Blues, Some of the Dharma, Book of Dreams, Wake Up, Mexico City Blues, and Visions of Gerard—creating a spontaneous bop prosody and original classic literature.... All these books are published in Heaven." Now it was time for Kerouac's manuscripts, written "in desolation & solitude," as he told his friend Helen Weaver, to be published on earth.

During the early days of 1957, Jack wrote two anxious letters to his agent, Sterling Lord, with detailed instructions about handling his manuscripts. Lord had loaned Kerouac forty dollars against his Viking advance to buy Christmas presents for his family. When Jack couldn't get another loan from his agent to pay for a bus ticket to New York City so that he could deliver On the Road to his editors at Viking and sign a contract for the book, his mother, Gabrielle, gave him the fare.

[Card postmarked January 1, 1957
Orlando, Florida]

Dear Sterling—

I understand how you're low—fortunately I'll get fare from G.—the ms. of ROAD is all ready for the printer, please tell Keith and Malcolm to have complete confidence in the libel-clearing thorough job I did on it ... they will be pleased ... I imagine they'll want to see it first, I'll show it them on Jan. 8 ... I am typing up the new novel DESOLATION ANGELS[1] (rich, good) ... Have you located "cityCityCITY"[2] and TRISTESSA mss.? I have to add to them. ... Till I see you, as ever,

Jack

Sat Jan. 5, 1957
[Orlando, Florida]

Dear Sterling,

Would you please take my 7000-word piece JOAN RAWSHANKS IN THE FOG[3] out of the file and mail it to Michael Grieg, PAPERBACK EDITIONS LIMITED, 1133 De Haro Street, San Francisco 10, Calif.

Enclosed are the stamps he sent me.

And make it clear to him that when he's finished with the typescript copy to mail it pronto back to you (altho I have the original in the main MS of VISIONS OF NEAL novel).

Although he doesnt pay anything, it will be good to get a piece of V OF NEAL published and start it a-rolling.

And as I understand it, we can always *sell* JOAN RAWSHANKS afterwards anyway. Tell him not to copyright it under anything but my name, of course.

I will be in to see you Tuesday [January] 8th, late afternoon, to join new addition to TRISTESSA and discuss Viking contract with you, and I'll have prepared MS of ROAD with me in a suitcase, along with other new MSS. SUBTERRANEANS is all ready for Don Allen ... it is 173 pages long, at

---

1. At this point Kerouac had written only Book One of *Desolation Angels*, describing his experiences as a fire watcher on Desolation Peak during the summer of 1956 and ending when he left Los Angeles on a bus bound for Mexico at the end of September. Kerouac completed Book Two of *Desolation Angels* in 1961, when he picked up his narrative where he had left it in September 1956, chronicling his experiences in Mexico and concluding a year later, just before the publication of *On the Road*.
2. A science fiction story written in 1954–1955.
3. An excerpt from *Visions of Neal* later published as a section of *Visions of Cody* (1973).

300 words per page, therefore it is no less than 50,000 words long and so worth $500 at 1c a word, tell Barney Rosset.[4]

Till I see you,
As ever,
Jack

While in Florida, Kerouac dropped postcards to his girlfriend Helen Weaver and the editor Donald Allen at Grove Press. Jack had moved into Helen's apartment in Greenwich Village after Thanksgiving 1956, and stayed with her until returning to his family in Orlando on December 20. In the last days of 1956 he exchanged several cards and letters with Helen, describing his Christmas, when he had "raced on bicycles with young nephew to go buy his present, which was Elvis Presley album, and he takes his banjo and closes his eyes and imitates Elvis to a T. . . . all the little boys love him. . . . so I was right about his singing like little boys."

TO HELEN WEAVER

[Card postmarked January 5, 1957
Orlando, Florida]

Dear Helen. . . . Will be home, call you, probably Wednesday. . . . Received your gone letter and Greg's [Corso's] note. . . . Glad to hear of various good times you had Xmas and NY's eve. . . . Funny about yr. dad digging Screamin Jay [Hawkins].[5] . . . Tho I'm sposed to be a lazy bum I havent done anything for the last 12 days but rattle this typewriter day and night tryna catch up with my wild handscripts writ in desolation & solitude. . . . money in the future bank for logs on the fire and scotch & soda and the late show and you in my fleecy arms. . . . Incidentally we are invited to a weekend in Old Saybrook, Conn. dont forget in a big victorian house oer topped by great old trees and with fireplace and jazz and toddies and wonderful couple Johnny & Shirley Holmes so save a January weekend for that, you and me and Pete [Orlovsky] and Allen [Ginsberg]. . . . I got nice letter from Don Allen, he is swell. . . . also a pretty Xmas card from English publishers, apparently Bob Giroux wrote them I was back. . . . (Eyre [&] Spottiswoode).[6] . . . I hope yr. 33 speed [phonograph] is fixt, I'm bringing back Chet Baker.[7] LOVE N'craint pas . . . Je t'aime. . . . Oui . . . X X X Jean.

---

4. Donald Allen, an editor at Grove Press, had advised Barney Rosset, the publisher, to buy Kerouac's novel *The Subterraneans.*
5. The singer Screamin' Jay Hawkins, best known for his rhythm and blues hit, "I Put a Spell on You."
6. The London publishers Eyre & Spottiswoode issued the first British edition of Kerouac's first novel, *The Town and the City,* in 1951.
7. An LP recording of jazz trumpet player Chet Baker.

TO DONALD ALLEN

[Postmarked January 5, 1957
Orlando, Florida]

Dear Don—

Your letter most charming, unexpected, & welcome.[8] Working like a dog down here trying to get those 2 new mss. typed up and ready. I'll be over to your place (call first) I believe Tuesday Jan. 8 in the afternoon and with me I'll have a suitcase containing six manuscripts some of them huge ... VISIONS OF NEAL (novel), DESOLATION ANGELS (novel), BOOK OF BLUES (poems long and short), BOOK OF DREAMS (long dream diary written in my "spontaneous prose" & quite rich), SOME OF THE DHARMA (a Pascal-Pensees of Buddhism probably more important than Pascal's and almost as well written), and TRISTESSA (novel, fairly short).... You can peruse them at yr. leisure while I'm in NY and after I'm gone, it'll just be a question of getting them delivered somehow back to my agent Sterling Lord ... okay? Visions of Neal and Some of the Dharma are the books I really want you to dig. Also, let's make a date to go out and hear some jazz. Your new friend,

Jack K.

On January 8, 1957, after riding a Greyhound bus from Orlando to New York City, Kerouac went to the Viking offices to turn in the manuscript of On the Road *to Malcolm Cowley. According to Helen Weaver, Jack told her that he bought a pint of bourbon and chugalugged it in the elevator before meeting Cowley, and then after leaving Viking he continued to celebrate with Allen Ginsberg, Peter Orlovsky, and Gregory Corso before coming back to her apartment in the West Village. Two days later Jack told his friend John Clellon Holmes that he would sign the contract with Viking "for sure" the next day.*

TO JOHN CLELLON HOLMES

Jan. 10, 1957
[New York City]

Dear Johnny—

All of us are agreed on the weekend of Jan. 19 for our visit with you & Shirley [Holmes's wife] in Ole Saybrook—Allen [Ginsberg], Peter [Or-

8. Donald Allen first read Kerouac's writing in 1953, when he copyedited "Jazz of the Beat Generation" for Arabelle Porter at *New World Writing*. He began to work as an editor at Grove Press not long after Barney Rosset acquired it for $3,000 in 1952. On July 10, 1956, Donald Allen sent a memo to Rosset praising Kerouac's work, especially *The Subterraneans*, which Allen said was "in a style that attempts to capture the moods, emotions, and stances of the hipster life. In this field he's way beyond people like Chandler Brossard and [John] Clellon Holmes."

lovsky], Helen my love & I—Dig February issue of *Mademoiselle,* our pictures are in it—wherein is called Allen Ginsberg a "bop pioneer"[9]—is date satisfactory? Drop note—

Excuse paper. I am alone in Helen's Hawthornian room, afternoon, it looks out on the White Horse bar & old cobbles & gables—playing St. Matthew Passion on box—I am sad because I flew into a rage over her Olivetti typewriter (they never work)—Signing contract tomorrow for sure with Viking—Sad because we live to be good but the bad works hard & works us down to despair—But I refuse to be bad!—Gregory [Corso] in town, alone, his Surrah's in Paris waiting—

I'm looking forward to sweet Shirley's fabulous cooking—hmm! I hope our visit won't leave you exhausted—Diamond Sutra say: "Keep your mind free and all-penetrating and calm"—

Tonight I drink with Lucien [Carr] alone in a blizzard—

Your friend
Jack

On January 11, 1957, Kerouac finally signed his contract with the Viking Press for On the Road. *He stayed on in New York City, waiting for a ship to Tangier the following month, the first stage of what he planned as a long sojourn in Europe. After a couple of weeks at Helen Weaver's apartment, she asked him to leave because she couldn't take what she later remembered as the "nonstop party" at her place, with Jack drinking "prodigious amounts" and Allen, Peter, and Gregory sleeping on her floor.*

For a few days Kerouac lived in a cheap hotel on Eighth Street in Greenwich Village, where he impulsively phoned his first wife, Edith Parker, in Michigan, after she sent him an affectionate letter. Jack wrote to Edie giving a forwarding address that was the West 113th Street apartment of a new girlfriend in New York, Joyce Glassman, with whom he stayed until he left for Tangier. Glassman, a twenty-one-year-old graduate of Barnard College and aspiring novelist who supported herself working at an office job in a literary agency, later published under her married name, Joyce Johnson. She told the story of her love affair with Kerouac in her memoir Minor Characters.

9. See Kerouac's letter to Sterling Lord on September 17, 1956, about the afternoon in San Francisco when *Mademoiselle* sent the photographer William Eichel to take pictures of the East Coast writers Jack Kerouac, Allen Ginsberg, and Gregory Corso to illustrate an article about what the magazine called San Francisco poetry. At the end of Part One of *Desolation Angels,* Kerouac described the photo session in detail: "We'd had our bloody pictures taken and had got drunk all as who would stay sober to have his picture taken and to be called 'Flaming-Cool Poets.' . . . " The other poets were cropped from the photograph when Eichel's striking image of Kerouac in a checkered shirt was used as the author photo on the back inside flap of the dust wrapper of the first edition of *On the Road.*

Monday Jan. 28 [1957]
[New York City]

Dear Edie,

That was a beautiful letter you wrote me. I read some of it to Lucien later on.

You know, before Joan [Burroughs] died, when I saw her in 1950, she said you were the greatest person (I think she said nicest) she had ever known.

As for Willy B[urroughs], he's queening around now but as ever he never bothers me with that. Instead we take long walks in the evening with hands clasped behind our backs, conversing politely. He is a great gentleman and as you may know, has become a great writer, in fact all the bigwigs are afraid of him (W. H. Auden, etc.) Yes, he knows we're coming in February late.

Allen never loses track of me even when I try to hide.[10] He does me many favors publicizing my name. Well, we're old friends anyway. But I cant keep up the hectic "fame" life he wants and so I wont stay with them long in Tangier. I'm going to get me a quiet hut by the sea on the Spanish coast, then join them in Paris in the Spring.

"Escaping reality to go into simplicity" is just what I do, except I regard reality as being simplicity. That is, God is Alone. Dont worry, I eat plenty. I have my cook kit in my pack and make delicious food wherever I go, when I have to. In NY naturally everybody invites me to big dinners in homes. But like in Spain and Europe, I'll make me pancakes and syrup with black coffee for breakfast, boil me big pots of Boston baked beans with salt pork and molasses, make salads, eat French bread, cheese and dates for dessert. Etc.

I'll write to you and you keep writing and if you suddenly get the impulse to see Europe I'll be there to show you around.

I have never left you either, and had many dreams of you, wild dreams where we're wandering in dark alleys of Mexico looking for a place to bang, etc.

I want to end my life as an old man in a shack in the woods, and I'm leading up to that soon as I dig the whole world including the Orient. I'm

---

10. Ginsberg had left the West Coast and was living with his father in Paterson, New Jersey, after the publication of *Howl and Other Poems*. When he learned that Kerouac needed a place to stay in Manhattan, he arranged for Jack to meet Joyce Glassman. Early in February 1957 Ginsberg wrote his publisher, Lawrence Ferlinghetti at City Lights in San Francisco, that Jack was involved "with Viking and Grove publication revisions and plans." Like Kerouac, Ginsberg was also planning to stay with Burroughs in Tangier, but he told Ferlinghetti that first he was "trying to get howl [sic] reviewed somewhere in NY, unsuccessfully." During this time Ginsberg took Kerouac, Orlovsky, and Corso to visit the poet William Carlos Williams in New Jersey and loaned Jack the money for his passage to Tangier.

invited to a Buddhist Monastery in Japan and will go within 5 years. Also other things. Make movies too, later. I'll have more money than I need. Or maybe only what I need. I'm glad to send my mother her reward, think eventually I'll take her out to California and get her a little rose covered cottage, and get me a shack for half the time, in the wild hills beyond Mount Tamalpais.

Hearing your voice at night over the phone, in a hotel where I'd gone to hide out to work, was like a strange & beautiful dream. You sounded warmer and more mature. You will always be a great woman. I have a lot of things to teach you now, in case we ever meet, concerning the message that was transmitted to me under a pine tree in North Carolina on a cold winter moonlit night. It said that Nothing Ever Happened, so dont worry. It's all like a dream. Everything is ecstasy, inside. We just dont know it because of our thinking-minds. But in our true blissful essence of mind is known that everything is alright forever and forever and forever. Close your eyes, let your hands and nerve-ends drop, stop breathing for 3 seconds, listen to the silence inside the illusion of the world, and you will remember the lesson you forgot, which was taught in immense milky ways of cloudy innumerable worlds long ago and not even at all. It is all one vast awakened thing. I call it the golden eternity. It is perfect. We were never really born, we will never really die. It has nothing to do with the imaginary idea of a personal self, other selves, many selves everywhere, or one universal self: Self is only an idea, a mortal idea. That which passes through everything, is one thing. It's a dream already ended.[11] There's nothing to be afraid of and nothing to be glad about. I know this from staring at mountains months on end. They never show any expression, they are like empty space. Do you think the emptiness of space will ever crumble away? Mountains will crumble, but the emptiness of space, which is the one universal essence of mind, the one vast awakenerhood, empty and awake, will never crumble away because it was never born.

> The world you see is just a movie in your mind.
>   Rocks dont see it.
>   Bless and sit down.
>   Forgive and forget.
>   Practice kindness all day to everybody
>   and you will realize you're already
>   in heaven now.
>   That's the story.
>   That's the message.

11. See Kerouac's *The Scripture of the Golden Eternity,* Section 51: "here I am dreaming that I talk about it [the Golden Eternity] in a dream already ended, ages ago, from which I'm already awake...." Also his unpublished prose piece *A Dream Already Ended* (ca. May 1954): "And now I know that life is a dream already ended. There is nothing to do but be kind. Death is truth. Death is the Golden Age."

Nobody understands it,
nobody listens, they're
all running around like
chickens with heads cut
off. I will try to
teach it but it will
be in vain, s'why I'll
end up in a shack
praying and being
cool and singing
by my woodstove
making pancakes.

Write again.... I'll be at this address
till our ship leaves, c/o J. Glassman
554 W. 113th St.
(right near Johnny &
the West End, Johnny
asked bout you the
other night.)[12]

Your eternal old man,
Jack

Before leaving for Tangier on February 15, Kerouac sent a last-minute letter to Malcolm Cowley, who had shown Jack his notes for an introduction he was planning to write for On the Road. *A month later, after reading the manuscript of* Desolation Angels *that Kerouac had typed up for him, Cowley decided to drop his introduction.*

TO MALCOLM COWLEY

Feb. 4, 1957
c/o J. Glassman
554 W. 113 St.
New York, N.Y.

Dear Malcolm,
Two things we failed to insert in your notes for the introduction.[13]

12. In Book Two of *Desolation Angels,* "Passing Through," Kerouac described drinking in the West End Cafe with Joyce Glassman a few days after writing this letter. "We finally get to Borough Hall and dive into a subway, Van Cortlandt line, takes us all clear to 110th Street and Broadway and we go in the bar where my old favorite bartender Johnny is tending the beer."
13. Dated April 8, 1957, Cowley's Acceptance Report to the Viking Press suggested his ambivalence about *On the Road:* "It isn't a great or even a likable book, but it is real, honest, fascinating, everything for kicks, the voice of a new generation."

(1) That as a "recording angel" however I have to do it in a necessarily birds-eye personal-view form of a legend, which is the DULUOZ LEGEND, to which all the books belong except first novel naturalistic fictional Town & City. "Duluoz" is Kerouac, as you know, but might note.

(2) We forgot to add BOOK OF DREAMS to the complete list of works, which is a 300-page tome of some excellence, spontaneously written dreams some of them written in the peculiar dream-language of half-awake in the morning.

If you have the time, let me know what you think literary-spiritually and then professionally of DESOLATION ANGELS, and if you decide for that or DOCTOR SAX as our next venture.

Hoping you're having a pleasant rest,—

as ever,

Jack

Along with Joyce Glassman, Kerouac's friends Lucien Carr and his wife, Cessa, saw Jack depart New York harbor on the Yugoslavian freighter S.S. Slovenija *to Tangier. They were among the first people to whom he wrote letters after he'd survived the rough crossing on the stormy North Atlantic Ocean. In Book Two of* Desolation Angels, *Kerouac described his excitement aboard ship, catching his first sight of the African coastal city:*

> *Then like seeing sudden slow files of Mohammedan women in white I saw the white roofs of the little port of Tangier sitting right there in the elbow of the land, on the water. This dream of white robed Africa on the blue afternoon Sea, wow, who dreamed it? Rimbaud! Magellan! Delacroix! Napoleon! White sheets waving on the rooftop!*

TO JOYCE GLASSMAN

[n.d. or place]

Dear Joyce—

As I write we're only 8 miles from the African coast & will be in at dusk—It was a good thing you didnt come back on the ship with me because it only went to big gastank barges off Perth Amboy—Also, because I went to Lucien's alone, they were able to squeeze me in at his mother's little dinner, where I ate a pint of vanilla ice cream covered with creme de menthe and been feeling good ever since—Our books turned out fine—Ten days at sea studying history & Kierkegaard have opened new cracks in my mind—I'm saving *Genji* for Spain—Fresh sea air, sleep, walking on deck, sun, & now I'm my old self again (the healthy Jack you never saw)—Rarin' to go to Tangier, the Blue Pearl of the Hesperides—the City of *vice!* whee!

This is also by way of being a greeting to Allen, Peter, Elise[14] and Carol—All during the trip I ate alone at a huge white tablecloth with one mysterious Yugoslavian woman Mata Hari—We had a dangerous storm 500 miles out & almost foundered. . . .[15] In all my years as seaman I never saw a ship bury its nose in mountain waves & plunge up into other valleys like a rowboat. . . . it was awful, we had to flee South & lose a day—During this ordeal I heard the words:

EVERYTHING IS GOD, NOTHING EVER HAPPENED EXCEPT GOD

—and I believed & still do. Kierkegaard & the storm together made me see this luminous peaceful truth—You must read FEAR AND TREMBLING (never mind SICKNESS UNTO DEATH, which is an abstract discussion of despair)—F & T is about Abraham & Isaac & made me cry.

At moments I was sad remembering your tears—We'll meet again.

TANGIER—Wow—Immediately Bill Burroughs took me to the Casbah where the veiled women pass—I was so high I thought I'd seen it all before—He lives on a hill overlooking the bay where even now I can see the *S.S. Slovenija* docked—We smoke marijuana right in the cafes, in public, it's legal—a strange wild Arab town—old as Time—Very excited I am—I'll get me a room of my own & write—bright sunshine this morning, cries of Arab peddlers, & tonight again the mysterious Casbah & that whanging music—Write soon & let me hear the latest. Love,

Jack XXX (X For Ti Gris)[16]

During the first days of March 1957, Kerouac received a letter from his editor Malcolm Cowley dated February 24, 1957, and forwarded to Tangier. Cowley wrote that he was turning down the manuscript of Desolation Angels *that Kerouac had typed in Florida describing the events of his life during the summer and fall of 1956. In Cowley's judgment, it wasn't the "sort of book" that Viking "or, probably, any other publisher could persuade people to read." Cowley felt that Kerouac had failed to create solid characters in his description of his adventures in California and Mexico with his friends: "it seems to me you go sort of soft about Allen and Gregory, all admiration and not much of that accurate vision you showed when writing about Neal-Dean in* On the Road."

The cool tone of Cowley's letter, and his negative response to Kerouac's latest autobiographical fiction, were a harsh rebuff to Jack's dream, as he had told his agent on February 23, 1957, of becoming "more powerful with the publishers." To

14. Elise Cowen was a friend of Joyce Glassman's who was in love with Allen Ginsberg. Cowen and Glassman had met as freshmen at Barnard College in the fall of 1951.
15. At the beginning of Part Three of *Desolation Angels,* Kerouac wrote that on his sea voyage to Europe, experiencing a "huge tempest" on the North Atlantic "put the fear of the world in me like an omen warning."
16. Joyce's cat.

add to his disappointment, he also received photostats of pages of his manuscript of The Subterraneans *after Don Allen had cut it and revised it into shorter sentences for Grove Press's magazine* Evergreen Review. *Kerouac couldn't do much to change Cowley's opinion that "Duluoz seems to be moving through his own reflections almost in a world of ghosts," but he asked Sterling Lord, who had sent the photostats, to intercede for him with Grove Press. Lord acted swiftly so that a different excerpt of Kerouac's work could be included in the issue of* Evergreen Review *devoted to the San Francisco scene planned for later that year.*

TO STERLING LORD

March 4, 1957
Hotel Mouniria [Tangier]

Dear Sterling—

I'd rather die than betray my faith in my work which is inseparable from my life, without this faith any kind of money is mockery—Photostats show common, halting, namby pamby changes that would definitely damage JK as a reputed natural writer—Offer TRISTESSA as is or as I personally shorten it, or 3 or 4 excerpts as is—(such as MANHATTAN SKETCHES plus OCTOBER IN THE RAILROAD EARTH plus JOAN RAWSHANKS IN THE FOG, app. 69 pages right there)—But THE SUBTERRANEANS is impossible in 69 pages—

This horrible castration job by Don Allen (who undoubtedly was ordered by Rosset) is a violation of the sanctity of prose and also the violation of the sanctity of a very careful large poetry & if I may say so myself the best poem in the issue. Make this clear, that my prose is a series of rhythmic expostulations of speech visually separated for the convenience of the reader's eye by dashes, by vigorous definite dashes, which can be seen coming as you read, so that some of my lines which get their temporary relief from commas can run far beyond the limits of one page-width (which is where my poetry becomes free of line-restrictions and is still prose thereby) and can run into three-page sentences if need be but are *definitely released by the dash*—Since all of this is executed in one spontaneous word-flow every bit of it belongs to every bit of it, and if it is drastically fucked-with as Don Allen did it loses its swing——and worse than that it becomes unutterably more *wordy* as though there were too many words after half of them were taken out—He has broken down the organic strength of the manuscript and it is no longer THE SUBTERRANEANS by Jack K, but some feeble something by Don Allen—He apparently thinks that I dont know what I'm doing, like a critic who doesnt believe that writers know how to write, only critics know—My whole believing heart is involved here—I can see it clearly, there will be no American Literary Renaissance unless the sanctity of personal speech is honored, that indefinable personal quavering sound of each and every writer.

11

Don Allen has SOME OF THE DHARMA, BOOK OF BLUES, (poems), TRISTESSA, and VISIONS OF NEAL—please get them back—

p.s. What's the news on Martha Foley money, New Directions money, the whereabouts of "cityCityCITY" & of my new excerpts?[17]—I hope to see you in Paris this summer & go to Olympia Press with you—

Cowley says: "Pretty soon your book will be set up in type and then the salesmen will go out on the road with "On the Road" and I hope they sell a lot of copies"—

The local gossip columnist in Tangier, "Barnaby Bliss," prophesies it will sell 70,000 copies!

Till I hear from you & the angry Groves,

as ever,

Jack

TO MALCOLM COWLEY

March 8, 1957

c/o Hotel Mouniria

Calle Magallenes no. 1

Tangier, Morocco

DEAR MALCOLM—

I was fairly certain you wouldn't cotton to *Desolation Angels* because of its (deliberate) formlessness[18] but I wanted you to see it anyway ... I guess it's a kind of Love's Labors Lost in my shelf, to be followed of course by the Macbeths and Hamlets of good luck and prime ... However I still feel soft about the whole thing ... The trouble is I've just got too much to write about ... John Duluoz wandering among the ghosts was precisely what was intended. Enuf of that. Now I want to say, that after ROAD comes out and we be able to ascertain the situation, I can quite easily write another just like it, that is, on a typewriter in 3 weeks time with cup after cup of black coffee ... The sequel to ROAD in fact, is all there, culminating in that sui-

17. Martha Foley had chosen Kerouac's story "The Mexican Girl" from *On the Road* for inclusion in *The Best American Short Stories* of 1956. It had originally appeared in *The Paris Review* (winter 1955). *New Directions 16 in Prose and Poetry* (July 1957) included another excerpt from *On the Road*, "A Billowy Trip in the World." *New Editions 2*, subtitled "An Anthology of Literary Discoveries" (1957), published "Neal and the Three Stooges" from *Visions of Cody*. Kerouac's sketch "cityCityCITY," retitled "The Electrocution of Block 38383939383 ...," appeared in *Nugget* (August 1959). Cowley had interested the editors of *The Paris Review* and *New Directions* in Kerouac's writing in order to convince Viking that *On the Road* was worth publishing as what Cowley called "the voice of a new age," despite other Viking editors' reservations, such as Helen Taylor's, about what she called Kerouac's depiction of "unrespectable" "hopheads" in the novel.

18. Reading *Desolation Angels* had dampened Cowley's enthusiasm for what he now called "the interminable Duluoz Saga" in his undated report on Kerouac's new manuscript for the Viking Press. Stating that he didn't find Kerouac's "pretty fancy writing" about his experi-

cide (was why I saved the suicide) ...[19] the story of Sal Paradise continuing to hitch hike and while Dean settles down to hectic marriage and picking up the threads of the others like Balloon etc. in the same vein of pure narrative report ... so dont worry, I wou'd do this in fact for the sole reason of justifying Viking's faith in your faith in me ... can do, will do. Because also of course I do need money to live on. The sequel to On the Road would also center on the great railroading days of Dean and Sal, a thing in itself ... The plot's side issues include Balloon's accidental shooting of his wife, Carlo Marx erupting as the poet of SCREAM and the San Francisco school, etc. really a large ribald story and with those marvelous new characters ...[20] In fact I'm all hot to go at it right now. As for Doctor Sax, I'm afraid to spoil it by adding or removing, and that special clear remembrance flower of it was something that happened to my mind in 1952 and cannot return, I mean the special magic recall that happened that month. The sequel (which should be called THE BEAT GENERATION to clinch down that title) would also follow the later development of Remi Boncoeur, Al Buckle, the whole thing (even many minor characters like Ray Rawlins and his sister) (who is now TB).... and it is significant that in the actual action of this Sequel, the Denver lawyer *is* out & gone ... It'll be another big tale, will run from 1951 to 1957 here in Europe ... also to trace the development of jazz since that time.

Here in Tangier I have a room with a patio facing the sea, for 20 dollars a month, and eat every day in a little restaurant in the native quarter for 35 cents. Paul Bowles is not here now but is a very good friend of Burroughs and returning soon. Burroughs did *not* deliberately shoot his wife, and I am one of the few who know it ... He has just written the most fantastic book since Genet's OUR LADY OF THE FLOWERS and it is called WORD

---

ence as a fire watcher on Desolation Peak at all "interesting." Cowley granted that "the story becomes livelier in the San Francisco passages," but he felt that "this ground has been covered in *On the Road*." Cowley also found the references to Buddhism "hard to take" and complained that "there are no plot complications" to interest the reader.

Writing Kerouac on February 24, 1957, to reject *Desolation Angels*, Cowley insisted on the importance of an author's developing his plot and characters in a novel: "The book doesn't have any plot—it's just Duluoz alone on the mountain.... One character, really. A book, a novel doesn't get started until one character gets mixed up with other people, gets into conflicts with them—and it ends when the conflicts are resolved, the situation changed." Disregarding his editor's advice, Kerouac told his agent to send the novel to New Directions. See letter to Sterling Lord, March 25, 1957.

19. Neal Cassady's lover Natalie Jackson fell to her death off a roof in North Beach on November 30, 1955. See Kerouac's letter to Sterling Lord, September 17, 1956, and Chapter 15 of *The Dharma Bums:* "She went up on the roof while [Neal] was asleep and broke the skylight to get jagged bits of glass to cut her wrists ... and when the cops ran out on the roof to help her that was it...."

20. Kerouac is referring to William Burroughs ("Balloon"), Allen Ginsberg ("Carlo Marx"), and "Howl" ("SCREAM").

HOARD . . .[21] definitely a great writer, and it will take time for the world to accept that fact because of the curious martyr streak . . . Together we take long walks over the green hills in back of the Casbah and watch the fantastic sunsets over Moroccan fields, where little burros trot, men in robes, women in veils . . . We even smoke opium and I find it distasteful (I thought I would like it) . . . We chat at international sidewalk cafes with the curious scum of Europe . . . We brew tea and have long talks, go rowing in the bay . . . I go alone on long walks along the sea and watch the ancient Arab fishermen, seven on each of two lines hauling in the nets from the shore with a beautiful slow rhythmic dance they all do . . . In my room at night I read Van Wyck Brooks' Melville & Whitman,[22] the New Testament, Genet, Time and Perspectives Magazine . . . I drink the most delicious wine in the world, Malaga, for 28 cents a litre . . . in my room I brew coffee over an alcohol stove and boil eggs . . . Little short on money for the beautiful veiled Arab whores who come to your room for 3 dollars but O they are passionate & sweet . . . Malcolm, if you write to Keith [Jennison], tell him we'll have that binge when I gets back . . .

As ever,
Jack

TO DONALD ALLEN

[March 19, 1957
Tangier]

Dear Don——(March 19)——Sterling Lord writes me that he sent back the manuscript of Subterraneans to you plus your cut version and that you will try to do it differently and then send the whole thing on to me for approval. I assume it's too late for Evergreen Review no. 2 but if not how can you possibly trim that thing down to 70 pages? The only way I can see to cut it is to remove one large block, the Flipping Confession of Mardou,[23] which was something I later added on *to make it a longer novel* and which is really therefore (by my own laws) superfluous and kinda poor too I think and so does Mardou herself[24] . . . that's about 40 pages right there, for in the original version there was no flipping confession and everyone read it and naturally didn't miss it. So that would reduce Subterraneans to its original artistic length of about 140 of my typed pages.

21. *Word Hoard* was the working title of the book Burroughs revised and published in 1959 with Olympia Press in Paris as *Naked Lunch.*
22. Van Wyck Brooks's *The Times of Melville and Whitman* (1947).
23. The pseudonym of Kerouac's girlfriend, Alene Lee, with whom he had a love affair in 1953 described in *The Subterraneans.*
24. On December 20, 1956, just before leaving New York City to return to his sister's house in Orlando for the Christmas holidays, Kerouac had written Don Allen that "The heroine of

This is all I can see, plus possibly the en toto removal of *other blocks* of narrative … but Don, I cant possibly go on as a responsible prose artist and also as a believer in the impulses of my own heart and in the beauty of pure spontaneous language if I let editors take my sentences, which are my phrases that I separate by dashes when "I draw a breath," each of which pours out to the tune of the whole story its own rhythmic yawp of expostulation, & riddle them with commas, cut them in half, in threes, in fours, ruining the swing, making what was reasonably wordy prose even more wordy and unnaturally awkward (because castrated). In fact the manuscript of Subterraneans, I see by the photostats, is so (already) riddled and buckshot with commas and marks I cant see how you can restore the original out of it. The act of composition is wiser by far than the act of afterarrangement, "changes to help the reader" is a fallacious idea prejudging the lack of instinctual communication between avid scribbling narrator and avid reading reader, it is also a typically American business idea like removing the vitamins out of rice to make it white (popular). American publishing has no criteria for evaluating popular taste other than what it preconceiving feeds the populace. Who's to say what people like? I say they have yet to see the sprung-free language of storytelling and poems that is to come in the American and World Literary Renaissance if the Big Castrating Scissor be only put away. As for me, that scissor doesnt exist. The changes you asked me to make for the sake of the magazine mails, taking out sexy words, spoiled the book enough I thought … & I looked forward to complete book publication. But now the whole thing is no longer the Subterraneans, the swing, the heartbroke sound, the blues style, the rush of lowdown confession that embarrasses no one but me, the crude glad (if-you-wish-Carlylean) personal quavering sound of my own voice which took me so long (15 years of writing) to find and tap and only after removing all that literary and grammatically-inhibited and unenlightened debris. It all ties in, the reader cannot fail to receive telepathic shock and meaning-excitement by same laws of self-utterance of personal secret idea-words operating in his own human mind. So I eschews 'selectivity' and follow free association of mind into limitless blow-on-subject seas of thought, swimming in seas of English with no discipline other than the story-line and the rhythm of rhetorical exhalation and expostulated statement, like a fist coming down ona table with each complete utterance, bang! (the space-

---

Subterraneans has finally signed the [libel] release form, but she did it on condition that I would let her make a few (disguising-type) changes (her mother dead, etc.) and also on condition now that she write up the chapter on 'flipping' she says it really happened and I can pop-bop-prose it from her version and she says it will be a much better book because of it and I believe her. Anyway I promised. So I am taking the *Subterraneans* ms. with me till Jan. 5th, to Florida, to incorporate these changes, and meanwhile her signed release is in your mailbox, sealed."

15

dash)[25] ... Like Lee Konitz in 1951 I want to blow as deep as I want,[26] for nothing is muddy that runs in time and to laws of time, Shakespearean stress of dramatic need, to speak now in own unalterable way or forever hold tongue, and never to afterthink to "improve" or defray impressions because the best statement is always the most painful personal wrung-out tossed from cradle warm protective mind TAP FROM ONESELF—blow!—now!—your way is your only way, it cannot be "good" or "bad" but only always honest ('ludicrous'), spontaneous, confessional, interesting because not 'crafted.' Craft *is* craft. We must allow the subconscious to admit its own uninhibited interesting necessary and so 'modern' language what conscious art would censor. Right now, language in literature is dead. This is more important to me than a few bucks, than success.... I see it leading to a tremendously interesting literature everywhere with all kinds of confessions never made by man before, leading to a cool future ... the strange future when it will be realized that everyone is an artist, naturally. And each good or bad according to his openness!

An excellent substitute for Subterraneans for your Evergreen No. 2 would be certain three excerpts of mine, now at Sterling Lord's office, which are authentic Friscoana ... (as you know SUBS is a New York story transposed to hide identities).... The three excerpts are, first, JOAN RAW-SHANKS IN THE FOG (which Rexroth likes a lot), the filming of some shots for a movie of Joan Crawford on the foggy top of Russian Hill (SF) one night, a great piece.... Then, from 'Visions of Neal,' NEAL AND THE THREE STOOGES, also Frisco scene.... and finally not least OCTOBER IN THE RAILROAD EARTH, all about Southern Pacific Railroad (when I was brakeman) and skid row Third St. of Frisco.... You couldnt have a better coverage of the SF scene. And what's more they add up, as is, to about 70 pages! If you'd only use them, as is, with no changes, they'd fit right in with Evergreen No. 2 poetry, be Frisco scene, and stand up beside that untouched poetry of the other boys (as SUBS cut does not).[27]

So this is my suggestion about a substitute. Now, if on the other hand you plan Subterraneans by itself (?) in a coming issue, and want cuts,

25. This description was later included in Kerouac's statement "Essentials of Spontaneous Prose."
26. In 1951 the alto saxophonist Lee Konitz worked with pianist Lennie Tristano to develop a jazz style free of the influence of Charlie Parker. Konitz's style was characterized by *The New Grove Dictionary of Jazz* (1994) as the creation of "long serpentine lines ... with varied sub-divisions of the beat, and a discreet, urgent sense of swing."
27. Don Allen eventually included the first half of Kerouac's "October in the Railroad Earth" in *Evergreen Review*, No. 2 (titled "The San Francisco Scene"), along with Ginsberg's "Howl," a story by Michael Rumaker, photographs by Harry Redl, and various work by California writers: Kenneth Rexroth's "San Francisco Letter," Henry Miller's sketch "Big Sur and the Good Life," Ralph Gleason's essay "San Francisco Jazz Scene," and poems by Brother Antoninus, Robert Duncan, Lawrence Ferlinghetti, Michael McClure, Josephine Miles, Jack Spicer, James Broughton, Gary Snyder, and Philip Whalen.

cut that Flipping Confession block, where it (about Page 25 or so) says (I think), "but I was a more serious listener etc. and she had to tell her story ..." all the way to where finally those two girls in the MG and Adam Moorad [Allen Ginsberg] interrupt coming in the pad....

I dont know what your plans are so let me know ... I feel (and know, in fact) that Subterraneans is a careful large poem and shouldnt be fiddled with (overmuch) any more than the shorter poems of Ginsberg, Corso, Snyder, Whalen et al, who wd. certainly have not been impressed with my heralded Subterraneans cut 60% like that and all sentence structure rhythm broken, like Satevepost nowhere tale.... Dont be bugged, I know what I'm talking about tho I may get drunk and act childish socially and tho my Zen name is LAZY LUNATIC.... I'm an artist, oldfashioned, devoted.

Please write. As ever
Jack

TO STERLING LORD

March 25, 1957
[Tangier]

Dear Sterling,

I feel that I definitely did the right thing in the Grove Press matter, that it will definitely bear fruit in the end. Hemingway went thru the same trouble in early 1920's and had he succumbed to the ideas of the editors there would have been no "Hemingway Style" at all and nothing great about the literature of the Lost Generation. Ditto Faulkner in the 30's. It's not that I have an arty phobia against money, as you know. I presume you are sending Gerard and Desolation Angels to New Directions;[28] you see, when I did write to MacGregor there I thought Grove was all washed up with the idea of publishing Subterraneans. Now is it true (as MacGregor mentions in letter) that Subterraneans will appear in a later issue of Evergreen Review as I have written it? And what is the excerpt Don Allen did take ... as substitute for No. 2 ... (?) .. "October in Railroad Earth"?..... Again, there, I naturally dont want any extensive useless changes that will disable the prose and render it Non-Jack.

---

28. On March 8, 1957, after receiving Cowley's rejection of *Desolation Angels*, Kerouac had written a letter to James Laughlin at New Directions reflecting conversations about literature in Tangier with Williams Burroughs. Laughlin didn't bother to reply for several months to Kerouac's statement:

> I am in the strange position of being able to offer various levels of my novels to various levels of publishers—not "novels" per se, but all my books are as it were poetry sheeted in narrative steel, a new kind of narrative which does not concern itself with discipline or dryness but aims at the flow of feeling unimpeded and uninterrupted

Allen Ginsberg just got here and mentioned you had offers from Esquire Mag. . . . what are you sending them? He also says that my friend John Clellon Holmes sold a jazz story to Parade(?) (West Coast) magazine for $600 . . . if so, that might be a good one to try, with any of my excerpts (Burlesque etc. Joan Rawshanks etc.) (or Jazz excerpts from Desolation Angels) . . .

I just wrote long letter to Don Allen extending my views and describing my prose theory and position etc. As soon as Black Mountain Review comes out sometime this year, with my essay on prose called "Essentials of Prose" and an example (from "Railroad Earth"), you wont have to do any talking, just show the article. . . . Malcolm Cowley completely disagrees with me, believes in extensive "revision" etc. and strictly entrez [sic] nous I would bet that my life span at Viking may not extend much beyond On the Road. Evidently the publishing world is turning over and in a few years I will be accepted on my own terms by companies that are growing more powerful now. But meanwhile, money wise, On the Road is our best bet. Please keep an eye on reprint offers, which may lead also to reprint offers for Town & City . . .

Please send me the $90 check for April[29] to me here at Hotel Mouniria and once I get it I'm off, alone, across the straits to Spain to France to Paris and London. I expect I wont stay overseas long, am already planning to work my way back on a merchant ship (have my sea papers) and move my mother and I out to California to new life (Frisco) . . . This summer, . . . if you are coming to Paris this summer, please let me know when, I wont leave till I see you there, though.

---

by the calls of a dead craft, for I believe that the "novel form" is dead, and the new prose literature of any originality and value will be cast in just that form, cf. Genet, Céline, and the new work of William Burroughs. I'm looking for a writer's publisher. I would, I will no more have my prose cut up than would Paul Bowles or Hemingway or any other conscientious artist.

29. In a memo to his agent the previous month, Kerouac clarified how he wanted to receive his thousand-dollar advance (minus Lord's 10-percent commission) from Viking for *On the Road:*

On acceptance of *On the Road,* please send bank draft or whatever form convenient, of initial $150 payment, to my mother

Mrs. Gabrielle Kerouac
1219 Yates Avenue
Orlando, Florida

We have joint account at the bank there.

Then, please send me the first $100 on the first monthly payment, at European address I'll give you.

After that, the following monthly payment to my mother. (She will notify you of change-of-address, if any.)

Alternating after that, to me, to her, for the six monthly payments mentioned in the contract.

I am very pleased you sent the photostats, by the way, I had no idea and was prepared by hearsay to let them go ahead ... It would have been a flop, I say.

As for Cowley and Viking, I plan to simply write the sequel to On the Road in substantially the same narrative manner, call it the Beat Generation, and make everybody happy all around. . . . besides of which the sequel is a vast terrible tale enough (shootings, suicides) but also comedic at high points ...

Oh well, that's enough gabbing ... just let me know what you feel is important. While waiting for my check I'm earning my living typing up Bill Burroughs' manuscript & he buys my meals in exchange.[30] Till I hear from you,

As ever,
Jack

While in Tangier, Kerouac wrote an air letter to Neal Cassady in Los Gatos, California. Kerouac had stayed with Neal and Carolyn Cassady for a few days the previous fall, but he'd left their house without saying good-bye after Neal had asked for a loan. Now Kerouac, who didn't have a driver's license and hated to drive a car, asked his "old buddy" to do him a favor: he wanted Neal to move him and his mother "lock stock & bullshit" cross-country from New York City to San Francisco. Jack also mentioned the fall publication of On the Road, *the novel in which he fictionalized his adventures with Cassady as the character Dean Moriarty, hoping that "no one recognizes you too much in that opus." Cassady hadn't written Kerouac in years, and he never replied to this letter.*

TO NEAL CASSADY

[postmarked March 25, 1957
Tangier]

Dear Neal ...

Last night me and Allen and Peter go out and wander into an Arabian hangout for guys playing checkers and drinking mint tea, young guys mostly, and smoking t[31] out of big long pipes ... We come in there & I see this weird hepcat wearing a black robe with hood, barefoot, sitting cross-leg on corner bench with weed pipe puffing and when he sees my eyes

---

30. In Part Two of *Desolation Angels*, Kerouac described typing Burroughs's manuscript of *Naked Lunch* in Tangier: "when I undertook to start typing it neatly doublespace for his publishers the following week I had horrible nightmares in my roof room—like of pulling out endless bolognas from my mouth, from my very entrails, feet of it, pulling and pulling out all the horror of what Bull [Bill] saw, and wrote."
31. "T," "shit," or "weed" were some of the slang terms Kerouac used for marijuana.

get big watching him re-load pipe out of big round bag of shit he has at his side, he says "come on over" and we go over and pick up, legal in Morocco ... He is regular guy like you, only difference his clothes and nationality, tells how little he's paid on waterfront, how he hurt his (bandaged) foot, his father was a worker on docks, he has sisters and brothers in the countryside farming with the meek asses & biblical wells ... We turn on ten pipeloads ... Not only that, he is so much like you the reason he commands respect in his nightly hangout is that he beats everybody in checkers! He plays weird loose game catching other hooded robed shroudy checkerplayers with smart fast moves, they gang around to watch big games, bang checkers hard, yell, meanwhile on radio is the Arabic girls singing hingya hingya and then long political speeches from Cairo and man I was hi. It, the place, is on cliff over ocean, near old Carthaginian stonewall fortress that Scipio and other Romans used to scale 3000 years ago. They are all hi, all wild, hep, cool, great kids, they talk like spitting from inside the throat Arabic arguments ... My hepcat there sold us some for 10 cents, for 5 cents but we gave him tip, enuf for 20 joints ... He just sits there with his papers rolling up packets that he sells around town, he is religious, says "It is as Allah wills," says "Believe without asking why," and slowly ponderously mumbles his lips over his favorite ragged books, which last night were these 2: poems of Catullus in Latin, and a French grammar ... His hero is the Sultan of Morocco, Ben Youssef, who wears dark glasses and blasts also ... I only wish you could have met this cat, my good friend Mohammed M., by name. His buddy is younger kid, intellectual, who had long talk with Allen ... Peter played checkers with other kid and got beat ... Meanwhile one mangy dog rushes around our feet playing with hats and shoes ... cats cut in and out, blasting ... music wails ... you should see Morocco and all North Africa to believe it, imagine a whole culture of t-smokers ... and these lil ole Arab gals with veils, that charge 3 bucks & pant and puff boy ... (no disrespect meant to Maw who'll read this (Maw) but wow what goils) ... unluckily am low in funds and just look mostly ... Well Neal, I have a proposition now to make to you. My mother and I wanta move lock stock & bullshit to California once for all and when I mentioned my plan to give you a week's railroad wages plus gas & oil plus expenses ($400) to come get us in Florida, you remove seats from Nash Rambler and we come back with me, you, my Ma and the TV set, clothes, my boxes of manuscripts, a box of books, clothes, a box of dishes, no more, we zoom back to coast, all done in one fast week ... would you like to do that? In other words, Carolyn gets week wages to keep up family, you get all gas and oil and expenses, and get good vacation trip, which is, hop from Los Gatos to NY and pick me up at my girl's pad on Columbia campus, then down to Florida, pick up my mother, then back via New Orleans and LA and up ... where, within days, I find good cheap pad like in Berkeley or even Telegraph Hill and move in and there we are at last with our permanent homes next to each other ... Like, I dont want to move my Maw to NY I've had that and I feel like I'm finished with that old frosty fagtown ... Would you do this, Neal? Of course no need for me to plead, or mention, or bugger, or say, that you will be doing me great great favor and kindly deed ... Money being the only objection and I have the money ... Now Neal I want you to give me your decision on this, write to me here at this Tangier address, soon as you can, if you're too incapable to write have Carolyn write the letter with your decision in it ... I'm sure Carolyn will be glad to hear that I want to move my home out there, we'll have occasional big family sprees in Chinatown etc. and sometimes you bring kiddies to my mother's house for big Sunday dinners, etc. Also you can use my bedroom for in-between railroad naps, any time day or night ... If you agree to this, my plan, I will hurry up and get a freighter work my way back with seaman papers to states this summer and notify you well ahead time & we make it ... Nice trip for you too, to see NY again free of charge, and see Florida etc. Anyway my mother says in her letter, quote, "It's a good idea to ask Neal, I'd rather he would come and help us"... (she means, rathern I get me a license and an old beatup truck and drive her & me out) ... with you much faster & surer ... So please write soon, don't put it off, besides you never never answer my letters anymore ... Well meanwhile Old Bull Burroughs is mad as usual, writing great stuff, WORD HOARD his new masterpiece putting Genet, Ginsberg, all ALL sex poets to shame once and for all ... I'm going to Paris in 2 weeks, alone, these guys (Bill, Allen, Peter) plan to go Casablanca south of here and work for American airfields ... I'll go dig Paris, Brittany (village of Kerouac), London (see Seymour Wyse) and Dublin and then find that ship and work back as deckhand ... Maybe I can put in a coupla months braking October and Nov[ember] this year for emergency money, in Frisco ... ON THE ROAD coming out in the Fall, I sure do hope no one recognizes you too much in that opus ... all been carefully culled for libelious [sic] or unpleasant touches, not only by me but by lawyers and editors ... might be a bestseller and we all get rich on third choice. My love to Carolyn & kiddies.

As ever,
Jack

PS: Dear Carolyn—I'm praying now that I'll finally make it to my true home.

J.

After Ginsberg and Orlovsky joined Kerouac in Tangier, they learned from Ferlinghetti that 520 copies of a second printing of Howl and Other Poems *shipped from England early in 1957 had been seized by U.S. Customs officers in San Francisco as obscene literature. On April 3, 1957, Kerouac mentioned the uproar in California to his agent, who had just sent him the first advance royalty payment from the Viking Press and informed him that* On the Road *had been sold to the English publisher André Deutsch.*

TO STERLING LORD

April 3, 1957
[Tangier]

Dear Sterling,

Hallelujah, and I was just on my way to London to stay with a friend and wait for a job back on a merchant ship! I'll look up Mr. Deutsch ... It's wonderful, Sterling, the way you have been making things hum. I am going to take advantage of this apparently prosperous year and come right home and set up my abode proper.

.... On the Road might go over big in Rock n Roll Hooligan England, just as it might in USA ... & thank God it doesnt teach *meanness,* but SOUL.

As soon as I cash the April check you've just more than promptly sent me, I'll take the packet to Marseilles and hitch hike to Paris, stay there about 2 weeks and go to London. If Mr. Deutsch is paying us in pounds how and what is the arrangement ... ? Any news and new letters you have for me send to *me c/o American Express in Paris* now. (I'll leave here tomorrow.) I guess Mr. Deutsch will tell me what to do (convert pounds)..... and if I cant get a merchant ship to work back on I'll just take the Elizabeth back, late May ... As you see I am not much interested in Europe (yet).... I realize it was the time to make that home for my mother and I and a place to eat and write for me in privacy ... I intend to move to Frisco, right away.

It looks like I'll be seeing you in New York long before you make your reservation for your summer jaunt to Paris!

I have an idea for a wonderful follow up for On the Road with Viking ... have started it and tell you more about it later, a narrative.

I'll write to you from Paris within 10 days.

Meanwhile I have been digging Morocco, today took a 10 mile hike along the sea, a swim, then up into the mountains, high, to alpine villages looking like the Khyber Pass, grass-and-stick huts on slopes, sheep, cattle, fierce looking herdsmen with dark faces and turbans and bare knees, and beautiful Berber women with enormous packs on their backs toiling up the grade ... Sat and sketched it in word and picture. Last night Ramadan, the annual Mohammedan fast, started here, with a blast of cannon shot in the bay and then, like smoke over rooftops at 2 am came the lonely sweet flutes of Ramadan, the saddest sound in the world ... All the Arabs fast from 3 Am till 7 PM the next day, and feast in between and play flutes ... In fact in the last 24 hours I've really absorbed all there is in Morocco ... The flutes under midnight rooftop stars, the nighted drums, then the alpine villages and wild slopes where I sat facing the enormous further mountains southward into Africa.... and on the long lonely beach-stretch the gulls, all together in a group by the sea, at the surf which is their dinner table, the head gull saying grace.... then the old robed Bodhisattva, old robed bearded realizer of the greatness of wisdom walking by with a staff and a shapeless skin bag and a cotton pack and a basket on his back, with white cloth around his hoary brown brow, the shrouded Arab by the sea......

Well, you haven't got time for all this, I just thought I'd describe a little bit to you——Thank you so much for all you're doing, and my mother is equally grateful. Till next letter:

As ever,
Jack

p.s. A big cause celebre in San Francisco now, the customs have banned Allen Ginsberg's HOWL because "unfit to be read by children" and already all the big intellectuals are on the radio and in the press fighting it....[32] (his book was being printed in England and was stopped in the mails)——Like being banned in Boston ...

p.s. By the way, has that Fletcher in Cambridge Mass. sent back LUCIEN MIDNIGHT yet? Just let me know, as I'll see some people who know him in Paris next week.

In another letter on April 3, 1957, this one to Gary Snyder, who was finishing a year of study on a fellowship in Japan, Kerouac expanded on what he was doing in Tangier. After Cowley's criticism of Desolation Angels, *Jack had decided to write a different kind of book for the Viking Press about his adventures on the West Coast the previous year. He mentioned parenthetically to Gary that he had begun "contemplating" his next novel,* The Dharma Bums, *which was going to be "mostly about you."*

TO GARY SNYDER

April 3, 1957
[Tangier]

Dear Gary,

I just got back from a long ramble.... 10 miles in all, up the beach, swim, then inland into the mountain country, where I climbed a minor near one and came upon quiet shepherd slopes, honk of asses & maaa of sheep

---

32. United States Customs authorities soon cleared Ginsberg's book, but in June 1957 Ferlinghetti and his clerk at the City Lights bookshop were arrested by the San Francisco police for selling it. The American Civil Liberties Union took on the case, and the trial was set for August 1957. See Kerouac's letter to Ginsberg, June 7, 1957.

rejoicing in vales and silly happy trills of crazybirds goofing in the solitude of rocks and brush swept by sun heat swept by sea wind, warm ulululations shimmering—Quiet brush-and-twig huts looking like Upper Nepal—Fiercelooking Arab shepherds and herdsmen dark, bearded, robed, bareknee'd—Distant African mountain peaks to the south—Quiet powder blue village below—Crickets, sea-roar—Peaceful mountain Berber village or farm settlement, women with huge bundles of green going down the slope—little teeny girls of 4 in shawls and robes twinkling along on little bare feet going "nglambedaha" and proo proo proo—browsing bulls—a Van Gogh, Cezanne, a Kerouac could paint these chalk blue powder blue huts, live here in unutterable mountain peace and paint, the vast green meadowlands far down and the chalkblue huts nearer and the big Mexican-like maguey cacti—far down, dry arroyos in the fat meadow country—sketched it by pencil And O last night Gary under the midnight stars, among the rooftops of Morocco, the flute of Ramadan, lovely and sad and sweet, I suddenly heard, accompanied by nighted drums, and I saw, because Mohammed had done it, fasted from 3 a m to 7 p m, a whole world would too, because of *belief* under these stars. I saw the true glory of religion once and for all; in these humble, often mean-to-animals people ... so now I'll never be able to tell what I hear out this window, the beat of the wind, or of the sea, or of the drums of Ramadan (the annual fast) (was lying in bed contemplating next novel THE DHARMA BUMS, which is mostly about you, my freight hop to Frisco in Fall 1955 and meeting you and the Gallery 6 poetry reading and our climb of Matterhorn with John Montgomery[33] and all about Avalokitesvara)[34] ... (the hearer and answerer of prayer always ALWAYS answers because his answer is the diamond silence which immediately answers once for all) ... Yesterday I sketched a diagram of my shack I want to build (or have Locke[35] build) in Marin hill woods ... just sold novel ON THE ROAD to English publishers for 150 pound advance which is enuf right there for down payment on lot and materials to build ... This will make you laugh but I'm already heading back to states to do all this, fuck the tired Old World ... leaving for Paris in 2 days, Allen will take over my lovely patio room with Peter ... Allen wants me to tell you the big news and *cause celebre* just happened in Frisco, customs banned his HOWL as "unfit for children" and Rexroth has already been on the air howling about it ... you'll hear full details from Allen & others, like being banned in Boston, poetry making the newspapers yet! ... (clipping in *Chronicle*)—

33. John Montgomery was a California friend who appeared as Henry Morley in *The Dharma Bums.*
34. Bodhisattva Avalokitesvara taught that the virtue of great compassion encompassed all the virtues of the Buddha.
35. Locke McCorkle was a friend of Gary Snyder's who lived with his family in Mill Valley. McCorkle appeared as Sean Monahan in *The Dharma Bums.*

Ferlinghetti planning to print it in States instead of England ... I suggested he should send out letters to all interested for one-dollar contribution to cover cost and his present loss ... On the beach today, the gulls all together, in a group, at their dinner table the sea surf, the head gull saying grace ... The microscopic red bugs/ in the sea-side sand/ do they meet and mate?— Trying to count a pinch of sand on the beach, knowing there are as many worlds as the sands in the ocean! O honored of the worlds!—then old robed Bodhisattva, old robed bearded realizer of the greatness of wisdom walking by with a staff and a shapeless skin bag and a cotton pack and a basket on his back, with white cloth around his hoary brown brow ... the shrouded Arab by the sea.

Now Gary, I leave Tangier in 3 days, go on packet to Marseilles, hitch hike to Paris, spend maybe 2 or 3 weeks there walking everywhere, then to London, to pick up English advance on On the Road, to wait for ship (wanta work back as deck hand) ... so if you want to write to me, make it c/o American Express Paris ... but I understand you write to too many people anyway so just do what you want ... tso [sic] no good too much correspondence, takes all yr. writing energy out of ya ... Start writing prose narratives of your adventures, I got an agent for ya (Sterling Lord) and plenty market for prose stories ... make em wild, like cat operator telling tales at bar stool in Jackson Hole Wyo.... thank you for telling me Avalokitesvara has never left me, that is good enu [sic] for me for a thousand year ... when write to Phil Whalen, send him my love ... Allen will write to you soon he says ... he is quieting down here and digging Arabia his own special way (noticing cripples, poverty, etc.) so that now he says "what importance is HOWL to these people? I gotta write something better more serious." ... Remember lil slip of paper about mercy I gave you for Japan? Last night I thought I should have written instead: "Forgive, for when it shall be shown to you the symbol of awakenerhood, there will be no meanness." Kowtow Known as Buto—POWPOWPOW

Jack

Within a week after leaving Tangier, Kerouac was in London, where he stayed a few days with his friend Seymour Wyse and collected some of his advance for the English edition of On the Road *from his publisher André Deutsch. Settling down in California with his mother was uppermost in Jack's mind, so before embarking on a ship back to New York City and turning his back on "sick old Buddhaless Europe," he wrote another friend, the poet Philip Whalen, who still lived in a cottage in Berkeley, to ask for help finding a place to live in the Bay Area. He also told his agent about his latest idea for subtitling* On the Road.

April 10, 1957
[London]

Dear Phil—(Write me c/o GLASSMAN IN N.Y.)

Just about to embark for N.Y. out of England here, dug Paris & London quite, picked up British advance here—

Am moving me, kit, kaboddle and mother to Berkeley & would like permission to give movers your address as temporary point. By the time they arrive I shall already have bungalow or flat rented in Berkeley & will redirect movers—

Meanwhile, would you keep eye open for place, bungalow preferred (3 rooms, even 2) I can rent? And definitely keep it secret, as I don't want noise but new quiet home to write in? (You might see John Montgomery, tell him same)—(he might know place too)—

So about May 10th I'll be bringing you my dharma bones to doorsill to say hello. Have lots to tell you about Europe—(dharma-bummed through Provence, etc. saw Corso in Paris, Genet's translator, & in half hour I go see "Anthony and Cleopatra" at Old Vic)—

My operation will not disturb the even tenor of your ways, just need address for movers & any suggestions that may move things faster—

Very glad to become neighbors with you indeed—

All's well with Allen, who is going to work with Peter in Casablanca airfields for Europe loot (I *detest* sick old Buddhaless Europe)—Saw Stupa sculpts in British Museum here, & also coat-of-arms of my old ancestral Brittany family with motto: AIMER, TRAVAILLER ET SOUFFRIR (precis of Town & City plot!)

Until,
Jack

[Postmarked April 20, 1957
London]

Dear Sterling—

I'm sailing today from Southampton on the New Amsterdam, will be in New York about April 27 and call you Monday 29th.

Cyrus Brooks advanced me only 68 pounds of the 150-pound advance due to the tax complication which he will explain to you by mail, a form I have to get notarized in N.Y. and then British Government will send remainder on. There are further complications, a personal loan of 5 pounds and another of 2 pounds, all of which I'll explain to you Monday. In any case, it was a Godsend because I wanted to come home now. Mr Brooks is

26

a wonderfully dignified old gent with a goatee, bowler, gloves, umbrella, and a smart flat on Buckingham Gate.

I didnt see André Deutsch, not much time, but it occurred to me maybe it would double the sales to change the title to *ROCK AND ROLL ROAD* or at least invent a similar subtitle, & also for Viking.

Hold the May 1st Viking check for me at office, therefore, & I'll see you Monday 29th & we'll clean up odds & ends and then I'll leave for my new home life in California—

As ever,

Jack

p.s. Paris even more unbelievable than I'd expected!—but I went broke there and it was your letter at American Express telling me about London that saved me—English Immigrations almost didnt let me through because they thought I was a tramp—

Back in New York City, where he stayed at Joyce Glassman's apartment, Kerouac described his travels in letters to his old friends Ed White in Denver, Philip Whalen in Berkeley, and Ginsberg and Burroughs in Tangier. Jack had taken a sample of the typescript he'd prepared of Burroughs's writing to Paris to show Bernard Frechtman, translator of Jean Genet. In Tangier, Ginsberg wrote Ferlinghetti on May 10, 1957, that he continued to work "on Burroughs' mss. with friend been in town a week name of Alan Ansen, type in relays and sit & bullshit, story conferences, revisions, etc. hanging together huge 1000 page mss."

TO ED WHITE

April 28, 1957
Jack c/o Glassman
554 W. 113 St.
New York, NY

Ho Ed!

Yes my good friend I got your fine letter in Tangier, Morocco less than a month ago and wanted to write to you from Dr. Johnson's house in London when I got there but got too engrossed in the British Museum and staring at El Grecos in the National Gallery so here I am back in NY and leisure to write you.... Very interesting, your notes about Buddhist art, in fact in the Brutish [sic] Museum they have a Stupa from the Deccan south India showing empty places for the Buddha in the old sculpture.... En route from Tangier to Paris ... well first, in Tangier are Bill Burroughs who has just written a great book WORD HOARD and Allen Ginsberg whose poem HOWL has just been banned in Frisco. There I had a room overlooking the straits, a patio, for 20 bucks month, and went mountain climbing to isolated Berber villages, etc. and smoked tea out of pipes with shrouded Arabs in cafés.... Then, after Marseilles, I tried to hitchhike through Provence, outside Aix, where Cézanne painted, ended up hiking 20 miles but it was worth it ... sat on side of hills and pencil sketched drawings of the Cézanne country, dull red rusty rooftops, blue hills, white stones, green fields, hasn't changed in all these years ... mauve tan farm houses in quiet fertile farmer's valleys, rustic, with weathered pink powder roof tiles, a grey green mild warmness, voices of girl, gray stacks of baled hay, a fertilized chalky horseshit garden, a cherry tree in white bloom (April), a rooster crowing at mid day mildly, tall Cézanne trees in back ... etc. just like Cézanne nein? Then a rattly old bus through Arles country, the restless afternoon trees of Van Gogh in the high mistral wind, the cypress rows tossing, yellow tulips in window boxes, a vast outdoor café with huge awning, and the gold sunlight.... I haven't had chance to tell you but I've begun to paint, hence all the excitement about painting, started in Mexico City last October, first with pencil, then chalks, then watercolor, then paint ... my first painting: God.—So I went to Paris and in the Louvre stuck my nose up against Van Gogh and Rembrandt canvases and saw they are the same person.... I dug Pittoni first, as I walked in, expressive gestures ... Tiepolo, *Last Supper,* perfect dog attitude at bone, the final white paint touches on Christ's face ... Guardi, always the Doge, insane for detail and architecture but Canaletto is the master for that (*View of Venice*) splashing light on building and plazas and on corner, one thin line on corner edge (the Venetian 18th Century school) ... and so on, and thru David, Girodet Trioson, Fragonard, Gros, and suddenly face to face staring at me, a Rubens! A big smoky Rubens (*La Mort de Dido*) which got better as I lookt, the muscles' tones in cream and pink, the rim shot luminous eyes, the dull purple velvet robe on the bed.... But ah, THEN, Goya's *Marquesa de la Solana,* could hardly be more modern, her little silver feet shoes pointed like fish crisscrossed, the immense diaphanous pink ribbons over a pink face, a woman a French workingwoman said "Ah c'est trop beau!"... but then, walking along thru Gentileschi's little Jesus and Castiglione who paints a raging Christ distantly in a blue robe scourging the vendors in the Temple, throatslit lambs on the floor, confusions of ducks, baskets, goats.... Ah then Brueghel! Wow! His *Battle of Arbelles* has at least 600 faces clearly defined in impossibly confused tight mad battle leading nowhere NO-WHERE like real life, no wonder Céline loved him! Complete understanding of world madness, beyond which we see thousands of clearly defined figures and swords, above it all the calm mountains, trees on a hill, clouds.... everyone LAUGHS when they see this insane masterpiece, they know what it means.... Then O Rembrandt! Dim Van Gogh like trees in the darkness of Crépuscule Château, the hanging beef completely modern with splash of blood paint ... with Van Gogh swirls in face of Emmaeus Christ ... the floor (in Sainte Famille) completely detail'd in color of planks, and nails, and shafts of light on Virgin's tit.... St. Matthew being Inspired by the Angel is a MIRACLE, the rough strokes, so much so, the drip of red paint in the angel's lower lip making it so angelic and his own rough hands ready to write the Gospel (as I will be visited).... Also miraculous is the veil [of] mistaken angel smoke on Tobiah's departing angel's left arm. Finally, not least, Van Gogh ... his crazy blue Chinese church, the hurrying woman, the spontaneous brush stroke, the secret of it is Japanese, is what for instance makes the woman's back, white, because her back is unpainted canvas with a few black thick script strokes (so that I wasn't wrong when I started painting God last Fall in doing everything fast like I write and that's it).... Then the madness of blue running in the roof of the church where he had a ball, I can see the joy red mad gladness he rioted in that church heart.... I have a headache from all this.... His maddest pic is of those gardens Les Somethings, with insane trees whirling in the blue swirl sky, one tree finally exploding into just black lines, almost silly but divine, the thick curls and butter burls of color paint, beautiful rusts, glubs, creams, greens, a master madman, Rembrandt reincarnated to do the same thing without pestiferous detail.... HISTORY OF ART: from Egyptians & wall cavers to Meissonier-types (where was finally mastered exact imitation of nature) (of DeHootch, Treck, Van Velsen, Kalf and all the Dutchmen and Italians who could do exact silver spoons and hams) back to Van Gogh and Renoir and Degas and Cézanne (Gauguin really a cheap cartoonist compared to these masters), (via Goya, Greco, Velázquez and Tintoretto this movement back), to exact *painting* (not imitating) of nature.... So I will paint what I see, color and line, exactly FAST ... Paint being the holy blood.... (St. Matthew's Angel with the smear red mouth MOVED when I lookt!!!)

And of course Ed I visited Notre Dame, Montmartre, etc. all
    that jive,

And so, Ed, another letter later, write to me,
    and I'll tell you more about Paris than
        just museums.... I had a ball,
   it is greater than I thought it would be
but now I'm going to

              California....
        if you want to write to me care
           of this address pronto, do it

                    by return mail as I am
                    leaving in 8 days....
            alas, won't pass thru
            Denver but thru El Paso.

            Till I hear from you,
                    as ever
            sir, your
                    humble
            servant

                    Jack
Regards to your loved ones.
How's Justin?
    By the way, you started whole new movement of American litera-
ture (spontaneous prose & poetry) when (1951) in that Chinese
restaurant on 125th street one night you told me to start SKETCH-
ING in the streets ... tell you more later ... this is big historical fact,
you'll see ... (weird sketches).
    And how in Dickens did you know always I wd. become painter
somehow?

TO ALLEN GINSBERG & WILLIAM S. BURROUGHS
                                            [Early May 1957
                                            New York City]
Dear Allen & Bill,
    Yes the manuscript safe in the hands of Frechtman in Paris. When I left
he hadnt yet read it ... Writing you this from Joyce's pad in NY preparing to move out with my mother, only waiting to see if Neal agrees, if not,
bus ... The 4th class packet is nowhere, never take it, take it 3rd class, I had
to scrounge around for my food like a stowaway, woulda starved without
my camp pots, slept on burlap mattress, among soldiers and Arabs, no
blanket even, and had to have my camp pots filled by surly cooks in the
kitchen ... Tried to hitch hike from Aix en Provence to north, no rides, no
good hitching in Europe ... However dug the Cezanne country and also
Arles, tell you more later ... Paris bugged me because no rooms and no fine
American friends could let me sleep on their floor, Mason Hoffenberg
could have but didnt want, Gregory was nix because of his landlady, spent
5 furious days digging everything on foot then went to London and pickt
up advance, bought boat ticket, dug all London too, including perf[or-
mance] of St. Matthew Passion in St. Paul's Cathedral, and saw Seymour
who is at 33 Kingsmill ... Last I heard of Gregory he was at Hotel des

Ecoles, Rue Sorbonne, Paris … He got me drunk and made me spend most of my money the first night, 's why I had to leave Paris so soon … Paris better than I dreamed, great, unbelievable, Allen you will love it … but do NOT live in St. Germain Montparnasse, go instead to old Montmartre where it's cheaper, children's carousels in the street, artists, beater artists, working class district … (not fashionable now, the idiot Americans all sit in Montparnasse cafes as if they didnt get enuf of that in the Remo & the Place ugh) … So live in Montmartre when you get there … Dont miss the Louvre, I saw it all there … voluminous notes on the pictures I saw, in my diary … In Paris even Frechtman wouldnt let me sleep on (apartment) floor … as a result, all I got were one-night hotel rooms, kicked out in morning, spent most of time sightseeing Paris with full pack on back, sometimes in hail rain and snow … But really loved it and this whole trip, now I'm back in NY, I see as having been worth it, worth the money spent and the hassles … Now I'm in touch with Whalen and ready to go out there. Latest news: in this week's Publisher's Weekly a long paragraph about HOWL banned, and invitation to editors and writers to contribute to the fight against the ban, the court trial coming up … Nothing wrong will come of it, and anyway American edition will then sell like hotcakes … I hear Viking is excited about On the Road, expect it to be a bestseller (old story, hey?) …

Bad news is that Joan is after me with the cops again already,[36] they think I'm in Europe still (I hope they didn't check boat lists) and are about to clamp on my source of income at Sterling Lord's and attach it etc. just as I'm struggling to move Ma to coast … What I'll do is order a blood test in a few months and settle it once for all … that bitch, and I was feeling so good because no lushing and happy thoughts of concentrating all attention on Duluoz Legend, damn her, she's like a snake snapping at my heels … She got some doctor to prove that she couldn't work and support her child, because of TB … She made sneaky calls to Sterling who dug her right away without my telling him and kept mum … So what I'll do Allen, when I get their roundabout letters, is answer them, mail the letter to you to mail from Casablanca, as tho I was there … And how is the deal in Casa, any jobs? Is Bill with you? Peter? Is Peter's cure working? Saw Elise who misses you so much, almost cried, told her what I could.… Even Seymour dint put me up in London because of some cunt in there who hated me, I'm gettin to be like Burroughs.… Seymour still slim and boyish but strangely unemotional, tho as we were strolling through Regent Park one evening and I told him he didnt have to be fooled every second (by false mind) he let

36. Kerouac's second wife, Joan Haverty. According to her, as she wrote in her memoir *Nobody's Wife*, their marriage broke up in June 1951, less than seven months after their wedding, when Joan learned she was pregnant and refused to get an abortion. Their daughter, Janet, was born on February 16, 1952. According to Jack's journals, he left the house at Joan's request in May of 1951; he never stated at any time that he had asked her to get an abortion.

out a shout of recognition.... He's alright but England not good for him, nothing but drear there.... Anyway good contact for you in London.... Go to the Mapleton Hotel in London and get a "cubicle" room, cheapest possible ... (Mapleton on Coventry Street) ... In Paris, Montmartre ... Be sure to dig the Cézanne country which looks (anyway in Spring) exactly like paintings, and Arles too, the restless afternoon cypress, yellow tulips in windowboxes amazing ... Whalen and [Kenneth] Rexroth and Ferlin [Lawrence Ferlinghetti] and [Jack] Spicer making tape recordings for Evergreen,[37] will dub yours and Gary's in ... I got letter from New Haven poet man, having BOOK OF BLUES sent to him ..."cityCityCITY" has ended up (unfortunately) free of charge with Mike Grieg in Frisco ... (NEW EDITIONS).

Esquire to write piece about you, I hear, and they want a chapter from ON THE ROAD.

Joyce is going to get $200 option for her novel from Random [House] and is coming out to Frisco to live awhile,[38] Elise also maybe coming to Frisco with her ...

I will see Lucien before I leave ... Don Allen still wants to "improve" SUBTERRANEANS, this is a secret (says Sterling) we will probably remove it from them and give to MacGregor (keep this secret he says) ... But they did take October Railroad Earth UNTOUCHED(!) to go with your poems in Evergreen #2 which is good and will make a sensational issue.

I feel gloomy and bugged and Gregory didn't help in Paris accusing me of gloom and bugginess, we did have one gay day drinking cognac in Luxembourg gardens with big gang of French girls and Irish queers on bikes ... and that night met all the Paris American hepcats and painters, Baird, and others ... I saw Jimmy Baldwin who also wouldnt let me sleep on his floor ... I simply had, was forced to leave Paris, in England the immigrations wouldn't let me in because they thought I was a bum (with seven shillings left) and suspected my big oriental stamps from Tangier as me being a spy ... awful ... till I show'd them Rexroth's article in Nation[39]

37. Lawrence Ferlinghetti and Kenneth Rexroth were featured on Fantasy Records 7002, "Poetry Readings in the Cellar," with a jazz group composed of Sonny Wayne, Bill Weisjahns, and Bruce Lippincott. Hanover Records released an LP of the "San Francisco Poets" (M 5001), including Josephine Miles, Michael McClure, Jack Spicer, Robert Duncan, Philip Whalen, Allen Ginsberg, and others.

38. Joyce Glassman had sold her first novel, *Come Join the Dance,* to Random House.

39. Rexroth's article in *The Nation,* "San Francisco's Mature Bohemians" (February 23, 1957), was revised and retitled "Disengagement: The Art of the Beat Generation" when it appeared in *New World Writing,* No. 11 (New York: The New American Library, 1957). In both versions Rexroth made positive general comments about Kerouac's work as "the most famous 'unpublished' author in America," but Rexroth later became a savage critic of Kerouac's books. See Kerouac's letter to Philip Whalen, January 7, 1958, after the best-selling success of *On the Road,* when Kerouac had learned that "Rexroth is down on me," and his letter to Joyce Glassman, February 4, 1958.

and the inspector beamed because Henry Miller had been to his home-town and written about it (Newhaven, England) ... So now I'm back, came on the Niew Amsterdam, don't ever take a "luxury liner" it's one big drag, in my jeans among fops waiters staring at me in the diningroom, old freighters are better, food not so sensational after all and who wants to eat at sea ... cost $190 ... Was planning to write you huge happy letter full of news about my trip but this Joan shot has brought me way down to utter gloom again, there's a subpoena out for me and everything ... just like be-fore ... How can I ever make it as a Bhikku?—Even if I prove it aint my baby, the expense, the hassle, having to see her horrible haughty face again, the judge might still make me support the kid because no one else will, then what do I do? Give up writing and bhikkuhood and get a steady job? I'd rather jump off Golden Gate bridge. And if I run away my mother can hardly make it on $78 a month and they'd come sneaking around for her little pennies even. In which case I end up murdering somebody, guess who. I have a machete too. I'll take the Prophet's advice. By their fruits ye shall know them. O god all my crimes have been big gentle crimes of omis-sion and at worst "subterranean sabotage" as Billy says ... What would everybody say if I suddenly exploded with a sword of intelligence? Noth-ing ... because nothing ever happened. Listen here Bill Burroughs when-ever you say that what I say "means nothing" that's what I mean!

Allen, when you leave Africa, be sure to take lots of cigarettes with you, cigs in France and England cost equiv. of 60 cents a pack and are no-where. Moment I hit New York I bought tobacco like a madman happily. In Paris, get a stove pad, because food on the street stalls dirt cheap and sen-sationally delicious.... pates, cheeses, head cheeses, unbelievable. The beautiful churches I saw, Sacre Coeur on Montmartre Butte, Notre Dame, etc. etc. Only thing I didnt see, go dig, was Eiffel Tower, which I'll save for you and me, within next 5 years. Montmartre will call me back ... and that was where Van Gogh, Cezanne, Rousseau, Lautrec, Seurat and Gauguin were, all together, wheeling their paintings upstreet in wheelbarrows....

And listen here Bill Burroughs whenever I say "I know everything" it is because I know nothing, which amounts to the same thing ...

Take it from there.

Write me, Allen, care of Whalen, where I'll be in 10 days or so.... love to Peter.... I waved at you finally from the Packet but you and Pete cant see that far and there you were on the windswept sea wall peering blindly to sea.... Love to good old Bill who is a gentle soul I say and fuck all his talk. Meet you all in Heaven.

Jack

On May 6, 1957, Kerouac boarded a Greyhound bus with his sixty-two-year-old mother to travel cross-country from Orlando, Florida, to Oakland, California.

Later in Desolation Angels *he wrote that it was a journey he dreaded since "hardly anything in the world or at least in America [is] more miserable than a transcontinental bus trip with limited means." On their three-day journey Gabrielle devised what Jack considered "a terrific trick to keep us in fairly good shape," aspirins and Coca-Cola fortified with shared pints of bourbon. After Philip Whalen helped them find an apartment in Berkeley, Jack sat down to write a quick postcard giving his agent his new address.*

TO STERLING LORD

[May 15, 1957
1943 Berkeley Way
Berkeley, California]

Dear Sterling,

Received forwarded mail plus London contract, thank you— This is my permanent address now, we found this excellent furnished apartment for $50 a month and utilities & intend to stay here for good and are both very happy—I am living quietly, writing new novel, so keep address quiet—When ROAD comes out I'll revisit N.Y. and settle affairs—

Let me hear the latest whatevers—i.e. Esquire, etc.

As ever,
Jack

Determined to make a home in California with his mother, who had just begun to receive her monthly Social Security retirement checks, Kerouac devised a way to avoid paying child support for his five-year-old daughter, Janet, by giving Joan Haverty the impression he was still living in Tangier. Kerouac sent Ginsberg a letter from Berkeley with instructions about how to keep his return to the United States a secret.

TO ALLEN GINSBERG

[May 17, 1957]
1943 Berkeley Way
Berkeley, Calif.

Dear Allen—

Please mail enclosed letter for me to Joan Haverty (Kerouac) in N.Y. who will then send me something to sign in Tangier for her Puerto Rican divorce (she says)—A subpoena out for me but everybody thinks I'm in Tangier still—When you get divorce paper, mail to me in Berkeley (at my new above address permanent home with my Ma) (a $50-a-month great furnished pad) and I'll send back to you to mail and that will do it—She says she wants remarry a guy who will adopt kid, says she wants no money just divorce—

Will get my typewriter soon & write you long letter— Neal's wife mad at *me* now for being bad influence on him, says at least you had "a motive"— flippy world—Whalen is well—Your name in local gossip columns HERB CAEN—Phil sending you clipping—Bill's [Burroughs's] book looks greater & greater—[Alan] Ansen,[40] I'm so sad I didnt see you but I had time problems—We'll meet again.

Have you heard from Frechtmann?

Don Allen very pleased with SATHER GATE[41]—& tapes too—

W. C. Williams is sore about a big con letter *Gregory* wrote from Paris asking for personal loan, I saw letter, *you* didn't say anything wrong—Any chance my getting MAD CHECKS like Peter?[42]—I saw Ronny Loewinsohn on Beach, he reminds me of [Philip] Lamantia—Al S. arrested for shop-lifting, [Bob] Donlin[43] a bartender in Monterrey—[Gene] Pippin asked for you—Hal Chase[44] left Berkeley—Neal still the same, borrowed money from me & yakked of [Edgar] Cayce—

Please rush Joan's letter on.

Love,
Jack

In May and June 1957, while Kerouac waited to receive the galleys of On the Road *from the Viking Press, he wrote several letters to his friends and his agent. He described his cross-country bus trip and gave an account of what it felt like achieving his dream, at the age of thirty-five, of making a home with his mother in California.*

TO GARY SNYDER

[May 24, 1957]
BUDDHA'S BIRTHDAY
[Berkeley, California]

May 24 at Phil Whalen's cottage ... gray day, cold, Golden Gate obscured in milk, roses and bushes bouncing and quivering, out one window red flowers, out another white, like the Marx brothers opening one door,

---

40. The writer Alan Ansen, who helped type Burroughs's *Naked Lunch.*
41. Ginsberg's poem "Sather Gate Illumination," named in reference to the old entranceway to the UC Berkeley campus, was published in *Evergreen Review* and *Reality Sandwiches* (City Lights, 1963).
42. In 1953, during the Korean War, Peter Orlovsky was drafted into the U.S. Army. After serving as a medic in a San Francisco hospital, he was discharged and had begun to receive veterans' disability checks.
43. Ron Loewinsohn, Philip Lamantia, Al Sublette, and Bob Donlin were writers and friends in San Francisco.
44. Hal Chase was a friend from Denver, whom Kerouac had met at Columbia University.

rain, then another, sunshine ... Dear Gary, Phil kept telling me to answer your letter and I said I didnt have a typewriter and we yawned awhile then he said "Use Mine, there's the paper" and he went off to work and here I am with nothing to say ... The story backwards: got here with my mother on a Greyhound bus, immediately found a fine furnished pad groundfloor Berkeley Way for 50 a month, my next step will be a hut in Marin hills ... Also, a hike in Matterhorn area in September to look for that cave ... Before that, I came from New York where I'd gotten on the Niew Amsterdam from England where England is dreary as dishwater from Paris which is the Queen of Cities indeedy from Tangier dreary Arabs where I left dreary Ginsberg and Burroughs where I'd smoked hashish with arsenic in it and ever since then every thing's looked dreary ... fah. Last Sunday Claude spoke at Buddhist Academy here and I met Mrs. Imamura again and that fine fellow Tsufura and they took us to a Japanese dinner of eel at Fuji inn, which I guess Phil told you, then to Locke's, who wasnt there to greet me I guess because crazy Montgomery told him I was hiding my address from everybody (from Peter du Peru, Bob Donlin, etc. yes, not from Locke)— Sean McCorkle appears to be a tremendously aware child, 's gonna be a great one ... I am bored in Berkeley because our stuff, typewriters, manuscripts, clothes, aint a-comin so fast but I've been painting (chalk scene of backyard, chalk of Virgin Mary and Joseph, housepaint called Vision of the Goatherds) ... and planning my next prose work which I guess will be called Visions of Myself and be my life story so that I can then, in 2nd half of my life, branch off into endless fictions like Balzac (made-up) ... Every time I start to write, lately, I end up painting, but I'm just an amateur painter ... tho I did a lifelike portrait of Phil in pencil .. "Buddha Red Ears" is title, because the red flowers in sun came into window and lit up his shell transluscent ears bright red, which I reddened on pencil sketch with red crayon ... I dont agree with Phil intellectually, i.e., he says Emily Dickinson was a pathetic old maid who didnt know anything bout reality but Gertrude Stein (that dreary old dike) was great ... but intellectualness doesnt make a Sage, and he hasnt got a mean line on his face, and besides he's hiding under a bushel of some kind ... he also accuses sublime Burroughs of writing about "tired old faggots" and doesnt seem to dig him ... well, as I say, intellectualness doesnt make a wise man ... but I wish you were here because I like to hear speech spat forth but Phil just hems and haws except when he's drunk when he spits forth fire diamonds ... fuck, I dont know what to say ... anyway, I saw Will Peters[o]n's[45] long cartoon letter to little girl Imamura, very classical work, and I dug the beautiful Hiro Imamura 16 year old daughter, what a musical name for a musical girl ... Soon I'm going to Laurel Dell camp for kicks and to eat another puff ball

45. Will Peterson was a friend of Snyder's who was studying Buddhism in Japan.

so I can live an extry 50 years ... Just finish reading Chinese Immortals and am amazed what drug addicts and winos they were, just like me, pity I dont drink any more ... I cant anymore[46] ... I'm 35 now and something's happened to my metabolism I dont need liquor anymore ... so I yawn all day and wait ... wrote a lot of haikus this week ...

> Nodding against/the wall,/ the flowers sneeze ...
> Suddenly the official/goes cross eyed/ and floats away ... That's an unencouraging sign,/ the fish store/ is closed ... The strumming of the trees/ reminded me/ of immortal afternoon ... Here comes/ my dragon— / goody!... I hate the ecstasy/of that rose,/that hairy rose ... All the wash/ on that line/ advanced one foot ... May grass—/ nothing much/ to do ... Straining at the padlock/ the garage doors/ at noon in May ... The earth keeps turning/ like a dreary/ immortal ... A pussywillow grew there/ at the foot/ of the breathless tree ... Gary Snyder/ is a haiku/ far away

BUSON: The nightingale is singing/ with his small mouth/ open (knocks me out, Buson, every time)

I dont pretend to be able to write haikus like that ... Phil washes bottles and says nothing ... when he leaves he puts his turtle on his back ... when he returns the roof flies off ... I just saw a whale swimming in the sky, guess it was him ... yawn.

There's no doubt about Avalokitesvara but he's hiding under a bushel called Dreary Time, I wish he'd show me his diamond face once in a while, I am sick of waiting for a vision ... I know that what I see in a golden field that's Avaloki, what I see right now that's Avaloki but I'm yawning too much ... that's Valoki ... The way these bleary tree tops wave in the upper Chinese Silk Void this morning, that's too blank ... that's emptiness for sure ... nothing ever happened for sure ... I remember old hangovers I had, how I suffered, and cant believe that it could have happened to anybody but a ghost ... an inexistent ghost ... and all the old joys happened to a ghost ... and all this boredom now happening to a ghost ... how can you stand to read such crazy.... I am gonna buy me a quarter acre of steep hillside in far off Marin nowhere and build the tiniest hut you ever saw, to which I'll pack a tiny woodstove and tiny kerosene lamps and huge groceries and be Gulliver ... Your Myths and Texts (great book!) must be with Don Allen and Phil will find it ... When you write your huge novel I will make Sterling Lord your agent, he's my agent, he's sold James T. Farrell's

---

46. In *Desolation Angels,* Kerouac described the party on his first night at his new apartment when he and his mother drank so much whisky they passed out: "in the middle of the night I wake up to hear Mémère's groan from the whiskey and somehow I realize our new home is already cursed thereby."

Studs Lonigan to MGM for $150,000. He'll make money for you too, for Zendo grounds and huts everywhere ... I have a blonde novelist following me from NY also a brunette (Ginsy's old girl)[47] who will liven up the North Beach scene maybe ... anyway, orgies ... After all this world travel I feel infinitely dreary and dont know what to get excited about any more and cant live without exuberance ... Maybe you got hints for me, about how to laugh at everything that moves? ... by Zazan. Those mornings when you used to bang the pan and sing Buddham Saranam Gocchami for breakfast, I just laid down on that straw mat rosebush grass of mine last Sunday, and remembered, we sure had it good in that shack. I have never gotten over, tho, since then, those inexplicable moments of mutual irritation we shared, which were dissipated like at Stinson Beach jumping down cliffs, and those sad nights discussing death ... Since then, tho I've come to agree with you, I too, now, read constantly, anything & everything, reading is good ... I think that you and Ginsberg and Whalen are Immortals and will reappear after your deaths and laugh in the shades of night trees ... why have you been laffing behind my back, Immortals? Teach me too!

Jack

TO STERLING LORD

[Note: Rec'd May 31, 1957]
[Berkeley, California]

Dear Sterling

I think I (and you, as agent) wont need to worry any more about my ex-wife, who says she wants to settle out of court, doesnt want a cent; just my signature to a divorce paper so she can re-marry a fellow who will also adopt the child. Her reason (she says) for having subpoenas put out is because she can never find me by herself. I'm negotiating the papers with her through Tangier, as tho I was in Tangier, through my friends. As soon as this is more or less settled, in a few weeks, I'll write a big letter to Keith Jennison and explain everything.

Meanwhile I've just started and am working furiously on a new narrative adventure (I dont write "novels," as you know), the title: AVALO-KITESVARA,[48] which is a picaresque account of how I discovered Buddha and what happened in my experiences, often hilarious, as an American Dharma Bum (or bhikku, wandering religious teacher).... It has all kinds of hitch hiking scenes, girls, new characters I've never written about (such as Gary Snyder who wanders in the mountains alone for months and comes

---

47. Joyce Glassman ("blonde novelist") and Elise Cowen ("a brunette").
48. Apparently an early version of *The Dharma Bums*. See excerpt at end of letter.

down to, among other things, organize Tibetan yabyum orgies with the girls), railroads, wine, dialog, the story of the San Francisco poetry movement which began one drunken night, my meditations in the North Carolina woods, all written in a wild undisciplined way which is consistent with the spirit of the freedom of Tao (the Chinese Way) ... Perhaps it'll take 10 years to publish it but we'll see how ON THE ROAD sells, from which it wont be too different except in style, to which people'll catch up—I just get possessed and write as I wist, which is the only way.

Meanwhile that Mike Grieg is bringing out NEAL AND THE THREE STOOGES in No. 2 of New Editions, next week ... and is giving "cityCity-CITY" back to me, which we can send somewhere else sometime ...

What is Don Allen going to do with THE SUBTERRANEANS?

And has Rust Hills taken any excerpt out of the ROAD galley?[49]

And do I get to see that galley for final proofreading?

Let me know what there is to know, at my new address, 1943 Berkeley Way, Berkeley Calif.

As ever,
Jack

Excerpt from AVALOKITESVARA: "Because the young Buddhist starts out he's fascinated by the teaching that everything is emptiness which is something he's suspected ever since he was 16 years old (he thinks) but actually since babyhood crib wise, and he goes out and as I did sat there in the railyards contemplating the railroad iron convinced it was marshmallow and so it would serve me right if the world crucified me by 18 hoodlums picking me up and holding me stiff straight out like a battering ram and ramming me straight on into a Pennsylvania Railroad coal hopper, even tho I scream as they rush me along: "Butwhether my body is wrecked, has nature added anything to nothing or removed anything from nothing?" But a young Buddhist (a Virgin Buddhist) becomes an old dry dharma-bone Buddhist and that is to say he becomes not-a-Buddhist, he becomes nothing, he becomes the mailman shouting hello to you at nine o'clock in the morning, he becomes like everybody else already was! He gets drunk with the butchers in the springtime!".........

A week after Kerouac arrived in Berkeley, two San Francisco police officers entered the City Lights Bookshop in North Beach on May 21, 1957, and paid Shigeyoshi Murao, the shop manager, seventy-five cents for a copy of Howl and Other Poems. *Shortly afterwards Murao and Lawrence Ferlinghetti were arrested and charged with violating Section 311 of the California Penal Code,*

---

49. Rust Hills, Jr., was the fiction editor at *Esquire.*

which condemns "Every person who wilfully and lewdly ... either ... writes, composes, stereotypes, prints, publishes, sells, distributes, keeps for sale or exhibits any obscene or indecent, writing, paper, or book, etc." On June 7, 1957, Kerouac described what he knew about the incident to his friends in Tangier.

TO ALLEN GINSBERG, PETER ORLOVSKY,
WILLIAM S. BURROUGHS & ALAN ANSEN

[June 7, 1957
Berkeley, California]

Dear Allen and Peter and Bill and Monsier [sic] Ansen—

Well, first, Allen, I got the divorce papers you nicely sent, had them notarized, signed, mailed registered mail, with all kindsa receipts to prove, & so I hope now I'll be left alone in peace so's I can build me that hut for solitude ... And I revealed my presence on West Coast, but said I was en route to Florida or Mexico or someplace (in case of big tricks to trap me) ... wee hee hee ha ha ... I did not ever think I shouldnt pay you that $225 because you'd waste it,[50] tell Bill to stop presupposing his own thoughts in my mirror, I only just dont have it but wait till October when big things will be popping in NY with publication of ON THE ROAD and maybe pocketbook offer and movie options and excerpts etc. so you ought definitely get it ere Xmas, dont worry—As for Neal, yes, Peter, he fine but he borrowed 10 dollars off me saying his children were hungry and then I had to go to Frisco one month later and trap him at his train but he only shoveled up 2 bucks and kept talking all the time ... He's just as mad as ever, cunthappy, but I got a big letter from his wife saying I was a bad influence on him because he was making progress in trying to change to the better things, she says (she defines Dharma as the RIGHT WAY, tho it really means "the meaning"). So Neal persuades me to spend the night in No[rth] Beach and line up some babes, I spent overnight with one gal, but she was a dike I'm afraid, N I met the magnificent Hubert Leslie who is just like Du Peru (who I saw also, he still the same) and Hubert in fact is even coming to visit me at my house in Berkeley (imagine Hube the Cube and my mother in the same room!)—Hube is a great painter, he used butter on his last work, he really is not so dumb, he knows PLASTICITY of painting even if he uses shit for his browns, that's as it shd. be)—Also Leonard H. and Doris are 2 very great people, Doris is Hube's "mother" etc. and they have big mad friends who come around and tiazurnoh with big neezzeedles ... However, first, let me report on HOWL:—the whole (case) thing was put down and laughed at in Washington by big hep customs inspector lawyers or whatever, so the local dumb Irish cops rushed up on their own

---

50. The money that Ginsberg had loaned Kerouac for his passage to Tangier.

initiative and bought HOWL in the store and arrested the nice Jap cat who was instantly bailed out by Civil Liberties Union but I went there & there were no more HOWLS on the shelf—Ferling was out of town and will show up soon to go thru formality of arrest and bail out—it's disgusting—what's worse is even some intellectuals are saying it's too dirty, I have a hunch the intelligentsia of America is really so gutless they might knuckle under the dumb fat Irish cops in time and it'll be like Germany, a police state. I'm really worried and Bill was always right— However, Rexroth is burning and there are some who won't be gutless so Allen do not worry—write a big poem called WAIL beginning "Wail for the cripples of Morocco crawling on their bellies in the Socco Chico, Wail for the homeless Arab boys sleeping on tables by the sea with their heads in their hands, WAIL for etc. etc." a big super World Fellaheen HOWL instead of just dumb America hepsters—Wail for the boys with their Catch Mohammed pants!—Wail for the outraged American Queers throwing dirty pictures to the wind!—Wail for the seven foot pederasts leading small boys up the hall!—Allen, I just wrote a mad poem and sent it to John Wieners,[51] yes Whalen and I sent him a big mad letter with Corso, him and me poems, and Gary too, all's set, we're all accepted and to be published in the next 3 issues! My poem went: "Pulling off the human drawers of girls!/ Leaving whole pussywillows unblown!/ Because I'm a breathless tree!/" which I read to Ronny Loweinson [sic] the other night in Place ... Wieners took 12 poems from MEXICO CITY & SF BLUES ... Mike Grieg of New Editions is publishing my NEAL AND THE THREE STOOGES in this issue, shall I mail him your GREEN AUTO now?[52] it's at Phil's round the corner ... it was turned down by prissy jealous Berkeley high school boys ... Tell Ansen I'll be seeing him within a year anyhow as, if I make loot this Fall, I'll meet you all in Paris and go to Venice ... I cant get over Paris and it was greater than you'll ever dream in advance!—so I'll meet you there within a year or two ... Allen G., that is so mad, so mad, Allen, that line "Ansen worked on the manuscript (of Bill's) like a great professional pedantic scholar with an unruly library full of dignified ancient manuscripts of the Venerable Bill"!—Gregory wrote a big letter to [William Carlos] Williams last March or April asking for money saying you and I were loaded but he was poor, but somehow it came out sounding like a con organized by us ... Yes, you shd. pick up on Ullman's offer and Florence is a gas ... As to my recent work: poems and some prose, trying to write a huge novel call'd AVALOKITESVARA but at

51. John Wieners was a Boston poet living at the Hotel Wentley in San Francisco. He published the little magazine *Measure* and was writing the poems later published as *The Hotel Wentley Poems.*
52. Ginsberg's long poem from 1953 about his vision of driving with his lover Neal Cassady in "The Green Automobile" was published in *Mattachine Review,* Vol. 5, no. 6 (June 1959) and included in *Reality Sandwiches* (City Lights, 1963).

the last benny sitting it bogged down in metaphysical discussions ... however I painted The Vision of the Goatherds, which is red shepherds looking at a creamy cross in the heavens, with swirling blue clouds around, and also painted (on peotl at P's cottage) more mad flowers exploding out of a (black) pot, and one painting of the yard that I dragged thru the grass like a mad bohemian modern (which I'm not) and painted Smerdyakov in the Garden (nowhere) and painted another flower and painted a girl in bed and finally a chalk of Mary and Joseph but I aint even started yet—O yes, a perfect drawing of Whalen sitting crosslegs with his pipe, called Buddha Red Ears, or did I tell you all this?—Allen, meanwhile, there are big rumors around town here that you were seen several times on the street and in The Place, as tho you were Hitler and nobody wants to believe that you're really "dead"—Also you were "seen" in New York even, and everywhere I go I'm introduced as "that guy that HOWL is dedicated to!" (you rat!)— Cant be famous on my own! So anyway HOWL was cleared in Immigrations Customs Court or whatever (let Whalen explain details) but now local police step in—Write to Frechtman for God's sake, show to someone else if he dont like it, like Cocteau or Genet himself—Al S. [Sublette] is in jail for shoplifting, he will be freed in 30 days for good—My visit to Gregory was a big story in itself—Yes, I will pick up the [Robert] Lavigne painting of Peter, wanta study it—"New Haven Poet man" was John Wieners—(he has already bugged Sterling Lord with his "illiterate" letters ... Gary sent Phil Whalen big Buddha robes—also, Gary's sister is in Mill Valley and I am going to latch on—Send Wieners your and Bill's material and Peter's too and he wants snapshots too, he's open to everything—I think he would be better for GREEN AUTO because I think New Editions is square—When I saw Lucien he wasnt drinking any more, quiet, had to quit, I drank, got drunk, he was very friendly and nice and I told him whole story of everybody and he laughed—In Paris latch on to American Girls at Bonaparte Cafe near the Deux Maggots Cafe near the church St. Germain de Pres, better than men like Baldwin etc. they have loot and wanta be loved, that's how Gregory makes it, but try to live in Montmartre only half hour hike—London nowhere, dont ever even go there, except unless you want to strangle boobies in the fog ... try to go thru Aix and Arles too, and dont miss Louvre, dont miss anything ... (you wont) ... wish I was with you ... now that my mother all settled and happy I feel like becoming happy too—but the 3 girls are arriving soon (Joyce, Elise, Carol) and Neal all blowing hot and big season to begin—New poet on scene, little incunabular Burroughs with glasses called Dave Whitaker ... (17) ... Send me instructions about GREEN AUTO, whether for Grieg or for Wieners. I hear there's a picture of you and Gregory and Laff[53] in new issue of Esquire (for July) and that dumb

53. Laff was the nickname of Lafcadio Orlovsky, Peter's brother.

Rexroth article is in New World Writing no. 11 where I'm "in his small way" peer of Céline and Beckett ... Esquire has turned down what we offered them after a big hasselous lunch where they wanted to stare at me the pricks ... I shd have shoved my prick in their mouth, that's what they really want ... I will write big separate letter to Pete now but also for everybody to read.[54]

Ti Jean

At the end of June 1957, Kerouac wrote to Gary Snyder and Sterling Lord that he realized he had made a mistake moving with his mother to the West Coast. Gabrielle missed her daughter and grandson in Florida, and she had to pinch pennies to make Jack's monthy royalty advance checks from Viking and her small Social Security pension cover the expenses of their three-room furnished apartment and their groceries at the supermarket. After six weeks in Berkeley, Kerouac felt increasingly oppressed by what he described to Snyder as the "general killjoy culture" in California. Since he didn't drive or own a car, he was dependent on his friends or on public transportation for rides, and since Cassady was also broke, they couldn't meet very often. To increase Kerouac's sense of isolation, it had been months since he had heard from anyone at Viking Press. When Cowley didn't send him the galleys of On the Road, *Jack began to worry that his editors at Viking might be so concerned about the obscenity trial scheduled in August for Ginsberg's* Howl *that—as he told Snyder—he "wouldn't be surprised if Viking Press got chickenshit about HOWL being banned and put off" publishing his novel.*

TO GARY SNYDER

[June 24, 1957
Berkeley, California]

DEAR GARY? Just saw dear gary that letter you wrote Phil about how you almost got here, why dont you try also to ship as a deckhand or oiler (wiper) or messboy on freighters or dont you have all these endorsements—lissen, however, by god, you must have forgotten something about California, I know what it's like. I was just in Europe mooning about California and rusht back here and spent all my money doing so and goddam it inside six weeks I remember and realize the real horror of this place

54. On May 31, 1957, Peter Orlovsky forwarded a letter that Joan Haverty had written Kerouac under the impression that he was still living in Tangier. Orlovsky assured Jack that "its going to work out OK for you for she wants to get married, so all your worrying and careful planning is no more needed. But if you still think she is up to some scheme to find your whereabouts theres a new serum that can change the color of skin from black to white or from white to black, you can do a disappearing act in SF."

with its TOO MANY COPS AND TOO MANY LAWS and general killjoy culture and general old dreary oldpeople horseshit. I tell you I dont think I'm gonna stay here at all any more now—not only what happened to me (three instances, Phil and me talking on Chinatown corner stopped by cops, Montgomery and me walking across street fined 2 dollars for red light, and on our way to work [cleaning Montgomery's house] with shovels to boot,55 me and Phil singing drunk in the streets happy interrogated in Berkeley) but what I hear from others and read in the papers and above all sense in the sinister air the very look and feel of this place, shit, how do you expect the Highway Patrol would ever let us go free enuf to putput into town in our little bikes and jalopys for food and wine and "heard you had gurls up there th'other night" and finally we get raided for no particular reason but killjoy and on top of that naturally guys like Rexroth and all dont take such shit, pretty soon there'll be a revolution in this goddam state revolving around whether people should enjoy themselves or not and it's likely to turn into a bloody one, me if I ever lose my temper I'll be the worst one of all, the worst murderer—I feel so goddamned degraded and depressed, and when I read your letter I realized you dont remember the crap of America, naturally you yearn to "come home" but what kinda HOME you think this is gonna be, just wait and see—I keep thinking if I am to build a little zendo for the good guys it should be in Mexico but we all know even the Mexicans are a pain in the ass in a different way, there you have to worry about thieves (least of my worries tho) but worry about tourist cards and going to border and general loneliness of being outside America, in short I just dont know what to do or say or write—with this HOWL and cop issue, I get to feel I aint got to write what I want anymore, even that they'll take away from me, I can always write for private readings of friends but come a day when they start banning my books and dont get money no more will end up scrounging pennies for cornmeal and cant get a drink—O I guess it aint as bad as I see it now—John White says he knows where

HO GARY . . . 10 days later . . . maybe I'm exaggerating things but nevertheless since wrote you this I was stopped yet once more again, for walking on Milvia Street at midnight . . . Boy I wish we could find an alpine-side-lake-cave for more than just summer for all year round and forever, I'd make runs with back packboard for all the wine & saltpork we need . . . well, I dunno . . . anyway these days I'm writing right along, continuing LUCIEN MIDNIGHT, and A DHARMA BUM IN EUROPE, and BOOK OF DREAMS, and typing up all my old sketches to form the BOOK

---

55. In *Desolation Angels*, Kerouac wrote, "We set off for work next morning on foot and just as we were crossing a small side street a cop came over and gave us two tickets fining us $3 each for jaywalking. . . ."

OF SKETCHES (printed as written on the little pages, shortline) so we can discriminate between written-verse and written-prose ... no time to gab about that now—yes, indeed, yes, why discriminate, anything pretty is a poem ... but wanted to tell you, you'd never guess, my prose has reached a new dimension. LUCIEN MIDNIGHT[56] broke it open and now I can tell a crackerjack narrative tale with all kinds of wild spontaneous yowks (as you'll see) in other words I'm getting even better, like Stan Getz the tenor jazz man—there is no real repetitiousness in my work, I've gone far beyond the things now being published in Evergreen and New Editions and etc. and as for LUCIEN MIDNIGHT it is becoming verily the writing of what I hear in Heaven ... I love to do it ... if nothing else, and with all the troubles of this world, I will have the work done ... but now Gary is it truly possible that we can go camp on some river's edge by starlight out by some starmad tablelands and cook up grub like in olden days in this silly Amerika?—I'm anxious to see your reaction to the new development, a Total Police Control creeping up on America and I doubt if Rexroth realizes how Total, I mean not in politics only but on poor bums who try to hop the Zipper or walk down the road or (as I say) take a walk at night ... Incidentally, my mother wants to go back to NY, to work a few days a week, so I'll be helping her back there long before Xmas and so will be in NY in the winter anyway ... I just dont know what to do, thinking of settling down in Mexico City, or out in the Mexican countryside which is of course free and wild wide open western oldtime country with ranchers carrying guns and swinging door saloons and Indians that dont care ... I didnt want to finish this letter, send it on to you, cause I dont want to disappoint you comin back to America ... let Phil [Whalen] judge. I see Phil every day, tonight I went over to drink with him in his shack but when I saw him so quiet and peaceful sitting with George Bernard Shaw wearing the Buddhist brown robes you sent him, I quiet like slipt away to let him enjoy his quiet Saturday evening ... He loaned me Lankavatara and I dig that line THERE'S NOTHING IN THE WORLD BUT THE MIND ITSELF, which gave me a shuddering sight of reality, not shuddering, but I SAW IT.

So maybe you might ask what's Kerouac gripping about? Well, now you tell me, what the hell's the earthly use of Buddhism to me or anybody else? since there's nothing in the world but the mind itself ... Question: what is the nature of the Mind? I know it's imaginary but is the question imaginary? Yes, I know the question is imaginary but if it's all Mind itself, what is the Mind? why call it the Mind? and as I know Mind neither exists nor

---

56. *Lucien Midnight* was published as *Old Angel Midnight*. In *Desolation Angels,* Kerouac wrote, "With my supply of Moroccan pep pills I write and write by candle light in my room, the ravings of old angel midnight, nothing else to do...." See also letter to Ferlinghetti, before January 8, 1958.

does not exist, what's there to do? I mean why on earth (outside sickness and hangovers) aren't people CONTINUALLY DRUNK? Gary, I want ecstasy of mind, nothing else ... why drink, drugs, etc. saltpork and dope as you said ... I want ecstasy of the mind all the time ... if I cant have that, shit ... and I only have it when I write or when I'm hi or when I'm drunk or when I'm coming— Anyway, Gary, if you do come back soon, I'm gonna be anxious to see you, as I was going to say, John White knows where we can get cheap lumber, etc. and has a truck ... but I'm really truly worried about the feasibility of forming our Zendo Bendo in California. Why not Mexico? or maybe I'm crazy ... besides I wouldnt be surprised if Viking Press got chickenshit about HOWL being banned and put off the publication of my book and leave me flat bum broke again ... I don't know, all I know is that I want to live a long time and become a laughing old man of art like Rembrandt and drink a lot and love a lot and smoke a lot and travel a lot, and not worry and be a worry wart.

Blacky Burns said that about you, guess I told you, said, "Whatever Gary does I know he'll always be having a good time"—Phrases from my Desolation diary:[57] "Eat your soup in little doleful bowlfuls and it will taste much better than in some vast tureen"... HEARD ON RADIO: "We're over at Ruby Road/ now, in/ the hay deal"–"I made raspberry jello/ the color of rubies/ in the setting sun? (and stored in snow)–"A mad raging sunset pouring in sea foams of cloud through unimaginable crags, with every rose tint of no-hope beyond. I feel just like it, brilliant and bleak beyond words ... pow ... awful ice field and snow-straws on Jack Mountain"–"To the east it's gray, to the north it's awful, to the west it's raging mad, to the south my father's mist"... "Jack Mountain, your thousand fold precipice overlooks a hundred football fields of snow ... Shull, you lose yourself in the Golden Horn of Bleak"–"Poor gentle flesh, there is no answer"...

Well, Gary old pal, hope to see you soon, and dont let me discourage ya, there's been many a discouragin word in the west afore, yea? Equally empty, equally to be loved, equally a comin Buddha.

Jack

TO STERLING LORD

June 26, 1957
1943 Berkeley Way
Berkeley 4, Calif.

Dear Sterling
    I got the June check from Viking okay.
    Sterling, can you arrange to have Viking put out the last two checks (for

---

57. Kerouac had used this diary as the basis of the first fifty chapters of *Desolation Angels*.

July and August) simultaneously on July, that is, $200. I hate to admit that I'm a fool and long ago admitted I was a bastard, but made another mistake taking my mother out here, too far from her daughter and grandson, she wants to go back to Florida and I want to go to Mexico anyway. If you can have Viking send the 2 checks in one shot this next week, we will be able to manage the move.

Also, do you have any idea when the English check will be coming (the back tax deduction)?—if that were coming real soon, we wouldnt have to bother Viking. You said it would take time.

Also, Sterl, I'm real worried because you never write any more, as tho something was wrong, or is just my imagination? I wrote a long letter to Keith Jennison, also no answer. Is ON THE ROAD going to be published? And if so, what about the final galleys I have to see, and what about the picture of me, and isnt there some kind of promotion or business going on I should know about. I tell you I am lonesome and scared not hearing from anybody. (Needless to say I've gone mad.)

I would appreciate hearing from you, settle my mind and let me write my new book without this eerie silence from everybody.

Anxiously,
Jack

Early in July 1957, after an excerpt of Visions of Cody *titled "Neal and the Three Stooges" was included in* New Editions, *a small press magazine published in Berkeley, Kerouac sent a copy to Malcolm Cowley along with a letter asking his editor when he could expect to see the galleys of* On the Road. *Apparently while in the process of writing Cowley, Jack received a box of the finished books from the Viking Press. He was so overwhelmed he didn't protest that he hadn't been given the opportunity to see the editorial work on his manuscript. Instead, Kerouac tried to get Cowley to agree that "ROAD ought to soften the public" for what Jack envisioned as "the real business at hand," the recognition of his larger aims as an experimental writer. Jack even agreed with his editor's earlier criticisms of* Doctor Sax *and* Desolation Angels *in order to remind Cowley that he envisioned* On the Road *as part of the series of books comprising "the Duluoz Legend." Kerouac also compared himself to Joyce, Balzac, and Proust in the hope that Viking would support what he was trying to do.*

TO MALCOLM COWLEY

July 4, 1957
[1943 Berkeley Way
Berkeley, California]

Dear Malcolm:

Thought you would be amused to see my "untouched" prose in print [in *New Editions*] ... only trouble, the printer made several confused mistakes with long parentheses and other things. As you may remember, this excerpt is from VISIONS OF NEAL.[58]

I got an encouraging letter from Sterling Lord saying the review copies are ready and promotion is underway for ON THE ROAD—when do I get to see the final gallies? Do you know what photo will be used?[59]—Received my copies.[60]

I've been reading DOCTOR SAX with amazement, I can hardly wait to see *that* in print. ROAD ought to soften the public for the real business at hand—If you really want me to write further childhood scenes to insert in SAX, will do—

I'm thinking of writing the second half of DESOLATION ANGELS and can all the sentiment and give those "angels" the works, the subsequent shoddy events all the way to Paris ... when it's all put together and we've removed some of the surplus chronological heaviness (which even I don't like) it will be another "Road" picaresque. This item will take care of 1956–1957 in the Duluoz Legend. After that I want to take the 19-year old novel VANITY OF DULUOZ and give it a twirl to complete the Lowell picture within the Legend ... the last scenes in Lowell, when I was sports writer on the paper and Lowell is seen from another, a kind of Bloom-Dedalus angle. In 1942. Then a big major one about my Pa, to cover the years roughly 1940–1950, including the saga of the "young writer" writing TOWN & CITY and getting published etc. After that all the Duluoz Legend will be complete except for the future years. It will fit right nice on one goodsized shelf after I'm gone; a modern subjective Comédie humaine, a running Recherche du temps perdu.[61]

58. The book was published as *Visions of Cody* by New Directions in 1959 (excerpts) and by McGraw-Hill in 1973 (edited by Joyce Johnson).

59. Kerouac crossed out these two questions in the letter.

60. At the end of *Desolation Angels*, Kerouac described how Cassady and his friends arrived at the Berkeley apartment while Jack was unpacking "a crate of advance copies" of *On the Road*. At the time Kerouac had a guilty sense of being "caught red handed" with the book. Jack handed the first copy to Neal, who was "after all the hero of the poor crazy sad book," but he felt that Cassady "failed to look me a goodbye in the eye but looked away shifty-like." See also letter to Allen Ginsberg et alia, July 21, 1957.

Later Cassady stated explicitly what he thought about his friends Holmes, Kerouac, and Ginsberg taking him as the subject of their novels and poetry. In prison for possession of three marijuana cigarettes in the spring of 1958, Neal sent a letter from the California Medical Facility in Vacaville on August 14, 1958 to his godfather, Fr. Harley Schmitt, a monsignor in Denver. In this letter Cassady described his pride in becoming a legend in his lifetime as a major character in Holmes's *Go*, the hero of Kerouac's *On the Road*, and what Ginsberg called "the secret hero" of "Howl." See Cassady's *Grace Beats Karma: Letters from Prison 1958–60* (New York: Blast Books, 1993).

61. Kerouac later said that unlike Proust in his sickbed, he wrote his memoirs "on the run."

Please try drop me a note with news or without news, you've made me very happy as it is.

As ever

Jack

p.s. Did you write that introduction or will you make it just an article?[62]

p.p.s.s. Incidentally, from Mark 13.11—"Take no thought beforehand what ye shall speak, neither do ye premeditate; but whatsoever shall be given you in that hour, that speak ye: for it is not ye that speak, but the Holy Ghost." (spontaneous language)[63]

As Kerouac described in Desolation Angels, *he and Gabrielle left California in July 1957 "the same wretched way" they had come there, trekking back across the country to Florida on a Greyhound bus. Once he had settled his mother in Orlando, Kerouac made plans to go to Mexico City to escape the Florida summer heat. He typed a postcard to Sterling Lord before leaving Berkeley, and sent another one a week later to Philip Whalen from his sister's house in Orlando.*

TO STERLING LORD

[July 5, 1957

Berkeley, California]

Dear Sterling.... Thank you a million times over, got checks for July *and* August—Also your letter cheered me up more than you can realize—Next week you'll receive an envelope from me containing a new short story for the men's magazine (baseball story), and "cityCityCITY" (which was re-

---

62. Kerouac crossed out this question in the letter.
63. In Cowley's condescending reply on July 16, 1957, he didn't explain why Jack had never been given the opportunity to see the galleys of his novel. Instead Cowley began by commenting on the appearance of the dust wrapper of *On the Road.* The jacket design was by Bill English, a small red, blue, and black abstract cityscape printed on a black background which struck Cowley as "handsome" and "chaste." Cowley said, "I don't know whether it looks more like a devotional work or a handbook of applied sociology. But that's just the appearance it ought to have if it is to receive the sort of serious attention it deserves and we want to get for it."

Cowley suggested that for Kerouac's next book for Viking, he should lengthen *Doctor Sax* with "some more scenes of your boyhood" and submit it by October 1, 1957.

Then Cowley concluded his letter with several sentences of advice. Commenting on the quotation from Mark 13:11, Cowley told Kerouac, "If the Holy Ghost is speaking through you, fine, fine, let him speak. Sometimes he turns out to be the devil masquerading as the Holy Ghost, and that's all right too. Sometimes he turns out to be Simple Simon, and then you have to cut what he says. A good writer uses his subconscious mind and his conscious mind, one after the other, and uses them both as hard as they can be used."

jected by New Editions magazine), and a copy of New Editions Mag. with
NEAL AND THE THREE STOOGES published in it.

On Wednesday my mother and I moving, she to Florida, me to Mexico,
from where I'll write & give you my new address, meanwhile mail will be
forwarded from Berkeley—

Wednesday morning I'm being interviewed by the San Francisco Examiner, for a review of *On the Road.*

Christmas I'll visit my mother and then run up to NY to see you Xmas—
Meanwhile, keep me in touch as you see fit.

Jack

TO PHILIP WHALEN

July 12, 1957
c/o 1219 Yates Ave.
[Orlando] Florida

Dear Phil—

Well, I saw worried Mémêre all the way and today finally we found
a perfect pad for $45 with plenty room and a big shady yard so now I'm
leaving for Mexico in 2 days, where I'll arrive with only $50 but satisfied
that all is well ... the new address will be 1418-½ Clouser St., Orlando, Fla.
so send next letter there, twill be forwarded to my whatever-Mexico address ... Don Allen (occurs to me) thinks the VISIONS OF NEAL novel
he saw is the material from which magical editors at Viking plucked out the
ON THE ROAD book ... tell him they are entirely different alright, being
2 different novels[64] ... Viking publicity dept. asks me now to write an article explaining Beat for Harper's or Sat. Review ... ugh ... have to do it for
tortillas, will go brood by candlelight in dobe hut now and do it. Will write
letter soon—Regards to Les—Avalokitesvara sure made a long world.

Jacko

*In the publicity department of the Viking Press office in New York City, Patricia
MacManus began promoting* On the Road. *Kerouac enjoyed corresponding with
MacManus. She was a devout Catholic and, unlike his Viking editors, she didn't
patronize him. Instead, MacManus wrote him on July 10, 1957, that she'd "joined
the band of Viking enthusiasts who go around buttonholing people and thrusting*

---

64. Kerouac wrote John Clellon Holmes on June 23, 1957, that the Viking Press edition of
On the Road was "just about as originally written." It was the text of the manuscript Kerouac
had typed on the roll of taped sheets of paper in New York City in twenty-one days in April
1951, which he said he had revised very little for Cowley. Some of the confusion stemmed
from the fact that over the years Kerouac had shown editors two different manuscripts with
the title *On the Road.* The second was the experimental "spontaneous prose" book about Neal
Cassady that Jack wrote after *On the Road* in 1951–1952 and retitled "Visions of Neal"; it was
published as *Visions of Cody.*

advance copies of On the Road *into their hands." MacManus asked Kerouac to regard her as a "potential reader" and write her an article explaining the "who, where, what and why" of the beat generation, asking him, "Is it a cohesive segment of the populace—such as ex-G.I.'s? Or is it a whole cross-section encompassing a certain age-group?"*

Kerouac wrote an essay for MacManus titled "About the Beat Generation," which he enclosed in one of his letters during the summer of 1957. It was his earliest and most lucid essay on the subject, defining beat as meaning "down and out but full of intense conviction." Jack also requested an advance on royalties from Malcolm Cowley so he could stay in Mexico City to complete Doctor Sax *under "the conditions" he had started the book there in 1952.*

TO PATRICIA MACMANUS

[July 19, 1957]
c/o 1219 Yates Ave.
Orlando, Fla.

Dear Miss MacManus:

I will write the article and deliver it to you on or before August 15 for sure, the best I can do. Explaining the Beat Generation will be a pleasure and you'll be surprised how much of the concept derives from the New Testament.

Some of those worthwhile birds you're trying to flush out with regard to ON THE ROAD, you might tell them it's not fiction at all but a completely true story. Thank you so much for being an "enthusiast." I was an "enthusiast" for it myself when I wrote it in 3 weeks in 1951 ... have you seen the hundredfoot roll it was written on? Then, when I read it myself for the first time, the other night, I thought it was a very funny book.

As to Life magazine,[65] it seems the English woman in charge of the article just didn't want to believe that I was one of the San Francisco *poets*. She said I might as well have my picture taken with them because I was "cute." But actually I am a poet (as well as prosist) and Ginsberg will probably admit I'm the best in the group ultimately. MEASURE is bringing out my poems soon. Anyway, they just didn't understand that I had written poetry too but they have a slew of pictures of me. I told them about ON THE ROAD but they didn't hear me. I'm afraid I'm not cut out to be a self publicist and will have to rely on someone experienced in the field. They have pictures.

---

65. MacManus had written Kerouac that *Life* had prepared a "picture-story" on the Beat writers, "on the poets, mainly," but that Jack was included in the photographs. She added, "I can't understand how in their dealings with you they failed to ask you anything about your writing ... Time-Life and their vast research apparatus indeed!"

Allen Ginsberg, c/o American Express, Boca de Piazzo, Venice, Italy, has pictures, snapshots that is, a whole dozen or so.

I'm arranging to have a local photographer here take my picture tomorrow night and (if so) you'll have them by July 25. I have no snapshots here now ...

Before leaving Frisco to bring my mother here in Orlando to re-settle her with my sister, I had lunch and interview with Luther Nicols of the SF Examiner, a nice guy indeed, so that's done. I missed Hogan and Caen[66] and a gal from Vogue who was looking for me.

Review copies: Suggestion: William Carlos Williams,
                        9 Ridge Road, Rutherford, N.J. (good friend)

        Carl Sandburg
            Flat Rock, N.C. (?)   (good friend)

        Patrick Henry
            Radio KROW
                Oakland, Calif.   (disc jockey, with
                                          radio plugs)

Incidentally, that famous young photographer Elliot Erwitt has a lot of photos of me taken in 1950 some of which may still be in the publicity files at Harcourt Brace?—Anyway, article on the way.

Thanks for your letter, which relieved some of my loneliness.... (Keith and Malcolm don't write) ... Till later,

                                    Sincerely,
                                    Jack Kerouac

p.s. Am leaving for Mexico City this week, will send article from there ... with my new address.

TO MALCOLM COWLEY

July 21, 1957
[Orlando, Florida]

Dear Malcolm:

Received your fine letter and yes, the edition of ON THE ROAD is excellent—I had many favorable reviews of THE TOWN AND THE CITY and the book didn't sell anyway, so the unfavorable reviews you anticipate probably won't harm the sales and spread of it—I approve of the few cuts you made, too, since it will fit into pocket editions & anyway the story is well-nigh undecimateable [sic].

---

66. Bill Hogan and Herb Caen wrote for *The San Francisco Chronicle*.

Now, Malcolm, I'm depending on you—in order to recreate the conditions under which DOCTOR SAX was written, that is, by candlelight in a solitary dobe hut in cool summer Mexico City, I am going there tomorrow and will arrive just about the time you read this (Tuesday) with only $33 in my pocket, and will start right in on those extra childhood scenes for DOCTOR SAX, as well as an article "explaining the beat generation" for Patricia MacManus for Harper's or Sat. Review—You *must* arrange to have a small sum of about 80 or 100 dollars sent to me, either as an unofficial advance on SAX, or a subsidiary further advance on ROAD, or anything, I am completely at your mercy & that $33 will last me a month and no more, making the absolute deadline Aug. 23—

All my money has gone into resettling my mother in Orlando, in a $45 apartment backyard under huge old trees, my room of my own with typewriter & papers, all settled once & for all, it was worth it to hear her say, "I'll never move again, I'll die right here in Paradise"— This makes me a writing-place & home to come to in the winters, right now it's unbearable *heat* & I can't write at all & as I say I must go to Mexico to simulate the conditions of Sax Childhood, the childlike simplicity of Mexican people reminds me of Memory Lowell uncannily & I want absolute solitude to compose that & other new work—I'm writing Sterling Lord, he will call Viking this week, please Malcolm pave the way for a little food money since we all agreed my advance was a small one—As I say, I don't need much, and God knows how much money there'll be for me in September!—we *know* the book'll sell at least 5,000 copies which means another thousand for me anyway—I predict a sale of twenty thousand and over anyhow—

So Malcolm please assist me on this new work on DOCTOR SAX and have them send me, as a loan or anything, something to feed me in Mexico City till we see the light in the Fall—This is no hoax, I'm taking a chance, being penniless in Mexico is dangerous business not like USA—But I'm going anyway, I feel the call.

Write to me care/of this new address & my mother will forward.[67]

As ever,
Jack Kerouac
1418 ½ Clouser St.
Orlando, Fla.

Leaving on bus with a raisin bread, a pound of sass meat, a pound of cheese, still "on the road" . . .
OCTOBER 1st deadline can do. . . .

67. On July 23, 1957, Cowley assured Kerouac that "there would be no difficulty sending you a little money through Sterling Lord" and wished Kerouac "good luck with your Mexican venture."

Before leaving Florida for Mexico City on July 23, 1957, Kerouac wrote a gos-
sipy letter to Ginsberg, Orlovsky, and Ansen in Paris. He asked his friends if they
wanted Viking to send them copies of On the Road, *and then took particular*
care to warn Ginsberg about the description of him and Joan and William S.
Burroughs as the "fictional" characters Carlo Marx, Jane, and Old Bull Lee in the
novel.

TO ALLEN GINSBERG, PETER ORLOVSKY, & ALAN ANSEN
[July 21, 1957
Orlando, Florida]

Dear Allen & Peter & Alan—

Finally re-settled my mother for good in nice pad here in Orlando,
which has my own room—Cost me hundreds of dollars and's left me desti-
tute but all is set, she says she never wants to leave here & cheap rent of
$45 she can make it herself on her social security monthly checks—So to-
morrow I leave this heatwave horror for cool plateau of Mexico City where
I will arrive with $33 and must write despairing letters to Malcolm Cowley
and agent for money—If Garver[68] is dead, and my rooftop room is taken,
I'll go to 7-peso-a-day Hotel Solin where Esperanza[69] liveth & buy candles
& holy weed & alcohol burner & potatoes & write second half of DESO-
LATION ANGELS—Allen, crafty Cowley wants me to write more childhood scenes for DOCTOR SAX and deliver them by Oct. 1st and I suspect
he will yank phantasie [sic] out of it without my permission, as he yanked
much out of ON THE ROAD (review copies of which are out) (ON THE
ROAD undecimateable unlike SAX) without my permission or even sight
of galley proofs! Oh shame! Shame on American Business!—So I may get
SAX publish't as is by Mike Grieg for the record (free) & let Viking fuck
SAX?—You are very famous now, Allen—incidentally I will be getting money
this Fall undoubtedly & will send you cashier's check for $225 before Xmas
I hope—Reprint people ought to take ROAD any week, it's only 305 pages
as published hard cover—Wild book, by the way—(first Dostoevskian pure
novel in America)—Evergreen Review No. 2 is also great, "Howl," "Railroad
Earth," good Gary, McClure, everybody blowing, nice cover—Elise came to
Frisco mysteriously, Joyce in N.Y. wondering where I am, has $500 to
travel—Rather be poor than bugged—Received your Ansel postcards from
Spain—If all goes as it should, I ought to meet you all in Paris in May—Have
to explain *Beat* for Harper's or Sat. Review, big article, by Aug. 15th—
LuAnne[70] & Neal & Al Hinkle[71] floated into my Berkeley door just as I was

68. Garver had been Burroughs's friend in Mexico City.
69. Esperanza was a morphine addict whom Kerouac wrote about in his novel *Tristessa.*
70. LuAnne Henderson had been Cassady's first wife.
71. Al Hinkle was a friend of Cassady's.

unpacking boxfull of ON THE ROADS from Viking, all got high reading, LuAnne wanted to fuck me that next night, Ow, had to leave (bus tickets)— Saw Stanley Gould[72] & Al Sublette in one mad night that exhausted & scared Elise—Tell Gregory I wrote him letter but where mail it?—Lafcadio brooding in N.Y.—Desolation Angels all scattered—Is Bill alright? will you see him in Paris? does he know I love him? (I mean, in my letters, I never mention him affectionately)—Shall I have Viking mail you copy of ROAD?— dont be bugged by what Cowley wanted put in, on page 6 or so, about "intellectualism" of you & Bill & Joan as against Neal's hard-on hungry purity—Cowley thinks I'm Simple Simon, I'm a fool alright—who will really justify us shits?

Peter, I didnt get that LaVigne painting, no time—Peter, write a mad story, Mike Grieg wants to publish my "hidden geniuses"—you, Jack Fitzgerald, Huncke,[73] Laff, etc. in his NEW EDITIONS—How about a nice essay on Portuguese Baroque by Sr. Alan Ansen?—Don Allen came to Frisco with Jonathan Williams,[74] Whalen doesnt like him much (he's contemptuous of so many things including my way of writing, says "On the Road *ought* to be a good book, the Viking editors spent 3 years revising it")—and Rexroth saying at his big get-together "We who have power with publishers" like, they're all getting hungup on the power poetry gives, not poetry itself—Rexroth says ROAD is great & sent me message saying so—Even Mark Schorer[75] tried to reach me—Anyway, spending all my money *before* I get rich so now I can make me fine pad in MexCity & come home winters, all's finally settled—Now for Panama Street—write to me care of here till I send you Mex address—I'll write long letter soon to all of you—Are you going to file for Guggenheim now, deadline Oct. 1st—I will—Gary coming to Calif. within months, it seems, on freighter—Well, end of sheet.

DIAMONDSHATTERING BULLSHIT

Jack

While in Orlando, Kerouac tried to explain to Joyce Glassman why he had left California after he offered to help her get settled in San Francisco, and why he had been too drunk to befriend Elise Cowen (who had already moved to California from New York) when he saw Elise looking lonely and lost one night in the shadows of the Place, his favorite bar in the city. Joyce had planned to join Elise in San Francisco and live on the money she had been advanced from the sale of her first novel to Random House, but she decided to meet Jack in Mexico after receiving this letter.

72. Stanley Gould was a Greenwich Village hipster.
73. The heroin addict Herbert Huncke was a friend of William Burroughs in New York City.
74. Jonathan Williams ran Jargon, a small press.
75. Mark Shorer was a literary critic and professor at the University of California in Berkeley.

July 22, 1957
1418 ½ Clouser St.
Orlando, Fla.

Dear Joyce—

I moved my mother back to Orlando, leaving me with $33, which I think is a big joke in the family, since she wound up around the corner from where we started & everybody comes around every night to laugh—The review copy of *On the Road*'s unread on the shelf—and now, beyond the bugging stage, I'm becoming enraged so I'm going to Mexico tomorrow on the chance Viking will feed me down there—I saw Elise in Frisco, I was too much for her with drinking gangs behind me—Everything exploded—I was afraid to write to you—But here's your enraged bum—Are you going to Frisco anyway? P'haps you should spend your money on fixing a new pad in the Village, or come down to Mexico & join me after Frisco—Write to me care of here, I'll reply from Mexico City—In the next 6 weeks in Mexico City I want to write by candlelight in a solitary room, think & stare thru the wall—My Buddhist friend Whalen advised me to this noticing I was being set upon too much by family obligations—it's what I was going to do anyway, check vibrations—

So, sweet Joycey, decide what you wanta do—If you care to join me in Mexico City in September or so, come on down.[76] You can buy a Greyhound ticket straight thru from N.Y. to Mexico City, check your luggage straight through—Lush apartments for $20 a month, I'll be in an $11 hovel myself—Frisco was too much, but maybe you shd. dis[h] it & Elise is a little lost, I think—She thinks I'm irresponsible but NO! I'm just SICK! We got a letter from my sister and had to leave or lose the pad—Now I'm broke but conscience-free and ready to do some writing—

I'll write to you next week from my new address—You got a good advance! In a year we'll both be rich & corrupt!

Jack

P.S. $500 can last you 10 months in Mexico & write all you want.

After Kerouac left Orlando for Mexico City, Gabrielle didn't hear from him for nearly a week. Over the radio she learned about an earthquake in Mexico City, and in her anxiety for Jack's safety she wrote a letter to Philip Whalen, asking if he had any news of her son.

76. In *Minor Characters,* Joyce wrote that the morning after she got this letter she gave notice to quit her new job in Manhattan at Farrar, Straus and Cudahy. She told editor-in-chief Robert Giroux that she was going to join Kerouac in Mexico, where she planned to finish her novel, and she bought an airplane ticket to Mexico City for the following month.

TO PHILIP WHALEN
FROM GABRIELLE KEROUAC

July 29, [19]57
[Orlando, Florida]

Dear Phil,

Bless you for a nice letter. I was happy to hear from you. If I'm a little late in answering I was so busy getting myself put up out here. I have a cute little place. It looks more like a camp than that big house I had in Berkeley, but it suits me fine and I love it. One good feature about this place is my very big yard. It's very big and we are blessed with 9 orange trees, 5 grapefruit trees and 4 tangerines. So you see we are well supplied with citrus. The climate has been rather hot, but nights are really cool. Nice to sleep. As you know, the heat got Jack and he left for Mexico on the 23rd. And I fear for his safety now. When he travels he usually sends me cards or letters on the way. So far all I had from Jack was a card from Tallahassee, Florida. I'm really worried. I was thinking he might have stopped to see you again on his way. If so won't you tell me if you have seen him. We talked to the Red Cross but so far no news. If you should hear from Jack, please write to me right away. According to the news that earth quake was pretty bad. Please help me locate Jack. And Phil I was so glad and grateful to you too for getting me a little bell from Gary. I cant hardly wait for it and please thank Gary for me. Tell him I'll treasure my little bell[77] all my life. And now Phil if you should here [sic] from Jacky before me and know his address please forward it quick. I have a pile of mail for him here also checks.

Give my best to Leslie and good night Phil.

Sincerely, Mémère

Kerouac survived the earthquake in Mexico City in his rented room, a place he described to Sterling Lord as "an old 1910 whorehouse built of solid marble & tile & not one crack in our walls." There he wrote his article "About the Beat Generation," which he sent to Patricia MacManus. Soon afterwards he told Ginsberg and Whalen about it, saying he showed that "beat" was a religious movement prophesied in Oswald Spengler's Decline of the West. *Kerouac took with him to Mexico City the copy of this book that Burroughs had given him in 1944, telling him "Edify your mind, me boy, with the grand actuality of fact."*

77. Snyder had promised to send Mémère a bell from a Buddhist temple in Japan.

[August 9, 1957]
Hotel Luis Moya
Mexico City, Mexico
[Postmarked Brownsville, Texas]

Dear Allen—

This is by way of being a letter to Bill also, to tell him that Bill Garver is dead, buried somewhere in Mexico City with Joan [Burroughs], died last month or so—That was the first catastrophe, then I went to Esperanza's hotel, & she's disappear'd, then that night the earthquake which made me tremble and hide under the bed in this hotel room with a 20 ft. ceiling (woke up from deep sleep to what I wordlessly thought was the natural end of the world, then I said "It's a giant earthquake!" and waited as the bed heaved up & down, the ceiling creaked deeply, the loose dresser doors moansqueaked back & forth, the deep rumble and SILENCE of it in my Eternity Room)—One horror after another as usual in Doom Mexico—

Now, a few days later, I walk & see the building that used to say "Burroughs" on it is divided in two, all the windows broken and only "Burrou" left of the name in front—Anyway I wrote the article they want, EXPLAINING THE BEAT GENERATION, all about our visions, yours, mine, Bill's, Philip Lamantia's, Gregory's visions of "devils and celestial Heralds," Joan's, Huncke's, Gary's, Phil's—even Alene's and the Times Square Kid of the Second Coming—I hope they publish the article, in it I show that "beat" is the Second Religiousness of Western Civilization as prophesied by Spengler— I also mention Neal's religiousness and Lucien's attempt to gain asylum in a church, which is really the most Gothic mad event of all—Also, I'm writing new scenes for DOCTOR SAX but I've decided to showdown with Cowley by inserting a clause in the contract against removal of (Gothic) phantasie and, in fact, against extensive editorial fucking-up—I have $17 left, however, and am waiting to be saved—Will start back Sept. 15 and so to New York in October—Joyce wanted to join me here—

I keep thinking of Bill Garver . . . and of November when we were all together here—Have no typewriter and thinking of looking up old painter Alfonso for one, or Donald Demarest of the Mexico City News who mentioned you & Denise Levertov last Sunday in a review about a painter's autobiography (the painter, Lester Epstein, is an "aficionado" of yours & Henry Miller, it says)—I asked Viking to send you copy of ON THE ROAD—O what a lonely room I have, 20 foot ceiling, whorehouse mirrors, no windows, right downtown—Except for writing-work, I haven't got a single reason in the world to be here, especially since Catastrophe No. 3 was my visit to Panama Street, the whores have been driven off the streets *completely* apparently by spreading Cancer of Americanism—And I'm without my holy weed too! WRITE TO ME IN FLORIDA, AM LEAVING

Jack

LATEST LATEST NEWS—I GOT ASIATIC FLU & GOING HOME.
(1418 ½ CLOUSER ST. ORLANDO, FLA.)

TO PHILIP WHALEN

[Mid-August 1957
Orlando, Florida]

Dear Phil,

Got your letter about the malefic flashes and forms just in time to stick them into my article ABOUT THE BEAT GENERATION where I catalog the visions experienced by members of our generation to try to show the general religiousness of "beat" (including Lamantia's and Allen's and all)—(my own, Gary's, etc.)—Well and yes I lived thru the earthquake, which I see by the paper coincides with the birth of Gina Lollobrigida's baby boy who must be a new bosom Buddhy—(maybe Avalokitesvara)—But it was no joking matter as I lay there in my 20-foot ceiling hotel room resting comfortably from the bedbugs of an earlier hovel, and all of a sudden it starts to sway me outa my dreams, creak, crack, up and down, like a ship at sea, and like all the other Indians in Mexico City I get the big feel of God's puttin an end to the world then I hide under the bed and tremble—damage was much worse than advertised so's tourists will come again—Goddamit, been meaning to write to Gary all that time, too, but had no typewriter, then got sick on some kind of infection and barely staggered home, in fact when I got to Orlando I took a cab home and Mémère wasn't in so I curled up and went to sleep in the grass because I couldn't sit up (fever, swolled balls, all)—elephantiasis, my dear—Turns out I had something like strep infection which wouldn't have amounted to anything ner swolled ma balls if I hadn't been dehydrated from not drinking enuf water for 3 weeks (none at all, in fact, just cokes, leery of dysentery)—so that's all for Mexico for now. Did enjoy the churches, good t-bone steaks, movies, especially long whole days spent in my cool windowless room just staring at ceiling and reading Spengler and writing the article—The article is weird, I dunno if they'll even publish it—but I wish you could read it and comment on it for me right now—At least, before a thousand phonies start writing about the beat generation I wanted (as originator of phrase) to sneak it in that it means religiousness, a kind of Second Religiousness (that Spengler spoke) which *always* takes place in late civilization stage, i.e., as corresponding examples, Dionysianism and Pythagoras-ism coming in late stages of Graeco-Roman civilization, and Tao coming in late stages of Chinese civilization, and Buddhism in late stages of Indian civ. etc.—The 2nd Relig. is sublime, it takes place during the coldhearted days of big city skepsis [sic] but it is indifferent to that because it is a reappearance of the

59

early springtime forms of the culture and as such well-rooted—Our Second Relig., whatever it will be, will be rooted in Gothic—greatest example (I name no names) is that amazing Lamantia who was a cool hepcat and then the Angel knocked him off the chair—or take Neal—even you and Gary, tho it is in the name of Buddha you pray, there is that Gothic holiness outcrop of old cloisters in yaw bones, me too—and now finally Burroughs who originally gave me that copy of Spengler, saying "edify your mind, me boy" and "Such a pride is not the pride of a Roman" when I objected to Spengler, saying, "The sea instead of the paintbrush, techniques instead of lyrics!" now finally Burroughs' reception of the word that he is the One Prophet—Anyway, Harpo's Bazaar or SatReview may publish that.—Another bit of work: a chapter for Doctor Sax, for Cowley (he asked), I wrote up that hilarious story of Mémère's about the drunk priest and the sprinkling of pubic hairs in the porkchops,[78] I assure you not nearly as well written as she told it—(how could it be?)—Mémère is stickled to death about Gary and the bells from Japan, and also she wants me to invite you over here of course—if you ever make that trip to N.Y. just include a southern swing on your itinerary—Funny about your and Allen's dreams of [Robert] Duncan as evil wizard—Well, what's new ben hapnin in Frisco with Don Allen, Evergreen No. 2, Rexroth, the [Howl] trial, [...] By the way, if you meet anybody that might possibly have taken snapshots of me (like Lehrman, etc.) tell them Viking Press wants some [unfinished.]

In mid-August 1957, after Kerouac had returned from Mexico City to Florida, he wrote an apologetic note to Joyce Glassman explaining that he'd been too sick in Mexico to wait for her to join him. She recalled in Minor Characters *that "Jack was gone from Mexico City a week before the date on my plane ticket." Still broke, Kerouac asked her to send him the bus fare to New York City so he could be there for the official publication date of* On the Road *during the first week of September, promising not to interrupt Joyce's work on her own novel. Kerouac also sent a brief report to Malcolm Cowley along with new chapters for his novel about his boyhood,* Doctor Sax, *crediting his mother's stories about Lowell, Massachusetts, as the source of some of his new material.*

78. See *Doctor Sax*, Chapter 24, for Kerouac's account of his parents at a party at Salisbury Beach, where Father Duquette "comes up in his bathing suit, plucks pubic hairs from under his trunks and sprinkles them into the sizzling pan [of pork chops] saying, 'They need a little spice'—so that the gang laughter rang by the sea...."

Sunday Aug. 18 '57
[Orlando, Florida]

Dear Joyce—

I barely got home with high fever and unable to walk, which I've since sweated out in the endless heatwave of Florida August—It wasn't Asiatic Grippe but some kind of streptococcus infection that wouldn't have amounted to much except I was dehydrated from not drinking water in Mexico (says my old neighbor doctor)—Anyway, Mexico didnt seem to want me this time and drove me right out.

Well, Joyce, since you have writing to do, you should do just that, now, establish yourself wherever you like and start working, and I'll come up to see you as soon as Viking sends me more money—I already asked them if they needed any "personal appearances"—I'd sure like to be in N.Y. when ROAD comes out! Unless you'd like to ship me $30 and I could take a bus & come stay with you a month—During that month I'll surely collect $ on *something*, perhaps the BEAT GENERATION article for *Sat. Review* which I just sent in—I'd like that, Autumn in New York!

Even the Yorkshire Green Room[79] sounds good to me—I could take long systematic walks every day during your writing-hours—It'd be pleasant to see Lucien, Cessa & Helen Elliott again,[80] or go to the 5 Spot with you—If you really have the money, and you were going to send me some in Mexico, go ahead, send it, and I'll be up—I can easily pay it back this Fall—It's so hot in Florida now I dont do any writing anyway.

Someday you'll see Mexico, right now I just couldn't sweat it out sick and alone—it might very well have removed you so far from the concerns of your present novel as to "demoralize" you in a way. As to Frisco, that would have been a waste of money. Save your money for writing time, then when rich go to Paris—

Well, let me know what you're going to do—all I can do now is wait around.

As ever,
Jack

79. Trying to save money before she left New York to join Kerouac, Glassman had rented a room in the Yorkshire Hotel. She moved to her own apartment on West 68th Street in the first days of September 1957.
80. Helen Elliott had been Helen Weaver's roommate and a friend of Lucien Carr's.

[Mid-August 1957]
1418-½ Clouser St.
Orlando, Fla.

Dear Malcolm:

Here is the first of a series of new chapters for DOCTOR SAX, and where it should be inserted. In 2 weeks I'll send in another, longer one, also based on new anecdotes my mother's been telling me about oldtime Lowell.

I'm back in Florida now recuperating from some damn sickness I caught down in Mexico, one disaster after another sent me staggering home.

If any outstanding publicity or other business should require my presence in New York, and Viking can arrange transportation, I'm ready.

As ever,

Jack

After Joyce Glassman generously sent a thirty-dollar check by return mail for his Greyhound bus fare to New York City, Jack wrote her a grateful and affectionate letter of thanks. With the official publication date of On the Road *only a few weeks away, he was beginning to sense a stir of interest in his book. In his letters the last week of August and early September 1957, Jack told Joyce and other friends that Ginsberg had written from Venice that he'd given Kerouac's address in Florida to a* Time *magazine reporter interviewing him about the* Howl *trial.*

TO JOYCE GLASSMAN

Friday Aug. 23 [1957]
[Orlando, Florida]

Dear Joyce,

Just received your letter, and it came just when I felt better again, and it made me so glad to see the check and hear about "our" apartment, what a good time we can have in there September! ... And dont worry about money I'll get some and I'll pay you back too. What I'll do then, is stay home another week and see that I dont have a relapse, and leave for NY around Sept. 3 so I can get in the day of my publication (get into N.Y. and look at Charles Poore's column) (he gave me a tremendous review in 1950). —So, also, you'll be in that new pad when I get in and I'll go straight there. Meanwhile I got a letter from Peter and Allen in Venice, TIME wants to interview Allen and me, they had Allen fly to Rome so they might conceivably have ME fly to N.Y. so that's another thing I'll be waiting for all next week then I could have your check intact to give back to you. I'm writing to TIME today telling them where I am and that I'm broke.—Say, I wonder if you could do me a favor: call up Viking Press, ask for Pat MacManus of publicity, tell her Jack K. is wondering if she got the article ABOUT THE BEAT GEN. in the mail and what she did with it: tell her it's the only statement I ever made about the Beat Generation, and that is the only statement about it ever made by the *originator* of the idea (3 or 4 people have already written about it) and that tho my article may seem deceptively light-headed it really is the score (immense historical forces carefully considered and the "beat generation" carefully placed therein)—Otherwise there'll be all these impostors having their say-so about the Beat Generation, all except the originator of the term and the idea, which is silly. The article will be understood a little later than now because it has a profound basis. (I compared beatness to the Second Religiousness prophesied by Spengler, an idea that might not go over in Sat. Review of Lit. or Harpo's Bazaar, with their contempt for "rock and rollers" but it's TRUE.)

If TIME doesnt send me a ticket, I'll cash yr. check at my sister's bank and come up anyhow. Meanwhile send me the new address and phone number. Just wait at the pad for mo, I'll let you know app. when I'll be in, just have a drink ready to pour, we're gonna have a ball.

I got a message from Elise, about Frisco newspaper man wants a letter from me, but that's all I heard, message thru Allen G. in Venice. But she must be okay. Oops, that was thru you.

Your parents oughta be pleased you're staying in NY. By the way, are they going to let you publish under yr. real name? I hope so. Your reputation will be no more lurid than Virginia Woolf's after all.

Oh, please write and tell me in detail how and where you met Bob Creeley and what happened and what he said and what he's going to do.[81] You know, he's a mysterious figure and everyone was wondering where he was. Publishes Black Mtn. Review. Is it out yet? the new issue with me in it?

Jai and Kai records, ah, I can hardly wait till I get "home".—We'll have a great time and I always feel better in the Fall but I feel extry fine now because I was so sick. I dont think I'll catch flu or that you'll catch anything from me. I feel too good now. —Well, write to me right away, and I'll answer right back. I can hardly wait till I have you in my arms.[82]

                                                                          Jack

---

81. Glassman wrote in *Minor Characters* that she spent an "uneventful evening around a table" in the Cedar Bar with Robert Creeley, Fielding Dawson, and other poets from Black Mountain College, listening while they discussed the poet Charles Olson's theory of projective verse and "rehashed Black Mountain softball games until two o'clock in the morning."
82. In *Minor Characters*, Glassman recalled that as a lover Jack "wasn't fierce but oddly brotherly and somewhat reticent." She described what usually happened after they made love: "Jack leaves me. He goes into the small back bedroom where I never sleep because there's no radiators there. He pulls the window all the way up, closes the door, and lies down on the floor in his sleeping bag alone." In *Desolation Angels*, Kerouac gave Joyce Glassman the pseudonym Alyce Newman and said that they "were wonderful healthy lovers."

On September 5, 1957, Kerouac was staying in Manhattan with Joyce Glassman when On the Road *was reviewed by Gilbert Millstein in* The New York Times *as an "authentic work of art" whose publication marked "an historic occasion." Jack and Joyce bought a copy of the paper at a newsstand on Broadway just before midnight and read the review together at Donnelly's Irish Bar on Columbus Avenue before returning to her apartment to go back to sleep. Joyce remembered that "Jack lay down obscure for the last time in his life. The ringing phone woke him the next morning, and he was famous."*

A few days later, the Village Voice *reviewer took the novel as "a rallying point for the elusive spirit of the rebellion of these times." With this auspicious beginning, reviews of the book surfaced, as Jack said, "everyfuckingwhere." Most were unsympathetic, as when* Time *accused Kerouac of writing a novel that created "a rationale for the fevered young who twitch around the nation's jukeboxes and brawl pointlessly in the midnight streets."* Newsweek *described the character Dean Moriarty as "a frantic-animal-like delinquent ... a kind of T-shirted Ahab of the automobile," and then praised Kerouac's "fast-tempoed, bop-beat prose." In* The San Francisco Chronicle *Rexroth read the book as a description of "the delinquent younger generation," but he also recognized that* On the Road *was "full of a new language," and he felt that the book was "pretty sure to be the most 'remarkable' novel of 1957." In the swirl of controversy,* On the Road *moved onto the best-seller list for a few weeks, alongside* Atlas Shrugged *by Ayn Rand and* Peyton Place *by Grace Metalious, another French-Canadian novelist from New England, whose book stayed on the list for nearly a year.*

Kerouac found himself besieged by interviewers wanting him to explain the Beat Generation. In late September he appeared on John Wingate's Nightbeat *TV show, feeling, as he said, like "a kid dragged up before the cops." There Jack told millions of viewers that the Beat Generation was "basically a religious generation" and that he was "waiting for God to show his face." In mid-September Ginsberg sent Kerouac a letter from Paris saying he'd seen Millstein's review and "almost cried, so fine and true—well now you don't have to worry about existing only in my dedication [to* Howl and Other Poems*] & I will have to weep in your great shadow." In Lowell, Stella Sampas wrote Jack telling him her response to reading* On the Road.

TO JACK KEROUAC FROM STELLA SAMPAS

Sunday, Sept. 15 [1957
Lowell, Massachusetts]

Dear Jack,

I have just finished reading your book, "On the Road."

Needless to write that you have and are fulfilling all the faith and hopes of the people who have loved you.

In all humility, may I offer my congratulations?

Were only Sammy alive to see how well you have fulfilled his faith in you.[83] "The brotherhood of man in all its glory!" Let's pray that he knows.

That boy whom Sammy loved so—believed in—could live, love and write with such intensity.

Time has improved you.

The boy is a man now and it takes so long to grow up.

The whole family takes pride in congratulating you.

Jim is now in Washington with the Department of State. He is now what is called "2nd Secretary" (big position) and studying law nites.

Michael is in Lowell with his wife and children—working in Bedford V.A. Hospital as a social worker.

Tony is helping Dad at the barroom.

Nick is now married to a German girl and living in Germany. Still with the Army.

Little Helen and her family are living close by now.

Both my mother and father are well and everyone is happy with your success.

Again my sincerest congratulations on the completion and success of "On the Road." May you have many, many more.

Fraternally—
Stella Sampas

Still in New York City at the beginning of October 1957, Kerouac wrote to Ginsberg (who had gone to Amsterdam with Peter Orlovsky to visit Gregory Corso), describing the previous month of drunken "roaring parties" and public appearances. He also dropped a note to the Gloucester poet Charles Olson, who had been rector of the influential arts program at Black Mountain College and a close friend of the poet Robert Creeley.

TO ALLEN GINSBERG

Oct. 1 '57
New York

Dear Allen,

Of course now in a position to send you your $225 sometime this Fall ... Did you see Gregory in Amsterdam? I writing to him separately ... First, you must tell Peter that I wrote him a long beautiful letter about the Russian Soul but mailed it c/o Orlovsky instead of c/o Ansen, Venice, so it's probably still there and he must send for that letter for sure ... it was to you too ... important you shd. read it. Everything's been happening here,

---

83. Sebastian Sampas, Stella's younger brother, who died in World War II.

including this last satori weekend[84] with Lucien and Cessa and kids and Joyce at his upstate country haunted New England house with birds peeking in the holy windows, a big blurred Dostoevskyan party with socialites where I was the Idiot, etc. so mad in fact I could write a novel about just this last weekend, Lucien and I went mad in moonlight haunted house yelling coyote cries and gibbering and seriously insane sitting in our shorts in the old parlor as girls tried to sleep ... then when all sleep I played 4 hours massive musical suck-out of everything in pump-organ incredibly long sonatas, thundering oratorios, shoulda heard ... A guy called Leo Garen (who you better meet, 20, hepcat) will produce a play about Neal if I write it, offers me a weekend in Taft Hotel in room overlooking Broadway with free sandwiches and typewriter if I knock it off, which I might (big play about Neal, horses, the night of the Bishop etc., with you and Peter in it)—But another guy called Joe Lustig backed by money also wants a play about Neal—Meanwhile Hollywood somewhat active on Road, Marlon Brando's manager (his Dad) I heard was interested—Italian publishers bought Road—Grove Press bought Subterraneans on new hard cover bigtime basis—Esquire bought casual baseball story for $400 (all spent now)—Pageant bought articles on Beat for $300—I wrote intro to a book of photos by Robt Frank, to be trans[lated] into French for the English edition (Delpire publishers)—Ferlinghetti getting my Blues by mail—Letter from Charles Olson saying I am a poet, he says, from reading Ontario stuff and "3 Stooges" (by the way, I sent you a copy of the "3 Stooges" New Edition to Venice, did you get it?)—Bob Donlin was in NY. (with evil Hittleman) got photographed by Playboy with me kissing me on street, after photo I fed him hand to mouth in Cedar bar Creeley artist madbar—Donlin and I fell on sidewalk in Bowery, I also fell on Bowery with Stanley Gould

—Unbelievable number of events almost impossible to remember, including earlier big Viking Press hotel room with thousands of screaming interviewers and Road roll original 100 miles ms. rolled out on carpet, bottles of Old Granddad, big articles in Sat. Review, in World Telly, everyfuckingwhere, everybody mad, Brooklyn College wanted me to lecture to eager students and big geek questions to answer ... Of course I was on television big Interview bit, John Wingate show, mad night, I answered angelic to evil questions, big letters poured in saying I was beloved, finally a phonecall from Little Jack Melody[85] ... I had nervous breakdowns, 2, now

84. Kerouac and Joyce Glassman went to upstate New York to stay with Lucien and Cessa Carr and their children. When Jack became so obstreperously drunk that he interrupted a doctor who was prescribing flu shots for the children, Cessa Carr told him "Shut your big mouth!" and he was shocked into what he called a "satori," or brief moment of sudden awakening, what he regarded as a "kick in the eye."
85. Little Jack Melody was one of Burroughs's acquaintances in New York City in the 1940s. Melody was arrested with Ginsberg, Huncke, and Vickie Russell in 1949 after a $10,000 theft of jewelry and furs.

I got piles and I lay up read [Dostoevky's] *The Idiot* and rest mind ... I had final evil flips of evil spirits and most insane dreams of all time where I end up in leading big parades of screaming laughing children (wearing my white headband) down Victory Street Lowell and finally into Asia ... (parade is intended to cover me up from cops, when they look kids surround me hide me singing, finally cops join parade happy and it ends big blur of robes in Asia)[86] ... I been preaching Peterism, on TV too, about love, preaching Nealism, everything, I have just made big final preachment in American that wd. flip you if you knew details ... big roaring parties finally where I see old enemies in a blur, shouting round me—(Bill Fox, etc.) ... news that Norman Mailer pleased with me, telegram from Nelson Algren praising me, etc. etc. in short we dont need press agents any more (I told Sterling to leave minor details of our poetry & Burroughs to us, he is busy with contracts and $$$ and bewildered by yr. innocent demands, you being poet do not realize the madness of NY)—You will when you get back— NOW LISTEN VIKING WANTS TO PUBLISH HOWL AND YOUR OTHERS AND ALSO GROVE. THEY RACING TO REACH YOU FIRST. TAKE YOUR CHOICE. I THINK HOWL NEEDS DISTRIBUTION. IT HAS NOT EVEN BEGUN TO BE READ.[87]

TO CHARLES OLSON

Oct. 12, 1957
[New York City]

Dear Olson—I preened up like a turkey cock when I got your letter—[88]

"O peace, mother, for the mammothness
of the comings & goings of the ladders of life"

86. Kerouac included this dream in his *Book of Dreams:* "I had a white bandage on my head from a wound, the police are after me around the dark stairs of wood near the Victory Theater in Lowell...."
87. On October 10, 1957, Ginsberg assured Ferlinghetti, who was traveling to New York, that he had no intention of switching to a Madison Avenue publisher. He urged Ferlinghetti to look up Kerouac "even if he's drunk in Bowery & hard to reach," because City Lights should publish all his friends' work: "If you follow Corso with Kerouac & Burroughs you'll have the most sensational little Co. in US, I wish you would dig that, anyway—we could all together crash over America in a great wave of beauty. And cash." On February 27, 1958, Ginsberg again reassured Ferlinghetti that he would stay with City Lights: "Best put book out in cheapest & simplest possible form as before, City Lites [sic] Pocket series is both eccentric & distinguished, as is."
88. Shortly after the closing of Black Mountain College on September 21, 1957, Olson relocated with his family to Gloucester, Massachusetts. There he had written to Kerouac that he'd been impressed with the prose sketch "Neal and the Three Stooges" in *New Editions* and selections from the prose poem "Old Lucien Midnight" in *Combustion* magazine. Olson also said he had spoken highly of Kerouac's writing to Don Allen, "claiming ... you as a poet, on the basis of that Major Hoople swag in *Combustion*.... It's a tight form—and delicious."

is surely mighty poetry.... so you too be poet.... We sent all my perms [poems] (200 pages) to Ferlinghetti to publish—others now in [John] Wieners' pubs (Measure?)—Big N.Y. poetry readings being arranged by big press agent Joe Lustig OR 9-0768 (phone) unless you feel the renascite [sic] of English poetry shd. be confined to the humble ones[89]—when I get my typewriter I write you proper letter—In writing give my love to Robt. C[reeley].

Jack Kerouac

By mid-October 1957, Kerouac was back in his mother's cramped apartment in Florida. Gabrielle gave Jack the small bedroom while she slept on a couch in what he told Joyce Glassman was "the kitchen-livingroom-bedroom." Kerouac set to work writing a play and planned another book about his childhood, Memory Babe, *for Malcolm Cowley. Despite the excellent sales of* On the Road, *Cowley remained unimpressed with all of Jack's unpublished manuscripts. In September 1957, the same month Cowley wrote a favorable review of James Gould Cozzens's best-seller* By Loved Possessed *for* The New York Times, *Cowley described* Doctor Sax *in a Viking Press memorandum as "an exercise in self-abuse." Cowley also rejected* Tristessa *as "even more (if possible) impossible. It raises the question whether Jack has been completely ruined as a publishable writer by Allan Ginsburg [sic] and his exercises in automatic or self-abusive writing." In October 1957, after turning down the manuscripts of* Desolation Angels, Doctor Sax, *and* Tristessa, *Cowley wrote curtly to Sterling Lord that what he wanted from Kerouac was simple. Any book would do, "so long as it was a story and about people."*

Receiving no encouragement from the editors at Viking, Kerouac sent a flurry of notes to Pat MacManus in the publicity department. She wrote back describing the parties he was missing and told Jack that she sensed "an overtone of slight melancholy" in his letters.

---

89. Early in 1957, before Ginsberg had left for Tangier and was, as he put it, rushing around New York City trying to connect "everybody up with everybody else" to get small press poetry books written by himself, Creeley, and Denise Levertov reviewed by the influential New York journals such as the *Partisan Review* and the *Hudson Review,* he had contacted Olson to explain what Kerouac was doing. Ginsberg wrote Olson from Paterson, New Jersey, on February 18, 1957 (erroneously dated 1956 in the Olson archives at the University of Connecticut Special Collections Library), that

> Jack's material is not historical saga [like Olson's *Maximus Poems*] but personal. The only way I know to stay solid is to keep my individual firsthand feelings & what I've seen & fucked; or goofy imaginations of Poe in attic, still strictly personal, actually each poem a confession, for Jack each novel a confession or vision—of someone he loves usually.

[October 15, 1957
Orlando, Florida]

Dear Pat—

Well I'm back home and have already written that 3-act play they wanted on Broadway. Later activities of Dean. Funny. Now all I need is a good fast new typewriter to write the new novel about childhood for Malcolm.[90] That'll take a month [strike-out] 3 months. Then I be back in NY with my Maw. The play, if you wanta see it, will be at Sterling Lord's inside 10 days, typed. How is Keith [Jennison]? Tom [Prideaux]?[91] Just wanted to say hello to you.

Jack

In October 1957 Lawrence Ferlinghetti was acquitted of the charge of publishing and selling obscene and indecent literature when Judge Clayton Horn ruled in a San Francisco court that Howl *had redeeming social value. About to publish Gregory Corso's* Gasoline *in his City Lights Pocket Poets series, Ferlinghetti asked Kerouac for an endorsement of Corso's poetry. Jack sent Allen, Gregory, and Peter Orlovsky a letter quoting what he had written about Corso, and telling the "Gang" about the play he had just completed. Kerouac followed this letter shortly afterwards with one to Neal Cassady, going into more detail about the play and telling Neal that there were parts in it for all his friends.*

TO ALLEN GINSBERG

[October 18, 1957
Orlando, Florida]

Dear Allen and Gang—

I've just sent in my 2 cents to Ferling on the subject of Gregory's poesy as follows: "I think that Gregory Corso and Allen Ginsberg are the two best poets in America and that they can't be compared to each other. Gregory was a tough young kid from the Lower East Side who rose like an angel over the rooftops and sang Italian songs as sweet as Caruso and Sinatra, but in *words*. 'Sweet Milanese hills' brood in his Renaissance soul, evening is coming on the hills. Amazing and beautiful Gregory Corso, the one and only Gregory the Herald. Read slowly and see."

(Okay?) As you know (or do you?), Ferling asked for my BLUES from Sterling and we mailed them to him ... I told Ferling if he follows up to

90. Later Kerouac put aside this novel, *Memory Babe*, when Cowley indicated that he didn't want to read another book about Kerouac's childhood after *Doctor Sax.*
91. Tom Prideaux, like Keith Jennison, worked at the Viking Press.

call my book BLUES ... nice sequence, HOWL, GASOLINE, BLUES!!! Meanwhile I typed up "Zizi's Lament"[92] and sent it to Don Allen, who crossed me in the mail with your preface to GASOLINE which is alright, in fact rather good ... especially "hip piss." So all's swinging ... but here (I think, I hope) is the truly great news: I wrote a play, a 3 act play for Broadway or off-Broadway, *one,* definitely Leo Garen will produce it in his 2nd Avenue Yiddish theater but we also have Lillian Hellman and big producers on the line, big press agent Joe Lustig who is also going to organize such immense poetry readings in the Spring that it will be worth all your while to come home early Spring and do it ... he wants to do it with jazz and I'm going to tell him definitely to play a number, let a poet read a poem, play a number, let a poet read a number, but NOT mixup jazz and poetry together like SQUARES OF SAN FRAN. Joe will take all our advice, he is nice Yiddish saint, in fact Allen you must ally yourself with him and advise him, to have people like Chas. Olson and Gary read instead of Richard Howard and Popa Ididoud (tho he sounds like he might be interesting). The play will be called BEAT GENERATION and is only the beginning ... meanwhile too Leo Garen is eager to see Gregory's plays; you can reach this mad little (director) cat thru Joyce Glassman, 65 West 68, get on ball. Plays! Productions! Leaping from the author's box to the stage to make flower speeches! Homburgs! Operas! Red linings to black cloaks! Millions! Money! Cunts!—Drunk on the Bowery like Jack Dempsey![93] Falling on our head with Stanley Gould in the Ritz! Early morning whiskey sours in the White Horse! Throwing garbage pails at Caitlin Thomas![94] Kissing the feet of Nuns!—Do you rats realize that the Fathers of St. Francis of Assisi Church 34th Street New York are actually saying a Mass for my spiritual and temporal welfare, at the request of 2 secret Dostoevskyan nuns in a Connecticut monastery, because of what I said on TV!—I wrote my play in 24 hours, no less, couldn't sleep till it was done, there.—All argues in favor of spontaneous.—Here's the big news I wanted to say: ALLEN! You will play Allen Ginsberg in the play! Rush to NY and become big actor, scream Rimbaud on the stage, sprawl between the Bishop's mother and Aunt in Neal's imaginary livingroom! It's all about the Bishop Night, preceded by a day at the races and a first-act scene in Al Sublette's kitchen with big Al Hinkle and little Charley Mew! A Comedy! The dialog pours like waterfall across the pages!—big part for Peter as Peter, Peter singing "Can't recall the hours, flowers" (Peter, please send me title and words of that tearful rock and roll number so I can insert it in playscript in

92. An unpublished manuscript.
93. Jack Dempsey was a boxing heavyweight champion.
94. Caitlin Thomas was the widow of the Welsh poet Dylan Thomas, who died of alcoholism in 1953.

time for big producers to understand with cigars in mouths—big part for Peter finally Peter Allen and Jack start screaming holy holy holy in front of Bishop ... I have a hunch I've re-done the American Theater with this one ... it's not even typed! I just finished it! Leo Garen is driving to Florida to see it! Airplanes are flying overhead!—When I get back to N.Y. around New Year I'll take up business on Burroughs ms., meanwhile Don Allen has it, I had Joyce Glassman call Philip Rahv, answer forthcoming.... Peter's gazeelee on Moon beautifull ... all beautiful, Gregory, Allen, all ... My latest poem is: "Flesh the payer/ spirit bills." (I call them little ones "Emilies"[95])—very latest poem: "I wooed her with the soft young glue."— ooo— (meaning America, me young once)—I wrote a poem "Too ashamed to show my asshole to Jesus Christ" and next day I had piles.

Jean-Louis

P.S. You won the trial in SF.[96]
My money not in yet—soon!

P.S. Germany just bought ON THE ROAD, Rowohlt Verlag Publishers. Allen—My money so far has been one short story loot—but more coming & in January $8,000 royalty check! When & how & where you want your loot? (Rumor in N.Y. that I dont want to pay you!)
Peter—Did you send for that big letter c/o Orlovsky in Venice American Express? You must get it—Also, be sure to send me title & words of the "flowers" song (you sang to Lucien with tears in yr. eyes)—

TO NEAL CASSADY

[Late October 1957
Orlando, Florida]

Dear Neal—

Come on you ole sonumbitch and get on that typewriter and write me your first letter in 5 years, if not to me, who?—Tell me what happened after I left, LuAnne, etc.—My mother and I rode 4 days and 4 nights on the bus to Florida and got a $45 a month pad a week later then I went to NY for publication of my book & everything exploded—To the point, where, for instance, Warner Bros. wanted to buy On the Road for 110,000 dollars with me playing part of Sal Paradise and my agent turned it down because it

---

95. Brief poems in the manner of Emily Dickinson's lyrics.
96. Ginsberg, Orlovsky, and Corso had followed the coverage of the *Howl* trial in *Life* magazine. On December 3, 1957, Orlovsky wrote to Neal and Carolyn Cassady from Paris that he and Allen had seen Neal's picture in the *Life* article about "how Allen's Howl was progressing, just the side of your face with your hair back, yes it was you, Gregory just discovered it. We all said together, ha Neal was there seeing how things was going."

wasnt enuf money or something[97]—Everybody asking me "WHO will play Dean Moriarty" and I say "He will himself if he wants to" so boy maybe truly you can become movie star with luck (tho my girl Joyce says not to wish that fate on you)—Allen in Amsterdam with Gregory and Peter writes that you should play the part yourself, and him Carlo, and me Sal—But meanwhile I was asked to write 3-act play for Bway, which I did, just sent it in the other day, big shot producers reading it, again a part in there for you, for me, Allen, Peter etc. It's the story of ACT ONE You and Al Hinkle walk in Al Sublette's kitchen, play chess while Al and I toast Khayyam tokay and Charley Mew figures horses, Connie standing around, finally you and Charley and me play flute solos straight off that Visions of Neal tape of 1952 ... crazy scene. SECOND ACT: You and me alone at races, playing third choice, Pulido, dreams, talk, Cayce, girls, beer in cartons, etc. including the horse that spilled in the backstretch and nobody cared—ACT THREE[98] the night of the Bishop with Donovan, Bev, Carolyn, Allen, Peter, you, me, Bishop, Bishop's mother and aunt but all of it changed to Lynbrock L.I. to New York Scene and the Bishop is "of the New Aramean church"—nothing incriminating—I mean only grayfaces wont like it—Meanwhile magazines demanded shorts, so sold Baseball tale to Esquire for 500, article on Beatness to Pageant for 300, blues tale to Playboy for 500, and sold book [*On the Road*] to German and Italian publishers—Appeared on TV, John Wingate's NIGHTBEAT before 40 million viewers and talked about God monstrously had Wingate fluttering thru his prepared questions sweating I sprung God on him and he sprung dope on me—went out got drunk with him after show—Little Jack Melody phoned me at TV studio—Had hotel room with publishers drunk rolling out my roll-Road-ms. on carpet for screaming interviewers—Bway producers bring beautiful models sit on edge of my (girl's) bed, ugh, wanted to make it so much with so many—Went on 2 wild weekends with Lucien and wife and two kids to upstate cold nippy Fall red-apple country, drunk—Everything happened and I was wondering: what has all this done to you, are people bugging you & chasing you in Frisco? Man, that Mercedes Benz ride of ours to Mexico City on El Paso Hiway not far off, I already (come next year) got enuf money to buy one!—Main thing is movie sale, Marlon Brando definitely interested, soon's he crawls outa bed and reads ROAD he buy it, meanwhile Paramount and Warners bickering—gossip columnists report that Slim Gail-

97. Warner Brothers had offered $110,000 for the film rights to *On the Road*, but since Paramount and Marlon Brando were also interested in the book, Sterling Lord hoped to get the studio to raise the bid to $150,000.
98. Act Three was improvised and filmed in January 1959 in a Lower East Side loft studio with Allen Ginsberg, Peter Orlovsky, Gregory Corso, Larry Rivers, and others. Photographed by Robert Frank, co-directed by Alfred Leslie, and narrated by Kerouac, it was released as the short film *Pull My Daisy* later in 1959.

lard[99] will play himself in movie version! (we gets to get hi with Slim!)—This time I no make faggot scene, but girls, girls, girls—only a few feelers from a few faggots in mail—Went out drank ate with Henri Cru,[100] Bob Donlin (who was snapped by Playboy)—everything happened—I was drunk all the time, no more wine, just whiskey, which by the way is much easier than wine—All the time wondering, "What is Neal thinking?" and if I sell movie this Christmas, as likely, as I pray, for will convert 150,000 into monthly trustfund checks like Burroughs, not squander, will shoot right out to Frisco, go stay with you at Los Gatos pad with money to burn on groceries, kicks, etc.—Promised Buddha would go meditate whole month in Mountain solitudes eat no meat if sell movie, spend whole month praying for all living creatures—Fathers of St. Francis of Assisi church 34th St. New York saw me on TV talk about God and Francis, and are giving a mass for my spiritual and temporal welfare—I also correspond now with mad nuns at a monastery who love me—Write! I tell you more! Buddy as ever

Jack

P.S. After brot [sic] mother to Florida I took foolish trip to Mexico City just in time for earthquake. Went to find Esperanza couldnt, she must be dead, went to find Garver, he dead, died in July, alone.... Finally old Garver dead—I cried in Mexico, alone.... got drunk in Mexico, alone, stayed only 10 days and rode that bus again and again thru nightmare New Orleans again and again—Didnt even green [smoke marijuana], or looked for any, put it down now—Saw Dick Hittleman in NY and he says "Come on man go down to Mexico and make it with Diane, she needs somebody like you" I said "You tryna kill me man?"—wow—Had for awhile swollen balls and no sex, suddenly got letter from Gary Snyder in Japan saying "I pray to Avalokitesvara Buddha and you be well quick" and suddenly as I read letter my balls went down and I been straight ever since and went to NY and balled with chicks and am straight again—???—The chick I really need is Gary's sister Thea—questionmarks mean: How come Buddha answers all prayer? Man on TV (Wingate) said: "Can you tell us to whom you pray? and I said "To my brother Gerard, my father Leo, Jesus Christ, Avalokitesvara Buddha, and Our Mother in Heaven." Meanwhile, man, here's what: when I get check for $300 every month trustfund, I travel and ball all over world, to India, Japan, racetracks, Mexico, Europe, Paris, all over, I move fast and

---

99. Slim Gaillard was a jazz guitarist, pianist, and singer best known for his duets with Slam Steward as "Slim and Slam."
100. Henri Cru was a friend Kerouac had met at Horace Mann Preparatory School, who had introduced him to his first wife, Edie Parker. Edie was also in New York City during the official publication of *On the Road*. She remembered that Jack took her to a book party, but he got so drunk on whisky highballs that he fell on the street outside a Village bar and then forgot that she was there. She didn't see him again for several years.

when I make a million my monthly check will be $8,000 and that's when you and I make time in your old plan that Lazy Charley was gonna bring you, no Lazy Jack is the system.

Please give my love to Charley Mew, Al Hinkle, and Al Sublette hey—if you see them—I saw Jane Belson at a mad party in NY too—She was scared of me, I was drunk—My exwife Joan got divorce in Juarez and now wants me to sign adoption papers so her new Arab husband Aly adopt ... I will move me and my Maw back to Richmond Hill, Long Island next spring and then build me a log cabin on Lucien's land upstate and them will be my headquarters.

Now come on, Neal, reason I didnt see much of you in Frisco this last time was shortness of money ... no other reason—so write and let's get on the ball here, HIBALL

JACK

At the end of October 1957, Kerouac wrote his old girlfriend Helen Weaver, whom he'd seen wearing a striking dress at one of the parties he'd attended with Joyce Glassman the previous month. Kerouac told Helen that he'd been so drunk during his interviews he wondered if he "screwed up" his chances of making On the Road *a best-seller. Jack also wrote his friend Lucien Carr, asking for the phone number and address of his second wife Joan Haverty, who had remarried.*

TO HELEN WEAVER

[October 22, 1957
Orlando, Florida]

Dear Helen,

When I got the package from Farrar, Straus I thought it was Giroux sending me a book—when I saw the cigars I laughed and knew who it was— It was very sweet of you and they're damn good cigars.

When I saw you at Bob Merims' party I wanted to talk to you alone, even go off with you, but J. was watching me like a hawk and I didnt want to make her cry. I dont wanta hurt anybody. You hurt me when you took that damn psychoanalyst's advice and said I couldnt stay, it should have made no difference to you. But I also understood your point of view. You'd do a whole lot better goin to confession than going to those fakes, and confession is free. Ho ho. I'm not tryna proselytyze you, I dont even go to confession myself. But can I see you when I come back to N.Y.? I know where you live from Henri Cru showing me your door. We can sing "My Fair Lady" again ... I'll sing you my new version of Sinatra's "Chicago." [....] On the Road is slipping off the bestseller list, I was wonderin what went wrong ... Steinbeck, Mailer, [James] Jones, were all raging bestsellers. I guess I'm really made to be a poor Zen lunatic, which is alright with me.

But I do want to sell the book to the movies, it's in the works and looks good, then I'll establish a trust fund and be free to wander anywhere I want anytime and help feed my companions. Wanta go to India and Japan ... write books about it. Also to work on the screenplay in Hollywood, they even asked me to act in it as Sal, so's to write a book about Hollywood ... my book about Hollywood I promise you would be the end. Marlon Brando's father, his manager, is interested and calls my agent. Etc. You looked lovely that night at Merims'—in that lost generation dress. I was very drunk. I was sposed to appear on further tv shows but was too tired from drinking ... I wonder if I screwed up my chances of making it a best-seller ... well, trying to get as much as you can is infinite perturbation ... I like poetry better than nervous wealth.

I'll be in New York around after New Year's and I'll call you at Farrar or at home. This time I'm staying with my mother in my aunt's house in Brooklyn ... Till I see you

As ever,
Jack

p.s. Tone of letter tight but that's because aint talked to you for long time.

TO LUCIEN AND CESSA CARR

[October 22, 1957
Orlando, Florida]

Dear Lou & Cessa—

If you still have Joan Haverty Aly's phone no. send it to me ... I presume her address was on it ... you remember I crumbpled [sic] it and threw it away in yr. livingroom ... I just wrote to her as Joan "Kerouac" at her old address hopin it all be forwarded ... since Cessa and Jerce[101] think I should get it over with.

We forgot our greatest joke of all, Burroughs' limey joke:

Two limies were sitting in the front row of the burlesque when a big blonde come on undressing and Limey number one sez: " 'Ey, ow do you like *er?*"
Limey number two sez "Oi've ad er." ...
Then comes the redhead bombshell. "Well, what about
ER?" "Oi've ad er." ...
On comes the brunette.
"What about er, Archie?"
Archie: "Shh, I'm *aving* her naow."

---

101. Joyce Glassman.

A good one for Blair.

If everything works out, movie sale etc. I'll be livin in Richmond Hill again next Spring, I hope. Then all's I gotta do is build me a lil cabin in Rensselaer valley up yonder, around the mountain from you . . .

As to Al Hendrix of the Post, call him up and tell him Jack says not to mention you . . . you're not supposed to be mentioned,[102] his talk about you was after the interview was over, when Pat MacManus Obregon O'Toole and I were talking about where to go that night. But if you want, tell him I said to keep it cool about you . . . Besides, they haven't run that story yet and proly won't. But I'm pretty certain he won't mention you and understands.

Jerce says On the Road is off bestseller list because they don't have enuf copies in stores but I think it's just old Kerouac luck . . . it really shoulda been a bestseller like Mailer, Jones, Steinbeck,[103] just as good a book— Enclosed is AP article might amuse you about beep-beep. Hoping erl is well, Cessa, Simey, Caleby, and Potchki Dribblerbottom. Since ben back home bought 5 quarts Schenley and 10 cases coca cola and drink nothing but Rye and Coke now, great drink.

Wrote a play, Lillian Hellman Productions wanta see it. It's too short. I dunno if it's any good. Dialogue good. Got big letter from Pat MacManus opening with "Querido Amigo (as we say in the old country)"—

Getting to know you

Jack

In October 1957 Kerouac wrote to Stella Sampas, who still lived with her parents in the family home at 2 Stevens Street in Lowell. She had sent him a batch of clippings from the local newspapers that she thought he would enjoy.

TO STELLA SAMPAS

[Postmarked October 25?, 1957

Orlando, Florida]

Dear Stella

Just wrote a big mad insane letter to Charley[104] he can cull from for his column or just keep for momento or just as letter from friend. . . . I told him I was coming to Lowell early this winter February or so and I'll go to 2 Stevens street and look you up, Stella . . . and all the others you want me to

---

102. Lucien Carr didn't want to be part of the interview with Kerouac.
103. Kerouac was referring to Norman Mailer's *The Naked and the Dead* (1948), James Jones's *From Here to Eternity* (1951), and John Steinbeck's *The Grapes of Wrath* (1939).
104. Stella's oldest brother, Charles Sampas, wrote a column for *The Lowell Sun.*

meet—I'll have to get me a warm coat for that trip, Florida is mighty warm all year round—Many things we can talk about—I got your clippings and enjoyed them. When I first heard about the beep satellite I laughed, it's just a toy, and even if it ever becomes a manned satellite with war-controlling instruments, well war is just a toy too, big men play with toys.... In the freedom of eternity who cares? Dont you know the world is uncreated and therefore eternal? Havent you read the Lankavatara Sutra?—Read the books of D. T. Suzuki,[105] they have them in our library on Merrimac St.... Every night I thank God that it's only a show in His mind. Since thought is unthinkable, and the world a thought in God's mind, what world is there? Think of your dead ancestors, now did they really truly appear and then disappear? T'would seem to me that the nature of appearance and disappearance is in conformity with the nature of non-appearance and non-disappearance.... Go to the source for your spiritual comfort. The world is a primordial mystery and never even happened. Five falling stars every minute on a dark night mountaintop I saw. The name of the mountain was Desolation Peak. I was in bliss. My only friends were deer. Two nuns just offered a mass for my spiritual and temporal welfare, to be given by the fathers of St. Francis of Assisi on 34th Street Church N.Y., and I wrote to them: "Reverend Mothers, Pray for all living creatures." And there are living creatures more numerous than the sands of the ocean out in space ... not only out in space but within into your own body.... there are innumerable living creatures infinitely in every direction in and out (!) Rest and be kind.

I wrote a poem called Prayer:

> God, protect me!
>   See that I dont defecate
>   on the Holy See
>
> See that I dont
>   murder the bee
>
> God, be kind!
>   Free all your dedicate
>   angels, for me
>
> Or if not for me
>   for anybody
>
> God! Hold fast!
>   I'm dying in your arms
>   delicately

105. Eminent Buddhist scholar.

Ah God be merciful
to Princeton me

Ah God alack a God,
nobody farms
amnesty

As ever
Jack

Regards to the folks

After the furor over the publication of On the Road, *Pat MacManus had tried to place Kerouac's article about the Beat Generation with* Esquire *magazine, which had already contacted John Clellon Holmes for a piece on the subject.* Esquire *had bought a Kerouac baseball story, "Ronnie on the Mound," from Sterling Lord for their May 1958 issue, and they agreed to run Kerouac's essay (retitled "Aftermath: The Philosophy of the Beat Generation") in their March 1958 issue, to follow Holmes's "The Philosophy of the Beat Generation," scheduled to appear in February 1958. Holmes wrote to Kerouac about his article, saying that he intended to write about* On the Road *and asking permission to quote from some of Jack's letters to him. Primed with "a snort of whiskey" followed by black coffee, Kerouac replied with a letter describing his life in Florida, where he was using his new Royal standard typewriter to copy a Buddhist scripture onto a roll of Teletype paper.*

TO JOHN CLELLON HOLMES

[November 8, 1957
Orlando, Florida]

Deal Ole Daddy John—
    Liz[106] had the wrong address, it's CLOUSER not Culver.... Mr. Clouser himself after whom the street (shady little dirt road) is named is now out there on his ladder pulling down ripe grapefruits—In my own yard ($45 a month backyard apartment) I have grapefruit, oranges, & tangerines—and one particular holy tangerine that fell on my head, square on the middle noggin, as I was reading the Diamond Vow of God's Wisdom (vajrachedikkaprajnaparamita) [sic] with a little change by J.K. the Buddha-Dog........ copy of which, I'm typing on a 30 foot roll, scroll, will show you this early spring or wait a minute, around New Years.... are you coming to NY for NY's eave? Under New Years Eave sleepeth the Firestone Tire babe his candle put aside.... Well John, hope you can wade thru this sea of fun, just had a snort of whiskey and now blackcoffee....

106. Holmes's sister.

Yes, go ahead and do whatever you want in the article, I trust you to represent me as I am and as you know me, all the quotes are okay ... I hope you expand the Hemingway quote to explain what I meant by "fool," i.e., a bull dies a big death, too big to snicker over or call "spectacle"....[107] And as for the "rattling" trucks they dont rattle any more being big wellbuilt diesels by now, you might mention I meant the Forties Trucks.... I'm dying to see the article in toto and by the way I had no idea somebody'd taped the Nightbeat interview, can you tell me who the crewcut *Esquire* guy was who had it? Would that be Clay Felker or Rust Hills Jr.? (Rust Hills Jr. reminds me of your "appletart autumn rare brief smoky thoughts".... How beautifully you write.... "It fills one with rare, brief, smokey thoughts and old imaginings" and where you say "addled by the sun" (after red wine nap) you sound like Old Hawthorne with the unmendable hole of his mind, a big New England Giant turning over in the hot sap wine apple cider haystack sun ... I meant to say, there, you were a Giant Hawthorned [sic] turning over to sleep in the sun that turns apples to cider & gets ants drunk.... I havent got Liz's letter yet but Viking forwards.... Have you got Stan Getz's LOVER COME BACK? I just bought "Trombone for Two" with J.J. [Johnson] and Kai [Winding] but I dont have a box to play it on, the first number whiffenpoof song is the end. Last night I heard [P.P.] on TV wailing on a great tune I never thought of, I'M SHOOTING HIGH.... Never will forget the time Neal and I were glumly sitting before his living-room TV in Los Gatos Calif, where he has his ranchstyle home bought from the railroad-broke-his-leg payments, I say "Boy look at that [P.P.], what is she thinking?" and Neal snuffs down his nose and says "Blows spades"— Speaking of Neal, I've just written my first play, 3 act, Marlon Brando asked for it, he's reading it now in Hollywood, I wrote him a letter yesterday commanding him to pick up *On the Road* also (which he read but says it doesnt have movie structure) (told him I'd write the screenplay myself making one vast roundtrip voyage if he wants) and the new play is also about Neal, whom I call ZEAL, title is "Beat Generation" (which would look good on play page as title) and Lillian Hellman also reading it but it will definitely be produced if Brando & Hellman dont like, by Leo Garen in his 2nd Avenue Yiddishe [sic] theater with wild young new actors like Don McGovern and Kelly Reynolds (Kelly looks just like Neal, he's insane, he pounced on me in the Remo[108] and had me turning everywhichaway

107. Later Ernest Hemingway gave only a condescending nod to the Beat writers when he described his early story "Big Two-Hearted River" as being "about a boy coming home beat to the wide from a war. Beat to the wide was an earlier and possibly more severe form of beat, since those who had it were unable to comment on this condition and could not suffer that it be mentioned in their presence." See Hemingway's unpublished preface to a student's edition of his short stories he compiled in 1959; this preface is in the Ernest Hemingway archives at the John F. Kennedy Library in Boston.
108. The San Remo was a Greenwich Village bar.

trying to explain the non-explanation of diamond sutra and I saw he is an intelligent Irish Catholic like Neal for sure) (I mean, the part of Neal should be played by someone with intelligence not just a dopey hotrodeer) (right?)— Did *Esquire* tell you they, O I told you myself, that baseball game [Alan] Harrington and I play'd in your livingroom, I turned the cards over and play'd a game and typed it up as I went along, with all those mad names of Seymour Imagination appearing in *Esquire*, remember Herb Jangraw, George Kolek, Babe Blagden, and my own names Ronnie Melaney, Homer Landry, Tommy Turner and his brother Oboy Roy Turner, and Leo Sawyer at short, etc.—

John, has P.E.N. club asked you to join—I dont wanta join anything. Besides I dont like the names on their list: Charles Rolo, Robert Pick, Ralph Ellison, David Dempsey, B. J. Chute, John Brooks, Saul Bellow, Elmer Rice, John Farrar, the only people I like on their list are Robert Frost and James Putnam and William Cole. I really dont wanta be bugg'd by joining silly clubs. I simply wont answer, hey?

That was a great description of Thelonius Monk night and Melba Liston (wow). . . . I went to hear Monk with Gilbert Millstein & wife in Sept. but I dragged Gilbert out to a Bowery bar for boilermakers & later fell on the sidewalk with Stanley Gould & last I heard of Gil was "Take care of him for godssake"—and Monk was still Pure! like you say!—As to Dizzy [Gillespie], he also has a corny remote, whattayoucallit, radio dance hookup where he sounds just like a poor danceband at a Lake (and I saw Diz on Madison Avenue and we yelled hello at each other for some reason) (and that same day I spied Horace Silver on Central Park West and waved at him and he made some kind of gesture with his head)—

Yessir I'm looking forward to revisiting Saybrook in January—by the way, I think you can sell a jazz story to *Holiday*, write them, to John Knoles Assoc. Editor, *Holiday*, 5 Independence Square, Philadelphia, and tell him I suggested you write a jazz story for them as they asked me to pick out jazz or travel, I'll spin them the tale of Desolation Peak in the High Cascade Mountains[109]—Meanwhile, I've been getting lousy new novels about hypes & jazz from publishers, expecting me to rave, I sent back very cautious quotes, I wont rave about anything that isnt great—After reading SOMEWHERE THERE'S MUSIC by George Lea I went to your GO and was immediately struck by the fact that you knew how to write a sentence and he didnt, so my comment was: AN INTERESTING STORY ABOUT THE COOLER COLLEGIATE CROWD and it took me 2 days of conscience-stricken ness [sic] to decide to throw in "interesting" which it isnt—The trouble with all this is that I want to be a buddha lunatic of poems & tales & adventures, dont wanta get entangled in the Publishing Business &

---

109. Kerouac's story "Alone on a Mountaintop" appeared in the October 1958 issue of *Holiday*.

worldly affairs, fuck it, I'm praying Brando buys for the movies, I'll establish a trust fund and become the biggest happiest free bum in the world. . . . and anyway I'll do that anyway . . . I'm getting sick of spending all my time thinking about details & technical questions. . . .

Yes, I'll bring my mother [to Holmes's house in Old Saybrook], we'll come over en route to Lowell on the NYNHH [railroad] or whatever they call it, or else a nutty weekend with my favorite doll Helen Weaver who isnt mad at me no mo. . . . sends me cigars. . . . beautiful girl, but Lucien doesnt like her. . . . I think because he cant snowjob her and also she doesnt like to get drunk . . . but is mad.

Further news: the book [*On the Road*] was bought by Rowohlt Verlag in Germany, by Frangipaniaoaloudkdk [sic] in Italy, and by England . . . also I wrote an intro to a book of photos, good ones, a mad intro. . . .[110] I'm supposed to get 300 dollars some day from each of these remote sources (the photo book is France)—Sold an article on BEAT G[eneration] to *Pageant*. . . .[111] My theory of prose and an example coming out in BLACK MOUNTAIN REVIEW the next one—[112] Ferlinghetti will publish a book of my poems, BLUES. . . .[113] Pieces of my wild FinneganWake book rave language LUCIEN MIDNIGHT wanted by a young press run by Mike McClure in Frisco. . . . I wrote a jacket-blurb for Gregory Corso's new book of poems GASOLINE (Ferlinghetti) (City Lights)— Next novel is THE SUBTERRANEANS coming out Grove Press March, I have the terribly messy galleys here—New Directions wants to do VISIONS OF NEAL[114] (letter from Laughlin) either a little cut or just uncut selections for $7.50 thin private edition, dirty. . . . latter may be best. . . . and so on, things I cant even remember, O yes, a spread about me in *Harper's Bazaar*, picture & story, and a spread of pictures in PLAYBOY soon (banned in Orlando) color shots on streets with bums & pals & in Cafe Bohemian where my God John I sat there all alone at a rickety little table with a whisky sour with no whisky in it watching a cool group of white musicians and being watched

110. *The Americans*, photographs by Robert Frank with an introduction by Jack Kerouac, was published by Grove Press in 1959. The previous year it was published in France by Delpire.
111. "Lamb, No Lion" appeared in *Pageant* in February 1958.
112. Excerpts from "October in the Railroad Earth" and "Essentials of Spontaneous Prose" were included in *Black Mountain Review*, No. 7, autumn 1957.
113. Ferlinghetti didn't publish Kerouac's *Book of Blues*, telling Jack it was "prose, not poetry," but various blues choruses appeared in several little magazines over the years, including two excerpts from "San Francisco Blues" in *Ark* magazine (winter 1957) and four choruses from "Mexico City Blues" in *Measure*, No. 2 (1958).
114. At this time Kerouac wrote James Laughlin at New Directions that he was "still smart enough as a hobo-wanderer and general Dharma-bum to ward off money-temptations & keep my literature clean." Jack also had a premonition that some day *Visions of Cody* "would be clutched underarm by young American writers like some kind of bible. . . ."

by all the customers all cool as mad Jerry Newman photog bent and leapt around flashing me, but all I did was dig the jazz anyway as tho as of yore I was alone which I am anyway.... Saw Jerry Newman went to his studio heard his new [jazz] sounds he mad as ever he will do my albums later ... sweet Jerry ... goatee, gray ... Send Shirley a kiss from me, she is sweet, almost as sweet as her sweetpotato & marshmallow....

Well, yah, go ahead John and send the article.[115] ... and as for Europe, if you do go before I get to see you, Allen is c/o American Express.... Seymour [Wyse] is at 28 Cochrane Close, St. Johns Wood, London.... reachable by subway, Picadilly line.... in fact I walked aback from Seymour's pad to Picadilly, about 2 miles, right down Baker Street. BUT WHERE WAS SHERLOCK HOLMES?
YOUR OLDER BROTHER SHERLOCK?

LATEST PERM
Oi the lone woe of Lee Lucien
... a basketa pittykats ...

Comme toujours,
Jack

Please forgive me for showing off, but I have the urge to write to Hiram Haydn[116] and advise him to take yr. book, I'll make it sound okay, I shouldnt have told you but I was looking for a p.s.

The first weeks of November 1957, Kerouac spent five days correcting the Grove Press galleys of The Subterraneans, *an "exhaustive overhaul" for his editor Donald Allen (the entire book had taken Jack three nights to write in 1953). Then he made another false start on* Memory Babe *before he plunged back into* The Dharma Bums. *Despite his absorption in his novel, Kerouac found time to write Hiram Haydn at Random House recommending Holmes's unpublished novel about a jazz musician,* The Horn. *Jack also told his agent about a firm*

---

115. Kerouac was disappointed in Holmes's article "The Philosophy of the Beat Generation" because he thought that Holmes—like Norman Mailer in his essay "The White Negro" (1957) in Dissent magazine—stressed the antisocial image ("beat") of the hipster instead of pointing out the religious significance ("beatific") of those people whom Kerouac called "a generation of crazy, illuminated hipsters" in his article. On November 13, 1957, after City Lights published Mailer's essay with the subtitle "Superficial Reflections of the Hipster," Ginsberg advised Kerouac to "play down the Beat Generation talk & let others do that, it's just an idea ... let Holmes write up all that ... You only get hung on publicity-NY-polemics-politics if you let them or be encouraged to beat BEAT drum...."
116. An editor at Random House.

offer from James Laughlin to publish excerpts from Visions of Cody *with New Directions, and advised Lord about how to negotiate the movie sale of* On the Road.

TO DONALD ALLEN

Nov. 11, 1957
[Orlando, Florida]

Dear Don

I've just finished five exhausting nights correcting the galleys of THE SUBTERRANEANS restoring the original freeflowing prose according to the original manuscript which I had here, with the exception of a few deft touches you'd made that were in excellent and wise taste.

Now Don, if this exhaustive overhaul is going to cost money in the printing plant please charge it up to me. I want this book to be an artistic triumph for myself as well as for Grove so that we can publish my later books, *comme ils sont.*

I assure you that the manuscript is now ready to publish, in the galley I'm sending, including all mistakes in spacing made by the linotypist and even places where the print was dull, faded, and all the grammar is straight, all the commas to my satisfaction according to the original rhythmic-paragraph-swing, and the whole thing a mighty strange and astonishing poem.

Hemingway has nothing over me when it comes to persnickitiness about "craft." Nor any poet. And why not?

Again, if it's going to cost money to restore the manuscript-galley the way I had it and want it, charge it up to me. You know how I feel about my prose and about the future of prose.

Let me know if everything is straight.

If by any chance my galley-correction is unacceptable then we're going to start hassling all over again for nothing so let's go ahead with this little bomb, this scorching *novella,* especially while I'm on the bestseller list.

By the way, Don, New Directions is interested in doing VISIONS OF NEAL either en toto with sex-cuts & libel-cuts (as in SUBS) or as it is in selected small edition for private $7.50 volumes. I've asked Laughlin for an outline of his hesitancies and will decide. I wanta get these masterpieces of mine published before everybody gets sick of me.

As ever
Jack

p.s. How much you wanta bet Allen Ginsberg will be in NY before Christmas? a hunch.

Jack Kerouac
1418 ½ Clouser St.
Orlando, Florida
November 11, 1957

Dear Mr. Haydn

I dont want to butt in your business, Mr. Haydn, but as a friend of Clellon Holmes I'm naturally interested in his welfare and do hope you accept
his new book. But what I wanted to say besides that, was, I should think
it's a very important book and should make a graceful addition to your list
along with Miss Joyce Glassman's book ... (my other friend.)

Publishers have been sending me the latest "beat generation" books
and boy they aint nothin compared to Holmes, who knows how to write a
virile sentence.... and who has a big heart and doesnt pose as some cool,
careless, agnostic-type fancypants. Holmes is a great good writer and a
great sweet man and I hope he winds up with you.[117]

Sincerely,
Jack Kerouac

[Postmarked November 23, 1957
Orlando, Florida]

Dear Sterling—Mr James Laughlin of New Directions has written that he
wants to do an uncut selection from Visions of Neal in private edition. This
is fine with me and his letter was very polite and intelligent. Accept his
terms because for me this is more of a prestige occasion than a money deal.
He says then, later, he could publish the whole book in its proper form after softening the audience. He'll be calling you soon to come to an agreement. I'm very glad about this development concerning my best book.

Meanwhile, the only book that I can hope to make money out of, is
Road, and I hope you can swing a movie deal. On reflection, I think your
idea about the west coast writer who would take it on option and write
screen script and sell it, and give us no lower than the minimum you mentioned, is splendid (because now I dont think I want to get into the tin-
horn Hollywood act myself). So contact that writer if you see that outright
sale of the book is out. As ever,

Jack

p.s. Did you receive HIGH CASCADES & BULL FIGHT story?

---

117. Random House published Holmes's *The Horn* in 1958.

The last day of November 1957, weary after fueling his long sessions writing The Dharma Bums *with Mexican Benzedrine, Kerouac responded to a letter from Ginsberg in Paris containing what Allen described as "first lines of a great formal elegy for my mother," the beginning of the poem that later took shape as "Kaddish." Jack replied in two exuberant, drunken letters from Florida to bring Ginsberg up to date on his plans to read his work to jazz accompaniment at the Village Vanguard in New York City, where he'd been offered $500 a week at the end of the year.*

TO ALLEN GINSBERG

[November 30, 1957
Orlando, Florida]

Dear Allen—

Your poem very beautiful, especially "eyes of Ma Rainey dying in an ambulance."[118] (why dont you spell it "aumbulance" which would mean aum-vehicle....)   well, and Greg's "sweetleys in sun arc" indeed amazing ... I'm very drunk as I write this, forgive, I too have a thousand new poems but I'm tired & too tired to send you some ... later. I'm going to NY in 3 weeks to appear twice a night at Village Vanguard nightclub to read my prose, starting with Road and later I'll stick in Visions and Pomes ... at plenty money a week I'll do it and if this doesnt make me a drunk, nothing ever will ... actually I look skeptically towards this adventure but the money is necessary. Hollywood aint buying my book probably at all, Brando is a shit, doesnt answer letter from greatest writer in America and he's only a piddling king's clown of the stage, I bugged, so your $225 I'll send as soon as I can probably December or January when I get royalties, dont worry, and it'll be your return fare security anyway. Like you paid my

---

118. Lines from a section of what would become part IV of Ginsberg's long poem "Kaddish," mourning the death of his mother, Naomi, which Ginsberg had sent to Kerouac in a letter from Paris on November 13, 1957. Ginsberg wrote Kerouac that he "sat weeping in Cafe Select, once haunted by Gide and Picasso and well-dressed Jacob, last week writing....

    Farewell
    with long black shoe
    Farewell
    smoking corsets & ribs of steel
    Farewell
    communist party & broken stocking
    o mother
    Farewell...."

Ginsberg's biographer Barry Miles has written that Ginsberg composed "many pages of material labelled 'Elegy for mama' in his Paris journals but none of it appears in the final ms.— perhaps it was not to hand when 'Kaddish' proper came to be assembled [in New York City in 1959], only the section quoted to Kerouac survived, presumably in ms. since it is not in the journals."

way over to the other shore, I'll pay your way back.[119] Without movie sales I really only have not much more than T[own] & C[ity] loot, which is a shame. You guys were all het up about nothing. I be bhikku till day I die. But I hope to meet producers et al as nightclub performer, and I will come on like a cool SOUND MUSICIAN like Miles Davis and not drink too much I hope. I'll be living at Henri Cru's pad which is 307 West 113 St. in 3 weeks. [Paul] Carroll at Chicago Review askt me send him stuff, I sent Lucien Midnight poems (new ones you didnt see, wrote em last night in fact) and other pomes. Jay Laughlin is going to do a selected edition of VISIONS OF NEAL, maybe 100 pages, of best prose, in fancy $7.50 thin volume private edition, he says to begin with, is very nice and polite in letters and sent me little brochure of his really most excellent pomes. He's very good poet. I am afraid of this coming New York trip but I was getting fat and bored down here. I'll probably end up in the Bowery this trip but as Esperanza used to say I DUNT CARE . . . No, Gregory, I wont go cry on Lucien's floor, Lucien makes me laugh happily. Lucien is my brother. I'll this time find Laff and take him under my tutelage when he hits town. With loot from Vanguard I'll buy oils and paint more holy pictures of Virgin Mary my mother, and your mother, mother. I am vast endless nakedheaded giant cloud making no sense even to members of the nut ward, what a fate for a simple footballplayer! I got a nutward letter from a certain B. Zemble and am sending him back a spontaneous poem so crazy Gregory would flip over it, in which I say "science statement in million years over owned by pens as treacherous as Aga Arnold of Good Day Biddy Father Uptown—see? I'm a fool! I love reverse! I got hidden Moo-Flutes in my horn cow. I did it dad because I dood it money—I am Governor President!"—etc. and it ends with "My conscience is all snow. In fact my conscience is coldspot."

In other words I have discovered Gregory's secret because I'm so smart and crazy. But I dont care. I'm rather good novelist now, my in-progress work is THE DHARMA BUMS about Gary and 1955 and 56 in Berkeley and Mill Valley and is really bettern ON THE ROAD, if I can only stay sober enuf to finish it now that I know I'm going to make big fool of myself with evil Gilbert Millsteins ain New Yoik. If I can swing the sale of Road to movies, on this jaunt, Brando may come dig me in nightclub, I'll

119. Initially Ginsberg didn't hassle Kerouac about repaying the loan, though he was often short of funds in Europe. By August 21, 1957, Allen had spent the $200 stipend from the National Academy of Arts and Letters that William Carlos Williams arranged for him. Ginsberg told Ferlinghetti that he was "broke & can live on about 2 bucks daily comfortably" with Orlovsky, who shared his monthly fifty-dollar veterans' disability checks. At the end of September Ferlinghetti sent royalty advances and fifty copies of *Howl* to Paris for Allen to sell after Ginsberg generously offered to finance a City Lights book of Kerouac's poetry out of his own royalties. On October 9, 1957, Allen told Jack he was in no hurry to get the $225—"SAVE YOUR MONEY!!!!! God knows what oblivion we'll wind up in like unpopular Mellevilles [sic] when Russia gets to Moon & world is bugged with U!S!...."

make a trust fund and disappear on Zen Lunacy Road and you can all join me. That's my purpose in this blear deed. "All of Medieval Europe in a Shakespeare inch," I wrote last night, "where says: 'Poor perdu' thin helm!'" Wow. Also I'm reading Don Quixote which is probably most sublime work of any man ever lived, thank God for Spain! All living creatures are Don Quixote of course, since living is illusion. Ho ho ho ho ho ho ho ho ho ho ho ha ha aha ah woeieield! So I'll send your money soon, Al, dont worry, Allen, did you get the letter I sent you to mail to Burroughs a month ago? Well, I'll write later. I am bugged and sad and mad and writing a great novel, THE DHARMA BUMS, wow, wait'll they read that one! How great Gary is in it, and Whalen ... you'll see. Meanwhile all I gotta say is: We're all going to die. Neal dont write. Neal great. Neal says "Ha! I shall now suc- cumb to victory" as he plays chess with me, satirizing where I'd said to him I let him win chess games because I a bodhisattva ... I wrote great play about Neal, too, which was mentioned in Herald Trib and now 4 produc- ers reading it, but it's wofully short, but that's all right you sweet daddies please pray that I can join you in Paris in April because I want to em- brace you, poor perdus. Well, this is John the Roi saying, Dont step on the candy gal.

John Perdu

TO ALLEN GINSBERG, PETER ORLOVSKY, & GREGORY CORSO

[December 10, 1957
Orlando, Florida]

Dear Allen & Peter & Gregory ...

Just got your wonderful letters today and havent even had time to re- read and digest them but I want to leap up and answer right away with blah blah blahs ... Wanta tell you, I just finished writing my shining new novel THE DHARMA BUMS all about Gary, the real woodsy vision of Gary, not surrealistic romantic vision, my own puremind trueself Ti Jean Lowell woods vision of Gary, not what you guys will like particularly, actu- ally, tho, there's a lot of Zen Lunacy throughout and what's best: all the tremendous details and poems and outcries of the Dharma Bums at last gathered together in a rushing narrative on a 100 foot scroll ... So I wrote Cowley and told him, and if Cowley dont want publish it, someone else will, as it's like ON THE ROAD, real muscular prose ... But when SUB- TERRANEANS comes out February I'll be so proud that a real sweet poem of mine is finally out, and the next drive is for DOCTOR SAX. On SUB- TERRANEANS manuscript I labored days undoing the wreckage of Don Allen's commas and dumb changes ... so it's now as original, shiney, rhyth- mic, bespeaking future literatures by great young kids ... May I say, Peter's poems about red footprint in snow is real great poetry, I now pronounce Peter Orlovsky a great American Surrealistic Poet of the First Magnitude. Peter, I hope you do come back to New York within a month and as I say, I'll be at Henri Cru's but be SURE NOT TO COME THERE. Henri has laid down a strict law with me that I can stay there PROVIDING none of my friends call, so just telephone me there, CHelsea 3-1528, and we'll make our meets wherever we want, Fugazzy's, Helen W.'s, Joyce's, anywhere, in fact Peter why don't you take up with Joyce at her new address 338 E. 13, phone GR 3-3932 where she has full huge pad with big kitchen and all where you can stay because I want to make it with Helen W. I just wrote big letter to Laff telling him I'll see him. Yes, Al, I know reading will be fiasco-ish but I think I'll make them vibrate just so's I can be held over an extra 2 weeks and send you your money and also set some aside for my own triumphal visit to Paris (bleak, meek on the street) in March where I'll rush up and find Burroughs, Ginsberg, Corso, Orlovsky, Ansen and Cocteau all in one bed of rocks I was going to say Roses, I mean all in one stew, I mean all at one time—besides Gallimard has just bought ON THE ROAD and advanced me francs and it will be published in French in Paris 1958 so now Genet and I have same publisher. Frankly, last 2 months, I havent been interested in anything but peace. You know what Christ said when he entered a house, "I bring you my peace," or, leaving, "I leave you my peace." That is the greatest kick of all. Just sit all day doing nothing, enjoying cats and flowers and birds. My swift finger in writing poetry is swift finger but Gregory you're right, beauty is slow, but you see, if you dont speak now your own blurt way you may forever hold your tongue, this was Shakespeare's law, how do you think he wrote so fast and so much and so sublime? The hawthorne sleet of Lear fool and the dancing fool and Edgar in the moor, was all fast wild thoughts. O, I've pissed more water as a sailor of the several seas than sallow's aphorism will allow, and had I written slowly and deliberately, might you call me Sallow then. Aphoristic Lionel Trilling deliberating like Henry James over his imaginary sentence structures. Poetry is "Ode to the West Wind"? Wake Up. Poetry is Shakespeare and nobody but Shakespeare and don't Pound me no Tolstoy me broach me no rejoinder! Shakespeare is a vast continent, Shelley is a village. Why do you insist, Gregory, on being DIFFERENT and chosing unlikely Shelley for your hero, why do you be afraid of being like everybody else and admitting the Supreme Greatness of Bard Will Shakespeare? How, ask Burroughs about Shakespeare, he spent years with the Immortal Bard on his lap ... Burroughs in fact bespeaks himself like Shakespeare. Listen to Burroughs talk. Don't be fooled by Mighty Burroughs. Gregory, you are about to come in contact with the greatest writer alive in the world today, William Seward Burroughs, who also says that Shakespeare is the end. Apollinaire is a veritable cow's turd in a meadow in the continent of Shakespeare. The greatest French poet is Rabelais ... The greatest Russian poet is Dostoevsky. The greatest Italian poet is Corso. The greatest German poet is probably Spengler for all I goddam know. The greatest Spanish poet is of course Cervantes. The greatest American poet is Kerouac. The greatest Israeli poet is Ginsberg. The greatest Eskimo poet is Lord Bleaky Igloogloo. The greatest Burroughsian poet is World. Well, boys, I'll be seeing you in March in Paris and don't flog your dummies, and save some girls for me, and some harry, and don't upset the tables, and don't worry, I don't give a shit what I saw, when I sawyeouek what I sawk wouet, and that's that. I'm drunk. You can see I'm writing this letter drunk. Okay. Tell Alan Ansen to go to that queer bar on the same street as Cafe Napoleon about 5 blocks down where they all sit around listening to classical jukebox sipping coffee and vermouth, I went there with Irish motorcyclist from Dublin. Or is Ansen yearning for long haired youths from nature boy caves? Poor Ansen? Bless his eyes, kiss his eyes for me! Hello Ansen! Hello Burroughs! Hello out there you mothers! How are you? Hello Allen! Eyes of Ma Rainey dying in an ambulance! There are sweetlies in sunarc! the little purple women monsters are straddling the sun! The black cowboy! The cottage without bacon! Hello Peter Brother, how are you son, kiss the ground you walk on! Hello all you Franciscans! Hello out there! Have another cognac! Hello you miserables.... end of magnificent message, end of blah hoard, see you all in Paradise Paris in March when we'll light the torch of saint.

Allen, you know why I said I was greatest American poet and you greatest Israeli poet? Because you didn't pick up on Americana till you read VISIONS OF NEAL, before that you were big Burroughsian putter-downer of Americana. Remember Hal Chase and the Wolfeans and the Dark Priests? You suddenly saw Americana of Neal and all, and picked up on it, and made a killing on it, but your heart's in the mountains, O Tribe of the Mountains, the Mountains of Judea! Am I not right? YOU KNOW I'M RIGHT. Burroughs' own Americana is effortless, it's Brad coming on their redleather seat, so he is intrinsically Americana, like me (with teenage poems to Americana) but you only got in the act later. This is pure vision of Ginsberg's poetry history. Because you are not an American, you are a Magian man, and belong to the yearning new culture of the 21st century, which will be Magian, Orthodoxy, Cavern-feeling ... s'why old tired Western Franciscan monks of Italy can't convince you, because you are really an Arab and above all an Aramean Russian Motherlander. Jews and Arabs are Semites, and Jews and Arabs and Russians are all Orthodox in the deepest sense. If you want further information, mail 25c for booklet.

And Gregory, you have the nerve to tell me that you're not Italian at all but pure Gregory No-Name, pure Gregory-Stick, pure ogre monster dwarf of Gregoryhood! Ach! Don't you know that your lyric line is pure Romance Lawngwaj? Do I deny my Keltic crack words, their sources? Isn't Peter a pure Aramean Saint? Isn't Ansen a tired Western loser of sources? Isn't Burroughs the return of Faust? Well, then, read History and see! Ansen gave up, Burroughs forged on, but Ansen is as sweet as the Good Samaritan who helped the wounded man, and in historyless reality of God, nothing's greater.

Well, this was a strange letter but it's all true ... When I come to Paris in March and get drunk and pass out you may all stomp me to death in the gutters of St. Denis and I will rise going Hm he hee hee hee he ha ha and be Quasimodo and run down the bloody flowery streets of Sacred Heart and tear little girls apart from limb to limb, my dear, and then you'll have to trap me on top of old Smokey with Lucien and we'll dump molten buckets of Wilson Rye whiskey on your beholden heads and crown you with garland gain. See?

In a mood of elation after finishing The Dharma Bums, *Kerouac sent off some notes and postcards in early December alerting his friends in New York City that he would see them soon.*

TO STERLING LORD

[December 10, 1957
Orlando, Florida]

Dear Sterling:

Here are the contracts signed. I'm so happy about France, that was my secret desire all along. Now I have a good reason to re-visit sweet Paree. The advance is very substantial, too. When I was in Paris in April 100 francs was a quarter, so 250,000 francs would be $625. Gallimard also publishes the mighty poet Genet.[120]

Allen Ginsberg wisely suggests that we try to publish On the Road with the Russians. He says they pay better than anybody else. If you know of anyway to contact Soviet publishers or Soviet literary agents, try it. He says the Soviet are looking for raw stories about the real America. The claim that we are softies certainly wouldnt stand up in the sufferings and endurances of Dean Moriarty.

Enclosed, also, is the Book Find slip.

I'll telephone you late in the afternoon Tuesday Dec. 17th fresh off the train eating pizzas near Times Square.

As ever,
Jack

120. Gallimard also published French translations of most of Kerouac's novels.

TO PATRICIA MACMANUS

[December 12, 1957
Orlando, Florida]

Dear Pat ...

I worried, did you ever get that Christmas story I sent you to forward to Leslie Hanscom?[121] Please let me know. I'll be "opening" at the Village Vanguard nightclub Dec. 19 reading from my manuscripts with jazz group: Sterling has all the details. Therefore I'll be available also for any publicity work you want me to do between Dec. 20 and Jan. 20 or so. Sterling says my appearance, with attendant publicity, & coinciding with magazine pieces in January, should get ON THE ROAD back on the bestseller list. Meanwhile, I'm going to write a long letter to Malcolm Cowley in a few days describing the new novel I've just finished on a 100 foot roll again.

As ever,
Jack

TO LUCIEN CARR

[Postmarked December 14, 1957
Orlando, Florida]

Dear Lou,

Doubtless you've heard, highborn one, that I'm going to read from my dusty books at Village Vanguard nightclub beginning night of Dec. 19th and running to Xmas day, at $500 a week by the way (that oughta make your eyes gleam), with if successful, extry 2 weeks at same. So I'll be in town before you can say Jack Carr or Simon Says and I'll call you. I'm going to be holed up in a room in the YMCA to make sure I can sleep all day and lay off lush till job done, as I never used to drink on job on railroad. New Years Eve I will be with you, God willing; I hope Cessa okay. I've just written new novel you'll like, about Gary Snyder, about doublebitted axes and pancake breakfasts in North woods, and mountaintops, very nice: I'll type it up at Henri Cru's pad between Jan. 1 and Jan. 20 so I'll see lots of you-all. I had a Christmas story in World-Telly Dec. 5, dja see it? ... Burroughs leaving Tangier for Paris, says T. is hotbed of virus hepatitis makes for asexuality ... Jadis bientot

J.

In New York City on December 28, 1957, Kerouac wrote two of his last letters of the year to Allen Ginsberg and Elbert Lenrow, who had lectured on American writers at the classes Jack had taken at the New School in 1948–1949. After the publication of On the Road, *Lenrow wrote Kerouac on December 23, 1957,*

121. "Not Long Ago Joy Abounded at Christmas" appeared in the *New York World Telegram and Sun* on December 5, 1957.

praising the novel by quoting Rimbaud's definition of a "visionary" and concluding, "I suppose he would have liked your people, 'the mad ones.' And you've got their quintessences." But Lenrow also raised a question about the final scene of On the Road, *when Sal Paradise got into the car driven by his friend Remi Boncoeur's bookie, to go to a Duke Ellington concert, leaving Dean Moriarty to walk off alone. Kerouac had written:*

> *So Dean couldn't ride uptown with us and the only thing I could do was sit in the back of the Cadillac and wave at him. The bookie at the wheel also wanted nothing to do with Dean. Dean, ragged in a motheaten overcoat he brought specially for the freezing temperature of the East, walked off alone, and the last I saw of him he rounded the corner of Seventh Avenue, eyes on the street ahead, and bent to it again. . . .*

Lenrow's question, "Since when is a bookie more important than a man in a motheaten coat?" prompted one of Kerouac's most passionate defenses of his view of himself as a writer. Jack's outburst was fueled by his disappointment that his gig reading poetry accompanied by a jazz pianist at the Village Vanguard on a double bill with the J. J. Johnson Quartet was canceled after a week. Kerouac expanded on the subject of the attacks on his writing in a letter to Ginsberg at the close of the year.

TO ELBERT LENROW

> [Postmarked December 28, 1957]
> [Return address on envelope:
> c/o Lord
> 15 East 48th St.
> New York 17, New York]

Dear Mr. Lenrow,

Almost like a child you incensedly cry to me "Since when is a bookie more important than a man in a motheaten coat" (concerning the last scene in the book) as tho it was my own MORAL IDEA, as tho I was a spokesman for such ideas, instead of an American Novelist working in the field of Realism. You might as well ask Frank Norris "Since when is the money of Chicago more important than the wheat of the West?" And everybody has been attacking me for On the Road as tho I was God-Who-Allows-Such-Things-To-Happen, everybody's forgotten my PEN. So I read in a nightclub for $500 a week because the book didnt sell and I want more money to support my old Maw, and so I can teach people how to read in an age of TV, so they describe my sweating face, they sneer at the crowds that came to hear me because they run the gamut from Steve Allen to bums with rucksacks, they accuse me of wearing a necktie on opening night,[122] etc.

---

122. Kerouac wore a Paisley tie chosen by his mother on his opening night at the Village Vanguard.

92

etc., of slurring over the "Beautiful lines"... in Nation they even deplore the fact that I read the Daily News and smoke cigars... daily the indictment grows... and all the time I'm just an old motheaten storyteller of America asking for no more than a living so that I can eat my bread in sorrow from the sweat of my face... Wouldn't it have been better if I'd never written, then? Then I would have laid low like a river, I would have never have popped up to be slashed down, laying low like a river I would have had power because then I would have been the quiet valley of the world ... like when I'd creep into the backseats of your class at New School and nobody noticed and I enjoyed what you said about American writers because you spoke so beautifully. Wasnt there a time when American writers were let alone by personality mongers and publicity monsters? But I had to publish my stuff because my mother couldn't go on working forever and nobody else to help her. It was her idea, the necktie, "You must look neat in front of Your Public." I guess it's time for me to sneak across the river in a boat and go find a cave. But I'll buy her a little house first. If I were as big as Tom [Thomas] Wolfe, Jay Laughlin or Charles Olson I'd rush around town kicking all the critics in the ass. Maybe next lifetime. Yet speaking truly there is no rebirth in this or in any other world, thank God.

But I am well loved. Every single woman I've met in the past week (excepting dikes) has wanted to make love to me (married or not), at least secretly. I am well loved also by almost all men. It's the SYSTEM that rejects me, and you, and all of us. The system of ignorance. It bears watching, that lil ole system. Enclosed is a five dollar bill you loaned me 5000 years ago in the Pure Land. I just called you on phone, you werent in.

Jack Kerouac

TO ALLEN GINSBERG

[December 28, 1957
New York City]

Dear Allen ...

Dear Alleyboo, I'm in Joyce's[123] kitchen and brooding at the table suddenly said (as she's cooking hamburg supper) "I wish Allen was here" and she said "That's right, we have enuf meat for another hamburger."

Mad pad in Puerto Rico 13th Street near Ave A ... where I'm hiding out, this afternoon I finally told everybody I was thru with publicity for rest of my life. I see where Rexroth says I am an "insignificant Tom [Thomas] Wolfe" (can he really say that about SAX?) Everybody attacking us like

---

123. Joyce Glassman.

mad, Herbert Gold,[124] etc. etc. you and me now equally being attacked. My mother says every knock is a boost. I saw your sweet sweet cousin Joel the other night, he gave me bottle vitamin pills, your father wrote, wants me come out Paterson "talk." O talk talk, I've talking to 1,500 people in past week. I read fine. Lucien said Yes, I read fine. Lucien said, admires my sticking it out, dear Lucien slept on my bathroom floor on 2 day binge. Wish you were here. Broke up with Joyce because I wanted to try big sexy brunettes then suddenly saw evil of world and realized Joyce was my angel sister and came back to her. Xmas Eve read my prayer to drunken nightclub, everybody listen. Lamantia was here and had mad days with him walking 5 miles down Broadway yelling—about God and ecstasy, he rushed into confession and rushed out, he flew off to Frisco, back soon, he got in big publicity interviews with me and was full of sacred eloquence. Great new poet: Howard Hart, a sheer Peter, a Catholic, Lamantia's buddy. I will write big novel about past week so you can dig the whole scene entire and to warn you about something. You'll see ... Excuse my last letter, paranoia lapse I guess ... I am funny kind of hungry fool. I hunger for final ultimate friendship with no hassles, like with Neal early days, not for part time sneer friendships like with Gregory. You have never sneered at me but I have sneered at you. Now why? I tell you this is the beginning of something great, let's do it, put it down, put down publicity, go underground for final great maybe caves of gold. With Gary and Pete. And Laff. And Bill. And if Greg wants. I say, I say fuck the monster. No more poetry for poetry sake, either, like word slinging, but actual me-to-you and you-to-me hey-listen hey-say saying like Neal Joan Anderson (re that, I see from Robert Stock article that Gerd Stern is now regarded as an SF poet so I figure Yes, he did steal Joan Anderson, let's get it back for sure now.)[125] ... Well, actually, I won't do anything, probably never see you again, don't know what I'll do, I just dig peace. You come see me in my cave. Wish I was talking to you on transatlantic cable. You're right, you're right, you're forever forever right. Right right right! You dont know how right you are. You're right forever forever you're right. Goodbye. God be w[ith] ye. Las ombras vengadora. DO WHAT YOU WANT DONT LISTEN TO ME

.... Jack....

124. Kerouac was referring to Herbert Gold's belittling review of *On the Road* in *The Nation*, as well as Howard Smith's "hip" review of his nightclub performance in *The Village Voice*, titled "Jack Kerouac: Off the Road, Into the Vanguard, and Out," which quoted someone at the Village Vanguard saying of Jack's drunken reading of poetry to jazz, "Well, Kerouac has come off the road in high gear ... I hope he has a good set of snow tires."
125. The previous year Ginsberg had lent Cassady's lengthy "Joan Anderson" letter to his friend Gerd Stern, who lived on a houseboat in Sausalito, California. Stern apparently lost the letter and told Ginsberg it disappeared overboard.

1958

In January 1958, living in his mother's small apartment in Orlando, Kerouac wrote his first letters of the year to his close friends Philip Whalen, Lawrence Ferlinghetti, and Allen Ginsberg while he recovered from what he told them was the "wildest time of all time" in New York City. He sent his typewriter off for a complete overhaul before starting to retype The Dharma Bums, *his novel about Gary Snyder, from what he called its "scroll manuscript" (a roll of Teletype paper) onto sheets of 8½ by 11 inch paper for the Viking Press, predicting that the book would contribute to a "sudden Buddhism boom" in America. Kerouac also looked forward to seeing the Grove Press publication of* The Subterraneans *early in 1958 with his spontaneous prose sentences intact. After* On the Road *made the bestseller list, Sterling Lord began to place Kerouac's writing in mainstream magazines such as* Playboy, Pageant, Esquire, *and* Holiday, *which paid well. On January 4, 1958, Ginsberg had written Kerouac from Paris telling him not to "yell at me so drunk & wicked as in first airgram from fla., it is actually very upsetting, I dont know how to answer." But in Jack's letters to his friends in the first week of January, he was still excited by "all that ROAD noise."*

TO PHILIP WHALEN

> Jan. 7, 1958
> Tuesday Kshanti
> [Orlando, Florida]

Dear Holy Old How'll Who'll Ya,

You brilliant diamondstar, shining on Oregon beachie ... You old bangle-gaving bo! (that was sposed to be gavel-banging) ... Goddamit I already lost your beautiful letter[1] which was the first thing I read for 1958, sitting

---

1. On December 18, 1957, Whalen had sent a Christmas card to Mémêre enclosing a letter to Kerouac praising *On the Road*, saying, "Now the best part of the book is the trip to Mexico, it really goes wild there, I like that real well. It feels funny, reading about you & Neal & everybody, so far away. Sometimes it reads like a letter from you." Whalen also told Jack that the San Francisco poet Michael McClure was also "crazy" about the novel "& says it's the best

sad drunk in gloom of room on edge of bed gray New York ... the human voice speaking to me, also the Buddha voice ... Got big letter from Gary, from ship, him shuttling back and forth Arabia to India to Italy, sent me his new poems, some of em ... there's no telling what an immense future he has, I mean, famous prose novelist Gary Snyder hiking off to Sierras & putting all publicity down (after one magnificent burst with him on tv) ... Saw [John] Montgomery at my Village Vanguard reading, I was drunk, we went out talked a bit, we didn't even smile at each other but I love him and he knows it ... but seems I only see Montgomery when everything is hectic, that is, when vibrations start, when God gives gift of prophecy to me, swirls of people surround me, suddenly here comes poor Montgomery and I never have time to talk with him, as I done when we were mad fools walking in the street ... O this fame is a bad bit, Phil. Watch out for yr future. Mémêre loves you and sends you her love all the time. Mémêre is now quite pleased because all our relatives begun to write us invite us, to Canada, New England, California, Kansas, lost lost uncles and such.... ere this, Mémêre and I were quiet unobtrusive dharma bums ... I just wrote The Dharma Bums, new novel, about Gary ... must type it this month ... then rush fly to New York in airplane do an album with Steve Allen of TV, him play piano behind me, him love me, he by the way a fine sensitive poet (no bullshit) ... I going buy Mémêre house, way out sand dunes of Long Island, nowhere town (I mean, within walking distance of stores of little town somewhere) cape coddy country, there I will also finish my own life be an old graybeard Jack Poet writing haiku & praying for deliverance of all living things to heaven, which, if prayer is earnest and desire is true, is not only possible, but done. I was asked to appear on TV with England angry young man John Osborne,[2] I was going to tell him I wasn't angry, I only prayed (as above) as only responsibility of a man, but I couldn't wait around New York ... Actually, from his pictures, I see he is quite a cat, an Englishman, vaguely familiar, I think he was a thief with me in previous lifetime in London 1750's ... (we picked Boswell's pockets) ... Rexroth is down on me, hey? He's a funny one, after trying to "take leadership" of "beat generation" and then this, calling me "insignificant" on radio, wow. Creeley not so dumb mebbe. Well well well well well ... things as they are, to look at things as they are, okay okay okay ... I am going to get Rexroth into heaven ... I am the son of Virgin Mary ... since Mary is said to be mother of all things, and God is all things, then who misses heaven? Use your Sanskrit substitute names as you will.... 1948 I mean 1958 will be

---

book written to date in this part of the world & says he ain't going to write any more until he can really blow like that."

2. John Osborne (1929–1996) was an English playwright, author of *Look Back in Anger* (1956) and *The Entertainer* (1957), plays that established him as the leading young exponent of British social drama.

great year, year of Buddhism, already big stir in N.Y. about zen, Alan Watts big hero of Madison Avenue now,[3] and Nancy Wilson Ross big article about zen in Mademoiselle mentions me and Allen and knows her Buddhism good, now with Dharma Bums I will crash open whole scene to sudden Buddhism boom and look what'll happen closely soon ... everybody going the way of the dharma, this no shit ... reached dead head block ... then with arrival of Gary, smash! watch, you'll see. It will be a funny year of en- lightenment in America. I dunno about 1959 but 58 is going to be dharma year in America ... everybody reading Suzuki on Madison Avenue ... that in itself mighty strange ... but I fear for Frisco, I fear for a coming silly stu- pid revolution with blood in the streets in that town of poetry and hate.... Jean McLean and such things only a harbinger of awful things to come ... did you know New York was a nation in itself, uncontrollable by the police and also incapable of revolution because the people are there, the rush of people too busy eating pizza to care about silly revolution ... one man hates you, another a step away loves you ... beware of California.... there is more hatred brewing in that town than I would care to tell a faust.... with witches ... ah, maybe not ... but duncan hates you and ginsberg, robert stock hates corso and the whole world, rexroth hates me and cas- sady, so and so hates so and so, you know what i mean.... there is malice in n y too but its too big to bite in ... but in frisco there is nest. imagine how broughton must hate snyder, or how jonathan williams must hate pe- ter orlovsky, i m just shooting names ... i m thru with all this criticism and hatred, i m going to be jolly old bilbulous [sic] story tellerloveseverybody. blah blah blah

Jack   Write!

On the Road was *not* edited (a few libellious deletions[4])—that was my "middle style" (1951) between Town & City and Doctor Sax—It was pub- lished as is off my ms. from the 120-foot roll—The rumor is untrue.

TO LAWRENCE FERLINGHETTI

[Before January 8, 1958
Orlando, Florida]

Dear Lawrence,
    Enclosed is a recent prose sample of Burroughs' he just sent me from

3. Alan Watts (1915–1973) was a prolific author who popularized Eastern philosophy for Western readers in more than twenty books. In the summer of 1958, his article "Beat Zen, Square Zen, and Zen" was published in the *Chicago Review,* along with an excerpt from Ker- ouac's *The Dharma Bums,* and poems by Snyder and Whalen.
4. On December 18, 1957, Whalen had written, "I wish ROAD hadn't been edited all to hell, but what there is is still great."

Morocco. The main body of his work (an endless novel which will drive everybody mad) is in the hands of Don Allen, 59 W. 9th St ... Write to him for the whole works. I think you would be doing a literary bombshell to do a prose copy of Burroughs whom Auden pronounced a genius and who is really the secret underground hero of world literature (Allen and I think). I wish I had time to cleanly type up this selection but my typewriter ribbon isn't turning, no return carriage, no nothin and it's going out tomorrow to repairs.

In MEXICO CITY BLUES you could have excerpted a consecutive series of choruses, say #100 to #150 but I see where you are taken in by my original lines that say "poetry just doesn't make it" or "this is prose not poetry" and false modesty like "but I cant write poetry just prose." You know as well as I do I'm a poet and these are poems and Charles Olson said so too. If you wanta change your mind later, and New Directions doesn't take em, okay. My Buddhism is extremely serious & sincere & I really believe that by nightly prayer for the deliverance of all living things to Heaven it will really take place and that is my idea of the ONLY responsibility of a man. (And I was going to tell that to John Osborne on a Sunday afternoon TV panel but I couldn't wait around NY.)

Now as to LUCIEN MIDNIGHT have you seen a sample of it I sent McClure? Because the typing of it (25,000 words approx.) will be a very big job for me now (I'm typing new novel, writing about High Cascades for Holiday,[5] etc.) (must do an album reading my works with Steve Allen on piano) and I'm afraid you might want to publish 25,000 words of raving prose a la E.E. Cummings' EIMI ... So take a look at Mike's sample, decide, and I'll do it and send it. ("Lucien Midnight"[6] is not prose, it's really a long one-line poem, like.) If I were to separate it into lines the poets would flip, but Lines Don't Make a Poet ... Frost's lines don't make him a better poet than the Thoreau of Walden. Let me know.

TO ALLEN GINSBERG

[January 8, 1958
Orlando, Florida]

Dear Allen,

My royalty check comes in February, I send you money then, in one

---

5. "Alone on a Mountaintop" appeared in *Holiday* (October 1958) and was collected in *Lonesome Traveler* (1960).
6. The original title of *Old Angel Midnight*. At an earlier stage Kerouac had considered titling this work *Sebastian Midnight*. He called it *Lucien Midnight* until it was published, at which time Lawrence Ferlinghetti convinced him to change the title to *Old Angel Midnight*.

lump.[7] Sterling tells me you and Gregory wonder about my riches ...
didn't he tell you I'm only going to get about $4500 from all that ROAD
noise? No movie sale, of course, & little dribbles from everywhere.[8] With
that loot I gonna make down payment on a cottage for me and my mother,
my later old age Emily [Dickinson] cottage of haikus, way out on Long Island, further'n Lafcadio Northport.[9]—Just sent Burroughs ms. (the one he
sent me about queer fuzz who calls counterman by first name & another
about Joselito) to Ferlinghetti, who askt, giving Ferling Don Allen's home
address so's to get all of NAKED LUNCH—Ferling doesn't believe
MEXICO CITY BLUES is poetry because I say so in it ... In Chicago Review I will be lead poem ("Quivering meat conception") and lead notes on
what is SF poetry, so there.... I told Ferling off about this ... Ferling thinks
like Gregory that I write prose (as I state myself), LINES DON'T MAKE A
POET ... Poetry is poetry, the longer the line the better when it comes finally to 2 page Cassady sentences horray. Big attack against me in Nation
saying I a fool boy poet and Richard Wilbur a heroic man poet[10] ... Do
guys like Wilbur and Gold stay up nights hoping we'll hurl critical attacks
at them? Geez. Everybody down on me for reading my heart out in Village
Vanguard careless of my appearance, my "poise," etc. Read like Zen lunatic
saint, like you said to do, would have anyway but you gave me confidence
ahead of time. Steve Allen will make album with me,[11] just wrote me. Your
cousin Joel was there, sweet, your father wrote me from Paterson. I had
wildest time of all time. Met great new cat Zev Putterman, from Israel, play
director. Saw Leo Garen again (your brother, he's like) ... Got heeazi [sic]
on your Paris kick but straight with Allen Eager. Had 3 girls in my bed one
night. Me and Philip L. orgied one together. Philip really wailing these
days, got in the papers with me, NY Post, made big Marian nervous
speeches to Mike Wallace tape. Tryna think of all thousands of details you'd
like. I should write novel about it all. I read last part of HOWL in the club,

7. Kerouac still owed Ginsberg the money that Allen had loaned him to pay for his passage
to Tangier on the Yugoslavian freighter the previous year.
8. Kerouac estimated that his income from his writing in 1957 was $3,650. See letter to Ster-
ling Lord, January 29, 1958.
9. Lafcadio Orlovsky was living with his mother in Northport, Long Island.
10. In Dan Wakefield's review in the January 1958 issue of *The Nation,* he ridiculed Kerouac
for dressing in what the reporter considered poor taste in a gold-threaded open-necked sport
shirt (chosen by Jack's mother). Wakefield also put Kerouac down for acting like an immature "boy poet" at the Village Vanguard, comparing him unfavorably with Richard Wilbur,
who had given a poetry reading a few blocks away at New York University earlier on the evening Wakefield heard Kerouac reading selections from his own poetry and Ginsberg and
Corso's work at the West Village nightclub.
11. In March 1958, Kerouac recorded "Poetry for the Beat Generation" with Steve Allen's piano accompaniment (Hanover Record HML 5000). The album included "October in the
Railroad Earth" and poems from *Mexico City Blues.*

it's mentioned in a newspaper. I also read "Arnold" the few lines I could remember and got big yoks, of course I repeated that it was Corso's, twice ... I even read one of Steve Allen's sensitive lil poems ... I even read Dave Tercerero's confession ... (Esperanza's old husband). The Negro dishwasher said, "Nothin I like bettern go to bed with 2 quarts of whiskey and hear you read to me," and Lee Konitz said I blew music, he could hear music ... At Brata Gallery I read your latest Mother elegy pome and Gregory's Concourse Didils and use use use to big audience of pale faced sober shits, at Phillip's and Howard Hart's request, but later, after I left, a wino stumbled in from the Bowery street and got everybody drunk and the reading was big success I hear (at same moment I was reading in club to big opening night audience & being photoed as I read and sneered at and thunderous applause and big swigs and long talks with hepcats in back). One young hepcat from Denver said everybody was going to start imitating Neal. In fact you shoulda been there, for all the handsome teenage boys came up to talk to me (hundreds). Trying to sleep days, my floor was covered with sleepers: musicians, editors of small mags, girls, junkies, it was a spectacle. Robert Frank is going to be our boy: Robert Frank is greatest photographer on scene, has already shot an experimental movie on Cape Cod with free nutty actors who only want wine, and is going to make a movie with me in May in New York wherein I will get my experience for later in the year when you come back we will begin work on our first great movie. He says it only costs about $200 to make a movie but we'll have sound too; he will get money from big Meyer Schapiro foundations. I already have an idea for a great movie about Lafcadio & Peter as brothers, Frank's wife their sister, and you the father, or you the father with your evil brother Uncle Willie Burroughs (incest) ... This Frank is no bullshit, a future Rossellini but refuses to write own movies, wants me to. I told him of our old dreams and plans. With Bill back in New York we could really in 1958 do Burroughs on Earth. Gregory knows Alfred Leslie,[12] don't he, and Miles Forst, they were in movie, Leslie technician, wildhaired subterraneans running off their holy movies against pockmarked walls of Bowery lofts is the scene. Then all rush down to Five Spot ... Poor, crazy, future moguls of Hollywood like D. W. Griffiths actually. I have discovered cat to play Neal in On the Road, Kelly Reynolds, Irish nervous Neal with blue eyes & imperious Neal look in profile and nervous Neal of 1948 ... (He's an actor, MCA) ... Got big letter from Gary Snyder shuffling around the world on a ship, India to Italy, etc, and back to India. Got big letter from Lenrow who told me [Archibald] MacLeish at Harvard praising my book.[13] Rexroth however is

12. Alfred Leslie was the New York artist in whose loft Robert Frank later filmed *Pull My Daisy*.
13. See Kerouac's letter to Elbert Lenrow, January 13, 1958.

down on me, called me an "insignificant Tom [Thomas] Wolfe" on KPFA, because, why? I'll write & explain to him I disassociated myself from his sphere of influence because I DON'T WANT NOTHIN TO DO WITH POLITICS especially leftist West Coast future blood in the street malevolence. (There will be a revolution in California, it is seething with incredible hatred, led by bloodthirsty poets like "Jean McDean" & Rexroth keeps yapping about the International Brigade etc. I don't like it. I believe in Buddha kindness and nothing else, I believe in Heaven, in Angels, I eschew all Marxism and allied horseshit & psychoanalysis, an offshoot therefrom ... beware of California.[14])

By mid-January 1958, Kerouac's mood had lifted in his letters to Joyce Glassman and his New School professor Elbert Lenrow. Lenrow had been taken aback by Kerouac's heated response to his question about On the Road *the previous month and tried to make amends in his next letter by saying that his "quip about the bookie [in the last scene of the novel] was meant to be ironic.... You made it perfectly plain in the context: both Sal and Laura felt badly, it was Remi who 'didn't like' Sal's 'idiot friends.'... I was really paying YOU the compliment of responding to your realism—of trying to show that I was moved, moved to 'care.' ...." Lenrow also reminded Kerouac of "that paper you wrote for me aeons ago, called 'The Minimization of Thomas Wolfe.' ... (a damn good paper!) Well, didn't you anticipate that there would be a 'Minimization of Jack Kerouac' also?" As Lenrow later commented, Kerouac's response to his compliments "evoked a reply that was decidedly more happy."*

TO ELBERT LENROW

Jan. 13, 1958
[1418 ½ Clouser Street
Orlando, Florida]

Dear Mr. Lenrow, "El,"

What a fine letter you wrote me. I immediately realized my mistake, thinking you didn't understand my impartial presentation of modern horror chapters, so I called, your maid said you weren't in, so I figured I'd just

14. In Ginsberg's next letter on January 11, 1958, he told Kerouac that he hoped his friend could immediately send "at least $20 or $25 to see me through end of month.... I really be starving otherwise. I've used all other dribbles of ready cash, hawked my book & Evergreen [Reviews] in various bookstores, spent my Xmas $15 family money sent me & am down to stamp money for this and one last lugubrious letter to Bill [Burroughs]...." A week later, after Ferlinghetti sent Ginsberg a hundred-dollar advance against royalties (*Howl and Other Poems* had sold 10,000 copies by October 1957), Ginsberg thanked his publisher "for check, they always seem to come in when I'm broke."

write long letter later, and for sure will see you this spring in NY as I see that there has been a general tone-leveling-down process in Ameriky in past 8 years and my old masters have the class. Your letter, in short, reminds me of how intelligent I USED TO BE, before all this flop phenomena, I mean all this twaddle now. Like, when I wrote ON THE ROAD I really didn't think much of it and still inclined to think little of it. Yes, the Myth of the Rainy Night is writ, and that's the book, that's the book I have which I'm proud to say to YOU is writ. I'm so anxious to have you read it. Would you like to? I'll arrange for my agent to mail it to you. It's called DOCTOR SAX AND THE GREAT WORLD SNAKE. Only [Mark] Van Doren has read it, said it had "crazy power," and Ginsberg is mad about it (and Clellon Holmes). Outside that, only my family's read it, frowning in perplexity. The prose is strange. But O I hope you read it soon.

Are you still lecturing at New School? If so, that will be nice, I would like to drop in, sit in back, hear you, then go off with you afterwards, if you have time. Let me know. If so, schedule. I did rush into New School to read prose to Mr Marshall Stearns'[15] class last month, on a whim, well, he askt me. I barely made it; half hour late. Nobody knows how many people were with me all that time. thousands.

HINCTY,[16] from what I gather, from what I know from Times Square etc. where such words originate, really fully means EFFEMINATE ANNOYANCE as well as suspicion, in short, I'll have to demonstrate, its a kind of SNIPPY PET. Women and homosexuals are hincty. "Hincty sweets" is really just a spontaneous burst, it were best spoken by a Carlo Marx. But whenever "hincty" was said, I remember, there was a little flip of the shoulders. I doubt if your sources can be very truly vulgarly or vulgately accurate, after all, because there is no organic relationship between the founders of words and the collators of words.

As for Archibald MacLeish, I'm grateful to hear that, and that I should hear it from a source like yourself.[17]

Speaking of "googing" and "hoorair" etc. in my new works, after 1950, I have invented so many new words it's not funny. I especially like "peotl grooking in the desert to eat our hearts alive." Allen Ginsberg wanted to know if he could use Grooking too. I said if you're a good boy[.] When I come back NY within few months I'll call you and see you. Pleased to sign your copy of ROAD, and of new book The Subterraneans. I have a new novel now, The Dharma Bums, typing it for Malcolm Cowley. Then, about 8 unpublished beauties likely to be taken up only by Grove Press and New

15. Well-known jazz historian.
16. Lenrow had inquired about the adjective in "wetting their eyebrows with hincty fingertip" in *On the Road*.
17. Lenrow had written Kerouac that the poet Archibald MacLeish praised Kerouac's novel to his Harvard classes.

Directions. Grove will do (they say) DESOLATION ANGELS, and ND will do a $7.50 private excerpt from VISIONS OF NEAL which is the great one. Visions of Neal is tears of gray rain, America mountains of used tires, mist, the West, snow and gray. It's Neal (you know old Neal).[18] It includes 150 pages of tape-recorded dialog of Neal talking to me high not-caring about machine and of parties etc. then it has a 30 page stretch IMITATING the sound of the tape, a la Joyce, or e e cummings of EIMI, and ends up with tears. My new theory of writing, my old original one of boyhood actually, is contained in Black Mountain Review no. 7 just out, which also has fine excerpt from works of "Wm Lee" who is William Seward Burroughs the secret genius of world letters, and other good things.—Also, I have a note about poetry, and 2 poems, in the next Chicago Review. We'll have a lot to talk about and I can hardly wait to see you. I hope you still have those rare monastic cheeses and do still sit at your desk and at the touch of a button play me Provençal boys' choirs in French. (Not to mention some good pernod.) . . . .

> Until I see you,
>> then,
> as ever,
>> your friend
>> & admirer
>> Jack

TO JOYCE GLASSMAN

> Jan. 13 [1958]
> [Orlando, Florida]

Dear Joyce,

Was more or less waiting for word from you but I'll write first now. Allen G. says you have a new letter, will you forward it later? I'm going to send him his money tomorrow, all of it, and be done with it and also give him a chance to enjoy Paris these next 3 months with no worries (unless he gives it away). I've been very miserable here, my in-laws annoy me no end, are worse than anybody ever dreamed. The details are too dreary (& repetitious to my Town & City days when they got that too.) (The money.) Now I'm wise. In fact I'm leaving this Fla. and moving to New York. When Steve Allen has me come up for an album, as he says he'll do, I'll do that then go out on the Island and find a house to put a down payment on,

---

18. Lenrow would hardly have forgotten Neal Cassady, whom Jack and Allen had brought to his Manhattan apartment on May 6, 1950. Later in Lenrow's memoir he wrote that on May 12 Neal broke into his apartment to steal his money and jewelry from the top drawer of the dresser in his bedroom.

maybe not so far out as the Hamptons, but someplace or other. But my mother expressly forbids me ever to bring either Ginsberg or Burroughs ever to my house, which sounds strange since I'm buying the house and I'm 36 years old. Anyway, may I say I enjoyed our last hours (and weeks) together more than ever, I find you to be the sweetest girl in the world and I want you to know that I respect you for that and even love you (as a woman, as a friend, as a anything). Somewhere or other, in the back toilets of nightclubs or bars and in the train toilets, I picked up a dose of crab lice which I'm getting rid of pronto with the proper medication. I might have left some on your toilet seat. If so I'm sorry.—It's raining, gloomy, I told my nephew[19] not to bring friends around so now the house is full of his friends in a kind of mockery of me in my own house (my mother probably whispers to them that I'm crazy, pay no attention). So I'm locked up in my own room, foolish. At least I can see everything clearly. I sprained my ankle playing basketball and am limping. My supertypewriter (this one) just came in partially repaired (a $27 complete overhaul, they said), the ribbon feeder works but one way and they forgot the "legs" but this is the smoothest typewriter in the world and now I type DHARMA BUMS, big job. I hope Keith and Malcolm like it, if not I'll take it to Hiram. I'm sure Viking will like it ... It has only one flaw, towards the end, a kind of anticlimax. It doesnt have a mad climactic moment like ROAD. I dunno. But the whole thing is enormously readable as they say, and in parts sublime, and the end is heavenly. Producer Jerry Wald is writing to me from Hollywood soon. Black Mountain Review is out, by the way, with Allen's AMERICA pome and my instructions on prose and other things, I have 2 copies of it, I can give you one when I come to NY.

Send your Elise [Cowan] poem (black leather road) to Rainey Cass, c/o h. Silver, 18 Cornelia, New York 14.... for Climax, the New Orleans jazz mag, if you want. Or any other poems you have, especially jazzy ones. Or even a piece of prose. Leo sent me photos, wild photos, by Jerry Yulsman.

Ah shit, I feel dreary, I'm telling you there are NO VIBRATIONS in Florida or anywhere in the south, the people are DEAD. Now I'm entering into a period of mingling with human beings again, and leave the quiet night woods awhile, I wanta be back in the Nation of the People, which is New York. I hope Leo or Lucien or Robert or Howard will have time to drive me around L.I. on weekends or something. O yes, Peter [Orlovsky] is arriving before end of month, Allen says. I gave Peter your new address and phone.

Any more yawks about my [Village] Vanguard reading, or anything, let me hear of it, Miss Grapevine.

Buy yourself some Petri Port and sit on the rug and play Sid[20] and light

19. Paul Blake, Jr.
20. Symphony Sid was a popular jazz disc jockey on AM radio.

candles. Do you know New York is full of electrical vibrations: that black sweater of mine I sleep in, it always crackles and bristles in New York, here it doesnt.

Mine cats are fine, bigger now, we'll bring them to Long Island and introduce them to snow next December. The other day I went to the super-market and bought six cans of Calo cat food, a jug of wine, and a bottle of aspirins. The check girls look at me suspiciously. What a dreary place it is, you'd never believe it. I'VE changed, tho, not Florida. I'm for NY again, and so's my mother. Nathless I'll have a quiet hideout in Long Island tho. I've been planning Rbt Frank's movie, possibilities of a great French Movie are enormous. POET IN NEW YORK, maybe, with Bellamy as Lorca....

In the hassle with my nephew, my mother doesnt want to bug little chil-dren, but she did finally quietly tell him to stop upsetting the house and my work room and t'other day the gangs of kids and dogs chased my little kitty across the car-zipping road up a tree which blew my top. What bugs me is that he doesnt obey me but stares at me arrogantly..., he is arrogant, indocile, perverse.... qualities, my dear, not good for 10 years old. Anyway, I feel like an old Scrooge and you know I'm not an old Scrooge, unless I am really (as Allen may think), I dunno. The movie I'd really like to do is of Henry Cru, Pat MacManus, Keith, Stanley Gould, Leo Garen, Don Allen, Lucien, Helen Elliott and Zev in his room.... what a vast French movie that would be, A DAY IN NEW YORK.... Anyway, I can write that anyway.

When I come back I'll fly, $5 more, last trip on train I had to pay $1.10 for a seat and got no seat.

Write!

Jack

Up all night drinking wine in mid-January 1958 while he retyped The Dharma Bums, *"Buddha Kerouac" in Florida wrote an air letter to Gary Snyder to ex-press his sympathetic feelings for Snyder on a "helltrip" on board an oil tanker that was making an eight months' voyage back to the United States. Thoughts of Snyder led Kerouac to reminisce about his merchant seaman voyages during World War II, and he assured Gary that he'd have lots of experience to write about later. Then, after urging Gary to "spin me a pome about that sea," Jack scrawled poems on the inner folds of the air letter based on the morning sounds he heard in Florida and a recent dream about his absent friend.*

TO GARY SNYDER

[Postmarked January 15, 1958
Orlando, Florida]

Dear Gary—

5 A M in the mawnin and here's your old dad writin you a letter from lonely old Orlando, hiccupin ... when I was much youngern you, 19, I went

105

to straits too, tight straits, names had Baffin, Desolation, Farewell, capes, impossible pearls of northpole, I wanted to jump over the side of the ship because the Negro cook wanted me re-mop the deck and there were knife fights by the cook-range like I never seed before or since, as in hell ... I collected 600 dollars, which is worth in 1958 what you're going to collect for your present helltrip ... words as swords ... and went to Harlem and did it up brown and found a young girl with tight thighs who spread her legs and threw em way back and I went in hard into her soft cunt boy and you know the winds blow cold against Harlem windows and cigarettes do kiss erotic lips ... I saw huge mountains in Greenland and dream'd of Thoreau, my boy, your boy [John] Muir and my boy Thoreau ... two of the same cloth ... what men, what men, Thea[21] is a great woman, I love her ... Gary hang on ... you'll be home soon with lots of loot to build your shack in Marin county woods, don't spend it on anything else.... we'll hang up 1250 bhikus and make em scream with 250,000 quarts of wine.... I read your letter about sappa creek crew, had same kind of crew long ago, we overturned waterfront shacks in Nova Scotia, novice socsha, and threw seamen in the water, deserted ships, ran out in bumboats, got robbed, but jacked off horses on Main Street, got thrun in jail, run out on limey baseball games, thru windows, it's all the same cut of cloth & boloney ... write to Rexroth, Creeley, make them happy—Gary, this is your year.... this the wheel turning dharma year that was prophesied by Dipankara without words, the year of the Neanderthalers.... cause I just saw big sane article about bussishm buddhismus in Mademoiselle of all places, by of all people Nancy Wilson Ross, who hated me in 1950 when I barged in on Artie Shaw's party with Frank Morley brother of Kitty Foyle and Johnonian [sic] and cab drives with talk under tunnels and the EYE A TORTURED BRIDEGROOM says sweet Mike McClure [sic] or sha ... Oshay ... now look, Gary, I drunk, now can hardly run typewriter keyes, could never be purser on ship because who could make out lists of payment fights on fist block stewards room.... I know captains whispered to me in stateroom clean up with mop you slobs of the kitchen sea, I got sea stories make your Conrad hair split ... not even typed ... but I am Chico Sea. You talkin to old seaman now seamea seaman now boy, see, semen seaman known sea, sea is my brother, see, and all's quill mighty well with germanic scholars singing in high tree. See. You understand. The Dharma Bums, my new novel, all about you, your name is Jpa ? Japhy Ryder, make you famous, I can hear it now, folk songs about Japhy Ryder, Japheth M. Ryder, of East Oregon woods, yay.... so I say, and got all your pomes, fine permns, eeeeeeifne, fvery foog; perms, gary hang on, come home, this is your year, the year of the dharmy. I know. Alan Watts now big hero of New York pub-

21. Kerouac had dated Snyder's sister Thea.

lishing scene, has turned WISDOM OF INSECURITY everybody on Madison Avenue bespectacled welldressed fine Westchester executives on to Buddhismus, of New York Library fame, return all stolen books please, me too, and this is your year, year of the dharmy.... I know whats I talking about boy because I no lie made the universe, with you, and Whalen at your heels, you flying dharmy bums you. Big drunk letter writ late at night drunk on wine, so who cares, I can handle, wont even bother with upeer a case, but jjstu write as I sees fit to you jgary, this is your year, hang on child. i am your father, i love you, nothing can harm you as long as avalokitexsvara knows your re heaere inthis endless pearl void, and kcand dyou see bug it will all be done bke zcau bi am the pjrusrser of this havenship, and this ship cant miss port. youbttou abieie cas slong as this ship is run by angels, and angels it all is, dh army bums, dont worry gary, now try come home soon as you can, see you so in home world heaven land, that s be very soon, if i die do bury me on the lone prairier. youddi di I die. and remember gary the lord said speak spontaneousloyo, o that s the way all the tathagatas in all 10 quarters did indeed make it, so come on gary, stop worrying, paint thsoe ebunkers, and be sur eplenty hershey bars in the lifeboats, and as for the red sea, spin me a pome about that sea.

Your ever loving ever admiring and ever weeping yourthufl firned
Buddha Kerouac
And thats o ly proper fittin and right.... but as for those seaman, whelek you go out find nice plynesian columbian girl pre columbian cunt make her hair stand up hyell, I be with you in spirit, if theres anytying I like in this world its the tinkly tinkly fellaheeen sound of gereat port-cities at night, you hi on majoun, or on gangee, listening to the sounds coming in your hotel window and you barely make it back to your shisk but bumake it back to your shi, that s good, I captain, I am captain hansen. I am camptain buddha field, a new field, an old field, a goo field, what other fields you features. So Gary hang on, I love you, soon see ya

Jack

Gabrielle sends you Belle-s of love (never met you) (fine chick) (Trueheart)

Morning birds
        sounds mighty strange
                whats all this shit
I got yak birds
        where's my little bluebirds
            of morain older than time
        I mean, this noise of yak
                    yak, florida
                    muckland

                    yok yok
                        nightclub
                            floriday
                                nighttree
                                    birds, wow
                        what a sound to have

        But at least I got a letter writ to my Gary

            I dreamed of Gary,
                        you know, about a month or two ago,
                        he was sittin in moroccan sand
                                musing over his pack
                        like a young kid
                                worried about
                        raisins and peanuts,
                            and I thought
            "Ah, no Buddhism, there, just pure
                            raisins and peanuts."
                                And I realized how
                                good that was,
                compared to all that buddha

        On Desolation Peak
            in Skagit Country
        Whenever I sang
            "When the Whole Wide
        World is Fast Asleep"
            I cried,
        And deers cried too

In the second half of January, Kerouac sent a postcard to Lucien and Cessa Carr,
telling them he planned to move with his mother to a house near New York City
in the spring of 1958. He also dropped several notes to Sterling Lord, keeping his
literary agent informed about his plans to record poetry and jazz, and sending
the retyped manuscript of The Dharma Bums.

TO LUCIEN CARR

                                            [January 16, 1958
                                            Orlando, Florida]

Dear Lou & Muzz ...
    As you see I barely crawled to my train and made it back, if I'd gone to
your place one more time I'd still be there ... Anyway now I'm going to

move menage (maw and cats) to N.Y. for good this spring so be seeing lot of you ... Cessa, would you tell that host of our New Year's Eve, the guy in the dinner jacket, it was positively greatest party I ever went to, I mean when we all started to leave and stayed a couple of hours that's when party good ... Don't even know his name or address but tell him I thank him for his hospitality, wit, sandwiches, etc. and showerbath ... Miss you both, would rather be in your livingroom right this minute than in all your Floridas ... Say hello to my fine macho friend, my rough-hewn rock of a man, De Onis ... Might see you soon'n poof, because Steve Allen album I fly up big heap airplane fast ... Things looking up in movies, got big intellectual (classic) letter from big producer who wants big socko ending where Dean crashes & dies, utilizing myth of James Dean on ROAD story,[22] I dunt care.

TO STERLING LORD

Jan. 29 '58
[Postmark: Orlando, Florida]

Dear Sterling,

Yes, I would like to make that record with Bill Randall and Norman Granz whether or not Steve Allen sooner or later wants to make one with me, and the reason is the unreleased Parker tape, which Steve Allen himself will well understand. So call Steve: and my hunch is, Sterling, that Steve's manager Jules Green is against the venture altho Steve is all for it, and that has been the cause of the delay, I think, maybe I'm wrong.

I've not made any previous recordings: I think you're thinking of a private recording I made with a friend's [John Clellon Holmes's] equipment which is now under the floorboards here, a kind of drunken uncommercial thing with swear words, etc.

Tell Randall I'm free, therefore, and ask him the date he wants to do it. If he can send me my $500 guarantee against royalties I can come up any time. He mentioned Los Angeles or New York as the site. With the guarantee I could even make it to L.A. (and see Wald at same time.)

Sterling, one final different item: Are you supposed to send me income tax forms-slips showing my total incomes for 1957? If not, I have it all noted down anyway and can file anytime. My tax will be around 3 or

22. Kerouac's novels appeared to some Hollywood producers to be tailor-made for the "B" picture, teen exploitation market fueled by the film *Rebel Without a Cause,* released in October 1955, a month after the death of James Dean, a teenage idol. Between 1956 and 1969 there were nearly three hundred rock 'n' roll films produced in the United States.

4 hundred. My income was exactly $4055, or that is $3650 after your 10%.[23]

Too bad I'm not in NY to take care of all these items over the phone in a jiffy. I'm really waiting for a concrete date from either Allen or Randall to come up there.

As ever,
Jack

p.s. Am sending you the new novel in a few days.
p.s. A warm note from Jerry Wald—long letter coming from him.
[on envelope: Sterling:—What's the spread in N. Y. Times?]

At the beginning of February, Kerouac wrote Joyce Glassman in more detail about his vision of the house he wanted to buy close to New York City. In the letter he mentioned their mutual friend, the brilliant young Swiss photographer Robert Frank, whom Joyce had met when Frank came to show his work to the Viking Press.

TO JOYCE GLASSMAN

Feb. 4, 1958
[Orlando, Florida]

Dear Joyce ...

Got your letter ... and the Times section same time, found a nice prospect and wrote to the realtor ... when I do get a house it will be about 50 miles out and I want to keep the address a secret from the general world including Edw R Murrow[24] ... like, when I tell you the address, I'll be expecting you to keep it a secret from various mad types or are likely on a whim drive out and burst in on my carefully planned solitudes and work schedules, right? Lucien is mad but I wouldnt mind Lucien my best friend bursting in, but but ... there are too many hipsters looking for me. One of them, you know Bob Donlin, keeps sending me elaborate expensive telegrams from Cafe Riviera telling me he's dead broke and needs money immediately ... I dont even answer, letting him think I'm gone from Florida ... he did this to Allen, too, last year, and Allen sent him $40 ... it could go on forever ... I can just see him cashing the telegram money or-

---

23. Kerouac was paid only $4,000 by the New American Library for the paperback reprint rights to *On the Road*, a very low sum. In 1949 NAL paid $35,000 for the reprint rights to Norman Mailer's *The Naked and the Dead*. In 1952 Holmes received an advance of $20,000 for the reprint rights to *Go*. (Fearing a lawsuit, Bantam Books never published *Go* as a paperback.) In 1954 NAL paid $100,000 to reprint James Jones's *From Here to Eternity*.
24. Famous television newscaster.

der and buying drinks for the house ... Meanwhile, Henri [Cru] has written me a rather nasty letter, in a way, that is, complaining because I showed up at his house with a "97 cent tokay" bottle and his girl June says I made him out a louse in On the Road, etc., so I've ceased to bother answering all such twaddle & foolishness ... just because I'm going to be rich doesnt mean I dont stick to my good old 97 cent tokay too.... In fact, in furnishing my new house, I'm going to go down Delancey street or old shoppes in the country and buy nothing but beat up old furniture, I want a happy ramshackle type home, that was my dream in the beginning ... old round mission wood tables, old easy chairs, old squareback piano, an old rolltop huge like Leo's, etc. etc. Actually I hope movies buy because if they dont I'll be hungup with that house, the monthly payments anyway to be guaranteed by my mother's social security but what about food in case my "boom" ends. I dont think it will end, tho, too many new manuscripts in the works ... I keep turning it out, they keep taking it, that's the way Hugo and Zola made it, and Balzac. Allen C. is mighty lucky his father's going to leave him a house, Allen doesnt put out enough work ... like you say, yes, a travel article about Europe.—When I mentioned Bobo's in a recent letter, I meant that Chinese restaurant we went to, you should buy a pound of that wonderful tea they serve, if you want real tea.—I'll be in NY in 3 or 4 weeks maybe 4, making my date for a Steve Allen album, he's already advanced more than my fare, and I'm going to make other albums too. I dont understand the Rexroth item in NYTimes, 'pears like Rexroth still wants to grab off the "beat generation" as his own invention & baby and you watch, he'll end up trying to turn it to politics and start rancors everywhere, I dont like him, and I dont trust him, and I wrote 2 weeks ago and told him I was disassociating myself from his sphere of interests and he didnt reply altho the rest of the letter was friendly (by "interests," I meant political shit.) I'm going to take very great care to stay out of sight of that old raging fud. Anarchist indeed. I guess you dont have to send any more NYTimes, it'll be better for me to show up at the realtors in their locales. Keith Jennison can drive me up to the country too, and I have an in-law in Jersey, and can go to L.I. with Howard or Robert Frank. No errands, just whatever you hear ... for instance last Sunday on the TV show the Last Word, with Garry Moore, John Mason Brown and moderator whatizname they discussed the word "beat" and me and my book at great length and I didnt even see it or know it, just heard about it. Same with something about me in Newsweek about 2 or 3 weeks ago or more have you seen, heard? can find? It doesnt really matter, like Faulkner I dont care anymore and as for Joe Lustig I wont bother with bits & patches of hope any more, I'm back in my starry element. I'm sending a nice prose piece about Buddhism from Dharma Bums to Chicago Review, the last chapter of Doctor Sax to Gregory Corso for German publication (in German language) and Lucien Midnight I'm typing up for anybody (since it's been lost) ... Allen is very happy in

111

Paris, got his money, Burroughs turned sweet & friendly instead of scarey (to him) and they went on a week jaunt to London I hear to see the angry young men who I imagine are a bunch of screaming fairies from the sound of it, English literatera [sic] being what it is (literatera?) lierrrateurs? "I'm just so *angry!*" I could just b-i-t-e the mall … I could djus sit and pee.… (lisp) … I mean, dearie, I'm djus so m-a-d … I living nice life now, playing my solitaire baseball game, which is a beautiful thing, you'll see it, and doing my work, and cats, and fullmoon nights in my yard, and occasional home drunks, and good food, and much sleep & universal prayer. By universal prayer I simply mean, when I step out of the house and look at those cloudy worlds of stars, it comes awfully easy to feel compassion that this dream can be so sad & mistaken, you know what I mean … mere thought is a prayer, dont worry I wont drag you to church with Billy Graham.

Write soon, Jack

Before leaving Florida to look for a house on Long Island, Kerouac sent a post-card to Robert Creeley, editor of the Black Mountain Review, *and letters to William Burroughs and Donald Allen. Allen had asked Kerouac to advise him on the contents of what Jack referred to as "a big hep review" of the work of the experimental writers associated with the Beats, the San Francisco Poetry Renaissance, and other groups like the New York poets and the Black Mountain poets. Two years later, Donald Allen's work as editor resulted in the groundbreaking poetry anthology* The New American Poetry 1945–1960 *(New York: Grove Press, 1960), which brought widespread attention to the so-called underground writers.*

TO ROBERT CREELEY

[Postmarked February 11, 1958
Orlando, Florida]

Dear Bob—

Glad to hear [Edward] Marshall digs me, I dig him. [Hubert] Selby wrote me, too. "The coming downedness" is a great phrase, please use it in a poem. [Robert] Duncan, give him my address and tell him to write.[25] I'm sending one of my copies of B[lack] M[ountain] R[eview] to Allen G. & Bill Burroughs in Paris.… I may come thru Alameda sometime this year: only

25. Edward Marshall was the author of a poem circulated in manuscript about his mother's mental illness, "Leave the Word Alone," which influenced Ginsberg's writing of "Kaddish." Hubert Selby, Jr., was the author of the powerful collection of stories, *Last Exit to Brooklyn*, (1964). Robert Duncan was an important San Francisco poet. In a letter to Kerouac on January 31, 1958, Creeley had written that Duncan had praised *On the Road:* "there is a sense in which Kerouac touches everything with his own life, so that this reader will go anywhere with him." Creeley added a postscript after he finished the novel: "it's a beautiful solid & completely heart-open thing."

thing is if we go driving let me do the driving. What are you planning for next BMR? Incidentally, Ed Dorn's story in [BMR] #7 is certainly the end.[26] "He was called Tiny for the usual reasons ..." Really the best story in the issue. Re SOUND (1956 pome):–"... who wants to hear/ about the aniards and breast plates of warriors of the/ Medieval Ages/ I wanta know about the people/ on the street, what they doin?/ And what the high art/ hark squambling in his quiet/ temple moonlit jambymoon/ writing jingles and jongles/ for the pretties on the square"....

Kicks, man, kicks.... Kiss the kiddies for me

Jack
Shit Kerouac

TO DONALD ALLEN

Feb. 11th [1958]
[Orlando, Florida]

Dear Don,

Yes, about time for a big hep review.

First, yes, I'll type up a few meditations, and poems, and prose from something. From "Lucien Midnight," my wildprose book, maybe.

Allen Ginsberg: a little prose from his magnificent letter (to me) about Spain, no need to say it's a letter, just prose, would look good alongside his mad new poetry and also introduce his considerable prose ability. Either, or a statement of belief.

Corso: New poetry of his.

Peter Orlovsky: Ginsberg says he has just started writing exceptional and exceptionally strange little poems, Allen is happy about it and says Heaven oped. Allen has these poems in Paris.

Gary Snyder: New poems and a little prose, you might in fact write to Gary (c/o USNS Sappa Creek, Marine Transport Lines, 11 Broadway, NY 4 N.Y.) and ask him to compose a prose explanation of Zen Lunacy which is the backdrop for the Snyder hep shot, very great shot.

Philip Whalen: His address is c/o Judge Richd. Anderson, Lincoln County Courthouse, Newport, Oregon, and he has scads of brilliant poetry and by the way his prose in letters shines. Gary just wrote me and said: "Phil is turning into a beautiful landscape sentient & vast."

Will Petersen: Gary says of him: "Will Petersen is transformation upon transformation, a diamond onion or maybe a growing jewel tree like the Sukhavati says; him & his remarkable wife named Amiko. He wrote a huge stack of letters about love, cooking, No drama, house-cleaning, & his wife's

---

26. Ed Dorn was a young writer who had studied at Black Mountain College.

funny winter-girl wool underwear." Maybe you could write Will for something more informal than the Ryoanji garden.

John Clellon Holmes: He is now in London I think, and he has great vocal ability to explain beatness & hipness, maybe you could write him ask for some prose about what he saw of "the angry young men" in England or something but I dont have his English address. His home is Box 167, Old Saybrook, Conn., his mother or sister will forward. His new novel The Horn now being printed at Random, Hiram Haydn's his editor.

Philip Lamantia: Scads of beautiful stuff of all kinds, and he will urge you, as I do, to also publish his brother-poet-ecstatic Howard Hart, a fine new poet. Philip's home is at 1045 Russia St. San Francisco.

Ed Dorn: A brilliant writer indeed, I'm glad you dug him, he can be reached thru Creeley or Jonathan Williams I guess. Also a great poet, get both prose & poems from him.

Selby Jr.: He's in Brooklyn, our veritable little old Genet tho I've seen greater homosexual prose descriptions etc. by Allen and Burroughs. But Selby is a brave fine writer and his address is 626 Clinton St, Brooklyn.

Robt Creeley: Care/of Gen. Delivery, Alameda, New Mexico, the heppest and very strange writer, tell him to write something about the "new downedness" he calls it. And some poems.

Neal Cassady: I have some prose of his from old letters, describing bums on the railroad, better than mine. (He is "Dean Moriarity")

Mike McClure: Has many strange hep poems, of course, and willing to join in this.

Bill Burroughs: Some weird little piece of his massive work, that would fit in, completing a very hep issue.

Write to me and let me know if, with my own contributions, you want me to send assorted lil pomes by Creeley, McClure, the Cassady prose, the Ginsberg prose, etc. etc. that I have all bundled up here.

See you week of the 24th and give my love to Barney [Rosset]. What I'm glad about The Subterraneans is no hepcat's gonna come up to me and say it's nowhere, it's impossible to call it nowhere, the ordinary readers of course may object to its esoteric style etc. Till I see you,

Jack

Why dont you also try to get Koch, O'Hara, Ashbery,[27] and the Marshall of *BMR* #7 and even mebbe a poem by Larry Rivers & a picture of his & a picture by Iris Brodie and a poem by Anton Rosenberg.[28] hep hep one two three!

27. Kenneth Koch, Frank O'Hara and John Ashbery were poets associated with the New York School.
28. Larry Rivers, Iris Brodie, and Anton Rosenberg were New York artists and writers.

Well, them's the ideas
We're living in a wonderful literary
time, actually
(O yes, also I could send you a little masterpiece prose description of the
end of the world by Herbert Huncke, the mysterious "Junkey" we never
found on Times Square in On the Road, the "Ancke" of Holmes' Go, it is a
gem only Ginsberg & I have read & treasured) (Being a down word from
the horse's mouth, writ in subway at 5 a m)

A
lil
beato
pome
by
Bob
Lax[29]
Mebbe
too

After typing up a sample from the opening pages of Naked Lunch *and a description of William Burroughs and his writing for Donald Allen, Kerouac sent
Burroughs a different version of his description (possibly an early draft of his letter to Don Allen) with a brief note and some choruses from Kerouac's work in
progress, "Orlando Blues." At this time Burroughs was in Paris with Ginsberg
and Orlovsky, trying to interest publishers in the manuscript of* Naked Lunch.

TO WILLIAM S. BURROUGHS

[February 1958
Orlando, Florida]

Dear Bill:

DAYDREAM OF THE DISK

I have taken the pains of typing up this excerpt from Burroughs' massive manuscript. Because he cant type himself his manuscripts are well nigh
unreadable. I thought it would be a good idea to call this a daydream, because Burroughs writes what he calls "routines," which are big mad funny
satirical daydreams he acts out in front of his friends. In Tangier he never
touched a drop till exactly 4 P M, then had his brandy, and started acting
out his routines; in the morning, on a little majoun, he would then record

29. Robert Lax was the editor of the Catholic magazine *Jubilee.*

last night's routines. And because he is a great aristocratic master of the English language, and is really "The Forgotten American," which I can explain later, and because he's been everywhere and done everything, to read his prose is to get a first bird view into the latest accomplishment in human utterance. (I think Burroughs is being put down by publishers for the same reason that he was put down by Peggy Guggenheim[30] and Mary McCarthy[31] when he met them in Venice, he's too frank for society.) Daddy Long Legs Burroughs is my way back daddy. He is every bit as great as Céline and greater than Genet, almost. He stands tragic alone in a sea of facts. He is tall, with thin lips, spectacles, wears gray felt hats and walks down the street with a vigorous pump of his arms like a mad German genius of the 19th century, thru casbahs, medinas & Mexico Thieves Markets of the world. Aint nothin Old Bull dont know. Especially now, circa 1958. Ginsberg announced that he has become a Quiet Flowery Sage on top of all that. Like that other serious benevolent scientist, [Wilhelm] Reich, Burroughs is likely to be put down for 100 years. Burroughs is the scientist who has found out the secret of how to control dictators by telepathy. Telepathy of the People—He is also a great sad George Sanders[32] of the movie of our minds, says Phil Whalen among other things, the Great Ultimate Sanders-of-the-River.

Bill, this is what I'm doing with your stuff in the upcoming Beat/Hip Review by Evergreen. I am trying to make them cop. I think they will. I hope I didnt fuck up everything by naming you with Reich who is banned by U.S. government. I think maybe the Reich Institute raises too much of a hysterical liberal fuss, as tho medical dogma were any worse than literary dogma. "Old dotin old fuck," I just said, hearing a TV father whining to his daughter.

Say hello to Allen and show him these 2 new poems of mine from OR-LANDO BLUES, writing every night by candlelight, with windows open to moony yards & trees of Muckland Central Florida in Febiary [sic].

Chorus #32

HOORAY FOR ZOOT SIMS JAZZ
Listening to a guy play
tenor saxophone &
keep the tune inside
chords & structures,
as sweetly as this,

---

30. Peggy Guggenheim was an American heiress who supported the arts. Burroughs, Ginsberg, Orlovsky, and Corso had been turned away from one of her celebrity parties in Venice.
31. Mary McCarthy was an influential American writer who later championed *Naked Lunch*.
32. George Sanders was a movie actor specializing in sardonic, sophisticated roles.

you'll experience
  the same
    fitly thrill
      you got from Mozart

It is pure musical beauty
  like a musicale
    among wigs

People who dont understand
jazz are tone-deaf
  & dont understand
what tone-deaf &
  simply deaf
  meant to Ludwig
  von Beethoven

Chorus #33

Can diamond cut iron?
  Diamond cuts glass
    glass links

But can it cut
An iron link?

Nirvana means Cut-Link

If diamond dont cut glass
  or iron dont count,
              hey?
    maybe the wisdom Vow
    of the Diamondcutter
    may have made it

> Love to both of you,[33]
> Jack

*Early in March 1958, Kerouac and Joyce Glassman drove out with Robert Frank
to look at houses fifty miles from New York City in Northport on Long Island,*

33. Kerouac addressed the envelope to both Burroughs and Ginsberg:

Mr. William Burroughs
c/o Allen Ginsberg
9 Rue Git-le-Coeur   #25
Paris 6, France

where Peter Orlovsky's brother Lafcadio lived with his mother. Kerouac bought the first place the realtor showed him, an old shingled house with small front and back porches at 34 Gilbert Street located next to the athletic field of Northport High School. He expressed his happiness to Philip Whalen, writing him the day after the publication of The Subterraneans. *Jack also heard of the positive response to the typescript of* The Dharma Bums *from the novel's first readers at the Viking Press. Kerouac composed a blissful note to Keith Jennison there, who had told him that the editors at Viking, hoping for another bestseller like* On the Road, *were putting the book into production immediately.*

TO PHILIP WHALEN

[Postmarked March 4, 1958
c/o Glassman
338 East 13th Street
New York, New York]

Dear Phil,

Received your 2 welcome warm wild whoopee letters (excuse my tawny port) & had no time to reply soon or in length till I'm settled down in a month, did a lot of things, including wild interview at Brooklyn collidge [sic] before 2000 eager young students spitting back Zen answers to their intellectual queries and at one point even answered with fingertip to lips, brl, brl, brlbble ... My ms. about Gary you & me & Dharma Bummies has flipped Madison Avenue over, they plan it for the Fall with full trimmings ... they all read it twice not once ... it is loaded with bodhisattva magic, nagically [sic] ... a must book on the list of every freelance ghost, etc. etc. "I really dont want to listen to all this" ... I got house for Mémère, too, she coming soon ... about as big as that whole Berkeley Way house, but cheap buy ... now I broke[34] ... but glad in wisdom wine & love you.

J

---

34. Kerouac used most of the money he earned from the sale of his writing to make large payments on the houses he bought for himself and his mother, hoping to make her feel more secure about the future (he had promised his father that he would always take care of Gabrielle). Jack put $7,000 down on the $14,000 house and paid off the mortgage within a year. As a result, he left himself so short of cash that he often felt pressured to come up with new funds for their living expenses.

TO KEITH JENNISON

Dear Keith,

Thanx for warm report on *The Dharma Bums* ... I wrote it thinking of you, that you'd love all that outdoor business we did ... I pictured you and Malcolm [Cowley] chuckling over it, I didn't know you'd cry ... But since I cried when I re-read it (don't know why) I guess you can cry too ... See you soon, wherever you'll be, which I hope'll be

INNISFREE
Jack your friend

Three weeks after his thirty-fifth birthday, Kerouac was in a less exuberant mood when he answered a letter from John Clellon Holmes, telling him "the whole beat generation scene is a pain in the ass after 35." Kerouac had taken a vow to remain sober for six months after having been attacked in Greenwich Village by three men who followed him out of a bar when he was what he called "stumbling drunk." They left him on the sidewalk with a broken nose and arm, a large gash in his forehead, and a concussion.

To add to his troubles, The Subterraneans *was greeted by a chorus of spiteful reviews, though the novel sold over 12,000 copies in its first month of publication. David Dempsey in* The New York Times *said that the story "seeps out here, like sludge from a leaky drain pipe."* Time *concluded that Kerouac "is not Rimbaud but a kind of latrine laureate of Hobohemia," while* Newsweek *dismissed the book as a "tasteless account of a love affair between a white man and a Negro girl." In* The San Francisco Chronicle, *Rexroth sneered that "the story is all about jazz and Negroes. Now there are two things Jack knows nothing about—jazz and Negroes." Rexroth patronizingly concluded, "We've just got to realize we have another Thomas Wolfe on our hands, a great writer totally devoid of common sense."*

Holmes had been kind enough to praise The Subterraneans *after its publication, though Jack had portrayed him unflatteringly in the book as the character Balliol MacJones, a "midtown sillies world" writer who had made a lot of money writing* Go.

TO JOHN CLELLON HOLMES

[April 13, 1958]
34 Gilbert St.
Northport, N.Y.

Dear John,

Your letter really warmed my heart, because I thought, after long silence, you'd read SUBTERRANEANS and been bugged by references to "Balliol MacJones"—The editor, Don Allen, wanted to remove further confessions there, about our "fight" over "beat" and I wish he'd left it in, woulda been recorded how we made up over that nothingness ... Anyway, in writing it, I felt I was in the tradition of [Dostoevsky's] NOTES FROM UNDERGROUND, FULL confession,[35] there was much more about Mardou's cunt they had to cut out ... this is for the future, huge confessions about EVERYTHING. (Like in Neal's great letters.) Anyway, yes, I want to go out to Saybrook soon's I get this new house of mine & my mother's furnished and fixt up, etc., the owners only packing today ... The owner's wife is Mona Kent, who wrote "Portia Faces Life" for radio from 1940 on ... They good folks. Write to me at this address & let me know when you're driving to NY on business. It might be too soon, "late April," but we'll see how works out. Lotsa things talk about. I don't souse anymore, just a few cocktails for dinner, because I was really going Bowery way for a while there & one night when stumbling drunk got set upon by 3 hoodlums & knocked out twice and didnt even fight back but laffed like Cannastra.[36] This is dangerous to my health. So now I am deeply absorbed in nice sober thoughts. I feel much much better. I'm tired of all that jazz and smoke and want to go the way of the dharma bums, now, clean mountains and clean meditation and pine needles and woodfires. Next step for me is to buy a shack or lodge in the mountains in Adirondack or Mohawk or White Mountains or even Laurentian Quebec country. Movie ain't sold yet but Brando and Kubrick discussing it together. I guess Jerry Wald is out since I told him I absolutely refused to let any cruelty be injected into a movie version of the ROAD.[37] His idea was very cruel. Fuck these killers of the world's heart. Money's good but I was sent on earth for a prior reason. I think. I feel that, anyhow. Yes, and it's spring in Northport too (North shore, near Huntington but on the water and looks like a Maine fishing port town).

I have my cats, my mother, my typewriter, my work, and finally have reached that enviable position you have in Saybrook Old, of being in nice home & officially committed to the tender art of writing artistic literature.

I knew Sonny Rollins would make it big, there's another tenor called

35. In his preface to the Norwegian edition of *The Subterraneans,* Kerouac expanded on his idea that his book, "modelled after" Dostoevsky's *Notes from Underground,* "was a full confession of one's most wretched and hidden agonies after an 'affair' of any kind. The prose is what I believe to be the prose of the future, from both the conscious top and the unconscious bottom of the mind, limited only by the limitations of time flying by as your mind flies by with it. Not a word of this book was changed after I had finished writing it in three sessions from dusk to dawn at the typewriter like a long letter to a friend."
36. Bill Cannastra, a wild friend of Kerouac and Ginsberg, was killed in a subway accident in 1950.
37. On January 15, 1958, Kerouac sent Sterling Lord a letter to forward to Jerry Wald at 20th Century Fox studios, forbidding "any kind of brutality" in the filmscript of *On the Road.* Apparently Wald, trying to exploit the publicity around the recent death of James Dean, wanted Cassady to be killed in a car crash at the end of the movie. But also see Kerouac's "I dunt care" letter to Lucien Carr on January 16, 1958.

John Griffin from Chicago who's better'n Coltrane I think but not better'n Sonny. Pepper Adams is a mad new baritone, white guy, looks like you a little. Very friendly to me. But I dont go to clubs any more now I dont drink. The whole beat generation is a pain in the ass after 35.[38] Young Socialists League had a big meeting to discuss me. *Partisan Review* attacking me.[39] Rexroth (beware of that man) lied on TV saying I pulled out dope needles in front of his children BECAUSE I WAS DRUNK. How square can you get ... his idea of glibness. Doesn't even know that drunks can't take drugs from needle, chemical impossibility, yet has the nerve to say of me in his review of SUBS: "Now there's 2 things Kerouac doesn't know about ... Negroes and Jazz" (sic). & they tell me he never lets Negroes into his house, and he claims I don't realize that jazz is "like Rameau instead of just African drumbeats" ... I know what, we'll tie him down with rope and play him our Seymour [Wyse] jazz record, MEDITATIONS, what was the name of it?—Ah, once we only had to cope, you and me, with ignorance of the world in general, and now we're being attacked and misrepresented by the very people who were supposed to understand and HELP us in our fight to instill peace & tenderness in the world. Instead, all this malice.

38. In the May 1958 issue of *Esquire,* Dorothy Parker reviewed *The Subterraneans* from the perspective of someone over 35 who, from firsthand experience, could compare the writers of the Beat Generation with those of the Lost Generation:

> It says, on the dust-cover of *The Subterraneans,* that the Beat Youth believe that how to live seems much more crucial to them than why. (I don't know why they need give themselves such airs about it; if memory serves me, that is the way most generations believed.) But the "how" of the Beat Boys and Girls is of an appalling monotony....
>
> I think, as perhaps you have discerned, that if Mr. Kerouac and his followers did not think of themselves as so glorious, as intellectual as all hell and very Christlike, I should not be in such a bad humor.

39. In the spring 1958 issue of *Partisan Review,* Norman Podhoretz attacked Kerouac as the leader of a pack of "Know-Nothing Bohemians," stating that Kerouac's "tremendous emphasis on emotional intensity, this notion that to be hopped-up is the most desirable of all human conditions, lies at the heart of the Beat Generation and distinguishes it radically from the Bohemianism of the past." Podhoretz believed that "The Bohemianism of the 1950s ... is hostile to civilization; it worships primitivism, instinct, energy, 'blood.'"

In the summer 1958 issue of *Partisan Review,* LeRoi Jones took issue with Podhoretz's article in a letter to the editors:

> I have read a great many of these scathing rants that are being palmed off as objective critical studies of the "New Bohemianism," and almost without exception they have come from the small coterie of quasi-novelists or *New Yorker* suburban intellectual types of the late '40's and early '50's which represents [sic] so much of what Beat is a reaction against. It seems to me that Beat is less a movement than a reaction. It is a reaction against, let us say to start, fifteen years of sterile, unreadable magazine poetry.... And Beat is also a reaction against what Randall Jarrell calls "The Age of Criticism." ... There was neither Bohemianism nor any great intellectual rebellion in the '40's, and there was no poetry to speak of.... As with Dada, Beat represents a line of departure rather than a concrete doctrine.... [Like *Howl, On the Road*] breaks new ground and plants new seeds.

Ginsberg also has been attacked by these very people (Village Voice etc. etc.) who should appreciate him. Now, of course, Rexroth attacks poor Allen. I say, and what I've been doing, not answer any of them, my mother says silence is the best answer, the most painful. I can just see Herbert Gold tossing in his bed at night hoping I'll write a return attack against him, right?

Well, write and tell me date of yr next NY visit. . . . we'll arrange a weekend, me alone or with Joyce. . . . . . .

Allen lives in Paris off HOWL money, they sold 30,000 of em you know. . . . but he poor. . . . he's with Burroughs & Corso. . . . Did you dig that fine Burroughs writing in Chicago Review? "calls Nedick counterman by his first name," just like Harrington might have said, or Jimmy Cannon.

Love to Shirley, tell her to keep the mashed yams and marshmallow ready.

"Maybe Eden ain't so lonesome, as New England used to be"—I'll give you 2 cents if you tell me who wrote that masterful magical line.

Baron Jean-Louis Lebrice de Kerouac,

Gentilhomme et Roue,

J

John: Keep my new address a dead secret from everybody you know, thousands of nuts want to come out and bother my poor elderly mother, please keep address in yr hat.

In the spring of 1958, Kerouac settled with his mother into their house at 34 Gilbert Street in Northport. There he wrote a series of letters to Philip Whalen and Gary Snyder while recovering from the injuries he'd suffered in the assault in Greenwich Village, aware that his mental state had "changed a little" after suffering a concussion in the brutal beating. Determined to stop drinking, he stayed close to home. He played with his cats and watched the budding shrubs and trees outside his bedroom window, and he bought a pair of overalls to wear while he helped his mother plant a vegetable garden in his "big grape arbor" backyard on Long Island. When work on Memory Babe, *his work in progress about his childhood in Lowell, went slowly, he offered to type up a clean copy of* Doctor Sax *for Barney Rosset, who was still considering whether to buy the novel for Grove Press. Kerouac also finished several commissions for magazine articles, like the one he wrote for* Life *describing his trip with Robert Frank to Florida in mid-April to move Gabrielle and her two cats from Orlando to Northport.*

[no date or place]

Dear Phil,

Just wrote to Thea hoping Gary's back and gave them my new address but warned them not to divulge it to anybody but you because of crap & thousands of horseshit that have already started ensuing, such as demands for money as tho I was rich, etc. etc. so you keep address in your little pointed head too

34 Gilbert St

Northport, N.Y.

And write to me soon as you can, tell me your plans, you're welcome to stay here anytime you come N.Y. and meanwhile Gary has suggested we go dharmabummin & hikin up the Dharma body coast to Wash. this summer sometime which I think I will do, by that time Mémère's new house will be underway with furniture etc. It's a great house, 50 years old, with big yard.

Beautiful spring day in Long Island, buds, grape arbor, etc.

Spring day—
    in my mind,
Nothing

Life is finding your way thru nowhere.

God or Tathagata couldn't be so cruel as to have made a REAL world of REAL life and death, right?

Was drunk 2 weeks ago, got beat up by hoodlums, stopt getting soused, feel great. . . . sobriety is really an absorbing contemplation. Have changed a little, tho. No joy. No sorrow needer. Well, all I need is some more of you and Gary this summer. Someday when I'm rich us 3 go to India and trek. Gary could be rich too if he just wrote spontaneous accounts of his mad life and just changed names, like I do. I got him all lined up with Viking and my agent. Bussei was great, also Measure Magick, also Chicago Review. Did you see my baseball story in Esquire this month?[40]—that's written off my self-invented subtle card baseball game I never showed you . . . o wait a minute, I did too, only I improved it in Orlando from words to symbols. . . . I have a really beautiful piece in Holiday Mag. coming up about the Skagit adventures, called "High Cascades" and really too good for Holiday.[41] Doing another one for them now on Tangier to London trip.[42]

40. "Ronnie on the Mound," *Esquire* (May 1958).
41. "Alone on a Mountaintop," *Holiday* (October 1958).
42. "Tangier to London: A Beatnik Pilgrimage," *Holiday* (February 1960).

Went down South to get Mémère and cats on Life Mag photo-story assignment, what pictures that kid took![43] If successful; we'll drive out on another one to Calif.

Ecrit moi!
Jean

TO PHILIP WHALEN

[n.d.]
34 Gilbert St.

Dear Philliboo,

Yes I'm thinkin that idea of all four of us going hiking this late summer would be good. I already bought my Austrian lightweight mtn. boots and also a pair of sneakers to complete my rucksack. Are you really going to make the mountain lookout this summer? or next?

Just got long letter from Allen, he's showing your long poem around (the 50 page one?) ... Have you sent in yr poems for the Don Allen anthology? Well, old bean, Gary is back and it does seem strange, when he was in Japan I thot of him as a strange Buddha far away, and now I know he's puffing his pipe in paw's garage I feel he's Gary again and soon we'll be sweating on trails.... The only trip I'm going to take ere late summer to SF, will be to Lowell next month to walk around and remember scenes for projected novel Memory Babe (my boyhood nickname, I could remember everything then.) Or did I already tell you this? If I had any knowledge of flowers and trees I'd tell you about my yard, the grape arbor, the gnarly Japanese tree that my cat sleeps in, the strange flowers, the dogwood tree, the two pines, two spruces, not a big yard but full of trees and bushes and I'm going to fix it up like a millionaire's mansion someday by putting a 10 foot wire fence clean around it, crawling with ivy, to hide inquisitive neighbors so I can relax in my own grass. So far so good here Mémère is very happy and keeps wishing you could visit us. Someday you will. I watch Dracula and the Warewolf of London on TV at midnight, alone in dark parlor. Then I go out and dig stars and meditate under my pine. Planting tomatoes, onions, potatoes, corn, cucumbers, beets and radishes. Bought shovel, rake, lawnmower etc. Living quiet bhikku life and at night every night get fine visions from Sakyamuni. Will write big final Sutra, "Supreme Reality," and get that phase over with. The years fly by in twos. Just wrote thing for Holiday, about Tangier to London, quite rich. Rather listless, tho, about

43. "That kid" was Swiss-American photographer Robert Frank. *Life* never used Kerouac's essay about their trip to Florida. It was published posthumously by *Evergreen Review* (January 1970) as "On the Road to Florida."

poetry etc. these days, for first time in my life reluctant to write letters and only answer you and Gary and Allen & business. Am not as rich as sposed to be, in fact owe 10 g's on this house and no prospect of selling book to movies even now. Gypsy once told me I'd always have enough money, not lots. In fact you can tell from tone of this letter how rather listless I am. I can't even provide you with interesting notes & outcries any mo. Forgive me. Ah well, it's all a damn shame anyway, ignorance & existence. Who really cares? Diamond Sutra's finally sunk into me into very bones and I am grown completely neutral. Hope Gary won't be disappointed. 'course, a little benny, or wine, would wake me up to silly old self again.—Thought the strange phrase the other pine-night: "The inexhaustible vows of fertility...." Wa? is THAT what dem buddhas doin?

Pomc	Little bird in your nest
	in the tree of blossoms
	at night in the rain,
	what made you peep?
	—Your mother's soft breast
	or the bleak endless rain?
	If the Universe is Your Mother
	Is She like a blossom?

Simple enuf ...

Few Haikus	Late April
	dusk bluster—
	Lions & lambs
	The trees are putting on
	Noh plays—
	Booming, roaring

And one night the words:

A star waving in the sky like a lamp in the wind
and I'm not drunk....

Okay, maybe I'm not so
listless arter all, really
need long talk with you and G.

Jean

Early in June 1958, after Viking Press sent Kerouac the galleys of The Dharma Bums, *he was shaken out of his "listless" mood by seeing the number of changes that the copy editor had made in his typescript without consulting him. Sterling Lord set up a meeting at Viking, and Jack took the commuter train to Manhattan to try to persuade his editors to set the type of the book all over again, working from his original "scroll" manuscript. Since Malcolm Cowley was in Paris, Jack's editor at Viking was now Helen Taylor. Her response to the meeting was to write Kerouac that "it's obvious that you've restored to the original certain things you agreed to change on your first visit here. . . . We cannot read your mind as to what you will or will not accept, and so you must tell us." Taylor refused to abandon the set of galleys and asked him to mark it "exactly as you want it."*

Kerouac corrected the galleys carefully and returned them to Viking on June 18, 1958. After reviewing his revisions, Taylor wrote him on June 24, 1958, that "this has been quite a brouhaha, hasn't it, but now we know." When Jack told his friends what had happened, he considered the encounter with Taylor as a personal victory, despite the fact that he was so upset by it that it brought on a "2 day binge" that started his heavy drinking again. At the Viking Press the incident had confirmed the editors' sense that Kerouac was unprofessional because he insisted on restoring his prose to what he had written before they had imposed what they called their "house style" on his manuscript.

TO JOYCE GLASSMAN

[Early June 1958
Northport, New York]

Dear Joyce

Will you please forward this to Hiram Haydn, I just dont have the Random House address in the house.

Be sure not overlook this . . . the statement is good for him. Also you can ˎ write Haydn a note while you're at it telling him about the state of your novel.

I had to go to NY the other day mad as a hatter to contest Viking's shitty idea of making as much as 4,000 corrections on *Dharma Bums*. They said copy-editing hadnt hurt ROAD but that was a short-sentence style that couldnt be hurt. They agreed first to start all over again, I told them at my expense too, to prove to them I meant it, now after I'm back home they start to hedge and want me to go over the galleys and make my 4,000 restorations to the original (hardly any room in the margins) and finally now the damn galley aint arrived in the mail from them and if they are trying to sneak over their ersatz version of DB on me they've lost a writer.

They sorta laffed at me, not really understanding what I tried to explain about prose. . . . they spoke about their "house style" and all such sickening crap. Tom G[uinzburg] was not disturbed at all and looked to me like it suited him, but Helen T. doesnt seem pleased at all, I really let her have it, the speeches; . . . Sterling was sitting behind me. While all this was going on he got a call from MGM in Hollywood, they take out small option on Subterraneans and if buy, give 15 g's (not much but completely unexpected). Meanwhile Jerry Wald writes me he's disappointed I didnt sell Road to HIM! crazy. So I have to correct galleys now, when they get here, and rest up from the 2 day binge I went on, calling Leon 5 million times and he was never in and just as I suspected that TV movie would kill me, its just too complicated this New York world of telephones and appointments. So I'll see you when I come NY again with galleys, next week. I have angle for piano here now so dont worry about piano. Jerry Wald I think wants me to try a screen original for him but I wonder if I really would know how—Anyway I STILL haven't got going on Memory Babe? See what I mean? I should have got a house in Virginia or someplace.—On top of that George and Mona trying to get me to meet thousands of girls around here, that would really be the end of my Memory Babe work so I refused.[44]—— I'm working on Memory Babe right now this weekend. See you soon.

Jack

Shortly after Kerouac's pivotal editorial conference at Viking, he heard a rumor that Neal Cassady had been arrested in San Francisco by federal agents for possession of three marijuana cigarettes. Drunk on sweet white port wine, Jack dashed off a note to Philip Whalen, asking his friend, "What has happened to Angel Neal?"

TO PHILIP WHALEN

[Before June 12, 1958
Northport, New York]

Dear Old Phil—

The wind is blowing thru the trees, the music on the radio is sweet, and I am drinking wine. Hooray for Phil Whalen! Hooray for Zoot Sims! Hooray for Lou Holz! Hooray for my hair!

Are you okay now? Was this a hernia operation?—You know, I'm afraid to come to Frisco this September, supposing an old junkey friend rushes up to me in the street & the cops swoop in? What has happened to Angel Neal? Why did Rexroth say I had "pharmaceutical equipment" when we busted in on him with white port? Lucien says Rexroth would destroy me if he had a chance. I can just see him ordering my head cut off in a revolution. However, if I do come out, which is likely due also to developments in Hollywood (MGM just took option of Subterraneans up), I can always steer clear of the Beach. I may drive out in a truck with my old boyhood pal Mike Fournier (of Lowell).

---

44. On June 4, 1958, Kerouac wrote Glassman that his mother had banned all weekend visitors "except relatives like her sister and daughter because it always ends up with her being bothered all weekend with extra meals and extra linen etc. and what is this if it isn't a home? not a hotel. So I told her I'd separate my own life from the life in her house, and go see my friends in NY instead of having them come out.... When I come to see you ... will you try to get bennies from your doctor for late night work, I'll pay you."

Trees cant reach
          for a glass
Of water

I think American Haikus shd. never have more than 3 words a line—

The Dharma Bums was ruined by Viking Press, they put in 3,500 commas & changes in my swinging Mark Twain prose so I am denying them the right to publish yet I'm afraid they're going to try to sneak it through (laughing at "boyish" Jack) so there'll be mess of troubles and here I had handed in a perfect holy ms., all they had to do was print it—I had you read some of yr. poems at Gallery Six chapter & they were afraid of that even—Gary is a great new American culture hero, you too (in his background in book)—Anyway, I'll have my way on Dharma Bums, dont worry—Meanwhile, be lovey. That is, love me too!???

PAL Jack

TO PHILIP WHALEN

[Postmarked June 12, 1958
Northport, New York]

Phil,

Just got galleys from Viking, for me to restore to original, so theyre not going to try to sneak something over in [sic] me, i.e., a fucked-up manuscript not even mine anymore.

Your Corvallis haiku recently, "where does the weather turn off," was so strange & real, it seemed I'd seen it before, in my gray mind of you-dreams, us.

When you write to Gary tell him what I said about truck ride, etc., but you know I'm afraid I aint got enuf bodies to keep up with everything I should be doing. But when Dharma Bums comes out I'd like to be out of New York and out of cities and especially SF and be up in the mountains. If. Oh well, maybe I'll suddenly go to Paris.

I have a slew of girls in NY now and screwing em all and wish Gary was here to help, just too many. One night I was in bed with 3 girls. I'm getting too old for this. I try to serve the Bodhisattva's role for them but this ole bodhisattva getting tired.

Have you read the long tirade against us and me and Allen in Partisan Review, by [Norman] Podhoretz, about 2 months ago? Gad.

Also, last night on TV, on Jack Paar show, they did a parody of me based on what I did when I went to their show as a spectator, with Steve Allen, and suddenly Steve yelled "And now, presenting JK" and I was rushed on-stage before millions of viewers and the dumb shit said (Jack Douglass, Paar's writer), "What is the Beat Generation," and I answered:

"Nothin."

Then I reached for his lighter and quietly lit up, and he said, "O, I use morphine myself." I said, "Aint you tried H yet?" So last night here's this parody of me with sloppy sweater saying "Nothin" and lighting up cigarettes. However, Steve Allen and Jayne Meadows his wife had a big mad talk together in their pad, ending in great laughter, and they know I'm not like that. My album with Steve coming out soon, is, I think, the best poetry reading recording since [Dylan] Thomas ... you'll see yourself, when you hear it? I really blew in our best Milvia Cottage tradition, drunk, loose, even with glaring mistakes, but what music? Meanwhile Steve plunks pretty chords on background piano. The 3 albums I made for Norman Granz are being listened to by Shorty Rodgers and Jimmy Giuffre, and then they're going to compose scores over it. That will be about a year, I guess. I did what they asked me to and cut out, drunk. 4 goddam albums in one week.

Jerry Wald of 20th Century Fox wants me to write a screen original; the money will be fantastic; I think I'll try it and lay off all other shitty small-time pestiferous offers like a TV movie with Benny Goodman, a story for Film Magazines, or interviews with Mike Wallace headlined "Why are Modern Writers Amoral?" Hey? Almost every night I meditate under my pine and it all comes back to me, the inescapable bliss of the golden eternity, and since no one can understand that save you and Gary and mebbe Will Petersen, why bother to try to explain what to them is unexplainable, besides they just want to hear themselves talk and go on being fucked by samsara. I've only got one body and one mind. Pray to Amida get me 1000 transformation bodies to do the wheel-turning we prophesied. Mebbe it'll happen. You should come to New York with Gary this fall and I'll get you all lined up for wheel-spinning, via Mike Wallace, TV interviews, publishers, novels, etc. etc. really. Meanwhile, when caterpillars shine for you at night, you're happier than I am.[45]

Jean Louis Le Fou

45. Kerouac might have had in mind attacks like the one in *The New York Times* by J. Donald Adams in his "Speaking of Books" column on May 18, 1958:

> Reading Mr. Kerouac's *On the Road* or *The Subterraneans*, I am reminded of nothing so much as an insistent and garrulous barroom drunk, drooling into your ear. The sentences sometimes run to as much as a page and a half, and are formless. Faulkner at times writes sentences as long, but they are built. These are just so much slaver.

Adams thought that the term "Beat Generation" writers should be renamed "bleat generation," since "bleating is a monotonous sound, and I think that as a sleep-inducer the writings of this group are more effective than the long-recommended prescription of counting silent sheep as they jump over a stile." In Adams's column on October 26, 1958, he had a change of heart after reading Kerouac's "Alone on a Mountaintop" in *Holiday* magazine. Adams decided that "I find it necessary to revise certain opinions.... Offhand I would say that when Kerouac sets his mind to it he can describe the world of physical experience better than anyone since Hemingway."

June 18, 1958
[Northport, New York]

Dear Helen,

Here are the galleys exactly as I want them published. I want to be called in to see the final galley and check it again against my original scroll, since I'm paying for this and my reputation depends on it. I want to make sure we put out a book we can really be proud of. Just leave the secrets of syntax and narrative to me.

You were right about Hozomeen not being in Canada and about Highway 1-G instead of 17-A; I've fixed all that.[46]

Galley 80, "Happy and Wally didn't put on anything and just rode wet with heads bowed." The commas after "wet" practically destroyed one of the finest sentences I ever read.

Dont laugh about enclosed clipping,[47] be serious, note carefully how Associated Press refuses to muddle up its leads with commas for the sake of the average reading eye. SHOW THIS TO TOM.[48]

Galley 52, "instantly in my closed eyes" I saw a vision, not "before" my closed eyes. Example of misunderstanding by copy editors.

Galley 57, I explain one of my restorations on the basis of natural-born instinct concerning narrative.

Galley 58, when you say something like "Inside I saw the so-and-so" you don't say "Inside I saw *again* the so-and-so"—you're just bugging the reader's eye.

Galley 63, somebody insisted on making my "mild picnic" a "wild" picnic.

My "goodbye" (the spelling of it) is based on the philological theory and my own belief that it means "God be with ye" which is lost in machine-like "good-by."

Galley 34, "America *will* be"—I mention this to prove I dont always abbreviate "will," like in "it'll," for nothing. There's method in my madness.

Galley 40 and others, Heaven not capped? WHY?

Galley 41, "woik" was colored preacher's way of saying "work."

Galley 46, one fast ride from Mexicali to Ohio, was in one fast sentence with a minimum of marks, or pauses, just like he drove. That particular sentence was inexcusably misunderstood and ruined.

Galley 51, I changed "sentient weedhood" to "living weedhood" because sentient means "having the power of conception." My own error.

---

46. Two factual errors in the manuscript corrected by Helen Taylor.
47. The clipping was an excerpt from a newspaper article about the Dwight D. Eisenhower administration that consisted of eighteen lines without commas.
48. The editor Tom Guinzburg.

Galley 52 I was seeing the white light everywhere everything, not the white light everywhere, everything. . . .

Galley 83, "I felt just like it, brilliant and bleak." Like the hope, that is, not the "clouds," somebody had inserted "THEM" to aim at the clouds. Misunderstanding.

Galley 78, "Who does he think he is speeding on government property." No questionmark in that sinister laconicism. This explains one of the changes I made from questionmark to comma or period . . . questionmarks indicate a kind of "whining" sound, or implication.

Helen, sometimes when I came across a period and wanted to insert a comma and then a lower case (restoring to original), I made a mark like this: /

If this is not correct, please make proper marks for printer. I think it's all clear, actually, especially where I laboriously spelled out my instructions in the first part before you sent me your signs.

Anyway, now I'm starting on new novel MEMORY BABE and when I hand in the neat doublespaced ms. I want you to go over it for the ten or twelve "mistakes" or "serious problems" in it and we'll thrash out, but no more irresponsible copy-editing of my Mark Twain Huckleberry Finn prose. With freedom in mind I can write a book for every October.

See you soon, and mucho thanks.

Jack

Writing to Gary Snyder about The Dharma Bums, *Kerouac again described his revisions on the galleys for Viking Press, returning the book "to its original fresh-ness and purity of dharma bum way of talking." He insisted that all his friends could have commercial success if they wrote fictionalized autobiography the way he did, and he offered to collaborate with Snyder and Whalen "screaming over wine typewriter" to create a* Holiday *magazine article about "California Bud-dhism." In a parenthetical aside near the end of the letter, Kerouac casually asked Snyder for news of Neal Cassady, who had been sentenced on June 14 to five years to life in San Quentin.*

TO GARY SNYDER

[June 19, 1958]
34 Gilbert St.
Northport, N.Y.
June June June June June

Dear Gary-O

. . . One swoled ball? Must be the same thing I had, mumps, also Lucien had it (he just had his third boy) so dont worry. I just prayed to Avalokitesvara to make your swoled condition go away right away! Soon as you read these words you'll be better. Just returning a favor, a respect, really.

Well old shitface I had the same problem with Viking Press and the ms. of THE DHARMA BUMS, that I had with Grove Press and the ms. of SUB-TERRANEANS. I had to have a showdown and take the galley and restore it 3,500 places to its original freshness and purity of dharma bum way of talking. Now its in perfect shape again. The only technical error in it, I think, is in my estimate of the height of Matterhorn camp, that is, our big concave rock: I said 9000 feet, and the height of the little alpine lake at the foot of Matterhorn itself, I said 12,000 I'm afraid, and the height of Matterhorn Peak itself. Can you send me that and I'll rectify. I had other errors like Hozomeen in Canada, which it aint, and Highway 1-G off 99 goes to Sedro Wooley, I had 17-A hitting 99 which it dont. When you read that book you will really see what can be done with the likes of our common-type adventures. It's much more rollingprose than ON THE ROAD, which I wrote in 1951, you know. Old Montgomery comes out fine in our climb to Matterhorn chapter, in fact funny, a new comic character in my gallery, but yet I give him his due. I even have your father dancing wildly at Locke's house your farewell party but to hide him a bit I said he lived with his sister, no wife. I have him living in Mill Valley, and Locke (Sean Monahan) his shack is in Corte Madera. You are Japhy Ryder (Japheth M. Ryder), Whalen is Warren Coughlin, Allen is Alvah Goldbook, Rexroth is Rheinhold Cacoethes (cacoethes means ill habits that befall men of letters! hor hor) Montgomery is Henry Morley, Neuri is Psyche, Blackie Burns is Burnie Byers, Andy the Packer is Happy the Packer, Will Petersen is Ron Sturlason, etc. etc. Jinny is Princess and has yellow hair and gray eyes and lives with her mother. I covered everything fine. I'll show you this technique when I see you this year. Anyway the novel is just now on the way, first class mail, ready for the linotypist to make those 3,500 corrections and then it will soon be sent out fresh and pure and when I get review copies you get the first one, just like Neal got the first review copy of ON THE ROAD, naturally.

Miss ya, pal, and wish you were here. It may be I'll drive out to the coast with my old boyhood buddy Mike Fournier, a cross between you and Neal, in his big road truck, and see you this summer. About climbing I dont know. What I really wanta do is get me a shack now, somewhere in the eastern mountains, and spend that month of promised prayer in October in it while the book is coming out. When a book comes out people dont leave you alone, you end up panting in bed at night wondering if you're going to die: you'll see someday. I had nightmares last October. My apartment phone kept ringing incessantly; big parties came to a head every night; I fell flat on my head in the Bowery with Bob Donlin; I finally went home to winter Florida and recuperated in time to write DHARMA BUMS. Beware of the fantastic hordes of "admirers" that come clutching at your hand.

Their motives ... Oho, their motives, my dear.——I'd rather stick to my old lightning clique.—Just got a card from Mike McClure who's very happy, just wrote a new book of poems in creative old Mexico, go see him, he's one of the best on the scene I'd say. Ferlinghetti I never could smell and especially now, telling me, after reading my BLUES, that I wasn't a poet, and then out comes his new poems with New Directions using all my images and style[49] ... Would Ferlinghetti have dared to write poetry about tincans and wino alleys before me and Ginsberg's manuscript came under his scrutiny? No, he would have stuck to the old Richard Wilbur line, like all poets who consider themselves "educated." Rexroth is a great poet, however, no matter how much he hates me. I know this now, everybody says no, but I remember you too said he was a great poet. I think we're right. Tell him to go fuck himself anyway.

Meanwhile I have American Beauty red roses growing in my rock garden, corn growing, melons growing, grapes coming squeezed out of arbour joints (that's right), a chair in the sun every morning to read the Diamond Sutra in (I'll show you the new transliteration), two blue spruces out front, a Japanese tree of some kind, a big old barn big enough to make a movie studio in, an extra room with eaves in which I'll splash paint and paint divine paintings (my own way), a room to sleep in, with treeleaves swishing in the screen, and a room to write in ... but an old house about ready to fall down, tswhy I like it. An attic, even, I never used it yet. I'm burying the frigging "mortgage" with a cash buy next week ... Got 25 g's from Hollywood and another 15 g's for SUBTERRANEANS from Pandro S. Behrman at MGM coming in 6 months if he takes it (after option)[50] ... Got lotsa cunt, imagine them beautiful things with ivory soft thighs throwing their legs back over their shoulders and you slip in your hard rod in all that squishy softness and kiss their lips and they say "I'd forgotten how nice it was." Whooee! But I'm still not a lecher. No shit, I stay home and write and think most of the time, admire the stars of night, play solitaire, wait, working out the plot of one weekend, one typical weekend in my childhood (1935) to make MEMORY BABE out of this summer ... (they used to call me memory babe, the gang, because I remembered everything.) "Working" means I pace up and down the dark yard and sing.

49. Ferlinghetti's *A Coney Island of the Mind* was published by New Directions in 1958. He took his title from a phrase in Henry Miller's *Into the Night Life*. By 1998 there were nearly a million copies of Ferlinghetti's book of poems in print, including foreign editions.
50. When MGM also announced plans to make a film titled *The Beat Generation*, produced by Albert Zugsmith, Kerouac threatened to sue the studio over the title, but the movie was released in July 1959. It was advertised as "the title with $1,000,000 worth of publicity." In June 1958 *High School Confidential*, also produced by Zugsmith, was the first film to feature a Beat poetry reading and a performance by John Drew Barrymore as a compulsive hipster. It is now a camp classic. *The Beat Generation*, starring Steve Cochran and Mamie Van Doren, with cameo appearances by Louis Armstrong, Ray Anthony, Vampira, and Charles Chaplin, Jr., was

Are you telling letters to Allen in Paris? Tell him I expect to see him this summer in NY and I dont want to write any more silly letters, I'm sick of letters to Paris. Tell him to bring Burroughs who can make some money for once in his life if he plays it cool in NY. Burroughs, you know, is a superduper Rimbaud-type Raymond Chandler and could make money ... that is, in his "commercial" opuses, when he really goes, like in THE WORD, there's no writer in the world can match him, not even you and me. He told me he was the ONE PROPHET.

Somehow we'll meet this year, whether I come out in a truck or a pullman later. I told Whalen in a long letter the other day I'm genuinely actually no shit afraid of walking down North Beach and all of a sudden some old buddy rushes up with pockets loaded with shit and the cops swoop in. SF is absolutely silly with cops. In a hundred years it will have been a mark of distinction to have been a "hepcat" in this time, but right now I want fresh air, no dungeons for me, I've had enuf of those in previous lifetimes. Neal saw me off to the railyards last time I saw him, November 1956, and said "Reason why you wanta ride open flatcars and drink whiskey as you fly down that coast on the ghost is because ina previous lifetime you were in dungeons and never got enuf fresh air ... and explains why you have a metabolism that abhors indoors." (The "ghost" is the firstclass zipper freighttrain leaves five times a week 3rd and Townsend 7:30 PM and gets to LA 7:30 AM). (Find out about Neal, can I write to him is there any way I can send him jail money—if it's a jail sentence he may start writing his great book THE FIRST THIRD again. That guy is really a very great writer but he refuses to write.)

O yes, how about you and me and Phil Whalen getting together this summer or fall to do a piece for HOLIDAY magazine about "California Buddhism," they want ME to do it but I'm willing to do it with you 2 guys and split three ways ($1500 for the whole thing) and we'll investigate further scenes after Berkeley Bussei scene etc. In other words, money for doing what we usually do, I thought this would be a nice gesture to Phil who has no money. It's a dead cinch ... we'll gather the material, write it together screaming over wine typewriter, and all collect and spin the wheel of the dharmy. Holiday wants to send me to Quebec first, on expense account, then to California. Next year they want to send me to Japan and India etc. I just sold them a story about, a travel article I mean, called "Tangiers to London," a gasser. Keep your boots greased and straighten your tie!

---

reviewed by *The New York Times* as "contrived and downright embarrassing.... These greasy little characters are seen sitting around, writhing to 'noise' records or noisier music, and raptly listening to what passes for poetry." Zugsmith was also credited as the author of a Bantam Books paperback titled *The Beat Generation*.

I'm still with you, hardon! Don't forget what we promised Kwannon! Don't ever ever ever get mad at me for writing about you as I've done, I did draw my breath in pain.

Jack

Work on the revision of The Dharma Bums *galleys completed, Kerouac tried to get back to* Memory Babe *with the help of a local doctor's prescription for the stimulant dexamyls and frequent glasses of his new favorite summer drink, iced white port. Newspaper articles about him had publicized his Northport address, and since it was an easy drive from New York City, a stream of uninvited guests continued to show up at his house. Responding to a card from Phil Whalen, Jack brought his friend up to date on the film sales that were pending for* On the Road *and* The Subterraneans, *anticipating the security of an income from his writing for the rest of his life. But Kerouac's recognition as a novelist came at a high price: Jack also described the personal attacks on him in television programs and his disturbing fan mail, and told how he and Mémère had hosted four local fans who invaded his privacy when they "came stealing up to sit with me and ask about Beat."*

TO PHILIP WHALEN

[Early July 1958
Northport, New York]

Dear Philnik,

Just got your card, glad to hear you're well. Try standing on your head 3 minutes a day maybe, for general healthy circulation of all your organs not only your lungs. It's done me wonders, not only rid me of thrombophlebitis as you know, but common colds, etc.—only sinus and bursitis I think unaffected by that type-circulation therapy.

Your poem in Chicago Review best thing in Review, with possible exception (well who compares poetry to prose?) of Gary's marvelous clack-clack sesshin description.[51] Now Gary will start getting attention he deserves from publishers & critics. Other things good in there, it's really a Holy Issue. All except Watts—no bodhisattva ever carps at other bodhisattvas, right?[52]

---

51. The summer 1958 *Chicago Review* published Whalen's "Excerpt: Sourdough Mountain Lookout." The issue also included Snyder's "Spring Session at Shokoku-ji" and Kerouac's "Meditation in the Woods," a section from *The Dharma Bums.*
52. Alan Watts's essay "Beat Zen, Square Zen, and Zen" was also in the summer 1958 *Chicago Review*. Watts found "Beat Zen" to be "always a shade too self-conscious, too subjective, and too strident to have the flavor of Zen.... Furthermore, when Kerouac gives his philosophical final statement, 'I don't know. I don't care. And it doesn't make any difference'—the cat is out of the bag, for there is a hostility in these words which clangs with self-defense."

It is a good idea for me to come out to Newport instead of Frisco but still I want to stay home till the Fall, till my new book is finished, in fact I wont ever leave the house to go to New York. I only hope Gary doesnt leave before I see him. Something'll happen. I'm enjoying this house ...

Full moon—
　　　old pines—
Old house

Also I make it behind the barn with local young chicks at 5 A.M.

I watch old TV movies, sometimes double features, Clark Gable and the Marx Brothers ... I sip my iced white port. I shoot baskets, sweat, take showers. My zendo is right here. Last night Lucien came with the Chronicle article about Beatniks and we batted out an interview for United Press that will go over the wires Saturday July 5th I think. It's a pip, in a way, and it gets me off the hook as "spokesman" for murders. I've turned down TV appearances and more Mike Wallace interviews and anything of that nature. I got 25g's for On the Road, not much, but pay for house. The Dean will be Mort Sahl, a cynical New York yiddishe comic but intelligent. Sal will be Cliff Roberts. Screenplay by a DuPont. Tri-Way Productions. Anonymous angel bankrolled it, probably Max Gordon owner of the Blue Angel and Village Vanguard nightclubs, N.Y. Probably Brando maybe. Jerry Wald was just about to buy it for 20th Century when we sold it.[53] But I get 5% of the movie profits, which I wouldna got from 20th Century Fucks.

Also, Subterraneans about to be bought by Pandro Behrman at MGM, for 15g's. Not much again, considering, but on Dharma Bums we'll hold out for a fortune and I gets to buy a hacienda in Michoacan for Lucien and zenbos and me. Residual money after taxes will go into a bank at $3\frac{1}{4}$ percent, compounded quarterly, like say, if I can stash 20g's I get a check for $160 every 3 months for groceries. That's the extent of my wealth, and no rent. Property tax: $480 a year!

I oughta open up a liquor store but you wouldnt catch me running it. In other words, I will be modest in my means and ways, as ever, but secure. The drawback is these fucking college students who keep looking for me and sometimes finding me: last Saturday I was sitting on the lawn when two girls and two boys came stealing up to sit with me and ask about Beat. It ended up with a screaming drunken midnight supper my mother setting out a whole roast beef which was all devoured (week's meat) but one of the boys was French, Pierre, and she kept kissing him, you know her. But then she was sick for 2 days and so I wrote and told all these fucking

53. This film deal for *On the Road* fell through. The film of *The Subterraneans* was made by MGM and released in 1960.

broads and queer magazine editors not to come here any more, it's the refuge of an aged quiet lady and a quiet writer Buddhist. Right?

Actually, I dont do anything any more, and dont care, trying to still the waves and find the water for what it is, etc. Some assy zazen sometimes under moonlight pine midnight. Same message of Lotus Pundarika. Solo tu, says Italian singer on radio.

Meaning, God

is

Alone.

Imitate him. Will go west coast when Fall falls.

With The Dharma Bums *in production, Kerouac sent a brief note to Viking Press editor Tom Guinzburg, enclosing the copy he had written for the dust wrapper of his book. Soon afterwards Jack also sent Gary Snyder a page from* Publishers Weekly *advertising the novel and alerting Snyder that Viking Press would be contacting him to obtain a libel release.*

TO TOM GUINZBURG

[Early July 1958
Northport, New York]

Dear Tom,

See you soon.

Jack

MODEL FOR DUST JACKET OF "THE DHARMA BUMS" BY JACK KEROUAC

Dharma is the sanskrit word for Truth. It may also be translated as The Duty, or The Law. "The Dharma Bums" is a surprising story of two young Americans who make a goodhearted effort to know the Truth with full packs on their backs, rucksack wanderers of the West Coast hiking and climbing mountains to go and meditate and pray and cook their simple foods, and down below living in shacks and sleeping outdoors under the California stars.

Although deeply religious they are also spirited human beings making love to women, relishing poetry, wine, good food, joyful campfires, nature, travel and friendship. The hero is young Japhy Ryder, poet, mountaineer, logger, Oriental scholar and dedicated Zen Buddhist, who teaches his freight-hopping friend Ray Smith the Way of the Dharma Bums and leads him up the mountain where the common errors of this world are left far below and a new sense of pure material kinship is established with earth and sky. Yet it is the ancient Way of all the wild prophets of the past, whether St. John the Baptist in the West or the holy old Zen Lunatic Han Shan in the East. Japhy and Ray adventure in the mountains and on the trails, and then they come swinging down to the city of San Francisco to teach what they have learned, but the city will not listen. "Yabyum" orgies, suicide, jazz, wild parties, hitch hiking, love affairs, fury and ignorance result but the Truth Bums always return to the solitude and peaceful lesson of the wilderness.

In this new novel, Jack Kerouac departs from the "hipster" movement of the Beat Generation and leads his readers towards a conception of "continual conscious compassion" and a peaceful understanding truce with the paradox of existence.

The Dharma itself can never be seen, but it is *felt* in this book. It is the strangest of tales, yet an honest, vigorous account depicting an exciting new Way of Life in the midst of modern despair. The rolling pages of the novel are filled with original descriptions of the High Sierras, the High Cascades, the Northwest, the South, the desert, and the American road. There is also an account of the night of the birth of the San Francisco Poetry Renaissance.

Through these pages pass hoboes, blondes, truckdrivers, poets, hunters, Negro preachers, Mexicans, librarians, hound dogs, children, janitors, forest rangers, loggers, cowboys and Zen thinkers in a bewildering and delightful variety as the story races true to life to its conclusion.

Read slowly and see.

TO GARY SNYDER

Monday July 14 [19]58
[Northport, New York]

Dear Gary,

I'm sending you this page from Publishers Weekly, which will be the dust jacket of the dharma bums novel, to show you a general idea of what it will be like. As you see, I've got you down pretty accurate but I made some changes in your personal life, girlfriends, etc. mother-in-law etc. to throw off the scent. For instance, your father lives with his "sister," Jinny is a blonde living with her mother, Nancy C. is a divorcee living in Burlingame, etc. and the shack is not in Mill Valley. I make no mention of the Reed College trouble, at all. It's really irrelevant since you're a Whitman in this book. In other words, you'll find that there's no danger in signing the release Viking Press will soon send you, the same kind of release Allen signed for Road, a "libel" release meaning you would never sue me or the company for "libel" because your counterpart is too close to home. At first Viking's lawyer gave the green light but now, since they know you're back from Japan, they figure they might as well get yr. signature. Actually it's not very important since the lawyer felt there was no libelous matter, anyway. So do what you want.

I got a long letter from Allen the other day, very beautiful, he's coming to NY within a month but my mother wrote him a letter herself telling him to leave me alone. I sortav agree with her, his ideas of what "we" should do when he gets back, such as getting Julius Orlovsky out of madhouse (Julius eats his own shit) or starting trouble with the cops over Neal (who never took my advice about heat & fuzz), are really silly and hysterical and the ideas of a politically-minded man. I have retired from most of Samsara and I'm very happy in my solitude. I'll sneak into NY and see Allen once in a while, but even then I anticipate trouble. My mother told him to leave my name out of his affairs, stop howling my name wherever he goes. You were a witness to his "well then go!" in 1955 so I'm not being mean, after all. I got a long letter from Phil too. I guess I wont make your summer climbs but I'll see you probably in Fall or Winter, or mebbe even reach you in Japan in 1959 (they say you're going there again). If things develop so, we can do our Buddhist *Holiday* piece in the Orient maybe, if we want to.

I still haven't got my Hollywood money so still haven't bought this house and I don't know what's going on. Maybe something went wrong. My agent says no. I'll invest residual monies in bonds at 5%, like my sea-man friends do. I'm not spending but staying home. I want to establish a life of freedom from money-cares, thats more important.

Say what about that mad Alaska? Someday I may go there and claim a mountain that can be kept forever for real, and no "foreign country" hassles.

Whalen's poem in Chi[cago] Review very great. Your piece too. Whalen says Watts wanted to establish the fact he was the Buddhist authority in America. I think YOU are, not Watts. I didn't understand that editorial foot-note crack about you going Square. Anyway, so it goes.—I'm getting a little stale lately, tho, I'm not writing, I see no reason to write anymore. It'll have to be a religious or personal heart reason I guess. I watch TV at night and scribble poems about the shows, drunk. I'm planning a huge novel about childhood, a "solitudinous halo for Doctor Sax," as Allen suggested, but I wish Sax were published first. There's a stop-Kerouac movement at Grove Press, I'm afraid, and for sure in the Village where I saw a pencilled scrawl in a shithouse "Kerouac Go Home." So I'll get me a shack in the Adiron-dacks and forget about it allanyway. I zazan often under my pine and it's always the same assurance of Okay. But in the days I get bored and wisht I had something to occupy my mind, asof yore. I just dont care any more, like I said. But I always bounce back with imagination works. Let me know how long you'll be in Lockes shack so I can figure when to come later in year.—Lots of mad young girls after me these days, this Fall I'll go a fucking. Too hot now. Give my love to Locke and tell him I said the Devil doesn't exist and for him not to put stock in dreams or omens ever.

Jack

After John Clellon Holmes invited Kerouac to visit him in Old Saybrook, and conveyed some Hollywood gossip about the filming of The Subterraneans, *Jack sent his old friend a letter describing his life in Northport and praising Holmes's recently published jazz novel,* The Horn.

TO JOHN CLELLON HOLMES

[July 21, 1958
Northport, New York]

Dear John,

Looks like you know more than I do about Subterraneans. Can you tell me where you read about Arthur Freed, Vincent Minnelli and the Duke Ellington? Apparently in Variety or Billboard? My agent doesnt write often and is very busy and all I read (from Hollywood) is Louella Parsons. No, I'm not rolling in dough because they haven't paid me but $2500 for ROAD so far (a "binder").[54] And the option on Subs never even in yet. But it's all coming, of course. I already have this old house-heap almost half-paid now. My mother and I don't spend at all, really. I never go out. I made a vow not to go NY all summer. I feel happy in my overalls in the yard, like a Lowell Child again, tho late at night whango whango at the refrigerator chilled white port, or sometimes whiskey and ice water, or beer. Alone in front of TV digging. You've been missing great Channel 13, their Art Ford Jazz Party has Billie Holliday every Thursday night at 9 ... she's so thin & beautiful too, but her voice cracked. She sure does have a hip sneer, like I said to you in that letter in 1952 from Mexico.—I'm going for Holiday to Quebec in September so that's I guess when I'll stop at Saybrook, yes. You're right about Ted Patrick arranging it, and a guy called John Knowles who goes prowling the Brooklyn waterfront with Truman Capote. Ginsberg's Siesta in Xbalba, you know, was written in 1954 in Mexico jungles of Chiapas before Howl. Yes, he's living in small hotel at 9 Rue Git le Coeur with Burroughs and Corso, they all have separate cells with a concierge and all. Ginsberg returning to NY in August, however. He just wrote me a very great letter. Burroughs is really a great writer now, he tells me, and Gregory a great poet; some in NY think he best. I am turning down a movie I was to make superimposed on Benny Goodman session this summer, and

---

54. When Tri-Way Productions bought the film rights to *On the Road*, Kerouac was to have received $25,000. He was paid only $2,500 before the company went out of business.

Mike Wallace further interviews, and Wingate further interview "ad libbing with a strip teaser." I was really funny on Jack Paar and other shows last spring, even Giroux was pleased. I would say anything that was on my mind, any moment. I've changed considerably since that short time ago. Become very quiet, and fat. Must get rid of the fat but not the quiet. I'm going to get me a shack in the mountains this Fall ... remember I told Time magazine I'd pray a month if book sold to movies? in woods? This means simply sitting on the earth, under tree, stars, every night (in poncho cape in rain), and simply concentrating on God's compassion for all living creatures. Cynical as I am I still know that to be there. Hell is the inability to love God. The inability to love Cod is simply the loss of contact with the knowledge of his eternal compassion. Know why God is compassion? Because the world ain't real. If the world was real, then we "beings" would really be in hell. Tell it to Ivan Karamazov, that pale faced shit. (God bless Ivan Karamazov.) I'm trying to write a book about childhood, a big super job around Doctor Sax "bole of flower," a solitudinous halo around the Soul of the Child, maybe I'll start tonight. Hiram Haydn says my puff can't be published anyway because book dedicated to me he says (& others) so that's okay because I can't be making unqualified rave statements about any contemporary author except Céline. I told this to Mr. Gallimard, he is passing the great news of this humble statement of mine to angry-faced Céline. I really love Céline and better than Burroughs or Genet too, he's a man. He spits out with such barroom frankness. But John, by the way, your DIALOG was surprisingly perfect in THE HORN. I gotta hand it to you there. Again, as always, I was bugged by your slightly analytical prose passages but remember (don't pay attention to just me) I've met a bunch of college kids who are all fascinated by you and want to know who you are and some of them even accused me of stealing "beat" term from you because ROAD came out 5 years later. These kids are really interested in you. And the reason is, they WANT analytical prose passages, they want certain things explained, which I dont satisfy in my narrative eagerness. So okay. See you Sept. Write again soon. I'm looking forward, I'll bring Zoot [Sims] album and my new Steve Allen poetry reading etc.

J.

John, please remember to keep my address a secret. I'm much more exposed here than you are 100 miles out.

At the end of July 1958, as Ginsberg prepared to return to New York from Paris, Jack wrote a letter explaining why his mother refused to let Allen visit their house in Northport.

July [24?] 1958
34 Gilbert St.
Northport, NY

Dear Allen,

By now you must have gotten my mother's letter to you, which she wrote and mailed before telling me and thus only put a 6 cent stamp on it? did you get it? Anyway, whether or not, it's nothing new from 1945 Ozone Park hangups only now I more agree with her not because what she says, but I have withdrawn (as you saw me begin to withdraw in Tangier & Peter objected, recall) and want to live my own kind of simple Ti Jean (whatever you may think of it) life, like in overalls all day, no going out, no weeping mobs of Asia under my midnight Buddha pine, no "horde of silver helmets" (that alright for great historian & poet Corso who is a Romantic like Shelley)—I am just a Buddhist-Catholic and want no more shit nonsense and roses—What does this mean? O by the way I wasnt angry by your earlier letter, I've just been pondering what to say to you, it has nothing to do with that or with anything you've done since you never change, it's ME that's changing—Outside of a few calm visits with you in NY or preferably Paterson at your father's house I dont want no more frantic nights, association with hepcats and queers and village types, far less mad trips to unholy frisco, I just wanta stay home and write and figure things out by myself, in my own Child mind—This means of course I wouldnt dream of interfering with Julius shitmouth or Neal's fall, how many times have I in fact you told him to cool it, it was no longer feasible in California or anywhere in USA and on top of that he goes and pushes for the sake probably of saving a dollar for extry breakfast, poor N always did save a penny to spend dollars. He may write the first third[55] now, by the way, I think— what else do? as long as it aint a dostoevsky-siberian term in hard labor snow—Carolyn may be wrong about the fuzz knowing Dean but in any case whats the real connection? in fiction, as it says on jacket, and Dean never pushed.... I read all about the Frisco horror suicides & murders and Lucien came over and had me bat out a UPI interview to disassociate me from such shit—I agree with my mother on the point of your not using my name in any activities of yours (other than pure poetry & prose) such as politics, sex, etc. "action" etc. etc. I'm retired from the world now and going into my mountain shack later and eventually just disappear in woods as far as it can be done these days. Thats why I've made no effort to see poor Peter or even Joyce anymore, Lamantia bugged the shit out of me in the spring using me

55. The title of Cassady's work in progress about his early years. The book was published by City Lights in 1971 as *The First Third*. Ten years later Ferlinghetti wrote an introduction to the expanded edition describing Cassady as "an early prototype of the urban cowboy who a hundred years before might have been an outlaw on the range."

to publicize his poetry readings rushing into Joyce's with screaming Howard Hart (was fun for awhile) then vanishing as tho nothing happened anyway, he really a con man ... Very beautiful about Bill's great new Proustian sick-in-bed aesthetic millionaire genius, hope they do something together like India, because where can Bill go now? He said Portugese East Africa last time. Does Gregory know that he was mentioned in Danton Walker's column (NYdaily news) saying "While [Beat] Generation writers are raking it in in night club readings, Gregory Corso, who originated the idea years ago, starves quietly in Paris." Also Robt. Frank the great photographer thinks he's the greatest poet. Also there's a girl I know (20, rich) who's in love with him already. Yes, I'm beyond the idea of falls and orients and masses, the world is big enough to right itself, Sax said the universe disposes of its own evil, and so does History. You underestimate the compassion of Uncle Sam, look at the record. I know it will all come raining down in our paranoiac minds but maybe not in nature. As for a peaceful wiseman America I think you got that now. I just believe it, I have no facts to back it up, like Einstein dont have no facts to back up what Buddha knew in full (electromagnetic-gravitational ecstasy). Well Burroughs, okay, Great Teacher, the universe is exactly 2 billion years old—as for the 2,999 other Great Chilicosms guess. Dont get mad, Allen. I'm not screaming at you. I'm just like Lucien now, a quiet family man, of T[own] & C[ity] solidities again, and not rolling in dough at all. No money from movies yet, and royalty monies gone in house ... but I wanta figure it out by myself from now on in ... I tired of outside influences. I'm getting at something in solitude halo. Besides I'm only interested in Heaven, which is evidently our reward for all this screaming and suffering going on. When you come back we'll discuss in detail all the publishing items for you and Bill & Greg ... Be careful of NY this time, you know I got beat up almost killed when drunk by Henri Cru's enemies and people write on walls of Village shithouses "Kerouac GoHome" ... that dont leave me much stomach for the same old shit of past years, man. Me for midnight silence, and morning freshness, and afternoon clouds, and my own kind of Lowell boy life. As for the Freudian implications, or Marxian, or Reichian, or Spenglerian, I'll buy Beethoven.

O why dont I shut up, always showing off ... Your letter very great and I'm sorry and yet glad that now we'll have new quiet [Professor Mark] Van Doren type relationship. Lucien by the way approves of you altogether, says I'm nuts, and says all women afraid of manly queers who put shoulders to wheel but aint afraid of swishies. My own reason is: Peace. And the Dove. In my ceiling crack, the dove. George Martin[56] dying in the kitchen. Base-

---

56. George Martin was the pseudonym for the fictional character based on Kerouac's father, Leo, in *The Town and the City.*

ball games. *Memory Babe* my new book big RR Earth[57] run on Lowell memories. I'll see you around September, wont leave house till then, according to June vow, for work reasons. Alas, Allen Goodnight

When the editor Donald Allen at Grove Press asked the writers whose work would be included in his anthology The New American Poetry 1945–1960 *for statements about their poetics, Kerouac sent along his "Belief & Technique for Modern Prose." He told Don Allen it was an "early piece" that was "wilder and stranger" than his "Essentials of Spontaneous Prose." On July 30, 1958, Jack passed on the manuscript of his book of poems* Mexico City Blues, *hoping that Grove Press would publish it.*

TO DONALD ALLEN

July 30, 1958
34 Gilbert St.
[Northport, New York]

Dear Don

Here are the poems from Mexico City Blues listed by Allen Ginsberg[58] minus a few I didnt like, which I replace with some I did like.

On the roll, of course.

Enclosed also is the whole book of poems "Mexico City Blues." I heard you in my demarol trance say you were going to publish whole books of people's poetry: hope you do this one, entoto, as is. Will Petersen and Mike McClure have written me mad happy letters about these Blues. Nothing too good since then, so I havent sent you any more recent poems.

Enclosed also find Allen's letter from Spain, in red ink, it is one of the greatest letters in human captivity, like, and I hope you send it back to me and that the linotypeist has no trouble with it.

I tried to write a review of Holmes Horn but I cant do a decent job on it because I really dont want to be identified with his particular cloistered view of the sufferings of actual musicians, although it is a great work of hope & prose in itself. Allen might be able to explain to you why I cant vouch for it in a review. I really tried.

Forgive me for that. I'm no critic.

Finally, we are completely right in doing Doctor Sax next. I just re-read it. It is so much greater than Desolation Angels. Let me know when you're (we're) ready, I might have to make some name-changes for libel reasons. See you later.

Jack

---

57. The experimental prose sketch "October in the Railroad Earth."
58. In the dedication of *Howl*, Ginsberg had listed *Mexico City Blues* among the titles of eleven Kerouac books "published in Heaven."

Writing Philip Whalen in August 1958, Kerouac included some details about Neal Cassady's arrest for possession of marijuana in San Francisco that Jack had learned from Ginsberg, who had been corresponding with Carolyn Cassady. The news of Neal's arrest and conviction had contributed to Kerouac's decision not to visit California in the fall.

TO PHILIP WHALEN

Aug. 4, 1958
[Northport, New York]

Dear Phil,

All the money I'm sposed to have hasnt come in, for instance the Road movie people have reneged now and offer 5 grand instead of 25, which is mystifying and sounds to me like they must feel that since I'm "beat" I wouldnt know any better.... it's a property worth 20 times that much. However I have a good agent. And no word from MGM about the Subterraneans. But anyway I'm planning on having some money and the very first thing I'm going to buy is the whole 24-volume set of the new Encyclopedia Britannica.... just think how great that is, sitting down idly to read, to read anything, and idly turn to antiquities of vases or world war II campaigns or biographies of great men. Of course I'd prefer the 1911 edition and do you know that crazy Cassady used to have it, en toto, and sold it so he could buy an Americana 1953!—incidentally, re Neal, I know all the details now, from letters his wife is writing to Allen, it seems everything is better ever, Neal is meditating and writing and happy to make a comeback in jail, Carolyn has come out of her shell and is painting again etc. and both of them reverent as hell and praising God and people, nabors, pouring money and food to their door in a big civic campaign of some sort I find very hip for suburbia!—they read in the paper and they seem to think it's the shits, just for a stick of T. Turns out the agents got the stick of T from Neal in exchange FOR A RIDE HOME! That's the end ... But nothing can keep and keep a good man and good woman down.—Just heard from Gary, he's going with Locke now to Kern river headwaters and Kings Canyon, then back to Mill Valley mid-September, then up to Newport. I am all involved in my great new novel MEMORY BABE and in cleaning up the purchase of this house and furnishing it etc. so I wont come out.[59] What I'll really do, actually, in 1959, probably, is go out to coast, see you, then ship in a freighter for Japan and go dig Japan and Gary there. But right now I'm

59. Kerouac told Joyce Glassman that he'd bought a round maple kitchen table, an AM-FM Zenith radio "that plays big Matthew Passions all day with a big round tone," and a three-speed Webcor phonograph "that plays my poems and albums booming deep."

very happy being quiet and writing.—When I read your koan my immediate spontaneous reply was: "If the ground's disappearing around my feet, how can I reach that blazing furnace?" Also wrote a nice haiku:

> Glow worms
> brightly sleeping
> In my flowers

... I'm writing my book the way you should begin yours. That is, just exert yourself to explain, simply and sincerely, what's on your mind, and dont pre-think what critics or readers might think of your "awkwardness," since your "awkwardness" you'll see will turn out in the end to be the true meat of your style & story. Even tho I know this I myself sometimes hesitate, but knowing the rules I plow on mindless. It's good to chuckle over your own manuscript as you're pouring it out from the typewriter. It means you don't give a shit about critics. It means you're really art-ing it ... not hack-ing.—Allen has arrived NY, is very quiet, sad, takes too many demarols for his kidney stones, we spent quiet day at Don Allen's discussing publishing plans etc. and then went to Lucien's where Allen lay on floor and talked in low voice with Peter as the party raged. Allen tried to sneak up and look at my house here but is afraid of my ma who said she wd. call FBI if he ever came around. Actually I'm glad, in a way, to make it on a new level with Allen because I feel he may try to go political soon and get me and everybody in hot water. Or if not that, some premonition I have in myself. . . . Actually Allen seems pure, says he wants to be poor, will turn down opportunities to make a $1000 a month lecturing, he says, and just look for his soul new poetry. There's by the way a great new young poet in Chicago called Stan Persky who sent me his tremendous outcries; being only 17 he imitates us a lot, but he will be great. I referred him to Don Allen. . . . I get fan letters all the time, one terrifying one recently from a fag in Chi who wants to attack me apparently amorously. . . . Also a lot of others, like yours from Sepulveda, asking if I'm sincere. Since I get hundreds, I answer none, like Subhuti I'm going to abide in "silence and tranquility" or "neutrality." I rejoice in that and let the slanders and misinformations go by the board, like one recent slander about my father used to beat me, that's why I was beat, shit my father never raised a hand at me and never even chastised his poor little pets once, cats, dogs ... I hang around the yard, one day I saved four drowning insects from my full pail. . . . One ant's back broke when I lifted it out on my fingertip. . . . Beautiful fullmoon Augustcool night the other night when my 2 rows of corn looked like a throng standing behind Jesus who is pointing up at the moon to show their upward gazes the entrance-light of the Angels.

Ho! (means dharma) Bo! (bum)

Jack

In late August and September 1958, after Ginsberg settled into an apartment at 170 East Second Street in New York City, Kerouac continued his habit of writing letters instead of using the telephone to contact his friend. Since Jack and Gabrielle didn't install a telephone in their house at 34 Gilbert Street, Kerouac told Ginsberg he still had "to walk halfmile to phone after all."

TO ALLEN GINSBERG

[August 28, 1958
Northport, New York]

Dear Irwin[60]

Gone from the earth to a better land I know, I hear their angel voices calling Old Black Joe.... I'm coming, I'm coming.... for my head is bending low.

That's a nice song, now playing on my FM talkless Sunday music program. "Why do I sigh, that my friends come not again ..." And that was the song I played on the zither on a stage before huge audience at age 11. My favorite song, I see now.

Yes, Edw. Marshall is a fine poet. But havent you discovered Stan Persky yet? I'll bring in his work next time.

Carolyn put me down in Berkeley last year so I'll just stay quiet. Neal has money enuf I know. He never writes, if he does write to me that'll be different because I'll never forget the time I brought him candy and magazines in the hospital and he told you I had "descended on him." Bleakjawed Neal was mad at me and one day I jumped off the engine at Bayshore and suddenly saw him, and he drove away guiltily.

You're probably right about rights for On the Road getting more valuable, but I want to see what happens with this mess now, they want Joyce Jamison to play LuAnne and that would make the picture a hit and I get 5 percent and Mort Sahl said he wanted the picture to hew very closely to the book, that's better than MGM. Meanwhile MGM making a movie called Beat Generation with Jerry Lee Lewis, havent even consulted me about my copyright of that title in 1955 (remember, Jean-Louis New World Writing #7, from a novel-in-progress BEAT GEN. copyright 1955 Jean Louis etc). So Sterling will sue for copyright payoff. I also have Holmes article attributing coining of phrase to me, & other stuff.[61] They are really crooking me in H'wood, The Subterraneans for peanuts etc. Imagine Sloan Wilson getting a half million dollars for A Summer Place. I dont want all that but certainly fifteen grand is nothing in H'wood, or the 25 offered

60. Irwin Allen Ginsberg was Allen's full name.
61. Holmes's article "This Is the Beat Generation," published in the Sunday *New York Times* magazine, November 16, 1952.

then reneged for Road. This sounds silly to you in your poverty but if I ever get an income (trust fund) started I'll have money for you once in a while, gratis. Not for everybody, not for voracious Gregories and Neals, but for kindly poet saints cooking lung stew in east side quiet palaces. No I dont have burger's disease, I have a good doc called Rosenberg, I had boils and I guess they came from poison ivy getting right into my system from my constant retrieving of basketball from poison ivy patches. No, no phlebitis, nothing. My real problem is drinking. I drink alone and sometimes too much even alone. I take dexamyls to write and they not healthy (prescription). Do you remember that wonderful benzedrine used to make us shit and sweat and piss and lose weight and get holy high, this dexamyl constipates, fucks up, screws, agh, ugly depressions worse than benny. Our prurient medicos, wouldnt give me benny. They got goddam codeine in those dexamyls, bet you any money, causes constipation. So I'm still fat.

Glad you have long quiet talks with Lucien. I wonder how he can stand all those shouting visitors including me? poor dog has no life of his own. He is really and truly a gracious aristocratic man. He said that my Lucien Midnight was pejorative about him, shoulda been majorative. Cant even find words in dictionary! I just wrote long letter to Joyce describing my current work, ask her to read it to you, if you want idea. I'm bugged and bored by it, but I was bugged and bored by Dharma Bums too. No more fun in writing for me. Blah. Bought a Webcor 3 speed and played my own record albums, my Norman Granz 3 albums are greatest poetry records since Dylan Thomas and I do think Granz is not going to issue them at all from prurience. I really read like a bitch. Nice low voice, too. Steve Allen album said to be coming out with Hanover Records, it is quite a little gem too. If you have a box I'll bring them in. My own box weighs ton. Yes, and did Hart fight Lamantia physically or what? If you have big free poetry reading with Gary et al please dont urge me to join in, I'll just listen like in Frisco. I have offers to read for money all over country and reject em all. Too bashful, goddamit I dont like to be on a stage. If Gary does come, and Phil, it will be strange wont it. If you want to get to Bob Lax, he's phone Twining 9-1323, and lives at 3737 Warren St. Jackson Heights. He just sent me a letter, an empty envelope (!) (?) Great day in the morning, I go die now, I feel awful (dexies). See you soon. They wanted me write commentary to Norman Mailer's Hip and God talk, he says God is dying, etc. kinda nonsense tho he is nice serious kid. But I dont wanta get involved with him & his gang. They also wanted me to talk on stage with Max Lerner for $100 honorarium at Brandeis Univ., dont think I'd like that, big gray faced Liberal sneers . . . goodbye poor $100. When you and me and Bill have ALL our work published they'll be no more talk about Nabokovs and Silones.[62]

62. Ignazio Silone (1900–1978) was an Italian novelist and left-wing intellectual.

What a long time it will take, and when it comes, it never matters anymore, and then we go into eternity and dont care anyway. And so it's already eternity and here we inward tomb bliss our sleep.

Meanwhile Jonathan Williams sent me his awful list of dissident piss-poor intellectual wrecks, that whole B[lack] M[ountain] gang is full of shit if you ask me ... big abstract conceited tracts about nothing.

Following each other,
  my cats stop
When it thunders

And as for Alan Watts, I call him Arthur Whane in Dharma Bums, which is Old English for horsefly, but the way he bit us in Chicago Review. Ah, Heaven will respect us. In fact I'd better start respecting poor Mr. Watts. This fame shot makes you gripe more than blow, doesnt it. Adios

Jack

[Irving] Rosenthal at Chicago Review wants you to send him *prose*[63]—Will write you c/o Paterson soon—Send him letter excerpt.

P.S. I decided to accept that Lerner invitation and buy full set of oils & canvases. Royalty check just came in, ½ of what I expected.

TO ALLEN GINSBERG

[September 8, 1958
Northport, New York]

Dear Allen,

Got your letter about the dentist's gas satori[64] ... or maybe supreme enlightenment I guess ... yes, and if you want to follow up on the words on the subject, you know where to go ... Surangama Sutra, Lankavatara Scripture, Diamond Sutra, the MAHAYANA WRITINGS (not Hinayana earlier crude moral stratagems) (tho Mahayana even more moral) ... so, just get Dwight Goddard's Buddhist Bible in Library unless they havent replaced the copy I stole) ... we'll talk about it anyway. I dont want to leave my unpublished Some of Dharma etc out of house and Don Allen (if you want see) has Mexico City Blues Sutra at his pad now. Anyway, dont worry. I just

---

63. Irving Rosenthal was the editor of the *Chicago Review*, whose winter 1959 issue was suppressed by the University of Chicago after readers objected to what they considered offensive material in the excerpt from Burroughs's *Naked Lunch*. Rosenthal started a new magazine, *Big Table*, with the poet Paul Carroll to print the contents of the "banned" issue.
64. See Ginsberg's poem "Laughing Gas," written in the fall of 1958, beginning "High on Laughing Gas/ I've been here before." See also Ginsberg's poem "Aether," written on May 28, 1960, after another appointment with his dentist. In November 1958, Ginsberg wrote Charles Olson that he was beginning to understand what he called the "illusory fab-

wrote big letter to Gregory praising him to heavens for making me cry at last, after all these years since Neal's great letter. How sweet it is that a word-slinger can sling in prose or verse, hey? What mighty prose it is, what sounds emanate from his gregorytongue! Just as good as Neal. Both better than me, except I guess in SAX where I gets supernatural assistance and prose-tricks ... but prose-tricks dont add up to sighing tears prose. Poor great Gregory, and Jesus how he suffered! Well, we'll discuss that too. There's a girl here, J.L., rich, sexy, thin fucky, who went with me to visit Lafcadio [Orlovsky] last Sat nite and we saw him wandering in the moon and went in and talked in drear kitchen with Marie and looked at his paint-ings, his "simple" ones, that is, I know that he's going thru a strange little rococo phase of his own ... so we gave Marie her number so when you and Peter come you can call her and she comes in big car and gets us all for big moonlight swims but actually now it's almost too late, she going to Yale school now anyway. Did you see new *Horizon* magazine where you and me raked over coals again by another columbia trilling fink?[65] But every knock is a boost and we sure gets boosted knocked raked and everything in this. Once more accused of fomenting teenage murder atrocities. That, my friend, you can lay back to Mr. Holmes who said in Esquire that it was ex-tremely "significant" that a little cretin pulled the knife out of Michael

---

ric of this existence": "Recently after decade pining after God had all that undercut by some experiences in a dentist's chair with Laughing Gas [....] I experienced sensation that this life really is a dream in the void—began to understand (so late) Gary, Phil & Jack's hang-up with Buddha." Ginsberg had joined the company of many distinguished people who reported "metaphysical insights" under the influence of drugs, such as J. A. Symonds, poet, historian and biographer; Sir William Ramsay, a 1904 Nobel laureate; and the American philosopher William James, who wrote in *The Varieties of Religious Experience* (1902) that after experienc-ing "nitrous oxide intoxication," he had learned that "our normal waking consciousness, ra-tional consciousness as we call it, is but one special type of consciousness, whilst all about it, parted from it by the filmiest of screens, there lie potential forms of consciousness entirely different."

65. The September 1958 issue of *Horizon* (Vol I, No. 1) included Robert Brustein's attack on the Beats titled "The Cult of Unthink," quoting the start of *The Subterraneans* and the open-ing lines of "Howl." As a young lecturer at Columbia University, Brustein berated the Beat writers for "belligerently exalting" their "own inarticulateness." He saw them as assaulting "order, analysis, form, and eventually coherence.... The result is a style like automatic writ-ing or an Eisenhower press conference, stupefying in its unreadability.... Kerouac, Ginsberg, McClure, and the others fling words on a page not as an act of communication but as an act of aggression; we are prepared for violence on every page."

Brustein was sensitive to the shift of consciousness in postwar American culture, but in his article he dismissed the work of Abstract Expressionist painters such as Jackson Pollock, Franz Kline, and Robert Motherwell as well as the Beat writers, since he thought that "in this new art it is often difficult to distinguish between self-expression and self-indulgence." Brustein concluded that "Taken together in their inarticulateness, obscurity, and self-isolation, the assorted bearers of Beat Generation attitudes in the various arts in America show an increasing reluctance to come to grips with life."

Farmer's chest and said "Thanx, man, I wanted to see what it was like." How a man can make irresponsible statements like that from his cloistered position I shall never know but anyway it appears these Trillingers seem to think WE said such a silly thing and that's 2 critics now lay murder at our feet ... and you and me who dont even hunt or even fish. They have our pictures, our poems etc., they print the first page of Subterraneans saying and showing nothing because the book got rolling 2, 3 pages later ... Is it really true that Phil and Gary are coming? Let me know. Sterling is dying to nab Gary for his future novels ... and Phil. (O yes, the murder hints from Columbia from Trilling I just realized today pretty soon they'll be digging out Lou. If they do that they might have another murder on their hands.)[66] Kingsland wrote me letter from Philly said he would drive to Northport and drop in, I told him it was my mother's house, I guess he'll be bugged, imagine huge swishy Kingsland walking into my mother's innocent rosy kitchen.[67] Paranoiac rosy kitchen but she did rise at 6 A.M. for a decade while I was allowed (believed in utterly) to stay home write my saxes & sexes so dont forget that.—If you see Leo Garen by any chance, producing Genet this Fall on Lower East Side, tell him I called him twice in answer to his telegram and that damn Broadway yak was on and line was busy, I have to walk halfmile to phone after all ... Also, I turned down Monti Monitor radio tape with Holmes with F.S., an AA ex-drinker who nearly drove Lucien out of his mind with AA pamphlets and talk, but I will go to Max Lerner stage talk Hunter College Nov. 6th. ($100) where also you remember that guy Z.P.? will be, the guy in Jerry Newman's pad the night of Allen Eage, Z. is quite a cat, you should know him, his father is a Rabbi who cried when he read on the road and forgave his son for being a hipster. Z. on Bill's kick. In fact his rabbi father got married after reading road.

Z. was living in same hotel I had a room in (8th Street) when I was reading every night Village Vanguard, wanted to meet me, where was I? suddenly he discovered I was upstairs, he flipt and rushed up, I went down to his room, in his shorts he made big speeches and I puked out all the bile of one week's accumulation of alcohol, after billskick with 2 strange Garvers with big muscular forearms who took my advice and closed their eyes and dug nothingness ... it was silly, that whole week, gotta tell you, one night I had J. J. Johnson's rhythm section passed out on my hotel rug and in bed 3 girls ... No more! no more! Dont worry, I wont maddrunk bigscenes in yr quiet stately pad when I comes in, if I comes in ... ur ur ur ... be in soon few weeks. A ton coeur

Jean

---

66. Kerouac was referring to Lucien Carr's fatal stabbing of Dave Kammerer in 1944 while Carr was enrolled as a student in Columbia College.
67. John Kingsland was one of Allen Ginsberg's friends in New York City.

In mid-September, Kerouac learned that his editor Don Allen at Grove Press wanted to publish Doctor Sax, *the spontaneous prose book about his boyhood in Lowell. Jack had hoped that Grove Press would take his manuscript of* Desolation Angels *because it followed right after* The Dharma Bums *in the chronology of his Duluoz legend; he even thought of it as a "sequel." Writing Don Allen, Jack discussed the "serious question" of using pseudonyms in* Desolation Angels *to protect his friends, especially since there was speculation that Neal Cassady had been set up for arrest by federal agents after the publication of* On the Road. *Grove had included "Seattle Burlesque," an excerpt from* Desolation Angels, *in the* Evergreen Review *in 1957, but after Cassady's arrest they dropped the idea of publishing any more of this book, even though Don Allen had written a memo to Barney Rosset on December 2, 1957, saying that Kerouac's novel "gives some wonderful accounts of the S.F. poetry scene and especially of the sleeping-bag revolution in action."*

TO DONALD ALLEN

Sept. 16, 1958
[Northport, New York]

Hello Don my Dear,

Okay so now we begin work on Doctor Sax.

First, Sterling tells me now that since you chose SAX instead of Desolation Angels, which would have been a "sequel" to Dharma Bums, Viking and Tom G. won't mind your bringing out SAX earlier than next Spring, which is what I would like myself, like February or something, why wait around?

But there is a great deal of work for me to do. First, I'll have to re-type the whole thing because I'll have to change all the first names in the book, to avoid libel. Pete Plouffe's real name is Pete Houde, etc. etc. and the people of Lowell will be bugged to see their real first names. Or, if you have gone over it now, and feel that they won't be bugged and libel-conscious, then of course ... but no, like the first names of my relatives, it just won't do, there'll be a rumpus. Unless I simply insert the new names into the manuscript we have at your pad. Let me know, therefore, if you want me to insert the new first names into the old ms., or type up a new one (an onerous job but I'm ready to do it.)

So that's that and let me say how grateful I am to you and Barney to be so nice as to please so much bringing out my favorite book instead of Desolation Angels which bugs me (now) (maybe not later).

Now, as to those excerpts from Desolation Angels for Evergreen, okay with me about removing Laff to shorten the intro to the day at the races, just so long as we don't change the prose. In connection, by the way, with the question of excerpts for the Review, I've just sent in two excerpts from Doctor Sax to Sterling, THE FLOOD and another long one, if you should want any of that. It would plug SAX in advance.

The question of names in Desolation is also serious. Neal Cassady (Pomeray) is now in jail and I'm sure his wife would sock us with a suit if we used his real name. We should leave the names as is, except possibly Allen's name, Allen requests that I use his real name and doesn't care. Also Corso wouldn't mind. (Neal's wife is already saying that the cops recognize him as Dean Moriarty.) My name okay too, Kerouac not Duluoz.

Okay, so write me about preparing the ms. for the printer (name changes), and about an earlier date if possible, and I'll call you in town in about 10 days or so.

As ever

Jack

p.s. You asked me about my present work, well I wrote half a novel this summer and abandoned it because it was a dreary (to me) kind of repetition of Doctor Sax itself (it was going to be called MEMORY BABE but I'll do MEMORY BABE on a huger level later, like Proust). So I think what my next work will be, I'll get an advance from whoever wants to make it, say a grand, and go to Paris and write a huge halo for Balzac's Paris going around talking to dressmakers, apaches, whores, businessmen, I speak French, I really could do A HALO FOR PARIS real pretty.

Or no, SATURDAY AFTERNOON IN PARIS, that's it

As the date neared for the publication of The Dharma Bums, *Kerouac sent a cheerful note to his publicist at the Viking Press, Patricia MacManus. The day after the publication party for the book in Manhattan, Jack was so hungover that he told Ginsberg his exhilaration had changed to "mental exhaustion" as soon as he returned home to Northport.*

TO PATRICIA MACMANUS

[September 23, 1958
Northport, New York]

Dear Pat—

I did write back to Luther Nicols about where there are pictures and can send my personal snapshots if he promises to send em back. He'll wire. Re Podhoretz, it was very funny the other night we called him for fun and he came to Lucien's and we had him on the pan but he liked it. Pat, please send me that copy of *World-Telly* interview, I haven't even seen it, I'll send it back to you if you want it. I'm curious to know what Hanscom left in, and how it looks. (My critical debut. O) —I'll be in at Viking office on publication day [of *The Dharma Bums*] Oct. 2, with my mother, I'd like her to see a big publishing office and meet you and Tom et al. (She doesn't even read my books, however, because they're smutty. She's in some ways a Catholic

153

individualist in another direction like your Pa.) So see you then. Thank sweet Helen Taylor for me for sending the 2 novels of R. P. Smith.

Jack

TO ALLEN GINSBERG

[October 5, 1958
Northport, New York]

Allen—

Came home full of exhilaration which became mental exhaustion—I don't think I can do the Hunter College thing now—Like America I'm getting a nervous breakdown—I am going into exile—wrote Whalen big description of day—All these well dressed people looking at me with slitted eyes, why don't I just retire from the universe—Ah fuck it, I'm gong back to Li Po—I hate my beating heart—Something's wrong with the world—I'll be alright in the morning—Grandfather Night in this old house scares me with its black coffin. See?

Jacky

After the publication of The Dharma Bums, *Kerouac received an initial letter of praise from Gary Snyder, portrayed as Japhy Ryder, the "number one Dharma Bum of all time" in the novel.*

TO JACK KEROUAC FROM GARY SNYDER

12.X.58

Dear Jack,

Dharma Bums is a beautiful book & I am amazed & touched that you should say so many nice things about me because that period was for me really a great process of learning from you, not just your vision of America and of people but your immediate all-embracing faith. & thank you for sending me a copy. Philip [Whalen] forwarded it to me. Everyone is reading it.

Alan Watts is knocked out by the book & said so on the radio & is rewriting his "Beat Zen, Square Zen" article as a pamphlet for Ferlinghetti & entirely changing his opinions of you & Gins. [Ginsberg] et al. because he sees now truly religious wonders going on around him which he could not see before apparently the contours of wine-jugs bent the light he saw things in into weird burgundy colored distortions, but we were there he says. Behind the jugs. Claude & I are going up to the Sierras leaving tomorrow, for five days, we hope to hike 50 miles in & climb the BLACK KAWEAH & then hike 50 miles back out.

It is very important that you support Cardinal Agagianian for Pope & tell your friends to vote for him.

AGAGIANIAN FOR POPE.

The Zendo in the cabin here is all arranged as zendo, & weeknights people come & silently sit to the bell & clackers, real zendo style. About six cats regularly turning up.

I am going to slip away to Japan at the end of December.

How you bin boy? N.W. trip was great & Whalen is too beautiful & penetrating to believe; slept on Indian Olympic beaches of the ocean Queets Kalaloch

Gregory's BOMB the most![68]

Gary

Visiting Ginsberg in his apartment in the East Village in October 1958, Kerouac read the letters that Allen was receiving from Gregory Corso. Corso was still living at the Beat Hotel in Paris and asked Jack to send money so he could return to New York. Kerouac turned down the request for a loan, and then confided that after only six months in Long Island he and Gabrielle had decided that New York City was "too close for comfort" and wanted to return to Florida.

TO GREGORY CORSO

[October 13, 1958
Northport, New York]

Dear Gregory— Oct. 13, 1958—the other night I got drunk at my desk and scribbled you a long letter in pencil and then intended to type it up but now I see it's just a lot of repetitious drunken bullshit. I just read your latest letter to Allen about Zen-nutty and you're right, in fact I've not been able to "meditate" or make any buddhist scene now for a long time and have actually started writing catholic poems and sending them to Jubilee Magazine tho I'm aware that all the scenes are the same empty scene. Your criticism of buddhism in other words is fairly accurate but you mustnt let yourself be fooled every moment of your life into believing that there's any special "reality" to either life or death, you say people die real deaths but in a few hundred years who's to remember or notice that it was real death? Meanwhile where did yr bones go? I clearly saw the skeleton underneath all this show of personality. Meanwhile give my love to old Bill and tell him I look

68. City Lights had just published a broadside of Gregory Corso's poem.

forward to seeing him sometime next year wherever he'll be, even if in India I'll go find him and see what the latest news is. I guess Bill thought I was sore about his letter to my mother but not so, it's an old story, and her letters were correctly typed by him as insane. Actually my mother is just grinning up her sleeve about some insane something or other concerning allen and bill but lets forget all about this, it has nothing to do with me.... Now, goddamit, I still havent sold a book to the movies and have enuf money for, like, 2 years of grocery and rent and then what? so that if I had the money I should have, according to all my "fame and publicity" it wouldnt be any hair off my balls or sweat to send you your return trip money but I havent got anything like that yet, maybe will later. Allen says meanwhile Phipps will pay your fare. Allen and Lucien and I just wrote a huge mad article about the Beat Gen. and about us and you and Bill that will be very provocative and make everybody mad but it's a beauty. Will be published soon ... somewhere. For instance, one sentence:–"Though both myself and Mr Ginsberg have written puffs and introductions to the brilliant volume of Perms, Gasoline, by Gregory Corso, and tho Mr Corso has outstepped himself in beauty with his later greater bardic excellences (Power, Army and finally the fantastic Bomb among these) I have yet to see any general realization in the book columns, halls of English departments, or the pissoirs of the poetry publishing scene that we have in America a pure Dylan Thomas lyrical bard still in his tender years with the moonlight of immortality in his hair." Also, about Bill:–... That Bill Burroughs has the graciousness to write prose after all the horrors *he's* seen (nobody'll know what they are till his manuscripts forbidden in America are published), is (among others) a happy fact for which no credit is due or demanded. "These events" (this now is Lucien's contribution) "are better left unknown entirely, than made victim of the crepitation of a small but necessarily powerful clique of flatulent and undignified 'social critics.'" And Allen and I collaborated on this masterful sentence: "We last heard in 1910, at the beginning of a great literary revelation, enormous philistine charges of obscurantism, amorphousness, amorality, decadence, self-willed isolation, oddity,–we now have added perhaps an even less sublime contruct [sic] popularly known as 'maturity' which, as the truth is known, has come to indicate a ridiculous spineless New Testamentless (THOU MUST BE AS CHILDREN) desire to please old fairies."

etc.

Strange about your feeling about the skies of Stockholm because I wrote a perm about Stockholm 6 months ago about its skies, as follows: "Finally I was in Stockholm at last/Cold night/Dark in Swedenborg/Zeldipeldi my junkey friend/from N.Y. and Maldo/Saldo the hot trumpeter/from Nigeria, turned on/in the cold room overlooking/black rooftops of winter,/Sweden night skys February,/Om mani pahdme hom/I wanted to catch a train to the Capital/I was on a seacoast town,/the name of it was Fidel/or Fido/wow, mominu/you dont know how far/that sky/go."

My mother and I are leaving NY soon and moving to Florida where it's cheaper to live and also where I can write more and fool around less with a thousand repetitious parties and appearances in NY city which is too close for comfort to this my desk. When I wanta get laid I'll go to Havana, by god. Summers I'll live in a cabin probably in Lucien's two-headed-people valley up there east of Albany near Mt. Greylock. Also, if I get enuf guts, buy a jeepster stationwagon and bring full pack and drive to Montana and even Alaska and such summers. and mexico. The girl here who's practically in love with you is Jill Lippman grandaughter of John Golden but there are better ones even, for looks, shit you can get any girl you want, Allen read your Bomb to the ownders [sic] of Paris Review (Tom Guinzburg, Matthiesen etc.) and they loved it and said they would do something. Meanwhile that weird little bearded cat Rosenthal is mad about Bill's work. Well write soon and see you later.

Jack

In a postcard to Ginsberg ten days after the publication of The Dharma Bums, *Kerouac gave a sense of the hectic round of publicity events he was involved with in New York City to help Viking promote his book. Most reviewers were condescending, as when Nancy Wilson Ross concluded in* The New York Times *that "the new activities of Ray Smith-Kerouac and his fellow bums are rather more on the positive side than heretofore. Digging 'cool' Zen is clearly more adult than digging hot jazz, drinking tea is certainly healthier than smoking it." The* New York Herald Tribune *critic felt that "when narrator Smith-Kerouac gets away from North Beach and the nonsense, and goes up into the Sierras ... the lyric voice is authentic, the eye keen and morning-fresh." Some reviews were hostile, as when* Time *magazine said that "Jack (On the Road) Kerouac might have called his latest novel* On the Trail, *or How the Campfire Boys Discovered Buddhism."*

Most important to Kerouac was Henry Miller's generous response. Miller had been sent a review copy of the novel, and he wrote from Big Sur to Pat Covici, senior editor at Viking, saying that "from the moment I began reading the book I was intoxicated. . . . No man can write with that delicious freedom and abandonment who has not practised severe discipline. . . . Kerouac could and probably will exert tremendous influence upon our contemporary writers young and old. . . . We've had all kinds of bums heretofore but never a Dharma bum, like this Kerouac."

[October 15, 1958
Northport, New York]

Dear Allen—

What Whalen meant you hadn't written him about Suzuki,[69] so do. Meanwhile please try to do me a favor, go to Lou's before he leaves Thursday night at 8 for the country again & pick up my sleeping bag with its inside roll of pajamas, turtleneck sweater, first-aid stuff, razor, shaving brush etc. and take that back home to Second St. and after the Ben Hecht show Friday night I'll come over to sleep or maybe be hungup and show up Saturday afternoon. The show is definitely on, at ABC studios, wherever that is, I'm being taken by Sterling and Pat MacManus. OH YES AND ALSO DONT FORGET MY TWEED TOPCOAT AT LOU'S, it's gettin cold. Now this week I work on our article. When my Ma goes to Florida for a month next month I stay home all the time a whole month and take Lucien's advice and write more, like you should do. If you have time investigate Robert Lowry at 190 Bleecker St., he'll print anything you want printed. Say I'll see him myself later. Henry Miller letter real breakthrough for us. Later.

Jack

At the end of October 1958, Gabrielle left on an extended visit to Kerouac's sister, Caroline, and her family in Florida, leaving Jack alone in Northport. Disappointed that The Dharma Bums *didn't make* The New York Times *best-seller list, Jack was determined to raise enough money from publishers to pay off the mortgage on his Northport home, thinking this would make it easier for him and his mother to sell the Long Island house and relocate in Florida. Setting aside the unfinished manuscript of* Memory Babe, *he advised Sterling Lord to take* Doctor Sax *away from Grove Press and place it with any publisher who would pay a large advance. Meanwhile Kerouac told his editors at the Viking Press that he would revise the manuscript of* Visions of Gerard, *which they were reading, and substitute Catholic references for Buddhist references if they would buy the book.*

Writing to Ginsberg, Kerouac described what he called his "harried" existence at home without Mémère. At the end of the letter he mentioned a "new chick" in his life, the artist Dody Müller, the widow of the painter Jan Müller. Jack met her in October 1958 at Robert Frank's loft on the Bowery at Ninth Street. She offered to teach him how to paint, took him to art openings, and introduced him to painters such as Larry Rivers and Willem de Kooning. In Minor Characters, *Joyce Glassman described her as "another of Jack's dark women, older than I was." Joyce finally ended her affair with Kerouac later in the fall of 1958.*

69. See Kerouac letter to Philip Whalen in early November 1958, describing his visit with Ginsberg and Orlovsky to the Buddhist scholar D. T. Suzuki.

[October 28, 1958
Northport, New York]

Dear Allen—

Here's what I'm telling Sterling to do, and it's what I want: to get that new publisher to buy SAX for $7500 advance but without a single change; thereby SAX gets published, what does it matter who? or hard or soft cover? it's still publisht and read and can be reprinted in 5 years hard. I need the $7500 now to complete the buying of this house so I can put it up for sale, if I dont buy the house now I'll lose the $7000 already in it, by big defaulting suits. A hard and evil world. But SAX will be angelly published. if they make changes, no go, I give it back to Don Allen[70] ... Meanwhile, I'm insisting that Viking take and publish glorious VISIONS OF GERARD next. No changes except where I'm going to take out the Buddhist imagery and transfer Catholic since the story is about a little Catholic saint. There will be no theological difference ... The Holy Ghost is Dharmakaya (the body of truth). See? Etc. Dharmakaya literally means the Holy Spirit, or the Holy Truth, so what's the big tzimis? So I told them, okay I'll go to Paris but I wont write the book about Paris till a year later when I've had time to digest the events. Meanwhile, even, in fact, I think now, I know now, when I get to peaceful Florida this Xmas I'm going to write THE BEAT TRAVELER anyway about my trip to Burroughs in Tangier then on up France and London and back, and all the mad sea-writing around that, when I got caught in that great tempest and we had to flee south and almost foundered and I saw the white Jacob's ladder into the sea and saw Stella Maris too and thought NOTHING HAPPENS EXCEPT GOD which was the only thing I could think about because I thought we were all going to drown now ... O poor seamen.[71]

Okay. I think this is right. Meanwhile I'm sending LUCIEN MIDNIGHT to Rosenthal and if he rejects it he's crazy but he may reject it because also I told him to give me whatever payment he can, or wants to pay.

My hand is shaking so today, Henri Cru came suddenly as I was balling with my baby and the house then became full of local drinkers and if it hadn't been for the girl cleaning and cooking it would look like hell now. She's coming back Thursday to take care of things while I try to answer a thousand letters. So today I tried, alone, in house, to sit and write you big glorious poem about golden eternity and couldn't because I've so been

---

70. Donald Allen told Sterling Lord that Grove Press would match any other publisher's offer for *Doctor Sax*.

71. This account became Part Three of Book Two of *Desolation Angels*, continuing up to 1958, when Ginsberg returned from Paris and Kerouac was "back in New York sitting around with Irwin [Allen] and Simon [Peter] and Raphael [Gregory] and Lazarus [Lafcadio], and now we're famous writers more or less...."

importuned by this world lately I can't even push a pencil any more so now I know if I want to take Lucien's advice and write more I must leave NY, and will (not so much "importuned" but pleasantly partied, actually, but my god every day, every night, no rest, no solitude, no reflection, no staring at the ceiling or clouds possible any more). Big mad telegram, for instance, from Lucien, a British lord wants to rush out and interview me and I just GOT interviewed yesterday by *Herald Tribune* here in house, "millions of cool beautiful Marlon Brandos" I told him to say is what Beat Gen is ... and *Look* mag is sposed to be coming out to interview me too, and meanwhile I try to feed and mind my poor frightened cats, the yard full of cars. When do I find time to type up NEONS FROM NEAL. Allen, can't you go to New Directions office and type up whatever you want (and Laughlin allows). If you need note of intro and permission I'll send. Short of that, okay, I'll type up NEONS, let me know. As for poems, I just dont know which ones are forever eternal, goddamit, they the forever eternals I gave Don Allen on that roll but after all I got many more. Why dont I just send some and you judge, I dont know. Besides what's your deadline with City Lights?[72] Let me know deadline, that'll help prod me in ass.—Bruno never came back the next day, he probably went away saying Ah he's just another fag, you don't know how those characters are, unless you're right about river-of-shit I-dont-care-everything-lkokay—In any case, whenever I come on with fuck I dont mean it, it's just a zen joke. In fact it's the one thing I've never done, recall.

The situation about Tuttle etc. and Grove I just dont understand but let me know when time is ripe tho for krissakes yes I dont care but it's a good idea for Phil & Gary to get busy and blow out some poems. [....]

And to add to all the confusion of my book coming out and all this new spate of publicity and nervousness my sister had to go and throw HER complications in making my mother babysit for a month & here I am no time to shit & the house getting dirtier every day. If you do come, you could in fact come and browse among my msses. and type up what you want for anthology, come with in mind not to dirty house and Peter too, like I'm really harried. I wish you would come, like right now this weekend, fuck Norman Mailer he's trying to get in the act. Why wasnt he a hipster when it counted? why didnt he talk about God when everybody else was talking about Freud? On Friday night Nov. 6 I'll be at Hunter Playhouse 68th and Park and will drive back with Dody. I still dont know what I'll say. I'll talk a little, give them their money's worth of Kerouac Beat Generation,[73] then start reading [Corso's poem] Bomb I guess, unless you think of some-

72. Ginsberg was preparing an anthology of Beat poetry for City Lights Press in San Francisco.
73. Kerouac had written a new essay on the Beat Generation, "Beatific: On the Origins of the Beat Generation," which was published in *Playboy* in June 1959. *Esquire* had published his earlier essay as "The Philosophy of the Beat Generation" in March 1958.

thing else and new. (Because I dont really agree with Bomb world-apocalypse is good, I believe in people saying it wont happen at all because we evolve now and become smart human race. I hope.) (Microphone in heaven.) I'd rather read [Corso's poem] "Marriage," can you bring that for me? And do I shoot you question in audience? Will I be in the enemy camp on that mad night? Do I wear Mighty Goodwills? Am I Sirdanah the Mighty Goodwiller? Do I have to be smart? Do I even have to think? Can I drink beer on the stage or shall I show up quiet wordless sober? Will I address Dean Kauffman directly? Oh yes, dont miss my interview on the editorial page of Herald Tribune, by Ray Price, in which I said the old hipster saw, printed for first time now, "Wouldn't it be wonderful if Ike and Dulles and MacMillan and DeGaulle and Kruschev and Mao and Nehru should all sit around a table and smoke tea? What humor and openmindedness would result, what tender perception." He said he would make that his lead. When the fuzz comes to my house there won't be a joint or pill in the house so never bring any you and Pete. All I have is dexamyls by prescription from local doctor. Navaretta is very nice, is that Manuel? Yes, Portugese name. Yes, very nice and good man. Mike Goldberg was telling me how terrible you and Pete were in the Hamptons, says Joyce, I dont even remember, I was answering eagerly yes to everything he said (blind drunk) and Joyce said I sold you and Peter down the river and that I was a balloon and that I was always worried what the neighbors would think and etc. embarrassing her in public she added and really, now, when we went to Hecht show you remember we tried sneak out the back way. Is she demented?[74] I hope she doesn't shoot me before I see SAX in print, and GERARD next fall. As for new chick[75] (new, NEW, I had no old chick) Henri says because she Indian and French she knife me if I ever kid around other girl. O boy, here goes Leon Robinson into the ends of the night. What with being pulled apart on earth by you and my mother, in heaven by Buddha and Christ, none of whom can get together I dont know why except over my suffering carcase, wow, this will be the end of me, I always thought I was too strong to be Stephen Craned like Louis Simpson but it's almost happening and NOBODY IS RESPONSIBLE. You see Nobody is Responsible. Not even me. Not even my mother. I forgive myself first and then all of you for the original ignorance of wanting to be born in the first place but we're doing alright, especially you sweetie.

Jack

Laff just come. Sold me a painting for $10!

74. Joyce Glassman published her first novel *Come Join the Dance*, in 1962. That year her friend Elise Cowen, who had returned to New York City from San Francisco to live in the same apartment building as Ginsberg and Orlovsky on the Lower East Side, committed suicide after they left for their trip around the world.
75. Dody Müller.

On November 6, 1958, in a forum addressing the question "Is There a Beat Generation?" sponsored by Brandeis University (it was held at the Hunter College Playhouse), Kerouac appeared on a panel with Ashley Montagu, a noted anthropologist; James Wechsler, editor of the New York Post; and the English novelist Kingsley Amis. Jack read his essay "The Origins of the Beat Generation," and he later described the ensuing uproar to his California friend John Montgomery. Ginsberg, who was in the audience at Hunter College, recalled that the climax of the event "came when Wechsler shouted 'We have to fight for peace' (eternal quote) and Jack looked at him in exasperation, said 'Wha!? Don't you realize that doesn't make sense?' then sat down silent but with Wechsler's hat on his head." Ginsberg watched as "Wechsler got mad and angrily demanded his hat back! as if Jack were a barbarian just like he dreamed, taking his hat!—An old Zen koan, that lovely gesture was accounted in [The Village] Voice as a sign that Jack was 'inarticulate,' an uncouth drunk!"

TO JOHN MONTGOMERY

[After November 6, 1958
Northport, New York]

Dear Monty,

Old boy I'm going to endeavor to write you a letter tonight tho I am jess about dead drunk after 3 2 3 weeks of bingeing here in my own house where I had to stay and babysit the cats. That James woman[76] was here and helped me keep the place clean. When she read your note saying "Dont let that James woman make a gent out of you," her answer to you is: "Tell him for Jack Kerouac not to make a lady out of me." ... Many people came here as soon as they learned my maw wasnt here ... seamen, girls, dogs, poets, Ginsbergs, painters, neighbors driving over with cocktails in their laps, etc. and the place was a mess of jumping. However, the other night [November 6] I finally made my Brandeis University appearance which I didnt want to do, but they cried and sent telegrams and said I was letting the university down, so I had to go, but I was angry because it was a mess of communists and after reading my prepared article about Beat which was very good and funny (Ginsberg said I was "magnificent" which I doubt) I started to call them a bunch of communist shits over the microphone and warning them that if they get what they want, Sovietization of America, they will no longer be able to attend such meetings as we were at. There were boos and cheers. I tangled with James Wechsler and wore his hat and went off the stage and played the piano in the back and insulted photographers and generally acted like a mad drunken fool just off a freight train,

76. Dody Müller was also named Dody James.

which is precisely the way I am and precisely what I think of universities. I even pushed the Dean aside to yell shit over the mike. A lot of people were shocked. The title of the forum was "Is There a Beat Generation?" and the next day a press dispatch said that I had proved it. The James woman was there sitting on the floor backstage digging, and she is related on her father's side not only to Jesse and Frank James but to Jim Younger and she is a real Texas gal. And I've found my gal, pal.

Someday you'll meet her. Bishop Pike wants to finance me a plane trip to SF to discuss beat with him over the air but I know I'd never make it.... Anyway I told those communists off, and you can tell Gary.

There is a lot of freedom and prosperity in this country and lets keep it that way. Nathless, natch, I know, when Dody and I try to go to the beach at night the cops drive us away, but they do it politely and dont hit me over the head. Its private property and I buy that. I'll buy my own ocean, in fact.

Gettin drunker. So long.

Anyway John, I've placed your "Henry Morley" review of dharma bums in my "cream file" I call it and someday it will see print. If you have any really truly weird wild spontaneous poems send em to Allen Ginsberg, 170 E. 2nd, NY 9, NY, he is making an anthology for Ferlinghetti (big, 200 pages).

Do you ever go out to the foot of that cliff in Santa Barbara channel beach out yonder and cook hotdogs or fuck? If not oughta........ I wish I could see you, I cant write a letter tonight, I can talk but cant type. Anyway, good man, thank you for the kind letters, they are always amusing and lively and you are a prince or a shit one. I think youre a prince. But I'm a shit myself. So anyway say hello to the girls. Is the Goddard Buddhist monastery still in S[anta] B[arbara]?

I've seen all the interesting backyards of SB from the cab of a steam engine. When I was a red omnipotent brakeman on the SP. I even know conductor Kelly in the yard office down there. And I used to drink beer in a Mexican place on the street off the tracks there, lovely brunettes in there. Ruth Sasaki sent telegram to call her but I havent called because I dont know what to do with her, and Gary says she is a tourist type. I dont know. I'll call her Thursday when I go to the James Woman's loft and if she's still there at the Gramercy Park Hotel okay. I saw Suzuki, as I probably told you.

Anyway I'm sick, but after a 12 hour sleep tonight here in Long Island with windows open to softly falling November I'll be okay in the morning, just as good as new, and have two quarts of buttermilk in icebox and a sad heart. When you write go fast, I wanta see you write like you talk, never mind the protocol and tradition of the poetry youve already seen, send something that you rattle off, get a tape recorder, do something, but you're brilliant and you are not writing FAST and TRUE. Come on. Whatever you do when you do it fast, you dont like it except six months later. That's the secret . . . of Tu Fu as well as me or you. . . . goodbye.

Jack

In November 1958, Kerouac sent Philip Whalen a humorous description of a visit he had made with Allen Ginsberg and Peter Orlovsky to the home of the Buddhist scholar D. T. Suzuki, who had asked to meet them after the publication of The Dharma Bums.

TO PHILIP WHALEN

[Early November 1958
Northport, New York]

Dear Mr. Whalen,

I understand that the gentleman's committee of the Rosh Hashanosh has sent you their latest Koan, could you please transmit it to the blue worm? Or would some snails help you? Or a few vast funebreal consonant splowsh of bow-foams? Well now boy I really enjoyed that wonderful letter of yours all about karrrrrma and stuff and I wanta tell you somethin now boy if Allen hasnt beaten me to the punch or you didn't get it in a blue cloud vibrating shimmering over your pine tree, Allen and me and Peter, well, first, word came out that D. T. Suzuki wanted to see me so I called him on the phone, a woman answered and said (as Allen and Peter waited outside phonebooth listening with big serious faces of Dharma), "Well, how long will you be in town, when can we arrange the appointment with Doctor Suzuki?" and I said, "Right now," and she said, "I'll go tell Doctor Suzuki" and was gone into big back secret whispering chambers and came back and said "Half an hour allright?" I said "Yes" and we strolled down First Avenue looking for cabs.

It was a strange day anyway. Trucks looked strange, big fat trucks with piles of rock. We got out, walked along Puerto Rican slums and came to a door with a nameplate with his name on it and rang a long, long time. Finally I rang three times deliberately and then he famously came, walking downstairs, a small bald Japanese man of 80 and opened the door.[77] Then he (he had paneled walls, ancient tomes) (and eyebrows that stick out an inch like the bush of the Dharma that takes so long to grow but once grown stays rooted grown) led us upstairs to a room where he picked out three special chairs and made us sit just there and picked his own chair facing us behind a huge bookpiled desk. So I wrote him out my Koan, "When the

---

77. Later Kerouac wrote in the *Berkeley Bussei* (1960), "I rang Mr. Suzuki's door and he did not answer—suddenly I decided to ring it three times, firmly and slowly, and then he came— he was a small man coming slowly through an old house with panelled wood walls and many books—he has long eyelashes, as everyone knows."

Buddha was about to speak a horse spoke instead," and he had a funny look in his eye and said, "The western mind is too complicated, after all the Buddha and the horse had some kind of understanding there." I didnt remember your own answer to that Koan. Then he said, "You young men sit here quietly and write haikus while I go and make some powdered green tea." And we told him all about you and Gary and drank the tea in black bowls and he said it was weak, we wanted it strong, so he made another batch real strong and Allen said, "It tastes like shrimps." (Shouting, we had to almost shout as he's deaf, tho he did say "No shouting"), and when Allen said it tasted like shrimp he answered, "It tastes like beef" then he said "Dont forget that it's tea." And then he and Allen discussed the famous old print with "the crack in the universe" Allen said, which he hadnt noticed, so Peter pointed out that there was also a crack in the wall behind the Buddha on the mantelpiece and then we all got high on that green tea (which he brushed), he said he drank it every day, something has happened to me since then I think, and he said "Have you never seen the pictures of Han Shan and Shih Te?" We thought we hadnt, soon's we saw it we remembered and Peter laughed that funny moaning laugh and DT liked him now. I wrote a haiku for him:

> "Three little sparrows
> on the roof,
> Talking quietly, sadly"

and they wrote some too, Allen and I both wrote the same haiku in fact, in different words, about like this:

> "Big books packaged
> from Japan—
> Ritz crackers"

because of his big box of Ritz crackers on the shelf under big books packaged from Japan, and so finally I told him I'd had some samadhis lasting a whole halfhour or 3 seconds, and o yes, the great thing, when Allen asked him if he knew who was the Bodhisattva responsible for the building of the first Buddhist (non-Taoist, or not-Taoist) temple in Frisco Chinatown, he said "I thought they were all Bodhisattvas." I could remember lots more but this is the big climax (for me, A and P had theirs), as we were leaving I suddenly realized he was my old fabled father from China and I said, "I would like to spend the rest of my life with you, sir," and he said "Sometime." And he kept pushing us out the door, down the stairs, as tho impatient, tho it was me instituted the idea of leaving because we were late for Viking Cocktails (commitments all over that day) but then when we were out on the street he kept giggling and making signs at us through the window and finally said "Dont forget the tea!" And I said "The Key?" He said "The Tea."

Now, love for sale on your radio was just it, Radio Daddy.

Now, also, please send me John Montgomery's fucking address, he writes to me without return addresses then waits for my letters.

I got no new book, Mémère is fine, Mallory and Ervine yes, Mahalia yes (I first dug her 1947 in North Carolina rainywoods radio) and too bad you write to me NOW.

Jack

TO PHILIP WHALEN

[Postmarked November 12, 1958
Northport, New York]

Dear Phil,

A golden giant has finally pulled the dharma out of my eyebrows.

> A mother and son
>   just took a shortcut
>   through my yard—a leaf
>   danced by—
> My cat suddenly chased
>   a female far
> Across the neighbor's yard
> —I was trying to read
>   a letter!

>   No telegram today
>   —Only more leaves
>   Fell

Jean

While complaining to Gary Snyder "how horrible it is to be 'famous,'" Kerouac occasionally agreed to meet his fans, as he did when he sent off two postcards to Stan Isaacs, a sports reporter for Newsday *on Long Island.*

TO STAN ISAACS

[Postmarked November 12, 1958
Northport, New York]

Mr. Stan Isaacs
NEWSDAY
Garden City LI, NY

Mr Isaacs,

I'm extremely honored to've heard from a sports writer and a good one at that—I've always wanted to be a sports writer and now that I could be

one (offers everywhere) I havent even got time to go to Paris and see a
horse race, or time to p— however if you want to have drink with me at
Toots Shor's (I'd like to see that place) name a date in December or late
November sometime and I'll meet you—Now that I have enuf money to go
see a pro football game, or a world series game, or even a track meet, I cant
even get out of my mad life and so it's almost too late but when I was a kid
I kept big sports diaries with pasted pictures and I remember Kiki Cuyler,
Goose Goslin, Gheringer, Bill Werber and I saw Discovery and Equipoise
in person and also Grove and at age 11 predicted Louis' knockout of Brad-
dock to the round. Anyway

Jack Kerouac

TO STAN ISAACS

[Postmarked November 28, 1958
Northport, New York]

Dear Stan,

I was on a 5-day bender and got home long after the appointment you
made to meet Nov. 25 at 3. I've been asked to write a column every two
months for Escapade magazine and my second one will be about baseball ... Anyway if you travel around the Island, have a car, in the course of
yr. work, why not just drop in at my house 34 Gilbert St., Northport, but
let me know in advance, we can chat whatever you had in mind, I'm afraid
to go to NY anymore, too many acquaintances, parties, etc. I want to quiet
down now and write new novel. So I hope you come. Keep address secret.
Till I see you or hear from you

Jack

TO GARY SNYDER

[December 1, 1958
Richmond, New York]

Dear Gary,

I reckon you're going back to Japan soon now. Your knees'll get cold. In
a little hut in the winter hills. But a good fire. I haven't written because five
thousand sillinesses have kept me from it: emergency letters and gaddam
telegrams thrown on my doorstep noon and night and I have to answer
them all one way or t'other, emergencies that not only die in 3 days but 3
minutes probably. If you only knew how horrible it is to be "famous" you
wouldn't want it, in fact you don't want it. In the stress of everything, in
fact, Ruth Sasaki sent telly for me to phone her, I didn't have time. Why go
on like this, if I were to tell you everything that hap[pen]s you wouldn't be

interested and it wd. take 10 silly pages of names.—I am going to get a cabin in the woods for me and my gal. I am going to stop calling it samsara and call it vicious circle. Etc. I am not going to write another book till they publish Visions of Gerard and Doctor Sax. After that okay. Allen wants me to type up 50 pages of my stuff for his anthology. Publishers of Lolita sent the book and demand a blurb.[78] I need a new needle in my machine. I am writing monthly columns for Escapade magazine. I have to get a batch of typewriter ribbons. I haven't even had time to accept a $1200 writing assignment and trip from Holiday (to freezy Canady). I have to go over Visions of Gerard and stick in a few new anecdotes (true ones) my mother remembers. I have to get a new RCA transistor battery for the little radio I bought her. I have to get a desk. I have to get oils and canvases and start painting. I have to screw my love. I have to get my landlord's gun out of the house before the cops come (loaded .45). I have to get a tape recorder and take down Henri Cru's tales. And Allen's. And Peter's. I have to tell my lawyer Ann Sothern is making a TV series about the beat generation without consulting me. I have to get the fleas on the floor, my cat Tyke is tearing his neck out scratching. I have to get post cards and soft leads and candles. I have to call Lionel. I have to write to Gregory, Bishop Pike, Joyce, Garlock, Jill, Nin, Phil Whalen, Charles Mills the composer. I have to (I won't) pose for oil portraits by Raphael Soyer and Larry Rivers. Already posed for Lafcadio. I have to visit nuns and a mansion. I have to write to a friend's sick mother before Xmas. I have to mollify my publicity agent at Viking because I let her telegram fly in the autumn wind. I have to type up long excerpts. I have to get in touch with Harold Goldfinger who left me a note in the Old Landmark bar in the Bowery and it was there 2 months. I have to get some whiskey. I have just written a 20-minute screenplay[79] for an independent experimental group in the Village. I am asked to send my poems to about 10 different people (won't). I must love life no matter what happens. Up your ass, apology, I said in 1951. Art is the shape of the pisspot. I have just been maligned by a priest. I receive holy scarfs in the mail. I am invited to the dances of experimental interpretive fairies who get mad if I don't show up. Tonight I stayed home instead of attending a party of jazz-poetry given by 2 colored photographers in the Village and another 40 miles away in the woods on Sunken Meadow Road. I have to go to Kim Stanley's cocktail party and meet the guy who wrote script of Subterraneans for MGM. I have to buy this house Friday and write out a check for $7000. It's a bitter cold howling Saturday night, roar, crack.

78. Kerouac praised Nabokov's best-selling novel in a letter to Lawrence Ferlinghetti, June 15, 1962.
79. *Pull My Daisy.*

The mansion of the moon has hidden faces when the big black cloud rolls back from her.

> Frozen
> in the birdbath,
> An autumn leaf

I am full of ruthless rue. I had to go to Yale with Allen to read but didn't. I have to be kind to young painters. I have just been insulted again in Esquire who don't take my stories any more because I slept on the floor of their photography editor. At noon, drunk. I am full of human kindness. The moon is yearning to recover fairytale Mineola earth McLoughlin's gigantic ursh [sic]. I didn't sleep for 3 nights. I feel waves of evil vibration from New York. I am being pursued by the Irgun but just for idolatry. Maybe later bombs. Waves of spiritual ecstasy are passing through my physical madness. (I am abstracting and writing this all out of my notebook.)

I wanted to give you idea of what a crock of shit it is to have to satisfy every tom dick and harry stranger in the world. No wonder Hemingway went to Cuba and Joyce to France. I was in love with the world thru blue purple curtains when I knew you and now I have to look at it thru hard iron eyes. I will survive as myself just the same. I read the Diamond Sutra and I still know all about that self shit. A lot of courage and ecstasy is packed in a man's pants. Right? Write!

Jack

LOVE TO LOCKE![80]

After the Viking Press sent Kerouac a Christmas present of a copy of The Dharma Bums *bound in black leather stamped in gold with gray-and-white marble end-papers, Jack inscribed it to his mother:*

A third adventure to pay for the house,

the cat food, the brandy and the peaceful sleep.

From Dharma Bum Jack Ti Jean xxxx

Kerouac sent a thank-you letter for the book to Tom Guinzburg, asking to know if Viking had accepted Visions of Gerard *for publication. On November 29, 1958, Jack had written Sterling Lord that he was convinced that* Gerard *"is by*

---

80. The letter was addressed to Gary Snyder
                c/o[Locke] McCorkle
                348 Montford St.
                Mill Valley, Calif.

far the wisest next book for me because of present screaming about my juvenile delinquent viciousness." Lord had advised Kerouac to propose a travel book about Paris to Viking, and obligingly Kerouac told Guinzburg that his next book project was designed to show "how a 'beat' traveler always gets in some pickle or other." A few days after Jack's letter to his editor, Sterling Lord sent a selection of Kerouac manuscripts to Guinzburg, including the novels Maggie Cassidy *and* Tristessa, *in a final attempt to interest Viking in another book.*

TO TOM GUINZBURG

Dec. 12, 1958
[Northport, New York]

Dear Tom,

Thanx for the Christmas remembrance, the leatherbound copy of BUMS. The one of ROAD was beautiful.

Please let me know when you have decided on GERARD. This is a fine book, a gem actually, all it needs is for me to change the Buddhist references to Catholic, to fit the life & personality of the little boy my brother. I think it would be fine to publish that next and shut up the critics who say I'm not intellectual and full of brutal instincts etc.[81] It will be a feather in Viking's cap because it will attract attention from the church and from different kinds of people and critics this time. It has Shakespearean language, too, different from previous books. A change is in order.

As soon as I hear of yr. acceptance of GERARD I'll write a new novel for you for 1960. Does BEAT TRAVELER sound okay to you? It would be an account of my first trip overseas, on a Yugo freighter, to Tangier, from there (3 months among the Arabs, Americans, international decadents,

---

81. Attacks on Kerouac for publishing novels that celebrated "brutal instincts" and promoted juvenile delinquincy continued for years. In the *Saturday Review* on February 6, 1960, for example, John Ciardi wrote in "Epitaph for the Dead Beats":

> The fact is that the Beat Generation is not only juvenile but certainly related to juvenile delinquency through a common ancestor whose best name is Disgust. The street gang rebellion has gone for blood and violence. The Beats have found their kicks in an intellectual pose, in drugs (primarily marijuana, but also benzedrine, mescaline, peote, assorted goof-balls, and occasionally heroin), and in wine, Zen, jazz, sex, and a carefully mannered jargon. . . .
>
> Speed is, of course, another drug, the illusion of one more escape. In the kind of Beat who most resembles the late Jimmy Dean (who was most nearly a middle ground between the Beats and the leather-jacket hoods, and who finally found the big crack-up he had long been looking for) speed is some sort of death wish.
>
> It is, simply enough, a child's game without the easy freshness of the child's imagination. To the Beat, anyone over thirty is "The Enemy." One trouble, of course, is that by now most of the boys and girls Father Kerouac celebrated in *The Subterraneans* are over the line into enemy territory.

whores, fishermen, Berbers etc.) on the packet to Marseilles and a dharma bum rucksack hike up by Aix and buses thru Arles and Avignon, to Paris, a week in Paris with food, whores, frenetic friends, museums, loneliness, long walks, then over to England on the Dieppe boat and the customs in England wouldnt let me into the country because I looked like a bum and only had 15 shillings but let me in when I showed them a clipping about me and Henry Miller. Thence London, descriptions of the streets, the hotel, the friends, the little events, then the Dutch ship back to states when I was the only man in the diningroom without a tie and et with schoolteachers. Rushing thence to Mexico City just in time for the gigantic frightful earthquake. Showing how a "beat" traveler always gets in some pickle or other. If this sounds too much like my previous books, let me know. I could do a childhood book instead.

Or, with an advance from you, go to Europe anew (with girl) and write new book about Europe for 1960 publication. Go to Europe in the Spring 1959.

I hope you come to Northport meet my mother with Sterling, as he said you might. I have tape recorder now, and I am going to recite a play over it, playing all the parts, see how that works out. Maybe I'll have it recorded by the time you get here. If not, we'll join forces over grog and knock off a comedy. Anyway, see you soon. Merry Christmas to you and Rita and the little child in your crib.

Give my regards to Helen and Malcolm.

Jack

P.S. Ask Malcolm's opinion.[82]

Always a supportive friend, Ginsberg was alarmed at the direction Kerouac's career was going. After reading an advance copy of The Dharma Bums *in one five-*

---

82. In-house memoranda written in December 1958 suggested that despite the praise that Henry Miller had given *The Dharma Bums*, the editors at the Viking Press didn't take Kerouac seriously as a writer. After Sterling Lord sent over new manuscripts, the reader's report on the novels in a Viking Press memo dated December 22, 1958, began, "Actually, when you've had one of Jack's Lowell memoirs you've had them all." The reader thought that *Maggie Cassidy* was "the best of those I've seen," but that *Tristessa* is "plain awful, and should be suppressed if at all possible."

Earlier, on December 2, 1958, the same reader ("C.C.") reported that *Visions of Gerard* was pure bathos, somewhere between Charles Dickens and Harriet Beecher Stowe, and that "the fact that it's rendered in this phoney hopped-up-Zen-bedewed disjointed 'spontaneous' prose cannot . . . disguise the banality and self-indulgence of the subject matter." On December 2, 1958, C.C. concluded that Kerouac had no talent for "real fiction" and advised against publishing *Visions of Gerard* and *Doctor Sax*, because then Kerouac would be encouraged to "take refuge in self-fingering explorations of his childhood and the sources of his own unconscious patterns."

hour sitting, Allen had written Jack on September 10, 1958, praising the novel as "a great piece of religion testament book," yet adding it was "strange thing to be published ... You settling down in simpler prose, or just tired like you said?" Ginsberg feared that "perhaps Viking and Lord are neglecting your good books and trying to get you to write 'potboilers' according to their idea of what your writing career should develop like." Allen advised Jack, "Don't let Madison Avenue try water you down and make you palatable to reviewers Mentality by waiting on Wildbooks and putting out commercial travelogues."

When The Dharma Bums *attracted a spate of hostile reviews, Ginsberg responded with an article in* The Village Voice *on November 11, 1958, defending the book and giving what Allen called "a few facts to clear up a lot of bull." In Ginsberg's opinion, "It's all gibberish, everything that has been said. There's not many competent explainers. I'm speaking of the Beat Generation [of "new visionary" poets], which after all is quite an Angelic Idea." Kerouac was "the great master innovator" with his method of "Spontaneous Bop Prosody, a nickname one might give to this kind of writing—that is to say, read aloud and notice how the motion of the sentence corresponds to the motion of actual excited talk." Ginsberg linked Kerouac's prose experiments "with the half-century-old struggle for the development of an American prosody to match our own speech and thinking rhythms. It's all quite traditional actually you see. Thus W. C. Williams has preached the tradition of 'invention.'" Ginsberg also analyzed passages from* The Dharma Bums *to place Kerouac in the company of Céline and Genet, who "would have the freedom and intelligence to trust their own minds ... not censor it but write it down and discover its beauty."*

On December 16, 1958, Kerouac told Ginsberg about his work in progress Old Angel Midnight *and passed on Henry Miller's response to Ginsberg's* Village Voice *article.*

TO ALLEN GINSBERG

December 16 [1958]
[Northport, New York]

Dear Allen,

Just got Midnight[83] from Rosenthal, he doesnt like Jean-Louis so I decided once for all on Old Angel Midnight ... I'd stayed up all night trying to find names in Bible & Dictionary, gave myself a headache, listed down such names as Lauschen M., Listen M., Lumen M., Luscious M., Lablum M., TiJean M., Jean-Louis M., Jeshua M., Hezion M., Vision M., Grecian M.,

---

83. This spontaneous prose piece was published as "Old Angel Midnight" in *Big Table* magazine, edited by Irving Rosenthal.

Goshen M., Nimshi M., Ziphion M., Ninevah M., Neriah M., Misham M., Mishma Midnight, Misham Midnight, Leshem, Shelah, Shelumiel, Shelomi, Sheshan, Elishua, Enosh, Ephean, Eliatha, Shimeon, Marcion, Halcyon, Elysean, Love Midnight, Illusion Midnight, Motion M., and finally couldnt sleep and watched Charley Van Doren on morning TV show where he suddenly begins telling Ling Giggling Ling tale by Mark Twain about an "old angel" in heaven and it was like the magic of his father and I took it. So I'm sending it tonight with these changes, using Lucifer Moidner at one point since he's an old angel of light they say. Rosie says he has the $600 for the publication so it's all set.

I'm sending you enclosed in this letter your story we writ at Lucien's farm, which has bit poems here and there for you, of yours, and I'm going to quote you a letter I just got from Henry Miller:

"Big Sur 12/9/58 Dear Jack Kerouac—I dont know where Ginsberg gets his mail, so you write him a postcard, will you, and thank him for his letter. Tell him that the review he wrote of your D[HARMA] B[UMS] in the Village Voice (N.Y.) struck me as quite quite wonderful ... I felt, when I read D.B. that you must have written millions of words before—and I see, via A. G., that you have. Salute! P.S. Do you read French? I know, or hear, that you are French Canadian but—? Anyway, if you do, I'd like to send you 'Salut Pour Melville' by Jean Giono." etc.

I'm puttin down most everything, I've decided, except you and Dody and Peter in NY with a few exceptions, I really dont care if I ever see six million of those madcaps ever again... I'm really all up to here now. Have mad new great novel in mind I think I'll write after Christmas, beginning right after Desolation Angels in Arizona desert, to down to Mexico with Bill, you and Greg and Laff and Pete in Mex., pyramids, etc. floating gardens, etc. up to NY in that mad packed car, the Helens, WCWilliams, Yugo freighter, Tangier, Paris, Greg, Bill, London, ship back, Florida, mad bus trip with my ma to Berkeley, Whalen, back again to (after little North Beach anecdotes) Fla., back alone on bus to Mexico in time for earthquake, back to Fla., illness, then up to be "what you call October wave of beauty crashing over my head" publication of Road on up to nightclubs, readings, albums, interview, the whole mad scene in its entire nutty entirety (including Lucien weekends, Pat M., etc. etc.) showing how it starts I'm a rucksack bum in the desert trudging along not knowing I'm trudging along to European travel, fame and fortune and showing how fame & fortune is a crock in America. Think of a nice title for me.[84] Fame in America? Trial on Earth.

---

84. Kerouac titled this second book of *Desolation Angels* "Passing Through."

Through the Wringer. Love on Earth (the weight of the world is love indeed).[85] (O yes including the mad nun scene I made, etc.) A big epic book telling all the critics and reviewers how full of shit they are, right in their faces. Well, I'll write a book soon anyway, maybe get mad and just do Memory Babe childhood Town City reminiscences in real life non-fiction setting.

Meanwhile it looks like Viking okay for Gerard, and Allen (Don) wants Sax, and Jerry Wald interested in Road again he says. I'm being quiet and healthy and happy taking long walks in sub-zero I mean freezing yard in cold moonlight and have color and clear eyes, dont drink at home, do my exercises and feel great. Eat big meals in kitchen and sneer at TV and say to people on TV, "Oh, aint we smart!" which is my old original self okay. I mean, all this consanguine Diamond Sutra vow to be kind to every tom dick and harry & waste my energy & health. Kind to sportswriters n priests, kind to memo book salesmen and real engineers. O yes, have a tape, just recording jazz now, later languij [sic]. See you this weekend 19th and 20th and 21st.

Jean-Louis FOO

In Old Angel Midnight I put in, instead of "Chicago suicide attempt," which you deleted (and we'd stuck in "Irving"), I put in "Fireplace suicide attempt."

85. "Song–The Weight of the World Is Love" was a poem Ginsberg wrote in 1954.

1959

Kerouac spent a peaceful Christmas Eve in 1958 at home in Northport with his guest Robert Lax, who published an excerpt from Visions of Gerard *in the September 1959 issue of* Jubilee. *Lax remembered that Jack slept in his attic bedroom that night with the windows open to the freezing winter air, but on New Year's Eve, Kerouac went into Manhattan to celebrate with Lucien Carr, Dody Müller, Robert Frank, and others.* The Village Voice *photographer Fred McDarrah caught him stumbling drunk, blindly clutching a doll's head in his hand, as he left the Artists Club.*

Early in January 1959 Jack began working with Robert Frank and the artist Alfred Leslie, who were filming Pull My Daisy *in Leslie's loft on Fourth Avenue. Discouraged that there hadn't been a lucrative sale of the film rights to* On the Road, *Kerouac felt he should have made more money as what he called "the 'beat generation' originator," but Sterling Lord had negotiated the sale of* On the Road *and* The Subterraneans *to German, French, Danish, Swedish, Dutch, Italian, Spanish, and Japanese publishers, and placed* Maggie Cassidy *with Avon Books for a $7,500 advance. The second week of January, still self-conscious about his rowdiness with his friends during the New Year's Eve celebration, Kerouac sent off letters to Sterling Lord and Philip Whalen.*

TO STERLING LORD

Jan 8 [19]59
[Northport, New York]

Dear Sterling

Here are the contracts for Mondadori Italy, signed.

About Burroughs, the best thing is, I'll get his present address and you write to him just what you said to me, he's very practical and will send you spates of his work that are "publishable" like the spate in Chicago Review, or direct Ginsberg what to give you.

Gary Snyder now wants to know if you'll handle his book of poems, which is now with Don Allen. The reason this would be good, is, he's go-

175

ing to sea again and will write a sea-novel in Japan which would be Viking Press material. Gary's address is

Gary Snyder
340 Corte Madera
Corte Madera, Calif.

I would like to see you Monday (Jan. 12) to discuss our business soberly for a change. I'll also have with me 2 copies of the 3 act play. My typewriter broke down, thus delay. I'm worried because I lost the first act in the Cedar Bar which is full of bearded frustrated opportunist beatniks, one of whom (the stealer) could try to produce it on TV.

So I'll call you from NY Monday afternoon to meet you, and can stretch my time to wait for you.

As ever
Jack

because among other things I want you to know that I feel a great responsibility to my mother, house and cats, and want to get the money that's coming to me as "beat generation" originator this year, because it's being stolen from my hands on all sides. One kid the other day told me he saw a one-hour TV play in Vermont called "On the Road" and it was a version of the book! This is going too far. And my mother says Jerry Wald wont take On the Road at all, he would have before now. He's doing a new Peyton Place now. Yet everywhere you read, you hear of On the Road "sold to the movies." I dont understand it but I'm going to. I'm cutting down on drink this year to do just this.

TO PHILIP WHALEN

Jan 10 1959
[Northport, New York]

Dear Phil

Started to write you a letter the other night and was too drunk and threw it away crumpled, couldn't see the type ... It was all about how you and I are both "Keltic Boasters"—Well my life has changed a bit, Mémère is a grande dame in her home but she looks lonely as usual without her dotter. But she has a nice new huge bluescreen 21 inch TV and is now watching Lawrence Welk this very moment. I paced in the cold wind just now in the yard, and felt a little better. Last night I finished up typing my play in a spurt of energy. It's 3 act, full play, and going to producer readers this week, what I wanta do is make money either with a play or a movie and UCKYDUCKY, I want to CUT OUT FROM THE PUBLISHING SCENE and just write for myself, in fact I'll end up settling Mémère with my sister in Florida and go back to my old round of Mexico etc. Altho I do have a love now, Dody James, widow of Jan Müller the great young painter, a great gal, painter herself. A cabin with her by the sea somewhere sometime ... I just don't know, don't care, I'm fuddled. I mean, in my head, about prajna, I couldn't be less interested any more. I'd be ashamed to confront you and Gary now I've become so decadent and drunk and don'tgiveashit. I pulled a big Zen Lunatic shot at Brandeis University that got everybody gabbing and scared, only Allen thought it was great, and Dody, everybody else is screaming at me for undignifying my position, whatever that is. They all think writing is a "profession" that's their trouble. To me it's the day. Reason why I ain't writ to you is because I really don't know what to say to YOU ... I'm not a Buddhist any more, I'm not anything, I don't care. I do care about hearts. We're also making an experimental movie (me and Robt Frank and Alfred Leslie) and we're shooting this week, Allen is Allen, Peter Peter, Gregory plays me ... Larry Rivers painter, plays Neal ... etc. It's disgusting how mad we were New Year's Eve a party of mine 15 rowdying around town stealing bottles and books, nobody ever wants to see us again, even Lucien is ashamed (he was leading the way.) O Rip Rap.

I wrote the play by reciting it out on the tape recorder for 2 hours, then took it down word for word.

It's an original, unusual, natural play and therefore no producer will take it except for maybe off-Broadway types.

Gregory and Allen want me to start a revolution, Greg wants to be my "henchman." I told them I wanted to be a lonely New England poet. plet. Wanted to be Cervantes alone by candlelight. Which is why I'd like to go to Mexico alone soon and be just that. I'm not rich. Papers say I am. I have 3 g's in bank, that's all, and am almost daring this week to buy me a typewriter because mine own is finished. Imagine, every office on Madison Avenue has six thousand beautiful perfect typewriter machines ... Wish you were here, love you, see you someday on the rosy street. Henry Miller writes to me every week. Gary just wrote, he is depressed. Why does he go back to Japan and do so by being tired fucked-up screaming knife-slinging among those silly seamen? Why doesn't Gary just get a cabin in the Sur woods? Fuck Japan, it's all words. Fuck religion, it's all words. The only words worth anything are words that you think of when you see a butterfly. Or a big fat Negro lady. Or anything. Why bother? Bang your gavel, jedge, I'se guilty.

I'se guilty of no-more-a-yogi, BHRASTA. It was all prophesied on Desolation.

Anyway, I love you, I really do, and we'll meet again some day soon somewheres.

And when we do, embrace me.

Think I'll become a painter or something.

I like Dufy. I mean his colors.
I hear Lavigne[1] coming NY. Later

Bah
Jack

At the end of January 1959, imagining a sunnier and more peaceful life in Florida, Kerouac wrote his sister, Caroline, a bleak wintertime description of "cold and lonely New England around here" in Northport with his mother and their two cats, Timmy and Tyke. Nin had moved to Seattle with her son and her husband, Paul, who was employed as a radar technician. Jack disclosed a complicated plan he had worked out with Mémère to bring the entire family back together in Florida. As usual, Gabrielle added a handwritten note to her daughter on the back of Jack's typewritten letter.

TO CAROLINE KEROUAC BLAKE

Jan 29 [19]59
[Northport, New York]

Dear Nin,

Here's what: I dont want to be so close to New York, everybody is bothering me. I should be far away. (2) It's too expensive here, the taxes, heat, etc. (3) Mémère is lonely when I leave the house even for a few days.

So what I propose is to buy a few more lots around our Sanlando Springs lots and make a lot of private wooded area, and then go ahead and build one big eight-room duplex with two kitchens, two bathrooms, and one large patio for the whole family. Two kitchens is important, because of the cats, etc. and it would be cute when you are making your supper in one kitchen for Paul and Lil Paul, and Mémère is making her supper in her kitchen for me and the cats. (When I'm there.) I plan to be there most of my time but there's a lot of traveling I want to do and I cant leave Mémère alone in this big lonely cold house.

I have some money to help get this going. I can put up the house for sale as soon as we're ready to roll. If I knew when you are coming back from Seattle for good (I assume Paul is going to be stationed in Orlando for good), then we could decide and go ahead. [....] I have the money to go ahead. I have money *coming* this year, right now I have 3 thousand in the bank. The house here is worth fourteen thousand, all paid.

I may get a little jaloppy [sic] or a Jeepster stationwagon if we are going to live in the country. Mémère is all for this idea and so am I. So write to me and give me your ideas. I have to go ahead and write and type my

---

1. The painter Robert Lavigne.

manuscripts and publish and have a lot on my mind, so it would be nice if you took over the reins of handling this big final move while I work and make more money.

I'm willing to buy the extra three lots, and to put the down payment on the 8-room duplex, etc. so go ahead. I'll put my money in a family homestead.

If Paul can settle in Sanlando (Orlando plant) and go on with his job at Martin's, and make payments to Mémêre for his less-than-half share of the house, okay. We'll iron it out.

But this is important, and I want to go ahead with this, this year. Soon as you can. Timmy has been gone 4 days and we're waiting for him. Tyke is crying and doesn't eat. Mémêre is crying. It's a cold and lonely New England around here.

What more can I say? I leave it to you to figure the plan. I have the money. Let me hear from you. All I want is for Mémêre to be happy so I can be free to roam and work my way.

From what Mémêre said about Orlando last Fall, it was apretty lousy, but Sanlando Springs is another story and I want to be quiet in the country when I write. Blah blah blah. Write to me.

Your brother who loves you too,
Jack

[MÉMÊRE'S NOTE]
Dear Ti Nin—

What do you think of Jack's plan ... it may come in handy for you some day. I wont live forever you know ... let Jack do the financing. I want that money to stay in the family and not for the *Bums* around him here ... Now start the ball rolling so we can put this old barn up for sale ...

Mom XXX

Early in February 1959, Kerouac wrote to his agent and to Jeanne Unger, the production editor at Grove responsible for seeing Doctor Sax *through the press. He was looking forward to overdubbing the soundtrack narration for* Pull My Daisy, *which Robert Frank had photographed and directed with Alfred Leslie as a twenty-eight-minute film featuring Allen Ginsberg, Peter Orlovsky, Gregory Corso, Larry Rivers, Alice Neel, Richard Bellamy, David Amram, and Delphine Seyrig. The script was a loose adaptation of Kerouac's play* The Beat Generation, *but his mother complained to Nin about the new title* Pull My Daisy: "Jack says it's a poem and has beautiful meaning. Right now, it has a double meaning, that is if you think what I think."*

Feb 3 [19]59
[Northport, New York]

Dear Sterling

Here are the Swedish contracts for Dharma Bums, signed.

I'm sorry I missed you Friday night and in fact I'm getting awfully sorry and mad at myself for constantly missing you on our important and also impromptu meetings in New York, things have gotten even more hectic around me than ever (it seems ever since Hunter College, which by the way was the cause of the big NYPost spread now, ordered by James Wechsler himself) and I'm really now rapidly going to pot and on the verge of becoming a blob. My mother and I have written to my sister to go ahead with plans to build a family house on her lots in the woods outside Orlando and that is the only way I can be saved from the fury of New York and get some time to re organize my heart and mind and go on writing. And what bothers me is the way I have to constantly drink to put up with nervous appointments with everybody in sight, for one reason or another, and vast nervous parties where everybody is staring at me and fulfilling their preconceptions of me as a drunken fool. And the mail! whether pro or con it has a frightening intensity that makes me wonder if they simply dont want somebody to crucify or tear apart limb from limb like some sacrificial hero in their own minds. So, yes, and you were right, I must get out of the vicinity of NY and retire to the South and come here on business trips to see you. We'll do that this year. Meanwhile I notice you've been doing a tremendous amount of foreign sales of the books, so I can see other matters cant go as fast, like I dont know (didnt have a chance to ask you or you a chance to answer) what precisely Ria is doing now about the MGM title etc. But anyway here's what, first things first, I would appreciate if you could do for me. Okay?

(1) Contact Al Aronowitz of the New York Post and tell him to cancel the photographing of me in my Northport home because my mother doesnt want the spotlight on her home. Tell him there are plenty of suitable-to-his-subject photos at Robert Frank, 34 Third Avenue, and also with John Cohen reachable through same address. Aronowitz was here, N'Port, interviewed me on 2 hour tape, he got enuf.

(2) Could you send me the complete list of monies that came in, through your office, for me, for entire year 1958, so I can present it with my income tax. You remember last year I typed that up myself from your account book, but this year I doubt if I can do anything so rational. I'd be willing to pay Lee an hour's union wages (2.00) for this chore, if she wants. If not, I'll come in someday and type it up myself.

Okay. I'll write the Escapade column now, the Holiday article, correct the proofs of SAX and MIDNIGHT (just in), read off the soundtrack of the movie and quietly go mad. Imagine, I was going to write a new book this month!

But Florida will be the answer.

And so we will end up having a long and interesting career together and please dont think I'm as rude, brash, thoughtless or careless as I seem, it's all blamable on Fame and Barleycorn which have to go hand in hand when you're a naive Canuck like me.

I think you're a marvelous gentleman and I'm sure we will make the kind of money we're supposed to within the next 2 years, so in the end it'll be worth your while.

In about 10 days sending you manuscript of MAGGIE CASSIDY, as I said. Avon? Or ... anyway, I'll see you in about 10 days.

As ever,
Jack

TO JEANNE UNGER [GROVE PRESS]

Feb. 5, 1959
[Northport, New York]

Dear Jeanne:

It's now absolutely clear to me that it's a damn good thing you were there at this time, because ... well, here are my notes writ while proof-reading this ms.

(1) Doctor Sax was written and titled in 1952 (nothing to do with Doctor Zhivago title)
(2) Beautifully accurate proofreading sensitively on your part—you should be an editor soon
(3) Forgot to change "Cousin Raoul" to Cousin Noël ... and Ernie Malo
(4) I erased some of yr. penciled questioning notes where it was okay as is
(5) Found out in the British Museum records of Heraldic Brittany the name was "Lebris" not "Le Brice" (Lebris de Keroack) (old independent family spitting on the rest of France) (like Breton Louis Ferdinand Céline does today) (his real name's Destouches)
(6) Fix't some of the French but you fix't most 99% of it, you know French
(7) Turned "toy" to "tool" ("prick" too stiff)
(8) Marvelous job of linotyping second half
(9) Name of Book One in original handwrite ms. was "Ghosts of the Pawtucketville Night."
(10) Anyway congratulations on a wonderful job, I went through this ms. in ONE NIGHT it was so well done. Do I get to see the final galley?

181

My address is 34 Gilbert St.
If no mistakes are made the ms. is ready for publication.
See you,
Sincerely
Jack Kerouac

The day before Valentine's Day, Kerouac wrote Stella Sampas in response to her and her brother Charley's curiosity about how he described Lowell in Doctor Sax.

TO STELLA SAMPAS

Feb. 13, 1959
[Northport, New York]

Dear Stella

The reason I havent written to you is that I was getting so many letters it was impossible to answer all of them sincerely so I decided to answer none of them at all. Sometimes 50 a week and all *personal*. I was trying to get on with my work and not be swamped under other business which would have required a secretary and that's not for me. But right now the mail has receded, the storm is over, and I see where you and Charley are curious about DOCTOR SAX.

It's coming out in April, published by Grove Press, and will probably be banned in Lowell and Boston too. It's all about my French Canadian boyhood in Pawtucketville (with touches of earlier days in Centralville.) It's all about Moody Street up there, about playing ball in Textile field, about playing along the banks of the Merrimac, about the big flood of 1936. Sammy's not in it, I didnt know him then (age 14.) (only slightly, that is, as a friend of Steve Spaneas.) The main heroes are G. J. (Gus) Rigopoulos, which is you know who. Also some of my French chums. I make no bones about our pubertical interest in sex and alas there are many 4-letter words but it was because I wrote it in exile in Mexico in 1952 and didnt care at all (then) what people would think, I wrote it in honor of art. It is a strange work. The end is a fantasm in the boy's mind whereby a hundred mile long snake is made to emerge from below the Castle of the World (in Centralville hump hill that you see from the bridges) and all the forces of World Evil are gathered there and DOCTOR SAX (the hero, the Shadow of the Lowell and Dracut woods) with the help of the boy are on hand to prevent world destruction. It's wild. It's said to be the first real vision in America since MOBY DICK. The descriptions of the Merrimac in the 1936 flood are wild, the river foams and lunges like a snake thru my hometown. The full title, properly, is DOCTOR SAX AND THE GREAT WORLD SNAKE, subtitle FAUST PART THREE. It is the completion of the Faust

Legend and also a Gothic New England work with roots in Melville and Hawthorne. You'll see, in any case. It has nothing to do with the beat generation material I've published so far. I have two more books about Lowell after that, to be published, the first about my Centralville childhood and the death of my brother (VISIONS OF GERARD) and then my high school love affair MAGGIE CASSIDY. After SAX I will never dare revisit Lowell ever again but it is my deepest vision of the world, which to me was, and still is, Lowell. The Lowell of my mind satisfies my need for Lowell as I get older. The Lowell of my mind is my only Lowell. Lowell was a kingdom. Now that I'm sposed to go to Japan and India and everywhere I'll wait ten years before sneaking back to Lowell, with black slouch hat, and hear the laugh of Doctor Sax by the river again. The river is central.

Happy Valentine and good luck to all the family.

I hope you understand why I dont write, or visit. My mother is moving back to a small house in Florida now, with me, because it is too expensive in New York. I dont have as much money as people think. I didnt even sell On the Road to the movies yet but the movies are coming out soon with big pictures using the same theme. So I lost out and wont be rich at all. It's a shame but it always works that way. I dont need much money for myself, in any case. The awful abuse that I have been getting from critics resulted in the complete neglect of Dharma Bums. For some reason my name has become associated with bearded beatniks with whom I never had anything to do at all. I'm angry now, for sure, I'm going to Paris this spring and forget it all, and write something beautiful about Paris. When I'm an old man I'll at least have my jug of wine and a loaf of bread too.

Jack

In mid-February 1959, Dody Müller ended her affair with Kerouac, running out of patience with his drunken moodiness and his disruptive visits to her studio in Manhattan with crowds of hangers-on. She felt unwilling to settle for what she saw as Jack's "sweet self maybe one and a half days [a month] sober, plus Mémère." A few days later, at three in the morning on February 21, 1959, Kerouac tried to drown his sorrows at home with "Old Crow highballs" while writing to his sympathetic friend John Clellon Holmes about the good times he'd had with his "(ex)" girlfriend.

TO JOHN CLELLON HOLMES

Feb. 21, 1959
34 Gilbert St.
Northport NY

Dear Johnny:—

Not writing to you of late (altho you never write me impulsively but only answer me politely) maybe that's the reason but just hearing now

Lester Young new record (I guess it was Lester maybe Quinichette) I thought of you and your wonderful book THE HORN and you especially and the other day ran into Anatole Broyard too but that's not the point, here I am at 3 in the morning in my big wind-open house receiving all the northwest winds across the football field of Northport drinking my Old Crow highballs alone and sad and fucked after still another lost love affair, wishing I were with you by the fireplace crackle talk and Parker records and old remembers ... O Hawthrone, can I wear your glumly crown? As we become aged men of letters and disappear into our New England trees, we create but cease writing impulsive letters! We should live near Birdland! (not really)—What I mean is, how I would like to see you tonight! That's all! I'm not bullshitting! I get telegrams from Newsweek and tear them up, that's how busy I am! That's why I haven't had time to write, plan, prepare a 100-mile journey to Saybrook ever since I been back. And I would rather go alone than with screaming poets AllenPeterGregory, they scream and talk, they are very great, but we'd never get a word in edgewise ... I'm going to Paris this year, again, but with money this time, money for quiet inns I guess ... I'm moving this menage back to Florida in any case to get away from NY which is killing me ... My new (ex) girl was a painter and gad I got all involved in the painter set, gallery openings and so forth, mad, insane, my poets and all the painters and a slue of musical composers all screaming in the Cedars! Not only that but fantastic poetry readings with people trying to get in from sidewalks and fire escapes! Gregory and I and Allen reading our hearts out ...[2] Hoodlums, gangsters, cops, revolutionaries, Fidelians everywhere! I must leave, get out of town. And all the time what kind of quiet musical sad Dickinson life are you leading sitting in your gargoyle cubbyholes (what ya call those round window hole rooms?) writing your sad poems about Southern pianos. How is sweet wifey? with her yams and hams and fresh peas? ... All that's gone under the bridge now, Sinatra, Lester, Seymour, old wire recordings, long talks about Laventry and Huncke in your loft, Marian, Harrington, Red Harrington, those dolls whose names we forgot ... Neal in San Quentin for pot ... Right now I'm typing up Mary (now Maggie) Cassidy for publishers, probably Avon softcover, and remembering via my boyhood with G.J. and the gang my veritable boyhood with you and the gang... How come we don't hear from you much? Pretty soon you won't hear from me any more, when I get under the stars in that Carib splendor and sigh by pines, ai, ai, haik, bor-

2. Kerouac was referring to the poetry reading on February 15, 1959, at the Artists Studio in Manhattan, where Fred McDarrah photographed him on a stepladder reading a passage from *On the Road* dressed in chinos and a plaid shirt, arms outstretched—as McDarrah noted—"like a Christ figure." Also present at the marathon reading were Ginsberg, Corso, LeRoi Jones, Ted Joans, Edward Marshall, and Jose Garcia Villa. McDarrah's photograph of Kerouac was used on the cover of *The Beat Scene* edited by Elias Wilentz (New York: Corinth, 1960).

racho ... I'm drunk but you see I can type splendidly. I want a girl, I can get all the girls I want, but now I want to LOVE a girl, not just fuck, I've done enuf of that ... I'm getting old, I'm a fat tub now, 180 lbs., awful—too late—now I'll have to be kind and talented, no longer will it WORK just to be goodlooking and young—I'll go to Paris with a new sad raincoat and wait under the lamp for the beauteous whore of St. Denis? ... I'll meet amazing Italians in Rome? When do you come to NY? Let me know when you come to NY, have much things to show you/ anyway write when, if, how, which, can/ i hate miles davis/ cornball/ everytime I start to write you a letter i start off good and end up fucking up like this;/ '7#" I'm sorry dammit, I wanted to tell you long story about what happened, so much has happened, in fact, to Allen too, he doesn't even remember any more certain events of even poor 1948! —Oh well, it's all a big daydream

   and wisdom is a heartless occupation

adieu
Jack

Despite Snyder's praise of The Dharma Bums, *Kerouac worried that his friend really didn't like the novel. When he wrote to Snyder on February 23, 1959, Jack confessed that he was growing too soft to come out to California to practice his "rucksacking bummism." Snyder, who had returned to Japan to continue his study of Zen Buddhism, replied somewhat testily on March 10, 1959, referring to the glib comments about Buddhism that Jack had made in the book. Snyder wrote Kerouac, "I told you I liked it, but that doesn't make it right. What concerns me is* your mind ... Do *you* think you understand [Buddhism]? Nobody ever said anything against love or entanglement with women but you ... If you come here I'll put you to work hoeing my vegetables & cutting firewood on the hill—far kinder than hell, where they pull out the writer's tongue with red hot pliers." Later Snyder told interviewers that Japhy Ryder was a fictional character, not a realistic portrait of him, and that Kerouac's narrative about meeting him and the other poets in California in 1955 should be read as a freely embellished work of Jack's imagination.*

TO GARY SNYDER

Feb. 23, 1959
34 Gilbert St.
Northport, NY

Dear Gary,

   Hope you're not gone to sea by the time this reaches your father's house. Maybe you should have (or should now) come to New York to get a Japan-bound vessel. Much shipping here. In Baltimore too and Philly and Boston. Well, Viking Press is going to advance me a few bucks and I'm going to take a cabin on an American freighter or passenger vessel, just so long's it's one cabin for me to read and study in, en route to Paris, this time for a long time, and with side issues to Hamburg, Ireland, London again, Rome first time and so forth. Then, nothing could stop me too from taking a freighter to Japan sometime this year, from Europe. Anyway I'll write a book about the whole trip and it's on the house, Viking House.

Meanwhile, since Dharma Bums came out I feel that you've been silent and disappointed about me. I dont think the book was as bad as you think; when you look at it again in future years, when the world will've gotten worster [sic], you'll look back and appreciate the job I did on "you" and on Dharma Bumism. For Mrs. Sasaki to say that "it was a good portrait of Gary but he doesn't know *anything* about Buddhism" is just so fuckin typical of what's wrong with official Buddhism and all official religions today—woe, clashings, divisions, sects, jealousies, formalities, materialism, do-goodism, actionism, no repose, no universal love-try, no abandoning of arbitrary conceptions for a moment. Even Suzuki was looking at me through slitted eyes as tho I was a monstrous impostor of some kind (at least I feel that, I dunno). Why should the Japanese make the chief claim on Buddhism when it came from an Aryan Indian, and Bodhisattva Bodhidharma came from the West?

Anyway what's important to me now, is that I've become soft and have abandoned my rucksacking bummism, which is bad, and if I go to Japan and join you I would like to make it again, in the hills, or alone. I don't want ANYTHING to do with Official Zen and their monasteries. There are no Hui Nengs around there, left, I'll bet. But I do want to meet the old hillsmen thinkers and haiku writers and also lay some pretty girls and drink saki. We could proceed to India together after that. Allen and Gregory and Peter and Burroughs all four want to go to India with me (on me) but I don't have that much money yet and moreover it would be nervewracking all five yakking at the same time. Yet, if I should suddenly sell ROAD to Movies (or upcoming SAX) I would, could summon them, from America, send big fare. Allen's idea is really European, to get a big comfortable house on outskirts of Calcutta and come in on weekends, just like living in Mill Valley and coming into City, or living in Northport and coming into New York. I can see it now, my Calcutta would become another great Tea-High-Eternal-City-of-my-Imagination, Sravasti no more'n Mexico City! Mitt Cobras!

But anyway, Gary, if there's anything on your mind that has disappointed you, please tell me. I don't understand yr. cold silence after our rock dhyanas together. Really don't. I havent had time to pee, reason I didnt write to Phil much either. You have no conception of the enormity of the demands on my poor simpleminded time around here, I tear up telegrams daily, even the ones from Newsweek et al. I'm typing up clean copies of my remaining already written gemmy novels and we made a movie and I have to do the soundtrack by myself etc. and my girl was a painter and I was at art openings and drunk all the time, ow ... I'm goin. Write!

Jack

Give my regards to Thea and your Pop.
If thou didst never hold me in vain
But drew thy breath in vain....

[Poem enclosed with letter on separate page]
O Lord Tathagata
Or whatever gata
Make us free
To be gay
Let us all
   Grow old like Picassos
   with young wives
Laughing at our canvases
Drinkin wine
Singing in the moon
Like Li Po
Of dread majesty

O Lord Tathagata
Passer through
Are you suffering
Everything
We suffer?
For show?
What show?
The show a hint
Of your pity? And Heaven's soon
Compassion Yours and our Reward?

Throughout the winter and spring of 1959, Kerouac sent a stream of typewritten letters to his sister, along with his mother's notes urging Nin to agree to their plan to build a two-family house on the lots they had bought together in Florida. Mémère offered to take care of her eleven-year-old grandson, "Little Paul," while Nin consulted with the builders in Florida. Gabrielle also promised not to interfere in the family's plans, telling her daughter: "I have enough letters pinned on me as insane and frustrating."

TO CAROLINE KEROUAC BLAKE

[Before March 1959
Northport, New York]

Dear Nin,

What I'm willing to do [is] put down payments on both our houses and get the builders going. You could come to Northport now with Lil Paul (there's a grammar school right across the football field in back) or come in June when school's over in Seattle, and be nearer Orlando for a few checkup trips. With you and Mémêre and Lil Paul together in this house I could either stay home or take that trip to Europe the publishers want me to do for a new book. Also I *do* want to buy an extra lot or two, I'd leave most of the land just woods, for privacy in my yard from neighbors' eyes. I now have 6 thousand in the bank but I pay my taxes of about 3 in March. If you could be here and arrange everything, the lots, the down-payments, the building, I could be free to go on working in peace, make more money. Either now or in June, come on over, and handle it yourself. You're smarter than I am. Then, in the Fall, when Paul is sent back to Orlando, his home would be ready. Let me hear from you. As ever,

Ti Jean

Three days after his thirty-seventh birthday, unhappy at the thought that he had alienated Snyder by writing The Dharma Bums, *Kerouac sent an affectionate letter to Philip Whalen, Snyder's friend since their student days at Reed College. Unable to complete a new novel since* The Dharma Bums, *Jack had decided that his primary task was to organize and retype his old manuscripts for publication. He hoped that once readers had the chance to see the range of his experimental prose and poetry, it would be "a big 'avant garde' year" for him.*

TO PHILIP WHALEN

March 15, 1959
[Northport, New York]

Dear Phil ... A GREAT TIGER WAS FREED
FROM HIS COTTAGE
AND HE DISAPPEARED!

Is that You?

Just wrote long letter (2 weeks, 3 ago) to Gary, dont know if he got it, sent it c/o his Paw at CM.[3] Well I guess he's done with me, I guess like

3. The envelope was addressed to Mr. Gary Snyder
c/o Harold Snyder
340 Corte Madera
Corte Madera, Calif.

[Stan] Persky he thinks Dharma Bums not great book. It better than any of em as will be proven when those Sierras turn to dust.

I dont like Persky for the simple reason that after helping him last summer, taking off precious time to write to Don Allen etc. for him, he turns around and puts Dharma Bums down because it doesnt have that stupid bigcity bullshit emptyword sound of sad redbrick wobbling mills. Imagine if I had written long letters to Faulkner or Williams in my teen days writing in furnished rooms, and then after they got me started put them down. Blind. I would say he is jealous and unintelligent, which aint no nice combination. However, arbitrary conceptions wont get this letter nowhere. Buck fuck him.

In fact fuck everybody including you with your tigers and cottages. I cant come out to Frisco but I may if MGM gives me job as technical advisor to filming of Subterraneans there, so's I could see you and eat chinese food and also make how much a week? After income tax next month I have about 1 or 2 thousand in bank, which aint what the papers are saying about my bank account.

Mémêre sends you her love and wishes you could have come to see us, of course we all know 3,000 miles is too much for casual visits, same for me as for you. Yes, Dr Sax is coming out, beautiful job of printing by Grove, not one error, I do final proof next week. Also they're bringing out Mexico City Blues all 240 choruses, wow, a big poetry book. Meanwhile New Directions bringing out 130 selected pages of "Visions of Enal" (changed from "Neal"),[4] O my best prose there. To add to the all confusion, "Old Angel Midnight" ("Lucien Midnight" once) coming out Big Table, as you know. A big "avant garde" year for me, actually, I wanted to shut up the critics of Dharma Bums who said it was a commercial hackjob, which it wasnt essentially.

Starting to read "Diamond Sutra" again, had given it up since October, starting to nod my head decisively over it again. Had girlfriend, may not any more, mutual agreement, I too mad for normal woman, I want solitude. So, aside from a possible assignment to drive to Cuba with photog Robt Frank for Holiday or Esquire, my next trip may be … Paris or Mexico, alone, to just go again light quiet candles in quiet city or country room and write visions and blues. My work in NY past year and a half has actually been consolidation and preparation of all my past works for printing, that's the point, when that's done I am ready for "new" work. (I aint a movie actor and it aint or shouldnt be expected of me to "bring out my latest" as SRL[5] insists.)

4. This book was titled *Visions of Cody* when issued by new Directions in 1959 with a slip inserted by James Laughlin describing it as "a 120-page excerpt from the long novel of the same name, which is Kerouac's favorite but which is considered unpublishable at present. It principally concerns the character who is the hero of *On the Road.* …"
5. *Saturday Review of Literature.*

Do you correspond with Dada Montgomery?[6] He wanted my fan mail, I saw a great chance to get rid of it, sent it to him with $1 stamps, he reads it, sends it all back in cookie box full of crumpled crunches of cookies! He's actually a pain because he had newspaper interviews about me that were inaccurate and "square." Really. But Montgomery is better in Milvia Floweryard than in newspaper.

So nodding my head decisively over D[iamond] Sutra again and fuck Suzuki, fuck Sasaki, fuck em all. They think Buddhism is something apart from Transcendentalism, well theyre not Buddhists, theyre Alan Watts social philosophers and glad-to-meet-yas. They want "group meetings" to "discuss" "Zen" that's what they want, not the sigh. You on your Oregon beach with illuminated worms' better. Whalen know why youre a bodhisattva really? you're the only one who never yelled at me "for drinking too much." Think it over if hits Zen you wanta talk about. Fuck Ginsberg, fuck Corso, fuck em all.[7] I'm happy. I'm going away. Once more I be now

> Free as a pine
> goofing
> For the wind

Thats pretty free, I hope. Not that I want Nirvana for myself, no sir, just a good night's rest every single night, with window open, in silent night, and wake up to good cup of coffee. Late afternoon, mope, but who can help it? Dont want Nirvana for myself but will not accept Samsara for everybody's sake if they go on insisting on being ignorant gnashers and yakkers. I hate em all. I'm happy. I like myself when I'm buy [sic] myself. ... Sure wish I could put my arms around your big fat waist tonight and say Phil, how are you? Dont pay any attention to rest of this letter.

Jean

In March 1959, Kerouac collaborated with Ginsberg, Corso, and Orlovsky on an article for Holiday *magazine. Soon afterwards Jack wrote to them in Manhattan, saying that he was too busy revising the material to go to a reading with them at Harvard University. The previous month, in his Lower East Side apartment, Ginsberg had resumed working on "Kaddish," the poem for his mother, Naomi, which he had started in Paris. In this letter Jack told Allen that he feared a major change in his mental condition had taken place after the concussion he had suffered as a result of the Greenwich Village assault in 1958: "maybe I got brain damage, maybe once I was kind drunk, but am now brain-clogged drunk with the kindness valve clogged by injury."*

6. John Montgomery.
7. See Kerouac's reference to his "recent belligerent drunkenness" in his letter to Ginsberg et alia on March 24, 1959.

Kerouac was referring to his "recent belligerent drunkenness" earlier in the month. On March 2, 1959, during a poetry reading at the Living Theatre at Fourteenth Street and Sixth Avenue, he insulted the poet Frank O'Hara by taking offense at O'Hara's lisping speech and interrupting his performance by shouting, "You're ruining American poetry, O'Hara."

O'Hara snapped back, "That's more than you ever did for it." After the intermission Kerouac continued heckling O'Hara until O'Hara left the stage, telling the audience, "I just don't feel like reading. This may seem uninteresting but it's no more uninteresting than Jack Kerouac."

Ginsberg was in the audience and he felt embarrassed for Kerouac. Later Allen said he wondered "if O'Hara understood how great Kerouac was and what grief and fear and paranoia he was talking out of. . . . But I think the problem was alcohol, alas."

TO ALLEN GINSBERG, GREGORY CORSO,
& PETER ORLOVSKY

[March 24, 1959
Northport, New York]

Dear Allen, Gregory, Peter

It looks like I can't go to Harvard anyway because Holiday magazine wants those 2 articles by March 30th and it will take me several days to type them and also make bigger sentences out of our material. In other words I'm staying home to make your money for India and Crete. Besides, I'm tired. Hearing your Chicago Records (tapes) made me feel depressed all over again about poetry readings. Too much repetition of same material for new audiences etc. Too much the eagerness to be accepted. O well, you know how I feel and felt about that in Frisco.

Here's your check for 15 bucks I owe you. If I suddenly go mad and decide to go to Harvard with you anyway I will be at your pad at 3 or 4 on Thursday.

But then that would only be if I finisht and mailed off those two articles to Holiday by then. Almost impossible.

How do you like my new typewriter type?

American College Dictionary sent me their big square definition of "beat generation" and wanted to know if I would revise, emend or make a new one. Theirs was awful, "certain members of the generation that came of age after World War II who affect detachment from moral and social forms and responsibilities, supposedly due to disillusionment. Coined by John Kerouac."

So I sent in this: "*beat generation*, members of the generation that came of age after World War II–Korean war who join in a relaxation of social and sexual tensions and espouse anti-regimentation, mystic-disaffiliation and material-simplicity values, supposedly as a result of Cold War disillusionment. Coined by JK."

If I don't come to Harvard, read them this definition and tell them that I "plead work as my excuse for not attending the reading at Harvard, for every Massachusetts boy dreams of Harvard."

My mother (not wanting me to go get plastered so often in NY, and me too I get sick and dirty and don't work) invites all 3 of you to come out here any time you want, so after Harvard let's do our tapes etc. Also you can see my paintings etc. Also, Allen, I have copy of Jabberwock sent to you care of me, by big Scotland types, who want our work published there in fall.[8] & other items. Anyway, I'm not a liar. As to my recent belligerent drunkenness[9] I just noticed today it all began last April right after that bum pounded my brain head with his big fingered fist ring ... maybe I got brain damage, maybe once I was kind drunk, but now am brain-clogged drunk with the kindness valve clogged by injury.

More anon. Addio.

Jack

Kerouac had published a section of his experimental prose piece variously titled Sebastian Midnight *and* Old Lucien Midnight *as "Old Angel Midnight" in* Big Table. *After the magazine appeared, Lawrence Ferlinghetti offered to have City Lights bring out the complete work in San Francisco.*

TO LAWRENCE FERLINGHETTI

April 5, 1959
34 Gilbert St.
Northport, NY

Dear Larry,

Okay. And since you're using Al Podell's offset of OLD ANGEL MIDNIGHT perhaps then you wouldnt want a few new chapters already written, as Ginsberg suggested in order to give the City Lights issue a greater value than the Big Table one ...? Let me know.

For jacket blurb, or preface or whatever, I would suggest this following quote from me plus possibly a word from Allen or Whalen or somebody. Here's my quote which adequately explains the purpose of such a work to the customers who buy your books:

8. In 1959, The Scottish magazine *Jabberwock* published the 180th chorus from *Mexico City Blues*.
9. In October 1959, Kerouac, Ginsberg, and Orlovsky visited Frank O'Hara's apartment, where Kerouac used O'Hara's typewriter to write an apology for his behavior at the Living Theatre: "Dear Frank: the reason I was extraordinary that nite I was jealous of Gregory [Corso] liking your poetry.—J.K." See also letter to Ginsberg, June 20, 1960.

"Old Angel Midnight," says Jack Kerouac, "is only the beginning of a lifelong work in multilingual sound representing the haddal-da-babra of babbling world tongues coming in thru my window at midnight no matter where I live or what I'm doing, in Mexico, Morocco, New York, India or Pakistan, in Spanish, French, Aztec, Gaelic, Keltic, Kurd or Dravidian, the sounds of people yakking and of myself yakking among, ending finally in great intuitions of the sounds of tongues throughout the entire universe in all directions in and out forever. And it is the only book I've ever written in which I allow myself the right to say anything I want, absolutely and positively anything, since that's what you hear coming in that window ... God in His Infinity wouldn't have had a world otherwise—Amen."

Okay. I may at that show up with Allen in May in San Francisco, for nostalgic reasons ...

Yours,
Jack

P.S. For a cover, would you like me to send you a drawing of my own? Let me know. And can it be in pencil? My DR SAX drawing for Grove Press was in pencil.

A year after Neal Cassady's arrest in San Francisco for possession of marijuana, Kerouac wrote a friendly but subdued letter to Carolyn Cassady, telling her that he was willing to contribute to Ginsberg's plan to buy Neal an Olympia typewriter so he could work on his autobiography in San Quentin. Jack was anxious to make it clear to Carolyn that he hadn't been responsible for Neal's arrest by portraying Cassady [Dean Moriarty] in On the Road *as a man interested in drugs and "kicks." Kerouac was also concerned that some members of his family had told him that he had "disgraced the name of Kerouac" after they had read what he called "the disgusting abuse from critics" of his literary work.*

TO CAROLYN CASSADY

April 17, 1959
Northport, N.Y.

Dear Carolyn,

No, the prison authorities rejected my application to correspond with Neal, also Allen's. They are cruel in every possible way. Imagine that bitch Connie N. getting off with parole after murdering a human being in cold blood, and poor Neal with his pockets full of innocent loco weed that grows wild in Texas getting an indefinite term ... Do you mind if I say this in my next Escapade Magazine column or shouldn't I mention Neal's name.

By the way, Allen is coming out a few days from now, to Frisco, and wants to see Neal etc. I dont know if he'll help the situation or not but he will see you first possibly.

It's no longer possible for me to live in NY now, I'm pestered night and day by visitors most of them girls and college boys. I'll have to go to Mexico and hide soon. My mother and I have decided to move back to quiet retired Florida where I can work.

Is this Olympia a portable or a big brand new standard? Let me know how much you need and I'll send the check. The money will represent my debt to Neal for all the porkchop suppers we had over the years in your dear sweet kiddie kitchen, remember? (And all the pizzas). I dont want you and Neal to think my book had anything to do with his arrest, after all he was too reckless, people were telling him to stay away from North Beach years ago. If anything, if all the On the Road fans all over the world knew what had happened to "Dean" they would all be writing protesting letters to SQ about it. The only thing I'M sorry about, that is, with reference to what I did that was wrong, was the invitation to Neal in 1957 to drive to NY and fetch me and "meet the girls," which had made you mad and rightly, Carolyn. But I'd only said "to meet the girls" as a laugh, well, truly, secretly, to INDUCE the excitable Neal to come and get me, and that was sneaky. But O my book, On the road, isnt it a paean to Neal? I hope you think so.

Now be sure and get this typewriter to Neal because he wants to go on writing and also I can start publishing him immediately & pay you money, I've been made editor of an anthology, appearing 3 times a year or so, for 25¢ in drugstore newsstands, Beat Generation Anthology, I'd like to start with First Third the beginning and work on up each issue. Meanwhile N. continues work on the rest in SQ. Someday he'll be a successful writer, both artistically and commercially, and could have time to stay home and play with the kids and write by the pool, instead of torturing himself on railroads. For he's a great man indeed and as good a wordslinger as I am, which is the best. Encourage him to write, Carolyn.

The Aronowitz series[10] was frightening and yet I get the feeling it did a lot of good ... the best part was Neal's dialog about "pineal fire" etc. big Cayce Aurobindo mysticisms suddenly appearing on the page. And the picture you took of us at the San Jose farm.

When and if I ever come to Frisco, I'd like to see you again and have

---

10. The journalist Al Aronowitz interviewed Kerouac and Cassady and wrote a series of twelve articles about the Beats published in the *New York Post* in March 1959. The article on Kerouac was reprinted in *U.S. No. 3, The Paperback Magazine* (New York: Bantam Books, 1970), retitled "Would You Run Away from Home to Become a Beatnik If You Knew That the Man Who Wrote *On the Road* Lived at Home with His Mother?"

more pizza and wine. You'll find me jaded, compared to last time. Too much adulation is worse than non-recognition, I see now, except on the economic level. "Too much adulation" means also the disgusting abuse from critics, which has caused my family in Lowell to announce, for instance, that I have disgraced the name of Kerouac, when all the time the disgrace emanates from critics and press. Ah, it's all sad, like I said, like you said, like Neal knew. I shall certainly go to Heaven kneeling. I desire to remain in solitude, says Milarepa,[11] because much talk is of no avail. So you wont see much of me unless I get a solitary cabin somewhere in Calif. But I think of your sweetness and tranquility the same as ever. The other day I paid my income tax and had a $30 deficit in the bank! So you see, I'm not rich at all and I'm not lying to you. But I got a check today that enables me to get that typewriter for The Preacher, as I call Neal now.... I think that latter part of your lives will be prophetically blissful, so dont despair now. My mother is anxious to get out of hysterical New York but otherwise well. Give my love to Jamie, Cathy and Johnny.[12] Tell them I still have their poems and am going to have them published next year, along with poems of other little children. Well actually I'll put them in the very first issue of the anthology KIDDIE POPS, Poems recited to me by little children ... I've started painting with oils but I'm bored sort of, now, by painting, but I'm good.

Jack

Kerouac wrote a series of letters to Allen Ginsberg and Philip Whalen in the spring of 1959, after learning that Allen planned a trip to San Francisco to see Ferlinghetti at City Lights. Kerouac was working with Ginsberg on a Beat Generation anthology for Avon Books, as well as continuing to collaborate with Ginsberg, Orlovsky, and Corso on an article on "Beatnik" nightlife in Manhattan. It was published as "The Roaming Beatniks" in Holiday *(October 1959) and reprinted as "New York Scenes" in* Lonesome Traveler *(1960). Kerouac was also writing an article on hoboes with Corso, published as "The Vanishing American Hobo" in* Holiday *(March 1960).*

11. Milarepa (1038–1122) was a Tibetan yogi. See Kerouac's letter to Ginsberg, April 18, 1959.
12. Carolyn and Neal's three children. Their poems are included in Kerouac's *Some of the Dharma* under the heading "Kiddy Pops" (pp. 347–358).

[April 18, 1959
Northport, New York]

Friday
Dear Allen . . .

Here's check for $15 you loaned me. Will you please reciprocate by mailing me the anthology material I'd given Don Allen, including Neal, Huncke, Garver, my Sea-Storm-Tangier piece and whatever else there was.

Also, does Gregory want me to publish his long letter as "by Gregory Corso," I mean will he be embarrassed by private revelations with own name or what? Also, I'm getting through with Beatnik nightlife, they've accepted it, the "changes" they wanted were actually additions, to mention the Greek Bellydancer place and the Half Note, that's all, no changes, so they're actually quite hip at Holiday considering. So tell Gregory HOBOS comes next and I wish he would wait for his money from that source, I aint no goddam millionaire, my tax I paid the other day left me $30 short in the bank! and that aint being rich. I'm getting scared of all this demand from me . . . and hints. Like, I'm sending Neal's typewriter money this week. I wish I was poor again, and could remain in contented solitude. The other night I was about to write, bang, a girl in the door, stayed till dawn.

The Chinese scholar from Staten Island sent me translated (never before translated) excerpts from THE 100,000 SONGS OF MILAREPA (the Tibetan Tantric Buddhist), very very great. It's all about Milarepa dispelling hallucinations of demons and coming down from Lashi Snow Mountain to explain it to people! I dont understand it yet. The scholar says only 1/10th of Buddha writings yet translated. Lafcadio came the other night asking for his painting which he said "he gave me," forgetting I bought it, I gave it to him, he stood in starry yard pointing at sky, "See the flying saucers?" I looked up and saw a Cross of Light in the sky, I felt really strange. Then I said "Nothing is happening, nothing ever happened." He said "It's very quiet." Then he said "Do you know Allen Ginsberg wrote a poem called Howl!" He seems to be forgetting everything. I think he also asked me if I knew Peter his brother, etc. He said he contacts the saucers and they wiggle back, he run thru the woods waving his arms. He not paint at all, he says. He hinted strange things have been happening to him.

Dont forget my pipe at Norman Mailer's. (I like its lightness and cost 3 bucks.) I'm sad as hell . . . tired of life & love.

Jack

[Alan] Ansen wrote from Tangier, heat, they're fleeing to Paris . . . tell him I won't be there, their address is Paris Am.Exp. (Ansen and Bill [Burroughs], that is.)

[April 19, 1959
34 Gilbert Street
Northport, New York]

Dear Phil—I been made editor of a new anthology to be put out about 3 times a year by Avon books for 25¢ on newsstand called Beat.Gen.Anthology probably, I am final decider of all mss. —I want, I'll make it wild, of course—So send something and tell McClure, Loewinsohn, etc., anybody you like I'll really rely on your taste and tell MacClaine too (Chris)[13] but I'm not really interested because have own work to do but will get some good stuff broadcast awhile. Gary wrote from Japan that it's a good thing I'm not in a certain hell where "writers have their tongues pulled out" so I guess he won't send anything. Tell Persky send stuff too, I lost his Treasure Island address, he's good poet. I will publish esoteric things like Neal, etc. 18-year-old girl poets etc. Children's poems even, by children. Great opportunity for all poets. Prose too. Big Table Mag. is deteriorating after first great issue, as you'll see, and Evergreen Review is full of friends of publishers—my anthology will be great like Yugen.[14] Okay. My cat at his saucer—/ spring moon.

Jack

[P.S.]You gets paid, too. It'll be mass-distributed.

Apr 23 59
34 Gilbert St.
[Northport, New York]

Dear Allen,

Well your Jet [to San Francisco] didnt crash, I heard it reported over the radio, "Allen Ginsberg's Jet didnt crash."

Re Lafcadio: when he told me to look up and see the flying saucers, I had been looking at the house across the street which had a bright window with a cross effect in it from crossbeams etc. so when I looked up I saw the same cross effect but it felt eerie coming at just that moment and also I felt eerie feeling I could also see ephemera-saucers of some floating misty or bright-nightgown diaphanous kind. But Laff, for instance, thinks that blinking red tail wing lights of airplanes are saucers blinking at him etc. and I

13. Chris MacClaine was a San Francisco poet.
14. In 1959 and 1960, *Yugen* magazine, published by LeRoi and Hettie Jones in Greenwich Village, included Kerouac's poems "Two Blues and Four Haiku" (*Yugen*, No. 4), "Sitting Under Tree Number Two" (*Yugen*, No. 5), and "Rimbaud" (*Yugen*, No. 6).

had to explain that to him. But like Abraham he has complete faith in his own hallucinations and cannot be shaken and Kierkegaard says faith is faith, so all Laff needs is a message from his faith to go forth and do something beautiful which he will, if hospitals dont catch him for their own beauty-store ...

Tell Ferlinghetti I took his advice and during full moon nights have knocked off 3000 new words of Old Angel for him and will keep working (tho secretly) until I have another volume for him next year, but that the present new 3 or 4 thousand words oughta go just well with his City Lights OLD ANGEL MIDNIGHT Part I ... (he's going to do part II, III etc.) I feel silly writing Old Angel tho because it is an awful raving madness, could make me go mad, I'm ashamed of it, but must admit it reads great, I wish other writers wd join me I feel lonely in my silliness writing like this is space prose for the future and people of the present will only laugh at me, o well let em laugh. Like last night wrote: "Got shot charge Rebel joyous Georgian by witchcraft. Ah, & what lunchcart? The one with 69 year old daughters & 690 pound brothers & all the stars of Alex Manhole clar to Rubber O North Carolina Oklahoma Indian pips ..." See? SPACE PROSE. Only blue-eyed newphew spacement of the future will ever love my writing now.

Re Chicago: I was griping about you omitted me at the last minute apparently from IGNU, I am no longer in Ignu, I am no longer an IGNU,? I heard about the rest, yes, thanks.

My anthology is going to be fantastically great ... tell McClure, MacClaine, Persky, Whalen, Loewinsohn, everybody in Frisco send poems to me 34 Gilbert St. neatly typed, EVERYBODY GETS PAID, too. By Avon big rich types.[15] Dont have creeps send poems, tho. Prose too. My love to you, Phil, Pete.

Jack

And tell Ferlinghetti I am painting oil painting for him to photo for cover. P.S. Make sure about typewriter for Neal, by checking if Carolyn intends my soon check for house money or really means to deliver him machine.

---

15. The "big rich types" at Avon Books commissioned Henry Miller to write a preface for the thirty-five-cent mass-market paperback edition of *The Subterraneans* in 1959. Miller concluded with strong words of praise about Kerouac as "a passionate lover of language" in the era of the Cold War:

> This is the age of miracles. ... Day of wonders, when our men of science, aided and abetted by the high priests of the Pentagon, give free instruction in the technique of mutual, but total, destruction. Progress, what! Make it into a readable novel, if you can. But don't beef about life-and-letters if you're a death-eater. Don't tell us about good "clean"—no fallouts!—literature. Let the poets speak. They may be "beat," but they're not riding the atom-powered Juggernaut. Believe me, there's nothing clean, nothing healthy, nothing promising about this age of wonders—except the telling. And the Kerouacs will probably have the last word.

TO PHILIP WHALEN

[Enclosed with letter to Ginsberg
dated April 23, 1959]

[April 23, 1959
Northport, New York]

Dear Phil
            Blackbird—no!
                        bluebird!—peach
            Branch still jumping
OOOG!
ROOORGH!
BROOOOO!
Jean-Louis

A week after the publication of Doctor Sax, *Kerouac tried to explain to his pub-*
lisher Barney Rosset, who had also accepted Mexico City Blues *for Grove Press,*
why he never made it to the office for his book party.

TO BARNEY ROSSET

May 8 [19]59
34 Gilbert St.
Northport NY

Dear Barney
    On the day of publication of SAX I started out to visit Grove Press of-
fice but ran into a colored girl and got drunk with her. In fact, several times
I've tried to get there. I certainly don't want you or the staff to think I'm
upppiittitiitty or anything but my life is so complicated I'll have to leave
N.Y. soon to ever do any peaceful thinking and writing again. I guess there
must be at least one thousand people who want to get drunk with me the
moment they see me. My old wild enthusiasms are all bouncing back on
me now I'm growing old and can't keep up with em. Without the long
sleeps in my mother's house when I heal from binges, I'd be dead now, I
think.
    Got a card from Don Allen in L.A.
    I hope you have some reviews of SAX to send me, I haven't seen any
but the Sunday Times. How come a "major" writer who has been on the
"bestseller" list and who gets so much publicity free on TV and everywhere, is reviewed at the bottom of page 100 in one of those reviews where
the reviewer only signs his name at the end? Sterling and I were wondering about it. Also, we recalled that SUBTERRANEANS also was put down,
not reviewed in daily Times or anywhere, and only briefly in Time Mag.

But SAX I've seen nowhere. It seems to me the critics don't know what to say about SAX. Maybe they're waiting to hear what others say. In a year from now they will be talking about it more than now, watch. It is "rumbling underground" and will continue to do so for 100 years.

When do I get the galleys of Mexico City Blues? I'd like to check them, when time comes, very difficult for printer. —Are you going to premiere of our movie[16] (with Robt. Frank) at Museum Modern Art 11:30 Tuesday morning (May 12). —Found a typo in SAX, page 211, line 21, says "well night" for "well nigh" —Sent a long piece (Final Railroad Earth) to Evergreen Review. Well, be seein ya, and thank you for publishing SAX and taking the chance of being ignored, the ignoration won't last more than a few months ... I mean it's not of immediate but of eventual publishing fame.[17]

Jack

Regards to Jeanne Unger.

On May 19, 1959, Kerouac sent a letter to Ginsberg after Time *gave a favorable review to* Doctor Sax. *The magazine had panned Kerouac's previous books, hating his "ambisextrous and hipsterical" characters because they used drugs, but the anonymous* Time *reviewer praised* Doctor Sax *(which Kerouac wrote in 1952 while living in Burroughs's Mexico City apartment, as he later described it, with "millions of junkies coming in").* Time *regarded* Doctor Sax *as "an elegy to the warm, safe smells of a tenement kitchen and the dark mysteries of a city neighborhood" and concluded that it was "Kerouac's best book," possibly because it avoided "such adult concerns as marijuana, Zen Buddhism, or women." Earlier* The New York Times *had dismissed* Doctor Sax *as a "largely psychopathic ... pretentious and unreadable farrago of childhood fantasy-play."*

TO ALLEN GINSBERG

May 19 '59
[Northport, New York]

Dear Allen—

Please forward this to Neal, I dont know his "number" and also, when answering me, please, send me Neal's entire address. Read letter then seal. It's just a little note.—So much mail in my room I cant sit. Will you ask Fer-

---

16. *Pull My Daisy.*
17. In May 1959 Grove achieved "immediate ... publishing fame" by issuing the first unexpurgated edition of D. H. Lawrence's novel *Lady Chatterley's Lover* in the United States. Barney Rosset continued to challenge the country's obscenity laws by publishing Henry Miller's *Tropic of Cancer* (Paris: Obelisk Press, 1934; New York: Grove Press, 1961) and William Burroughs's *Naked Lunch* (Paris: Olympia Press, 1959; New York: Grove Press, 1962).

linghetti if 5,000 additional words of Old Angel enough? They are written and ready to mail, also the cover (ink and pastel, weird). But that goddam [Irving] Rosenthal has not gotten our release for Old Angel yet! And never paid me $50 token as promised! What IS Irving's ax address?—

Glad about typewriter.[18] Now Neal can work. And he will. I never saw NY Post review of SAX, musta been awful, but Time waxed good.[19] Time likes to be put down, Dennis Murphy threw them off porch and they gave him swell review. Had we ever mailed that mad letter to Lipscombe?

Didnt see Diana's Trillings,[20] heard much ick reaction everywhere even Wesleyan college where on whim went to accompany Gregory and had big fantastic time almost endless to describe. I danced with teenage girls in shorts, like a kid I was (they had shorts) ... [....] I was a bit silly. Mason H. drove us back in hotrod to Persia New Haven. I autographed 20 Saxes and Roads and Subs etc. with all weird poems in them and drawings by Gregory. I banged piano. I wrestled wrestlers in the grass. Gregory went to a picnic with 300 girls while I slept. We had to flee. The reading: G's "Bomb" reading made me weep (quietly), I read Doc Benway to roars of laughter, read just like Bill does. Also read last 2 pages of Bums. Got nice letter from Gary Snyderee. All's well. I leave for Fla. I don't know, 6 weeks or so, I guess, will see Bill in NY I guess. With Whalen also in town we better cool it, Gregory almost started race riot in 7 Arts when Negro slapped him, mad Italian rage, Lucien and Cessa were there. Our Movie (Frank) is

18. On May 7, 1959, Kerouac sent Ginsberg a fifty-dollar check to help pay for Cassady's typewriter.

19. Don Allen wrote to Kerouac on June 21, 1959, that 20,000 copies of *Doctor Sax* were in print. The novel, was "sailing along," according to the editor, helped by the good review in *Time.*

20. Diana Trilling, wife of Columbia University professor Lionel Trilling (who knew Ginsberg as a student), published an article in the spring 1959 issue of *Partisan Review* titled "The Other Night at Columbia," describing a poetry reading at the university given by Ginsberg, Corso, and Orlovsky on February 5, 1959. Diana Trilling was moved by Ginsberg's reading of "Kaddish," but she wrote that she wished that he had been born into the previous generation of political radicals who came of age in the 1930s: "it was surely a time of quicker, truer feeling than is now conjured up with marijuana or the infantile cameraderie of *On the Road.*" She asked, was it "any wonder, then, that *Time* and *Life* write as they do about the 'beats'—with such a conspicuous show of superiority, and no hint of fear? These periodicals know what genuine, dangerous protest looks like, and it doesn't look like Ginsberg or Kerouac. Clearly, there is no more menace in *Howl* or *On the Road* than there is in the Scarsdale PTA."

For *The Fifties,* Third Issue (1959), Robert Bly wrote a parody of Diana Trilling's essay titled "The Other Night in Heaven." Bly began, "My name is Diana Trilling, and I am very important.... How different it might have been for Ginsberg and his friends if they had been born ten or fifteen years sooner!... If they had, they could have sung union songs, played Mah Jongg, and been great rebels like us!"

The summer 1959 issue of *Partisan Review* printed Ginsberg's short, typically generous reply to Mrs. Trilling on the correspondence page: "The universe is a new flower."

best movie I seen.[21] Germans buying it. Also TransLux chain I guess. But it's all too much and I'm afraid now, we gotta get out of NY. Arch Wash Square on Sundays crowded with thousands of beatniks. Thru which Gregory and I and Persian and Stanley Gould walk highdown billkick. Why dont you write a new poem about Jet plane adventure for Avon anthology? Please tell McClure and MacLaine that I rec'd manuscripts and that anthology people at Avon are slow. Write new poem for me, or anything you want. Antoninus sounds great.[22] Reading at S[an] Q[uentin] a triumph of your prophetic soul, boy. You were prophetic right about SAX too, Sax instead of Mad Avenue Winking Wiking Pwess. Caw Caw. You're the hippest kid. If Irving Layton or whatever his name is, I mean Lawrence Lipton knew how hip it is to be hip like you . . .[23] ah shit, that book is awful, all about his own barefooted bearded non-working art friends who dont write but just talk and show off and the things about us who started it all are pejorative. *Holy Barbarians* is the first fullscale attempt by the Communist Party to infiltrate the beat generation, and please tell everybody I said so, if you want. I dont want to have anything to do with no Communists: tell them to leave my name out of it. And they even can get poor innocent pure jazz musicians in hot water: their awful hot water of hatred. You and I and Burroughs and Gregory and Peter believe in God and TELL THEM THAT, YELL IT! (Burroughs said so in Word.) (But why was it deleted from original ms. of Word, which I have here?)—God is what everything is. Everything is a vision in God's mind which is No-Mind. When people are shitty it's because they dont know. Dont know this. And God in his mercy gave me alcoholism instead of leprosy. Got big mad letter from Lamantia in Mehico. Also an enormous huge spread in Copenhagen Denmark paper with big pictures of me and Dean and Mailer (James Dean) and all about you inside and all in Danish. Saw John Holmes, okay, went to opening of awful "Nervous Set" musical by Jay Landesman,[24] music was good, story it-

21. *Pull My Daisy* was well received in New York. Jonas Mekas wrote in *The Village Voice* that it was "a signpost of purity, innocence, humor, truth and simplicity." *Esquire* critic Dwight MacDonald wrote that Kerouac's narration "kept things rolling along on a tide of laughter and poetry ... Kerouac shows an unexpected virtuosity at the American art of kidding."
22. The California poet William Everson (1912–1994), a.k.a. Brother Antoninus after he joined the Dominican order. In 1959 he published the essay "Dionysus and the Beat Generation: The Reemergence of the Dionysian Spirit in Contemporary Life."
23. Lawrence Lipton, author of *The Holy Barbarians* (1959), a best-selling account of the Beat lifestyle in Southern California. The book was advertised as "the complete story of the 'Beats'—that hip, cool, frantic generation of new Bohemians who are turning the American scale of values inside out." The popularity of *The Holy Barbarians* prompted a hostile article on the Beats by Paul O'Neil in *Life* magazine on November 30, 1959.
24. Jay Landesman had edited *Neurotica* magazine, a counterculture magazine that published writing by Ginsberg, Holmes, and Kerouac in the early 1950s. Jay and his wife, Fran Landesman, co-authored *The Nervous Set*.

self is middleclass play about lumpenproletariat beatniks. Condescension dripping from stage. The beatnik himself a silly fool. Jay was sad. But he will get his money back anyway, it'll run about 6 weeks. Why dont somebody produce my angelic play I wrote? Why dont Hollywood buy my angelic ROAD if they want beat movies? What's going on, Allen? It's not money I'm worried about any more, but the perversion of our teaching which began under the Bkyn Bridge long ago? Gregory and I also crashed in on Jay Laughlin, and on Richard Wilbur, and I got Samuel Greenberg pomes for anthology (from Mr Laughlin) ... I haven't even had time to write my new column.[25] I'm not going into NY anymore, except when Bill gets here. I have a broken leg. All day yesterday I was wearing a hat that wasn't on my head (tell that to Creeley).

Coombye. Don't steal that hat. I want it. Grook. Yak. Kitchen yakkings. Not important. Come on. Besides soon we'll part, later grow old, die, you won't even be at my funeral.... we'll remember with tears. I'm sorry I hurt you. Our lives are no longer ours. So we'll go home. Far away. Gold clime. Don't waste your energy on the frenzies of mediocrities. Genius is Calm. Whalen is a Genius. Caterpillar genius. Peter is a Saint. So sleep. Write hymn for me.

Jack

On May 23, 1959, Kerouac asked Stella Sampas to send him reviews of Doctor Sax *in local papers such as* The Lowell Sun.

TO STELLA SAMPAS

[Postmarked May 23, 1959
Northport, New York]

Dear Stella

Thanx for yr sweet notes. Can you send me reviews from SUN or anyplace, I'm really curious what Lowellians think of Sax/ Time magazine said it was like Tom Sawyer. I see no evil in it. Also see no references to Lowell as anything but my sweet hometown. Some reflections here and there reflect my old man's onetime bitterness. Remember, he used to run the Spotlite newspaper, Billerica News etc. and lost them and got sore and ended his life poor, like I will. But what does Charley think? By the way, I have old poems of Sammy's here and am going to publish them in an anthology and have the check made out to you. Just to resurrect a saint. Like Joyce Kilmer was resurrected. Unless you mind. Above address my home.

---

25. Kerouac had agreed to write a bimonthly column for *Escapade*. His first article in the magazine, "The Beginning of Bop," had appeared in the April 1959 issue.

Am leaving here in 6 weeks, to go live in Florida ... Then a freighter to somewhere.

Jack

In late May 1959, Kerouac wrote his sister, Caroline, and her husband, Paul, that he and Mémère had put up their house at 34 Gilbert Street for sale, explaining why they were so eager to leave Northport.

TO CAROLINE KEROUAC BLAKE

[Late May 1959
Northport, New York]

Dear Nin and Paul,

As soon as this house is sold I'll have $14,000 to divide equally among us to start building the two houses. Meanwhile we'll live in a rented house [in Florida]. Nin, if you find the house be sure to get one where the cat will be safe, not on a busy highway or street. Dont be afraid of paying $100 a month rent because we're splitting it. For the rental house dont worry about a room for me, for instance, because I'm going to Mexico anyway as soon as we move from here. I'll only join you in Fla. for a few days or a week. I have a 3000 dollar assignment to write about Mexico for Holiday Magazine which aint hay, and worth the trip. When I come back from Mexico in the Fall I hope to find the houses built or at least underway. I'll write out my personal plans for my own house (a concrete wall all around it, a private door to my bedroom, etc., a new basketball pole & basket etc.) and the rest is Mémère's choice. If I can buy another lot I will, there's no harm in sinking cash in land and it will make our homes private. The experience with the next door neighbor here, who threw a rock and hit Tyke on the leg and he was limping for 3 days, serves to convince me I'm through with neighbors. When I write in my yard in Fla. I want no one, no EYES to be staring at me all the time, like here [....] The reason I want to leave NY is because I cant write here because of constant insistent demands on my time by all kinds of people (big emergency telegrams almost every day). People know I'm only 40 miles from NY and keep bothering me; instead of assuming that I'm home writing, they insist I come into NY for this and that, publicity, etc. openings, etc. It's silly and hysterical. So remember when we get to Fla. dont tell anybody I'm "Jack Kerouac," the same thing can start there. Dont say anything. Almost sold a book to movies last week—if this happens we can go ahead even before I sell this house. If MGM takes up the option on *Subterraneans* next month June we can go ahead anyway, house sale or no house sale. So dont worry. If not, and no house sale, we can wait in the rental house awhile ... I'll have the loot by October for sure (from royalties and new books). Get those deeds straightened out and by the way ask them if there are any adjoining lots for sale, for me, Okay? See you soon. Love

Jack

During the early summer of 1959, while Kerouac helped his mother get ready to move out of their house in Northport, he continued to work on the anthology of Beat writing he was compiling for Avon Books. He wrote to Lawrence Ferlinghetti about the project.

TO LAWRENCE FERLINGHETTI

June 4 '59
[Northport, New York]

Dear Larry,

I have the whole additional 5000 words typed [of *Old Angel Midnight*], the cover ready, will pack it all neatly in big envelope with hardboard protection and leave at my agent's office till you send for them (I'm taking off in a month).

Meanwhile, could you send me pronto some wild poems of yours, new ones, or far-out ones you were afraid to publish, for my Avon anthology which will come out in October? The printer is ready to start the galleys in a few weeks. I contribute only a running commentary on the works and the workers. It will contain many interesting documents that I've collected over the years from thieves, poets, girls, hipsters of all kinds. Send me something you feel cant be published anywhere else. It will be a far-out anthology and I want it to be the best in the world: le meilleur de la plume, mon vieux, or something. It may please you to know that yr name is in new chpts. of "Old Angel" but not for anything but textual kicks— ". . . I will not rest no won't rest till Ferlinghetti's dog his day had . . ."[26]

Jack

In July 1959, when Avon Books published Maggie Cassidy *as a fifty-cent mass-market paperback, the fact that it was the sequel to* Doctor Sax *in Kerouac's Duluoz chronology was never mentioned. Instead the cover blurb announced that in* Maggie Cassidy, *"The Bard of the Beat Generation reveals a startling new dimension to his personality in this brilliant and profoundly moving novel of adolescence and first love." The ad copy continued on the first page of the book: "Maggie Cassidy was no longer a girl. The vibrant, demanding, thrilling, woman body of her splashed over Jack's life like soft spring rain, warming him, coaxing him, pushing him into life. . . ."*

---

26. Perhaps a reference to Ferlinghetti's dog Homer, the subject of his poem "Dog."

Kerouac lost the battle with his editor at Avon, Tom Payne, over the deletion of the word "fuck," which had occurred five times at the end of Chapter 38, but he was even more unhappy when reviewers like David Dempsey in The New York Times *found the novel "patchy and half-hearted." In the* Saturday Review, *John Ciardi dismissed it as "one of our boy's earliest scrolls." On June 10, 1959, when Kerouac wrote to Philip Whalen mentioning the publication of* Maggie Cassidy, *he also worried that the sale of Avon Books might jeopardize his Beat anthology.*

TO PHILIP WHALEN

June 10, 1959
34 Gilbert St
[Northport, New York]

Dear Philliboo

No room in the anthology left for anything as long as this prose of Stine's, tho it seems to me pretty terrific and he shd really submit it to publishers and get it printed. I dont see where Dennis Murphy has anything on him when it comes to sergeants.

The anthology will be wild. Yr. new stuff dazzles me out of my mind. I know at first reading I'll have to read it all over again several times and let it sink in. It is like Gary said, poetry like the horns on a hare. I'll have the lot printed in the anthology, together with an excerpt or two from yr old letters (one a particularly brilliant letter you wrote to Allen in 1956, no 1957, Feb.). A lot of the anthology is from letters, Neal's great letters, Gregory's one vast life-confession letter, etc., Allen's old letters, Holmes, etc. THE ONLY THING I'M WORRIED ABOUT IS AVON MIGHT CRAP OUT ON THIS DEAL BECAUSE WILLIAM R. HEARST JUST BOUGHT THE GODDAM COMPANY AND MAY NOT LIKE BEAT WRITING ETC. But we'll see. If so, they crap out, I can picture myself getting stoned by MacClaine, McClure, etc., but actually what I'd do in such a case is get it published by Grove or New D[irections].

You sound rather lonely. Didnt you get along with Allen and Pete? [....]

[Gary Snyder] sez he'll be in Kyoto at least 2 years, s'got a koan to work on from Oda Roshi. Sez "amazing process, dumb as a newborn baby."

Myself, the dharma is slipping away from my consciousness and I cant think of anything to say about it any more. I still read the Diamond Sutra, but as in a dream now. Dont know what to do. Cant see the purpose of human or terrestrial or any kinda life without heaven to reward the poor suffering fucks. The Buddhist notion that Ignorance caused the world leaves me cold now, because I feel the presence of angels. Maybe rebirth is simply HAVING KIDS. Am typing up my 250 page BOOK OF SKETCHES, sketches I wrote for years, took me all this time to catch up to my pencil,

Truman Capote notwithstanding (who said I was not a writer but a type-writer, the little faggot).[27]

Am getting wild outcries from Lamantia in Mexico who screams "Ver-rrra Crrruuu, man." Did you read SAX? MAGGIE CASSIDY next novel, July, Avon, is just as good almost, the sequel, sex etc. Poem in itself too. — Am reading Casanova's memoirs and wish I cd see the original "porno-graphic" entirety of that great classic. I guess Olympia Press will do it. This summer in Mexico (alone no contacts) think I'll write next novel BEAT TRAVELER about what it was like to be a bum in the desert in October 1956 and suddenly a bigshot a year later and the funny days of being best-seller author etc. Straight continuation of "Duluoz Legend" like Proust, Balzac, what else?

Or I wont write anything at all.

Here is sample page of my BOOK OF SKETCHES.

N.Y. State

Crows are insane in
the mist—America
 is thrilling on a gray
 day, Quebec non—
America has histories
 of wood & Robert
 Frost fences—
McGillicuddy'll
 make his comeback—
The Canucks are ignorant,
 vulgar, cold hearted—
I dont like them—
No one else does—

Straight from the little breastpocket notebooks, as writ, typed neatly in nice binder and for my own shelf & kicks. Latter was written on bus re-turning from Montreal to New York State in 1953.

O well, why not?

> After the shower,
> Among the drenched roses,
> Bird thrashing in the bath

---

27. Appearing as a guest on David Susskind's television show, Capote quipped that what Kerouac did wasn't writing; it was typewriting.

I applaud
the American Flag
And it bows
OK so long
Jack X

I like yr poem about Hui Neng letting the guy try to pick up the robe of
the dharma—I like it all and am mystified by such brilliance & PUNK

TO ALLEN GINSBERG

June 18, 1959
[Northport, New York]

Dear Allen,

Received all yr poems and everybody's poems Whalen's etc. (including
yr recent batch with Burroughs' letter enclosed) so all is set except the kind
of mad man who is the editor at Avon who keeps taking me out on binges
that always end the same way ... I keep getting the feeling the anthology
will never out, he'll kill himself or something [....] I told him and told him
to rush on this job because I'm leaving but he does nothing, so it looks like
I'll have to write my running commentary on the (now) 2 anthologies (have
that much material!) in Florida or even Mexico since I'm leaving Northport
here within a month ... actually might get it all done at last minute. Will
leave present pile at Sterling's. If this guy flips (and W R Hearst just bought
Avon Books!) & everything falls thru I will be accused by all the poets of
stealing their manuscripts! But I'll have to mail them all back at my own
expense. The trouble with these (like you sod) (said) guys in "business"
(P. is the guy who wrote that letter about the disastrousness of publishing
SAX at this time) is that they dont have the quiet serene sense of work-
accomplished that we "beatnik" poets have, they flip & let everything go to
pot!! I could have all this anthology, both of em, ready in 2 days if he'd simply send me his batch, which I would collate with my new batches, tack on
commentaries, and send to printer!—Anyway, we'll see—

Allen, Hanover records who made my Steve Allen record now want to
advance you $500 to make an album with them, in NY here, also they want
Gregory. So here's yr money you need! THAT could be yr last reading. The
address is Bob Thiele Hanover Records

O shit, I dont have address, any wait a minute,

Sterling is going to be yr agent in this deal anyway so write to Sterling
and get all the details. He SHOULD be yr agent or you'll get screwed on
subsidiary rights later on, so stick to him, he's been fiar fair and honest
with me, and he is willing to arrange for Gregory too. The guy looking for
you is Bob Thiele.

Everything is too much, I'm trying to run away back to my quiet soul now but so many things hanging, so I turned down another album offer (was to cut it tomorrow) and turned down even articles with Playboy etc., I am mentally exhausted and spiritually discouraged by this shit of being of having to do what everybody wants me to do instead of just my old private life of poesies & novelies as of yore.

I met Eugene yr brother on the train and said I wd like him to be my attorney in the closing sale of house but when I got back to N'Port it turned out the broker had arranged for local lawyer and I want to tell Eugene but lost his card and dont have his address or anything, so tell him? He did send me a penny postcard with a completely illegible return address.

Even Lucien came to get me last night for wild weekend in woods, cant do it, have to concentrate on packing and escaping all this. Lucien said I had become strangely philosophical. I saw a snapshot of myself taken recently in which I could see with my own eyes what all this lionized manure has done to me; it's killing me rapidly. I have to escape or die, dont you see. I cant get all hungup at this time on anything ANYTHING. So what I can do, as last thing, is ask Laughlin to write to Neal and offer him a job, okay. I haven't even got the spiritual energy to write a preface to VISIONS OF CODY like Laughlin wants.[28]

---

28. Kerouac wrote his preface before *Visions of Cody* went to press, and it became his earliest published statement describing the scope of his work in the Duluoz Legend:

VISIONS OF CODY *is a 600-page character study of the hero of* On the Road, *"Dean Moriarty," whose name now is "Cody Pomeray." I wanted to put my hand to an enormous paean which would unite my vision of America with words spilled out in the modern spontaneous method. Instead of just a horizontal account of travels on the road, I wanted a vertical, metaphysical study of Cody's character and its relationship to the general "America." This feeling may soon be obsolete as America enters its High Civilization period and no one will get sentimental or poetic any more about trains and dew on fences at dawn in Missouri. This is a youthful book (1951) and it was based on my belief in the goodness of the hero and his position as an archetypical American Man. The tape recordings in here are actual transcriptions I made of conversations with Cody who was so high he forgot the machine was turning. Dean Moriarty becomes Cody Pomeray, Sal Paradise becomes Jack Duluoz, Carlo Marx becomes Irwin Garden and so on in all of my work from now on, published and unpublished, (with the exception of the 1950 fictional novel* The Town and the City). *My work comprises one vast book like Proust's* Remembrance of Things Past *except that my remembrances are written on the run instead of afterwards in a sick bed. Because of the objections of my early publishers I was not allowed to use the same personae names in each work.* On the Road, The Subterraneans, The Dharma Bums, Doctor Sax, Maggie Cassidy, Tristessa, Desolation Angels *and the others are just chapters in the whole work which I call* The Duluoz Legend. *In my old age I intend to collect all my work and re-insert my pantheon of uniform names, leave the long shelf full of books there, and die happy. The whole thing forms one enormous comedy, seen through the eyes of poor Ti Jean (me), otherwise known as Jack Duluoz, the world of raging action and folly and also of gentle sweetness seen through the keyhole of his eye. Thanks to J. Laughlin for helping make this selection of 120 pages.*

Jack Kerouac

As for J.S., if he can write prose like subterraneans and has imagination to conceive a dr sax and the energy to write an on the road and the spiritual fervor to write a visions of gerard, I'll believe what Bill says about him. Sounds like he's hypnotized Bill, to me, what with all the drugs too. There will be a great writer who will rise above us but I'm sure he will be a young American kid in about 10 or 20 years, like after Melville and Whitman there came Twain. Dont be discouraged by talk like that from Bill, he sounds jealous now. I'm so sick of being insulted by every critic and everybody and now even by Bill whom I lauded so much and put over so well at Wesleyan! Fuck him. Besides no Stern Jackes can write a Bomb like Gregory, I can promise you that.—Have you seen Dr. W. C. Williams' weird statement about Peter Orlov?—that we have a lot to learn from Petey?—in that new magazine put out by Willard Maas' son? somebody stole my copy of it. Wagner College magazine.

Meanwhile, I hope I see you, when you get back just come with Peter to visit his mother and drop over, my mother wont mind and we'll say goodbye here. If you're too late, I'll see you in India or in Heaven ...

Hasn't it been awful? We were so swingy? And now young poets are sneering at us? And saying that we're merely mellow classics now? without even reading sax and Kaddish? In fact they're all screaming at the same time, how can they read?—Ho Ho!—I know what part of the blue sky I go to ... Ho Ho I'm happy

> I'm happy to be free
> again. . . . Ho Ho
> > fool him all
> Jean XXX

Cruseke.
Hello Mike! [McClure]

Packing up the house on Gilbert Street after it was sold in late June 1959, Kerouac wrote another letter to his sister urging her to help with the plan to build two houses on the family lots in Sanlando Springs. Since the new owner of the Gilbert Street house wouldn't take possession until August, Jack decided to camp out in its empty rooms through the rest of the summer after he arranged a ride to Florida for Mémêre so she could stay with Nin.

TO CAROLINE KEROUAC BLAKE

June 18, 1959
[34 Gilbert Street
Northport, New York]

Dear Nin,
The stage is all set. I'll transfer my money with me to Fla. and all we've

got to do is rent an unfurnished house. Since you'll be there first, just go to Mrs. O'Rourke or any other agents and get a house about the size of the one we had on Yates Avenue (I can sleep on the Florida porch, wont be there more'n a week anyway, and Paul will be gone too)—You and Mémère will have a car, the bank account, and can go ahead and build the houses to your specifications, at $7,000 apiece. The money will be in the form of a checking account, in my name and Mémère's name, everytime you need a check she'll write you one out and make a record.

When you and Big Paul and Little Paul get to Fla. take a motel room for a coupla nights or stay with friends, and go to Mrs. O'Rourke or anybody and rent that house. As soon as you've got it, wire me for the first month's rent. I'll send it. Move in.

Try to borrow a bed and some dishes from friends; camp in the house. Mémère and I will drive down with Tyke in Robert Frank's car and also bring a lot of dishes and blankets and camp in the house with you a week till the furniture comes. Then we're all set. Mémère and I cant leave here till the closing is done on the house [in Northport], and the movers have picked up all our stuff and taken off.

There's no reason for either one of us to go to Fla. ahead of the other. It's just a simple matter of finding the proper house and sending me a wire for the first month's rent.

Try to rent a house near or in Sanlando Springs so you'll be near the construction projects (and remember, a quiet place so the cat wont get run over).

I assume you'll be reading this letter when you hit Orlando. Well, just go out and find the house and send for the rent. Move in. Mémère and I still have to close on this house (it's now June 18th) by the time you get this we'll probably be set to leave, and go join you, and the furniture comes about a week after.

You have nothing to do all summer but overseer [sic] the building of the two houses with Ma. By October they ought to be finished. We'll move in. I'll be back from my writing-work in Mexico the first weeks of October. I have to work just as much as Paul but cant do it in our confused circumstances. I'm lending you the money to build your house without interest, all I ask of you is to rent that temporary household and we'll come (we have to have an address to give the movers). It's really simple. I dont know what good I would do there ahead of Mémère.... Rent any suitable house & send for the rent. And also, I have writing and publishing matters to conclude in these last few weeks here. You're the only one, Ti Nin, who's really free to do this, rent that house. Concentrate on just that, and the building of the houses. You and Mémère and Lil Paul will have a lot of fun this summer, I can see that. Okay. Mémère writes on the back of this page. Love to all

Jacky

[Mémère's note]

Things are popping around here. Jack took a lot of assignments and we are rushing to get everything straightened out real quick. The people who bought the house should have been here to close the deeds last week but Jack was in New York now we have to wait a bit. Jack done real well—and of course money is the thing to take care of first. But cheer up, sweet. I'm all packed up waiting for Mr. Roberts to close the deed—but Honey I need an address for my transfer of social security. They dont relay checks. We got to go and give them an address just for the records, I guess. Jack has an awful lot of work to take care of too but honest Honey, we will be there as quick as possible . . .

In the summer of 1959, living at 34 Gilbert Street after the movers had emptied the house of furniture, Kerouac sent off a flurry of notes and postcards to Donald Allen and the production editor at Grove Press, where Mexico City Blues *was in its final stages.*

TO DONALD ALLEN

June 30 '59
[34 Gilbert Street
Northport, New York]

Dear Don:—

This is the best I can do now, the movers are coming today for my typewriter—

Later

Jack

TO DONALD ALLEN

[Postmarked June 30, 1959
Northport, New York]

Dear Don—The "digest of Buddhist writings" I showed you would be much too long for LeRoi's purposes also it's old-fashioned Hin I mean Indian Buddhism in this Zen craze time what I suggest is LeRoi do "Scripture of the Golden Eternity" with wide margins and big line-spaces and big print, to make it truly a scripture format, anything else added to it would spoil it. And the "digest" is not of my own composition, just copies I had intended to roll in rucksack and take to riverbottom camp. (Under separate cover I am sending you my contributory poems to yr anthology, all that you asked for except 3 long ones, one of them already publisht in White Dove, movers

212

taking this machine away now no time to type anymore). My mother was very pleased with you and her invitation stands. We'll have permanent address October. Okay. I think the "Scripture" wd. make a weird thin volume and also it has enlightening properties proper to the turning of the sick wheel.[29] I say sick because look what Lucien just wrote—" Pessimistic old wartbrain wd rather a nibble at the meringue of here & now than all the eternities of

Etc.

Jack

Sent you about 8 poems, long and short

TO DICK [GROVE PRESS]

July 28 '59

[Northport, New York]

Dear Dick:

Wonderful galley. Give it to the printer please for these final minor points.

CHORUSES

99th Chorus	Misspelled my father's name with a "v"
138th Chorus	Insert "Culiacan" for "Culiao" because at the time I was afraid to mention "Culiacan" for fuzz reasons but now it's all under the bridge.
160th Chorus	Delete that capitalized line "LOOKS UPON THE BEAUTY OF THE SUN" ... It was the only afterthought in the whole spontaneous book and, as always, afterthought is an avid mistake. Please do that for sake of purity of whole book.
217th Chorus	A very important comma missing
225th Chorus	Delete apostrophe and insert comma, so that it reads

Mother of Buddhas,
Mother of milk

230th Chorus	Insert comma

Okay? I took so long to return this because my life is in a turmoil but I finally got a quiet moment this Sunday morning. Thanx again for fine job. Regards to Jeanne.

Yours,

Jack K.

---

29. Corinth Books in Greenwich Village published *The Scripture of the Golden Eternity* as a ninety-five-cent paperback in the spring of 1960.

Soon after writing to Ginsberg and Orlovsky on August 19, 1959, Kerouac learned that the family plans to build two houses in Florida had fallen through. Jack gave up his idea of a trip to Mexico City at the end of the summer and instead quickly found another house to buy in Northport at 49 Earl Avenue.

TO ALLEN GINSBERG & PETER ORLOVSKY

[August 19, 1959
Northport, New York]

Dear Allen and Peter—

Hope you can come out here this weekend, my last weekend here—The kid from Northport said you were waiting for me to "invite" you—Shucks, Paw—I miss you both—I'm itching to get down to quiet Mexico pad in mid-September and see if I can feel like writing big crazy sequel to Desolation Angels and return Thanksgiving—with big hardcover type novel for Viking, about time for that again now—O yes, Allen, please bring out that "Sound" article from Canada about me, or mail it right now[30]—Have new big philosophical synthesis, like, honest as Meister Eckhart—

And the quiet cat
  sitting by the post
Perceives the moon

ALLEN: "Watermelon." JACK: "Why?... Say wouldnt it be awful if students kept asking Zen masters why?" ALLEN: "Especially when the Zen Masters dont know why they said it."

Jack

TO LAWRENCE FERLINGHETTI

[September 22, 1959
Northport, New York]

Dear Larry,

Want to know what the progress is on publication of OLD ANGEL MIDNIGHT and would like to check on the final proofs since it is such a difficult text for the linotypist. And how does the cover look in black and white? And will you have just picture on front and title in back, or superimpositions? Let me hear. Sterling and I were wondering why we havent heard from you lately. Hope to see you soon. Send me order blank

---

30. Warren Tallman's article "Kerouac's Sound" was published in *Evergreen Review*, Vol. 4, No. 11. It had originally appeared in *The Tamarack Review* in the spring of 1959.

so I can order KADDISH, HOTEL WENTLEY and other new things of yours. Try to get a book out of Al Sublette sometime, he's good—I could also provide you with a book by Neal Cassady, from what I have here in huge old letters, all pure narrative confession of frantic Neal-type events in his own great style.

Jack

TO STELLA SAMPAS

[September 1959
Northport, New York]

Dear Stella: Poem?
    After the shower,
  Among the drenched roses,
   The bird thrashing in the bath

   After the shower,
    my cat meowing
On the porch

******

Please send me GJ's address,[31] which
you can probably find in the phone
book—If I do come to Lowell, GJ
is my first stop after you—
Thanx for the Sun clipping of the
beatniks in Moody St bistro, loved
it because it's like some old prophetic dream of mine, when Sam and
I used to visit Conny Murphy who
lived among the mills down there

Coming & going
   my door is open
Both ways
      —GARY SNYDER
        "Japhy Ryder"
       of Dharma Bums
. . . a poem he sent from Japan

Jack

31. GJ was George J. Apostolos, Kerouac's childhood friend still living in Lowell.

By October 1, 1959, Kerouac was settled at 49 Earl Avenue with his mother. He wrote Don Allen in response to a request for poems and a statement on poetics for Grove Press's The New American Poetry 1945–1960.

TO DONALD ALLEN

Oct. 1, 1959
49 Earl Ave.
Northport, NY

Dear Don

Keep above address a dead secret (only Allen [Ginsberg] and Sterling know it). Get too much screwy mail and screwy visits. My Ma prefers Northport after all. New little cottage. Florida was a flooded swamp all summer.

Somebody at Grove wrote me a note asking if I liked *MexCity Blues* appearance of edition,[32] and signed illegible name, so tell whoever it is that of course I love it. The name looks like Martha Schlier or Janet Skler. By the way (I'm out of touch here) let me know reactions to it, or whoever handles that, reviews, etc.

Dates:[33]

SAN FRANCISCO BLUES	1954
MEXICO CITY BLUES	1955
SAD TURTLE (MexCity Blues)	1955
MACDOUGAL ST BLUES	1955
TREE NUMBER TWO	1955
ORIZABA BLUES	1956
MY GANG (same)	
[ORLANDO BLUES	1957]
A TV POEM	1958
HEAVEN	1958

Sterling is going to let you have entire VISIONS OF CODY for next big Grove novel by me. Much better than just New Direction "Excerpts"— Plenty time.

I would like a new biography of me for this anthology. Here it is, followed by the poems I remember you also wanted.

---

32. Grove Press officially published *Mexico City Blues* on October 20, 1959.
33. Donald Allen had asked Kerouac to supply the dates for a list of his poems.

JACK KEROUAC BIOGRAPHY After my brother died, when I was four, they tell me I began to sit motionlessly in the parlor, pale and thin, and after a few months of sorrow began to play the old Victrola and act out movies to the music. Some of these movies developed into long serial sagas, "continued next week," leading sometimes to the point where I tied myself with rope in the grass and kids coming home from school thought I was crazy. My brother had taught me how to draw so at the age of 8 I began to produce comic strips of my own: "Kuku and Koko at the Earth's Core," (the first, rudely drawn) on to highly developed sagas like "The Eighth Sea." A sick little boy in Nashua N.H. heard of these and wanted to borrow them. I never saw them again. At the age of eleven I wrote whole little novels in nickel notebooks, also magazines (in imitation of Liberty Magazine) and kept extensive horse racing newspapers going. The first "serious" writing took place after I read about Jack London at the age of 17. Like Jack, I began to paste up "long words" on my bedroom wall in order to memorize them perfectly. At 18 I read Hemingway and Saroyan and began writing little terse short stories in that general style. Then I read Tom Wolfe and began writing in the rolling style. Then I read Joyce and wrote a whole juvenile novel like "Ulysses" called "Vanity of Duluoz." Then came Dostoevsky. Finally I entered a romantic phase with Rimbaud and Blake which I called my "self-ultimacy" period, burning what I wrote in order to be "Self-ultimate." At the age of 24 I was groomed for the Western idealistic concept of letters from reading Goethe's "Dichtung und Wahrheit." The discovery of a style of my own based on spontaneous get-with-it, came after reading the marvelous free narrative letters of Neal Cassady, a great writer who happens also to be the Dean Moriarty of "On the Road." I also learned a lot about unrepressed wordslinging from young Allen Ginsberg and William Seward Burroughs.

TO DONALD ALLEN

[Fall 1959
Northport, New York]

Don

My only possible statement on poetics and poetry is this:[34] Add alluvials to the end of your line when all is exhausted but something has to be said for some specified irrational reason, since reason can never win out, because poetry is NOT a science. The rhythm of how you decide to "rush" yr statement determines the rhythm of the poem, whether it is a poem in verse-separated lines, or an endless one-line poem called prose ... (with its paragraphs).

34. Kerouac's statement on poetics appeared on page 414 of *The New American Poetry 1945–1960*.

So let there be no equivocation about statement, and if you think this is not hard to do, try it. You'll find that your lies are heavier than your intentions. And your confessions lighter than Heaven.

Otherwise, who wants to read?

I myself have difficulty covering up my bullshit lies.

Jack

Shortly after moving into his new house in Northport, Kerouac agreed to travel to Los Angeles to appear on the Steve Allen television show to publicize his books and to earn the money to insulate his attic. In Kerouac's letter to Ginsberg on October 6, 1959, he described his pleasure at the prospect of visiting the West Coast again. He also tried to be funny about a vicious portrayal of him on television as "Jack Crackerjack" spouting a parody of "Howl."

TO ALLEN GINSBERG

[October 6, 1959
Northport, New York]

Allen—

Truman Capote notwithstanding, I'm still catching up with the stuff I wrote by hand, am only now (like you) typing up Orlanda Blues written in 57, also busy—Running the anthology isnt as hard as you think, I can answer Schleifer myself, in fact am doing so this minute, okay I can do whole thing by myself if you want—I thought you might need the money and ALSO have a better knack than me for picking up true gems and historical diamonds . . . more opportunity, that is, hanging around Village etc.—Let me know what you secretly really feel you want to do about working with me or not on Avon anthology—The second number is already well set with Ed Dorn's great new poems, his "Buck" story, with Donlin's great story, with Huncke's new gems you mentioned (Huncke, all he has to do is keep writing those gempy vignettes and then we'll have a whole BOOK and take it to Sterling)—(Peter too)—(you too)—Tell your story, you lazy bastards, people pay money for stories not just easy pomes rattled off couches—Yes we can have Avon send back what we dont want with big diplomatic notes by Preston or Payne, easy enuf—In fact, Schleifer already recovered his ms. and wants to bring it back again!—You dont have to visit Payne and bother him, do all by mail—As I say, I can do it alone—I am going to start writing longer smarter running commentaries for this material too—first time is short drunk notes—Time to get Tough, like Time Magazine—SO MAKE UP YOUR MIND ABOUT CO-EDITORSHIP.

What radio station will you be on with MEXCITY BLUES, when, date?— I am going to H'wood Nov. 12th in train for 2 G shot with Steve Allen, want to read railroad prose or something—or from visions of neal about west—

golden west—so won't leave NY till then, go to Mexico after—Got a note and a poem from Creeley, will ask him for stuff for second anthology—

The only way to detach yourself from all this frantic non-literary activity is go away, to Greece join Gregory write golden poems under fig trees of Crete—If you work like your father keeps yapping in Paterson you could fritter away in office desk—travel! That $100 you spent last week was half fare to Greece—When my on the road deal is set, if ever, I'll give or lend you the money for any trip you want ... We'll try to make a trip with Lucien to mtns. this October, okay?

Big Table sold 7000 copies of that mag., made enough money to pay me my measly $50 for "Old Angel," haven't done it, in fact have the nerve to write nasty notes to Sterling who's only doing his job, and then on top of all that hold back my Ferlinghetti deal,[35] just a bunch of greedy sneaky shits and you can shove them up your ass, and on top of that they use MY title ... Start a magazine of your own—why fiddle around with Paul Carroll—who is dying to put not only me down, but poor mc clure and whalen and lamantia, like a virago—who cares about him anyway? what has he done to command your attention?—and what's so great about the magazine? LeRoi [Jones] is starting KULCHUR and you have YUGEN and BEATITUDE, all those lil things will grow into big DIALS in time—

Okay for mescal,[36] be in soon, but waiting for you and Pete come out here like you said to pick up clothes and dig basement[37] ... altho, wait, then, I'll come out myself soon and bring the clothes a neat package ... Everything mixed up, in fact—movie men coming this afternoon, silly telegram just came, I cant even write letters, bulletins everywhere—

That's great about Gene's wife ... I didn't dream ... Virus gone now, except big cough like I had remember in January 1957 at the Helen's when we all had coughs from Mexico trip in car—Yes I remember spencer ... I dont have the dutchman's address—why dont I do that in yr kitchen, on white sheet ... That's nice the nice things you write about me ... In next anthology I will try to match that.

Just wrote the finger sutra, in my yard, t'other night, pod. Silly, I guess. Am kinda bored. Enclosed is a seminar where they lump beatniks with delinquents and drag what's left of the segment of America that's artistic into the criminal muck. Thought you might want to throw a bomb at them. This is the good work of Albert Zugsmith emerging, like last night a parody on me on TV "Jack Crackerjack" I leap up (hair pasted on brow) and start

---

35. The editors of *Big Table* had refused to give permission to Ferlinghetti to publish *Old Angel Midnight*, so City Lights never brought out the book. It was finally published in San Francisco by Grey Fox Press in 1993 with introductions by Ann Charters and Michael McClure.
36. See letter to Ginsberg, October 19, 1959.
37. The house at 49 Earl Avenue had a finished basement Kerouac used as a study before he insulated the attic.

screaming "I saw the best minds of my generation destroyed by naked hysteria ... kill for the sake of killing!" (Louis Nye the actor) ugh.

Jack

[On back of envelope] Finished typing entire BOOK OF SKETCHES, a mighty Pure Tome. Now typing up Tome: —TICS & DAYDREAMS. NEXT: "Various Poems."

While Mémère was in Florida, Kerouac had begun an affair with Lois Sorrells, a young woman from Northport who was working in Manhattan. After Kerouac experimented with mescaline in October 1959, he wrote up his experience as a 5,000-word "mescaline report" and told Ginsberg he could read it at Lois's apartment. A vision he'd had with the drug confirmed Kerouac's belief that he'd "been on the right track" with his method of writing spontaneous prose.

TO ALLEN GINSBERG

19 October [1959]
[Northport, New York]

Cher Alain—

Yes, but mescaline is not just "cute" because the very 2 hours when it really hits it's as strong as pure big fourbutton peote shot—if not more, because of compensatory chemical laboratory arrangements to cut out unnecessary puke nausea—altho there was much of that—Final strange vision, finally strange too that it came same time as Gregory's "final"—or Finale—I now no longer sad about sadness of birth-and-death scene because all that I had divined about the truth of Prajna Paramita Vajra Chedika (diamond-cutting splendor of wise ideal) was SEEN not just divined or known—I kept saying "Stop thinking, just look" and had my first fullscale samapatti transcendental visits and shows—O this world is One Flower a New Flower you're right indeed, but I knew it before but'd never seen it—What a waving ghost t'was—in fact I'm going to take a monthly mescaline and am rarin to try lysurgic next—I'll be in NY this Saturday Oct. 24th at Lois and Barbara (B. is hungup on Petey, by the way) and the phone is unavailable in my address book at moment—Anyway I'm going to spend 5 days at Lois' and Barbara's and among my projects is to go to yr. pad and write big letter to Neal whom I'm been afraid to write to before I learn'd of this parole good news—afraid to SIGNIFY—prison talk—big cheery or condescending or benevolent or malevolent letters all signify anyway—but now he's coining out of that mint it's okay and I ready to write him big letter and offer him big Avon job tho I know he'll go back on railroad—blesx hix hearx [sic]—And O boy that healthgiving mescal, if everybody in the world took mescaline but once there would be eternal peace—I trembled, I shuddered, I saw the earth opening up with light flashes and then I saw the assembled dancers in Heaven and you way up there one of the highest of saints ... whoever "You" is—and so ... I wrote a big 5000 word MESCALINE RE-PORT and will type it up and take it in for you to read Sat. or Sun. when-ever you come to Lois—Allen, please call up Tom Payne at Avon and ask him for Lois' number so you can call me and we can meet there or else-where to discuss my vision[38]—and for me to hand you the five thousand word report—Most miraculous of all was the sensational revelation that I've been on the right track with spontaneous never-touch-up poetry of imme-diate report, and Old Angel Midnight most especially, opening out a new world of connection in literature with the endless spaces of Shakti Maya Kali Illusion ...

High in the Sky
The Fathers Send Messages
From on High

I forget exactly how it went, the Blakean line, but I'll tell you.... if you had been here the day of my mescaline, I wd. have spent 2 days and 2 nights explaining everything to you two veteran mystics, Allen and Peter

Jack

ps. s. [sic] In other words, when the mescaline really hit me, 3 hours after ingestion, I went to bed in my whole bed with blankets and sheets and all the window wide open to haunted October moon and M E D I T A T E D
(no sentimental music, try it that way now, no music)
The secret is Samapatti
This is the whole visit
And how can it be a visit when you are God Yourself?
Like, I realized that Christ has a cunt, that Avalokitesvara has a cunt,

---

38. See Ginsberg's "Howl" (1955):
    I saw the best minds of my generation destroyed by
            madness, starving hysterical naked
    dragging themselves through the negro streets at dawn
            looking for an angry fix,
    angelheaded hipsters burning for the ancient heavenly
            connection to the starry dynamo in the machinery
            of night ...
    who drove crosscountry seventytwo hours to find out
            if I had a vision or you had a vision or he had
            a vision to find out Eternity....

Neal was right, and Jesus Christ and the black cunt are reconciled at last. Easy enuf. You dont know the half of it. I'll tell you. Big long talks. Starting Saturday. Call Payne for Lois Number. We'll eat in Chinatown, etc. I bring lot loot.

Ti Jean Louis

In other words, see you this Saturday weekend for big long talks—& Love to You & Peter

Jack (ALWAYS PHONE FIRST. WE'LL BE STEPPING OUT)

TO ALLEN GINSBERG

[Postmarked November 2, 1959
Northport, New York]

Allen,

Here is Herbert [Huncke's] check.[39] He asked for $25 on the phone[40] but this is a huge sum, I'm not Frank Sinatra. I would appreciate if he would pay it back when Playboy takes his story. Send "Hermaphrodite," they wont take "A Sea Voyage" because of queer scenes. Huncke's Sea Voyage shows that he is a perfect writer. (Also send "Cuba" to Playboy.) [...]

When I got home there were 30 letters and telegrams each one insanely demanding something. I see now clearly that I have to quit the whole scene for good. I dont want to see anyone or talk to anyone, I want to go back into my own mind. It's murder pure and simple.

One was a telegram from [the] Wm Morris [Agency] demanding I read at the monster poetry rally. The list would kill you. Demands for free prose and poetry, for me to phone at once, for me to attend receptions and Halloween parties, for me to write the publicity for MGM's Subterranean movie, for me to answer obscure literary points in England, for me to appear in public, for me to write columns I never planned, for me to send books to all parts of the world, for me me me in my one trembling body ... so I'm cutting out. After [Steve] Allen show in H'wood I'm going to Mexico and wont be back till my birthday March 12. Give my love to Huncke, Petey, Lucien. This is awful. I'm going OUT. There's nothing personal. I feel I need Gary's Way now. For a while, a long while. This is serious. I'm mad. There's no hope. Eugene Burdick was right when he said "bemused spectators crowding around have suffocated the beat vision." I know you have fun spending mornings answering letters but my prose work takes more energy. I have last part of Tristessa all set to do the Lu-

---

39. Herbert Huncke had asked Kerouac for a loan after having served five years in the penitentiary.
40. Jack and Gabrielle had installed a telephone in their house at 49 Earl Avenue in Northport.

cien story and if he changes his mind I'll hide it okay.[41] There is a dream of cold mountain ranges on a gray day with clouds that I always get when I've been home 2 days sleeping with open silent window. Cities and poets are repetitious. It's time for the world to change. Nobody believes in enlightenment, i.e. kind tranquility, kind silence. I know you and Petey are trying hard without phone etc. but get thee to that finca. Anyway, love as always & see you

Jack

[Handwritten postscript] I'm not a Messiah. I'm an artist.

TO ALLEN GINSBERG

[November 6, 1959
Northport, New York]

Dear Allen,

Lucien was just here, with Cessy and kids, and we tried to play your record from Fantasy but somebody creamed on it.[42] However, after Lucien left I woke up and tried it again and at least can get Kaddish n Holy. The record is covered with some kind of gook and is absolutely worthless. What they tryna do?

But I wanted to tell you that your reading Holy is the most beautiful thing I've ever heard. Too bad Lou didnt hear it. Play it for him at his house.

Here's my Hollywood address good till Nov. 17th and I'll ask Steve to forward to me:

JK
c/o Steve Allen
Bellmeadows Enterprises
1558 North Vine
Hollywood

Where I'm going after Hollywood I dont even know. I think I'll float like a Chinemen [sic].

---

41. Kerouac wanted to make another try at writing a novel about Lucien Carr's fatal stabbing of David Kammerer in 1944 (earlier Kerouac had collaborated with Burroughs on a book about the event, *And the Hippos Were Boiled in Their Tanks*). Carr objected, but Kerouac regarded the incident as an heroic act and kept after his friend to let him "do the Lucien story."
42. Ginsberg's reading of "Howl" was released on Fantasy Records LP 7013, along with his poems "A Supermarket in California," "America," "A Strange New Cottage in Berkeley," and selections from "Kaddish" and other poems.

Anyway, your Holy, Allen, is so very beautiful that I must say. It is covered with holiness. Dear Holy Allen, I shall certainly see you again real soon. Dont mind what people say about you. When men lie, men lie, but when men like Lucien and me love you (not to mention Nunkey and Iepety) well anyway, may God now lay his perfectest blessing on your suffering brow.

All ends well.

Isn't it strange that everybody goes to Heaven no matter what they do?

If you see Gregory, tell him I miss him.

And Bill too. And Whalen.

Anyway, Allen, the record the company sent me is useless almost. Lucien will tell you. I'll buy a new record in the store. You were hi on mescaline when you made that record.

I don't know where I'm going but I do know that there's nowhere to go, that's why I bought this home and spent 2,500 dollars fixing the attic row. But since the void is holy I'm holy too. The latest news is that the stars are fine.

Anyway, Holy Thou, see you very soon, and pray for me.

Jack

Kerouac's excitement before his trip to Los Angeles was partly due to his experience with mescaline, which he described to Snyder early in November 1959 on a postcard he sent praising Snyder's first published book of poems, Riprap.

TO GARY SNYDER

[n.d.]

Dear Gary—

RIPRAP is great ... apologies for that silly note I drunkenly sent you this summer—had mescaline and saw everything including your old peote vision of all the myths are real, indeed, saw the devil, saw God, saw all, the Tathagatas in fact were goofing showing me so much but I know now that nothing necessarily has a name—or even is—knew it all along, but SAW it on mescaline—Allen is going to follow up with lysurgic acid for me—Allen and I and Peter Orlovsky are really veteran mystics by now—we realize that the deprecatory press about us is irrelevant in the Samapatti worlds of Infinite variety, Shakti, Maya-Kali—In fact I reconciled Jesus with the black quonyt—Is that how you'd spelled it in a poem?—Will see you somewhere next year 1960 as I'm traveling—Whalen coming NY Nov 7 but I'll see him just briefly as I'm taking train to H'wood to get 2 g's on Steve Allen TV show to plug Dharma Bums too—Everybody is plugging books on TV now, mostly show biz autobiographies, so I gotta get on the horse and ride away the Sultan ... So what? Okay

(revisit old railyards anyhow)

Jack

On November 8, 1959, just about to depart for Los Angeles to appear on the Steve Allen television show, Kerouac typed a postcard to John Clellon Holmes, mentioning a plan to see Cassady, who was eligible for parole. Enrolled in a course in San Quentin in comparative religion taught by Gavin Arthur, Neal had arranged for Jack to talk to the class. Unfortunately, in San Francisco Kerouac overslept the morning he was to give his lecture, so he missed his chance to meet Cassady.

TO JOHN CLELLON HOLMES

[Postmarked November 8, 1959
Northport, New York]

Dear John—

Am now off to H'wood to do Steve Allen show (Nov. 16th Monday, watch me) and am playing Horace Silver album, met him the other night, what a sweet kid—His tenorman's name is Junior Cook—Eugene Taylor on bass—I will dig H'wood for the first time and get my material for the first chapter about H'wood—Almost came to see you last 2 weeks but my life tolerably intolerably hectic—In fact I'm half dead and should have got a house in the quiet country—Allen is fine, Burroughs is big hit literary lionized now in Paris, Gregory had a vision in Crete, and Peter writing great new batches of long mad poems—I will go to San Quentin prison and address a class in Comparative Religion for Neal, who wants to see me—Neal getting out six months, feeling good now—Have you ever (yes, I remember you did) the House of the Dead by Dusty [Dostoevsky]?—Great. —How's, well I'll see someday, Harrington?—Anyway, amigo, love and kisses—And keep thinking. Write what you thinking. Dont worry about nothin. Earnest eardla grabfunik. [sic]

Jack

After appearing on the Steve Allen television show in Hollywood, Kerouac went up to San Francisco, where he made two new friends, the poet Lew Welch and the Zen Buddhist student Albert Saijo. Welch offered to drive Kerouac cross-country back home to Long Island in his Jeep station wagon. Arriving in Northport at the beginning of December, Welch and Saijo stayed with Jack and Mémère for a few days, enjoying Gabrielle's dinners of clam spaghetti and Taylor port wine. Visiting the photographer Fred McDarrah and his wife, Sheila, in Greenwich Village, Welch and Saijo collaborated with Kerouac on a long poem while their host took pictures of them. Describing Ginsberg and Orlovsky's apartment in the East Village, Welch wrote Snyder in a letter on December 3, 1959, that Allen and Peter were living in "terrible squalor on 2nd St." in a state of total "dedication to being Beat and Art and Holy." Then, Welch continued, the gang returned "to Jack's house where all is love and simple and one can wash his car." On December 6,

1959, when Welch and Saijo went into Manhattan to stay with Ginsberg, Kerouac wrote his own letter to Snyder describing their "enlightening" cross-country trip.

TO GARY SNYDER

Dec. 6, 1959
[Northport, New York]

Dear Blarney Gary—

Extry added little note, Lew Welch and Albert Saijo gone off to city to stay with Allen and find Frisco friends and make it for a few weeks ... It was a great enlightening trip, by car, from SF to Vegas where Lew demonstrated his old gambling taxidriver personality losing 22 bucks at a gambling table before we dragged him home to the motel.... Albert sat in the back of the jeepster much of the way on a mat meditating. We turned up with various amazing little poemettes that I kept writing down on my lap in little yellow notebook notable for its sporting the color of the Sangha ... We first decided that it was the road was moving, not the car, and ended up in the last of the Bulls with the original that the road didnt move, the car did. Albert fresh from yr zendo wanted to see if it was possible to meditate away from the tranquillity of a zendo, see, thats why he took the trip. He sat there silently for hundreds of miles, under blanketed cross legs, as Lew and I hashed over all the good news of America including track, football, American literature, survival kits, kicks, everything. I had my survival hat, Albert had his, Lew had his freedom shirt ... We just rolled and rolled across that immensity road. It was refreshing for me because I've been quiet and placid and stale for 2 years staying home answering letters. I've decided to answer only friend letters from now on, and answer fan letters of exceptional purity only. I didnt visit your old zendo because I didnt want to see Sandy Jacobs who said The Dharma Bums novel was immature, I dont see why he said that.

We missed Whalen by a day. At that thumping mad 1713 Buchanan house where Joanne K.[43] clobbered Jay Blaise with a halfgallon jug of port which decided us not to wait for Thanksgiving turkey there but take off. However I must say in very honesty with absolutely no bullshit that Joanne is the most sensitive woman I've met since Joan Adams (Bill Burroughs' dead wife). But Joanne needs a good man to put her in her place, in the sack. We had an interesting banquet, a Pekingese banquet (Imperial cooking) with that Chinese Teacher who later brought a lovely 15 year old Japanese highschool girl to interview me and I said, "Okay, but only if you ask me something interesting," and she said, "How are you?" which floored me.

43. Joanne Kyger was a California poet who was planning to join Snyder in Kyoto.

Ole John Montgomery was there. Les Thompson. I enjoyed it but it was rough on my health, after 10 days in Hollywood on the TV show, visiting the Metro lot with the producer, watching rushes of SUBTERRANEANS, going out with H'wood types, dining at a table next to Norma Shearer, taking long 5 mile hikes on Dismal Sunset Blvd. in the Saturday night emptiness of Los Angeles. Etc. All to go in my next book which will be a full 600 page chronicle of everything that happened to me (of interest) since that night in October 1956 when I trudged down the Arizona desert road with full pack under a red moon, with Desolation money, and was surrounded by 3 squad cars wanting to know where I was going. "To sleep in the desert," I said. And showed em my good US Agriculture papers and they let me go and suddenly I got a truck ride to Mexico border. To go live in a candelit cell in Mexico City and write, penniless almost. The fantastic story of everything's happened since then, rags to riches sort of, or (since I don't have riches yet) obscurity to fame, and how awful it is to be "famous" (fame mouse) at least in America. . . . It was easier to chop wood for Locke and have wine and a good meal in the cabin.

Anyway Gary, as to going to see you in Japan, mayhap, and if so, okay, with Albert maybe, if I make movie money, but meanwhile Kwannon bless you buddy.

Jack

After missing Whalen in San Francisco because he arrived after Philip had left on a trip to New York, Kerouac also didn't get to see his friend in Northport, although Whalen came out to Long Island for a visit. In a letter written on December 6, 1959, after Whalen had returned to California, Jack explained what had happened. Then he dropped a note to Barney Rosset at Grove Press, asking for a copy of Mexico City Blues *to be sent to Snyder in Kyoto.*

TO PHILIP WHALEN

Sunday Dec 6 [1959]
[Northport, New York]

Dear Phil,

Why didnt you YELL my name in Northport night windows & bang door? Dammit, I was passed out (my ma too) after drinking waiting for you & others—We could have been wakened—And I go & miss you in Frisco by a matter of hours—Well, I'll see you soon because going to Lew's Rogue River mine next Spring-Summer—Lew & Albert are just great—We wrote long letter to Gary—Please tell Jay Blaise the 3 medals he gave us got us here safe & the St. Christopher medal will stay on Lew's windshield—He'll be back in 3 weeks—We also pulled out a death-by-the-roadside cross in Arizona, & gave it to Ginsberg—How come you're getting thin? Amphetomine [sic]–? Give my love to John & Les–I'll be back there 1960, the only drag was that scene of violence which is bad enough in men–But I do think Gary can direct Joanne's high fine sensitivity towards maybe maternity or something–maternity and shaktihood–I wish we could live to see the day when all women become Dancing Shaktis & men monks of Love & life is built around the sexes again, as in the beginning–Lew is terribly sexually frustrated–So is H.E.–"It wont do," as Eisenhower said when the Postmaster showed him the underlined dirty words in LADY CHATTERLEY–Turn off the radio, the television, dont read the papers & just think of Karuna in all its forms transcendental or otherwise–I am writing this in my attic I paid for on TV show–It was just an attic with beams, hot in summer, cold in winter, but now's sheetrocked, spackled & painted, Albert himself waxed the tile-type floor–2 new windows of light facing west pines–the basement was damp & bringing back my thrombophlebitis–So I have huge Handelian attic & play St. Matthew Passion & will soon write new novel of 1956–1959 events–Mexico to NY to Florida to Berkeley to Fla. to NY to Tangier to Paris to London to NY etc etc including this final grand trip with Lew & Albert–Might as well keep writing, nothing else to do (but I MUST tell this story, it will reveal things to me too)–and meanwhile "good french frieds, everything good."

Jack

TO BARNEY ROSSET

[Postmarked December 6, 1959
Northport, New York]

Dear Barney–

Would you call interoffice and have the proper person package a copy of MEXICO CITY BLUES to be mailed to Gary Snyder

Konoecho, Yase

Sakyo-Ku

Kyoto, Japan

and have it charged to my account?

Letters from fans keep saying they cant find copies of DOCTOR SAX. Quite a few letters state it is my masterpiece. The book will take root slowly.

My idea for our next book (if you want it) is, of course, the entire 600-page VISIONS OF CODY. Laughlin is bringing out a $7.50 limited edition of 750 copies, only a fourth of the whole, this month sometime.[44]

---

44. *Excerpts from Visions of Cody* was published in December 1959 by New Directions in an edition of 750 numbered copies signed by Kerouac. There was a bindery overrun of fifty-five books, not numbered or signed, used as review copies.

Don Allen wants it. Hope to see you soon in NY somehow by accident happily.

Jack Kerouac

The same day he wrote Snyder, Whalen, and Rosset, Kerouac made elaborate excuses to his sister to explain why he hadn't made it to Seattle to visit her. Pull My Daisy had been received with hostility at the San Francisco film festival, where Jack was so drunk he fell off the stage. As Kerouac put it, he was "drinking every night to stand the gaff with a smile." During the same week as the film festival, Life (November 30, 1959) attacked the Beats in a disparaging article by staff writer Paul O'Neil titled "Beats: Sad But Noisy Rebels" on the cover of the magazine, and "The Only Rebellion Around" at the start of the article. O'Neil began by describing the United States as "the biggest, sweetest and most succulent casaba ever produced by the melon patch of civilization," and likened "the improbable rebels of the Beat Generation" to "the hairiest, scrawniest and most discontented specimens [of fruit flies] ... who not only refuse to sample the seeping juices of American plenty and American social advance but scrape their feelers in discordant scorn of any and all who do."

O'Neil went on to deprecate Kerouac as "the only avant-garde writer ever hatched by the athletic department at Columbia University." He was "Beatdom's Grand Old Man," writing prose with a "goulash-like texture." The article castigated Allen Ginsberg for his "shameless exhibitionism" and his insistence that "U.S. citizens have a constitutional right to all the narcotics they want." It quoted Gregory Corso as admitting he never combed his hair, although "I guess I'd get the bugs out of it if I did." It referred to Neal Cassady as the "Johnny Appleseed of the Marijuana Racket" and revealed that he was doing time in San Quentin "for selling same." O'Neil marveled that "between agonizing periods of ineffectual withdrawal" from heroin, William S. Burroughs "has rubbed shoulders with the dregs of a half dozen races." Conceding that the Beat poets were powerful enough to "architect" a literary movement that "has attracted wide public attention and is exerting astonishing influence," O'Neil dismissed them as "undisciplined and slovenly amateurs," and concluded that "the Ginsbergs, Kerouacs and Corsos, like the dissidents who emulate them, are social rebels first and poets only second."

TO CAROLINE KEROUAC BLAKE

Dec. 6 [1959]
[Northport, New York]

Dear Nin,

I wanted to go to Seattle and started off good enuf going up to Frisco in a car but I had to stay there for publicity work on my little movie PULL MY DAISY and then my drivers were afraid to go to Seattle because we had to get onto NY and couldnt do so across the Montanas and Dakotas,

& I was sick anyhow, so we headed south to Las Vegas to avoid snowstorms & got to Mémère's a week later—Where I'm now sleeping and resting after 3 solid weeks of meeting 100 different people (no lie) and drinking every night to stand the gaff with a smile—I'm no Art Linkletter, you know, that can meet & talk with everybody & travel here & there—I'm just poor Ti Jean who wants to go home & go to bed when he's tired—And if it werent so, how could I have written my books with all my ideas burned out[45] among people—Mémère tells me you had a party watching my TV show—Anyway, I almost made it but I'll be seeing you folks later, I guess if you're transferred to Chicago—It sure is a crazy world in Hollywood, no one has any fun really, much less fun than you & Paul have, you bet—It's all business & they're all afraid of the next in rank—like slaves—so I just rushed around doing what I wanted & they looked surprised—I hope you didnt spend too much on your long distance phonecall from Seattle—Yes, Nin, it's much more fun to do what you like & be what you like, than to be a "celebrity,"[46] I'll explain it to you someday—And all I wanta do is write, anyway, & have fun, like I always did—Now that Mémère has her house & my savings account picks up the annual tax, insurance, & some of the heating bill, things are almost perfect for her—And I don't want to get into any "celebrity" spending habbits—So we have enough & not too much, just like a fortuneteller once told me—To spend your life trying to get as much as you can is to murder your life—Your life is supposed to be happy natural-ness in eatting, sleeping, going to the toilet, walking, talking, working—not

45. See *On the Road,* Chapter One: "the only people for me are the mad ones, the ones who are mad to live, mad to talk, mad to be saved, desirous of everything at the same time, the ones who never yawn or say a commonplace thing, but burn, burn, burn like fabulous yel-low roman candles...."
46. Carolyn Cassady described the perils of being a "celebrity" after the issue of *Life* maga-zine on the Beats appeared. On November 2, 1996, during a panel at the San Francisco Book Fair, she said:

> I had kept the fact that Neal was in prison both from my parents and my children, and good old *Life* magazine came out and announced it and my father read every word in *Life* magazine. They didn't actually tell me they had read it or knew, until my sister told me they had, and so I asked my mother if she'd like to know any more, and all she wanted to know was: is it true? And then she told me it would have been far better if Neal had killed every one of his children rather than disgrace them. If you want to get a period thing here [about what her life was like in the 1950s], "death before dishonor" was still very, very with it. So it wasn't always the best thing, that article.... I was subsequently disowned from the family after my parents found it. My brother had several children and I think one of them got busted for marijuana and the other one got a girl pregnant or something, and he said it was all my fault. And my niece said, "Well, how well do your children know Aunt Carolyn?" and he said, "Oh, they never met."

a nervous worry about how to get more, More, MORE[47].... But anyway I got home & will see all of you soon—We're going to have a small Christmas tree on the table & a nice turkey & that's enough—Once in a while I go into NY & see my wild friends & blow off steam—I may go to Oregon this spring to live in a cabin on the Rogue River & if so, of course, if you're still in Seattle, it will be a breeze to go see you (near Grant's Pass, Oregon)—So long keeds & have [a] good time. Tell Little Pauol [sic] to study hard so he can be a jet pilot—those jets are magnificent ships.

Love,
Jack

After the editors of Big Table *blocked their plan for an edition of* Old Angel Midnight, *Kerouac and Ferlinghetti continued to discuss other manuscripts that could be published by City Lights, as Kerouac described in his letter to Ferlinghetti on December 7, 1959.*

TO LAWRENCE FERLINGHETTI

Dec. 7 [1959]
49 Earl Ave.
Northport, NY

Dear Larry—

Thanx again for getting me the cash[48] ... We had a great enlightening trip, Lew Welch talked all the way & showed great knowledge of American

---

47. Acknowledging their readers' "morbid curiosity" about the Beats, *Life* illustrated O'Neil's article with a double-page posed studio photograph showing "the well-equipped pad" of a Beat with his "chick" and infant child. The photograph showed a couple of attractive young white models (the so-called baby was a rubber doll) dressed in sandals, black turtleneck sweaters, chinos (him), and black tights (her). They were surrounded by posters from old poetry readings and jazz concerts, a paperback library of Beat classics such as San Francisco African-American poet Bob Kaufman's *Abomunist Manifesto* (City Lights broadside, 1959), and a typewriter with a half-finished poem. Everything in the photograph, including the baby, was numbered and labeled for easy identification so that it could also be used as a blueprint of how to dress and set up an apartment (for example, naked light bulb, cheap espresso coffee pot, bongo drums, Miles Davis and Charlie Parker long-playing records, marijuana plant). Before the *Life* article, the Beats' "infiltration" into popular culture was relatively contained, consisting mainly of Beat characters in the radio soap opera *Helen Trent* and the inept, goateed, bongo-playing Maynard G. Krebs in the television show *Dobie Gillis*, as well as a few films like *The Beat Generation*, a trickle of exploitive paperbacks like *Beatnik Party* and *North Beach Girl*, and a scattering of espresso coffee houses and cellar folk music or jazz and poetry clubs in cities such as New York, San Francisco, Los Angeles, and New Orleans, and in student enclaves around university campuses. Boasting a weekly circulation of 6.4 million readers, this issue of *Life* (probably more than any Kerouac book) spread the new bohemianism throughout the United States in the beginning of the 1960s, preparing the way for the hippies as representatives of a counterculture lifestyle by the end of the decade.
48. Payment for Kerouac's poem "Rimbaud," published as a City Lights broadside in 1960 after its initial appearance in *Yugen*. See Kerouac's letter to Ferlinghetti on May 20, 1960.

subjects (dialects, lit., folk songs, logging, football, track, girls etc.) and Albert Saijo meditated most of the way. We wrote a joint book of poems called TRIP TRAP. Albert is like my guru now.

... Yes, send OLD ANGEL back to me, including the cover I drew, and I'll hold it for later. Meanwhile I can offer you the complete RAILROAD EARTH (final part upcoming in Evergreen Review), about 60 pages of prose, or the full text of my only play from the third act of which PULL MY DAISY was drawn. Or selections from BOOK OF DREAMS or from BOOK OF SKETCHES (these two books are 350 pages long by themselves) or selections from the 600-page SOME OF THE DHARMA (pensees on Buddhism). The trouble with the latter is all the typing I'd have to do, but can do (really). So write when you get back from [Big] Sur and will straight out. I'm seeing Al Leslie in 2 days re City Lights DAISY.[49]

Jack

Lonely after his new friends Lew Welch and Albert Saijo returned to the West Coast, Kerouac wrote an air letter to Gary Snyder in which he described his sense of himself in crisis as a "sick" and "drunk" author. Kerouac had hoped that Mexico City Blues, *his most substantial book of poetry, would make his reputation as a poet. He introduced it with the note,*

> *I want to be considered a jazz poet*
> *blowing a long blues in an afternoon jam*
> *session on Sunday. I take 242 choruses;*
> *my ideas vary and sometimes roll from*
> *chorus to chorus or from halfway through*
> *a chorus to halfway into the next.*

Back in Northport, Kerouac was devastated when he saw a review of Mexico City Blues *that Kenneth Rexroth had published in* The New York Times *on November 29, 1959. Rexroth claimed that "Someone once said of Mr. Kerouac that he was a Columbia freshman who went to a party in the Village twenty years ago and got lost. How true. The naive effrontery of this book is more pitiful than ridiculous." After quoting a few lines of poetry, Rexroth concluded with withering sarcasm, "It's all there, the terrifying skillful use of verse, the broad knowledge of life, the profound judgments, the almost unbearable sense of reality."*

---

49. *Pull My Daisy* was published by Grove Press in July 1961.

Other critics also savaged Kerouac as much as his writing. In the Saturday
Review, *the poet John Ciardi wrote, "Kerouac's latest excursion into let-it-spill
self-expression . . . is billed as poetry, a view of things to which Kerouac has persuaded Grove Press, but not me. Poetry, I insist, is not a jam session in which the
poet blows whatever comes into his head; and if it were, Kerouac is not musician
enough to sit in with the men."*

*Kerouac was so heartsick at his reviews that he felt too self-conscious to begin
work on a new book. He plaintively told Snyder that "I'm afraid because everybody's going to read every fucking word and I cant be myself any more."*

TO GARY SNYDER

[Early December 1959
Northport, New York]

Dear Gary me Bye—

If I'm a red-legged immortal where's your Dragon? Let's ride away to
that lake where they sell drugs a thousand years from now—Glad you got
Mexico City Blues—Rexroth gave it a terribly execrable review that was so
bad people wrote the Times to complain—He said I was like a wax figure
in a museum but even I was drinking wine in Phil's cottage I had more red-
ness in my nose than Rexroth paleness—I still think he's a fine poet, a great
poet in fact, I love Rexroth type poetry—He's mad because I said on TV,
when the announcer asked "Why did R. throw you out of his house?" "Because he doesnt like me?"—Rexroth even went so far as to lie on TV about
me in rebuttal, saying I took out a big heroin needle and gave myself a shot
in front of his children—Imagine—as if I knew how to do it even—I really
think he's off his rocker now—I hope he straightens out and realizes that
the beat literature is the literature he worked for so hard for years—Besides
he makes good money reading thanx to all the publicity—Aint gonna be no
future lives, Gary, for me or you or anybody: diamond say "No rebirth in
this or any other world" (unborn void sense)—if you mean in a buddha-
show sense, we return, okay, but aint even here now, tho you could butt
me like a goat now and make me yell but even the yell aint there—ah gary
dont you know that the universe is the only way a dream could take place,
atoms are universes and universes are atoms—Even you with all your
brains, how come you dont underSTAND it's all in "our" minds?—how can
you grasp at externals?—flowriver flower flower flow—And when buddha
pointed at a flower he had a river in his heart—and do you know how horrible it is to be a "famous" writer, I'm writing my new novel and I'm afraid
because everybody's going to read every fucking word and I cant be myself any more, I want to throw cocks and flowers at the reader and I hesitate and dont write in my novel such nice things as for you privately I just
wrote: flowriver flower flower flow—qwf—Lew Welch and Albert Saijo
greatest men I've met since you and Phil—Allen G. dont like Lew, jealous—

likes Albert, who doesnt?—Is that so?—Lew great—Lew and I big buddies—
What do you mean "mountains of merit?""? who needs it with a Goodwill
suit?—the embarrassing situations that will arise in my "future lives" have
already arisen and everything is very quiet here, in this universe they call
it—Yes Lew & Saijo gone back to coast, Lew writing his novel HARD
START at his mother's house in Reno and Albert repeating the life story of
Buddha in 1713 Buchanan kitchen—His version of Buddha's Life is best I
ever heard, I told him to write it—He says Buddha had to know EVERY-
THING including eunuch boys, etc., cuntsucking, etc. perversion etc., rare
dishes, rare ideas, etc. I cant even begin to explain but when Albert says it
everybody is fascinated—Albert Saijo is the Buddha who travels around the
world everyday in a chair—naturally—Creeley's in Venezuala—I dont prize
him like I do you because he starts fights but he is very intelligent but I'm
afraid of him really—I am—Sandy Jacobs, he said to Look mag. that Dharma
Bums was an immature book or maybe it was his Jap cunt—I dont see why
that book shd. be so immature as all that—at least it was fun—and turned
certain types on dharma—when I did meet Sandy one time he was very
funny & charming and we stood on our heads together, I dont get it—it's
like the British poet Geo[rge] Barker who had a big wonderful night with
my bars in NY with me and then went away and wrote a limerick satire of
me in an avantgardey magaziney—Why?—badly brought up? no manners?—
I like your Joanne, she is really in need of you and has great potentialities
as a loving human being—She hit Jay Blaise on the head with a bottle of
wine because she was becoming attracted to him, that's my enkelhoptic
[sic] theory, I guess that washes me up with Joanne—and You? no—after all,
you were too far away and Jay is nice—that was her way of getting married
to you—my girls are the same, or were—Anyway she's spontaneous—And
while I was swabbing Jay's bloody forehead in the bathroom he said, like
Dostoevsky hero, "it was all my fault."—Montgomery meanwhile was struggling in thru the streetdoor with a secondhand easy chair—And all the children slept, anyway.

Tell Furusawa to be sure to translate Dharma Bums, which somebody
Japanese bought recently—I have no control over translations—The German translators must be wild because they put my "Essentials of Modern
Prose" essay on the book jacket!—There are also Swedish, Danish, Dutch,
Spanish, French and etc. translations how can I keep up—everyday I get an
invite to lecture somewhere—I'm going to get a cabin in the woods and a
jeepster stationwagon this year or die—die probably—my new book is lousy
for me to write but probably will be pleasure for others to read—In the
great Goethean sense we have got to CONFESS our literature or no literature worth reading—Your sense of local deities, Saravasti etc. and Yase
etc. is straight, because sometimes I get weird messages from Jesus or Go-
tama just from askin em O goodbye

—I see you now, why shd. I go to Japan, and if I do go to Japan how do I get back home drunk on sake? in a jet? crashing in the sea drunk? goodbye?

Goodbye is all we got anyway/;///11//////////I'm sick, I'm drunk.

By the time you get this, I know how things work, you will have had your sesshin and wont be interested anymore in arbitrary concerns such as are contained in letters but here is a bit of Zen thought: when the cat got in wet from the rain he dried himself on one pillow and then went to sleep on another pillow and nobody can say ultimately, philosophically and prajna-wise that it is the same pillow.

NOT-TWO equals NON NOT-TWO.

Jack

[On reverse of letter, written by hand:]

Living at home with my mother open to daily invasions of all kinds (mail, callers etc) I'm slowly going mad.

I'm fat, dejected, ashamed, bored, pestered & shot. I must get a cabin or die, but getting a car for me is such a horror—I dont like driving—Mebbe I can get a cabin reachable by bus & foot, in the Adirondacks.

(Except winter, that's the trouble with the snowy eastcoast woods & mountains.)

I'm really in bad shape & in danger right down the line & *must do it* this Spring.

Shortly before Christmas 1959, Kerouac heard from his old buddy Henri Cru, who had been his friend at Horace Mann School. Cru was working as a merchant seaman and asked Kerouac to look after his cat, Mr. Fuzzynuts.

TO HENRI CRU

Dec. 21, 1959
[Northport, New York]

Dear Henrk, I mean Henri

I'm glad to see you got such a good job at last, it's much better than hanging around the Kettle of Fish upstairs—As you know, I can never take care of Mr Fuzzynuts for the simple reason that my cat Tyke is insanely jealous of other cats, he even drives them away from the yard and sometimes they come into the house via his secret cellar entryway and he has big fights with them in the kitchen over his Puss n Boots plate—which wakes my mother up and the enemy cats scat—I hope your mother's operation will leave you sufficient money to enjoy yourself for a year in NY thereafter and that you wont go throwing it away on the horses. Did you know that I had an invitation from Armstrong Racing Sheet to sit in the clubhouse sipping cocktails and if I had had time for that, I would certainly have insisted on your being invited also. Now that you just left San Pedro, remember the incident of the tumbling weed in the engine dept. foc'sle[50]—Now that you are in San Francisco, go down and have a good meal in Chinatown—[....] There's a chinese guy that hangs around there, forget his name, who will take you to an Imperial Chinese (Pekinese) banquet, Chinese food you never tasted in your life. Ask the kids about him. If you go into Barnaby Conrad's Matador bar on Broadway, tell him I sent you and tell him I said for him to listen to the story of the banana king (which I have here)[51]— Come to think of it, you wont have time for all this. Your ship sounds great and one of these days I'll see your room but you know how busy I am. I left Calif. 15 days ago, by car, driving with 2 guys, we had a ball in Vegas and especially in East St. Louis with dancing girls—We had a greater ball in New York than anywhere else—Give my regards to Shorty Man and tell him that as far as Baba is concerned, if I should STOP talking the world would come to an end.

There's a blizzard in New York tonight and it's going to be a White Christmas. I'm buying my mother a Polaroid Land Camera to take pictures of the cat with, and the house.

I had a ball in Hollywood with the comedians of the Steve Allen show, especially Gabe Dell who plays Bela Lugosi (Gabe Dell's real name is Gabriel Marrano, of the Lower East Side) and Dayton Allen (Why Not) and the others. I had a ball in Frisco too, but especially driving back cross-country and seeing the land again, altho I was almost arrested in Oklahoma for being high on liquor in a filling station. (a gas station).

Save some of the money from this trip and buy yourself a tape recorder to tell the story of your voyages.

Well, Hank, I'll be seeing you next time around in NY, let me know well in advance.

Ton ami toujours,
Jack

Met Ziggy on the sidewalk—also John Bates—Met David Niven in Calif. who said "Strike a blow for freedom"—(meaning, sexual freedom)

On Christmas Eve 1959, Kerouac put on a record of Bach's Saint Matthew Passion *and sat down to write to his old friend Allen Ginsberg, who had been invited*

---

50. This incident is described at the end of "Piers of the Homeless Night" in *Lonesome Traveler*.
51. Remi Boncoeur's [Henri Cru's] fascination with the Banana King is described in Part One of *On the Road*.

along with Lawrence Ferlinghetti and twenty-five other writers to a literary con-
ference in Santiago sponsored by the Communist Party to discuss recent events in
Cuba, where a revolution had brought Fidel Castro into power. Kerouac also
wrote a postcard to a fan in Brazil named Roberto Muggiati after Sterling Lord
had forwarded Muggiati's article entitled "Jack Kerouac and the Bop Children."
Muggiati later commented that he was struck by the postmark on the card from
Kerouac: "6:30 PM, December 24, 1959, in Northport. Quite a significant date for
a Catholic such as Kerouac used to be. And think of his loneliness on Christmas
Eve!"

TO ROBERTO MUCCIATI

[Postmarked December 24, 1959
Northport, New York]

Dear Mr. Muggiati

I received the page from the paper and I sorrowed that I couldnt read Portugese as well as I can read Spanish but got 50% of your meaning—It is only regrettable that you quote what other writers with other interests say about me or the beat generation—I assure you that the beat generation is an honest movement, and if the criticism is "Where are you going?" the answer is "We will get there." Naturally. Someday I will visit Brasil and see you, my dear sir, and look forward to it. If I get nowhere else, I will get to Brasil. Meanwhile continue with your work and have faith in your own joy or maybe in your own joylessness. (in the Latin tradition) ... Lawrence Ferlinghetti and Allen Ginsberg are going to Santiago Chile in February and will visit Brasil too ... But I am staying home to write a new novel. Salud, hombre

Jack Kerouac

TO ALLEN GINSBERG

Christmas Eve 1959
[Northport, New York]

Cher Alain,

Just concluded an amiable wrangle over TRISTESSA and am going to have it published just as it is (no additions) just like Lucien and Cessa said it should—

Seduction after all, doesnt make a book sexy, or dithyrambs.

It is such a short book that I myself gaze with amazement at the few words she spoke (you never read the whole thing tied up with the second year of composing so you dont know what I means.)

Am playing St. Matthew's Passion as I write this, marveling at your taste when I came to your cottage in the Western night in October 1955 from Mexico and nobody home I played your St. Matthew and waited for you hi on benny, remember?[52]

Well, and I got big letter from Grove Press girl asking what I planned to do in Chile, I never GOT no invitation to go to Chile, did you intercept it for Peter's use? If so your schemes mell with my rhyme because I dont want to go anyway ... am happy in my attic with the bat. The only explanation I can think of is that you bit your lip, tweaked your beard, and took my invitation and gave it to Peter, which is okay with me. Who wants to go south of north? But write to me from there and also find out why I didnt get an invitation: am I too crude? Too crude to be a Mahatma? I, the ponsell dinker?

Drama aint nowhere without poetry (see Broadway), and poetry aint nowhere without drama ... s'why I write what you call PROSE, novels, see? My model is Shakespeare. In the interests of which I advise you, really, to plan now a big Miltonesque dramatic poem for your next pook. Boog, I mean. Imagine you getting hungup on big modern Shakespearean city tragedies using long line, short line, prosody, ellipses, etc., see. I decided this when looking over my poetry and my "novels," which have better lines in em.

Karl Paetel is giving Sterling a bad time. What is he, a German con man? a sinister Burroughsian debt collector? a slinker? Sterling only claims that in every beat anthology I shd. get "premium" payment because they cant make it without my name ... thats all. I got with Sterling because I've had a long talk with Albert Saijo who reminded me that "money is poetic" (viz. Balzac, Shakespeare, etc.) and shd. not be put down per se by per se william. In fact, I intend to make a million and when I'm sixty I'll give it away and walk away with rucksack, grayhaired, across the roads of America, everybody will be amazed. Imagine, like, if Hemingway did it tomorrow. No cops would arrest him. Everybody would listen. S'why Buddha was born a KING, a Maharajah. Only trouble is, I aint got no message.

Well sweetie, anyway, I'll see you New Years Eve at Lucien's or around Lucien's orbit, me N Lucien never miss a New Years Eve.

I hope Peter out of doldrums. Saw Laff in the road, at night, stalking, looks happy. Anybody'd be happy with all that good star of solitude.

I'll get you a copy of my new album when come to NY, you and me go together maybe to Hanover Records 57th St. and pick up 4 or 5 and hand them around. Free. Money for Tristessa will be 7500 dollars and's going right in bank.[53] Wont start spending till I have 50,000—like I mean on crazy

52. Kerouac described hitchhiking from Santa Barbara to San Francisco high on Mexican Benzedrine in the fall of 1955 in his story "Good Blonde." See also his description of Ginsberg's "rose-covered cottage" on Milvia Street in Berkeley in Chapter Three of *The Dharma Bums*.
53. Sterling Lord had sold *Tristessa* to Avon Books, which published it as a thirty-five-cent paperback in 1960.

things. Am still Canuck and smart. Never draw money out of the bank unless I put MORE in. That way I can always write a check with confidence. Nothing to do with American ideas. Got Xmas card from Neal.

Only writing this to wish you big happy welcome holiday
Anyway writing it
Write me note
Ton Jean
Jean Louis

At the end of December 1959, Kerouac wrote to Don Allen asking his editor to supply him with Benzedrine and phenobarbital tablets so he could "get going" on his next book, Beat Traveler.

TO DONALD ALLEN

[December 30? 1959
Northport, New York]

Dear Don

This is a strange request in a way but not so much considering I'm one of your most successful writers and you a hip editor. As you know, I wrote Subterraneans on benny, Desolation Angels on benny, much of Visions of Cody etc. For 2 years now since I've been in Northport I've been out of my usual Mexican or Moroccan supply and havent been able to get going on a new novel. I went to one local doctor who was afraid to give me anything but dexamyls either because he thought I was a gloomy writer who wanted to commit suicide or was too notorious a public figure to take a chance. All I want is oldfashioned white bennies and a supply also of oldfashioned white phenobarbital tablets to offset the benny depression 8 hours after ingestion (after 8 hours of writing). I would like to know if you know a doctor who would fill out a prescription for these 2 items for me so I could write my new novel BEAT TRAVELER (story of a penniless author becoming successful overnight and the hilarious adventures thereof) (blurb). If so, I'll come into N.Y. and pay him a visit, once he's told what the purpose of this prescription is. (Also, by the way, I would like to lose some weight.) I didnt get a chance to get some in Mexico and besides the border is rough. I'd rather have a prescription anyhow. Dexamyls are nowhere at all; cause constipation, depression, and not high-making. With good white benny tablets I can rattle off amazing narrative chapters and be *interested* in them as I go along. If you get me this, I'll give Beat Traveler to Grove: a simple narrative on the order of Road and DBums. Okay? Let me know soon. I want to write that book this winter. In the spring pack my rucksack and go to Oregon woods with Lew Welch and Albert Saijo, possibly Whalen and Snyder too.

You can tell this doctor that I've been using this combination most of my adult life and understand how to use them without damaging my health. As a doctor he'll know that Phenos one pheno are a perfect antidote for two benzedrines . . . taken with hot milk and honey.

Maybe Barney [Rosset] knows a doctor also. In any case, let me hear soon, and also anything else concerning our work next (anthology etc). By the way, I got Huncke sold to Escapade on Xmas eve!

As ever
Jack

1960

After the New Year's parties in Manhattan with Lucien Carr, Allen Ginsberg, and other friends, Kerouac returned to his house in Northport, hoping to start a new book he was calling Beat Traveler *about his trips in 1956–1957, before the publication of* On the Road. *As before, he stayed in touch with Ginsberg and Sterling Lord by sending them letters, letting them know that he planned to get to work as soon as Don Allen supplied him with a fresh supply of Benzedrine, which, Kerouac told Ginsberg, wasn't a "drastic demand."*

TO ALLEN GINSBERG

[January 4, 1960
Northport, New York]

Dear Allen,

Got your long letter which I put away in my new INTERESTING LET-TERS folder. I have a FAN LETTERS folder, and a CREAM FILE, and BEAT ANTHOLOGY folders and that is a good way to despatch.

Not that yr letter wasnt cream file but it was your new poem which is very good & will be published.

Enclosed find $40 to cover taxi fare, other taxis, bottles and part of Chinese restaurant bills.

I got a long letter from Lew Welch, a funny card from John Montgomery who is actually a pest because he wants me to send him albums, books, and puts down MEXICO CITY BLUES ("low material").

I am home safe now for a thousand years.

I want to write. I dont want to write letters (I got big huge letter from some Brierly type saying Neal isnt as great as Jerry who stole from private homes and got elected president of high school class and why dont I write about HIM instead of Neal) (isnt that awful) (Neal who read the Lives of the Saints and never stole anything PERSONAL from poor people)—

So I'll stay home 1000 years now and write Beat Traveler fast (soon as Don Allen comes through with my needs) (which arent drastic demand)

and one slow book about something probably Harpo Marx vision ...
Me and Harp and WC Fields and Bela Lugosi hitch hiking to China
together ...

Note, send me note before Chile.

Or not ... or from Chile ...

I tore up all the other letters today tho there is one smart kid called
Dave McFadden who says "Now when Spring comes along, as she does
every year, she grabs my/ melting heart with her warm lily-fragrant message: of the budding/ eucalypti on the Riviere du Loup highway, and the
greening of the/ grass" ach I cant type it, but its good. so long.

Jack

TO STERLING LORD

Thurs Jan 14 [1960]

[49 Earl Avenue

Northport, New York]

Dear Sterling

Enclosed find the Panther softcover contract signed & witnessed.[1]

I got your fine letter and think we can accomplish all that in 1960.

My new novel is going to be BEAT TRAVELER but I'm waiting for my
supply of benzedrine to start on it. Once I have the benzedrine it'll be done
in 10 days or less. I have it all plotted out, the "rags to riches" plot of me
with rucksack in the desert road 1956, to the Steve Allen Hollywood
scenes. As usual, there'll be dozens of characters seen through the narrator's eye who is just the focal point for stories. The traveling includes the
whole United States, Mexico city earthquake, Tangier to London, etc. ending Hollywood.

I havent had any benzedrine for 2 years and I realized that's why I
havent written any new novels. Wrote SUBTERRANEANS, DESOLATION,
TRISTESSA and most of CODY on benzedrine. Wrote ROAD on after-
dinner black coffees but I was younger and stronger (physically) then: 29.
I asked Don Allen to get me a prescription and he's doing so. I promised
BEAT TRAVELER to him, therefore. But we'll get a big advance this time.
And we can give ANGELS9desolation0 [sic] to Tom Payne. I tried to get
my writing-pep supply around here but the doctors are afraid of me. The
work's got to be done. I think it's great of Don Allen to come through
for me. He's a fine editor and man. I hope my agreement with Don is okay
with you.

1. Panther Books issued the first British paperback edition of *The Subterraneans* in January
1962.

I knew Morgenbesser would never give me a prescription.

Got a lot of questions to ask you when I see you, among them I want to see our accountant soon for new tax. In about 2 weeks I'll come see you at the office, and we'll go over items.

As ever

Jack

A good idea for Playboy now would be to submit Act Two of the "Beat Generation" play, or SLOBS OF THE KITCHEN SEA.

Also, dont forget we're raising the Escapade column fee.

Come to Northport any time you want.

J.

Writing to Philip Whalen, Kerouac composed playful letters responding to Whalen's latest poetry and sending him haiku, excerpts from old diaries, and sketches of "kids dancing" that Jack thought might entertain his friend. He also kept Whalen up to date about his involvement in Buddhism and asked for news about his West Coast friends Lew Welch, Albert Saijo, and Gary Snyder, who would marry the poet Joanne Kyger in Kyoto on February 23, 1960.

TO PHILIP WHALEN

Jan. 18 [1960]

[49 Earl Avenue

Northport, New York]

Dear Phil,

Your new poem strange. Especially that pencil and chair bit. What's with Gary these days? And did Jay Blaise receive the copy of Mexico City Blues I had Grove mail him? or not?

I'm sorry you're cold. I'm cold too, in my attic there's no radiator so I sit up here writing with extry clothes on. Today as I was falling asleep in a nap I heard myself think "Black voices hear the dent in the hail." What the fuck can it mean. Yes, getting big letters from Lew Welch who sounds like he's going to be a great new goody novelist.[2] He certainly told me an epic on

---

2. Lew Welch's unfinished autobiographical novel, *I, Leo*, was published posthumously in 1977 by his literary executor and editor, Donald Allen, who wrote in his preface:

> Lew Welch's resolve for 1960 was to sit down in his mother's house in Reno and write the long autobiographical novel he had been thinking of for some years. Conversations with Jack Kerouac during their drive to New York in the previous November, and Jack's literal example, convinced Lew he too might become a successful novelist and eventually a self-supporting writer.

In November 1960, Welch wrote Kerouac that he decided to abandon his novel because he felt it was "badly written and (therefore) dull."

the way over in his car. And why in hell should Albert [Saijo] be stumped in his writing?—tell him for me I know why and if he'll write I'll tell him. Oh Ho. Did you see where Alan Watts (in an "impertinent interview" in the Realist magazine) said I had Zen flesh but no Zen bones. It made me shudder. "No Zen bones yet," he said. It must mean that when I have a bellyache I moan. I cant stand pain, I admit it.

I'm about to write a new novel, BEAT TRAVELER, all set to start Thursday, when you get this just about. Have my pills at last (didnt have proper supply of workpills for 2 years). When I go out to stay at Rogue River mining camp this late spring I will see you, dear Phil. We'll have a ball if you can come to Rogue River too, and Albert too. By "ball" I mean big starry nights with wine by rushing creeks under trees. No mad city scenes. I'm completely sick of mad beat city scenes at last. I quit that for sure, right now, I am going to exert my will from now on. Most of my lushness arises from having to be with bores like locally, I drink from nervousness and ennui, social and everyotherway they're bores. Lew and I lushed driving east but it was to relax the driving nerves. I love Lew and Albert too. For some reason Allen G. doesnt like Lew (maybe jealousy like little boys) but Albert loves Lew as I do and I remember you were the one who first told me about him. I like his optimism and wit. He has fits of depression that are worst than mine almost.[3]

I've been reading the new book Suzuki and Erich Fromm (phoney shit) and the brilliant De Martino, a book about Zen and Psychoanalysis. God, I cant understand how charlatans like Fromm can build up such enormous reputations for repeating what everybody else said and in gray dull language at that. Also reading Proust etc., still only in middle of Volume II, breaking Neal Cass[ady]'s record of spending 3 years on Proust (I've been at it now for nine).

Yes, do sit down and write everything that happened last year and you'll have a great book and make some money and be able to buy yourself a lil car and a cabin in the Oregon beachie woods. Just write honestly to yourself, to close friends, clearly, telling what happened, reader will but know. Dont let invisible Critic peer over your shoulder. Remember how Aurora Borealis shimmy'd bright. Found this in my old Desolation Peak diary:

"The void is limited
        by any kind of conceiving;
It shrinks to imitate
        your silly kind of thinking."

3. Lew Welch apparently committed suicide in May 1971 after disappearing with his .30–30 rifle into the mountains near Gary Snyder's home north of Nevada City, California.

I said it better in 1950 waking from a nap:

"A nuder think changeth the sea."
                    Ah so, hiss
                    Love to Albert my boy
                    and love to you my father
                    Aplustard[4]
                    Jack [TURN]

(Later) P.S. Tried to start a novel last night and I was stumped too! Tell Albert advise me!

A big fat flake
    of snow
Falling all alone
        —KEROUAC
        1922–2000

Eternal Recurrence
    is a story,
not a philosophy,
& stories last forever.
        JEAN-LOUIS

Unable to concentrate on Beat Traveler, *Kerouac wrote his new girlfriend Lois Sorrells about his dreams and his wish to escape to a cabin in the woods where she could join him on weekends. Jack was resolved to break the destructive pattern of the last couple of years after the publication of* On the Road, *blaming his mother for not keeping unwelcome visitors away. A month later, feeling lonely, he sent a postcard to Ginsberg in Chile and invited Ferlinghetti to stay at his house, saying "My mother loves handsome Frenchmen, etc., good food, drinks, etc."*

TO LOIS SORRELLS

Tues. [January 19, 1960
Northport, New York]

Dear Lois

Just woke up from big 12 hour sleep feeling happy because I had dreamed of giant blue men hugging skyscrapers and turning into statues, a new kind of dream for me possibly presaging my new decision to exert my own will from now on and not just follow everybody like I been doing

4. "I'll see you later" in French.

since I was caught so by surprise in 1957 with on the road book success—I am now a giant blue man hugging my will—They were twice as big as King Kong and not destructive at all—As soon as they hugged the skyscrapers lovingly they turned into blue bronze statues—A big panoramic shot of New York shows them squatting on top of skyscrapers and halfway down—turned solid blue limestone.

And just now as I was pondering your new poem idea I SAW a haiku, out the window.

> A big fat flake
> of snow
> Falling alone

Send your girlblue poem to Tom Payne and tell him (also send others I liked and those you like) tell him not to goof and lose it but either insert it immediately into the sheaf for the linotyper for anthology number one, or, if anthology number one is already linotyped, for him to place it in beat anthology number two folder. Then tell him which one you want removed, also. I still dont have Tom's number, I never see him, it will be better this way. Anyway the beat anthology has already been advertised in advance in that Sunday pocketbook review. You will be in second one too.

Yes, I saw Town and City. I get half the royalties in the next royalty statement from Harcourt Brace who sold it to Grosset & Dunlap without telling me because I had no agent for Town & City in 1950. Now I do, put Sterling on it. Incidentally that book is in my mother's name, beneficiary, as an old gift when I thot I was going away forever to Tibet in 1954. So she's going to get big royalty statements and feels all excited.

Yes, I yearn for last summer too, that rainy midnight football field, that wonderful double mattress on the floor, the shower upstairs, the big empty dark house, the chairs on the porch.

I've definitely made up my mind: when I'm ready this spring I'm going to get a license, driver license, and then buy a $1600 new Volkswagen, then go (write to realties) and see what cabins or "hunting camps" fit my needs, buy that. So that on Friday nights when you come out of work I'll meet you and we'll drive 100 or 150 miles to the cabin and stay there with trees & brooks & stars till Sunday noon and drive back. That will be the beginning.

On other occasions, I will be there for 2 week stretches and you can come up probably out of a port authority bus and I pick you up somewhere near.

Meanwhile, I'm having a radiator put in this attic so I can sleep with windows open and also write comfortably and in March the stockade fence, so that I can enjoy my stays at home also. See? I'm going to exert my WILL.

No more being dragged around by big Colin MacLachlans to places I hate and where I have to drink because I'm bored or nervous. I drink by myself always sensibly, always eat right, it's only when I'm overwhelmed by bores and non-bores I dont wanta see that I get myself sick. I'm going to go back to my old ways of following my own will.

Because when books suddenly sold I got woozy and began being dragged around by millions of "admirers" and followed them blankly wondering what to do. This has been going on 2½ years. I saw it all clearly.

I dont have to put sign on door rejecting goofs, I'd told my mother to simply tell everybody I had an apt. in NY and wasnt home any more but this weekend she was mad at me (and lonely) from that fight so she let them in and now they have big plans for a swell spring with me being dragged around. But I'm re instating that thing: my ma tells everybody (except you, Sterling, Victor) that I have a pad in NY now and aint home. My mother okay now.

Standing on end
on top of the tree,
The Big Dipper

(I start my novel Wed. (tomorrow) or so, in fact probably tonight, will see you in NY in at least 2 weeks, or, if you come here, any time you come)...........

See you soon, kissy one.

As ever,
Jack X X X

TO ALLEN GINSBERG

[February 20, 1960
Northport, New York]

Dear Allen—

And I have dreamed of flying horses,[5] I'm in some Mexican village and look up and see the hundred-mile-high mountain of "Mien-Mo" (Burmese name for the "World") and tho everybody ignores and says they're only birds I can tell with my own horrified silent eyes that it's horses up there, flying, pawing the void with their slow fore-hooves, with capes furling back over their infernal shoulders, a dream I had after a Chinatown dinner which will scare me for the rest of my life, I cant begin and have not begun to describe it ... Come back to NY some time soon, got a letter from Gregory and answered to him and Bill in Paris—I am very quiet now, never go to NY no more, am exerting my own will about what to do, i.e. Tao Nothing, so sweet—Made 4 false starts on Beat Traveler, about 40,000

---

5. See "The Flying Horses of Mien Mo" in *Book of Dreams*, pages 180–182. Also references to the "Mien Mo Mountain" in *Big Sur*, Chapters 8 and 36.

words in all, rolled them up and put them away, too tao to wanta write I guess. But we'll see. Meanwhile be gay, have fun, meditate, be made and grave, think of wilder gravestones (thornton) anyway I will always love you.

That's True, Alain. Regards to the Indios.

Jean

TO LAWRENCE FERLINGHETTI

[ca. February 1960
Northport, New York]

Dear Larry,

The hardcover people who want to do RAILROAD EARTH wanted to change my dashes so I told them they could only do it if they didn't touch anything in the original—It's still being decided by them—But I don't want you to think that I'm screwing you—It so happens that I have hitherto un-published material that might do better for your City Lights edition of my work that would be that much better because UNPUBLISHED—Like, as you may have heard from Allen, I have a one-thousand-page book on Bud-dhist and general Religious Philosophy or non-Philosophy called SOME OF THE DHARMA, parts of which I could type for you to make a City Lights Pocketbook—Also there's BOOK of DREAMS (250 pages), BOOK OF SKETCHES (same)—When you come to New York, it's obvious now, if you really want to do something with my work, come over to my house at 49 Earl Avenue (phone ANdrew 1-8973) and we'll decide after you've glanced at my typewritten unpublished manuscripts—which include BOOK OF BLUES (poems) etc.—It would also be pleasant for you to visit me, you can sleep the night here, my mother loves handsome Frenchmen, etc., good food, drinks, etc.—So don't be bugged at me—So many people have read Railroad Earth I really don't think you should bother with it ... Give em something new ... But if you still want Railroad Earth, there's a chance those hardcover people will crap out on my silly artistic demands.[6]

Later,

at least please write or call

hoping to see you

Amigo Jack
Jack

Writing a thank-you note to his sister, Caroline (now living with her family in Morton Grove, Illinois), on the day of his thirty-eighth birthday, Jack told her

---

6. Both Parts One and Two of "The Railroad Earth" were included in *Lonesome Traveler* (1960), published by the McGraw-Hill Book Company.

about his dream of buying a cabin in upstate New York on the Montreal bus route so he wouldn't have to buy a car. He also firmly turned down his brother-in-law's proposal to invest in a cattle ranch. Then Gabrielle jotted down her thoughts on the second half of the page.

TO CAROLINE & PAUL BLAKE

[Postmarked March 12, 1960
Northport, New York]

Dear Nin and Paul,

Thank you for sending me the birthday card with the potbelly stove—In fact that's exactly what I'm going to have pretty soon as next week (or two weeks) going upstate New York to see two large acre properties with hunting camps in the hopes that one is suitable to buy—Since I dont want to buy a car it will be good because on the Montreal bus route—3 mile hike—

Paul, I received that book you sent me, I guess you'll pick it up next visit, those are fine properties but as you know I dont want to get involved in no businesses because they take up too much time & mental anxiety for a writer. I just want a cabin in the woods to go to for several times a year for 2-week stretches, and for Mémère to have a neat little home where she isnt scared and can walk to the store—

I guess you're getting the big blast of winds all the way from Hudson's Bay across those Great Lakes in Chicago area—You know, it's much colder there than in New York or New England because the lakes let the wind in from the Arctic Circle—I guess you'll be glad to get out of there—

Give my love to Lil Paul and just look ahead to the future, I guess you'll wind up in Orlando? If it aint too hot, it's too cold, in this world—Maybe God made the world for lizards.

Let me know if and when you're coming to Northport again (April?)— See you then.

Love,
Jack

P.S. Paul, those hunting camps in New York State are cheap and all have spring water bubbling out of the ground, and private streams, etc. The one I may be buying borders thousands of acres of state land, too, and has 82 acres of its own, in dreary beautiful Mohawk Indian woods—I'll have to buy snowshoes and a doublebitted axe—They cant be reached by cars, new model cars, just rut roads—Good place to sleep. Jack

[Gabrielle's note:] Hello kids—
I tried to persuade Jack to go in the "Bull" business. So far no soap—but dont lose hope, he can change his mind he has that deal upstate. I dont think he'll go through with it. Some "nut" put him up to it and now I'm

working overtime to make him forget about it. It sounds awfully wild anyway. Keep fingers crossed. Jack has to learn the hard way—he'll soon get tired of having "to foot uphills" for miles. I only wish I could get him away from all those "crack pots" who's all-ways influencing him on silly deals—*"let us pray."*

Mom

After making four false starts on Beat Traveler, *Kerouac abandoned the 40,000 words he had written so far on his novel. Instead he gathered his magazine sketches into a new book published in September 1960 by McGraw-Hill as* Lonesome Traveler. *In April he congratulated Philip Whalen on a new book of poetry and went on to mention Allen Ginsberg's travels in South America after attending the literary conference in Chile with Lawrence Ferlinghetti. In the letter Kerouac also reminded Whalen that Neal Cassady would soon be released from San Quentin.*

TO PHILIP WHALEN

April 12, 1960
49 Earl Ave.
Northport NY

Dear Philly:

Rec'd MEMOIRS OF AN INTERGLACIAL AGE[7] and it's really some of the best poetry ever written in the world—I pasted your pencil drawing of Avalokitesvara into the blank second page—very good, father—"Delights of Winter at the Shore" worthy of Li Po if Li Po was suddenly cast into this particular American scene—The Swede boat Gandharva beautiful!—When you suddenly say "O rage, O desespore, &C." you make romanticism laugh at itself, well—Anyway it's good, I've been reading it on the toilet bowl—Where do you say that you're not worth anything, but just a poet, you make your whole infancy worthwhile, it was a good thing you were born to write a thing like that—There's a style all your own that no one can pin down or define—a style of Seeing and Saying—You're a definite poet definitely Whalenesque. You don't have to write novels if you don't want to.

If you ever do write dramatic pieces, try a play: write it like you did that dialog on the floor with that other guy in North Beach, that dialog I saw

---

7. Whalen published three collections of his poetry in 1960: *Self-Portrait from Another Direction* (San Francisco: Auerhahn Press), *Like I Say* (New York: Totem/Corinth Books), and *Memoirs of an Interglacial Age* (San Francisco: Auerhahn Press).

sometime ago. Just dialog. Your "wo I meant to say your "quotes" always so funny......

As usual, I have a sour stomach from wine, writing to you on a fullmoon mild April night..... my backyard now enclosed by six-foot tall cedar stockade fence, shadows of moon, my sleeping cat..... this afternoon I slept in the yard like Egyptian king, with wine glass spilled in grass........ Reason for wining: just last night finished preparation of new book for McGraw Hill, 65,000 words of prose LONESOME TRAVELER concerning railroad work, sea work, etc., travel, mountains, etc. smoking opium and hasheesh.....

O well. Please let me know in your reply where Lew Welch is and why he doesn't write ... I have so many things to do, I'd wanted to go to Oregon this summer but I think I'll go to Paris and Sweden and get away from my mail...... Imagine: I get such silly letters every day, high school students bloated up by the Parent Teachers Association demanding that I complete their term papers on "beatniks"—Or ridiculous requests that I appear somewhere to read..... Whether it's Oxford or shithouse college why should I get away from my wine moon chair of poesy? My wise chair.... Pussywillows in the moonlight ... Shit, Phil, it's awful.

I tried to explain it to Lew but he was so enthusiastic about answering every letter ... Newspaperman came to my door yesterday wanting a statement about why Rube Goldberg is a beatnik, for instance ... Strange sinister French Canadians come down from Montreal to film and interview me ... Steve Allen sends clippings in Christian Science Monitor where he acknowledges I can write, etc., that kinda stuff.

This morning on toilet bowl I also read McClure's "To Artaud," very good.

Allen Ginsberg bought a $30 Chinese print in San, no in La Paz, Bolivia, coming home with it ... Says if he had a lot of money he'd be in business, millions he says of great unknown Chinese prints ... Maybe they're only Chimu.

Neal Cassady coming out of San Quentin in May 1960.

By the way, I had mescaline last Fall, just about the time you should have shouted my name and banged my window, when I was drunk asleep, mescaline made me see new things: all's well, all's samapatti ...

How's Gary and Joanne? Well, what to say? Wish you were here so I (again) could hug youse ... See you somewhere sometime.......

The luirssant moon sends you love....
   What to say, sage?
      Just know this: I love you
          always will
          always did
       and don't slide sideways off

Remember all the old days? Meeting you and Gary and the F train station, walking to the place, I asked if you were Irish and you blew up? Ah, if we only knew......

O well ...

Love to all, Helen Elliott

etc.

MOTHER KALI DANCES THE DANCE OF LIFE WITH A THOUSAND ARMS BECAUSE EVERYTHING TAKES CARE OF ITSELF (KARMA)

Foutu

A Dieu, ton copain

Jack

A week later, Kerouac wrote a friendly letter to Carolyn Cassady hoping that she and Neal would "embark on a new road of love and wisdom now" after his release from prison on June 3, 1960.

TO CAROLYN CASSADY

4-20-60
Northport, N.Y.

Dear Carolyn

I hadnt written to you for the simple reason that someone had told me you were leaving Neal when he got out—

Allen and Aronowitz apparently thought that ... but now I see from your tone you intend to stick to old Neal ... because I had thought "If C. leaves Neal she wont be wanting to hear from *me*"—I think Neal loves you very much and always will and I'm glad you're going to stick together— I can't picture anything grayer than the thought of Neal in one part of the world, alone, and you in another, alone, lacking your intimate conversation between each other, which, as you remember from the last visit I made, even Gregory Corso couldnt interrupt ...

As for my books, they were published exactly as they were written years ago (CODY mostly in your attic on Russian Hill) so the only thing we'uns can say, you me and Neal, is that they were published ... You can remember, tho, from reading Cody, how much I loved that guy and his home and you and the kids—The only thing I regret is the time we fought over money in San Jose and you drove me to Al Sublette's where we spent that money anyway on wine....

By the way, in another forthcoming novel, about 1961 or 2 I guess, you'll laugh to read (DESOLATION ANGELS) about Neal and I at the races, etc., the Bishop, etc. I hope you and Neal embark on a new road of love and wisdom now, stop fighting, realize each other and work out your karmas.... My karma's pretty heavy as I'm loaded down with sickness now, a smashed elbow from drunken night, phlebitis in feets, hurting hands (neuritis), wow, and newspapermen hovering around my door for what I got to say about Ferlinghetti's poem on Christ. All I could possibly say is that I have written about Jesus in my own way but you can guess how it would emerge all twisted in the papers so I say nothing and my mother and I dont answer the door.... It was nice to hear from you, my darling blonde aristocratic Carolyn, and my next great moment will be when once again you and Neal and I sit in front of the fireplace with wine and the Television and laugh ... I'll be seeing you when I come to Calif. again—Show this letter to Neal when he comes out, tell him I love him, and by the way in the Italian "Life" Magazine (Successo) is a big picture of him calling him "The Santo" (the saint).... Peter Orlovsky and Corso's work ... but anyway happiness from now on for you two mystical greats (Love to the Hinkles too).

As ever
Jack

In the spring and summer of 1960, Kerouac sent a series of letters to Ferlinghetti about publishing his poem "Rimbaud" as a City Lights broadside along with his Book of Dreams.

TO LAWRENCE FERLINGHETTI

April 28, 1960
49 Earl Ave.
Northport NY

Dear Laurent,

Go ahead with the broadside of RIMBAUD. I'm sure LeRoi wont mind, it'll plug his *Yugen* ... I'm sending him a card this afternoon about it.

[...] As for book of dreams, before you have your selection type-set I'll have to change the first names to fit in with all the other books, like Allen isn't Allen Goldfinger any more, but Irwin Garden, etc.—and also libel—be sure to let me change the names or you'll be sued ... I have the real first names in there now ... ex-wives, etc. very dangerous ...

My elbow is better now, the one I smashed falling on the tile floor at Penn Station—everything takes care of itself, even the usual unreliable sources (I guess). Amitie

Jack

TO LAWRENCE FERLINGHETTI

[May 4, 1960
Northport, New York]

Dear Larry,

Just thought, why dont you let Whalen pick out the dreams, according to the number you want I mean the size of the book, and let him write a lil intro and give him some money for it. I think he might like doing it, I dunno. I'm sure he would. If not, send me ms. and I'll pick them out my-self and re-type them with new names.

You didnt bug me with L. I. profs.

If you see Rexroth tell him I never read that thing he said about me about "innocent lost heart straight" and had been so besieged at that time I couldnt read anything let alone sleep or think. Tell him, when they told me that crap on TV I should've simply told the story straight, about my bot-tle of wine screaming in his study. They asked me on TV why he "threw me out of his house" etc.

Jack

[May 20, 1960
Northport, New York]

Dear Larry,

I noticed you changed the paragraphing of RIMBAUD but I like to pub-lish my long poems as well as "blues" just as they appear on the page when scribbled in holy high, so I've restored the original paragraphing in my own way. There was only one typo, "degenerate lip" (not "degenerated"). And you see, about the paragraphs, I don't believe in changing one iota of the arrangement which my mind made while MOVING the poem, paragraphs, idiot words, all of it. Because God moves the hand that writes. Who's God? God is Everything, including you. It's just a convenient word to represent the transcendent and not transcendent temporary unity of all things, all an-imals, and all men including men of other galaxies. We must ride the way the waves ride. (them Einsteinian electromagnetic-gravitational waves, also words.)

So here's the completed galley proof.

As to BOOK OF DREAMS, okay, tell me how many words you want and I'll type long new manuscript. Incidentally I have some new dreams (1957–60) that I could replace or add (what I'll do is stick in the great new dreams).

Don Allen's anthology [*The New American Poetry 1945–1960*] is beauti-ful, isn't it? Also Fred McDarrah's photos in BEAT SCENE. On the cover of my own Beat Anthology, seeing as how everybody has wild party scenes, I'm going to have something different. Avon, 1960.[8]

There are some books I would like to buy from you. Send me big list: I have riprap, etc. already. Till I see you, Smiler.

As ever,
Jack

---

8. Apparently over the summer Avon backed out of its commitment to publish Kerouac's Beat anthology. See letter to Ferlinghetti on September 14, 1960.

[June 3, 1960
Northport, New York]

Dear Larry—

Received DREAMS manuscript, am lightly pencilling name-changes over typewritten material for the printer, will thenceforth mail it back surface mail 1st class registered etc. to you in about a week—Am deleting dreams you selected which deal with libelminded ex-wives etc., see?—only 3 or 4—am going to add fantastic new two or three dreams of recent and make exact 190 page City Lights Prose Series length—Am amazed to see how beautiful Dreams really are, like you said, had forgotten! No sense my typing out 250-page ms. for you, it would take over 2 weeks of useless labor and sweat and paper—I can later erase pencil marks from original blackbound onionskin private Dreambook—Picture of McDarrah's I want on cover[9] is with huntingcap looking down, in *Beat Scene*, looking right down on the words "In Arizona they put a cross beside the highway"—right after Saijo's last photo—it looks like I'm looking down into dreams—You could even have it blown up and printed in diamond form, that is, take the square picture and have it tilted to the left till the square is a Diamond. With DREAMS manuscript coming back pronto I'll send notes. Love.

Jack

Shortly after Allen Ginsberg's thirty-fourth birthday, Kerouac, intensely missing his absent friend, wrote him a long gossipy letter. Allen was now traveling in Peru, but Jack sent the letter to be forwarded from Louis Ginsberg's address in Paterson, New Jersey.

TO ALLEN GINSBERG

[June 20, 1960
Northport, New York]

Dear Allen—

Peter sent me your aether notes, I numbered the pages before they get screwed up and even tied a paperclip on but if you want me to type them

9. For the cover of *Book of Dreams*, Ferlinghetti preferred to use a photograph Kerouac sent him a few months later, one taken by Robert Frank on their trip to Florida, showing Jack asleep in bed. See letter to Ferlinghetti before October 18, 1960. For Fred McDarrah's photographs of Kerouac wearing cap, see Fred McDarrah and Gloria S. McDarrah's *Beat Generation Glory Days in Greenwich Village* (New York: Schirmer Books, 1996), pages 107–116.

up for you also, I will. I probably will anyway as I would like to read it en toto fast—Great new long poem of yours ["Aether"]—I havent really studied it yet, answering letter first—But it surprised me that when you were really hi on ether and heard the bells ("The sound of the bell leaving the bell," said Basho in a haiku) you thought of me, as I thought of you at the highest hi on mescaline last Fall—When on mescaline I was so bloody high I saw that all our ideas about a "beatific" new gang of worldpeople, and about instantaneous truth being the last truth, etc. etc. I saw them as all perfectly correct and prophesied, as never on drinking or sober I saw it—Like an angel looking aback on life sees that every moment fell right into place and each had flowery meaning—Your "universe is a new flower" is a perfect statement like that, as tho thought on real hiness—But I'm making no effort any more (like you) to get real high and write visions, it seems I have to wait right now, I'm a little exhausted actually from all those Angel Midnights of past few years when I went all out—But what I really must do is get off by myself for first time since On the Road 1957 so I'll take a secret trip this summer and live alone in a room and walk and light candles, in Mexcity probably, where nobody'll know me or see me—Have to have a holiday to rediscover my heart, like—These innumerable friendships of mine are too much—Do you realize what happened just this last week for instance and as example: Jack Micheline writes big nutty letter all dabbed with tears from Chicago finally asking for 10 dollars—Gregory writes Come to Venice at once! Money is my friend! (when I'd told him I might be sent there by Holiday on assignment)—Charley Mills and Grahame Cournoyer call me insistently from the Village for money and I have phone number changed—My sister wants to borrow a thousand for her house—(ahead of even the house)—Lew Welch hints he needs a hundred for his jeep—You invite me to fly to Peru, Gary to Japan, Ansen to Greece, Montgomery to Mill Valley to go live with him mind you, old Horace Mann schoolchums to reunion, art galleries to their art shows to buy stuff, etc. etc. I didnt put you in there because you belong in the battalion of money-askers (Look, if I complied with all these recent wishes, including the other ones, I'd have no more money! Always wondered why "rich" people were "tight" like Jay Laughlin or old 1945 Bill [Burroughs] now I realize it's because, it's NOT because they're tight but they're outnumbered by money demands (and saddened too)—Anyway how can I get into contact with the Nameless One by leaving myself open to all this? I must go and be quiet and alone, like God, awhile, again—To come back with something to write—Not that I havent written enuf and god I'm sick of poetry and literature—Maybe everybody else is and thats why theyre starting a war—Well I still havent shown you my mescaline notes of last Fall—I will when you get back—Much like ether—When we had ether with Jordan Belson in 1955 we were not alone to lie down and think and listen to bells and scribble, instead we talked and went to Chaplin movie—I only saw Peter once or twice since you left, and Laff, and Huncke, usual Chinese dinner—Laff told Lois he was a nice young boy blown out of a volcano with a gun—(quote)—I told her to write down notes of all he said, he talks to her a lot as they walk arm in arm to chinatown behind me and Petey and Hunk—Mainly I sit under the stars and realize the same old blooey samsara is nevertheless empty—Feel like going to Heaven, now, in fact—But I could really write a wild doosy book to knock out everybody—including myself—Don Allen's anthology was fine—Our own anthology I think Tom Payne is being fired for, he will go to Bantam books and work there with it and my future novels—Tristessa out this week—not a word changed—Good review by that penthouse Dan Talbot of West End Avenue we saw, remember, in 1957, the 2 Israeli girls night, with Sterling—Where he says that people who claim the "immense sincerity" of the beat gen. is a literary racket, is wrong—Anyway I'm bored with all this again, the whole present history of the world bruits on the horizon but I'm watching the freedom of eternity in the starry sky and wondering why the dream of life and history seems so real except to re-member old dreams (sleeping dreams) when a tree was thought real, an at-tacker was thought real, in fact, oh yes, Ferling is putting out Book of Dreams with all my great NEW dreams at the end including the Flying Horses I saw and a final great dream about shit—That'll be: for this year: Golden Eternity by LeRoi [Jones] put out: Tristessa, by Avon put out; Lonesome Traveler, by McGraw-Hill put out (I put together 250 pages of pieces from mags including our beatnik nightlife new york and gregory bums hobos and bullfight and statue of christ all new stuff about henri cru, mexico, railroad (all of railroad earth and new chapters) and things about mountains, Tangier, etc. not a bad book and to be on non-fiction list)—I now have 18 grand in the bank and not touching it—4 grand in checking for expenses—taxes took 16 grand last year—(this year paid)—not much compared to Senator Herbert Lehman and his half a million dollar dona-tion last week to the Zoo—

drear light of—

But my mother is guarding over my money, my health, L. comes to fuck and suck, Tom Payne (newly married) comes with new millionaire wife to get smashed—Has a cabin in Vermont I may live in soon—Think I'll just qui-etly sneak to Mexico (dont tell anybody especially Lamantia!) and get my visions in—

If perchance you will be in Mexico in late July or August on yr itinerary let me know, I'll have a nice pad with flowers in window, you can stay a week or so or two—That is, if I go—See, that's my life now, I never go any-where or do anything—My last run to New York was so awful, a month ago, I havent been back—I had nightmares, I saw ghosts—Bill H. scared me, Charley M. scared me, a big nutty trappist priest kept making me kiss a relic encrusted in rubies (but he did play me Bach for 2 hours) Everybody was smiling at me even Ornette Coleman, I was in torn blue jeans Lucien had torn, also had torn off all my underwear in front of Cessa in the house and I DIDNT EVEN REMEMBER THE NEXT DAY—There is a great deal of talk about Voodoo, too, in the village now, which scares me—People are sticking dolls—The police just closed down Gaslight and few other places for no good reason 'fire hazard'—Henri Cru is presently rushing back from Genoa to see me and tell me all about Fernanda Pivano the date I arranged for him with her and that will take up a thousand hours of energy could go on solitude visions, see?—And remember, remember, my introspective laziness not at all like your great social energy—Oh yes, John [Clellon] Holmes, they said in the Times that I was a disciple of his and [Anatole] Broyard and [Chandler] Brossard in 1952 (forgetting 1950 Town & City hipster chapters)[10] so Holmes get drunk and writes big sentimental letters about my boyish smile and "little Allen"—Is he crazy? I think Holmes is going crazy—Micheline is out of his mind—I enclose the letter he forwards you about one of his nutty woodcut visions (you know, remember those woodcuts we saw with Gilmore in 1945 showing "the young poet in New York"?) the sentimental view of the "youth" in the white shirt among dark towers—this is Micheline, his vision—I mean, dearie, strictly from Marc Brandel—

Dont hear from Burroughs but was pleased he mentioned I named Naked Lunch (remember, it was you, reading the ms., mis-read "naked lust" and I only noticed it) (interesting little bit of litry history tho)—James Wechsler has come out with his book Reflections of an Angry Middleaged Editor where he excoriates me (maybe you too) for political irresponsibility and complicating up American with poetry—Aronowitz will come out soon I guess, I got mad at him for million mistakes, I straightened out a lot of them (mostly about me but some about others)—

Well what am I living for? all I'm good for now is to graipe gripe gripe like this?—if I could only have a month alone, and smile and talk to myself quietly in French in a flowery sad Mexican midnight study, with a big garden wall with lizards maybe ... by god I'll do it! dont tell anybody! Of course, in the Fall, new energy will come to all of us. I'm really afraid to go to India because we may be caught here in a big Red Chinese invasion and wind up emaciated torturees in prison camps because we wont admit to insects in the snow—Now, no, I'll buy a 500 acre mountain and build a cabin

10. Anatole Broyard was a book critic for *The New York Times* and author of "A Portrait of the Hipster" (*Partisan Review*, 1948). Chandler Brossard had published the novel *Who Walk in Darkness* (1952) about hipsters in Greenwich Village.

on the southern slope of it—Tom Payne wants to go on a big gay Paris trip with Scott Fitzgerald women in the Fall, I dunno—I've been making wonderful tape records off the FAM radio jazz, FM, and have hours of jazz—Just wrote a column on jazz for Escapade all about seymour wyse— Previous column about Zen, mentions you and Peter—But mainly, I'd like candlelight novel now—But, you know, it seems I'm getting to be like the old Kerouac of 1944, when Lucien and you talked and I just sat brooding, remember, because I was bored and confused—Maybe thats better for rest of my life than silly Zen Lunatic yakking on Brandeis stages I dont really mean anyway—yes—but I love you, Allen, dont bug me when you come back to New York about all your enthusiastic plans to go here, go there (like the fiasco of taking me to the Living Theater when I wanted to go hear jazz and I got in trouble with Butch [Frank] O'Hara)—just a gag—but forgive me and love me, if I seem not to share your particular enthusiasms, and those of poor dear gregory, I just dont care the same way any more, I am going to become now a hairy loss old man with not-thoughts and no-talk almost—I'm trying to stop drinking—my soul is deeper than ever maybe because emptying—all you write in Aether is true and forever true—Pray for everybody, I guess—And Old Neal is out—wow—but I dont want to see him because, in the past he scorned me for being a drunken yakker, now he'll also laugh at me for making money at it (tho I know he has serious Jesuit undergarments where he knows I'm just a funny humble priest)—But here's to our Birthday! Much love

   Come back soon

Ti Jean XXX

The first week of July 1960, Ferlinghetti offered Kerouac the use of his cabin at Bixby Canyon near Big Sur. Jack welcomed the trip to California as a chance to flee the publicity surrounding the premiere of the film version of The Subterraneans *in New York City at the end of June. The novel had been rewritten by MGM with the subtitle* Love Among the New Bohemians *and starred Leslie Caron as Kerouac's lover Mardou (actually an African-American woman in Jack's life and in his novel). George Peppard was cast as Kerouac, and Roddy McDowall played Gregory Corso.*

   At the same time, Avon Books brought out Kerouac's short novel Tristessa *as a thirty-five-cent paperback, advertising his spontaneous prose narrative as "a new and hauntingly different novel about a morphine-racked prostitute" and illustrating their claim with a picture of a nearly nude dark-haired woman on the front cover. On June 19, 1960, the book was sympathetically reviewed in* The New York Times *by Kerouac's admirer Daniel Talbot, who wrote that "at times" the author "sounds embarrassing, even sloppy. In the end he is more truthful, entertaining, and honest than most writers on the American scene." In a mood of elation, Kerouac told Ferlinghetti that he envisioned his friend's cabin as a solitary retreat where he could spend the entire summer revising the* Book of Dreams *manuscript, which Whalen had typed for City Lights, and asked his publisher to keep his "presence there a secret."*

TO LAWRENCE FERLINGHETTI

7/8/60
Northport LI

Dear Lawrence (Laurence) (Larry) (Ferling) (Smiler) (Oopsy) (Poopsy) (Poopshack)

—Okay, I'll be out there in time for July 22—I can guess you can guess why I dont wanta go to Europe now because I'm at the end of my nerves especially now with Subterraneans movie opening in NY with big reviews[11] and Tristessa out at same time people starting to ring the doorbell for no good fucking reason in the human world—In Paris with Corso it would be MacDougal Street all over again in 2 hours time from arrival from Le Havre as you know—What I need now is a rest, is sleeping in my bag under the stars again, is quiet meditative cookings of supper, reading by oil lamp, singing, sitting by beach with note book and occasional wine—But seriously the other night I knew I was headed for a genuine, my first real mental breakdown if I didn't get away from everybody for at least 2 months—This includes even Lois who is sweet—even Allen who is coming in 2 weeks—I wd. like to spend a summer in that cabin, sleeping outdoors, visited only by you and on the occasions when anyway we kill 2 birds with 1 stone by finishing the book of dreams manuscript—Also I wd. welcome your visits because lonely and yet welcome them because you would keep my presence there a secret—When I "come out" of this delightful solitude and test in the Fall I will be so glad to hitch to frisco and meet Kirby wife[12] and Whalen and see the others of course—I'm going to come out now and call you from that motel or hotel at the proper time. Have your number home and office. This is no idle talk on my part, this can save my life, at least my sanity, as well as maybe I might write a book during those 2 months in Bixby Canyon—God knows there's enough to write about but I've got to be a lil bored to get around to it—Talking to admirers over Jack Daniels all

11. The MGM studio, according to actress Leslie Caron, wanted "to try something new" when it filmed Kerouac's *The Subterraneans:* "It was the new literature. It was the new style with the young people. It bombed."
12. Kirby Ferlinghetti was Lawrence's wife.

night won't lead to writing a new novel—which is what is happening here as slowly, slowly they're all finding out where I live and getting on my route—I'll have to sell this house (where you were) eventually and move to country and put padlock on driveway fence—My trouble is that my name is so fucking used everywhere people think they shd. merely SEE me and that's all they need (not read the books, nothing, not ask my opinion about letters, O no, just SEE me, some write and say they want to TOUCH me which makes me shudder and you too I'm sure).—It'll all blow over some-day and I'll be like old Bob Frost with my woods and can write—but I refuse to be taken in even now—I refuse to be fucked up and never did like being fucked up by what Others want—This is how I wrote all that I did write, by paying no attention to "what was expected of me" and just work-ing for Joy. This is what Wagner did—And Whitman—This is why I will never marry—

When I get there I can hitch hike to Monterrey (actually take train num-ber 78 the Del Monte) to Monterrey and buy a carton of necessary gro-ceries and get a cab to drive me out presumably up the dirt road up Bixby canyon from Bixby bridge (if you give me full description of cabin)—Because I'll also have full rucksack with sleepbag, poncho, pots, etc. etc. on my back—But once there with rucksack and carton of groceries I don't have to come out but once a week maybe and hitch into Monterrey or south to state store for extrys—

If you have time to drive me out there, and you will know date well in advance, we can do same in yr car and have one night of wine and moonlight talk and you leave in morning and as I sleep in bag in woods you have bunk—I think that would be best if you have time, because we have business to talk about anyway, and conversation in general—And is there a kerosene lamp? Is there kerosene? Is the water in creek to drink? etc. If I were Gary or Albert Saijo I would build you a tea house while there, but dunno how, but I will build you a pine bough bed where you can lay a sleeping bag under a special tree in the no-rain season—

And I wanted to tell you: when yr letter came offering me that cabin for a few months I felt like it was what I was waiting for, just a night before I'd despaired in nightmares and said, "O my God, I need outside help now" and you sent it.

Here are excerpts from Allen's new poem "Magic Psalm from Peru":—(so far untyped)

"Present my skull with its cup of light
   to the President"

"Yes Kerouac, you were right, I AM the Devil

with my Jewish smiles and horned feet
on feminine Persian rugs"

He has been taking ether and yage (telepathic vine) with local witch-doctors and has exploded with these 2 long poems scribbled in ink, mailed to Peter, who mailed them to me, which are here now, on the desk, only copy in the world, so I mail back to Peter special delivery. His comment on his own work and experience in Peru to Peter was, among others, "Hmm, but it's been a romantic visionary experience anyway." Till the 22nd

Adios
Jack

WANT MAIL EM *YOU* SPECIAL DELIVERY?—SHH.

Traveling by train to Oakland from New York City, Kerouac changed to the Zephyr *in Chicago and signed exuberant postcards to his buddies Ferlinghetti and Ginsberg, using the fictitious names "Richard Wisp" and "Fyodor."*

TO LAWRENCE FERLINGHETTI

July 21, 1960
[Chicago]

Dear Lawrence,
   I be in Saturday evening, call you at store or home from my motel—I buy carton grub Sat. night—Allen in N.Y. a week, is typing up his psalms & visions.

Richard Wisp

TO ALLEN GINSBERG

[July 21, 1960
Chicago]

Dear Allen—
   Hold the Mescaline Notes till I get back in Fall—Don't give em to my mother—Wandering midday Chicago Loop waiting for Zephyr[13] to Oakland Russet—I feel strong again—Death is holy ecstasy—Life is holy suffering.

Fyodor

13. See the opening chapter of *Big Sur,* where Kerouac described traveling cross-country:

> in a pleasant roomette on the California Zephyr train watching America roll by outside my private picture window, really happy for the first time in three years, staying in the roomette all three days and three nights with my instant coffee and sandwiches ... (all over America highschool and college kids thinking "Jack Duluoz is 26 years old and on the road all the time hitch hiking" while there I am almost 40 years old, bored and jaded in a roomette bunk crashin across that Salt Flat)....

Back in Northport after suffering a nervous breakdown in Bixby Canyon and re-cuperating at Ferlinghetti's home in San Francisco, Kerouac wrote ecstatic letters high on burgundy wine describing his California experience to his closest friends. A year later, when he drew on these events in writing Big Sur, *his account cul-minated in a harrowing description of his alcoholic collapse. He became "wide awake," as he wrote in the novel, to "the horror of all the worlds the showing of it to me being damn well what I deserve anyway with my previous blithe yakkings about the sufferings of others in books."*

TO LAWRENCE FERLINGHETTI

Sept. 14, 1960
Northport, N.Y.

Dear Larry—

The flight back was fantastic and almost worth the extra 69 dollars (which is tax deductible for writers anyway)—By the time the pilot was ready to say "Welcome aboard" over the P.A. system he was already over Donner Pass!—I wrote a few poetic notes about Nevada but I'm afraid some of them were really about Utah finally—Then out come the hors d'oeuvres and good St. Julien red wine, over Grand Junction Colorado I'd already downed my first glass, over Denver the second was underway, by the time we were over Wichita I was switched to white wine (by this time mellow and dont-know-where-I-am)—In front of me sat a Chinese woman with 2 Pekinese dogs, an elegant woman—I watched her elegant way of eating but saw she didn't know how to unwrap the Ritz crackers from the cellophane pack so I gave her mine saying "For the dogs?"—"No, for me."—She ate Ritz Crackers all the way, drank none of the great French wine, and turned out to be the wife of the ambassador to U.S. from Taiwan—I even asked her if she knew Mr. Wong but she wanted to know which Mr. Wong and I forgot Victor's father's first name—They trot out the steak above Wichita I think and by the time they bring out the champagne and the pastries I look down and see a huge city.—"Chicago?" I ask the hostess. "No, Cleveland."—Then I order more champagne and write a few more notes and it's dark and I write the hostess a love note saying "I love you because you're a simple brunette" (you can imagine how gassed we all were) and she sat with me and chatted (lives in Sausalito) and finally I say to her authoritatively, "Well, we must be over Indiana by now" but she jumps up as the "Fasten Safety Belts" comes on and she goes to the P.A. and announces to tie up, we're landing at Idlewild! That's how the trip was—ending with pastries and champagne. You should have seen the floor of like melted snow in March fog over the Gate and out into the Pacific—great trip, great approach to the airport with you and beautiful Kirby and Victor—All well—Now the only thing I miss is your control tower. Those 2 days at your house were two of the best days of my life—I think the whole trip was good—The nervous breakdown has taught me something—You taught me invaluable tips about drinking (burgundy, which I've been doing, without sickness)—The 3 weeks alone in Bixby Canyon taught me a whole lot—Best of all I have a new novel to write about all this now, reaching back to last November as the start—I may or may not write it but I feel like it—Everything is fine—And if nothing else, the trip was worth the friendship which I have developed for you (is that correct?) the great feeling I have about you now—I didn't know you before—great.

Meanwhile Beat Anthology was returned intact to Sterling, he sent it to Dial Press but I think Dial will want to delete the dirty words in it so if you really want it, and want to print it en toto (maybe with new title so's not to conflict with "beatitude anthology") let me know—0909685746374i000000–999999999)))))))))))))))))))) [sic] I can get it for you if you want it now—[14]

Waiting on pins and needles for my new books and especially for the encyclopedia from Henry Evans[15]—At last minute I thought "O shucks, I forgot to throw the Tales of Genji in the box!" Next time, another box! You'll notice that since I "made money" and have had the chance to travel anywhere, I've taken only 2 trips and both of em to California!—Okay. And on your swing to the eastern southern colleges to lecture try to come to New York and stay at my house—I have tape recorders etc. books you can read, study, drink burgundy, etc. go to NY with me etc. Even so.

Tell Victor not to mail me a hundred pictures but just ten, I like them anyway. Too much of a package.

I miss you and Kirby and Homer and Victor just like a lost family— funny. I also miss Lew Welch and Phil and all the guys. Funny. Wonder what I'll call this book?

Just let me know what you want from this end. Give my especial love to Lew Embree and tell him to get on his motorcycle and get his guitar and go a-singing in the wind a while. He'll be alright. He was feeling low. The pity of it I wanted to spend a lot of time with Embree. But you saw what happened: it's a big movie and I gotta dig every bit of it. Movie with a happy ending. A plus tard, mon copain

Jack

14. The anthology Kerouac edited for Avon Books was never issued, but his writing was prominent in a spate of anthologies published during the first wave of interest in the Beats: *The Beat Generation and the Angry Young Men* edited by Gene Feldman and Max Gartenberg (New York: Citadel, 1958); *The New American Poetry 1945–1960* edited by Donald M. Allen (New York: Grove, 1960); *Beatitude Anthology* (San Francisco: City Lights, 1960); *The Beats* edited by Seymour Krim (New York: Fawcett, 1960); *The Beat Scene* edited by Elias Wilentz (New York: Corinth, 1960); *Casebook on the Beats* edited by Tom Parkinson (New York: Crowell, 1961); and *The Moderns* edited by LeRoi Jones (New York: Corinth, 1963).
15. Henry Evans edited the eleventh edition of the *Encyclopedia Britannica.*

[Mid-September 1960
Northport, New York]

Dear Phil & Lew

First, Phil, here's your 2 bucks, you now owe me 25¢ for all eternity—I'll never forget that day in the park when by some magic I was allowed to sleep and only woke up to see you sitting smoking digging the world go by—And woke up long enuf to enjoy that walk with you arm-in-arm down the temple steps[16]—It appears like I had my first serious nervous or mental breakdown this time but now that it's over I wonder if it wasnt some kind of satori, because I've changed—to the better in the sense of quietness and drinking only red burgundy—aw well, fuck it, who knows—but the desperation and fear has gone, for awhile anyway—and I'm kind of making my home here my monastery now. (The Rev. Mother presiding.)

Dear Lew

I didnt want to thank you for driving me[17] to Sur and back in front of Lenore—Couldnt sleep even that night in the skid row room except about 5 and then all went well—Spent 2 good days at Ferl's—and now I'm home and so healthy I can hardly keep my eyes open. Trip back on Ambassador flight of TWA was one long cocktail-wine-champagne-dinner (white wine, red wine, everything) and at one point I'm confidently telling the hostess "We're over Indiana about by now" and she jumps up and rushes to the P.A. and says "Tighten your, fasten yr safety belts, we're coming in to Idlewild." "Some Indiana!" I yelled at her. She was goodlooking but dull. I wrote her a love note. But anyway thank you again and again for all the

---

16. In Chapter 30 of *Big Sur*, Kerouac described his visit to Whalen (named Ben Fagan in the novel), when Philip smoked his pipe in the San Francisco park from noon to 6 P.M. while Jack (named Jack Duluoz) slept for six hours in the grass. When Kerouac finally woke up, he and his friend had a talk:

> "Ben I think I'm going crazy"—"You said that to me in 1955."—"Yeh but my brain's gettin soft from drinkin and drinkin and drinkin"—"What you need is a cup of tea I'd say if I didnt know that you're too crazy to know how really crazy you are.... Duluoz it's good for you to drink in a way 'cause you're awful stingy with yourself when you're sober"—

17. In *Big Sur*, Welch ("David Wain") and his lover the poet Lenore Kandel ("Romana Swartz") drove Kerouac back to the Ferlinghettis' cabin in Bixby Canyon, stopping en route to visit Neal and Carolyn Cassady ("Cody Pomeray" and "Evelyn Pomeray") at their home in Los Gatos:

> But Dave is anxious and so am I to see great Cody who is always the major part of my reason for journeying to the west coast so we call him up at Los Gatos 50 miles away down the Santa Clara Valley and I hear his dear sad voice saying "Been waitin for ya old buddy, come on down right away, but I'll be goin to work at midnight so hurry up and you can visit me at work soon's the boss leaves round two and I'll show you my new job of tire recappin and see if you cant bring a little somethin like a girl or sumptin, just kiddin, come on down pal—"

driving you've done for me. If you'll read Hemingway's novel in *Life* magazine[18] you'll recognize old Jack sitting there at yr right. Hemingway is critical of bad drivers & ecstatic over good ones and always has his red in his hand, his cock of Spanish light (he calls them light & heavy). "Eeels are excellent," sez he gobbling up an entire generation of baby eels in a sauce in Madrid. Ferling by the way, Lew, a wonderful guy, showed me how to drink: just burgundy: which I'm doing. Lots of goodies in store for you as you rush along the way you've been doing, but get rest too. Love to Lenore. Give my love to Jay and Bob Miller also, not to mention the other angels there (Les, Tom etc.) Old Blubberpuss signing off ... a bientot ... goodman ... goodmen all ... bye

Jack

By the way, Lew, my mother wanted to know if you still had your beard because it spoiled your handsomeness

TO ALLEN GINSBERG

Sept. 22, 1960
[Northport, New York]

Dear Allen,

Yes, just got back, big TWA Ambassador flight, tax deductible, with wine and champagne and filet mignon and Chinese Tapei ambassador's wife in front of me etc.—New York seems cowed and nasty after anarchistic crazy freewheeling Frisco—Saw everybody—Neal greater than ever, sweeter by far, looking good, healthy—Walks to work in Los Gatos now as tire recapper—would be willing to play Dean in On the Road movie, anything better than tire recapping—SP railroad won't take him back but want ME back (Al Hinkle reports) (because all read "Railroad Earth," forgetting what a lousy brakeman I was)—Much to tell you about Neal and everybody—Gave Neal money in crisis, he very glad now, crisis was solved and he got fine new rubywine Jeepster with good motor—gave him 100—(for rent) (he was fired)—He got new job he walks to—Had love affair (I did) and almost got married with his mistress Jacky but I was drunk—Prior to drunkenness I was alone 3 weeks in woods in fine quiet fog with animals only and learned a lot—Have changed, in fact—Am quieter, don't drink as much, or so often at least, and have started new quiet home reading habits. For instance had 11th edition of encyclopedia brittanica mailed to me (35 bucks whole price) 29 volumes containing 30,000 pages with exactly 65,000,000 words of scholarly Oxford and Cambridge prose (65 million that is) and last night stayed up till 5 a.m. amazed in that sea of prose—

18. *Life* published Hemingway's narrative about bullfighting in Spain, "The Dangerous Summer," in three issues in September 1960.

looked up Logia where Jesus is reported to have said (on old Egyptian pa-pyri dating to 2nd century) that one must not cease seeking for the kingdom & WILL WAKE UP "A S T O N I S H E D" in the kingdom! (just like my bliss-astonishment of golden eternity faint)—Apocrypha, Shmapocrypha!—Thought I'd also look up bats as there was a bat in Big Sur kept circling my sleepingbag every night til dawn, was referred to Chiroptera (Chirop is Greek for "hand," tera "wing")—found what amounts to a small volume of complete technical explanation with pictures and diagrams—This is the prize of prizes! I've been waiting for this 29 volume edition since I first saw it age 16 in Lowell High library—It's possible to make complete studies in Theology of ALL religions, for instance, or study of all Tribes in the World, or all Zoology, all History to 1909, all Campaigns till then in detail, all Biography till then, all Mysticism, all Kabbalas and Shmabbalas, all rare scholarly treatises on Old and New Testaments, all about Buddha, Hindus, rare exotic Malayan religions, visions, all Ornithology, Optometry, Pastometry, Futureometry and in other woids ALL—I simply can't believe such an ocean as the Pacific any more'n this encyclopedia—so my new reading habits: also bought 50 bucks worth of books from Ferling and have those (Pound, etc)—and soberly studying now, writing new book (started anyway)—doing exercise (headstands, snake pushups, bent bow and knee bend and breathing)—feeling fine—lost 10 or 15 pounds—only got drunk once since home 2 weeks. Wanted to get new novel in or underway before calling you but made a false start. Had to keep Henri Cru away who went and got himself job as electrician in Northport (!) and wanted to inundate my life as usual with all the ridiculous trivialities of his fancy—so he mad. But I can't worry about every tom dick and harry who used to leave me alone to write visions of neal at my lonely happy rolltop desk in the early fifties.

Meanwhile, at Big Sur, I sat by sea every day, sometimes in dismal foggy roraring dark of cliffs and huge waves, and wrote SEA, first part, SEA: the Pacific Ocean at Big Sur California. All sound of waves, like James Joyce was going to do. Wrote mostly with eyes closed, as if blind Homer. Read it to gang by oil lamp. McClure, etc. Neal, etc. all listened but it's just like Old Angel, only more wave-plop kerplosh sounds, the sea don't talk in long sentences but comes in pieces, as like this:

No human words bespeak
  the token sorrow older
  than old this wave
  becrashing smarts the
    sand with plosh
    of twirled sandy
  thought—Ah change
    the world? Ah set
    the fee? Are rope the

angels in all the sea?
Ah ropey otter
barnacle d be—

(barnacle d be), rather, with the "d" all alone—Anyway this, and what Logia Jesus said about astonishment of paradise, seems to me much more on the right tracks of world peace and joy than all the recent communist and general political hysteria rioting and false screaming. Cuba Shmuba—I will come New York, open yr lock with key you gave me, wait if you not there, am buying rucksack etc., will see Lucien etc. so see you & Petey soon. Okay. Will come around the 28th—meanwhile please drop another line and enclose *Mescaline Notes* & *Gregory Letters* for the Cream File.

Jean

TO NEAL CASSADY

[September 1960
Northport, New York]

Dear Neal—

Well, love, a little typing practice here as I gets ready to write a new book god knows why but there just ain't anything else for me to do and certainly the story of the world as seen thru my eye is story enough to please enough readers in enough brown chairs over the canals of time from here to umpteen toot toot poop oopoopoopoop—rag rag and what is this i want to tell you, well let's see, first off (just typing practice you see) but with a message which is: i left frisco without seeing you because i was staying at ferlinghetti's house the last 2 days and he drove me to the airport in the morning, well to the store first, where i bought a crate of books, then to the airport and i knew you were walking in los gatos at the time—well there was just no sense wasting money or time to call—all i want to say is Everything is fine, everything is okay, i never was so glad in my life my little measly contribution to yr household turned out so good what with the new car, the new job, why man when you blatted open that door in big sur and stood there with yr various blondes and blonds it was amazing, i felt like, well it was dark in the cabin remember and me and mc clure was talking and you sneaked up and suddenly when the door was burst open all the light came in and you stood there all 5 of you like archangels but you most of all goddamit face it you looked like an archangel with arm extended as you had—

and then when you told me how beautiful everything had worked out and we walked down the trail bliazast to the fence (ing) it felt like the old days when things used to work out for both of us anyway no matter what happened—As to Jacqueline what can I say? I want to be a bachelor, she is by far the most sensitive gal in the world and too much for me she made me very nervous, the last few days with her were hell and that little kid is a witch for sure the way he kept getting on my nerves, he's no child at all, there's something sinister about him but how could I tell jacqueline beyond in monterrey in the bar I did say "He's a little cretinous" as she was asking me where to put him or put him away or which, that got her mother instinct mad naturally and she said "You're so fucking abnormal"—(me)—which I don't deny goddamit but I want to be peaceful, I couldn't spend the rest of my life with her beating him every hour because she does the fool thing of answering every one of his little questions, I tried to explain to her how to let the little bastards croon and have a good time unnoticed among their elders like the kids in Mexico—but it broke my heart because the mere sound of jacky's voice is enough to break any man's heart, man if she lookt as good or as completely good as the sound of that voice!—Tho when we went to the beach alone and she wandered off down the beach alone I couldn't help turn back the babbling words in my head (I had nothing but babbling words in my head for a week, i almost went bats) saying S T C A R O L Y N B Y T H E S E A and I wish now I had some book or other to look up and find out who that was and what she did—but Neal, Neal, the poor girl, and to think that fucking ass hole got to her first and knocked her up that very guy who lost your greatest work—so goes the dostoevskyan world—

anyway i just wanted you to know i left frisco without calling you because it really wasn't necessary just to blat over the phone, i knew i was just too exhausted to (or in fact to get anybody to drive me) down there, to los gatos, so that was that—but the thing that lifts my soul is that everything is back to normal, the way it should be, you and carolyn and the nice ranchito home and the kids happy and old uncle jack back in the fold—so that the next time i come to californy to look for used cars, orange ade coming out of fountains, to make a whole lotta money, dear okie, i'll go stay with you if it's alright because I tell you there's just too much balling going on in the city itself altho I love it of course—My next trip will be to Paree, after my birthday, March, and then I'll be headed back for californiay again—I'd like it if you could write me a letter once in a while, & Carolyn too, and thank her for sewing my shirt—Hold that shirt there! You can wear it meanwhile! when you come home all tired from the recapping used hole just ask carolyn to fluff you up some nice bacon and eggs, take a shower, put on a tea shirt, over that put on my magic sewn flannel shirt, you can even wear my pants tho they are too big for you and if you feel like it you can even sleep in my filthy old sewn torn sleepingbag—all magic garments and shifts with which I did make it while you were behind those iron bars for nothing—I don't blame you for looking a little stern and mebbe a little frightened the night i barged in there for my full pack with lew welch and lenore and jacky came in etc.—what do you think about your poor old buddy now? is he crazy? is he going to the dog? to hell? is he going to heaven on the arm of somebody he helped? he who helped no one?—

are you going to write or don't you have time? (books, I mean)

anyway send me letters now and then and tell me also what's with jacky inside and what's happening and what happened to jaime who they said was going mad the day I left—and who IS that jaime and what's the story? what books you could write about everything that's happened all yr life, like proust, like me when I write a book it's just a chapter in the whole story but there wd be no literature in the world safe to say i would rather read than yr own remembrance of things—

i've come to an impasse in style: shall i write like railroad earth? shall I write like dharma bums for everybody to understand (sailors chewing gum under the reading lamp in greyhound buses)—what'll I do? it's too late for me to write clearly like in dharma bums—o it's a terrible stew—

haven't seen allen yet—the trip back TWA ambassador flight was one long champagne and wine party with steak in the middle, a coupla hors d'oeuvres covered the distance between Grand Junction and Wichita mind you—was worth it. Enuf for now. Just to say, all's well and I love you as ever and Carolyn too and Johnny too and the whole gang. I even love the old potbellied cowboy at the rodeo hiss-the-villain playhouse because he made it possible for us to get out of there—and go meet jacky—ugh—to think that I kept calling her lucien—but there's a sobbing break in her voice (just like you say, Blubberpuss) that even anybody would understand is almost unbearable—i mean, i would tell Carolyn that—there's something so bad needs help there but not me! I wont do it! Whats going to happen to her? she said she was going to kill kid and self—i ran away—she said she was going to nunnery—Did I understand the papers to say we were eloping to Mexico? wow—

since I'm back home have been sleeping, eating, exercising, walking, having quiet time, planning new books, reading, having quiet ball as tho, and by god this is true, i am now making my home my monastery, Rev. Mother presiding—once in a while I jump the wall and go into N.Y. with my collar turned backward again—and Lois comes to see me on Fridays for non-nunnery type teachings naturally altho im sure carolyn would object—Give old steamy pants my regards anyway—And Neal, take it easy, enjoy home life, beware of watchers and finks mebbe around you mebbe—just stay home quietly in yr robe write letters to your old boy—By God we WILL end up 2 old bums in the alley! It's coming closer all the time! Silverplated garbage cans! Tuxedo bums! with velvet hoods and a moat!

A Dios
means
To God
Jack

Writing to Ferlinghetti about Book of Dreams, *Kerouac created a "Table of Characters" for his publisher to insert at the beginning of the volume. The table linked the pseudonyms of people mentioned in* Book of Dreams *with the names Jack had given them as characters in his three most popular novels:* On the Road, The Subterraneans, *and* The Dharma Bums.

TO LAWRENCE FERLINGHETTI

[September 1960
Northport, New York]

Larry,

This is the way I'd like the front of the book to look like. The table is useful, literarily charming, etc. and connects BOOK OF DREAMS to the excitement of the novels.

That green sleepingbag cover in yr. cabin is not mine, probably it's Lew Welch's.

Still haven't put on weight since I got back, following your advice about burgundy, cheese, fruits, etc. and Kirby's advice about dark bread (rye or pumpernickle). But the same old sad moon of Autumn. Going to New England this weekend in car with 2 guys to dig land for sale north of Laconia N.H. for future cabin. "Ma" doesn't want to move back to Lowell, neither do I, actually, because old friends & relatives would ring the doorbell all day thinking I have millions of dollars to give them, really. Tho I may do it, move back "home," in my old age, in cabin anyway. "A thatched hut in Lowell."

When you come east don't forget you stay at my house a few days, browse thru record collection jazz, 11th edition of Henry Evans, etc. Love to sweet Kirby. I just got nutty letter from Joanne Kyger Snyder from Japan telling me all about Jacky Gibson in earlier days. Gary himself is meditating and didn't put in a word.

Just sent off my answering drawing to Victor Wong. Better ones en route as soon's I buy Yellowjack felt tips.

I think these 3 pages are fine for frontbook format. Let me know. Meanwhile send galleys for me to correct. I'll send you a copy of ($4.50) (free) LONESOME TRAVELER[19] this month so you send me HER[20].

Hope all's well with yr. cabin, no unwelcome visitors and all clean and quiet. Okay. Soon

Jean Louis
Jack

I'm seeing Allen tomorrow—I'm enjoying Beckett's books.

19. McGraw-Hill had commissioned a drawing of Kerouac by Larry Rivers for the cover of *Lonesome Traveler.*
20. Ferlinghetti's first published novel.

Sept. 24, 1960
[Northport, New York]

Dear L:

From Stormonth's *Dictionary of the English Language:* "CACOETHES,[21] n. (Gr. *kakos,* bad; *ethos,* custom, habit), bad custom or habit, generally applied to inveterate scribblers."

By the way, rec'd my wonderful 11th edition of Encyc. Brittanica and am having a big ball reading up on all mysticism etc. The articles are written in great old prose, by Cambridge and Oxford scholars. 65 million words! You oughta get one! Plus tard

Jack

Let me know when DREAMS proofs and orig. black ms. comin ...

[Before October 18, 1960
Northport, New York]

Dear Larry,

I *threw away* the first preface—but I had another alternate I saved, which is all I can send you now & you can use it for blurb notes—No, I don't wanta write the blurb because it wd. take me weeks of anguish, these things are harder for me than writing "artistically." Here is the preface I saved:

"BOOK OF DREAMS was the easiest book to write—When I woke up from my sleep I just lay there looking at the pictures that were fading slowly like in a movie fadeout into the recesses of my subconscious mind—As soon (one minute or so) as I had assembled them together with any earlier dreams of the evening I could catch, like fish in a deep pool, I got my weary bones out of bed & through eyes swollen with sleep swiftly scribbled in pencil in my little DR notebook till I had exhausted every rememberable item—I wrote nonstop so that the subconscious could speak for itself in its own form, that is, uninterruptedly flowing & rippling—Being half awake I hardly knew what I was doing let alone writing.

But an hour later, over coffee, what shame I'd feel sometimes to see such naked revelations so insouciantly stated—But that is because the subconscious mind (the *manas* working thru from the *alaya-vijnana*) does not make any mental discriminations of good or bad,

21. Kerouac's pseudonym for Kenneth Rexroth in *The Dharma Bums.*

thisa or thata, it just deals with the realities, What Is. It is only with our conscious mind (the *mano-vijnana*) that we judge and make arbitrary conceptions, that is, that we arbitrate and lay down laws about should & shouldn't be written or done. So I wrote these dreams with eerie sleepingcap head & now I'm glad I did.

Everybody interested in their dreams should use the method of fishing their dreams out *in time* before they disappear forever."

Larry, I thought it was Lew Welch had your key when I left. If Cassady had an extra set of your keys, write him at 18231 Bancroft Ave., Los Gatos, to mail them to you or drop them off at Jacky's or your store.

I like the Beatitude #17 and the anthology too (starting off with Peter was a stroke of genius)—I'm mailing you 2 copies of Lonesome Traveler tomorrow (one for Lew Embree)—your *beatitude* mag. so much better printwise, too—You could contact Allen for future material: Huncke, Wieners, etc. etc. He has a kitchenful of writings from everywhere.

Phil Whalen coming to see me here soon—

I feel guilty about all those mixed up keys—Montgomery just sent me a photo of the Bixby Bridge—I sure wish you come to NY but I guess you wont—Have a good time in the Carib isles (Haiti too?)—I'm reading HER, it is on my toilet shelf, I have red rings around my ass from sitting on the bowl reading HER—

I hopes you can use above notes . . . It may be too late, but Robert Frank has a picture of me *sleeping* that would have been perfect . . . still time? I can get it. Love,

Jean Louis

TO LAWRENCE FERLINGHETTI

[October 18, 1960
Northport, New York]

Dear Larry—

Waiting for Dreams, ready to proof them, will correct Table of Characters, write better shorter intro. & send whole works back to you together with a copy of Lonesome Traveler in one package—Am writing to a man about a log cabin in Vermont—My "Lowell" dream was of hills to the north—Anyway, if you go Cuba be careful, they'll say you invading—As to cabin broken in to, two 18 year old short 5-foot kids once approached yr place and yelled "Is anybody home?" & said they were trapped, didn't know how to get out of canyon, said their car was parked above near bridge, I showed them how to go round back to bridge via Alf gate, when they got overhead on pass they threw rocks on your roof, missed me—lookt like reform schoolers—Might be someone like them—I also saw big gangs of Sunday hotrodders climb down to beach on Sundays but they climbed back again while two shorties went through creek path—So watch for two shorties, 18, little prigs—almost hit me on head—Wanted to know if I was "hunter," I shoulda said yes—HER is very good, will surprise lotta people, is strange long thinlegged shadow Paris sidewalk dream of birds

Jean

In November 1960, Kerouac read an M.A. thesis on his work written by Granville H. Jones, a young instructor at Carnegie Tech. Kerouac was so impressed by the thesis that he wrote Jones a long thank-you letter, admitting that he "was becoming terribly discouraged by the scandalous lack of critical fairness" shown by reviewers of his books.

TO GRANVILLE H. JONES

[November 22, 1960
Northport, New York]

Dear Granville

Your thesis was given to me by Jas. Benenson. It is such a neat volume, I mean the typing, the exhaustive bibliographies, the whole works. It is the only thing too that has made me happy in three years, since the publication of On the Road and the subsequent sickeningness of "being famous" (being used by everybody and his uncle) and of course the nausea of phoney criticisms and even worse the nausea of false enthusiasms based on the wrong reasons (as for instance those who "admire" me for being so "wild & irresponsible" etc.)

What you've written about me has restored my faith in my own writing. What you say, I knew (not being vain), always knew. But no one ever said it out loud, or cared to say it. And I was becoming terribly discouraged by the scandalous lack of critical fairness.

All my fellow writers look at your title page green with envy. Now I'm really going to get it from ALL sides. But as Jimmy B. says, it's the Academic recognition that will really take care of me in my old age (beans money & beans love), NOT the temporary admiration for the wrong reasons coming from the wrong thinkers.

The vision of America is being destroyed now by the beatnik movement which is not the "beat generation" I proposed any more but a big move-in from intellectual dissident wrecks of all kinds and now even anti-American, America-haters of all kinds with placards who call themselves "beatniks."

What you've written about let's say is the work of Kerouac the Younger. What comes now, after this, is that of Kerouac the Elder. It will be quite different, harsher, bitter at times, not any bitterer than Wolfe's later things in You Cant Go Home Again or the "bitterness" of poor Whitman in Specimen Days. But I'm changing. I'm middle aged now and no longer an enthusiastic college boy lyrically feeling America. As Joyce says, first comes the Lyric, then the Dramatic, then the Epic. I hope for me too.

Well, I only wanted to thank you and thank you and thank you and also for restoring my love of America which has finally come around to discovering one of her real lovers, but I rambled on like this. But thank you, and for the fine copy of the thesis, which I treasure on my shelf, and I hope you get it published with some university press someday.

Yes, and my "individuality" is such, today, that I fear for the worst between the camps of America-lovers & America-haters so called, the communists who hate America, the FBI who "love" it. Ouch. But fuck em, I'll go on scribbling. And get a cabin in the woods too, where I just admire and don't get involved in discussions about "society problems"—where I just admire that same old eve star ... which droopeth on Iowa tonight just as ever, right? no matter what I talk about in this sad letter of beholdenness & shame (shame that I might not live up to what you wrote about me) [....]

Later
Jack

At the end of November 1960, Kerouac heard from his sister, Caroline, in Orlando, Florida, who offered to work as his secretary. Kerouac was feeling euphoric after another good review in The New York Times *by Daniel Talbot, who found* Lonesome Traveler *"vintage Kerouac" because "his adventures, although slight, [are invested] with an incredible animal word-energy.... Quite obviously any 9 to 5'er in America would throw over his I.B.M. and inkpot in a second to do what Kerouac has done, if he had sufficient courage and anarchy." Kerouac politely turned down Nin's offer, explaining, "I want to go on being a bum: that's the secret of my joy, and without my joy there's nothing to write about." His mother— as usual—added her own comments in a postscript.*

TO CAROLINE KEROUAC BLAKE

[Postmarked November 26, 1960
Northport, New York]

Dear Nin,

You see I'm probably the only "famous" writer in the world who pays no attention to his mail—A lot of it I just throw away, a lot of it I just file away in my Interesting Letters or Fan Letters files—When I get embossed invitation from Sherman Billingsley to attend the Celebrity Party at the Stork Club I'm hep enough to know (1) He only wants me to get in the habit of spending $200 a night for drinks and steak in his joint, (2) His reasons for inviting me are not because of what I wrote but because I'm a "writer" so I just file the embossed invitation away and dont answer him at all. (Then he's not offended, he thinks I've never gotten it)—See? Or when the committee for a Better Africa invites me to Nigeria as a goodwill ambassador I simply pretend I'm out of town for a long time by not answering. (This is what [Marlon] Brando does, he simply doesnt answer his public type mail, he didnt even answer me about filming ON THE ROAD three years ago, he's smart. He goes about his business, which is making movies, period.) Me too, I just go about my business of writing and trying to stay home as much as possible and playing with the cats and eating with Ma and watching TV and studying my books, like I always did. Otherwise I'd let myself be snaked into the position of great writers like Steinbeck who lost his greatness because he did everything everybody wanted him to do: attended dreary luncheons, lectured around the country, joined pestiferous Lit'ry Guilds with more luncheons, more talk, more kudos, wrote articles when asked (as though he had written *Grapes of Wrath* on order like that!) and finally deteriorated into a businessman with a secretary and piles of mail. I want to go on being a bum: that's the secret of my joy, and without my joy there's nothing to write about.

Remember when in North Carolina in January of 1956 when Ma went to Manda's funeral in Brooklyn, and you and Paul were working, and I was feeding little Paul during the days, and I wrote *Gerard* on the kitchen table after you all went to bed? Did I get millions of silly letters then to interrupt me?

Thats why I dont need a secretary. But if I could deduct off my income tax the price of a secretary, I'd do it. But you cant deduct that, Ti Nin, can you? I'll ask my wonderful accountant Mr. Barton G. Hocker in February see what he says. He knows everything about taxes. Mainly I dont want to complicate things: like Paul's idea to start a cattle ranch in Alabama was fine but think of all the complications, the bills, the gear to buy, the vet bills, the thisa and thata, I'd rather just live quietly because you see the writing of a novel may take a few weeks but the thinking out of a novel takes years and years of quiet sitting in a chair. With no worldly distractions.

The first thing I shd. do is get me a Jeepster stationwagon ... well, that's easy, what I need is a license—and then I could go find a good property in the New England woods and build a cabin by carpenters ... and also like drive to Montana in the summer and park my jeepster in the sheep hills and sketch the scene and sleep with the flap out, in sleepingbag, and be free.... This summer in Big Sur (I got there via the California Zephyr train, riding all the way with my own lunch and coffee in a roomette) I learned my old woods life again: making coffee on a woodfire, the fire quiet and glowing, the creek gurgling ... suddenly in the peace of day and night and day and night of that I began to write again ... What I need is not more money, not more complications, but a return to the Ti Jean who hid in his room on Sarah Avenue and drew his cartoons, his gloomy comedies, while Pa and Ma and Ti Nin had fun downstairs ... and then remember my long blizzard walks on Sundays to Pine brook? See ya later Ti Nin, and mon amour

Ti Jean x x x

[Mémêre's note] Honey—

Well here it is. He sobered up some. Anyway I knew the answer. Really Honey he dont need a secretary he has plenty of time to take care of his little Business. I wish it could have been otherwise and have you as a helper for Jack. But maybe latter [sic]. As he keeps writing it's possible he'll get Bigger then he will really need help and he wants me to tell you he'll remember you and take you along with him because here's his very words. You are very well-informed on finance and tax business and a very good accountant and he has nobody else in mind that would be so good and helpful to him, so sooner or later, he will ask your help. Just wait and see. But right now he can manage. Gosh Nin isn't that picture awful [Robert Frank's photograph of Kerouac in a cowboy hat that accompanied *The New York Times* review of *Lonesome Traveler*]. Some crazy artist plunk a hat on his head and made him look like "Jessie James." I offered some real nice pictures of Jack taken in North Carolina. They said they were too good looking so they cooked that one. With no *apologies*. Today, day after Thanksgiving, this house has been overflowing with people and the phone rings every hour on the hour.[22] And I'm plump [sic] tired. It's now 12 midnight I'm in my room—and six people are up in his room. Wish they'd go home. So write me soon. Love to all of you.

Old Mémêre xxxx

In response to Philip Whalen, who sent a Christmas card and a second copy of his Auerhahn Press volume Memoirs of an Interglacial Age, *poems written in Oregon in 1958 and 1959, Kerouac dropped his friend a postcard describing the plans for his holidays with Mémêre at home.*

TO PHILIP WHALEN

[December 16, 1960
Northport, New York]

Dear Phil—

Rec'd MEMOIRS & Christmas card—Thank you—But now that I'm sober I know why tape recorder *whistled*—I was too drunk to let it *rest*, cool

---

22. One of the telephone calls that day was from Allen Ginsberg, who phoned Jack after taking his first LSD with Timothy Leary in Boston. According to Leary, Allen shouted into the telephone that Jack and Gabrielle should join him: "Allen says he is the Messiah and he's calling Kerouac to start a peace and love movement." See Timothy Leary's article "In the Beginning, Leary Turned on Ginsberg and Saw that It Was Good," in *Esquire* (July 1968).

off the motor—Trading in, getting a German Wollensack—so next time we
make good records & move huge steaks—How's Les?—Welch?—Mémêre is
fine:—Xmas tree, manger, sock of pingpong balls & winding toys for kitties,
Turkey for Xmas to be immersed in quart of sherry basting, & I buy her Polaroid camera for quick kitty pictures.

Love
Jack

1961

After a quiet New Year's Eve at home with his mother, Kerouac was alarmed to learn early in 1961 that his former wife Joan Haverty Kerouac Aly, now separated from her second husband, was suing him in New York State Superior Court for child support, claiming $20,000 to cover what she said was Jack's share of her expenses caring for their nine-year-old daughter, Janet. Joan told reporters that Kerouac was earning $50,000 a year, a greatly inflated figure since all of Kerouac's hardbound books issued by mainstream publishers after The Dharma Bums *had been remaindered, including his latest book,* Lonesome Traveler.*

Mémère wrote her daughter, Caroline, on January 25, 1961, that the lawsuit was an "awful strain on Jack and me too.... Jack says it makes him so sick to see his name in every paper and never anything good.... I just hate to go to 'shop' [in Northport] everyone stares at me and I feel like I want to crawl in a Hole." Four days later, Gabrielle wrote Caroline that there were so many newspaper stories about the lawsuit that she was "fit to be tied. My nerves are a wreck. And Jack is no d-am help. He keeps himself 'stewed' to forget his troubles. There's always someone at the door. I guess some of them are reporters. I dont let no one in. I dont even answer the door. But all this goings on is killing me." Gabrielle confided to her daughter that her spirits had been lifted by an article in Time *magazine on January 20, 1961, mentioning that "while Jack Kennedy read American history, Jackie wolfed down four or five novels, ranging from Colette to Kerouac, a week." Mémère concluded, "The First Lady of the Land reads Jack's books: well it makes us feel good inside and I believe this little plug of 'Kerouac' might help to publicize a bit. We've got to have some good in between, eh."*

On February 2, 1961, Kerouac wrote Philip Whalen about his legal problems with Joan Aly. He also described a recent dream that he was dying, perhaps prompted by memories of the LSD experience he had in January 1961 at Ginsberg's Lower East Side apartment. Dropping acid with Allen apparently convinced Jack that psilocybin-induced "instant" enlightenment was impossible, and he insisted to Ginsberg and Timothy Leary that "Walking on water wasn't built in a day." Jack resisted the idea of hallucinogens as a panacea, arguing that the Communists had used them for brainwashing American prisoners of war in Korea. Later Leary wrote in Flashbacks *(1980) that*

Throughout the night Kerouac remained unmovably the Catholic carouser, an old-style Bohemian without a hippie bone in his body. Jack Kerouac opened the neural doors to the future, looked ahead, and didn't see his place in it. Not for him the utopian pluralist optimism of the sixties.

Kerouac ended his February 2, 1961, letter to Whalen encouraging his friend to keep on writing what Philip called his "Goofbook." There Whalen attempted to practice Kerouac's method of spontaneous prose before preparing his dinner of "mitloat [sic], baked acorn squash, spuds, salad, new pot of coffee, cheese & fruit."

TO PHILIP WHALEN

[February 2, 1961
Northport, New York]

Dear Phil

Things all fucked up on this end, as you may've heard, about an ex-wife wants all my money and Mémère's.... so today Mémère and me and my lawyer (Allen G's brother) go out to arrange finances ... But all this will prove unnecessary as soon as I get a blood test proving the daughter isnt mine (wait and see) (I remember circumstances) ... which puts me in the mind of never having anything to do with women any more. Not even Lois. And certainly not predatory Jackies.

Read your goofbook, it is you at youse best, Allen wants to see it to-morrow. Right now another guy is reading it (a fan of ours from town here). The drawings are terrific: do more drawings, you're a natural artist. Hey! why don't you start writing haiku with drawing beside it, like old Japs.

I liked goofbook bettern foogbook, which was stuffy-er..... And of course I was highly honored by youse addressing it to me.

I wrote drunk letter to Ferling calling him funny names like bastard, I think he took it seriously, tell him not to..... I was calling him down on his sympathy for Cuban Firingsquad Raoul Che Guevara Murder Revolution.

O well. But I love Ferling ... just wrote him.

Les comes across funny in Goofbook, the way he keeps coming in with latest news or latest question, & meanwhile you have 12 separate stews on the cover over 12 separate days of takes. I miss you.

Pome on back of this is by Robert Lax, a Jewish guy who is Catholic convert of a sort, in any case a strange wonderful laughing Buddha. Laughs all the time. Is Editor of Catholic Magazine Jubilee, and best friend of Thomas Merton the Trappist Divine.

I sent postcard to Lew Welch saying just "Hello, fish prayer" and he wrote back postcard saying "Small sentence for driving yourself sane on any occasion, deliberately, with emphasis, 'So it's ALL come to this!' yum yum Leo"

Allen was here and made crazy records, tapes. So did Lax and others. I have fine collection.

Allen and Peter going to join Gregory in Greece next month. Want me to come but I'm in hot water with supreme court, taxes, etc. and drinking myself into ugly ghoul.

Drinking Christian Brothers Port (tawny) on the rocks, day in day out.

Almost died t'other night in a dream ... wow. Dreamed I was dying suddenly and screaming for help but no sound came from my voice and suddenly I gave in, gave myself up to GOD (altho it was dark there it was God) and when I gave in, gave myself and soul up utterly, I woke up and what did I see? a portrait of John Kerouac on the back cover of Town & City absolutely and truthfully floating across the darkness of my room. I guess my eyes were rolling, like dying men's eyes roll. I followed the floating portrait with rolling eyes. Never saw such a thing. At least it was a dark haired man's portrait.

Clear as day.
    Awful.
        Hate it.
            No wonder sentient beings fear death.
        What we gonna do?

Buddha was right. I'm going back to Buddha.

An absolute stranger came in the house t'other night wanting to borrow $150! It's sinister. Everybody wants money; they're all doing ANYTHING for money. It wouldn't be so sinister if it hadn't been for the fact that I did NOT write my books in expectation of ever even publishing them let alone making money. Bell's ringing. Allen's brother Eugene is here, I'll mail this off to you and write to you later, soon. We're going out to bank. Love you, Phil, and keep writing that goofbook.... We'll do something with it, like Evergreen or something, altho since Don Allen left it not so hot magazine any more. Love now, see you soon

Ti Jean
Jack

TO JACK KEROUAC FROM PHILIP WHALEN

[February 1961
San Francisco]

[excerpt from Philip Whalen's "Goofbook"]

When it's warm enough in here (I've lighted the gas oven, our only heat)—I'll take a shower, I enjoy washing & inspecting my body, my skin is very fine.

The thing is, I've just discovered, I'm not WRITING much of this, I'm putting down what I think or see or hear inside & outside my head—the pencil is writing & I am, I guess, elsewhere, or feeling/thinking something which doesn't show here, isn't yet broke through onto the page—except maybe in the case of those flowers, ducks &c. above. Question mark. I keep forgetting that this is paper & graphite—the "modern" painters from Cezanne to Picasso have complained that the academic & historical painters were trying to make the viewer forget that he was looking at something made of canvas & paint, tried to make the audience imagine it was looking at real persons or seeing out of a window. Maybe I think the reader as he looks at this is looking at me instead of words? "A fearful error, my dear!", as Burroughs says,

So I shall write a word.

(& immediately, I'm stuck, can't think of a word—but suppose I put down one that I like) . . . . (long pause to think)

P E C U L I A R

& I suppose I could arrange a whole lot of such words into pieces like Stein's TENDER BUTTONS, but that isn't what I want to do, seeing that it is possible & already been done. Likewise, telling a story is out of the question, I can tell a story in a couple of pages & get bored with it. (I don't throw it away afterwards, I keep everything I write, but there it stays & I forget it) & poems are a nuisance, I write lots of them, some people like them but the poems seldom tell all I must—only what must be written right then.

Same with book for you. I think, "where will it go from here"—& "isn't this the end of it?" & "9 pages of handwriting, a great deal of space taken up with pictures, quotes & pompous essay isn't a book" & I am resolved (I tell myself) not to stop until I come to the end of "words I want to put here."

Doing this & WRITING—same difference as between indiscriminate balling, jacking off &c., & fucking with a woman you love & who loves you in return. One is momentary pleasure; the other is making it, a high, a breakthrough.

MORE   MORNING   A TURNING
VISION
NOT ocular,
knowledge/feeling/instant: THIS IS THE WAY IT IS
TATHATA ("SUCH")
as music, what it is
(I guess) when you're digging Sinatra
TOTAL POSSIBILITY FREEDOM SHAPE WORLDS NOW YES
all kinds worlds
happening happy all directions—also gone by & nothing

changed nor even started

OK

in any case

I'm fond of saying

"A RARE DELIGHT"

Like all the people I love I think you suffer too much or anyhow more than necessary & in that aspect you're a meathead—while realizing that you're very great—in fact almost anybody is got more on the ball, more brains, compassion &c than I

*

& now I stop & cook dinner

*

& wait for it to bake

*

PRAJNAPARAMITAHRIDAYA MANTRAM: GATE, GATE, PARAGATE, PARASAMGATE, BODHI, SVAHA!

i.e.;

"Dinner wil be ready sometime. Mitloaf, baked acorn squash, spuds, salad, new pot of coffee, cheese & fruit. SVAHA!" Thitherwards my heart is yearning. Also my belly....

On February 15, 1961, Kerouac answered a fan letter from Bill Michell, a student at the University of Pennsylvania, with a testy postcard insisting, "I am a Catholic Conservative."

TO BILL MICHELL

[Postmarked February 15, 1961
Northport, New York]

Dear Mitch

Whattayou mean my "status"? If you cared I would care less. In answer to specific questions (1) *The Town and the City* is my first book, youthful book, influence of Thomas Wolfe, while *The Subterraneans* is a later book patterned after *Notes from the Underground* of Dostoevsky ... and yes, like you say, "simply a case of different situations for different styles." (2) Yes, I'm a "stay-at-home" but I have jazz, booze, visiting girlfriends, friends, etc. dont like to go in public any more, too many blandishments all of em false hearted.... "Original members" of Beat Gen. means it started out in 1948 as a group of poets, beardless, with no political beefs, no idea of "nonconformity," just poets. Today's "beatnik" cant even recognize Stan Gets [sic] when he hears him, or even tell the tune he's playing, etc. "Beatniks" are Henry Wallaceniks jumped on the movement for leftwing reasons. I am a Catholic Conservative.

Jack Kerouac

On April 14, 1961, Kerouac dropped a postcard to Ginsberg in Paris on the first stage of a two-year trip around the world. Jack praised the new volume of Kaddish and Other Poems, *Number 14 in the City Lights Pocket Poets series. Kerouac and his mother were in the process of moving back to Orlando after they decided that public opinion was against them in Northport because of newspaper stories about Joan Aly's child support case. Joan also sold her story to* Confidential *magazine, which titled her ghost-written article in its August 1961 issue "My Ex-Husband Jack Kerouac Is An Ingrate." Before leaving Northport, Kerouac wrote Philip Whalen on March 30:*

> *Old committees of Northport ladies go around removing my books from local book racks. Why should I purchase anything in N'Port? Getting out of here. They say, "There's a nest of beatniks around here and we're going to drive them out." Meanwhile "Gun Girl" stays on the rack, first paragraph all about how she eases her bra off, lip lick. I wish I had Ferlinghetti's boundlessly delighted enthusiastic strength.*

When a new air-conditioned house at 1309 Alfred Drive, two doors from Nin's tract home close to a supermarket, went on sale ten miles outside Orlando, Kerouac bought it. He facilitated the sudden move, he told Lucien Carr, by giving all his old Northport furniture "to Nigra garbage collectors" so he and Gabrielle could buy new furniture in Florida.

TO ALLEN GINSBERG

[April 14, 1961
Northport, New York]

Dear Allen—

Just read narrative section of *Kaddish,* which has impact of Dostoevskyan novel—The whole package, with later visionary poems, makes one explosive book—No reviews yet, as tho they just wanted to wish you out of existence, the big Wilburs and Hollanders[1] weeping in their pillows—no reviews either of course of Book of Dreams—Time for us to quit the literary scene & talk to none of them any more, I say—Things okay here, Gene doing good, we move soon, me free soon—me prayed also to cut lush, prayers answered so far—When have time give me rundown on latest Gregory soulmind—Yr. early prevision of police-cabaret-beatnik troubles coming true—big political out-in-the-open battle now with John Mitchell coming on like Mayor—I studying Kant, Schopenhauer, Spinoza etc. all great minds agreed

---

1. The contemporary poets Richard Wilbur and John Hollander.

with Buddha—Lucien & Harry Smith[2] called me high on phone—Why Bill "fled"?—Infinite Swarming Light—Bill's Hassan Sabbah says there is no Time and no Thing in Space—Well? he no agree in 1957—Oh Hum, vanity is a bore—Brand new world a-coming—Hello

Jean-Louis

Peter got a knish?

Once more settled in Florida, Kerouac wrote Sterling Lord and his California friend John Montgomery in early May 1961, describing his new house and neighborhood and telling them that he felt as if he and his mother "shook off the gangsters of NY, so to speak, and went back to America."

TO STERLING LORD

May 5, 1961

[Orlando, Florida]

Dear Sterling,

It was great to get out of NY and suddenly as if "coming back to America." All's set here. We have a guest room which we got to call "Sterling's Room" so don't miss it! Two twin beds. Patio screened, soon. A private park a quarter mile away for residents of this "exclusive" tract, with tennis courts! And I already lined up a good player for you, Bill Brumley of these builders.

And now that I'm out of N.Y. I don't feel so hounded by that court case, forget all about it, and am ready to return to N Y to clear it up anytime. I hope to go to Mexico City first, however, for 2 months, to think, walk, write, alone, in a lil apt. Because that's one thing I haven't done in 3 years, is sit alone & think for months and work out the next novel. It will work out like this, probably: the Duluoz Legend: ("Jack's" Lifetime):—

1922–26	VISIONS OF GERARD	
1926–32	MEMORY BABE	(to be written)
1932–37	DOCTOR SAX	
1937–39	MAGGIE CASSIDY	
1939–43	VANITY OF DULUOZ	(to be written)
1943–48	VISIONS OF JULIEN	(to be written)
1948–50	ON THE ROAD	
1948–51	VISIONS OF CODY	(partially published)
1952–53	RAILROAD EARTH	

2. The ethnomusicologist and filmmaker Harry Smith.

1955–56	TRISTESSA	
1955–56	DHARMA BUMS	
1956–57	DESOLATION ANGELS	
1957–61	UNTITLED NEW NOVEL	(to be written)

(and the non-story fill-ins like
MEXICO CITY BLUES
SOME OF THE DHARMA
OLD ANGEL MIDNIGHT
etc.

So you see what the plan is. Now, more travel, more adventures, and future "chapters" of the legend in novel form.

If I can, I'd like to go to Mexico in a month or so, so let me know your plans. It's already hot down here but our air conditioning sends coolness from vents in every room of the house.

As ever,
Love,
Jack

P.S. I got the checks.

TO JOHN MONTGOMERY

May 9 1961
P.O.BX. 700
(c/o Blake)
Orlando, Fla.

Dear John

Glad to hear from you. Yr new place sounds great and when I come out to SF this summer I won't miss you this time. I'll sleep in the grass in my bag if I stay a few days, as always perfect in summer SF nights. And in Neal's yard too, and in Albert's yard . . .

Write to me this address, tell Ferling too, & Phil etc. . . . my sister's address is now my mailing address. I shook off the gangsters of NY, so to speak, and went back to America. Staying at my sister's and getting ready to go to Mexico, El Paso and SF this summer ending in NY, my usual North American Triangle.

Allen and Gregory Corso and Orlovsky are in Cannes, wondering on beaches, and will join Burroughs in Tangier or Spain. When I do go to Europe (next spring?) I want to go alone and just dig waiters and whores for companionship, what's the sense of going to Milano and being lionized by thousand Italian-speaking hornrimmed bohemians in Fiats. Milano is apparently wild over Beats, they write me.

Chas. Laughton read my prose in Boston Symphony Hall, along with Wolfe and Whitman! I'm trying to get his address to send him an autographt Lonesome Traveler or Tristessa or something. It said in Boston paper that he had "taken (me) to his ample bosom." Woo! No bosom biggern Bodhidkarma's? That thar Laughton bosom with all its captain Bligh connotations is too much even for Whalen I bet.[3] Maybe he'll have a hiball with us in yr new Panoramic Hiway patio?

How's [Alan] Watts? When you see him, will you tell him that I think his Way of Zen is terrifically valuable and accurate and fine. I have some interesting things to tell him about my experience with "spontaneous prose" when I see him, I hope to see him in MV when I see you. What happened was, as soon as I had made a formal discovery of spontaneous prose, it wasn't spontaneous any more! just like he says! so that way out was to simply be "deliberately" spontaneous, which Watts accurately said is ALSO spontaneous. Because what happens is what happens, or wha' happens. But it was tough. In fact I think I've forgotten how to write by now. 4 years without a book, a million visitors. Only the good ones came once a year, I F, Ferling, Phil etc. Allen etc. The fuckin strangers came every week till familiarity bred contempt, I guess that's what they came to my door for, to contemn. I spent 4 years bitterly defending myself. Till I lost my original gladness, like the silly gladness of that day in Corte Madera with you.

But now I intend to get back on the ball. By means of much travel & solitude. And selecting my visits & sojourns & shootouts.

Is Ginger by the way a folk singer?

I'll see Albert Saijo also I hope this summer. My next book is going to have him and everybody else in it.

Including Lew Welch and our drive east with Albert. Hollywood experiences. Last summer, Big Sur, etc. In-betweens. . . . Another nutty saga, why not? Including this summer too maybe whatever will happen.

Whatever happened to Jackie Gibson?

It's all really like a huge interesting Dostoevsky novel. The Possessed I think is the greatest novel of all time.

Gossip is the soul of Dostoevsky . . . Corso almost destroyed me when he accused me of "gossip, not poetry." . . . But now I see his motive.

Story-telling is harder than poetry. I mean simple storytelling, like Trotsky said of Céline "he walked into literature like a guy walking into a bar telling a story to the whole bar as he sits in the stool"—(semi-quote)

3. Charles Laughton starred in the role of Captain Bligh in the film *Mutiny on the Bounty*.

So Trotsky gets the alpenstock
Céline ends up in a Danish prison cell
And I get a kick in the ass from JOHN

MONTGOMERY

JACK

P.S. i.e. Gregory's motive was Shellyan, i.e., I shd. write about Adonais not Charles Gurk

On May 9, 1961, Kerouac answered a letter from Carroll Brown, a college se-nior at Perkins School of Theology at Southern Methodist University. Brown had written Kerouac two months earlier asking him to clarify the theme of On the Road, *but never got a reply. When Jack's letter arrived the day after Brown re-ceived a grade of C— for his analysis of the novel for his seminar on theology and modern literature, Brown discovered that Kerouac supported his interpretation of the book. Brown showed the letter to his theology professor and later recalled, "With letter in hand I swung out of class with an A or A plus."*

TO CARROLL BROWN

May 9 1961
[Orlando, Florida]

Dear Carroll

The hero of ON THE ROAD (whose real name is Neal Cassady, of Den-ver) and whose name in the book (a true story all the way) is Dean Mori-arty, was born in 1926 or so in a charity hospital when his parents were driving west to find the golden land of California in a poor old 20's jalopy. His mother died when he was an infant. His father was a wino hobo. They hopped freights together. But part of the time "Dean" stayed with his mother's people and went to Catholic church and became a choir boy. Years later when I was walking down the Denver streets with him a priest rushed up and embraced him & asked him where he'd been all these years. This wasn't in the book because it hadn't happened yet in the years (1947–50) covered by the book. I've since written further about this great man. It's my contention that a man who can sweat fantastically for the flesh is also capable of sweating fantastically for the spirit. Goethe said "The pathway to wisdom is through excess" and it was later quoted famously by the mystic William Blake. The quote (and the spirit of the quote) relates to the famous thought that "God loves sinners best of all" (because I guess he has more to forgive there).... Dean was a sinner because he had no chance to go straight. Outside of that he was a kind fellow. You'll notice that in ON THE ROAD, unlike the Television cheap imitation of it called "Route 66," there are no fist fights, gun fights or horror of that kind at all.

You'll notice that Dean picked up the most helpless hitch hikers he could find. He said it was "for kicks" but nevertheless he always managed to pick up the wretched, needy kids on the road, and they always came out fine, they always told us something intensely near-divine about one thing or another in their experience. Dean and I were embarked on a tremendous journey through post-Whitman America to FIND that America and to FIND the inherent goodness in American man. American Man and Child.

That we loved girls is another matter altogether. That we stole a little bread and cheese and one time a whole tank of gas, was simply because we had no money to MOVE ON. We did not steal from individuals who would suffer. Because of these few scenes about "criminality" so-called the book was branded as being a kind of Marlon Brando Anarchy "Wild Ones" hoodlum blackjacket thing, which you know it was not. It was really a story about 2 Catholic buddies roaming the country in search of God. And we found him. I found him in the sky, in Market Street San Francisco (those 2 visions), and Dean had God sweating out of his forehead all the way. THERE IS NO OTHER WAY OUT FOR THE HOLY MAN: HE MUST SWEAT FOR GOD. And once he has found Him, the Godhood of God is forever Established and really must not be spoken about. Thus Dean never spoke about it since. I wrote about it. Dean today is on the way even further: he says he's going to become a Preacher. He kneels (for instance) before Oral Roberts on TV when Oral asks every one to kneel and pray! (in front of his kids) (sweating). He's a very energetic and sincere man. I wrote about him in his youth. The story's far from over. And some of the most interesting "religious" thinkers in the country have written me asking about him, Dean, Neal, specifically. Actually he doesn't want to see anybody but his wife and kids and an occasional buddy like me (and girls) (he still has his various mistresses and insists on it, and they are all extremely intense girls too). I can't write you two pages, but just this one page, and hope it'll help you in yr assignment. Don't ask me to do it again, man, I can't find time to write my new books. I get thousands of letters like yours. I answer most of them in silence, some by penny postcard. But I thought your job and motive was strong in this case, and here's luck to you (and hope you can make something of what I say.) Mainly: Dean Moriarty is FREE OF HYPOCRISY...... and would never have been whipped out of no Temple by no sweet Jesus who Loveth him

Yours
Jack Kerouac

Writing Ferlinghetti on May 25, 1961, Kerouac rationalized his decision to stay at home instead of traveling abroad with Ginsberg and Orlovsky, who had left Paris for Tangier to join Burroughs for a few months before visiting Greece,

Turkey, and Israel en route to India. Then Jack explained to Ferlinghetti why he had no sympathy for the American peace marchers protesting the proliferation of atomic submarines during the Cold War. Earlier, when Ferlinghetti had asked Kerouac to lend his support to the Fair Play for Cuba Committee, Jack had also refused, telling Lawrence, "I've got my own revolution right here in Northport— the American Revolution."

TO LAWRENCE FERLINGHETTI

> May 25, 1961
> JK c/o Blake
> Box 700
> Orlando, Fla.

Dear Laurent,

Thanks for that beautiful card of Bixby Canyon & Sea.

It makes me wanta go back there this summer, this time for 6 weeks' solitude, with grub, instead of just 3. (Bring jello this time.) But you may have other visitors, or arrangements. Let me know. I feel like going to the coast again, to resume the "legend," that is, to see what happened next to Neal, Lew, Phil, you, Mike Mc[Clure] et al. & See Henry Miller this time.[4] (*and* ALF!)[5]

I've been pondering your request for a "statement" and I really can't think of anything more important than this verse from "Desolation Blues," a fairly (12-chorus) poem I thought I'd lost in the mountains and just found last week in the bottom of my papers. (Mémère and I just moved to Florida, next door to my sister, nice new house with wall-oven, shower stalls etc.) I let my Ma do as she wishes and Grace comes to me anyhow, thereby (see?). I happy & contemplative here. If I were with Allen, Gregory, Peter & Bill in Tangier I'd be distracted from my thoughts. And besides my main writing drive or campaign now concerns the west coast scene. American thru & thru me, mebbe. (Stories about Europe by Americans are really boring anyway.)

Here's my statement (unversed):—

KEROUAC SAYS: "We're hanging into the abyss of blue—In it is nothing but innumerable and endless worlds more numerous even (and the number of beings!) than all the rocks that cracked and became little rocks in all that rib of rock that extends from Alaska, nay the Aleutian tips, down through the High Cascades, through to California & Ensenada, down, through High Tepic, down to Tehuantepec, down the rib, to Guatemala & on, Colombia, Andes, till the High bottom Chilean & Tierra del Fuego O

---

4. Kerouac had missed his appointment to meet Henry Miller at his home in Big Sur.
5. Alf was the mule pastured near Ferlinghetti's cabin at Bixby Canyon.

yoi yoi and on around to Siberia—In other words, & all the grains of sand that comprise a rock, and all the grains of atomstuff therein, more worlds than that in the empty blue sea we hang in, upsidedown—Too much to be real."

But, & incidentally, as to the Peace Marchers, I think they should now endeavor to get permission from the Soviet Government to march in Russia in the name of the same peace plea. Have you ever thought of that? And if so, why not? Isn't it because the "Peace Marchers" are essentially marching *against america?* Why? There were no Belsens here, no mortal purges, no decimations of population by starvation. There *was* trouble but there has been humanitarianism more than anywhere else in the world . . . (considering how evil everybody is anyway.) (And the guys who wanta climb the sides of U.S. Naval ships protesting the Polaris Missile in Scotland, why dont they get permission to do the same thing at the atomic sub bases of the Soviets in the black Sea, or in Archangelsk?)

How's Victor Wong? . . . Well, let me hear. We could have a ball this summer. What's yr next trip? How's Bk of Dreams selling? & being rec'd by the intellectuals & poets?

Ah the tears of things, incidentally . . . I've all these two days spent filing old letters, taking them out of old envelopes, clipping the pages together, putting them away . . . hundreds of old letters from Allen, Burroughs, Cassady, enuf to make you cry the enthusiasms of younger men . . . how bleak we become. And fame kills all. Someday "The Letters of Allen Ginsberg to Jack Kerouac" will make America cry.

Old letters starting "Cher, Cher Jean . . ." etc. And O all the youngish preoccupations!

Cassady's letters are wildly beautiful and full of Irish Celtic verbal zing. Burroughs' old letters contain the same dry humor, like "H.C. is sailing away in a boat with a sail to match his blond hair. Enough to make a man spew."

Well, let me know about yr plans for the summer. And how Book of Dreams came out. Allen wrote from shipboard that it was a great book, naturally, it is and of course he knows it. And Whalen wrote and said it would live as long as American prose.

. . . Silly lil girls who dug On the Road meanwhile write saying it bugs them, they want stories about "Dean" . . . Well, they'll get em, but tempered with lacrimae rerum I guess . . .

While we're still young we should all join hands but not in politics, in God's name, in POETRY (or whatever you call it) PROETRY.

We were right in the beginning, I mean the beginning of the Fuss in 1955, and are still right . . . But have you seen the flow of venom from the academies and the press? Ugh . . . And what about that silly [Kenneth] Tynan article abominating Neal's name (in *Holiday*)? Those Angry Young Faggots.

They come over here expecting to find bicycle curls on our knees.
    (Hey!
                a pome!)
See ya later, mon cher Laurent fort.

                                                            Jack

I'm glad to hear you adopted a child. I'm sure Kirby is having a ball. She
is such a maternal & lovey type. Peace on your house.

*By the end of May 1961, Kerouac's elation about relocating in Orlando had
worn off. He described his new house in a letter to Lois Sorrells.*

TO LOIS SORRELLS

                                                    May 31 1961
                                                    [Orlando, Florida]

Dear Lois
    A little letter for Lois
    Alittleletterforlois
The house is great but the naborhood is dreariness itself. In fact there's
a woman across the street who is in a coma, no apparent illness, just
doesn't wanta be awake. The naborhood is not bad really but it was nice
till now because of big wilderness field & woods in back and now they're
building 20 houses there, model homes. But I'm quiet and happy here. Play
my jazz tapes, scribble, showers, read in sun, have own private door to
backyard which is enclosed in 6 foot fence. Huge yard. Will plant orange
and shade trees and grapefruit and lemon & lime trees in it in January, time
for planting. Will have money by then and buy big trees already 6 foot
tall, too.
    House is ranchito one-story with terraza floors, that is, like marble
floors, so we have wall to wall rugs and rugs and I have big new reclining
chair cost 120, solid wood with soft huge pillowings to lean in, in fact I fell
asleep in it twice at night. Chair is alongside bookshelf for immediate reading. My encyclopedia is on top of big shiny wood executive desk, making
scholarly look shot, and big swivel chair of wood. Extra chair in office is
Danish, soft. Two bedrooms are great. I got new Royal Comfort mattress
and box in my old wooden Northport bedstead, sleepy like log. There is a
guest room with twin beds and rocking chair, lamp and closet etc. There is
an inner yard within the larger yard, also fenced in with red-stained basketweave 6 foot fence, with concrete patio, chairs, and garden of perennials . . .
(rubbery tropical perennials). There is heating and air conditioning unit,
works both ways winter or summer, with vents in each room of house, all
you do is adjust button. I have new fan to wave coolness around my office.

TV is now in small television den, with rug, wood rocker and old N'Port easy rocker chair, and Japanese TV redlamp, kicks. Kitchen has miles of formica top bars, wall oven, stools for bar, endless cedar wood closets. Dining area has our old wooden set, all nice on rug, with wood chairs (maple dinette set) and looks great. Livingroom is too fancy for anybody: early American furniture on wall to wall rugs, the wall is gray, the rug is gray, and the furniture is orange and gray, cool. My mother has new writing desk. Sofa, etc. nice livingroom, which opens thru sliding screen and floorlength, to patio etc. Front is lawn, porch, plants, 2 pines, and across the street big boring Americans looking for togetherness. But won't get it from this old seadog.

Anyway this place fine for Mémêre who has Ti Nin 2 houses away to go shopping with in big white airconditioned 60 Pontiac and her husband has little English sprite to go sportin in with me. Mostly to bars. In fact I stay home more now, nothin to see but moonlight on lakes, who cares. I got moonlights & lakes right here in my dreamhead. Now that all this is set, I free to travel, see? and next thing I buy is cabin in Big Sur, maybe 50 miles down the wild south coast, get away from Carmel, way way down, maybe. So I come to NY soon for blood test and call you and see you.

If you travel with me this summer you'll lose your LeBlanc's job, what about that? Maybe 2 weeks vacation, we jet to [illeg.] Anyway, we see soon. (Woke up in middle of night tonight, saw bright full moon, said "O shit, I'm sick of mystery") (Strange?)

Jack

Early in June, Kerouac sent a sequence of poems titled San Francisco Blues *to Donald Allen, hoping his editor would publish them as a new book. Allen turned them down, and they finally appeared posthumously in 1995, when Viking Penguin brought out Kerouac's* Book of Blues.

TO DONALD ALLEN

June 10 1961
PO Bx 700
Orlando, Fla

Dear Don

When I got your letter I promptly started typing up San Francisco Blues in proper chorus form (like Mexico City Blues chorus form) and it was a hell of a job, 79 choruses. I also wrote an introduction explaining the "blues poetry form." The manuscript is dead perfect without a single mistake in it & even contains original lines that I had tried to erase and write over of in 1954! (that's an art in itself)

But, reading the manuscript now—I see it is a beautiful unity. And wouldnt want to send it to you if you only plan to use sections or excerpts of it. As a whole book of poems, it stands right by Mexico City Blues, original, strange, & neat. What do you plan to do with it? What kind of book are you preparing? Something like the Evergreen Anthology? Let me know. Because I hate to see San Francisco Blues be taken apart in pieces. (If you want pieces tell me *how many,* and I could send those—separately.)

Desolation Angels ... Sterling has it at the office, we're just holding up on any publication this year (1961) to give the critics a chance to stop saying that I publish too often and give the other books a run. I also have Visions of Gerard (novel) to publish, my best in fact. Gray Williams said he cried when he read it, but wanted "new" novel—. Barney offered a measly $1000 advance for Desolation so we just stored it away. I also plan to print Desolation from the point where I actually sat down to narrative discipline, and remove the first 50 pages which were after all only a mountain diary. This will make Desolation a good package for any publisher. It's after all a big inside novel about Allen, Gregory, Neal, Peter, Lamantia, Duncan, McClure and all, and about North Beach, the Cellar, etc. Ruth Witt Diamant is even in it.

My news is that my mother and I moved to Florida a few doors away from her daughter, my sister "Nin," so that I can be freer to travel. And to get me a cabin in the woods somewhere in America soon. We have a brand new house, a private yard with big fences, a supermarket to shop in down the way. These new Fla. houses have wall ovens, heating & airconditioning units, shower stalls, terraza floors, real fawncy and comfortable. You can visit us any time. My mother never forgot "Don"—Mémère, that is. . . . Yes, I may go to coast this summer. I just missed you in that bar last summer when I sat that little cat on my lap all night ... I had a ball that summer time, but overdid it & went a little schizo. (I thought I was being "poisoned by The Subud Cult")!

Don, can you send me a copy of that Ark that already has 2 SF Blues in it? And let me know if you plan to print all 79 choruses of SF Blues, all 40 pages that is. (I've never seen that Ark book). Write soon, I'm taking off right soon (Mexico or someplace). May see you in SF in July or August. I always yearn to go see what old "Dean Moriarty's" up to again. . . . .

Ton ami
Jack

And yearn for Sun Hung Heung's wonton—(& Phil Whalen too) (& Lew Welch)

Allen G's in Cannes with Peter & Gwegowy—headed for Tangier & Burroughs

Jack Kerouac: SAN FRANCISCO BLUES—In 79 Choruses

San Francisco Blues was my first book of poems, written back in 1954 & hinting the approach of the final blues poetry form I developed for the Mexico City Blues.

In my system, the form of blues choruses is limited by the small page of the breastpocket notebook in which they are written, like the form of a set number of bars in a jazz blues chorus, and so sometimes the word-meaning can carry from one chorus into another, or not, just like the phrase-meaning can carry harmonically from one chorus to the other, or not, in jazz, so that, in these blues as in jazz, the form is determined by time, and by the musician's spontaneous phrasing & harmonizing with the beat of the time as it waves & waves on by in measured choruses.

It's all gotta be non stop ad libbing within each chorus, or the gig is shot.

—Jack Kerouac

[in pencil]   Don—

> This is a carefully worded intro to explain, hence revisions—Hope you take good care of these & of yourself

Jack

Restless in Orlando, Kerouac replied to an inquiry about his boyhood from Bernice Lemire, a French-Canadian woman from Lowell who was writing a biographical study of his work for a degree at Boston College. Jack wrote his first letter to her on June 15, 1961. He continued to answer Lemire's questions for her essay on "Jack Kerouac: Early Influences" in a second letter, on August 11, 1961, after he returned from spending a month in Mexico City. There he stocked up on Mexican Benzedrine and phenobarbital and wrote 50,000 words of Part Two of his novel Desolation Angels, *which Sterling Lord submitted to Grove Press to fulfill an option.*

TO BERNICE LEMIRE

[Postmarked June 15, 1961]
Jack Kerouac
c/o Lord
15 E. 48th St.
New York 17, N.Y.

Dear Bernice Lemire

Yes, you have my permission to look over my Lowell High School records. I was on the Honor Roll for awhile. (1938).

At the time the Headmaster was Mr. Ray Sullivan.

My English teacher in the senior year was the best teacher I ever had, with the exception of one favorite: he was Mr. Joe Pine. He took great interest in me and in my appreciation of Emily Dickinson and general American poetry. (This was 1938–39 year).

My "favorite" teacher was a Miss Dinneen at Bartlett Junior High School, my homeroom teacher in the 8th Grade, 1935–1936. She was also fond of my sister Caroline Kerouac.

Also at Bartlett J. High (which, as you know, burned down the night in the winter of 1939–1940) was a marvellous Miss Mansfield who ran the library, whom I call "Miss Wakefield" in DOCTOR SAX recording how her house on White Street was engulfed by brown floodwaters of the 1936 flood (March). She later became a literary confidante of mine and Sebastian Sampas' and Ian MacDonald's. Ian MacDonald lived in the Highlands and was the biggest intellectual in Lowell at the time (1942). Another literary confidante from Lowell at that time was Edward Tully, later went to Tufts. Also Cornelius Murphy, now a physicist, who lived on Race St. High school friends of mine included James "Harper" O'Dea, I guess he's now D.A. of Middlesex County, but he wanted to be president of the U.S. and was on the Kennedy staff in Boston for years.

Others were Roland Salvas (the "Lousy" of Doctor Sax) ... Jim Cudworth of the Highlands (the "Bloodworth" of Maggie Cassidy) and a girlfriend Margaret Coffey (the "Peggy Cole" of Maggie Cassidy). Maggie Cassidy herself is Mary Carney, and still lives in the same house (with her mother) (or did, in 1954). (Has 2 daughters now.) (Her husband abandoned her.)

I was born March 12 1922 at 5 oclock in my mother's bedroom (that's 5 PM) at 9 Lupine Road in Centreville. We moved from there to Barnaby Street, then Beaulieu Street, then Hildreth Street, then corner of Lilly and Hildreth, then West & West 6th, then to Pawtucketville 11 Phebe Avenue and later to 33 Sarah Avenue. When my father lost his business in 1937 we lived for a time in the tenement on Aiken St. across from St. Jean Baptiste church, top floor facing church. Then moved to top floor corner of Moody St. & Gardner, over Pete's Textile Lunch (still there). After that we moved to Gershom Avenue, 34 Gershom, front steps go up steep.

After a short stay in New Haven, where my father itinerant linotypist, we moved back to Lowell in 1941 at Crawford St. (forget the number) which is where we were in 1943 when the Navy drafted me and I never came back to live in Lowell.

My father: Leo Alcide Kerouac, his father was Jean-Baptiste Kerouac of Nashua; his mother Clementine Bernier. All from Quebec. (Riviere du Loup)

My mother: Gabrielle L'Evesque, her father was Louis L'Evesque of

Nashua. Her cousin was Dr. Raymond Harpin of Lynn, Mass. All from St. Pacôme.

The "Joe Fortier" in Doctor Sax (all my books are true stories 100% with only the names changed) is Michael Fournier ... The Fournier family was our great friend. Michael's father, Mike Sr., ran the Merrimack Valley Supply Co.

My father Leo ran the Spotlight Print. You can look it all up in old archives of 1920's Lowell, the Spotlight Print, etc.

The mistake you've made is that you failed to realize that my totally 100% true biography is right there in my writings about Lowell: in Doctor Sax, Maggie Cassidy. Only the names were changed.

If you care to study the books themselves, I'll be glad to send you the real names of the characters, and then you can check at will.

For instance, the G.J. of the books is George Apostolos, the "Scotty" is Henri Beaulieu, etc. etc. They're all still in Lowell. The "Iddyboy" is Robt. Morrisette.

etc.

Okay

OTHER CLOSE LOWELL FRIENDS

Ernie Noval
Bobby Rondeau (LHS)   Well, that's all
Leo Nadeau (LHS)   for now
Eddy Sorenson
Pete Houde   I hope this'll help you
Armand Gauthier
Roland Dufresne
Barney MacArthur (LHS)   A Granville Hicks Jones
Louis Eno (St. Joseph's School)   wrote a Masters Thesis
Maurice Paquette   on me at Columbia, so I'm
Odysseus Chiungos (LHS)   used to this
Herve Kerouac (cousin)   (but I'm very very proud)
Robert Fournier
George Dastou Jr.
Louis Morin (LHS)

                                                     Jack (Kerouac)

August 11 1961
Jack c/o Blake PO Box 700
Orlando, Fla.

Dear Miss Lemire

In answering yr questions

(1) Yes, you certainly have my permission to read my teenage letters to Geo. Apostolos and tell him to find the blushingest ones possible? George, tell George it's okay. And tell Geo. I dare him to write me another letter now, he hasn't written to me since about 1942, altho I wrote to him in 1954. Stella Sampas tells me he has malaria, where the hell did he catch malaria: on Moody Street? I know he has an ulcer. Or had. I know how to cure it. Tell him to stand on his head 3 minutes a day. I remember his older brother, whose name I forget, who was very sick and died young. Tell George I love him as much as ever. After all, he IS an "Apostle" and who wouldn't love Apostles?

(2) "The Town and the City" is a typical "novel"-arrangement of experience, like Wolfe's "Web and the Rock".... What I did there was separate myself into three personalities: Joe, Peter, and Francis, with their younger counterparts Charley and Mickey. It is "fiction." And nothing could be worse than fiction after Proust & Joyce.

(3) The "Martin house" is no particular house, I just located it on the river for the sake of River Fiction. One critic, Warren Tallman of Ontario, said I satisfied all the demands of Thirties Fiction there. After that I discovered true stories. No, there is no Martin House in "Galloway" any more than there is a Castle on Lupine Road.

(4) In the Book of Dreams I just continue the same story but in the dreams I had of the real-life characters I always write about, including George (Gus Rigopoulos) or Ginsberg (Irwin Garden, his own invention for his name)—They, by the way, are much alike except Geo. isn't queer like Ginsberg. But they have the same way of impressing me with their big dark thoughts. So, "the same story that I always write about" is like Proust and his Remembrances, or Joyce, the people I knew.

(5) "Faust Part Three" simply means this: Goethe wrote Faust Parts one and two, ending with dull Canals, and I just wrote Part Three of the Faust Legend about the soul of the West. Faust sold his soul to the devil but Sax rushed in and called Faust a bastard. Consult Spengler on the "Faustian Western Soul" ... take a look at what Spengler said about Faust, and how Faust led up to Space Missiles because he believed in the "endlessness of the soul."

(6) Fifth grade teacher at St. Joseph's was a Brother, but I don't remember his name, tho when George and I and Salvey and Scotty Beaulieu were swimming at Pine Brook he suddenly appeared one afternoon and took a swim too. Was a great curly haired man. "Joseph?"

(7) No, Doctor Sax is not the "Satanic Doctor" of Rimbaud. Doctor Sax fights against satanism, he doesn't buy it. Doctor Sax is actually William Seward Burroughs, and me too, a Faustian hero (consult Spengler on Faust). Also consult Dowson and Marquis de Sade. Sax is not the Wizard Faustus, he is the enemy of evil. But, he is also "The Shadow" (Lamont Cranston). Ask George about "the shadow."

(8) Miss Dinneen must believe that St. James is the brother of the Lord. St. James was known as "Ya'akob" and on the road the accuser asked James for forgiveness. James was either the son of Zebedee or of Alphaeus, probably the son of Joseph. Was called a "son of thunder." His other brothers were Jesus, Joses, Judas and Simon. Was called "Oblias," "the just."

I know another nun, Reverend Mother Benedict Duss of the Benedictines, who cried when I told her that the "Universe is a Woman" (round).

Jack

THE TOWN AND THE CITY		MAGGIE CASSIDY	
Rose	Claire Fournier	Vinny Bergerac	Freddy Bertrand
Ruth	Carolyn Kerouac	Zaza Vauriselle	I Forget Zaza's name
Elizabeth	Margaret Coffey(?)	Billy Artaud	Bobby Rondeau
	Later: Vicki Russell of	Mrs. McGillicuddy	Alice Stickney(?)
	Grosse Pointe, Mich.		dont remember
Joe	Michel Fournier	Mr. Nedick	just a name
Francis	Actually	Mrs. Faherty	just a name
	Wm. S. Burroughs		
Mickey	Peter as a boy		
Charley	Mike Fournier as a boy		
Tommy Campbell	Billy Chandler of		
	Lowell, died on		
	Bataan		
Scotcho Rouleau	"Hank" Beaulieu		
Danny Mulverhill	Geo. Apostolos	DR. SAX	
Jimmy Bannon	Charley Connors	Shammy	Charles "Shabby"
Mary Gilhooley	Mary Corner(?)		Charbonneau
	Yes indeed	Dicky Hampshire	Billy Chandler
Ernest Berlot, Jr.	George Dastou, Jr.	Paul Boldieu	Hank Beaulieu
Wilfred Engels	Gerhardt Eisler	Sonny Alberge	Skippy Roberge
Buddy Fredericks	Seymour Wyse	Gene Plouffe	Pete Houde
	(now of London)	Joe Plouffe	Mike Houde
Judie Smith	My first wife,		
	Frankie Edith Parker		
Kenneth Wood	Lucien Carr		
Leon Levinsky	Allen Ginsberg yes		
Will Dennison	Wm Seward	BOOK OF DREAMS	
	Burroughs	Rudy	Ernie Noval
		Jeannie	/What page?

Books:	Roland Bouthelier Armand Gauthier
	Order or date written
The Town and The City	"Town and City" 1946–48
Dr. Sax	"On the Road" May 1951
Maggie Cassidy	"Visions of Cody" 1951–52
On The Road	"Doctor Sax" 1952
The Subterraneans	"Maggie Cassidy" 1953
Tristessa	"The Subterraneans" (1953)
Lonesome Traveler	"Book of Dreams" 1952–55
The Dharma Bums	"Tristessa" 1955–56
Book of Dreams	"Mexico City Blues" 1955
Mexico City Blues	"Scripture of the Golden
Scripture of G.E.	Eternity" 1956
Rimbaud	"Dharma Bums" (1957)
Pull My Daisy	"Lonesome Traveler" 1957
	"Rimbaud" 1958
	"Pull My Daisy" (1959)

On October 9, 1961, three hours after completing a new 60,000-word "narrative drama" titled Big Sur, *Kerouac described the ten-day process of composition to Sterling Lord while high on Mexican Benzedrine. Completing the book made Kerouac "feel so glad" he could still write after four years of frustrating attempts to complete a new novel in the Duluoz Legend. Emotionally drained by the physical and emotional ordeal, Kerouac realized that he was injuring himself by "taking enormous overdoses of benzedrine," but he was proud of what he thought of as his "greatest contribution to modern writing . . . the idea of spontaneous notation of the mind actual while writing." Complaining to his agent that avant-garde literary magazines credited Ginsberg as the originator of the idea of spontaneous prose composition, and that popular television shows like* Route 66 *about two buddies traveling cross-country made stars out of Jewish actors and producers, Kerouac wondered half-seriously if he shouldn't subtitle his new book "Another Idea for the Jews to Steal."*

TO STERLING LORD

Oct 9 1961
[Orlando, Florida]

Dear Sterling

Well here you see this strange paper which is the end of the teletype roll I wrote Dharma Bums on 4 years ago, I just now 3 hours ago completed new novel "Big Sur" on other (last) (here) said half of roll, a new 60,000-word narrative drama which was written with more excitement than Dharma Bums, is probably a better "novel," doesnt preach, sometimes run breathless like On The Road, surpasses Tristessa for sad misery, has flashes of the greatest prose of Visions of Cody and Sax, but at present is just a 60,000 word teletype roll in singlespace the net value of which I cant determine because it s too soon for the psychological blocks to clear away (that is, the blocks I now have that would warrant the "disliking" of the manuscript whereas in 2 months they, the psychological blocks of just now, will evaporate, and what'll be left is a sudden clear strange manuscript.)— in other words, news i've been trying to write you for four years, that i wrote a new novel, herein find said news, and I feel so glad i can still write.

But O so sad, this story, i vow my next book will be a Comedy and nothing else.

The doublespace typing in duplicate will take as usual longer than the composition; writing on this took ten days or so but of course a year of mediating and meditating and even practising long thrownaway excerpts on the story—For instance I preceded this novel with a reject of 24,000 words— But I can have this ready before Christmas in case anybody gives us any bluff guff about Desolation Angels we now have this ace in the hole which is nothing else but "Kerouac'[s] new major novel" (I'd say)—(objectively)— Lots of characters, lots of description of woods at Big Sur (and beach) but above all fantastic love story ending enough to make De Beauvoir and Sartre pale for its hopelessness (the love affair)—There's also the question of libel but I'm going to check up on principle loveybirds and loveybird associates—and of course can change circumstantial material to alter surface realities—

So we have ace in the hole—let me know what Grove s doing about Angels—which, compared, to this, is a lark—(classy poetic lark, incidentally a clever blurb idea for Desolation is to say that it is a composite portrait of the major SF poets from Duncan, McClure etc. to Ginsberg, Corso, Orlovsky and also Ruth Witt Diamant the San Francisco lady poetry boss who set up all the readings, i mean, it's historically if not just poetrically [sic] valuable as a document) ... Big Sur is the sequel but much more horrible events. . . .

Sterling, I feel that Route 66[6] and Al Zugsmith and all that represents the fact that my ideas are being lifted left and right, depriving me of maybe a million, and just between you and me being lifted by Jews, I should really subtitle Big Sur: Another Idea for the Jews to Steal—But of course I wont— dont wanta be blackballed—tho if they ever tried that there'd be a war on— okay, suffice it, we both know whats been stolen and how, and how it cant be legally explicated—like when Zugsmith had the effrontery to tell Al Aranowitz [sic], "I'M the one who copyrighted Beat Generation as a title,

---

6. *Route 66* was a popular television program in the 1960s and also the title of Bobby Troup's hit song, which predated *On the Road.*

what's Kerouac got to do with it?" or now when Route 66 has jazz and hip talk and the white line feeding into the car (a tip I gave jerry wald in 1957 and maybe he knows Herbert Leonard and Sterling Silliphant the "creators" of Route 66) but I'm going to beat them all by bombarding them—I have a final great idea for the next 10 books:—to take special trips to visit various characters like Allen in India, Visions of Bill, Gregory in Paris, Peter Eating Fish or something, G.J. Later (in Lowell), etc. and coming back home to write a complete report on them (for me a complete report includes the poetry of drama within the drama of poetry, what else, I mean what good's poetry without drama, or drama without poetry)—so we'll bombard them—by the time I'm dead they'll still have 12 ideas to steal—It's really disgraceful—why is everybody so mute about this obvious horror/—I'm not going to sit and take it—my greatest contribution to modern writing is the idea of spontaneous notation of the mind actual while writing, but this idea now belongs of Allen Ginsberg according to the small journals—so that it s been happening on all levels, theory or plot or format, everything belongs to the thief—And do you know also for instance that the idea of Clellohn [sic] Holmes' Horn, of creating imaginary great jazz charcters [sic] and writing fictionally about them, was my idea in 1952 in a letter I wrote to Holmes?—Finally it boils down to where Phil Whalen says "O well, you ve got so many ideas what do you care?"—That could be my final decision, too——But I've been thinking about all this and you know as well as I do it's all true—Paranoia they can yell at me, to cover up the truth—but I'm wise to that—My father warned me, my mother still warns me—At the rate I'm going taking enormous overdoses of benzedrine to write my novels i probably wont live long enough to enjoy money anyway but there will be heirs—So I hope you and Cindy as a team will be glad to receive a new novel from me, and keep your eye on crooks, and come visit when it gets cold and damp, come to sunshine state and play horseshoes (I built wooden boxes around pins, with clay in boxes, regulations, but I havent had a ringer in days)—sorry about my anti semitism but it s sadly true, keep an eye on that, I wont go overboard and become a big ranting fascist, I just want to know why my main ideas have been pilfered by one particular breed among all the idiotic breeds of man the least idiotic of which is Lord and the most the Kerouac.......Got Czech check, strange they must have railroads there too, how they gonna translate that prose? Incidentally if you can do anything to relieve my literary isolation here, like having Evergreen reviews and my own albums and all sorts of things like that sent, please do so—when you want me to come to New York? No particular reason now, I think ex wife is afraid of bloodtest which wd rob her of her fantasy that her daughter is of my blood—I wish my father were alive and you woulda met him—adios for now.... also send me transatlantic review, all those things, there're not even Grove Press books down here, nothing but Pres Kennedy and Alexander King on sale

Have you heard of the great new critic Roger A. Priori?

> Jack
> (idiot)
> (but good writer)

*In mid-October 1961, Kerouac told his California friends Philip Whalen and Carolyn Cassady that he had written a new book in which they "figure"—*Big Sur. *He also dropped a note to Tom Guinzburg at the Viking Press expressing his enthusiasm for Ken Kesey's* One Flew Over the Cuckoo's Nest, *which the publisher had sent him in galleys.*

TO PHILIP WHALEN

Oct. 17, 1961
[Orlando, Florida]

Dear Phil Was thinking of writing you when your letter came, telepathy—Your EEEEEeeeeek expresses just about the way I ben too—Spiritchally, that is, Parson—Physhically to—That's Fiszhically—too much sauce—Well but the sauce suddenly overcame me after about 6 weeks' beautiful control reading Balzac grand Dostoevsky and sipping good brandy very slow like Jimmy Vahey in a quiet moment and taking only half beeny a day—benny—But suddenly I exploded angrily outa my (outa mah chair) and wrote my first novel in Five friggin years—to be called Big Sur—Then, in the flush of triumph, I got drunk to "celebrate" but got sick for weeks—Got from a healthy tanned and 20 pound lighter handsome jack to a big glooby blob of sad blufush—In no time.

But the book is written. You in it. Lotsa goodies. Bettern Dharma Bums for drama. The Prajna too may be better, that is, no phoney idealist, easy-out concession to woids. Lew's in there, the main image of the book in a way is Lew driving Willy and me sitting in right front broken seat swigging. Then I got that day you sat smoking pipe as I slept drunk in Jacky's park all day: followed by our arm-in-arm walk to temple museum, closed, re-member: followed by little exchange, of woids, not too good but I just raced and threw down anything I thought you might have said and I might have said so that's Zen anyway. Also, other events, like the morning I read you Dr. Johnson on Buchanan St. and Big Sur woodchopping contest with Ferlinghetti and Neal and Lew and Victor Wong and McClure and day at Nepenthe and drunken failure to visit Henry Miller and etc. Gonna be a good one. My feeling Phil now is this: IF THE CRITICS SAY MY BOOKS STINK THEY ARE ACTUALLY HELPING ME BECAUSE THEN I'M FREE TO WRITE WHAT I WANT.

See? which leaves me complete freedom to write anything I want ANY-WAY in spite of my fear of critics, see? a strange nice humble position lead-ing to endlessly complete books.

303

Mémère is very happy here tho as usual she complains. Well, there are some complaints, like all summer you gotta have the airconditioner on or die (I wouldnta moved here without it) which makes you cough—But next summer if she'll only just sweat in the yard a half hour a day, at flowers, lawn, etc., cough will go away—also, tho, most horrible, one of these modern tracts with endless rows of perfect new houses but all of them without exception full of flat housewives looking out the window when someone dares to try to walk to the stores which are too far away anyway under broiling sun in flat treeless waste, ugh. But my sister is next door and there's family fun for old Mémère, which is bettern waiting for me under cracking old boughs of New England's November, really (with all its witches and graveyards).

If you ever come here, I play you fine game of standard horseshoes in back yard where I planted steel stakes inside regulation boxes, and each shoe weighs 5 pounds, standard, and really wears you out. Also, outdoor grilles, etc. steaks. But I'll probably see you out Calif. way soonern you get here.—How come you aint gettin money for collidge lectures? you could make a living just collidge lectures—Sometimes they pay hunnerds of dollars—You'd be a knockout in Utah or at Brown, you know—Get lecture agent! But that wd. ruin you as Phillyboo Whalen the guy who says Fuck You—

Tao Yuan Ming greatest poet in China—(his name means Way John Vase)—Influenced by this marvelous humble farmer poet I just wrote the greatest fucking haiku of all time, that is to say, a few lines, not haiku really, I've been writing Chinese type light poetry (Karumi light—I said the other dawn, sob,—"

"There go the birds, flying west a moment
—Who's ever going to know the world
Before it goes?"—TAO JACK KEROUAC MING

But, feeling high on brandy, it is a pretty lil poem, end of a longer one, show it to ya later—They used to say Li Po's main fault was the FACILITY with which he could knock off poems so don't worry about your new idea of writing a lot. I guess we'll still have to go down the Yellow River and see.

While taking big shits I keep reading Memoirs of an Interglacial Age which is some memoir to try to flush down the drain that down thar ain't memoir'd, shit, tryna get funny, but I like it better than ever and did you see what Sorrentino said about you in KULCHUR how you grow on people? It's really amazing how that mad Ginsberg knew all that at first. McClure is growing into such a gas too, and Gary was always wild. I can't understand how Allen sorta picked you and McClure and Gary out of the scads of poets out there and brought you to meet me as I sat there remember guzzling wine like all good poets do. But at that time I had no idea you were actually discussing the Dharma, I guess. O I knew it. Remember that first afternoon at Lafcadio's, you just down from Sourdough saying Poetry is Shit,—we were looking at Mexico City Blues. O grand days, the old poets are still here, I only wish we all lived on a magic mighty huge mountain in separate little huts that take days to visit, with wine and poems. Ah. Shit what an America. As you know for awhile there buried in the alcoholic pessimism of New York I was saying Ah Shit on Poetry but now I see it as just a gentle little concern with our lot, why not/ As they say in Black Mtn Review, "/"

Black Mountain Review: a Poem

///;//;;////;;;/////;;;/;p/pfft/

Power just went off, builders around here piling up more horror in what was my huge empty back field wastes of piney barren—Fuck it, I'm going to my cabin anyway, soon enough.

Thanks for Claude's address. He always did say we shd. go to Nepal together. Well I aint got time to goof around all over the world with everybody even Buddha. Glad to hear Creeley askt about me because I thought he thought I was "commercial" or something. Shit, man, take what they can give ya. "And put it in one basket, keep your eye on the basket, and don't change the basket"—Andrew Carnegie, actually said that—He meant put it in the bank, savings account, and don't spend more than you need like all these sports car enthusiasts and cunt enthusiasts—Wine and beans is enuf even for a rich man—and a poor man too—I've just finished a fucking fifth of Martell Cognac and here I go make another drink. In France Cognac is called "The Grape" but I guess the poor man only drinks 5 Star Poorboy. (Tho Tao Yuan Ming made his own wine, you know). But that cognac, after years of horrible hopeless nightmares, I see that Cognac as being at least the only drink in the world, with soda and ice, that won't actually kill you. Lew used to mention that too. So if you wanta borrow a hunnerd dollars from me for a coupla cases of Cognac or a sad return trip to The Dalles where there's nothing but insane ex mental patient Indians, writela. That's Jewish. Writella, Phillela.

There's a really good new novel by a certain Ken Kesey who says he's half Indian and from The Dalles, book about a madhouse, CUCKOO FLEW OUT THE CAGE or something. Viking Press. I can send it to you, I got the galleys, bound. But no post office within 12 miles tho. I will write to Creeley. My marvelously beautiful fat lion faced cat lies on my new mahogany executive writing desk with an expression of Fuck You, I'm The Lion Beauty (tho he's too humble and really old grandpaw to care how really beautiful he is, the Vet fell in love with him.) I won't see McClure in New York (and family) because I'd like to see him alone but I haven't got time for all these endless friendships of mine that as you know I keep extending endlessly for days ending with endless new friendships that come thru the door, ending I never be happy, get any poems or plops written, right?) But I'll see McClure when I'm thru with what I got to do and can be free go down get drunk with the butchers in the town. (By God, this makes me realize I'm still chasing that Ox.)

Allen's last note from Athens, going to India he says, to catch Malaria? I don't know. The slums I described in TRISTESSA and the people therein are not a whit different from Bombay or Calcutta or Delhi or Benares slums, smells of dead dogs, human shit, banana peels & mud.

You might tell Albert, if see, that I wrote an elaborate description (harkening back) of our marvelous trip east with Lew Welch in Willy Jeep in 1959, and greatest of all, a complete description of my visit to him at TB hospital in Tulare (?) last year when Albert and I kept waving goodbye till it was a game—that ended with little jokes in the bushes from far away—little final waves that were not the last—well, Albert will enjoy it—also long chapter about Albert's theory of dirty ass holes—also long chapter on Albert's theory of the Buddha Charita.

Also, long chapter on Phil Whalen reading Lankavatara Scripture in cottage at night as me and Mémère sneak up on him in the grass of milvia.

Smiling over Lankavatara, he was.

Les and Albert have "blonde ladies," you say? No brunettes out there. Jacky. Missus Cassady. Joanne Kyger. Valeria McCorkle. Except for that lovely brunette who sat on my lap in the queer bar and wrote a poem about it. Remember her name? Loves Marlon Brando? Confessions of a New York Youth? Hangs around men's johns ... Forget his name, can't find it in the Beat Scene, which has the gall to say I didn't name the Beat Generation: boy those Jews in NY are sure hungry to use that what they call "Norman Mailer's silken cunning" to take ideas away from Honest Sweating Goys and Boys ...

Bob Miller, is he the blond guy with a boy, carpenter or painter worker, with big boots, has hi fi jazz next door at Buchanan, drove the getaway car? Well tell him I wrote a half a chapter about him showing me how to drive a getaway car. He is a great guy.

John Montgomery writes me these annoying letters sometimes I can't understand, the last one said "So you're going to make the gene scene?" I understood that but he should be more friendly. After I've had a New York Supreme Court order a blood test, I'll throw a little gene and john will get it, gee.

Quit smoking is good. When I had to, in 1951, I suddenly could smell the actual dim pollen dust of Autumn in Long Island, it was beautiful. It was that damned Creeley got me smoking again in Marin-An in 1956, damn him and his beard and his New England.

You say now that you know that the inside of your head is also outside, that sounds exactly like what Bodhidharma told the 2d Patriarch: "Don't pay any attention to the pantings of the mind, make your mind a wall," meaning of course, "don't let inside thoughts or outside distractions do anything but bounce against the wall of your mind."

Truer words?

Nevair.

Jean Louis

All love to Ferlinghetti—

TO CAROLYN CASSADY

Oct. 17, 61
Jack c/o Blake
PO Box 700
Orlando, Fla

Dear Carolyn

Not writing this because I dreamed of you last night, and quel dream! but I was planning for weeks to write and explain my months-long silence.

But first, Ed White of Denver says Neal left a note there on somebody's door and I was wondering "What? did he break his parole or something?" Is everything okay up there in Los Gatos, Carolyn?

Your long letter of last summer scared me. I was then trying to concentrate on nothing in the world but packing and going down to Mexico City to write a new book for the first time in 4 years. I did this. In Mexico City in a dismal dusty streetdoor apartment I wrote 50,000 words by candlelight. But just as I was going to finish the novel the Mexicans moved in on me, friends, etc., finally some thieves stole everything suitcase and all (rosary and all) so I came home disgusted and also the 50,000 words disgusted me (tho I see now I'll use them as harkening back material later novels, so no waste.)

I in fact wrote you a big letter from Mexico City saying "How about me coming up to Los Gatos?" but I tore it up because the Mexican fiasco made me wonder I might get all hung up in Frisco again instead of just at home with you and Neal. So came home. But that too was favorable in the stars because after 6 weeks at home thinking and reading Balzac and working and throwing away writings suddenly, boom, I just finished my new novel, Big Sur, about the summer of 1960 you remember.

In it, as a matter of fact, I sort of answer your long letter! You know, that old idea about you and me meeting in Nirvana later at which time Neal will be perfect etc. you remember. Anyway, pretty romantic.

I just want you to know that I cherished your letter, and cherish you, in that special way you'll realize when you read the book. Later I can send you excerpts off this typewriter, if you want, in November. Like when we all walked down the Big Sur path to the sea, you and I in front talking as of yore, and Neal had his new magenta (?) jeepster stationwagon, and the kids, and McClure, and then that awful night I brought Jacky to your house. So ashamed of that I never came back for my old shirt you'd sewn for me so sweetly (as I say) but you never were even mad.

Anyway at this time, naturally, having just written a book in which you figure (and dont worry, you come off just like you are, which is moral and clean) (as a contrast to all the big lewd Lew Welches and Jacks and Paul Smiths whoopee) you're so on my mind I wish you'd write. Not only telling me every detail whatever you wanta say, about you, me, but I want to know if anything's wrong with Neal. And news of Jacky would interest me and might help me put the final touch in there. You see, if I were a big Russian novelist writing fiction it would be so easy. I hope you appreciate the fact I feel well, shamed? awful? shitty? for writing about everybody as they are. I always make an effort to clean up the mess by changing names, times, places, circumstances. But in years from now noone no one will see a "mess" there, just people, just Karma, the raging Karma of all of us. And in this case, of you and me, the soft and gentle Karma that aint even started. (wow, that dream last night) But Carolyn forgive me also for intruding on your gentle home life and for all I know you've got something new to absorb you but just write me letter on typewriter like old days. I'd like also to come out Calif. right soon. Sigh, pain in the ass jack

In fact wait a minute, I aint finished. The story starts I sneak out of skid row all drunk and sad and hurry to Big Sur at night in a cab (from Monterey) and suddenly wake up clean and refreshed by that burbling crick, thereafter spending 3 idyllic mystic weeks alone. Then I go to the city and get drunk for 3 weeks. The swirl of events, Lew Welch, driving me to Los Gatos the first time, the second time when I brought the hundred and you let Neal go off with me to the cabin, the third time when we brought Jacky, all the other events (including other people you dont know who were in raging dramas at same moment). Climaxed by the most marvelous sudden booming open of the cabin door allowing golden light to burst in on me and McClure and what do we see but five angels, Neal the archangel standing arm outspread, you next, golden hair, the kids, the jeepster outside, that surprise visit? The talk and walks, and that funny evening I got thrown out of the Hiss the Villain play?

Boy, do you realize how many books I could write?

Well, your part in the story is you talk to me quietly and sadly about Neal, about the old days, the new, I describe the children, what you're doing for them, your home, but there's that undercurrent of strange muted romance between us. So please dont get mad.

What I'm really worried about (about somebody getting mad) is Jacky: I come right out and say she bores me whereas you (Evelyn) never do—O it was horrible.... well ... it ends up that terrifying night of Sept 3 1960

308

when I went mad for the first time, while Jacky slept, her kid slept, Lew and Lenore slept, but I had nightmares the likes of which I only barely can describe ... It was the night of the end of Nirvana, in fact—I realized all my Buddhism had been words—comforting words, indeed, but when I saw those masses of devils racing for me—but Buddha did ward off devils under the Bo Tree before he knew and understood—but I'd like to tell you all about it when I see you—At least, one of these days, we'll have one of our old quiet religious arguments by the fireplace as Neal sits there playing self-chess saying "Hm, yass, got ya dirty pawn" "You old Queen"

Give my bestest regards & deep real love for that marvelous Al Hinkle and that marvelous Helen

And, A Dieu

or as the Mexicans say,

Okay, Memo

Jack

TO TOM GUINZBURG

October 19, 1961
[Orlando, Florida]

Dear Tom,

Publishers send me at least a book a week to comment upon. I just finished writing my new novel "Big Sur" so you can see I'm busy. So sometimes I just glance at these novels, and if I see the prose is bad I dont answer, if the prose is interesting I send a post card. If the prose is really very good I write a little more. I have my own work to do.

But I've just read all of Ken Kesey's book, because I'd thought at first glance the prose was unusually good ("talented and honest," remember?) but now I see I have to make a truly honest statement about this here Ken Kesey: "A GREAT MAN AND A GREAT NEW AMERICAN NOVELIST!"

Tom, this guy is no doubt the Columbia Gorge Indian himself, apparently "Kesey" is his wife's name, Tee Ah Millatoona's probably his real name, which would certainly be a better name that [sic] a phoney name (I wish he'd used it) (but I understand he's ashamed of being identified with the "deafmute" hero himself).

Not only that but this Indian has a great sense of language, of American lingo, and gets it down on paper. And it's a powerful novel. MacMurphy is a great character and so are George the Swede, the girls, the Big Nurse and others. It's just real good. I gave you my "statement" up above but I tried to make it brief for blurb purposes: you can extract anything you want from this letter, in any case, for a blurb you might combine yourself.[7]

---

7. Viking Press used one phrase from Kerouac's letter on the front flap of the dust wrapper of Kesey's novel when it was published in 1962: "A great new American novelist."

(He sure is right about that "Combine," isn't he? And incidentally that's real Wester[n] Indian talk, the way they pronounce "Combine" even when they're just working on harvests). Anyway, tome, this guy is great. And it will be of great interest for all of us to see his second novel. Tell him not to be ashamed of the dignity of his experience as a man in the world, the hell with the rest.

Jack

The word Great in above letter, same old Jack, but I mean it Tom

By return mail, Carolyn Cassady replied to Kerouac's letter of October 17, 1961, telling him about her life in Los Gatos after Neal had been released from prison.

TO JACK KEROUAC
FROM CAROLYN CASSADY

Oct. 22, 1961
[Los Gatos, California]

Dearest Jack:

How sweet to get a long lovely letter out of the blue from you. All full of kind thoughts which are so eagerly received by one who can't seem to find a niche lately with any group of people.

First to reassure you all is well in L[os] G[atos]. Neal had a two week vacation in August and went back to Denver (with permission) to see his father and revisit old memories. In Denver I gather Neal had a good revealing reconnaisance, tho it was none too joyful. He saw his father a lot, who never quite believed Neal was really his son, but I believe Neal is finally satisfied that his Dad is in the right place and well off in his way, taking the burden of responsibility and guilt off Neal. Naturally he saw Bill and had his first fist fight with same. I was glad he took his notebooks with him and reviewed some of the scenes he'd planned to write about. Doesn't seem imminent he will do so, but anyway that's something.

He's being a very good boy at work and home, but still depends on his weekends with the party gang where he can ogle the girls, sometimes get artificial stimulation in one form or another, and swap metaphysical theories. I imagine the latter is the least of it all, however, and from what he tells me it's all pretty much like the old days with some of the edge off. Many of them are Stanford kids, the new crop of young rash self-centered aimless souls, feeling superior to anything tried and true, and seeking kicks for the physical realm, while swallowing spiritual insights in pill form or smoke. Luckily grandma Cassady doesn't have to participate and has gotten over caring if papa does. It may not be the best way for us to live, it may not be anything more than hanging on until his parole is up, but if this can be done anyway, we can consider other ways and means when that hurdle is over. I vacillate from one group of people to another, seeking distraction from becoming too involved again with Neal, but knowing all the time that's all it is, trying to keep up different kinds of fronts to suit the different roles I'm supposed to represent ... mother, neighbor, citizen, wife, artist, but in reality nothing more than a post for Neal to lean on when he wants to, an artist to be exploited by those who've made me indebted to them, and a completely ineffectual everything else. At the moment I'm completely dissatisfied with myself on every front ... so I shouldn't be writing to you now. What I should do is throw it all up, get a regular job, join the mob from nine to five, and at least guarantee my children the same front enjoyed by all their associates of pretty clothes, pretty cars and regular alcohol for mom and dad every night. As it is we are doing more drinking than we ever have, so we've made the grade there, but unfortunately haven't enough money for the rent each month as it is and can afford it less than ever. I fully intended to do this last fall, but got trapped in another vision of promise named the San Jose Opera Association, which is supposed to bring me fame and fortune, but when and if it ever will, it'll be too late, unless I get a job also in the meantime. Ah me, why can't I be sweetness and light all the time, lovingly indifferent to one and all and guide my children with love and wisdom, like I wanna. Well, I can see it's time to get back to the inspirational books again and find some time for the quiet meditation that erases all this sea of discontent. It's been a long time since I have, but time is even harder to find now. Actually I realize I'm one of the luckiest of mortals, and usually keep my mind on all the blessings I do have. ... it's been a long time too since I felt blue as I have the last couple days ... so don't take all this seriously, you know how it goes, but thanks for letting me use you as a target ... it will save Neal's poor overworked ears. Today he has taken Johnny down to Laguna Seca for the big race and ecstacy for both, leaving us four girls (you know my 23 yr old niece Judy has been living with us for a year?). We're all lolling about in our bathrobes, watching movies on TV, or they are, I'm doing my costumes (aren't I) and it's like a girls' dormitory. We're going to have steak for dinner too ... but we're out of wine ... oh, oh. Judy and I have discovered Madeira. The recipes always call for it, but I've never tried it till one day we decided to. Discovered it's only made in Portugal, hence as expensive as it is, but it does have a delicious taste ... can't drink much of it at a time, tho.

What I was going to say was ... we have been looking for you ever since August and hoped you'd come up from Mexico. But when Lew Welch said he'd heard from you that you were coming, I knew it wouldn't be a nice quiet time together if he and the SF satellites knew of it, much as I enjoy Lew. So I'm kinda glad you knew best, yet still hope you'll come someday soon and not tell anyone until after you've been here awhile. Then we and you can open you to the public again if you like.

You've made me terribly anxious to read "Big Sur" and I'm really so touched you've included me and in a way to mean something to you. I've always felt the love we did share was so wonderful it was too bad it wouldn't "sell" like your other romances, yet I've been glad too and grateful that you've kept it out altogether, unless it could be immortalized and not sullied . . . not by you . . . but by what people read into things when they read about other people, of which I am guilty as anyone. And that's as it should be, or rather it isn't important, as you say, in ages to come it will just be people in a story as life is anyway if we didn't get our tender egos and emotions all tangled in it. But we've known some real wonder and beauty which would be exceedingly difficult to get across with words and have them interpreted in the way it felt. Yet I think you are the only writer I know of who has a better chance of doing just this than any other. I guess this has been my biggest frustration all these years and thruout all this fad of beatnikitis . . . having known the unearthly, extra beautiful and gentle values of you and Neal, and seeing no one interested or aware of any side but the self-indulgent one with imitators by the score of all the parts you're both truly ashamed of without having the depth of knowledge or experience to know that anyone that's moving in a negative manner must have extremes in the other direction too . . . which is why you two are justified, etc., but why the imitators are so sad and deluded. They don't even know you don't try to do these things, but they just happen because you're living men, and they're notable because they're part of the rich fabric of life you are eager to live bla bla bla bla. You're so sweet to apologize to me I could bawl and I don't blame you for anything except perhaps for not pointing a better way to your flock since so many are worshipping your words of describing what is as a proclamation of what should be, minus the counterweight. But if you don't want to be a philosopher or a Christ you may have to wait for your true recognition of your true stature until later day critics or philosophers begin analysing your works and finding the germs of the real truth and explaining it to the public for you.

Jacky has gotten married to a colored "cat," as they say, and Neal has only seen her once to talk to, I believe, since her new spouse doesn't encourage old lovers visiting . . . can't think why. And that's all he knows about her. See—one big change in Neal and me I'd like you to register is that he is real open with me about his doings now and talks about Jackies etc. I never ask questions, so maybe that's it, but actually he tells me more than I want to hear anyway. But you remember the old secrecies and lies and things I brought on myself by my possessive attitude. You've probably had a lot to do with this by abstracting much of it to an objective viewpoint in fiction.

It really has been difficult not seeing you and I've gone over every memory so many many times, they're threadbare. I'm so excited about the book [that] I hope you will find time to send excerpts but I know how hard that is to do. Better still, bring some, read them to me. How I wish you could be writing one within our walls again and get to look over your shoulder as it progresses and hear your thoughts between the lines as of yore. Gee, heaven. Why couldn't we have gotten that cute little trailer for you out in the back yard, or why can't I earn a vast amount and make the garage into a room for you where you could lock the door and have a view of the beautiful hills.

I'll go now, back to work. Ahhh, you've helped a lot; I'm all cleansed now and feel much more like creating. Now maybe I can get that opera on the boards and a great one, and it'll be the most gorgeous Christmas Nutcracker ballet anywhere!

Thank you, love, for being, forgive me for tying up your great mind so long with my little one, and please find a way to come let us bask in your aura some more and receive your blessings. I wish you and the children could become close again; that was a feature that really saddened me last time. John, by the way, has been writing terrific stories for school (even tho flunking otherwise), so who knows, maybe you'll have a true name sake yet.

A dieu, ti Jean, I love you,

Carolyn

Neal said Sat. nite at a party a funny thing, said he was just a dirty old man—we know better. Et tu, Brute?

Later in the fall of 1961, Kerouac wrote frequently to Ferlinghetti about various writing projects.

TO LAWRENCE FERLINGHETTI

Oct. 23, 1961
[Orlando, Florida]

Dear Lorenzo . . .

Yes, I'm still here but going to N.Y. within 10 days just for visit . . . You might send the legal copyright of BOOK OF DREAMS to Sterling . . . I hope Outsider takes dirty asshole poem . . . America needs it . . . Eau de Cologne scented commuters all sitting together in the 8:02 from Millbrae looking guiltily over their newspapers at other dirty assholes . . .

You ask WHAT YOU DOIN DOWN DERE ANYWAY, well I'll tell you, pops, I just wrote a huge full length novel about your cabin in Bixby Canyon . . . Hor hor hor . . .

Everybody in it (of course I won't call it Bixby Canyon and won't make it 18 miles south of Monterey, etc.) even Victor Wong is in it, fact quite a lot ... You in it, of course, tho I was going to have lots more at the "end" when I come to your house 706 but suddenly saw the novel should end at the cabin with Lew Welch and Jacky etc. Gotta type it up now ... It's 60 foot roll singlespace ... Will type it up late November ... Is my first novel since Dharma Bums written Nov. 1957 ... FOUR YEARS of bugged non-privacy was the cause ... Now, suddenly, alone in Florida, bing, a novel ... More to come, too.

Like a novel about Allen, a novel about Peter, a novel about Gregory, a novel about Burroughs, a novel about G. J. in Lowell, a novel about ci pi ca pi toutes les coigns ... (Djever hear "pi" used in Normandy stead of "et") (for "and"?)—shortened "epui"

Well, Lt. Commander Ferlinghetti, and what name shall I give you. I've decided on Harold Albigherti for the time being but if you can think of a ancienter Italian ghetto name? Marco Polo? Pops Feltrinelli? Harry Albighetti? Jimmy Spaghetti? Roger A. Priori? Arapahoe Rappaport? Leonardo da Levi? Per Se Williams? Carl Cunt?

Novel covers story from skid row hotel Mars of first getaway, to finding you in woods by accident, to back to city, etc. the whole shot—I had a detailed chronological chart of all the events but lost it in Mexico this summer; however, I got a memory like a pisspot. Anyway, tho sad, lugubrious, etc., there are some funny scenes throughout.

After I come back from N.Y., type up new book, spend Christmas here, I then take another trip. Where to? To Japan via 3 weeks in Frisco? To Paris for a garret in Montmartre? Anyway, somewheres. I in fact dreamed of being in a big Japanese city the other night walking down a shopping boulevard buying strange groceries and watching people on bikes waiting at red lights but with big huge canopied umbrellas much too big for bike to hold—well, I often dream ahead a time, anyway, s'why I mention.

Now that Old Angel Midnight is no longer barred by Post Office, are you ever going to make it into a nice lil old pocketbook? Or a BOOK OF HAIKUS with my drawings, like this, see (casual, Karumi-lightness):

Hurrying things along,
   Autumn rain
On my awning

Ah well, let me hear from you—tell Victor i am dying to see him again—give my love to henry evans and tell him find my volume 20 of Ency. Brittanica—greetings to lew embree, shig, homer, virgil and dante.

Jean-Louis

[November 1961]
JK c/o Blake
Orlando, Fla.

Mr. Lawrence Ferlinghetti
   (Serlingheppi?)
      (Lorenzo Monsanto?)
         CITY LIGHTS BOOKS
         261 Columbus Ave.
         San Francisco 11, Calif.

Dear Larry,

Lorenzo Monsanto[8] it is, fine name ... I call it "Raton Canyon" (which means Raccoon, doesn't it?)—Book will please you in many ways—Lots about Victor but only one word about Homer—Ends on last day in canyon so I didn't get to write about fine visit for 3 days on Wisconsin—Endings of stories always come to me in a flash altho I'd intended to carry story to Wisconsin—Neal emerges again great—Also Lew Welch, of course, and Whalen—Later—Am typing it up—Off long scroll—Later we can talk about any new book from me you might want—BOOK OF HAIKUS not collected yet but my latest haiku the best:

Chief Crazy Horse looks
   North with tearful eyes—
The first snow flurry

If so, would collect all my haikus from notebooks and put together for a book—Later—Now is business of prose muscles—I drinking whisky and typing slow—I Li Po and I you good amigo

Jack

Transcribing Big Sur *in early December 1961 from a roll of Teletype paper onto conventional sheets of typing paper, Kerouac put a few wishful thoughts on a post-card to Gary Snyder, hoping to rendezvous with him, Ginsberg, and Orlovsky in India in the coming year. Instead Jack made a brief trip to Vermont, looking for land on which to build a cabin, and when this mission was unsuccessful, he visited friends in New York City.*

TO GARY SNYDER

[Early December 1961
Orlando, Florida]

Dear Gare—Would conceivably meet you in March for Himalaya climbing and scenes like that and then return to Japan with you—Let's start

8. Ferlinghetti's pseudonym in *Big Sur*.

arranging that—I could fly to (Benares?) whichever, with full rucksack—Don't like hot snaky Ceylon anyhow—Me Mahayana coward of North—

> Autumn—Geronimo weeps—
> No pony
> With a blanket

Really mean it, for northern India meet—So you and Allen send post-cards set up meet—March or so—Am now typing up new big novel BIG SUR you will also like bettern DBums ... because honester—Recently hurried from Penn Station to lower west side NY waterfront with full rucksack while swigging wine in cold wind, so think I can still climb mtns.—Was recently drunk 30 days so can still swig mtns too—Gettin stronger, or weaker, ONE ... But love you

Jack

In the last days of 1961, Kerouac wrote Ginsberg and Orlovsky in Israel, describing his "30-day biggest drunk of all" on Canadian Club whisky. Allen and Peter had split up as a couple in Tangier, but they reunited in Tel Aviv. Jack mentioned to Allen that William Burroughs had come to New York City for a brief visit but hadn't made an effort to contact him or Lucien Carr. After the publication of Naked Lunch *by Olympia Press in Paris in 1959, Burroughs became involved in his "cut-up" literary method with a new group of friends.* Naked Lunch *was published by Grove Press in March 1962. A few months later the novel was the subject of heated controversy at the Edinburgh International Writers' Conference, where the acute critic Mary McCarthy gave her support to Burroughs's writing. Her prestige helped to establish an audience for him as an important contemporary author, winning for Burroughs the respect from literary critics and academics that Kerouac had always sought as a writer.*

TO ALLEN GINSBERG & PETER ORLOVSKY

December 28, 1961
Jack c/o Blake
PO Box 700
Orlando, Fla.

Dear Allen & Peter—

Glad to see you're together again. Why split out? Be like Boswell & Johnson, or Auden & Kallman, or Petronius & Ascyltus—Han Shan and Shihte, really—Or is all that moonlight faded away even from you—I can't even take refuge in the Tao or the Dharma anymore, have forgotten all about them, and can't think of anything more tedious than becoming Ker-

316

ouassady again—Pretty soon I might start yakking about moats and velvet drapes & Yseult, like Gregory ... Lucien was furious in N.Y. because Bill was in town and didn't even look him up, or me (I left message, but too late, with Barney Rosset)—Lucien was affronted real aristocratic like & we simmered together about that before our weekly wrestling match the last one ending in a horrible battle in Jerry Newman's sound studio with ripped coats, shirts, down to t-shirts, almost pants, blood, lost wallets—In the country as he sat talking in kitchen I calmly three times lifted my big Gary boots and knocked his chair over on his back, slowly, like ringing slow three-time Suzuki TripleBody doorbell or Trinity gong—I sorry now—His theory about my never getting mad all shot—I mean, never getting *mean*—We all woke up at sunny Indian summer morning to hear Jacques Beckwith playing pan flute on furry hill, high up in a tree—Me and Jacques journeyed to Vermont to buy land so he build me a cabin on it, greedy idiot Vermonters would only sell land AFTER they cut all the timber down to 8 inch stumps—to sell for few bucks—So me and Jacques come back, I was on 30-day biggest drunk of all—Getting worse all the time, whiskey yet—Almost got busted by cops who frisked me at 3 A.M. as I carried huge board to Jacques' loft—They thought I was going to hit somebody with huge board like crazy spade—But I wrote my best haikus that trip: "Chief Crazy Horse/ looks tearfully north—the first snow flurry"..... "Autumn night—/ the Whippenpoofers/ singing on the train"..... "In Autumn Geronimo/ weeps—no pony/ with a blanket."—

| "November—how nasal the drunken Conductor's call." | "November's New Haven baggagemaster stiffly Disregards my glance." | "Big drinking & piano parties—Christmas Come and gone— |

But despite boozing a la worse than ever, I did manage to type up whole huge manuscript of Big Sur novel, with carbon, and corrected it, not one mistake, and mailed it to Sterling before Xmas—all done in ecstasy, in fact (with bennies)—Also ate 12 SMushrooms in one afternoon and wanted to send telegram to Winston Churchill something about an old Baron crying for his hounds in his "weird wield weir," thinking, on psilocybin, one baron to another he'd understand—Gad, how self-aggrandized you get on S[iberian] M[ushroom]'s—Last time, remember, I was Genghiz Khan—I incidentally wrote Timothy Leary and Pearl that I think this is the Siberian sacred mushroom used by Brainwash-inventor Airapatianz to empty American soldier prisoners in Korean brainwash program—Because if you become so emptied you don't even care if you're Kerouac or Ginsberg or Orlovsky, and what that meant to you before, then you're ready to become anything at all, for any reason, even perhaps an assasin?—Serious business—I'm against it definitely now—I wrote nothing of value on it, or painted anything good, just vainglorious POOPOOS ... I'm terrified to hear about

Lafcadio & your mama, Peter—or don't tell me you haven't heard about it?—
If so, tell me right away, I have clippings about Laff now in Asylum etc.—
If Marie's trying to hold this back from you then I've made a blunder—Laff
let his hair grow down to his shoulders, full beard, never left Main Street
tenement apartment and began howling like an animal and taken to jail
where your mother tried to stab him so they wouldn't put him away—Can't
figure why you didn't mention this in recent postcard from Sodom—But if
you do NOT know about this, rest calm, Laff is alright and the authorities
sympathize with yr Ma—I hope they let Laff paint in hospital now and learn
good work habits make him big future DeKooning millionaire playboy &
buy your mother house on Gilbert Street—It can be done—At age 5 I also
was terrible all-day-chair-sitter catatonic artist genius—Even at 21 a bit—
and especially at 24—Now look at me, I big happy international wreck—
With nothing to look forward to, believe me—But maybe a big miracle will
happen—Maybe the angels will come to get me but give me just one week
to write big final hymn and type it up, and go—or I get Angel typist to do
it while I lecture and recite pompously—Maybe just ordinarily get Swiss
cabin in Alps side mountains over village—Maybe go to a bell bingbong
monastery in France and be winepresser & get small brushes and become
illuminated manuscript maker—Very curious, Allen, but now I understand
why you never wanted to meditate even in exciting 1955 yelltimes ... altho
Ben Gurion now meditating ... I tried it recently, had it, perfect, to a T
Bodhidharma's thing about let nothing from outside come in, nothing from
inside yak out, but I don't care any more even about nothingness ... hmm.
Write long letter from India, maybe I could join you in Nepal in March as
I say for mountain climb ... I can see the disastrous dénouement even now,
tho ... & maybe miracle not.

Jacky

*In a last letter in 1961, Kerouac wrote down his favorite Québécois recipe for
Jacqueline Stephens. He concluded by describing his favorite food for cooking in
the woods using ingredients from his rucksack.*

TO JACQUELINE STEPHENS

[Late December 1961
Orlando, Florida]

Dear Jacqueline Stephens,
    Briefly, here is just about my favorite recipe: oldfashioned Quebecois
cortons, a kind of *pate de porc gras.* Ingredients:

2 pounds of ground Boston pork butt (with all the fat)
2 onions
2 garlics
teaspoon dry mustard

Simply immerse the ground pork butt till water just covers it, in pot, with onions & garlic chopped in, and salt and pepper, and dry mustard. Let simmer slowly (say, 5 hours).

Spoon & level into bowls; chill bowls in ice box.

Next day, use as sandwich spread on crackers (preferably good French bread).

It has been sensationally received by all non-French Canadians I made it for.

In the uncomplicated solitude of the woods, I often make yellow corn-meal Johnny cakes by simply making a batter out of yellow corn meal, chopped onions, and salt & pepper, and tablespooning out into sizzling corn oil, turning over to brown both sides of each cake.

With this, in the woods, I always make my favorite soup.[9] Ingredients:

Package Lipton's Green Pea soup
Bacon
Onions
Salt & Pepper

Simply fry chopped bacon till the pieces are crisped dark brown, then throw the onions and spiced soupmix into bacon and sizzling fat, and stir. Let simmer a minute for excellent pea soup.

Goes as good in vast silver toureens. [sic] Really very good. [....]

Seriously & sincerely,

Jack Kerouac

9. See *The Dharma Bums*, Chapter 29: "At dusk Japhy lit a good big fire and started supper.... He made a soup that night that I shall never forget.... This was nothing but a couple of en-velopes of dried pea soup thrown into a pot of water with fried bacon, fat and all, and stirred till boiling. It was rich, real pea taste, with that smoky bacon and bacon fat, just the thing to drink in the cold gathering darkness by a sparkling fire." See also Chapter Six of *Big Sur*, where Kerouac described another favorite meal of "potatoes wrapped in foil and thrown on the fire, and coffee, and hunks of Spam roasted on a spit, and applesauce and cheese."

1962

Early in January 1962, Kerouac realized that he had forgotten to answer the letter Carolyn Cassady had sent him the previous October.

TO CAROLYN CASSADY

Sunday Jan. 7, 1962
[Orlando, Florida]

Dear Carolyn:

Kindof in a state of dotage where, during past 2 1/2 months, I determined at least 25 times to sit and write answering your long letter of Oct. 22nd and by nightfall had plum forgot, drunk—Then suddenly when my mother reminded me this was the first year I'd failed to receive a Xmas card from Cassady's I said, Ulp, I still havent answered that letter—which however oughta be a lesson to you to write to me anytime whether or not or if as yet I've answered you, see?—just write when you feel like it, I too—

So dont consider this an answer to your long letter, bust just a letter (bust just that)—See, drunk already and only 2 o'clock, altho I have no more booze now—

I never did get to see that PM West show, they dont carry it in Florida—Since October when I wrote to you, after finishing writing Big Sur I just rolled it up and put it away and went to New York to visit Vermont to see about buying cabin land—I should have gone around Bennington or something, but no I went near the Conn. river where all the idiots are cutting down trees before they sell you any land—Disgusted I came back to NY and went on a 30 day drunk, awful—But I had a marvelous time and saw everybody and met new great people—I was in despair tho, because I do need a retreat cabin somewhere sometime soon—My next go at it, might go see what they got in the Carolina smokies, huh?—Hot sun and cool nights, I imagine—

Big Sur is being read by publishers and no word yet ... When I got back from NY I had to spend a month typing it up double-space carbons—No

321

secretary, you see—What I really need is Carolyn the secretary and Neal the chauffeur which wouldnt be a far fetched idea if I ever get at Hemingway's income level ... which is possible—But I think Neva Dell Hunter's reading might reveal that I was a Negro slave quite recently (as you once suggested) so I better stick to beans—I really would enjoy a reading and maybe someday we'll synchronize everything—We'll probably find out that in Atlantis, when I was the court astrologer, I was in love with you and we ran away to the desert, and Neal was the King and had me beheaded—More likely he was stealing paddlewheels on the riverfront—Allen Ginsberg was probably dancing over the rooftops in pink tights—Neal was probably really the King's right hand man—The King was probably a strange queer—

Actually, as I said to you before, I definitely remember being a footpad in 1750 England running a gang of queer boys—who got money from rich lords and gave me the proceeds—and I fell in love with a London girl dancer and murdered her with an axe and got hanged—But I wish I could remember with equal facility when I was Balzac or somebody nice like that, or Raffaello—

Dont worry about the "beatnik" lies about Neal—It seems people are still lying about Joyce, and here he's been dead 22 years—Even Shakespeare-haters still hate Shakespeare, so—How did your Christmas Nutcracker suite come out?

If I ever do live in yr yard, I'll pay for the trailer myself; that would be nice at that. I could have a small refrigerator with ice cubes, butane stove, etc. and go there yearly just to sleep in yard in sleepingbag and write an annual report on Neal, like Boswell and Johnson—Have you noticed there's nothing "evil" and "Beat" about my writing about Neal, it's no different than Boswell annotating Johnson's days.

I'm glad Jacky got married ... she needs help. She really drove me crazy. You'll see a good description of how in book. I had to send out both copies but would love nothing better than January fireside readings with you tonight ... I understand she also drove Neal nuts after I left, and Jaime too.... The book outlines the possibility that she's a witch. It's being read by a Playboy editor who wants whole edition of Playboy devoted to just the novel, like Life done with [Hemingway's] Old Man and the Sea, remember, and being bandied back and forth by competing publishers Viking and Farrar Straus and Grove, really saddens me in a way I dont have one reliable friendly publisher but have a dozen all angry.

On that 30 day binge in New York I stayed at the lofts of two painters and we got drunk and tacked up a huge canvas and proceeded to paint a vast Pieta which started out okay with my white dove in a black sky, on the right over the cross, and then the Cross was designed by me but re-designed as a crooked tree-type-cross by one of the painters, then came the figures, the whites, blues, then we started another new long canvas to be called "Ohio River" or "Dark Laughter" where I drew man and woman loving on sawdust by river and we worked at that, going up big stepladders, in aprons, I think I'm going to be a painter someday. I love to go up big stepladders in an apron with brush and paint pot. We finally ended up ruining everything with gobs of wet paint turning shit brown, as you know. It was just for laughs. One of the painters was a Swiss, Hugo Weber, tall and lovable drunk, tho not as drunk as everybody thinks, who says I should get a cabin in the Swiss alps. I met several interesting girls that visit him and stand on stepladders looking around at all the canvases. One of them was Yseult Snepvangers, who plays Beethoven by ear and calls me Tristram. Another was Van something or other, and an Armenian girl, and my own girl Lois, but I was so drunk I made love to nobody but a 65 year old ex-movie star across the street so now I'm even with Neal and his palm tree affair with the palmist in San Jose. (Women dont change at 65)—The reason I'm talking like this is that here in Fla. I have no girl friends, no men friends, nobody to talk to, nothing, I'm just alone with my books all the time, so it's a big event when I go to NY and see people, or Calif.

Now that I'm free to do anything I want, I've deliberately imprisoned myself, like a hair shirt, I dunno why. And the months roll by, and turn into years, and it's amazing to realize I havent seen you and Neal since summer 1960!

Here it is 1962.

I'm 40 years old now. Because of excessive drinking my cells have changed so often in daily hangovers that I look younger than I did at 30. Like Dorian Gray, underneath it I may start cropping a corpse. No, actually I exercise, drink good booze, get sun, do allhealing headstands and am Okay. But my mind is dotty. Like, I actually did forget to write to you for a whole month. What I'm actually doing is WAITING FOR SOMETHING. Something's gotta give. I'm very happy with ma and the cats, three cats, but it's not enuf for a grown man, of course. Next week I have to pack for New York again for big awful court scenes where I spose the newspapermen will be watching how I shuffle in my seat or something. I'm going to get a blood test, if not, appeal for one, till I get it, and prove that child is not of my blood. I even have an extra lawyer on the line in case Eugene Ginsberg Brooks doesn't override the objections of ex-wife's lawyers for a blood test. Why the objections? Because she knows damn well. But it's going to be horrible: and at the same time negotiations on Big Sur will be on hand, and I have to write the documentary narration for the film on Paul Gauguin, Rebel in Paradise, which I cant pass up (several thousand dollars) considering how the money situation is closing in on me. I can do as good a job on that as any artist ever did on patronage. That's not the point. I'll have to find a peaceful hotel room in midtown manhattan and go to bed alone and sober at night till it's all over. Then by god I'm going WEST!

Karma is a strange thing, alright. It's so sad that apparently Neal, for instance, has had deeper friendships than he had with me, since we ran around together, and you too in a way, how we've fallen apart ... Allen in India.... Lafcadio in the madhouse ... Burroughs so grumpy he wont even call Lucien and me on the phone.... Gregory grumpy too.... etc ... Jack a drunk.... O, and the old visions of ecstasy ...

Just write to me soon about anything, also transmit any message of N's.... I'll just sweat it out, life in general, I mean.

Jack XXX

By mid-January 1962, Kerouac's editor Robert Giroux at Farrar, Straus and Cudahy had bought both Visions of Gerard *and* Big Sur *for what Kerouac considered the "princely sum" of a $10,000 advance. Kerouac wrote Giroux and his editor Tom Guinzburg at Viking about the sale.*

TO ROBERT GIROUX

[January 15, 1962]
J. Kerouac
c/o Blake
P.O. Box 700
Orlando, Florida

Dear Bob

I want to make sure that before any linotypist tries to linotype any portions of either Big Sur or Visions of Gerard, that a dash goes like this (–) and a hyphen goes like this (-).

When editor Don Allen of Grove Press went on a vacation to Peru in 1959 and left the editing to another guy, they came up with the awful dashes (--) of Doctor Sax that I think are so indistinguishable from the hyphens (-) as to've thrown everybody *off* that book–The same thing happened with the shoddy printing of Book of Dreams by Ferlinghetti's City Lights.

"The Subterraneans" was correctly printed, with dashes so (–) long, and hyphens so (-) long, creating no confusion as to my meaning–As I told you, the reason for the dashes is to give the reader advance visual warning of the impending end of a sentence which after all is a rhetorical expostulation based on breathing and has to end, and I make it end with a vigorous release sign, i.e., the dash–This has now become my trademark anyway ... (I mean, apart from their original purposes as visual separation signs).

Others have tried to imitate it but they don't know how–Walter Gutman who financed Pull My Daisy movie tries to use dashes he thinks the way I do, in his newsletter, but he only uses the dash as a kind of lackadaisical separation–I mean to use my dashes as definite separation of definite whole statements–In fact Gutman (and others) try to use dashes to separate clauses

WITHIN a sentence which is not what I mean at all—For the separation of clauses and statements WITHIN a sentence I use parentheses, as you know.

If there's any point in Gerard where dashes separate clauses within a sentence, I agree with you about turning that into parentheses—I doubt there are any, or many—As to ending paragraphs with a dash, that also can be arranged and changed there into periods.

As I told you, Gray Williams then with McGraw-Hill tried to put periods before my dashes in Lonesome Traveler and it looked just as awful as inadequately long dashes.

Why don't you read my "Essentials of Spontaneous Prose" printed in Evergreen and reprinted in college textbooks for a full explanation of how I discovered, since the days you were truly my mentor, that altho I had to learn to handle the reins I still needed the horses—I mean by that, critics have failed to realize that spontaneous writing of narrative prose is infinitely more difficult than careful slow painstaking writing with opportunities to revise—Because spontaneous writing is an ordeal requiring immediate discipline—They seem to think there's no discipline involved—They don't know how horrible it is to learn immediate and swift discipline and draw your breath in pain as you do so—And you'll notice that I know perfectly well where commas should go, nathless their horseshit ignorant criticisms—

I'll see you sometime in February to hash all this out, our manuscripts prepared for printer, etc., and I'm glad to be involved with you again as literary magicians—I look forward to great conversations and quiet suppers, this time I can even pay for some of them—We'll go to Sweets' and have lobster, hey?—Please give my regards to Roger Straus and tell him I apologize about asking him about Dick Kelly so insistently: now I remember it was Farrar who knew Dick Kelly.

Drop me a note whenever you can—Tell me a little about yourself & recent life—Still with the Opera Club etc?—Alas, lachrymae rerum, yet how good it is that everything'll vanish eventually—(some people, it makes 'em mad) (but it makes me feel god) (how just is God).... how clever.

Hasta la vista
Jack

Visit Florida at my home at will—

TO TOM GUINZBURG

Jan. 17, 1962
[Orlando, Florida]
Unmailed letter to Tom Guinzburg

Dear Tom,

Sterling tells me you feel very sad about the BIG SUR business—But as I told you, when FS & Cudahy took Visions of gerard, which Malcolm

Cowley rejected summarily, they exercised their option on the next work, which is Big Sur—Now remember if you will, for instance, that Malcolm rejected Maggie Cassady as a full whole work by itself and wanted to publish it with miscellaneous short stories because as a novel it was "too thin"— Nevertheless Avon Books bought it whole and entire, as a novel, and advanced $7500 on it (this was before Hearst bought Avon books and subsequently stopped the distribution of my books there, as far as I can gather from never seeing it anywhere) (or the other $7500 novel, Tristessa, which was also turned down by Malcolm). Malcolm just turned down everything: Gerard as well as Doctor Sax and The Subterraneans as well as Desolation Angels which is the last available novel I have (already written) in my desk— And he even had Dharma Bums mutilated beyond recognition and I had to pay you $500 to have it restored to the original condition I wrote it in, receiving the bill from Viking which says "Alterations" when the bill should have read "Restorations." But my point here is this: first, would your editors have accepted Big Sur? and secondly, would they have advanced me the princely sum FS & Cudahy advanced for it? (biggest I ever got), and with the understanding that not a word is to be changed? Goddamit Tom, I had a rough time even after the social bomb of On the Road getting as much as a $2000 advance on Dharma Bums! (I realize you weren't the boss then, I don't mean your father but the old literary men in there who never even shook my hand because they thought I was a hoodlum.) They were more excited about Dennis Murphy. That was because he wrote more like the 1920's than I did. My business is not to write like in the 1920's but to make a new literature, which I've done. You wouldn't have a Ken Kesey today without somebody breaking the ground & springing personal storytelling loose from "fictional" devices.

From what Sterling says you feel real bad—If you want a definite promise from me, in writing, as here, for the option on my next book, which I'll write late 1962 after traveling around, here it is. I made no definite promise about Big Sur, I just wanted to show it to you first because I liked you personally and I wanted to go back to firstclass publishing and figured things might have changed since you took over the reins of the company. But when Straus offered me that juicy offer I figured I needed the money. Everybody is making money off my ideas, like those "Route 66" TV producers, everybody except me so when they offered me ten grand advance I took it. (Besides, as you know, I have old associations and memories with Bob Giroux from 1950 when he edited The Town and The City rather badly but not from any mean motive.) It seems no publisher wants me to exceed 490 pages tho everybody else is allowed to do so. Ah, it's a disgusting business, I'm sorry about how you feel, your feelings mean something to me ... I remember the party at MacManuses' and what you said there ... would it really make things up if I promised you my next novel? Really, tell me, frankly, let me know ... And would you've honestly advanced ten grand for Big Sur? Now, come on, tell me. Let's straighten this out. Sterling is very concerned I think for personal reasons mostly. It all happened in a flash over the phone, I was joking with Giroux about a huge advance and he said "Okay"—(we were phoning about Gerard manuscript)—It's not against my principles to offer you my next novel because I can offer the one after that to FS & Cudahy according to their own optional demands. As for "Desolation Angels," that was rejected by Malcolm, and is wanted by Grove, but we don't want to offer it just yet so's not to clash on publishing dates. Meanwhile Tom please assure me in a letter or note, goddamit, that my main business is WRITING books, after all ... after all, I'm not a businessman. My father *was* but he also wasn't a novelist. If novels you can call them. Narrative sections of one long life story is what my "novels" are ... Well, finally, if you have to show this letter to Malcolm, tell him for me that I will always remember how he helped me get published in the beginning but he shouldn't have expected me to write like his 1920 heroes after I got On the Road out of my system and hit out on my own style ... I've nothing to do with Scott Fitzgerald and much to do with Joyce and Proust ... Please answer something, Marine Jack

During the first half of February 1962, Kerouac wrote Stella Sampas and Robert Creeley about his quiet life in Florida.

TO STELLA SAMPAS

Friday Feb. 9 62
[Orlando, Florida]

Dear Stella

Yr soft pretty description of domestic happiness with your mother is innocent of the fact that you are happier than most people in this world—You might want to be here, to be there, but it all amounts to nothing—I too've been living a quiet domestic life at home for ten months now except for a trip to NY and to Mexico earlier—I just get up, read in the sun, eat, watch TV, walk and write till 6 A M—Florida peace has been good to me because I finally wrote a new novel, as I think I told you—Incidentally Farrar Straus & Cudahy will publish the next novel about Lowell in Sept. 1963, *Visions of Gerard*—I'm enclosing *Book of Dreams*, which is mostly about Lowell, in case you or Charley or Pertinax never heard of it—It's a little risqué because it was written as a private dream diary with no intention of publication but some descriptions of Dream Lowell are worth it to me—Some allusions to Sammy & Charley here and there—Did you know about the existence of this Book of Dreams? t'was published early 1961—Bad job of typography—

As I grow older I more and more come to the life of a kind of literary monk—I'm alone all the time, except for family—No friends, no girlfriends either down here, on purpose—I'm just happy to be alone & studying—I'm reading everything, history, poetry, philosophy, the works—I don't get drunk any more except on special occasions—I'm actually entering a happy phase of life at 40—I'm now a confirmed bachelor—Later, a hut in the hills—somewhere—maybe Calif.—even maybe France—or Switzerland—History rolls on, people rage, but domestic silence is best of all—Ask the Church Fathers Orthodox or otherwise—

I'm going to visit Lowell this spring on the sly, and after I've been there walking around old scenes for a few days I'll call on you—Tentatively (I may have to go to Hollywood First)   Jack

TO ROBERT CREELEY

Feb. 16 1962
[Orlando, Florida]

Dear Bob

I just sent off a poem to THE OUTSIDER about how everybody dies and how sad it is (for us, anyway, not for the void) (if there is such a thing as the void, what is the void? a Jewish word? the word for word in Jewish? who ever heard of such a goddamn thing as a VOID?)—Cassady says that deaths occur sometimes in tiny infants because of previous Karma on the part of the parents who must pay for something incurred in a previous lifetime—Certainly, that's about the only way I can explain for instance my brother's death at Age 9 which made my father stop gambling and staying out late for the rest of his life—I thought I was dying last summer when I started throwing up blood but I decided then and there in bed I didnt give a shit about anything but heaven anyway—Which is also a "decent happiness"—Chacun a son goof, as my wisecracking friend Henri [Cru] says—But, and always remember what Buddha said to the woman who brought her three-day-dead infant to him in her arms and asked for him to bring the infant back to life, he said "Okay I'll do it if you now go to the city of Sravasti with its two millions of inhabitants and find one family which hasnt had a death in the past 20 years and when you do, bring me a mustard seed from that family."

He actually said "5 years" but in those days . . .

Certainly I would love to see you but I havent got any way of stopping off at Albuquerque when and if I ever go west which may be soon or not at all and I'm expected in Paris by old buddy Burroughs—I'm sure we'll meet soon somewhere, maybe all of a sudden we'll both roll in drunk at some cocktail party in the Berkshires. Or in Framingham! or Malden or Lynn!

Be sure, yes, to send me copy of your new book of poems—Not that I'm cheap, I just cant even find an Evergreen in "Orlando, Florida," man—or even an "On the Road" for that matter (banned)—No books at all except drugstore books about Exodus and Jackie Kennedy and James Jones—Not even one measly collection of English poems by Untermeyer available—[1]

If I only had a wild chauffeur to drive me to Albuquerque to see you, then to drive on say to Mexico City to see Lamantia, or to Frisco to see Whalen, or to wherever Dorn is (I think his poem about the plumber by the river with his daughter is one of the most mysterious yet clearest poems in the world)—Some wild chauffeur ... if I could only become rich like Sinatra and be a Chairman of the Board type with a private limousine with built in bar and TV and jazz records and go visiting poets, hey?—I don't even drive, myself—But as to "pulling you out" by seeing, by my seeing you, you'd probably end up socking me in a blind drunk or tackling me like you done Dorn that night ... no, just kidding....

So, meanwhile, let's have your long poem now, your Paradise Lost ... I'm going to New York tomorrow to get sued by an ex wife, just swell, I can just see the stuffy court room now and people staring at me to see if I really do twitch from all that dope and alcohol ... My mother says if I feel sick to just puke right there in front of them. I'm having a blood test to find out if the alleged daughter is really biologically mine: three previous bloodtests were arranged but wifey never showed up with so-called daughter; having conceived said daughter AFTER she threw me out in '51:—so we'll see: and you can bet your sweet life I'll never contract a "legal" marriage again: they dragged me outa grassy Whitman fields when I was 15 to "go to college and grow up and get married" for this.......... I'll see you shit or high water soon, look out

Jack

If you wanta continue writing to me at present time, which I hope you do, because I enjoy your letters, send next one or two to me c/o Lord, 75 East 55, NY 22 ... Allen G. is now in Bombay meeting Paul Bowles and Gary Snyder for trip to nepal ... where I was asked to be ... but shucks on that smallpox scene ... I've seen enough dead dog mud alleys in the slums of Mexico to last me awhile

p.s. Let me know in future letter if you've read TRISTESSA or even seen it or heard of it ... I sold it to Avon Books before Hearst bought the company and he has stopt distributing it ... Love to you, Bob   J

In mid-February 1962, Kerouac flew from Florida to New York City to meet Joan Aly and her ten-year-old daughter, Janet, on February 20 for lunch with his attorney in a Brooklyn bar where the corner television set was tuned to the astronaut John Glenn in a space capsule making his third orbit of the earth. Joan had taken

1. The poet and translator Louis Untermeyer (1885-1977) compiled anthologies that sold widely, including the influential *New Modern American and British Poetry*, revised with Karl Shapiro and Richard Wilbur in 1955.

Jan to a beauty shop to get her hair curled before her first meeting with her fa-
ther. As Jan described her impressions of Kerouac in her memoir Baby Driver
(1981), she could see why her mother "had been attracted to him. He was so
handsome with his deep blue eyes and dark hair hanging in a few fine wisps on
his forehead."

After lunch Jack and Jan took blood tests, and then he went back to Joan's
apartment on the Lower East Side to meet her twin daughters from her second
marriage. On the way Jan led him to a liquor store on Tenth Street for a bottle of
Harvey's Bristol Cream sherry, and she kept the cork as a souvenir when Jack fin-
ished the bottle at the kitchen table. In court the next month, the blood tests were
inconclusive, showing only that it was possible Jan was Jack's daughter. The
judge awarded Joan Aly, then supporting her three children on her earnings
as a waitress, a payment from Kerouac of fifty-two dollars a month for Jan's
expenses. Back in Orlando at the end of March, Jack explained to Sterling
Lord and Robert Giroux why he had missed his last appointments with them in
Manhattan.

TO STERLING LORD

March 28 1962

Dear Sterling

I hope you realize when I was in Long Island that last day, not far from
Idlewild, coughing and choking on bronchitis, it were better for me to grab
the first plane out, which I did—I fully intended to see you the next day in
New York but I think that after a few more days in New York I would have
wound up in a hospital there.

Now the hot sunshine has cured my cough and the remnant of your pills
have allowed me to calm right down back to normal, and I'm fine, mowing
the lawn etc. Incidentally, how much do I owe you for those sedative pills?

Enclosed is a letter to Tom Payne. Mail it on, please, to his New York
PLAYBOY address—I almost caught him there last week but he got drunk
himself and didnt return to the office after I'd talked over the phone with
Hefner's brother.

Is the PLAYBOY deal really a possibility now?

In the last check you sent me it says $25.00 for Little Brown payment
for use of ALONE ON A MOUNTAINTOP to be included in RETURN TO
READING by Randall E. Decker but underneath it says $12.75 for "bank
discounted at 4 1/4% $300 check from Canada 12/18/62"——I just dont
know what that is, a check for $300 is coming next December from
Canada? Can you explain?

I was anxiously waiting to hear from you all week. Also, is everything
okay at Farrar Straus? I settled the editing techniques with Giroux, as you
know.

I'm turning down countless new requests for "free" material, from Columbia magazine, others, etc. No more of that. And if you really feel the Hungarian and Czechoslovakian and Yugoslavian deals are boloney, just TELL me and I'll listen and agree.

You still have time to escape harsh April damps and take the sun here ... invent some "business" trip connected with PLAYBOY deal! tax free—Today for instance the sun was red hot but the air was water cool ... I already have my tan back ...

Let me hear the latest. I can do that Gauguin film, as I say, if they want to bring it down here, show it to me on a silent soundtrack 4 or 5 times. I can do it right here before they leave and go back. It's simpler than they think. Away from home there're too many complications now for me to write anything, whether it would be NY or Hollywood. It's amazing how people expect writers as prolific as myself to be valet, secretary, social secretary, traveling secretary, chauffeur and man-about-town all at the same time (and student of souls and cities all night long)....

As ever, dear Sterling, (write soon)
Jack

TO ROBERT GIROUX

March 31 1962
PO Box 700
Orlando, Fla.

Dear Bob:—

You'll appreciate why I plumb forgot our birthday luncheon date when I assure you that I even forgot my birthday itself!—It was a rainy day, remember, and it was my day in court, down around Chambers Street, a nervewracking day—Only later that night when I looked at the paper in the train to Long Island (to my attorney's home) and saw the date "March 12" did I realize it was my birthday—And after the "trial" was over (a trial in the Judge's chambers, of sorts) I felt a gnawing need to call either Lucien or you for I needed friendship that day, but I thought you were still in Barbados, and I didn't call Lucien either.

Another thing that helped confuse me was an earlier telegram you'd sent me, before I popped into your office on that February day, a telegram my mother kept writing and calling about, "Giroux wants to see you!" but I knew you were in Barbados—

The confusion was compounded by the fact that I had a nice little hotel room where I could sleep and refuse calls and clean up and straighten my mind out, but Negro visitors came and finally a girl and the hotel had me thrown out and there I was with my suitcase opened on people's couches drinking day and night—I did call Roger Straus once but I was drunk and asked him to sign another check but he just said "How are the boys in Chicago?" (the gang)—(It was 5:15 PM anyway)—

So that I did forget our luncheon birthday date, damn it, but you'll forgive me please because I even forgot the birthday—It was a horrible month, for one entire week I didn't sleep one wink, drinking and talking with hundreds and hundreds of my acquaintances day and night, in shifts—I ended up needing Sterling's personal help, he brought me sedatives to a sick bed—

I had a wonderful time in a sense, making another rash and riotous study of the city and all the dramatis personae of Duluoz Legend of course, but I really this time wanted to have quiet moments with you and as of old we could go eating in pleasant restaurants like Sweets and talk over literature—

But you know, Bob, you can invent a crisis and say you have to jet to Florida to my house to see about last minute details, like you done to Denver—We have a guest room here waiting for you, never been used by anyone—(Sterling came for only 4 hours with his wife Cindy)—We cook rare steaks on flaming coals—You can sit in the sun in yard chairs on a nice lawn surrounded by a 7 foot tall complete fence—You can sit your drink right there and read Boswell and listen to the mockingbirds—At night, if the wind is right, you can smell orange blossoms whole counties of em borne by the breeze from miles away—Quiet nights—If you're going to try to do that be sure to come before too late in May, when it starts gittin hot—

But don't worry about my forgetting the luncheon date—This I do now more than ever, I drink and drink like a maniac, like Frank Morley in his heyday in fact, and I am only guilty of a vice, not of lacklove for you my sweet brother. (Incidentally, in the impossible confusion of no hotel room, no place to rest, I forgot the Morley and Singer books but they're being mailed to me by a good friend.) I'm anxious especially to read the Morley.

How great it is to have an editor who finally understands the "Duluoz Legend" scheme! You're the first! Turn to next page now for details about enclosed galleys:

In the capitalized list of "Books by JK" "THE DULUOZ LEGEND" insert (in capitals) "LONESOME TRAVELER" and "BOOK OF DREAMS" (right after "VISIONS OF CODY" as I marked it there) because they are part of the Legend and have the uniform names (except in "LONESOME TRAVELER" my own name is "Kerouac" which was an idea of Gray Williams' at McGraw Hill). It'll still be alright because all the other names are like those in "BIG SUR" etc. If you've never seen a copy of "BOOK OF DREAMS" I'll send you one, I have two or three left (published by Ferlinghetti's City Lights Bookshop in 1961).

The only serious problem in the galley is page 26 where, in typing the manuscript, I skipped one whole line about how a tree grew out of a fallen treetrunk. Couldn't the printer just kill the one paragraph spacing on the page, shorten the dashes an em maybe, and find some way to stick the extra line in without too much trouble?—or even have that one page one line thicker than the others?

The other corrections are all duly marked—I don't know the official way to proofread with proper marks, but I'm sure it's clear to you and you can always red-ink the proper marks after mine which are in pencil ... (or over them.)

I doubt if there's one serious mistake left in the galleys now. One or two of the linotypist's "mistakes" I left in for their charm: there IS such a thing as concatenation *splendide*. Such as one point where Dave Wain the westerner says "Monsanta" instead of "Monsanto" which is precisely the way a westerner would pronounce the name in the heat of conversation.

Forgive this longwinded dull letter but I felt like talking to you.

When it starts getting hot here in late May I might go to California or to meet Burroughs in Greece or best, BOTH, and probably pass thru New York enroute and see you. But as I see, come on down here on some business trip. I am a hopeless paralyzed drunken mess and I don't know how long I'm going to live, if I keep on like this. It's not my liver or anything like that, it's my brain getting soft and paralyzed. Yet I have such a good time when I'm drunk, I feel such ecstasy, for people, for books, for animals, for everything. It's a shame there's a string tied to everything, huh? Yet I felt even happier when I was absolutely sober in the woods. Oh well, my next book will certainly not be any more of this boloney about "me drinking" etc.—I wanta try something new.

By the way, did you see "DESOLATION ANGELS" yet? If you want to see it, ask Sterling. That, and Gerard, runs out my string of "dray-mahs" now. I do have a huge philosophical work called "SOME OF THE DHARMA" which is the favorite of my sharpest friends: a philosopher from Fordham, a Japanese Zen master, and Ginsberg, for instance. And I have another book of poems like "MEXICO CITY BLUES" and I have other things even, on to infinity—

My plan re Burroughs is to spend time with him in Europe, go to London and Vienna with him, and write VISIONS OF BILL when I get back—I could go join Ginsberg in India and write IRWIN IN INDIA but I don't feel like it—

Incidentally, tho I still don't believe it's my daughter, the supreme court makes me pay $52 a month to her mother who is incidentally pregnant from a man who is not her present husband, so history repeats itself, but I can afford the $52 at least right now. The Judge was very funny and kept winking at me and saying I was an "exponent of a new philosophy" and almost came out to have a beer with me but I was afraid to be impolite and invite him in front of the clerks. etc. Écrit souvent

Jack

p.s. Roger Straus figured I would just blow that new $100 in bars on bums, I like him very much and hope he wasn't hurt when I said he looked like a Hood, at least no more than I do!

pp.ss. I met Edgar Varese during the binge, he said I spoke perfect Norman Medieval French (after some Parisians laughed at my accent, at a Gallery)

On April 4, 1962, Kerouac gave Donald Allen his impression of what was happening on the current literary scene.

TO DONALD ALLEN

April 4, 1962
P.O. Box 700
Orlando Fla.

Dear Don

Thanx for sending [San Francisco] Blues, I promptly bound them in my Book of Blues and will leave them there—Funny how they look so old-fashioned now, they were written in '54 but now everyone writes like that (with that fuckyou freedom)—Allen assures me now the avant garde is putting me down, which is a laugh can be heard even up on Mount Malaya (which is the mountain where Buddha laughed so much he busted his sides, before he could settle down and deliver the Lankavatara Scripture back-and-forth with) (who was it?) (Mahamati?)—

All this stuff about your anthology ideas evaporating, in favor of what new concerns? Lawrence Durrell, William Styron, Snodgrass, Richard Wilbur, Willard Maas, John Ciardi, Robert Frost, Jack Kennedy, Barry Goldwater and William Fulbright not to mention Herbert Gold, Gore Vidal, Katherine Anne Porter (good writer) and Liz Taylor?

God, the whole poetry racket is full of fickle girls.

I'm not interested in what Rumaker's done that I've seen so far but I do love Selby Junior, Huncke and Rechy too, and always thought Persky wd. be fine—Creeley's "For Love" I have, there's not enough swing in it, I think Peter Orlovsky much better with his harebrained snale graves with grass growing out of his cock and the grass always greener on the body in the next graive.

But that'll all come out in the wash, like Smart done, and Blake—Fox had his day, but Blake groaned on.

Colin Wilson has had to reverse his whole "Outsider" theory to stay away from me and Allen and Peter and Bill Burroughs because he probably realizes we'd only pour whiskey in his hair in the King Lud or King Lull pub ...[2]

2. The English author Colin Wilson had published *The Outsider* (1956) and *Religion and the Rebel* (1957), studies of alienation.

Writers are so evil, nasty, virulent, jealous, shitty—This letter must sound like an outrage from Jack Spicer or that asshole [George] Barker—At least [Brendan] Behan is an honest drinking or non-drinking companion with songs—

Robert Giroux, at Farrar Straus and Cudahy, and I, are together again so we had to bypass Tom Guinzburg as well as your excellent Grove Press associates—It's just a personal old relationship between two old Catholics and I really Don feel good about it—Besides Allen assured me Barney was off me as a writer—So let him publish Jack Gelber and Jerry Tallmer—

Hey! if you have time, send HEAVEN rollscroll poem back too if you can find it, if not, send it back when you get back—This summer I'll be alone in Cornwall (where my ancestors are from, Cornish language is "Kernuak") writing sounds of the Atlantic ocean at Land's End shore ... then Brittany, Paris, Milano, etc. Funny if we suddenly meet in a Flamenco bar in Cadiz, hey?

Here's to you, sweet Don, and dont stop loving me as I love you, good.

Jack

Mémêre sends regards to "Don."—

Writing to Robert Giroux later in April after mailing back the corrected galleys of Big Sur, *Kerouac reminisced about the first time he met his editor a dozen years before and rationalized his dependence on the stability of his "mother's clean home."*

TO ROBERT GIROUX

April 12 1962
[Orlando, Florida]

Dear Bob

I mailed off the corrected galleys on Monday April 2nd and hope you got them okay on the 4th, as requested. It occurred to me afterwards, though, that the mail might have been slower than I expected.

The other night I got drunk and wrote you a very silly letter I didn't mail. Well, I tried to mail it but my mother wouldnt let me because it was stained with oil paint and pastel chalks after a crazy silly night on liquor and benzedrine drawing pietas and writing outcries to you about Yeats and Joyce and Eliot etc. My final reason for not sending it to you is that I deny that Yeats is greater than Joyce, as I said in the letter. Joyce worked much harder, in bulk, scholarship AND linguistics.

I hope you understood my letter about the birthday lunch. It's quite true and quite tragic.... I cant help but laugh to think of the way I was

335

when I first met you, with careful photos by (who was it?) (Andre) some-body and I was so punctilious and sat there in Alfred Harcourt's office with a necktie, and went with you to the Opera Club. I even got thrown out of an art theater in the Village last trip for drinking in the seat (the Japanese version of the Lower Depths but none of this non-vicarious shit for the pro-prietors, hey?) (*Or* the audience who glared at me as I left up the center isle (aisle) with my loyal hooligans.) Too, there was a time when I could type a letter without making a single mistake. But this is no Scott Fitzger-ald cracup, thanks (see? *crackup*) to the fact I can sleep and eat in my mother's clean home—A year "on my own" in any city of the world and I'd be dead. This is because of my continual insistence on the ecstasy of liquor. (Yet Fitzgerald never wrote better than after his "crackup," in The Last Tycoon)—Ah Bob I just want you to accept me as I am and love me.

As for you, M. Distinguée, write more often. Jack

In April, Kerouac wrote a letter to the Swiss painter Hugo Weber, whom he had met the previous December in New York City. Trying to cheer up his friend in the hospital, Kerouac revealed what he considered an important "turning-point" in his development as a writer when he was hospitalized in the Bronx for phlebitis in 1951.

TO HUGO WEBER

[April 1962
Orlando, Florida]

Dear Hugo,

Aside from the pain & discomfort, I think you'll find your stay in the hospital very useful & beautiful—A chance to sleep, to think, to eat and to *read*—You'll come out of there feeling *great* & should paint right away—

I hope your May show in Chicago will go off as scheduled & get you some money for occasional retreats to the Maine coast or someplace, or oc-casional jets to Switzerland—

My stay in the hospital in 1951 was actually the turning-point in my system of narrative art—It was there, day after day in bed thinking, that I formulated all those volumes (16) I've written since (most of them save six so far published). But I mean I was *so happy* in the hospital. Don't be afraid to accept sleeping pills, but only ONE, every OTHER night—hear me? no more!

And have books brought to you—Don't accept too many visitors . . . read and rest—Make your plans for a great golden painting of the River Alph—Or a great black painting of the River Styx—Or a great brown painting of the Yellowstone River in Montana—

Let me know if there's anything special you think I could do for you, if you feel like writing—If not, I'll write again soon.

Jack

Kerouac filled John Clellon Holmes in on more of the details about his day in court with Joan Aly, including his "protest" which was left unrecorded by the court stenographer: "I do not admit that I am the father of this child, only that she bears my name."

TO JOHN CLELLON HOLMES

April 17, 1962
[Orlando, Florida]

Dear John

Yes I was in New York but in that Supreme Court business where they simply dictated to a court stenographer what they wanted me to say, because "it is the endeavor of the supreme court of the state of New York to disavow illegitimacy" so that's that—Joan's lie was one sin, one adultery, but now the sin is doubly compounded and *I* am supposed to be the liar—Because of the marriage license of 1950, and the various legal loopholes (all having nothing to do with blood itself) there was nothing I could do short of a trial in front of a jury of angry women who would have tried to strip me of my life earnings—Luckily, Eugene Brooks (Ginsberg) has an ace up the sleeve that prevented any big grab of my money (her present husband willing to testify that HE had supported the so-called "Janet" "Kerouac," not Joan)—So both attorneys went off with a total of $2500 of my money and left $12 a week for the girl—the court stenographer did not take down my protest, which was this—"I do not admit that I am the father of the child, only that she bears my name." It didn't appear in the newspapers anyway.... Joan will go thru the rest of her life knowing she lied and had that sin placed on my head, and she will go to the grave knowing this. And I don't really care because I know Karma works automatically.

Why don't you and Shirley come down stay a week with me at my home in Fla.?—Before it gets too hot, before late May?... If you bring your car I would even be willing to go on a jaunt with you to New Orleans, for chicken & gumbo. I have a double bed guest room for you, never been used. Big yard with trees and bushes to sunbathe in, and talk and drink in. Just pay yr gas and oil, I'll pay the rest (that is, i.e., booze and steaks and Shirley make me ONE dinner of ham and yams with marshmallow) ...

You shd. never have sent your excerpts to Esquire, they are a bunch of arty faggots there ... Try Playboy ... Change to Sterling Lord for yr. agent and he will send yr piece directly to Thomas Payne there, my buddy. Spectorsky has the final say but he was the one, remember, who published my

"October in the Poolhall" to perfection without one typo error, in Playboy [a] few years ago . . .

If you plan to come here, let me know and I'll send you full instructions on how to get out here 10 miles outa Orlando.

When I got out of New York in March, on my birthday, it was all I could do to drag myself to the airport . . . drunk, sick, nervous, coughing . . . wreaked [sic] . . . Originally I'd planned to call and go to Old Saybrook, see.

As ever

Jack

P.S. I signed that "freedom to read" paper, if you want to also go ahead—notice Wilson's name on bottom—
Return to

Barney Rosset
Grove Press
64 University Pl.
NY

In June 1962, after rereading letters from John Clellon Holmes about his trip to Europe in 1958 and receiving long letters from Ginsberg describing his adventures with Orlovsky and Snyder in Nepal, Kerouac wrote his agent and his friends about his plans to travel in France, revealing that his application for a credit card had been rejected.

TO STERLING LORD

June 2, 1962
[Orlando, Florida]

Dear Sterling

Sorry to be late with everything. Here's BOOK OF DREAMS contracts. Please make a notation to translate the title *THE* BOOK OF DREAMS (El Libro de Dreams) instead of "A" book of dreams (Uno Libro de Dreams) . . . LE LIVRE DE REVES. OK?

Meanwhile, tell HOLIDAY I'm honored to be invited to write travel stories for them all the time but to wait till I write about my trips to Cornwall etc. this summer because I have absolutely, sincerely nothing to say about Florida . . . since I never leave the house, have no car, it's too hot, there are no mountains, etc. I just make my studies here. Okay? I can write maybe three articles for them this summer. But please make it clear this time, huh, for them not to make their dopey changes on my prose, none whatever, unless mistakes of technical nature, or they might just as well ask Richard Rovere, Malcolm Muggeridge and Per Se Williams and even A. Priori Deft . . .

338

I mean why should they want my stories if they're going to be like some-one else in the editorial dept. would like to write them?

(Knowles ignored this point of mine and changed my stories anyway, on the sly) which is why I'd quit the *Holiday* setup.

Thank God for Giroux now, we finally have a first rate editor.

Dont worry, I mean I'll write something truly original about Cornwall etc. . . . First I'm waiting for my passport with some uncertainty: Diners Club turned me down as a member because I have no credit rating (because I buy everything cash and have no debts). Dont need Diners Club anyway. Can always consult my address book for local publishers & agents in round-the-world capitals, what?

Travel Bureau will probably route me right outa Miami so I'll probably see you in the Fall return trip, in NY, unless you come out there this sum-mer either to see Deutsch or Sherlock Holmes or Arsene Lupin or E. Power Tripp, author of "The Failure of Shakespeare."

Waiting for further notes from you, meanwhile, sir, I remain,
        your humble ser't etc. as ever

                                                            Jack

TO JOHN CLELLON HOLMES

                                                    June 8, 1962
                                                [Orlando, Florida]
TO:
Mr John Holmes
FROM:
Mr John Kerouac

Dear John:—Just now re-read your letter of Feb. 26, 1958, a long one about your trip to London, Paris, Avignon, Alps etc. while I was in the process of filing all your letters under the heading Holmes (the 'eading 'Olmes) in my brand new 4-drawer file cabinet which has now, neatly filed, some several million words of letters since 1939 in prep school and all my own loose writings I used to keep remember in old dusty boxes? and all childhood scraps, athletic clippings, in brief, a gold mine of information for scholars of dust—And if I ever was to wish ya a happy birthday or a happy New Year, I'd wish ya the power to stay as happy as you were the day you wrote me that glowing glad letter with all its perfect descriptions of streets, mountains, cities, restaurants, ships, seas . . . people . . . Someday when you can come visit me you can browse all you want through the thick Holmes file. It might even be of great use to you someday . . . unless you've simply carbon copied ALL your letters—Some of them you may not have.

The value of these great piles of now neatly arranged millions of letters to me from you, Allen, Burroughs, Neal, Corso, Peter, Whalen, Harrington,

339

even Tony Manocchio, Lucien, Roger Lyndon, Ferlinghetti and on and on is that I can always find some lost detail about who did what, which might light a spark of my own rememberance—Really, you oughta see it, I'm a genius of organization—I should have been a charcoal suit.

But the main purpose of this letter is to tell you that I'm off now, on a trip to Britain and the Nordic countries, God knows why, really just to get out of the swampy heat of Florida for the summer and get some reading done in lonely beds far away, some walking and bicycling too I hope— Most of all I wish, I hope I could rent a lonely cottage on the moors of Cornwall—I'll try—I'm even going to Finland if I'm not too lazy—I'd like to see the old light of the old north as I remember it in Arctic Greenland summer of 1942—shining on Finnish fishvillages—and fjords—I'm no stranger to fjords—I'm bringing my full rucksack for any eventuality but in London I'll buy a real long pockety ratatatat raincoat anyway—

Anyway, my point is, if you happen to be going to Europe too this summer let me know—Write care of here, my mother & sister forward—I might look up Colin Wilson who invited me 4 years ago to his place in Cornwall— I'll look up publishers and others but only after weeks of solitude and walking and reading—I want to cook for myself slowly and peacefully most of the time but wanta hit a few good restaurants—Burroughs expects me in Paris and Tangier but I wanta go North this summer, will see him later— Allen and Peter have just returned from Nepal with Gary Snyder, and are now with Paul Bowles in Calcutta, and preparing to go on to Japan (and Gary again) with Corso soon—They traveled from Paris to India via East Africa and a boat—They even visited Sodom—Burroughs and Ginsberg are feuding again, or that is B. is—refused to see them in Paris—Just a note of gossip—Myself I've just been sitting here reading and continuing my diary scribbles, sold Big Sur to Farrar Straus as I think I told you and next year they'll print Visions of Gerard (also in September, like Sur this year) so I have 2 years to mull over Visions of Bill or Allen, or any other spate of the Duluoz Legend past or present to handle—(like good old Faulkner with his Yoknphawta Yoknaphawta county carrying on and on without intellectual comment)—(I also admire Nabokov now for turning down big windy seminars and saying why)—(and of course Faulk too for not kowtowing up to the White House)—Anyway, the gist of the letter is, I will see you if not in Europe, in Connecticut or Manhattoes in the Fall—Remember to check with Bog Biroux at Farrar Straus for my whereabouts—Old Bog has turned out to be the best editor of them all, and I'm not surprised, after all what other editor turned me on to Dickinson and Yeats and Puccini?

Class outs, and Bob's now showing his class by agreeing with me 100% not to touch one hair of my prose, or of my story structure, nothing whatever, and also giving me my biggest advance so far (five times what Grove had offered, and Viking was about to offer) (Bob advanced 10 g's, and

$1500 for Gerard which is not a "beat generation" type potential commercial brickbat) ... Altho I feel the critics and book public won't care much about Big Sur even then, anyway—They're all sick and tired of this beatnik business and it's their own fault since they started it and pumped it up themselves—

When I come back, if I come back ("Give my regards to the boys when you get there ... if you gets there," says Laughton in Sanders of the River, removing a toothpick from his mouth) I'll hit New York and see Bob, you, others, Lucien, etc. might even find you in Saybrook and stay two nights ... and then I plan to go west and look for a cabin in the pines by a tumbling brook and buy it for my new semi-permanent hermitage later to become a final restingplace I hope, because as you know the pace, the so-called "pace," the fucking HORROR of being a writer in America with a limited amount of sauvee faire can lead to premature worse-than-death exhaustion of every decent sincere little instinct you were born with ...

So write me here, I'm leaving round the 20th I guess, jet outa Miami, maybe come back boat, and let's see you now really hit out the big book everybody's expecting from you ... You're a slow starter, like Whirlaway ... I mean in the field of narrative storytelling ... Don't revise so much, just tell what happened next ... Do like I do, tell true stories and just change the names ... If you weren't on the scene where characters are talking, admit that you're only imagining what was said ... Don't be afraid to inject yourself as the author-Eye, and blast off with long talk about what happened and what you felt about it—

Feeling is the essence of intellect, because without feeling nothing can be KNOWN, Goddamit! ...

So write how you FEEL

You have a heart as big as a house: open it to your typewriter: try lighting a candle just when you start a batting-out-session and blow it out just when you're through! (there's a lil magic to it)

Don't be afraid to try benzedrine: start writing about 30 minutes after you've taken benzedrine, have mucho hot coffee, cup after cup, beside you (a Samovar!) and your cigarettes right there at hand ... and write almost with your eyes closed, not thinking of punctuation or capitals or anything, that comes later when you type up doublespace for manuscript neat.

In London I hope to take a flat, my dear, and walk to the British Museum every day and read Tolstoy's "My Confession," look up the Kerouacs of Cornwall, and make notes (that is, sketch) about what I saw in the streets ... Then maybe a train to Penzance and then the moors ... Did you know what Kerouac means in Brythonic Celtic? Ker means house, ouac means moor.... House in the Moor

341

And Jacob is Aramaean for John

Yours

Jakey Moorhouse

Jack

Love to Yam Shirley
and Marshmallows
and Nunnery Stew
and Ecstasy Pie

TO LAWRENCE FERLINGHETTI

June 15, 1962

JK PO Box 700

Orlando, Fla.

Dear Larry ...

I'm glad that was just an anonymous crank thing instead of an item in the paper, et cetera.[3] Just got fantastic snapshot of Allen, Peter and Gary Snyder sitting with Tibetan robes with backdrop of Nepalese snowcapt mounts—Also a 10,000 word masterpiece letter from Allen, neatly typed, detailing all the adventures from Paris on thru Middle East etc.—Incidentally Fernanda Pivano, girl who translates us beats in Milano in Italian is at Stanford tending sick husband, guess she'll look you up—I'm going now in three days on plane to Paris, then boat-train to London, then cottage on moors somewhere, even Ireland, later Helsinki etc.—And next year Japan I guess—Just read Nabokov's Lolita which is one of the classics of world literature and ranks with Joyce, Proust, Mann and Genet in the divine solipsism of modern literature ... My opinion of him, earlier formed by critics, was low ... and so there you have our marvelously competent American critics.

Jean Louis

(See you Nov.!)

Instead of a trip to France, Kerouac fled the intolerable summer heat and humidity of Florida by taking the train to Maine, Cape Cod, and New York, where he unsuccessfully looked for a house by the seashore, enlisting John Clellon Holmes's help when he got back to Orlando. He was desperate to leave Florida, he wrote Holmes on August 8, 1962, because he felt that he and Gabrielle were "dying by degrees" there. Tension had developed between them and Caroline's hus-

---

3. Kerouac had seen a newspaper clipping about his alleged connection with the John Birch Society in San Diego.

band, Paul, who had borrowed money from Jack to build an addition on his house. Jack promised to buy his nephew Little Paul a car in two years for his sixteenth birthday, but in the meantime he was dependent upon his sister for rides to the liquor store and the post office twelve miles away.

In August after Lois Sorrells wrote Jack about the death of her mother, he invited her to visit Florida. Later Kerouac wrote to Robert Giroux about his impotency during the drunken week when Lois stayed with him and Mémêre in Orlando.

TO LOIS SORRELLS

August 8 1962
[Orlando, Florida]

Lowie

I just got back from a tour of New England seacoast looking for possible home-near-water for me and Mémêre, and Mémêre meanwhile had not opened yr. letter, so I only read your letter yesterday about your Mother. I wish you would accept my invitation to come down to my house in Orlando for a rest, I'll send you the fare. Maybe meanwhile Paul can go visit his relatives, or even come here with you for a rest. Besides I wanta see you and have a long talk. My father practically died in my arms when I was alone with him in the house and now you and I understand together. I must have had a premonition of your letter on the train down here when I suddenly remembered my father's death and cried in my dark roomette, cried for the first time in many years. I realized how frilly & silly I've been. You have never been quite as frilly & silly, I see now. So come and see me, very easy 3-hour flight and cab. When I hear from you I send check for fare and the house address is 1309 Alfred Drive, Orlando Fla. We'll plug a loophole in eternity. I came home all exhausted from another senseless 10 days in Manhattan (thinking you were not available for visits at B & C Hollow Road), another 10 useless days talking with everybody, but as usual this keeps me up to date for writing purposes, writing being my livelihood after all, and I did also make one new great friend (Jim Benenson of Atlanta, stayed in his apartment). Jim wouldnt let me spend a cent when I was with him because he said I was his guest. Others not only accepted endless drinks but stole my pencils, notebook, dark glasses, all the same old story, and I was even barred from the White Horse etc. I see now they're really only laughing at me but when I'm dead they'll tell how much they knew and loved me, the same as happened to Dylan Thomas. I am really only TiJean who used to fall in love with young nuns, from afar, many of whom looked just like you. Anyway, answer right away if you can, and remember I'm waiting for you and still love you. I'll do a pink Virgin Mary as soon as I play my Solemn Mass at midnight, tonight.

A toi mon coeur
Jack

Aug 17 [19]62
[Orlando, Florida]

Dear Lois

I'll pay your return fare too, but am waiting now in case I travel back with you.

Telephone a reservation with National Air Lines or Eastern Air Lines at Idlewild.... NAL is about $57, Eastern is big jets at about $67, direct to Orlando. When you get to Orlando you tell the driver (cab) to take you to "Kingswood Manor, 1309 Alfred Drive"—All the houses look alike but different colors, mine is light grey.... Kingswood Manor belongs to Orlando, a big dreary subdivision I hate, 8 miles from town: you might have to tell the cabdriver it's at Lee Road and Edgewater Drive. The cab will be 2 or 3 bucks, and you'll be here.

I might go back with you and I'll tell you why: thinking of moving back north.

I ben [sic] drinking and drinking and feel tremendously dejected—you will do me as much good as two months on a mountaintop.

O yes, there'll probably be a car in my driveway but it's my brother in law's.... I just took my nephew's bike and went pedalling to the liquor store on the highway ... Let's have a good time ... If you get this letter and check Saturday try to get the earliest flight possible, why wait? It'll be just like when I used to wait for you on pins and needles 10 o'clock Friday nights in Northport, only this is longer run.... I just made the run in a train roomette (O I told you)—I dont know where I am.... I dont think I never did know (ever).... shmever ... I have a copy of *Big Sur* to give you ... Piano, new tape recorder ... I tape recorded my new piano sonata "God Rest Ye Merrie Gentlemen"—You can tape your own first sonata—You'll be the first to use my guest room, pink—I tried to draw you a pink Virgin Mary last night but you stole all my pink chalk, I cant find it.

Hurry up
Snuffy Snuff

Sept. 3 1962
[Orlando, Florida]

Dear Bob

Received the three books you mailed me. Robert Lowell certainly went to town on Villon, Baudelaire, Pasternak (who *is* great, huh?) and others. The cat story by his ex-wife too cute, I think cats are *grave* and so does my mother and she says SHE will write a book on cats to make people understand cats once and for all. I offer to help her by leaving her alone in a room with my tape recorder to tell the tale, then I'll type it. The Flannery O'Connor book is an interesting story-content but the prose is too ordinary and done-before to really keep my attention. Really, Bob, you can't have a literature with everybody writing the same way, in the SAME VOICE, like "he jerked his thumb at her" etc. I never seen nobody jerk his thumb: how do you that? try it!

But the Lowell book a prize treasure in my growing library (my old library in the hands of Philip Whalen in California, he doesnt know what to do with it and also all his own books).

Completely trapped here I dont know what's going on, when Sur's coming-out date is, or reviews if any so far, or what. So please office-phone "Natasha" and tell her, yes, I do want *all* my reviews sent to me: she wanted to know if I wanted just the good ones, medium ones only, or just the bad ones.

My delay in answering you about the present of books was because a girlfriend visited me here from N.Y. (her mother'd just died) and I was drunk a week because she actually makes me nervous, but aside from all that I was inable, and sad about that.

Baudelaire & Villon aint seen nothin yet when I get started excoriating mankind. Wait, Bob. My next book is going to mark the end of my "experimental" period of "spontaneous prose" and I'm going back to the careful writing of Town & City only this time with more experience about how to make non-spontaneous prose look spontaneous.

Anon.

Oh yes, please, few years ago Ginsberg and Paul Bowles and others wrote a rather almost nasty confusing letter to Robert Lowell and had me sign it with them (all I threw in were a few toy names like Arapahoe Rappaport etc.)—Give him my respects and tell him I think he's a great poet and not to mind that letter at all anyway.

As ever
Jack

Published on September 11, 1962, Big Sur *was tepidly reviewed by William Wiegand in* The New York Times. *In the* Saturday Review, *Herbert Gold smugly concluded that after his California breakdown, Kerouac was "on the right road at last." Jack was so "sick and tired of being insulted by critics," he told Carolyn Cassady on October 21, 1962, that he "just about decided not to publish any more. . . . They make me sick with their Jew talk. . . . They'll go around vaunting their Philip Roths and Herbert Golds and Bernard Malamuds and J. D. Salingers and Saul Bellowses, whilst the bestselling is being taken care of by Micheners and Wouks, and my only clientele are kids who steal my books in bookstores." On September 14, 1962,* Time *added its ridicule to the chorus:*

What can a beat do when he is too old to go on the road? He can go on the sauce.... In the end he settles for a howling emotional crisis—which on a grown-up would look very much like the DTs.

A child's first touch of cold mortality—even when it occurs in a man of 41—may seem ridiculous, and is certainly pathetic. In Kerouac's case, though, there may be compensations. Think of the books, man, a whole new series: The Dharma Bums Grow Up, The Dharma Bums on Wall Street. *Who knows, maybe even* The Dharma Bums in the White House?

On September 15, 1962, Lawrence Ferlinghetti wrote a letter to Time *in Kerouac's defense, but the magazine did not publish it.*

TO *TIME* MAGAZINE
FROM LAWRENCE FERLINGHETTI

September 15, 1962
City Lights
261 Columbus Ave.
San Francisco 11, Calif.

Dear TIME:

Your snide, sneering, condescending, semi-literate, semi-dishonest, spiteful attack on Jack Kerouac and his latest book, BIG SUR, is disgusting. The fact that you've concentrated on Kerouac himself more than on his book makes your review particularly despicable. Since TIME is the Protestant bible to millions of Americans who receive your so-called literary criticism as from a godhead, don't you think you should at least try to consider authors as human beings rather than as fodder for your advertising men and copy writers? (I believe the Kerouac review was written by your advertising copywriters who got off at an editorial floor one foggy morning by mistake, or perhaps, by design, knowing that no one would be able to tell them from editors anyway.) Typical of the distortions and untruths in the article is the statement that Kerouac is "an adoring pantheist" and that at 41 he has just discovered Death. It happens Kerouac is a Catholic, and Death has been an insistent presence in all his books, from the earliest ones such as DOCTOR SAX onward. Your cruel, oh-so-clever annihilation of him only brings Death that much closer to him, and to us, and to America.

Perhaps this is just what you had in mind. For you are all great experts in the killing of the spirit, and here you have killed another great one. Cart the carcass off gleefully to your slick cemetery and pour yourself another dry martini. On the rocks. And ask for a raise. You're a clever fellow.

Lawrence Ferlinghetti

After Gabrielle begged Shirley Holmes to help Jack find a house in New England, saying that he'd "be a very sick Man" if he stayed in Florida, Kerouac got back on the train to Old Saybrook to stay with John and Shirley Holmes in mid-September for another unsuccessful house-hunting session. When Kerouac decided to visit his old friends back in Lowell, John mixed him a large brandy and soda in a mason jar, Shirley phoned for a taxi, and Jack went off on a sixty-dollar, 150-mile ride through Connecticut and Massachusetts to his hometown. He stayed in Lowell until September 24, 1962. When he returned to Orlando he sent a quick note to Tony Sampas and Stella Sampas before writing a long letter to Holmes about his drunken "fantastic" adventures with members of the Sampas family and his "5th cousin" Paul Bourgeois, who claimed to be "the Chief of the Four Nations of the Iroquois in the Arctic circle."

TO TONY SAMPAS & STELLA SAMPAS

[Postmarked October 2, 1962
Orlando, Florida]

Dear Tony & Stella—

Goofed around N.Y. for about 10 days, then brought Cousin Paul Bourgeois to Florida and goofed some more—

Now he's gone back to his mother in Lowell & I'm now sending check for $280 I owe you, Tony—

And I dont only love you because you are Sam's brother—

Longer letters later, Tony & Stella.

Jack

Tony, please tell Chief to mail me my *tape* as soon as he's re-recorded it—

Give him my address

—Say hello for me to Mousie, D.J., Vu, Billy Koumantzelis, Spence, The Cat, The Weazel etc. etc.

Jacques the Cock

TO JOHN CLELLON HOLMES

[October 9, 1962
Orlando, Florida]

John

I'm really overjoyed that you're not sore—By the time you read this I hope I'll have received Shirley's letter from the White Mountains.

My mother and I still so desperate to leave here, we've written to Northport again—I have a dull feeling about Northport respecting the same teenage and local scene invasions, tho—I still like the Saybrook idea best and by the way I like that doctor of yours—You know, he's the kind of guy, if you tell him "Don't bring visitors with you on your social visits" I think he'd understand, right?—He could also supply me with materials necessary to write long novels in 7 nights straight.

If I do come back to Saybrook (like a maniac rushing back and forth) to again "look" for a house this time I won't goof, and it might be long before Spring, and if you're working on your non-fiction book, why, what's the harm in just me and Shirley driving around to look, and with realtors etc.? Also, I might be there in time to do your tape-recording-questionnaire a la mode.

No more cognac, for me. I find it depresses worse than anything except Irish Whiskey. O John, I'm so fucking sorry, there I was right in Saybrook and didn't do a damn thing. You know, living here, when I get to see the North and my friends again I go crazy. Here I just don't see anybody or do anything and I can't go out, it's too hot!

I think in fact it might even be a good idea for me to live in a Motel in Saybrook UNTIL I find a house! In Motels I make my own coffee with a wire gimmick, and read, and don't drink, see—and therefore walk around and look for myself also.

Some people lie in bed with broken legs suspended over them for 6 months, some have cancer of the gall bladder, some have paresis, some have Banti's awful disease, some murder, some break rockpiles for life, or walk in chains, and all I have to worry about is the relatively carefree simple matter of finding another house for me and my mother and my cats in New England: so what the hell am I complaining about? Alcoholism is by all odds the *only* joyous disease, at least! (Unless you throw in the Laughing Sickness.)

No, no, no I can't goof on like this—we've had our three day preliminary talk which went on for 7 days, this time by God I WILL stay in a motel till it's done. Because when you and I get together a kind of bell rings in my head that says GLUYR TIME FOR A DRINK ... Same of course applies to when I see Lucien, etc. etc. a thousand guys.[4]

---

4. In *Visitor: Jack Kerouac in Old Saybrook* (1981), Holmes transcribed his journal notes describing Kerouac's behavior during his visit on September 13–16, 1962:

> Jack sits in torn blue pajama bottoms, a rank tee shirt, grimy socks and Japanese slippers, unshaven in nearly a week, his hair never combed till 5:00, growing headier & headier in the armpits, smoking his little Camels, fixing his brandies & soda, padding around with stiff, faltering old man's steps, talking in torrential gusts.... He drinks a fifth of Courvoisier every day, plus rations of scotch, beer & wine.... Sweet & tentative when sober, he becomes truculent, paranoiac, garrulous, stiff-jointed, wild-eyed, exhaustless, and amnesiac when drunk. Booze alone can seem to produce in him the "ecstasy" he needs to get thru time....

My adventure in Lowell was fantastic: I stood poor Lowell on its head: when asked to go onstage of rock n roll club to be introduced instead did a 7 second cossack dance—signed a thousand autographs—held up traffic they tell me one night on Moody Street as I recited poetry with a jug in my hand (this I don't remember)—when I left, my original favored bar of 8 bookies was suddenly a bedlam of 250 people of all kinds including photogs, teenage girls, whores, musicians, garage mechanics, elderly interview ladies, lawyers, took off fast with 2 new Lowell buddies and drove to Lucien's in the Village arriving just in time to see Lucien crash a whiskey bottle on another newsman's head (no hurt him, tho)—truth—Really HAD to leave Lowell—saw G.J. only one day, also "Maggie Cassidy," the works, stayed in Sebastian's[5] brother's bachelor cottage, had ball.

Love,
Jack

P.S. My 5th cousin was there, is Chief of the Four Nations of the Iroquois in Arctic circle, Four Nations are Sirois, Bourgeois-Ogallag, L'Evesque and Kirouac! (more anon on this, probably explains why British Holmes and Iroqouis Kirouac argue so)!

(L'Evesque is my mother's name—)

Got preliminary material for 2 new books on Lowell trip. (1) About present swing Lowell, and (2) About the last of the Iroquois, pushed up to hopeless Prince of Wales Isle (look it up on map!) because they were independent hunter-trappers who scorned tradesman lives & are now living with their own law & order, no Royal Mounties even! (strict moral law and order too, thieves get hands cut off, etc. tell you all when see you)

In other words, don't you see, the Iroquois squaws turned Montcalm's soldiers into mad savages within a generation, some of them at least, while other soldiers prevailed and resumed their middleclass Norman tastes—explains how some Kerouacs became farmers, carpenters and printers, and some Kerouacs are still wild in the north—The Four Nations was a Confederation formed by the Seven Nations of the South, to keep the Iroquois Nation (Tribe) going; an anthropologist in NY told me and the young Chief (who came with me) that the "four" were formed to symbolize a Tree that would flower. Man, I'm gonna get my mitts into this. I'm not invited to visit the 4 Nations for 2 more years, due to certain political preliminaries, but the only reason I'm invited at all is because I'm a cousin. None but cousins can go there (and live).* The chief himself is Bourgeois-Ogallag. You can see how there's so much French blood intertwined the whole thing is but

---

5. Sebastian Sampas.
*i.e., pow! [J.K.]

a political shadow of a former racial tribe. But the amazing thing is that the Confederation still exists, is called Iroquois, they have records of all the names on skin, and they have been pushed so unbearably far north it's unbelievable. (closer to Russia than to New York!) The Chief, Paul, is only 34 years old and is a wild young hepcat because when he first visited Lowell to see relatives, at age 17, with long oil-fish-hair and full face beard, some Greeks bought him a zoot suit and he hitched a ride somewhere and the car overturned and the drivers ran away in the woods, the cops found the 17 year old son of the Chief of the Four Nations snoozing in a car full of guns and stolen jewelry! so he spent 7 years in Massachusetts can and therefore knows English and all American items well. Himself speaks only a touch of Iroquois. And of course the same Canuck French as all over Canuck Canada from the Gaspé clear thru Alberta to the Pacific and on up to those far off arctic isles way north of Hudson Bay. More anon. My book will aid him in bringing his people down, because in winter they're snowed in over the log-cabin roof for 6 months: and other dreadful developments are starting, relating to Polaris radioactivity destroying fish and amphibious game. Keep this under your hat, the chief will kill me. (I almost brought him to Saybrook on the trip back, we were driven by a Portuguese Lowell hepcat, I felt we'd better get on to NY and get laid, which we did etc....) The Chief is, in effect, sort of Mayor of the Chiefs of the Four Nations, he himself Chief of the Bourgeois-Ogallag ... It is the saddest story I know ... All they are, is, after all, the "tough guys" of the Canucks pushed north by "self respecting Canucks" mind you. And don't think for a minute they're not religious, tho, they wear crosses around their necks and Pere Morain is there with them (O.M.I. order) ("Obligation of Mercy to the Individual" I'm pretty sure it means.) So, later.

Wm. Burroughs = 9 Rue Git le Coeur
Paris 6, France

Allen Ginsberg = c/o American Express
Calcutta, India

On November 13, 1962, Kerouac wrote Robert Giroux that he had bought another house in Northport, blaming Florida for making him "so silly" when he lived too far from New York.

Nov. 13, 1962
[Orlando, Florida]

Dear Bob

Fairly silly for me to try to do any work on a day like that—I'll correct and proof read VISIONS OF GERARD when I'm settled back in North-port, around the first of the year, I'm sure that's no too late for Sept.63 publication right?

I found a house and am moving back to Long Island and that means we can be in closer contact for business—I wont be always so silly, I wont have to be if I live 40 miles from my crazy New York.

And of course my mother and I look forward to visits from you—I'll have a fireplace—It's easy to get to by Long Island R.R.—

I rec'd a marvelous critical kudo from an Oxford Scholar (Wadham College)—

Call you just before Christmas, meanwhile same address.

As ever
Jack

Later in November, Kerouac wrote the long letter to Stella Sampas that he had promised her before he left Florida.

Oct I mean Nov. 17 1962
[Orlando, Florida]

Dear Stella

I didnt call "Mrs. Apostolos" at all! Is there some guy in Lowell calling and saying he's me? I'm sure that if the call had been to George Apostolos, her husband, George would have known it wasnt me.

And of course not, no, I'm not mad at you. Dont you realize how busy I am? I'm moving my mother and home back to Long Island. I just returned from there, negotiated everything, and got drunk to boot and met hundreds of new people and got sick and flew back and got poured off the airplane in Orlando.

Meanwhile I have endless business with 7 American publishers and about 30 foreign publishers, many letters, I have no secretary, I have to handle everything by myself and sometimes the legal papers concerning taxes, deeds, shmeeds get me so down I just get drunk and let it all pile on my desk. Somewhere underneath that horrendous pile sometimes I find a few humble letters from you. I only have one body and one soul and cant handle everything at the same time. Do you know that at any given moment as I'm going down the street in New York or San Fran or for that matter

Paris (and Lowell) I can be hailed by one of the some 5,000 people I know with whom I can end up an all-night conversation and all my business goes down the drain, i.e., what I was going down the sidewalk for, maybe just to go buy me a new pot for my camping rucksack, or a book, or a phone call? You think it's glamorous but I think this "fame" is all a big interruption of my original simple soul. If I want to go to Lowell and see Tony, you, Paul Bourgeois, Huck, the guys at SAC's, I'll probably end up intercepted somewhere else by a thousand raving maniacs at Yale, Brown and Harvard, that's the way it is.

This is by way of explanation of why I just cant keep up with your heavy correspondence. And believe me I enjoy your letters and I file them away. I also, by the way, have all Sammy's letters, with poems therein, filed away.

Incidentally, I'm going to call him "Savas Santos" in the next book, where he's mentioned in the first chapter. Is that okay? Later on, a full book about him, at least in relation to a book about my father, who knew Sammy and had long talks with him.

So we're packing and moving back around Christmas and I wont be able to get to Lowell till January or February and I'm looking forward however to get back to Lowell for a visit. I'm going to cut out the whiskey and go back to my original love, wine, 20$ sweet wine like sherry, port, etc. The whiskey has started to break my health down.

Thank Tony for calling me and explain to him that when he called me that day (from SAC's) I was very sick and trying to hide it. He knows how sick I can get: semi delirium tremens.

Tell your mother, that when I come back to Lowell, to make some more of that spinach and goat cheese pie. It sure is delicious. My sister sends her regards.

Tell Tony his Marlboro has gone out and all he's got in his mouth is an unlit filter (he always does that) (he's great)

Jack

During Kerouac's last weeks packing up the house at 1309 Alfred Drive in Orlando, he wrote to Philip Whalen listing the more than twenty times Gabrielle had moved house since 1922, the year he was born.

TO PHILIP WHALEN

Dec. 13, 1962
[Orlando, Florida]

Dear Phil

Seems a long time since me and Mémêre sneaked up on you as you sat in the Milvia cottage smiling over the Lankavatara scripture in the night

Same feeling now, as we've got several days before movers come to take furniture north, we follow in train with three cat cages (nice compartment room with bunks, for cats to sleep on with us)

Since I was born on Lupine road in 1922 Mémère has moved & changed household furniture 26 times ... Lupine, Burnaby, Beaulieu, Hildreth, Lilley, West, Sarah, Phebe, Aiken, Moody, Gershom, West Haven Conn., Crawford, then Brooklyn, Ozone Park, Denver Colo., Richmond Hill upstairs, Kinston N.C. [sic], Richmond Hill downstairs, Rocky Mount N.C., Orlando Fla. (2 addresses), 1943 Berkeley Way Berkeley Calif., Clouser St. Orlando Fla., Gilbert St. Northport, Orlando again, then Earl Avenue Northport, then Orlando again (here) and now we go to Northport again in best house Mémère ever had with 2 baths, fireplace, 24 trees in yard, completely finished basement all of it a rumpus room with wood panelling and kentyle floors, big workbench shots where I can paint, easy walk to A&P store and paper store and all fine ... and the air divine ... my good old winter air.

I hope it don't become a "Hatter's Castle" I can't afford: big $165 monthly payments on mortgage, and that bitch in New York who got knocked up by a Porto Rican telling the supreme court the child is mine (born 1952) so there goes another $52 a month and she's hinting for more—Big Sur's been published and nothing much happened, no big sales, no movie offers—I coulda been a Bhikku but I wanted to make good home for Mémère—So St. Mary'll probably help me anyway.

Last, well the summer of 1961, in Mexico City, I scribbled a whole novel which includes the Berkeley Way scenes with you and Mémère, someday you'll enjoy it: might call that book BEANS & WINE ? # 'cause those were my beans & wine days, nay no sirloins and Canadian Clubs then ... well that's where I'm going back to, beans-&-wine ... I'll have to.

Say, why didn't Lew Welch write to me about Big Sur and where the hell is he and is he SORE about "Dave Wain" portrayal? Do you know? Please let me have his address. I didn't send him a Big Sur copy because I only had ten and they were all gobbled up by NY friends around me (Lucien etc.)

No word from Allen lately, I'm wondering if he mightn't be on his way to Gary in Japan now, what with the war and all ... time to go to Japan anyway, for him. He sure has passed me up in traveling. Years ago I used to vaunt my great voyageuring at him (Arctic Greenland, England, etc.) but now, wow, he's even been to Sudan. He tells me "Scripture of Golden Eternity" was translated into Bombay dialect, "Parmathi" ... also "Old Angel Midnight," strange.... "Docteur Sax" just published in Paris, reads like Rabelais, good translator M. Autret.... I'm proofreading "Visions of Gerard" novel writ in 1956 January after I left youse-all in a huff in Dec. 55, recall?, will be published by Fall 1963 and will be ignored I guess, or called pretentious, but who cares.... Old Li Po feelings I wish they'd come back ...

Time limps under them pure stars and we gloop about.... I still have your Goofbook and Googbook.... I just spent 24 hours careful working on a dangerous boil in my eyelid, it going now thank God ... Had big bandage over eye two days wondering about poor Creeley ... Mémère got your card today but I was going to write you a month ago anyway ... If you come to NY don't forget, come to my house, big steaks, new cesspool, and lissen, I will send you address when I get it, meanwhile write to me care of PO Bx 700 in Orlando till I get new Northport box.... Am reading Hugo's mighty "Ninety Three" and T. E. Lawrence's "Pillars," all big military stuff I guess ... O well, yawn, O hum, the void lets you sleep.... I wonder what we'll be doing in ten thousand years? Think I'll get a new typewriter.... Who goes there? The GHOST Why?

Apple Jack

On Christmas Eve 1962, Jack and Mémère and their three cats in carrier cages arrived at the Long Island Rail Road station in Northport and moved into their new home on Judyann Court. Shortly afterwards, Gabrielle sent off a Christmas card to Philip Whalen with her new address. She signed it "Mrs. G. Kerouac & Son Jack," and included a note to Whalen inside the card.

TO PHILIP WHALEN FROM GABRIELLE KEROUAC
[Late December 1962
Northport, New York]

Hello There Phillip,
    Here we are back where we come from. Sorry to say Jack was not to happy here in Florida it was to Hot for him. Besides I got kind of weary of the Fuzzy face Castro—people out in Florida now are really scared and many has left back to the North. We are fine how about you. Best wishes,

Mémère

1963

Trying to settle in Northport, Kerouac discovered he couldn't escape the feeling that he was stalled in what he called the "Autumn" of his life. He wrote in his journal that

> *ROAD was learned in my Springtime, & prepared incredible work of summer (CODY, SAX, MAGGIE, SUBS, GERARD, ANGELS etc.)— Then came Autumn, to which BIG SUR belongs & all my present unhappy exhaustion of harvest time—For next 10 years I'll be harvesting & winnowing chaffs but with no great mindless purpose of summer—*
>
> *Then comes Winter, when I'll be a silent hermit writing only haiku, like Hardy, or at least haiku-like quiet last sonatas & conclusive technical spiritual symphonies without youth's anguish.*[1]

At the beginning of the New Year, he described his depression to his friend Philip Whalen.

TO PHILIP WHALEN

Jan. 14, 1963
[Northport, New York]

Dear Phil

Yes, me and Mémêre are most comfortably moved into our new home, which is really such a great pad I can't believe it and just sit in a more or less drunk stupor staring at it—fireplace, etc. It just goes to show that when you get what you always wanted, it's maybe too late.

A vast lassitude, an 'orrible indifference, a sickness, a shit Rilkean sorrow, a something-or-other, tho I'm alright really, kek kek, just feel strange. If Oh Lord Sweetheart God took me now I wouldn't be surprised at all except I can't leave Mémêre. I hang on a string waiting for you. I don't even have a phone, or know where Allen is, or what Gary thinks of me, or Creel, or you for that matter, and especially poor Lew Welch whom I love and

---

1. Excerpt from journal entry by kind permission of John Sampas and Viking Penguin.

always loved. As for Neal, what ancient histories. And all my lost girls. It's weird, like a revolution inside nature. I don't think Gertrude Stein really understood Scott Fitzgerald when he complained to her that he had "changed," she said; "Oh no one ever changes except they change and that's good" or something like that and here he is writhing in torment in Connecticutt-I-guess beds as she dikes ahead in Paree, I mean, the joy of the Good Dyke. As a matter of fact I'm a Dike myself and my Joy is so fast I can't keep up with it, or keep track, and thus this Complaynt.

Dragons anyone?
Latest Perm:

Run Ship Run

RUN
The Run

—Making the Run—

Nothin says nothin
like somethin
from the ovin
and Pills Bury
sells it best?
(And this is my new 10¢
red-inkpen, Much Better)

The infinite thing
is the infinite
Nothing, in which
it exists

Nothing is TRUE:—
Therefore I'm gonna
Keep my money,
Chuang Chou

Title:—   Uncut Edition

I Never rode
bareback
With an Indian Girl
upon a bareback
Tree

Said Peter O'Toole, star of "Lawrence of Arabia," on TV
Interview: "One cardinal is sinister, two are funny, but twelve are pretty
fast." (!)

          Not to put "religion"
         in people, but to
           bring out of em—
               All that wasted
               sweetness disunified—
               Little Lord Fauntleroy
               was an Angel and a
               Saint, like Myshkin

Ginsberg has a
marvelous imagination

After Deluge:
Christ Mass

S N O W H I L L

We live with
many a Santo
  or Santa
in the Stellar
  Electron Mystery
  (said the Carthaginian Sailor)
               "As tho I were
               abbott staggering
             under the vile
                 Centuries since
                     Paradise"—MELVILLE

                         There ...
          Yr most respectful friend & almost Servant,
          (if you want a drink)
                 Jean-Louis
                     i.e., *Servant* Jack

*In mid-February 1963, Kerouac told Robert Giroux that he was beginning to
think about starting a new book about his father. Jack's memory had been stirred
by the experience of unpacking old family letters, photographs, and newspaper
clippings after the move from Orlando back to Northport.*

Feb. 19 [19]63
[Northport, New York]

Dear Bob

Am now starting on VANITY OF DULUOZ by first studying all letters, photos, writings and memory-stuff of that time (1939-to-1946) and making notes.

The novel already written, called PASSING THROUGH, that I said I'd type up for you, I'm leaving untyped in the drawer awhile (it covers 1956-to-1957), because it's not in the mood that I'm in now and would only interfere in what I want to do now.

PASSING THROUGH is the sequel to DESOLATION ANGELS. You havent told me whether you ever want to publish ANGELS; I suppose you will. It might be good to make it run from VISIONS OF GERARD 1963, VANITY OF DULUOZ 1964 (if completed), DESOLATION ANGELS 1965, and PASSING THROUGH 1966, tho of course I'll have something else written by then, referring to later events in Duluoz Legend.

Anyway all's well in my writing life. I had some stunning thoughts last night, the result of studying Tolstoi, Spengler, New Testament and also the result of praying to St. Mary to intercede for me to make me stop being a maniacal drunkard. Ever since I instituted the little prayer, I've not been lushing. So far, every prayer addressed to the Holy Mother has been answered, and I only "discovered" her last Halloween. I shouldnt be telling you this. But I do want to point out, the reason I think she intercedes so well for us, is because she too is a human being, who was simply chosen to suckle and care for an incarnated Barnasha, after all. Of what use would Jesus be to us if he didnt have to have a mother's care?

How's Dramheller's[2] drawings?

Listening to the Vespers of Mozart

As ever
Jack

In March 1963, Kerouac typed a long letter to his sister about how he and Gabrielle walked to town in mild spring weather to buy "all kinds of stuff" for their new home. Mémère added a few lines to his letter with her black ballpoint pen. The previous month Jack had written Caroline that he was worried because he had bought such an expensive house: "my money comes in slow, the rent is high, and taxes coming up." Nevertheless, he spent $600 to put up a six-foot Alaskan cedarwood basket-weave fence around his yard, paid for by unexpected royalties from the sale of his books in Germany and Finland. Kerouac turned down his

2. Kerouac is referring to the drawings of James Spanfeller, who illustrated *Visions of Gerard.*

agent's suggestion that he write an article on the Beat Generation for Playboy, *but in April he asked Robert Giroux for a loan.*

March 9, 1963
[Northport, New York]

Dear Sterling:

Concerning PLAYBOY MAGAZINE and the article they want me to write: I can write about the "beat generation" but it can't be from the vantage point of the questions they sent you since I don't know all 20 million individuals involved and what they actually do and think, I can only write about this from the vantage point of myself, my life, and what I've seen and thought. On this basis I can write in all honesty, that is, I'll have to talk about myself, spin anecdotes and examples, and ramble along and talk about others too. An abstract intellectual discussion is out of the question for all eternity. Therefore, ask them for their price first, and then their deadline, their length requirements, and I'll write it and send it. I require that the article and the title I give it be published exactly as I write it. If they want to reject it and the title at their pleasure, it will be their privilege and my freedom.

As ever, Jack

TO CAROLINE KEROUAC BLAKE

March 25, 1963
[Northport, New York]

Dear Nin,

Am sending you check for Joan, mail it right away and forget about it.

No action was taken on that "raise" she wanted before Christmas, I guess because, like Paul said, she cant go any higher'n the Supreme Court.

Mémêre and I went walking to town today in 76 degree first-day-of-spring airs, and bought a Big Ben clock for her bedroom, a pair of good big scissors (first good scissors in the family since 1940), her Easter basket stuff, and all kinds of stuff just for a walk. The house is coming along fine. The yard is really going to be something: I pace in it sometimes at 4 am in the morning, under the cold stars and the bare branches, thinking of my new book and how to write it (book about Pa). The lady who sold us the house left us a lot of valuable things, curtains everywhere upstairs and in the rumpus basement, cans of oil, water cans, a tool cart, a saw horse, even an American flag, rugs, mats, tools, wall pictures (framed), big sets of poker chips and cards, a perfect workman's tool rack, varnishes, stain removers, paint, wood all carpented: in fact I'm going to make myself a bookshelf and paint it.

We took that rackety back off Mémère's bed so that her bed is now like a Hollywood bed, and with her curtains, radio, books, crucifixes, pictures, etc. her room is really cozy and Doby's always sleeping in there day and night. My office I put my big bed in it to sleep near my work, so in the "den" we put the bookcase and the little TV and one of your couch-beds and all the framed pictures and a new wooden rocker, it's a cozy lit-tle den for watching TV and reading. In my office I have my own little half-bathroom with new wallpaper and when I sit on the throne at night I close the light and open the window and look out on the field in back of the house. Mémère's bathroom, however, is one like you'd like, with cabi-nets under the sink and a 5 foot mirror, all in pink and blue. The living-room is really "grand." The fireplace with the white mantel and the black and gold fireplace fixtures is the centerpiece. The early American furniture goes well with it, the piano, etc. When we pull the cord of the picture win-dow we see trees, cute little houses, and horizons of further trees and pines. The diningroom is small, cozy, with Mémère's writing desk and Timmy al-ways sleeping on the table. There too the view is of hemlocks, grass, etc. [....] The basement is so huge and clean Mémère hangs out all her wash in it on plastic ropes tied to beams. Her new hobby is feeding the birds, black-and-blue shiney starlings, and she's afraid they're gonna poop on her wash. They come by the dozens every morning. "Les tites poules," she calls them. Mémère misses you and when they have ads about Florida on TV ("Come on down on Eastern Air Lines, it's warm down here!"), she misses Florida, but outside of that okay and she's getting used to her new home. She watches TV. They have late late late shows here, and on Saturday night the late late late late show starts at 5:30 in the morning!

Also lots of good local TV, etc. Anyway, all's well. I have my girlfriend come see me but no more Lois and only the guys I really want to see, no one else.

Mémère'll write you a note on the back of this. (Tell Lil Paul I just made me a banana split with caramel and also chocolate sauce, over butter al-mond ice cream, with Top Whip sproosh on top.)

Ti Jean

[Mémère's note]
Boy, that's a wang [sic] of a letter Jack wrote you. I cant top it but here's my 2 cents worth ... Jack is weeding out the friends he dont want around so we can have peace. Now that the warm weather is here they all want to come out here. Mind you, when they come they stay 3 to 4 days and that's too much for me....

Love, Mémère

Apr. 18 '63
[Northport, New York]

Dear Bob

Thanks for loan.

Dont forget to ask Dramheller to either give me or sell me that pencil sketch of Gerard in the window with cat and birds.

I'm glad I got some work done and that we're all set to print. My books are never bestsellers because, as I can see from re-reading Gerard, they're too complicated for average readers. I think I hit just about the right commercial level of success to meet my needs.

I'll send PASSING THROUGH in a month or so. Some of it (wow, a great big boom of thunder just hit, 2 A M, scared me!) is like this:

"Hubbard (Bill Burroughs) also introduces me to his lover, a boy of 20 with a sweet sad smile just the type Bill has always loved, from Chicago to Here. We have a few drinks and go back to his room.

"Tomorrow the Frenchwoman who runs this pension will probably rent you that excellent room on the roof with bath and patio, my dear. I prefer being down here in the garden so I can play with the cats and I'm growing roses." The cats, two, belong to the Chinese housekeeper who does the cleaning for the shady lady from Paris, who owns the apartment building on some old Roulette bet or some old rearview of the Bourse, or something—but later I find all the real work is done by the big Nubian Negress who lives in the cellar (I mean, if you wanted big romantic novels about Tangier.) But no time for that!....

Well, à toute à l'heur

As ever,
Jack

On May 7, 1963, Kerouac wrote a note to Barney Rosset, enclosing a letter defending The Subterraneans from charges of pornography after it had been translated into Italian and published in Milan by Giangiacomo Feltrinelli Editore. The book had been banned in Italy since its publication in 1960, and the lawsuit was scheduled for trial. Kerouac's open letter, titled, "Written Address to the Italian Judge," was revised by Grove Press's legal counsel and printed in the October/November 1963 issue of Evergreen Review.

May 7, 1963
[Northport, New York]

Mr. Barney Rosset
Grove Press
64 University Place
New York 3, N.Y.
Dear Barney:

Barney, I wonder if you would read the enclosed letter and then, since you're versed in all the latest lore about defenses against charges of pornography, dictate a letter that can be sent to the people in Italy, in defense of THE SUBTERRANEANS, you being the original publisher a strong case in point, and I having signed all your petitions in favor of Miller and Burroughs.

No big hassle, just dictate a letter and forget about it, if you want, and I'll insist that it be published as the preface to any new edition of SUBS in Italian.

As ever,
Jack Kerouac
PO Box 385
Northport, N.Y.
(no phone)

After Gary Snyder sent Kerouac an essay analyzing The Subterraneans, *written by a woman student in the English language class he taught in Kyoto, drunken Jack responded with a blistering attack.*

TO GARY SNYDER

May 23, 1963
Box 385
Northport, NY

Dear Gary:

You should tell dopey little cunts like that presumptuous Miss M. that they are full of lil brown turds that all they wanta do is shit em out in the form of babies, and you may tell your female schoolteachers too—I told you sincerely in 1956 in Mill Valley shack and even before that in Berkeley Milvia Street cottage that I was serious, that I meant it, that I agree with Gautama Buddha that women are always attempting to show their form, turning this way and that, showing a tit-shape, a shoulder, an ass-form, and if they're not in your actual presence to be able to do that, why, they do it in the form of Freudian analyses of your writings and stick in little underlined-by-you references to holding cock in hand (when all the time it should be holding cock in mouth and even that bores me even if the whole of Zen Buddhism was blowing me I couldnt care a fuck)–(I was gonna say "even if all Madhyamikha Buddhism")–The fact of the matter is, Buddha was right and Zen is a corruption of his truth–Just as St. Paul was a corruption of the rightness of Jesus Christ–and the church that followed was a corruption of Jesus Christ–and the India which Allen described you and he and Peter saw there, IS a corruption, a very fucking degradation, of Buddha what-he-said–Yet because of your clinging, your greed for desire and the consummation of desire, your penchance (Pirates!) (Penzance) for discriminating of desires and fulfillments thereof, you go off like monkeys fucking asthmatic sick women against midnight death tables in the name of your pitiful dongs which are nothing but the dongs of monkeys ... And all the time since I met you I've been trying to tell you this, and now you wonder why I dont write to you, goddamn it Gary it's because I Know you're not INNARESTED in what I'm saying because you're so hungup on Samsara and the reason you're so hung up on Samsara is just fucking very *because* you've been taught that Zen heresy of Samsara being the same as Nirvana–Now in the ultimate meaning of the Mahayana of course it's the same but it's not for Monkies to decide that.... It's for priests who've purified themselves of the temptations aroused by the wiles of Mother Kali's host of Mara demons known as W O M E N.... Didnt you for krissakes ever read that section of Ashvhaghosha's BUDDHA CHARITA where 1250 monks are sittin in a field with Buddha and they sit there and here across the field comes about 1250 courtesans bearing gifts, incense, cundroms, tennis rackets, analyses, slanty eyes, blonde eyes, cunt eyes, cunts inside pearls, white thighs, Marx, Freud, Pavlov, anything they can think of, and he says "Now fellas before they get here across that long field, which will take approximately five minutes, I wanta warn you about one thing: better it is to fall into the net of a woman's plans, Man, than to fall into a Tiger's mouth" and he was talking about Bengal jungle tigers–Man eaters–Now I spose you're running around on your motorcycle with your little beard at dawn going to a "meditation" thinking that all that was just Mahayana queertalk–Superimposed by a desert monk–And that Buddha himself hadnt abandoned a harem, a wife, a father, a son, servants, and millions, just Mahayana queertalk that has no relation to the marvelous touristy attraction of modern Zen with all its cunts in dark glasses staring at you through microscopes which say "Your mother thinks she owns you but it's I who shall own you" and they take you by the arm to the Law who swears out a warrant, which is a mandate to the Court, for your arrest in marriage, whereby theh [sic], though the heavens of Avalokitesvara sigh again, a cock or cunt baby is born, and THE WHOLE THING STARTS AGAIN BUT NOT ONLY THAT L E G A L.... and you gets your head cut off (if you're a knifer like me) or gets it shot off (if you're a gunner like a Mafia) if you dont abide by this earthbound rule of Kali cunts ... this rule which has absolutely no relationship to what Bodhidharma brought from th'West.

As for that girl's paper, it disappoints me and makes me no more wanta visit Japan, because I see that the students there have also been stampeded and ridden by the Four Horsemen of the Modern Apocalypse, i.e., Pavlov, Freud, Marx, and Ignorance.

Her education is incomplete, poor, and she should go back to her father and ask him what to do now. If you think that the solution of either Occidental and/or Oriental problems be solved merely by Pavlov, Freud, Marx, or Ignorance, then why do you profess to Zen anyway ... which is sposed to mean Chan, which is sposed to mean Dhyana?

How can you sit there and be spanked on the ass by the flat soft boards of brow beaten crewcutted Jap idiots and not roar at them with a Sword of what you used to call wisdom? Or that is, how can the young girl, or even you now, understand, for instance, in this case, how much Western complicity in mediocrity of complexity went into the making of a DeFoean narrative like THE SUBTERRANEANS? I know Goethe, I even know Eckhart, I even know Basho, God I know Li Po, I know Pascal, Liebnitz, La Place, Dostoevsky, Tolstoy's KINGDOM OF GOD IS WITHIN YOU, and you let her write inanities about me who am so horrified by ignorance everywhere on this street in N'port as well as on yr street that I gulp and die, how can you be a teacher and let that happen? You Of The Dharma Forever, Forever Weeping?

Jack

Send me the Gift from India.[3]

Traveling in India with Peter Orlovsky since mid-February 1962, Ginsberg wrote Kerouac a single-spaced three-page letter from Benares on May 8, 1963. Allen enclosed a leaf from the Bodhi tree at Bodh Gaya under which he had slept while visiting the temple, (saying "all comes from that spot to the Lower E-Side"). Allen described his enthusiasm for Andrey Voznesensky and Yevgeny Yevtushenko's poetry and told of his harassment by the secret police after insulting the head of the English department at Benares Hindu University. Ginsberg and Orlovsky had joined the Delhi Peking Peace Marchers for a demonstration but left the group "angrily preaching peace" with a copy of Ed Sanders's Lower East Side mimeographed magazine Fuck You/A Magazine of the Arts.

While in India, Allen kept a notebook and watched bodies being consumed in the burning ghat on a colossal staircase leading down to the Ganges River. He also consulted various holy men, telling them about his Blake vision and closely observing their gestures and style: "tranquil hand gestures & head shakes & un-inflamed voice, voices always natural & calm rather tender in fact, eccentric little

3. See letter to Allen Ginsberg, June 29, 1963.

*voices with grandfatherly quavers." He learned from their example that he
"really should treat people gentler & not insult & drive them into corner so
they claw out in self-defense." Ginsberg planned to visit Angkor Wat before
going on to Japan for a reunion with Gary Snyder, and he thanked Kerouac for
sending copies of* Big Sur, *which Allen had left with "Hindi who admire the
prose."*

*On June 29, 1963, Jack answered Allen's letter, confiding his prevalent state
of depression and urging his old friend to "Come home soon."*

TO ALLEN GINSBERG

June 29, 1963
[Northport, New York]

Dear Allen—

Was hesitant to write to you care of damned India where letter might be
lost but hope you gets this anyway—Just now had a flash of understanding
what a gone friendship we've had really, not only all the wild letters we exchanged (I have all your letters neatly filed here in my new steel office file
& you can browse anytime & use them etc.) and all the wild adventures together on Bklyn Bridge, Columbia, Frisco, Mexico, etc. and elsewhere later,
but all that bombed-out literature we started (bombed-out-of-mind) & all
the swirls and levels, like just now I was sitting daydreaming of Burroughs
and Huncke finally meeting again in your 7th Street kitchen tomorrow and
you and I are wringing our hands with delight and winking at each other
as Huncke says, "Well, well," and Burroughs replies etc.—Which is just another way of saying how much I respect you and value you, Poit.—When
you come to my new house in N'Port it will be perfect if you dont have that
beard and long hair, who cares about that shit anyway? Let me see your
cherubic haircut. Just saw Eugene who just came to my house and I really
wanted to chat with him (have been conversing with Eugene a lot since
you left and find him highly intelligent, as much as you in a way), but he
brings a crazy Rabbi who wants me to rush around like Norman Mailer
renting out Carnegie Hall and going to Stork Club and getting in Winchell
because "great works of art" shd. be publicized etc. His name is Richard
something-or-other, actually nice guy but I don't want to abandon my solitude and reading and quietude for just a lot of horseshit showing-off in
public—Besides On the Road is finally contracted for a movie, I'll get 5 percent of the budget when shooting starts, 5 percent of the budget when picture released, and then 5 percent of the net profits of the company which
will be headed by the guy who will turn Road into a scenario and also direct: name of Bob Ginnet ... so I don't need to make money scenes, just
enough for me anyway, since as you know I always collect my change when
I leave a woman, & besides I hate the bitches now they're all such a bunch
of whores and liars like Joan doubly lieing yet—Lies about me that hold *me*

up to the world as a liar!—But to hell with that, I'm thinking of something else, it's just started raining! My new pad here is at 7 Judyann Court, off Dogwood Road, keep that address a secret and put it in your notebook under the name of The Wizard of Ozone Park, under "W," and when you come to N'Port, there's the house, 7 Judyann Court, off Dogwood Road, instructions, etc.—Best house I ever had with big backyard with 32 trees all around and 6 foot tall wood fence of Alaskan cedar, basketweave style, nobody see me as I read in sun or goop among tomato plants and my mother feedeth the birds and they thrash in the birdbath and in my room is groovy new Telefunken FM (West German) set with big Bachs and Mozarts or jazz anytime, and full finished basement with den and FM music and records and later maybe a pooltable—Nothing fancy, just right—Only problem is too much local visitings from bores—No Lucien come yet, no Allen, just pain-in-the-ass visitores, as usual—One new friend rather nice, Adolf Rothman, schoolteacher and clamdigger, learned and quiet—Jewish lenin face—But tonight, ugh, unavoidable visit from two teenagers who want me to go meet girls in dance bars, will not go but just play them music awhile—Please tell Gary when you see him, or write him, to excuse me for the enraged letter I wrote him drunk on a quart of Canadian Club whiskey in which I excoriated women forever ... tho I meant it, I didn't mean to be mean to Gary, who however didn't seem to mind and wrote back he was sending me a present. (Some dopey Jap cunt "psychoanalyzed" Subterraneans in school like a real square Vassar shot.) A "living woman" indeed, what do they want me to do, screw cadavers? All mixed up letter, this, I really ain't got my heart in it, had so much to say when I got on typewriter just now, well anyway this'll let you know I'm with you all the way, but I want you to know, no like writing letters any more, getting like Neal now, I dunno why, sure would like to see you instead. Having Giroux look at Whalen's new book of poems (very good), returned McClure's novel without comment (hated it, cheapskate beatniks with guns in their briefcases kicking girls and sitting around being dull on pot), am recording great library of classical and jazz tapes, saving letters, filing them, wrote letter defending Subs to Italian Judge in Milano where Subs being on trial for banning with bishops of Milano behind it with Montini was the bishop of Milano, my painting of Montini might be colorphotoed in Time or Satevpo. Just sold a chapter from new novel to Holiday magazine about "On the Road with Mémère" (me and my mother in Juarez enroute Frisco 1957), and generally I being calm and readable tho had to quit local bars because a big blond fag wants to shoot me with gun because I called him a fag, I guess, don't remember, cops watching me, local clamdiggers fucked up, my cousin Mooncloud came to see me here to tell me his story[4] was just a lot of shit (I still don't

4. See letter to Holmes, October 9, 1962.

know, we went Lucien NY and girls and scenes, all a mad mixed up mess whenever I leave the house so I stay home and this summer I think be nice go to Quebec and write that for Holiday and then in the Fall, when "Visions of Gerard" is out, take off for Cologne, Germany, London, Paris, Cornwall & Brittany altho I don't know, don't care much, all's in my heart HERE IN MY HEART, Ami.

In any case we take big trip together somewhere, or do something, sometime, again, copain.

I recently had horrible visions of the too-muchness of the world which requires really too much of our attention, our mind essence is completely blasted by music, people, books, papers, movies, games, sex, talk, business, taxes, cars, asses, gasses, yack ack etc. and I almost died chocking over this (choking)—Like, now I'm outs with Gregory almost, we had a big jubilant reunion in April or so and haollelujahd to write a big article for Playboy about Beat and so he'd have money for his wedding with Sally November who hates me I think, and it all deteriorated with Gregory rewriting the whole thing behind my back and cursing me and Luce and everybody as creeps, and him a "pure lyric poet" which is what Lucien told him the day before and it went to his head—Mainly, I had the sensation that Gregory is insane, because he kept me up and down all the time, making me happy with his kindness, suddenly browbeating, not brow beating but actually "beating" me on the head to make me sad, so I was up and down, and up and down all the time with him, suddenly realizing he's crazy and doesn't want to be friends with anyone at all, maybe wants to be punished for this? The article we wrote together, dictating to girlfriends of mine, etc., was ridiculous, not even an article but a drunken whiskey chain poem meaning nothing whatever—I think H is going to G's head really—That Sally of his is sullen, I think—But maybe they'll have a baby and coo quietly together and it might turn out good for poor tortured Gregory Corso—But on these visits to NY, worse than ever, I come back with visions of horror as bad as the Ayahuasca vision on the neanderthal million years in caves, the gruesomeness of life!—Yet all my future be bright, with On the Road gonna be a movie, a new novel in the Fall, 2 new novels not yet publisht (Desolation Angels and its sequel about you and me and Pete and Laf and Gregory in Mexico, "Passing Through"), and I see nothing ahead for me but ease and joy and yet my mind is so dark, and so lonesome sometimes I could cry on your shoulder or Bill's or Neal's any minute. And what of poor Neal? Carolyn marrying another man, couldnt I be a millionaire and make Neal my chauffeur? Do I need a crazy teahead chauffeur with broads hiding in the trunk? And Bill, how come I don't ever get to see him anymore and if I journeyed to Paris via Air France or Lufthasa jet would he be kind to me when I rushed up to him? or laugh at me for being fat? or WHAT? Where's Peter, why did you leave Peter? Why did you and Peter leave Laf to such a fate? How could you carry Laf around the world on yr shoulders anyway?

It's hopeless. How's Gary? I guess he/s alright. Whalen is very sad and neutral with big sad neutral blue eyes. Scares me sometimes. Lew Welch is spending his time in an isolated shack, naked, at Forks of Salmon, Calif. and says he's going crazy like Han Shan. Did you see Big Sur novel which I had sent to you? And what you think of the ridiculous denouement in THAT? All too true. Ow. Meanwhile all these subsidiary bores keep hammering at ya, Aquinas monks denying my theology in long silly letters written-likethiswith Joycean arrangements, or bores around Los Gatos assuring me I WAS of some importance while America needed me and thanks—nevertheless, Allen dear friend, I feel a strange ecstasy, right now, always in fact, always.

Holmes has been bombarding me with huge questions for his non-fiction book which will be about everything: I spent 3 nights answering his questions in detail, on typewriter, he oughta be glad right now. Book will be about you, me, Mailer, Baldwin, etc. whole scene ... But it's raining, great straight drops of sheet rain falling through glen dark tree glades ... very pretty day. A day for getting drunk on whiskey, in fact, but dammit I did that yesterday. A lost day. Wonder what Joan Adams is thinking ... Where's Huncke? How's Laf? What is Paul Bowles thinking, and where? And Ansen? And Walter Adams? How sad the garbage can! Anyway, when you get back here, I'll show you all the piled up papers relating to everything since you left, letters, poems of Gregory, etc. and let us hope that the great calm hearts of Melville, Whitman and Thoreau do sustain us in the coming hectic years of overcommunicating Americas and Telstars and other Galaxies ... What have we accomplished? Good new poetry, that oughta be enough. "Charming bedraggled little princes" everywhere on accounta you ... and sudden waves of intelligent teenage football players somehow. Somehow my ass. Incidentally I liked your "honking Eliot" dream and just now in fact was studying an old dream of yours in a letter from Chiapas, no San Jose, about Chiapas,[5] a dream you had there of Burroughs being photographed in a Rome trolley, and a dream of me leading tourist millions wandering in endless Brooklyns ... I just had drink dream that I was shitting all the time whether I was in the toilet or not, shit all over the floor, over my hands, shoes, over my face really, just shit all over, like balloons ... [....] I wanta go back to my simple Lucien and Allen and Bill. Anyway my present job is to write "Vanity of Duluoz" novel about 1939 to 1946, won't be easy, football, war, Edie, etc. Bronx jail, you, Columbia, etc. ouch. Come home soon.

Jack

5. Kerouac might also have seen Ginsberg's new book of poetry, *Reality Sandwiches,* published by City Lights in June 1963, containing his long poem about Mexico in 1954, "Siesta in Xbalba."

On July 29, 1963, Kerouac wrote Robert Giroux to thank him for sending copies of Visions of Gerard. *Jack and Mémère liked the James Spanfeller drawings that illustrated the book so much that they framed one—Gerard feeding the birds—and hung it on their living-room wall. Jack also mentioned that he'd had a visit from Neal Cassady, who stayed in Northport with his latest girlfriend and a buddy. Two weeks later Kerouac wrote Carolyn Cassady that Neal was as "sweet" as ever by himself, but that Neal's friends made him angry when they helped themselves to "expensive delicacies" in the refrigerator and parked a "hot car" in front of his house.*

TO ROBERT GIROUX

July 29, 1963
[Northport, New York]

Dear Bob

I got the Xavier Rynne book and thank you.

Also, ten copies of beautiful Gerard book, all of which are already gone: keeping three for myself, and giving one to my sister, my aunt, one to a painter, one to a concert pianist hopeful, one to boyhood buddy Mike, one to Gregory Corso, one to Neal Cassady (both rats who don't deserve them, at least the former) and the last one I can't even remember. They were all here in a succession of visitors and that's the reason I haven't answered you sooner, as I was also on nervous breakdown manic elative kick surrounded by too many people.

Meanwhile I've turned down silly things like hiring out Town Hall, and making record album with civil righter poets, etc. and intend to go to Gaspé Peninsula in a few weeks to write an article for Ted Patrick at Holiday Magazine, and be by myself in motel rooms at night reading, and visit the village of Kirouac in Quebec, said to be the blueberry growing center of North America.

So, let me know whatever you want me to know meanwhile.

For my next book, I'll have to think some more. Regards to Jean White & tell her to pay no attention to that joke about Milton the blind poet.

As ever,
Jack

p.s. As to Xavier Rynne book, my mother said, "Well, they can say whatever they want about you, but you got into the Pope's book."
Write soon!

Aug. 16 '63
[Northport, New York]

Dear Carolyn

By now Neal must be home. If he'd come to see me by himself, he could have stayed in my mother's house indefinitely. But he had these rude people with him, one of whom reached without invitation into my pantry & icebox for *the* most expensive delicacies, the other put his feet up on the kitchen table after eating & even threw bread around while eating to show what a great independent hipster he was. I disliked them very much, & had the D.T. shakes anyway.

But Neal, alone with me for 5 minutes, was as sweet & gentle & polite & intelligent & interesting as ever he was with me or anyone else he's ever liked.

I was also worried about a hot car connected at my mother's home.

As you can see, I've grown older & bored with the world.

Please tell Neal to let Allen G. fix his "First Third" manuscript for publication, this Fall (Nov. or Oct.), at will. Neal needs to be published at last, after all. No hesitation. There'll be money in it. . . . & probably my own publisher (shhh).

Good luck with your new marriage, which is probably for the best after all, seeing as how Neal keeps taking such chances as on this last run.

But my thoughts, believe it or not, occur daily about you & Neal, from habit, & from unchanged affection in *Thou.*

(All these hanger-onners, *NO!*)

Pay no attention to drunken letters I wrote last Spring, to your "spies," I mean *my* would-be spies Brownrigg & Durant.

Enough. I havent touched a drink since Neal left.

Jack

A month after the publication of Visions of Gerard, *Kerouac wrote an anguished letter to John Clellon Holmes responding to the hostile reviews of the book. The judgment of the* New York Herald Tribune *reviewer was typical:*

A text very much like everything else [Kerouac] has published in the past five years: slapdash, grossly sentimental, often so pridefully "sincere" that you can't help question the value of sincerity itself—and most distressing of all, disclosing here and there that the author is a man with a subtle sense of human nature and gift of language every bit its equal. . . . Set against dramatic New England seasons and in the bosom of a warm French-Canadian family, it is a tender, pathetic story of innocent suffering and harsh effacement, and in someone else's hands, it could have been moving. Even in Kerouac's own hands, it could have been good, if only he had made writerly demands of himself. As it stands, though, it just amounts to 152 more pages of self-indulgence.

Like Big Sur *and* Lonesome Traveler, *which had also been handsomely produced,* Visions of Gerard *sold poorly and was soon remaindered by the publishers.*

TO JOHN CLELLON HOLMES

Oct. 5 1963
[Northport, New York]

Dear John

Got your inspired description of Ioway. I've nothing really to say except I'm filled with that sickened feeling that comes after the reviewers have done with one's latest book. Now I'm a tin-eared Canuck instead of a golden-tongued Jew, says Newsweek, and others like that. The only decent review I got in fact was from a tin-eared Canuck on the Knickerbocker News in Albany who seemed to be the only one to understand the compassion I tried to convey. Compassion, in this time when Mailer is being called a "Radical Moralist" because of his public & political ideas, after having been so moral with Adele Morales, is a lost word, a lost, lost word, a lost, lost thought, a lost, lost feeling ... everybody's become so mean, so sinister, so hypocritical I can't believe it. So I turn to drink like a lost maniac. Why doesn't someone start a placard parade saying "We Want Compassion!" "We Want Everybody to Stop Being Sinister!" ... I'm really sick and tired, also of critics saying either that I must grow, or haven't grown, or did grow, them and their damned GROW, if I grew into what they are I'd stow myself in my pencil and drop it in a manhole in Manhattan down into the steam from which they come crawling at midnight to infest our culture, etc.

In fact one reviewer infuriated me by harking back to the last paragraph in Road about Iowa, you remember, "the evening-star sheds her sparkler dims across the prairie," the ass thinks "dims" is a present tense verb and therefore I'm being unrhetorical, all the time he doesn't even know (being a big sociological critical expert of literature) what "puttin on your brights" and "puttin on your dims" means in ordinary American car driving talk. So what am I going to do. They make me feel like never writing another word again. They pull cruddy cobwebby gray fud over my eyelids and make them droop, I assure you, or will continue to do so until I stop reading anything but great books and my own manuscripts and like they say Faulkner used to do, not even bother glancing at reviews etc.

I'm going to try to get Giroux to publish DESOLATION ANGELS next.

You read it, remember, in winter of 1957, at Saybrook. It's the logical next step in the Duluoz Legend presentation, after all. You'd laugh, tho, actually, if you knew how ANXIOUS I am just because I haven't got a book in the printer's works at last! I've run out! I'm done! Actually, Angels is okay but I wonder if Giroux will take it. He ain't said a word. If not, I can always sell it to Grove press, hor hor hor. You wonder how I got 13 books (volumes) published since 1957? By simply taking the mss. to the publishers who'd take them. When I see Allen's loyalty to one publisher, City Lights Ferlinghetti, and know how careful and clever he is, I wonder if I'm digging my own grave with the publishing business. Well, if I have, I'll simply spend the rest of my life w r i t i n g f o r m y s e l f something to read in my old age.

I'm reading SOME CAME RUNNING and find [James] Jones to be a great big earnest Wolfean Dreiserean American genius of the novel, don't let nobody tell you otherwise. His characters sit right on your shoulder. Everybody's losing sight of "character study" nowadays: pimply poor man's Jewish John O'Hara characters like in Roth are forgotten in a day. I think, in fact, the best way to judge contemporary American writing is to see who's getting panned the most (in which case Roth has just risen a notch, I guess). (I mention Roth because in the new Doubleday book "The Creative Present" they threaten to cross me off the list for Roth because I haven't "grown" tho I've "produced.") (produced too much? heh heh heh)

Amigo Jack

On November 18, 1963, Kerouac expanded in a letter to Philip Whalen, saying that he had slowed down on his letter writing to some of his friends because it had become a "huge chore involving 'arguments.'" He might have been thinking of the air letter Ginsberg had sent him on October 6, 1963, from Ferlinghetti's office above the City Lights Bookshop in San Francisco, where Allen stayed after participating in the Vancouver Poetry Conference with Charles Olson, Robert Duncan, Robert Creeley, and Denise Levertov. In the letter Allen told Jack that he had learned from living abroad that he was not a "hairy loss," the name Kerouac had called him in 1958, after Allen had come back to New York City from Paris. On October 6, 1963, Ginsberg wrote to Kerouac:

> *I's me, and me's nameless, but certainly not a bad feeling OOK like hairy loss, you put me under a spell for years, and Burroughs about killed me off with his cut ups—his cut ups fine since it cuts up the head but he wants to cut up his body feelings too, and that dont feel good at all—your hairy loss served to get me down off my high head too, but you coulda saved me faster by calling me tender heart, honey—*

Nov. 18 1963
[Northport, New York]

Dear Phil

Not a word from Giroux about your book of poetry since I sent it to him so I am writing to him today, you'll hear from him one way or the other within a week—He *is* knowledgeable about poetry, like, he explained Yeats to me (& Eliot) when I was 27 years old, in a nice & interesting way—Even Allen was impressed—If he doesn't take your book it'll be only because of financial reasons, like he turned down ON THE ROAD right after I wrote it in 1951, because "the sales manager would not approve of it."—(Adding, "but Jack, it's just like Dostoevsky.")

So don't get mad, and if Farrar don't take it, or the others, get it published by LeRoi Jones (Corinth) or Auerhahn.

It will be nice to start writing to you again. Actually I'm not writing letters like these any more but you're an exception. Writing to Gary and Allen is too much of a huge chore involving "arguments." I'm living very quiet life, actually, boozing alone at home, reading (just finished Sir Gawain and the Green Knight, and Tristan and Iseult, all about my Cornish ancestors), not going into N.Y. any more, sold a story to Playboy ("Good Blonde" is title, oughta be printed Christmas or later), planning to move my menage to New England in the Spring, am invited to go to Berlin to make a movie with Hansjurgen Pohland (?), visited Florida 3 weeks ago and hated it and got escorted to airport by the sheriff at my sister's instigation, don't remember the return flight at ALL, talked to Japanese sailor at airport bar lounge (U.S. Navy), goofed around New York for 5 days singing Boo Hoo You've Got Me Crying For You to Thelonious Monk, spent days with great Freddie Redd pianist and playing some for him, almost got mugged in the Bowery by Jaimie Pepergnan of S.F., (and his Apache Buddy Rego), bought James Spanfeller's pencil drawing of "Gerard in the Window with Cat and Birds" for $52 and having it framed with glass on top (to hang in livingroom over piano), was in trouble about paying my rent until Denmark bought Big Sur for $160, got a $13 royalty check from England, get letters from jailbirds asking for money, my brother-in-law Major Hoople wants thousands for his new invention, Gregory Corso insists I give him $250 for his new baby coming, this is what I get for being called a Messiah and Saint Jack, read Norman Mailer's brilliant "Papers" where I don't believe in his personal attack on Kennedy person but the "Essay on Waste" a Pope-Baconian classic and also piece on Liston–Patterson fight, had me published again in Evergreen Review ("Letter to Italian Judge" and the case is won, in Varese Italy, censorship of Subterraneans lifted), am sending OLD ANGEL MIDNIGHT Part Two to Rosset therefore, (that which Ferlinghetti rejected), found out that Villon's 16th (15th?) century French is just like Quebecois "patoi" (tué, mué, instead of toi, moi) and pronounced VEE-

LON and not VEE*YON), (a la like Pancho VEE LA), (so that the way we pronounce fish in French Canada, puéssons, is closer to pisces than "poissons"), see, and thought of this poem while walking home with beer "King Prat the Berber come running by today yelling 'Whee! November Pretty!' "——Decided that Communists are people who want to spread everyone's wealth but their own—Hungary bought Road for $150—and in a Sunday night hangover I saw the Spectre of a Loneliness in me so bad I would be afraid to take it with me to the grave.—Will send you a home made Christmas card.—Let me hear from you. Wish you were here.

Tristan the Sad
Jack

On December 11, 1963, Kerouac sent Holmes a blurb for his third novel Get Home Free, *along with a note mentioning that Ginsberg had returned to New York City. Jack had decided not to be Allen's friend anymore, angry at "his pro-Castro bullshit and his long white robe Messiah shot."*

TO JOHN CLELLON HOLMES

Dec. 11, 1963
[Northport, New York]

Dear John,

Here is my blurb for GET HOME FREE and every word I mean—I like it, and some parts of it are *great*—The sex scenes are very erotic without being offensive, which is an art—"It was Paul Hobbes!!" (on piano) made me realize you actually dream such drizzly stuff for your vision of America, that, in fact, you're a maniac—Sometimes when I get drunk and listen to Freddie Redd etc. I daydream it's really ME playing and all my old doubting friends are piling into the nightclub to see how mad and how changed I've become—Molineaux is good but I think the Negro-White party down south tops it, and the last scenes with Verger and Girl—I cant for the life of me understand why Burroughs' Mitchell (is it?) didnt take this at Scribners, or was it Viking too?—Anyway, congratulations on what I think will be a "new career" after this, and the non-fiction book too—

I like the quote about me you sent, use it.

Meanwhile, Allen G. is already here, I had no time to send him to you, as a matter of fact I dont even particularly wanta see him with his pro-Castro bullshit and his long white robe Messiah shot—I mean, actually, too much mixup, I wanta stay home and think and read and write—Enough talk I've had these last 6 years around NY—He and all those bohemian beatniks round him have nothing NEW to tell me—I am Thomas Hardy now and that's that, back to my moor and my house (Ker) i' the moor (ouac)—Period.

You must be having a strange time teaching—I've just taught a little Shakespeare to SHOW magazine via a 1500 word opinion on Shakespeare, I dont even know if they're going to print it after all, it's too dignified and scholarly for JACK CARRAWACK to dare print[6] ... anyway, too, I have a hunch they thought I was going to C R I T I C I Z E my bard? Broadway Sams all.

To Shirley, a Cajun 'allo from Swampfire Jack.

Jack

6. Kerouac's essay "Shakespeare and the Outsider" appeared in *Show,* Vol. IV, No. 2 (February 1964).

1964

Early in 1964 Kerouac wrote to Fernanda Pivano, an Italian translator of con-
temporary American writers who was compiling and translating an anthology of
Beat poetry for a publisher in Milan. A great admirer of Ginsberg's work, Pivano
disregarded Kerouac's tirade against his old friend and went on to include sev-
eral Kerouac poems along with many pages of Ginsberg's poetry in her bilingual
anthology Poesia degli ultimi Americani *(1964).*

TO FERNANDA PIVANO

[Early 1964
Northport, New York]

Dear Nanda—

I've just turned down $3,000 because I didn't want to be in the same
film with Ginsberg, please do not identify my biography with his, or with
Corso's. They've both become political fanatics, both have begun to revile
me because I don't join them in their political opinions (in person, this is),
and I am sick of them and all their beatnik friends. I want you to know that
VISIONS OF GERARD published last year is the beginning of my new
feeling about life, strictly back to my original feelings in Lowell, of a New
England French Canadian Catholic & solitary nature. What these bozos and
their friends are up to now is simply the last act in their original adoption
and betrayal of any truly "beat" credo. They have used "beat" for their own
ends, like Lawrence Lipton and even Miller have done. Why, I don't know,
except to point out they can't possibly feel the way I do about life because
their childhoods were distorted by madness and disorder, and mine was
not. Now that we're all getting to be middleaged I can see that they're just
frustrated hysterical provocateurs and attention-seekers with nothing on
their mind but rancor towards "America" and the life of ordinary people.
They have never written about ordinary people with any love, you may
have noticed. I still admire them of course, for their technical excellence
as poets, as I admire Genet and Burroughs for their technical excellence as

prose writers, but all four of them belong to the "keep-me-out-of-the-picture" department and that's the way I want it from now on. You may have noticed in my letter to the Italian judge that I was serious when I said I didn't want to offend people because I'm frustrated. I may be frustrated but I will not offend, ca c'est dans le sang de ma famille. Genet and Burroughs do not offend half as much, because they are metaphysically hopeless; but Ginsberg and Corso are ignorant enough to be metaphysically healthy and want to use art as a racket. Ginsberg was just on TV announcing the imminent "Fall of America," for instance; and Corso visited me last summer wanting "my riches," wanting to move his wife into my mother's house, wanting one of my adolescent novels to use as his own, finally announcing that I was as good as dead because I do not want to parade with him and Ginsberg politically. And I've felt this coming on ever since 1956. I don't know where they got all this, or what they do behind my back, or even say about me behind my back, but I've always felt something funny about the two of them "behind me" and Orlovsky too. I renounce them and I don't want you to publish my haikus or put me in that book. I hope you can make arrangements to publish me *by myself.* Otherwise, you will be doing me a disservice as an individual voice in America, and I do mean *individual,* i.e., ALONE.

Buddha's last words: "Be ye lamps unto thyselves." [. . . .]

Jack

P.S. Lois doesn't want me to tell you anything about her family background. She's very much like Emily Dickinson, from a good family, a quiet bored background, etc., and reticent about public. I know you understand. In Yellowstone National Park there's a giant geyser that spouts up every 64 minutes and is called "Old Faithful." Like "Old Faithful," I am going to keep faith with America, I'm going to be faithful to the land. You should know my ancestry: Lebris de Keroack is the way the name is given in "Rivista Araldica," with a motto, "Aimer, Travailler, et Souffrir" and "Un clous d'argent" on a blue field. "Originaire de Quebec," pioneers of Quebec, and they were from Brittany and Capt. Francois Alexandre Lebris de Keroack married an Iroquois squaw in the 1750's so that today one of the Four Nations of the Iroquois is named "Kirouac" and another "Levesque" (my mother's family name). So I'm proud of my ancestors and I will not defile their graves with denunciations of the very skies they suffered under, in the name of "Nouvelle Vache."

In the first half of 1964, during a time when it was clear to everyone around Kerouac that his drinking was again out of control, Jack sent a stream of letters to Sterling Lord. Negative reviews and poor sales of Visions of Gerard *fueled Kerouac's depression, especially after the reviewer in* The New York Times *accused*

him of debasing the pathos of his brother Gerard's death with his "garrulous hip-
ster yawping," and Time *sneered at "the self-indulgent gush of his prose." In*
March 1964 Jack was invited to read for the students in Lowell House at Har-
vard University, but he got so drunk he overstayed his visit and was called a
"clown" rather than a poet by the Harvard Crimson. *On April 22, 1964, Ker-*
ouac described the reading to Stella Sampas, and the following month he wrote
her brother Tony Sampas about repaying a loan.

TO STELLA SAMPAS

April 22 1964
[Northport, New York]

Dear Stella

Dont get mad at me and send me empty envelopes, you dont realize
how busy I am one day, how sick the next. I would like it very much if
Yanni is alright.[1] Tony tonight on the phone said he was. I dont think Yanni
felt too good watching my friends in N.Y. steal from me. Yanni was ready
to clobber them. I gave the poet Corso $20 for his newborn child and later
that night in front of Yanni he stole another $20. I gave Yanni only $20 for
the whole trip, by the time I was ready to give him more I had no more.
This is all money I borrowed from Tony, whom I'll pay in a few weeks, mailing the check to him c/you, at No. 2.[2] Yanni was great, believe me, and
without all that confusion I could have brought him to my house for a meal
and sleep and talk. He is a true Sampas, i.e., a gentleman of the old school.

I feel guilty for introducing him to a bunch of bums. Bourgeois is also
a great gentleman, by the way. But I took Yanni to Ginsberg's pad (after
hitting first the Jazz, at Birdland, the Half Note, etc.) Yanni was stoned out
of his mind. He drove and I talked. I drank. I am sick of life and that's why
I drink, but I am not sick of people like Yanni and Paul Bourgeois. Or you.
Believe me. I've suffered so much now from my frantic imagination, of
which I am the victim, I sound now like Billie Holliday when I sing, or
worse, like Homer. I hope Charles Scoopy and Pertinax werent mad about
Harvard, it was bad enough as it was without journalists and photogs from
Lowell to record it. I told everybody anything that came to my mind and
it doesnt matter what I said. I'm like Brendan Behan and Dylan Thomas,
determined not to have monuments built to me in Dublin or in Cardiff. I'm
an old time French *farceur,* which is a French word meaning honest goof-
off. I liked you when I saw you, as usual, and remember what I told you, I
dont write for television: what you see on TV that sounds like me is all

---

1. Yanni was Stella's youngest brother, John Sampas. In order of birth, the siblings in the
Sampas family were Charles (Charley), Nicholas (Nicky), Stella, Claire, Sebastian (Sabby),
Anthony (Tony), James (Jim), Michael (Mike), Helen, and John (Yanni).
2. Stella lived at 2 Stevens Street in Lowell.

stolen from my books. I'm worried about next month's rent, for instance. I'm going to have to move my Mother down back to Florida where it's cheaper to live. I'll tell you when I do that, in July or so.

Nicky Sampas was grand but I ran out on him for the sake of an empty hearted woman, from his bar. Tell him I should have stayed with his party that night. All the Sampases are fine. I know we'll all meet in Heaven and laugh. It's too bad you never met my father, or my brother.

The pork chops PLUS lamb chops your mother made for me were delicious.

Write to me and send the clipping of Pertinax's story so I can see what other kinda dumb fool made of myself in Lowell this time. I think New England understands, tho. If I had to work on the railroad and be sober again, you'd be bored with my grimy quiet company anyway. Every writer in NY wants me to quit writing and work on the railroad again but they got another think coming. Right?

Give my regards also to the German bartender, Nicky's father in law, and to Hank the German guy there. The father in law IS a great painter. I know painting.

I met one Sampas brother who looks just like Sammy, Jimmy I think his name was, notice how I hadnt time to talk to him, and didnt even have time when I went to Nashua on Easter Morning to see my brother's (Gerard) and my father's (Leo)'s graves. All I saw was filling stations, no bars, dull mean men in a rooming house, and I left, and we went to Lakeview to a Canuck roadhouse for cards, drinks, talk, dogs, cats, the Lake. I am amazed. I finally got Mozart's REQUIEM off the radio last night: this I've been waiting for for years: a tall man in black came to Mozart when he was dying and asked him to write a Mass for a dying noble; Mozart wrote it, thinking the dying noble was himself; he died before he finished it: turned out it was a big joke played on Mozart by some Nobles: but Mozart died, was buried in a pauper's grave, and today the Requiem he wrote stands as the greatest Mass ever writ.

Jack

TO TONY SAMPAS

May 21 '64
[Northport, New York]

Dear Tony—

I dont know how sore Stella is, I understand she called here & talked with my mother—I was gone—So I'm sending the check to you via Charley Sampas, being afraid she might goof in anger.

$20 goes to her, $280 to you for the loan.

The $20 was borrowed from Stella by Paul Bourgeois, who came here & just left back for Lowell. (My dumb idea over the phone to the Cosmo.)

Big mixup, but, if Stella gets her $20 from you, I've repaid everybody. Till the next time we meet, I remain, Sir, your affectionate friend,

Jack

Regards to Nick & Yanni
Tell Yanni things aren't as bad as they look

Arguing that Kerouac's visitors in Northport encouraged his drinking and that the house on Judyann Court was too expensive to run, Mémère insisted that they return to Florida in the summer of 1964. This time Jack and his mother decided to live in St. Petersburg, fifty miles from Nin's home in Orlando. Once again a Kerouac house in Northport went on the market.

In July, needing cash for a down payment on another new tract home in Florida, Kerouac sent Sterling Lord an article to peddle to Gourmet *magazine and urged him to sell the manuscript of* Desolation Angels. *On July 18, 1964, a reporter from* Newsday *described a visit to Kerouac's home in Northport, where Jack sipped boilermakers and showed his caller the calluses on his ankles formed in the hours he spent rocking in his favorite chair. He said that he never "got to the Village" anymore to see his old friends. "They don't like me. All the old timers are turning politicians, getting up petitions for civil rights and all that kind of stuff. It's politics, not art anymore."*

On August 27, 1964, a few weeks before leaving Northport for St. Petersburg, Kerouac had a final reunion with Neal Cassady even less satisfactory than the five minutes they had talked together the previous summer. This time Cassady showed up in New York City as the driver of a 1939 school bus painted in Day-Glo colors with the destination plate "Further," transporting Ken Kesey and his Merry Pranksters cross-country. The bus was named by artist Roy Sebern to inspire the Pranksters to keep going even if it broke down.

Proud that Kerouac had praised his first novel One Flew over the Cuckoo's Nest *(1962), Kesey invited Kerouac to a party in the Park Avenue apartment where the Pranksters were staying before they drove up to Millbrook to visit Timothy Leary. When Kerouac arrived he expected to meet Cassady and Kesey, but he was surprised to find that the meeting had been turned into a media event: the stoned Pranksters had set up the room as a recording studio so they could film what they regarded as a historic encounter between Kerouac and Cassady, whom they regarded as two authentic American heroes.*

Jack smoked some marijuana with them and allowed one of the Pranksters to snap his picture wearing a scarf printed in red, white, and blue like an American flag, but he drew the line at sitting with Neal on a real American flag draped over the sofa. In Kerouac's view, if he sat on the flag he was showing disrespect to his country. Cassady, now a principal player in the Prankster entourage, made no attempt to see the situation from Kerouac's perspective. They didn't talk much at the party, and they never met again.

381

By September 9, 1964, Jack and his mother had relocated to a modest air-conditioned new house at 5155 Tenth Avenue North in St. Petersburg. He described his first days meeting new drinking buddies in the "stimulating" city for Sterling Lord, who had helped finance the move by selling the reprint rights to Kerouac's books to publishers abroad.

TO STERLING LORD

Sept. 9 64
[St. Petersburg, Florida]

Dear Sterling

Hope you got my telegram in time for Tuesday's talk with Coward-McCann. Whole idea is okay. Only hope you get enough money to realize the 2 G's I owe you and THEN some, or mebbe just a little anyhow.

I lost some on my Northport house but we just had to get out of there and it was worth it.

This is a stimulating city. The first 10 days here, while we waited for our furniture on cots loaned by my kindly builder next door, Tex, I had nothing to do so kept rushing out, to baseball games, bars, pool games, beach parties, etc. etc. wild dances etc. etc. . . . never had such a wild time in my life because the fellows I met, who drove me around were every one of em gentlemen, one of them a sports reporter (two of em), one a 6 foot 5 soldier who tried to get me into St. Jude's church at 4 A.M. by knocking on the front door, another who holds down two jobs, etc. etc. and every one of them neat and spit to the teeth and courteous and helpful and fine.

Meanwhile Mémère stayed at her window, which looks out on a beautiful cypress and southern foliage backyard of a millionaire, and took walks up and down on the moonlit sidewalk at midnight without any fear at all. Stores 3 blocks away. Very hot right now but our central airconditioning is perfect. Wait'll you see it.

All's well. Superburgers, buckets of Kentucky Fingerlickin Good Fried Chicken, Braunschweiger sandwiches a full 2 inches thick, etc. etc. and by the way that ballgame (St. Petersburg vs. Lakeland) knocked me out. I hadnt seen a ballgame since 1949.

Enclosed find contracts for Catalan. Adds my 14th language to the list. That must be some kind of Quebecois version of Spanish?

Let me hear from you. I hope you can make this sale. Let me know anything else, like magazine offers etc. I'll be able to get back to work down here. Love to Cindy, and tell her that just before I left Northport I bought a painting from Stanley Twardowicz that will just knock her out when she sees it. We hung it over my piano. $100 I paid but friend Stanley was being kind to me. Etc. etc.

As ever
Jack

On September 19, 1964, Kerouac came home from drinking and shooting pool with his new friends in St. Petersburg to learn from his mother that his sister, Caroline, had died suddenly of a heart attack. After Paul Blake had left her for another woman, Nin had moved with her teenage son to an apartment in Orlando, where she did maintenance work in exchange for their rent. Nin was drinking coffee in the apartment with a friend when Blake telephoned her. Apparently she became so upset by what her husband said during the phone call that she suffered a fatal heart attack. On the day of Nin's death, Mémère wrote a note to Stanley and Anne Twardowicz, a painter and his wife who had been friends in Northport. Making the arrangements for the burial, Jack and his mother couldn't afford to put a headstone or marker on Nin's grave in Orlando's Greenwood Cemetery.

TO STANLEY & ANNE TWARDOWICZ FROM GABRIELLE KEROUAC

Sept 19 [19]64
[St. Petersburg, Florida]

Dear Stanley & Anne,

Writing this note in haste. My Daughter Died to-day. Just when everything was going to be fine and good for us all. My heart is broke. My only little girl gone. Please tell the other friends of Jack. I will write you all again later.

My best to you all. We do miss you.

Sincerely
Mrs. G. Kerouac

TO JOHN CLELLON HOLMES

Oct. 16 1964
[St. Petersburg, Florida]

Dear John

Glad to hear from you. Yes, Nin died and as time goes on I think about it more and more, in my own way. Up at night at 3 A.M. I sit and remember up a storm as tho I were still writing Sax and Maggie. There was a reason, tho, and I have nothing to do with it. Get older and you get more mystified. Youth has a way of sluffing off death and graves and even makes purple armpit poetry about it, as I did. But when in real life there's a red-neoned funeral parlor on the end of your street, and gloom hits you, yet, ah, I'll still not die in a stain coffin in Lowell, Oh, but maybe fall off Mount Sumeru (Everest). The trouble here is, Nin woulda had a lot of fun with me and my Maw here, picnics etc. a very stimulating city is St. Petersburg, you'd be surprised. The story is that her husband left her and broke her heart, period. (For another woman, a siren.) Nin had a loyal heart, which that cracker couldn't begin to understand. During a longdistance phonecall she was heard to say to him (from Orlando to Wash D.C.) "Alright if that's the way you want it," and had a heart attack right after. Who knows what he told her. But I harbor no grudge against the guy; and he is not really to blame; I think what caused her heart attack was the fact that her house (her lil apartment) was constantly full of visitors, her little son's buddies who came to have HER do their homework while they went out playing; visiting gossip women; endless this and that and no chance for her to relax in front of TV with a wine, or go to sleep catnap afternoons. Togetherness America. Nobody's gonna pull that shit on me. The last week of her life, because her husband wasn't sending support money (not court-ordered, just private arrangement), she was seen weeding and mowing the huge lawns of the apartment building, and her weighing about 90 pounds or less. To pay the landlady rent. Voila.

I'm telling you all this because I know you'd like to know. She was also making food money at the time "carrying a spear" so to say in a perf. of the Mikado. I had already extended myself to the tune of almost $5,000 to her house and home and husband, who took most of it on the sly and by guile, for himself and galfriend. I'm going broke at present unless something happens.

The last time I saw her I gave her hell.

On the money question and as Lucien did say "Ah you Canucks, the only thing you ever argue about is money!"

Well, meanwhile I'm trying to straighten out and get my football-and-war-youth novel written, Vanity of Duluoz. Will start in Nov. Meanwhile Sterling's sposed to be getting Desolation Angels sold to a publisher. What you read was the first half, I've since added the other half, later events. Long book thereby. Somebody is supposed to write a big preface. No contract yet. My income for this year has been so far $2,500! All of 1964. Most of it from Playboy and Show Mags. Big Sur lost money, Maggie is 6 grand in the hole, also Tristessa, and so forth.

But this new lil house in St. Pete, the rent is cheap, no phone bill, store around the corner and my mother feels safe from Long Island hoods who had gotten out of hand in Northport and converted me into an all-night guard of my own house with homemade tomahawk in hand in darkness, waiting. I'll tell you all when see you. Write and let me know about Midwest teaching jaunt. Give full description of Connecticut Autumn. How's non-fiction book coming? Had your reviews of FREE[3] sent to me and read them and commented to Sterling you were being treated like me . . . . down

---

3. Holmes had just published his third novel, *Get Home Free*. See Kerouac's letter to Holmes, December 11, 1963.

to the bone, publishing has been taken over by out-and-out con men who are the Mephistopheleses to your Faustian effort. No mind. Autumnleaf laurel you.

Jack

Strictly keep this address under your hat especially with Carr and Ginsberg et al

Jack

5155-10th Ave. N, St. Petersburg, Fla. 33710

Later in October and November 1964, Kerouac resumed his habit of writing frequently to Sterling Lord, asking for details on the foreign sales of his books, the mainstay of his income as a writer at this time.

TO STERLING LORD

Nov. 11 1964
[St. Petersburg, Florida]

Dear Sterling

The offer to write about 5,000 words about Pres. Kennedy:—I'm afraid there'd be no point in my trying that, I dont know anything about it. All I have is a brief dream of a few nights ago I couldnt possibly stretch into 5,000 words. Being an irrational dream it might look silly among the other stories. Wish I'd had a different offer.

We might be getting some new magazine offers after GOOD BLONDE in Playboy, so let me hear em.

If any copies of the Deutsch GERARD and TRISTESSA have come in, let me have a few? Anxious to see that.

Your check came in with all that fine breakdown of royalty figures. Thank God we made it at this time.

Hot sun and cool air here now. I've got a tan. Hope you and Cindy havent caught a cold, as I did, hot sun and all, few weeks ago! (virus)

Ye old scrivener,

As ever
Jack

Writing John Clellon Holmes on December 8, 1964, Kerouac filled him in on the progress of his novel Desolation Angels, *which Sterling Lord had sold to Coward-McCann at the end of September. His editor Ellis Amburn had asked Kerouac to recommend someone who could write an introduction to the novel, and Kerouac had advised against asking Malcolm Cowley, Norman Podhoretz, Alfred*

Kazin, or Leslie Fiedler, the leading contemporary critics who had panned his work. Amburn finally chose Seymour Krim, who was sympathetic to Kerouac's writing.

TO JOHN CLELLON HOLMES

Dec 8 1964
[St. Petersburg, Florida]

Dear John Boyo:

I've just finished reading the life of James Joyce and feel it's worthwhile after all to study and struggle through life and suffer and shit and sweat, while people laugh at you, rich or poor, famous or not-famous, and come to the margin of the sea at the end of life and say: "I've got my life work done, annaliviaplurabelle is the belle of all belles forever." Yowsah, John, it made me feel like getting back to my work.

As you know, I guess, "Desolation Angels" is going into galleys now at Coward-McCann's. Twice as long as when you [illeg.] read it (another novel added on to it, the sequel.) I think I told you all this. But now, in the peace of this, my new Florida study, I'm starting to churn for new work, to add to that long shelf Duluoz Legend, fill in the gap thar between *Maggie Cassidy* and *On the Road* and don't think for one minute that I feel inferior to James Joyce because my lifework arrangement is in installments that are eventually going to number in the twenties and that are cast as "narratives in time" rather than as universal and linguistic mellings in 2 long "poems" like ULYSSES and FINNEGANS WAKE. No sir, I got my lil old bangtail way, to arrive at the same sea margin satisfied.

Isn't it amazing how Balzac went about it and how different his way from Joyce's? or Shakespeare's? How come we love those blokes who make big one-shots out of their lifework? All of Dickens is Dickens himself, how strange. Dostoevsky you could recognize in a dark alley full of woodfences and Chagall cows. (Note: should it be of more importance to me that Chagall wanted to paint me in 1958 than that I love his fences more, by themselves and without having to see his ugly face? Hey! Paste that in my testimony for your book.) Isn't it amazing how *orderly* the lifeworks of Balzac, Shakey, Dusty, Joycey are! Talk about your housework! Even Emily! Even Walt! ! ! (Corso's exclamation points) ! ! Even Corso is orderly! read him sometime in entirety and see. Burroughs too, orderly in his shiney boots and crumbling burroughs. I like it, I like it, I tell you I like it literature. What a hell of a better way to do it than apply paint to squares and oblongs and pop out designs and worry about color or design. Have you ever noticed how the letters of famous painters and great painters were never so cherished as the letters of authors? I have here an order for a loaf of bread, written in Rembrandt's own handwriting in sixteen-O-Two-Two and I would rather have the one word 'Wa?' written by Joyce on toilet paper. (This is not a spontaneous letter: I haven't written on my typewriter in months.)

I've been drunk, John, drunk on Scotch and beer chasers. Enough, now I'm through with that and going back to my private philologies. I went to jail on Thanksgiving night for putting a bun on in honor of the pilgrims. The cops saw me piss in the street. First time in jail. Okay, so I ain't spending no more money on the businesses of St. Petersburg but staying home to work on my private philologies.

Hail to the writer! Hail to Holmes! Yes, your book is better if it's like a composite biographical study of all the writers, instead of just dry academic evaluations.

As ever
Jack

Keep my address secret—I'm too happy to be back with my books! J.

Material (thesis on me) being sent to you, by me, via Sterling, next week surface mail— j.

1965

Early in January 1965, Kerouac corresponded with his editor Ellis Amburn after he finished correcting the galleys of Desolation Angels. *Jack also wrote to Philip Whalen, explaining how he had gotten in with the wrong crowd of people, as usual, when he moved to St. Petersburg.*

TO ELLIS AMBURN

January 9, 1965
[St. Petersburg, Florida]

Dear Ellis

All I want you to do for me is go over the pencilled proofmarks I've made correcting these galleys [of *Desolation Angels*], and make sure to professionalize them where I missed the correct proofmarking technique, because I dont want the printers to make any mistakes that will have to be re-corrected in page proof and especially any mistakes that will come out in the published volume. After all, this is for "eternity" ... and it's all about eternity.

The only big items for your red ink may be:

(1) Where chapters 27 and 27 appear side by side. Go over my pencil marks there, where I simply joined a couple of chapters into one.
(2) Galley 55, where they failed to make a paragraph.
(3) Galley 84, where I cut out a whole line that is no longer necessary now that "Desolation Angels" precedes "Passing Through" as one whole book.
(4) Galley 114, where it's up to you to find out what the spelling is for "Schraffts," since I have no NY phonebook here to check.
(5) At galley 122, where the hangup about the *accent grave* on "Mémêre" begins ... use your own judgment ... I dont think it's important, I'd leave well enough alone, it's not a French novel anyway.

(6) At galley 127, where Cody reappears from "Desolation Angels," changes had to be made to avoid serious redundancy. Notice how I make the changes fit the line for the printer's convenience.

Other items: At galley 84 I just had to remove a line, it no longer fits for same reasons ("See what I mean about these cats?")

At galley 116 I had to put in a comma which was missing from my own stupid manuscript and had ruined a whole sentence (about the waiter and the German on the ship).

And finally at galley 128 I took out the word "sad" and put in "sunk" because how can I get from sad to sad: I was always sad: but I did get from sad to sunk, after all these drear events.

The chapter about the burlesque in Seattle previously appeared as "Seattle Burlesque" in Evergreen Review, and reprinted in Leroi Jones' anthology "The Moderns." The chapter about "On the Road With Mémère" was bought (under that title) by Holiday a few years ago. In case you have to know.

The transition from "angels" to "passing through" is uneven, as I knew it would be, and that's what happens when you paste two novels together, but the overall effect I hope overshadows this.... And now, all's left, I want to see the Krim intro and I hope he comes up with something other than the usual beatBeatBEAT. After all, what's "beat" about that opening prose on the mountain, hey? But, I've just discovered in myself that whatever people say about my work is of no consequence to my work, and of no consequence to my reasons for working, i.e., to keep from dying of boredom and diffuseness of heart ... (you know, the "who-cares?" that finally sinks in till you might as well be a snarling puky drunk in a gutter). So that once I'm thru with a book, I dont care what they think, and I gotta get on to another and keep up with the Heavenly Times. etc. So, till I hear from you,

Jack

TO PHILIP WHALEN

Jan. 10 1965
[St. Petersburg, Florida]

Dear Phil:

Got your card, and calligraphies,[1] hung one of them next to my reading chair, is very pretty on wall—Please, now, try to keep my new address a se-

1. A dedicated student of Buddhism, Whalen was awarded a grant-in-aid from the National Academy of Arts and Letters which enabled him to quit his part-time job in the San Francisco Post Office and move to Kyoto early in 1966, where he supported himself by teaching English at a YMCA school for sixteen months. After a brief return to the United States, Whalen stayed in Kyoto until 1971.

cret or it will get around and guys are always flying to Florida in carloads and don't know where to go to toss beer cans around in privacy—Had to leave Judyann Court Northport for this reason—Mémère couldn't even sleep nights as a certain gang of teenagers kept sneaking up in the dark and peering into our windows, looking for free beer which they assumed they deserved by false flattery as I sat there in my hopeless cups—Down here, it's been much better—As usual I made a mistake right off, getting drunk and shooting pool with "sharks" of St. Petersburg who turned out to be college boys—But the leader of this gang is the boss and lets no one visit without him, loves Mémère, protects her, and is okay all around—At last, here, as right now, I can run my typewriter in the middle of the night without fear of someone peeking in the window—After all, a 70-year-old mother's house is not a PAD for krissakes—Her house is a real home and they all wanta come and sit and shit all over it—Remember the little white house on Earl avenue? well things weren't bad there, all this new invasion of home privacy began around 1963 and is not so much a sign of my "celebrityhood" as of the times, people are starting to raid homes now and with great disrespect—(Think of it if you and I were still living in Berkeley and trying to study the Lankavatara in our rooms at midnight!)

Pah! Anyway I got "Desolation Angels" all corrected in galleys and off to the publisher—I look forward with great glee to your reading it—If they want a list of review copies sent out, I'll have them send you one—I especially want you to dig the beginning, about Desolation Peak, written up there in boredom and good health, a real gas of mountain prose done in full bloom of snowburn and windburn and Sourdough burn—"Ben Fagan" thereafter appears later on when I come down from the mountain and go to the evil city again—I describe that evening we took peotl and you meditated in your new robes from Japan while I painted in the yard, remember? (at your cottage)—

Correcting and re-reading this new book of mine makes me realize I'm on the right track with the Duluoz legend—I only wish, O sigh now, I could have used the same names for On the Road, Subterraneans, Bums ... a thing I'll certainly do when somebody consents to issue my collected works ... what a wild one-shelf that will be! But do you think it will bug everybody to suddenly pick up said collected works and look for Dean Moriarty and find only Cody Pomeray? Well, it'll be so far off from now might make no difference. But I'm on the right track. "Vanity of Duluoz" is next now, I'll write that in Paris starting next month or two, events from age 16 to 27, completing all events that are of any importance in the "Life" up to and including "Big Sur" events, tho a lot of people want me to stick in 1957–60 events to really round it out (events of being published and going to Hollywood and on TV etc.)—We'll see—But there are the events of the future to come—I've got to keep busy with my Legend or die of boredom and of neglect of my naturally worrywart heart—

I've just discovered Schopenhauer. He is a Buddhist through and through, did you know that? World as Will and Idea, world as "ignorance" and "delusion"/// ... when he says "thing-in-itself" he clearly indicates same signposts as "mind essence"—that's not surprising either, because much of his thinking derives from an obscure old French translation of a Persian original translation from the Sanskrit of the Upanishads! He talks of "Maya" right straight through, with perfect German philosopher calm, no sweat. I've often wondered why the name Schopenhauer had always sounded like thunder on the horizon, not only when I heard it, but when I heard others pronounce it, and now je sais.

It might be a good idea for me to revisit you and Neal and Monty and Lew (and Gary) some time this year later, and I probably will, and will warm you in advance. That phone talk with Gary, last Fall, was confused; I wanted to tell Gary he hadn't changed at all, meaning the same old Gary of bhikkuing with me, but Ginsberg, repeating it over the phone, made it sound like "same old shit" like. Anyway, prend ma main, ami.

Jack

At the end of January 1965, Kerouac wrote Sterling Lord that he had been "waiting & waiting" to read Seymour Krim's introduction to Desolation Angels *and feared that the publishers weren't sending it on because they didn't want Kerouac to reject it. When it finally arrived in February, Jack liked it and sent Ellis Amburn a few factual corrections. Kerouac also dropped a postcard to John Clellon Holmes, rueful that his royalty checks barely covered his household expenses and wouldn't stretch to cover the airfare to Paris. When two of his ribs were broken in a barroom fight in March, he postponed the trip indefinitely. To help Kerouac pay his taxes, Lord was trying to arrange for the sale of his manuscripts to the Morgan Library in New York City. Shortly after his forty-third birthday, Jack wrote to Stanley and Anne Twardowicz, trying to trace a missing notebook diary which had been stolen from him.*

TO ELLIS AMBURN

Feb. 11, 1965
[St. Petersburg, Florida]

Dear Ellis:

Krim's introduction corrected as follows:

(Page 3) Not "all" of my novels, but "most" of them, covered the beat generation.

(Page 7) My family was not living in N.Y. when I was 17 and attending Horace Mann, so I just crossed that out for biographical accuracy. I didn't get a "football" scholarship from Columbia, there were none at Columbia or any other Ivy League school, it was a scholastic scholarship.

Broke my leg, not my foot, in Freshman football.

Burroughs was never a department store thief but he did hold up a Turkish bath "for a Gidean laugh" in Cincinnati. This little item livens up the intro, is true, and ought to please Seymour.

(Page 8) Burroughs and Ginsberg and I met around 1943, not "before" the war. And I never was, or wanted to be, a homosexual, so I inserted the truth: our hero "compassionately include(d) non-participant acceptance of the homosexuality of his literary confreres." If this change is not instituted, Krim will have to give me satisfaction.

(Page 9) I sailed in the North Atlantic U-boat war *before* the Navy called me up, and inserted the details, which are interesting and will form the center of the next novel, "Vanity of Duluoz."

I add "North Atlantic again" to show that, though the Navy discharged me, I went on risking my life for my country.

I only went to that silly "New School for Social Research" for the G.I. Bill of Rights rent-money.

(Page 11) Krim says I'm not an original thinker in any technical sense but has just finished describing my invention of a new prosody: so I inserted "prose-theorist" to avoid his contradicting himself, and to set the fact straight about my technical original thought, which is my due.

(Page 16) Statement on Duluoz Legend made in 1960 edition of "Cody."

(Page 17) The "I" of Kerouac is always surrounded by appearing, disappearing and reappearing characters from book to book in the "Duluoz Legend," and there is, therefore, a chronological order which has to be vouchsafed. This is part of the intro I don't like, because while praising me for minor reasons of "charm" etc., the structure of my work, block by block, is being bulldozed (and why?)

(Page 18) "The *actual* speed of the mind" is what I try to convey, not easy. "Dr. Jekyll and Mr. Hyde" was read in woods at Big Sur, not on Desolation Peak.

(Page 19) Another silly rumor, that "Excerpts from Visions of Cody" was mostly tape recorded: only four chapters of it, on pages 95 to 108, were transcriptions of Neal Cassady's talk over a mike. (Correct title of book.)

(Page 20) As I told you over the phone, no need to have "dirty words" in an intro to a book that has no dirty words in it. Dirty words are no longer revolutionary innovations, but simple braggart vandalism now. For "jacking off" substitute "onanism" or, if you prefer, "masturbation." "Fucksack" is a dirty afterthought, we can substitute "sexsack" and mean same. This kind of stuff could also prevent "Desolation Angels" from selling widely.

(Page 22) Date correction.

Yours,

Jack (Kerouac)

393

TO JOHN CLELLON HOLMES

[March 2, 1965
St. Petersburg, Florida]

Dear John,

Just a card, nothing to report—How you coming along with nonfiction book? Spring melting the banks of the Connecticut? What do you make of Hicks-Jones' thesis?[2] How's Shirley? Any trips you planning? I just brooding stagnant angry relic of the past. I not big Jewish genius like Saul Bellow, Philip Roth, Irwin Shaw, Herman Wouk, Norman Mailer, Bernard Malamud, J. D. Salinger—I big tin-eared Canuck with royalty check of $1.37 last week, and $15.19 week before—I no have standing in American literature with above mentioned American Giants because I not really a "writer," just a phenomena and according to fan letters asking if I am real, unreal anyhow. I not "American" like above but some kind "nik."

Worked out fine by Podhoretz and swell critics and Van Doren great helpin' mentor also Cowley.

Krim say I immigrant like him, because my Pop come from 3 miles north of Maine.

J.

TO STANLEY & ANNE TWARDOWICZ

March 22 [19]65
[St. Petersburg, Florida]

Dear Stanley & Anne—

Say, Stash, I'm missing a pencil-written diary in my files and I'm hoping I drunkenly gave it to Northport Library instead of having it stolen by those teenage bums the last weeks in N'Port.

Can you tell me what else besides the "Town & City" type manuscript they displayed there?—Brown notebook "Further Notes?"

Here's a drawing of you—

I'm still grateful to Anne for arranging the new train reservations that last day! Thinking about it the other night, and what a drunk I've been, & a pain—

2. See Kerouac's letter to Granville H. Jones, November 22, 1960.

Sober here, & happy, & "working"—Yes, Stash, like you I'm going to call it WORKING—You were right!

Yours
Yashou[3]

P.S. I'm going to watch a Mets game next week at Al Lang field here.

TO STERLING LORD

March 27, 1965
[St. Petersburg, Florida]

Dear Sterling:—

Your letter about Keith Jennison and the Morgan Library idea made me feel great. And Sterling, you go right ahead with whatever you think should be done with my original manuscripts so that I can get that big tax deduction when it will count.

Here is the list of original manuscripts:

(1) ON THE ROAD, singlespace scroll in possession of Keith Jennison, and do tell him that I will be needing the tax deduction. (Typed editor's copy of ROAD here in house.)

(2) THE TOWN AND THE CITY, original singlespace typed manuscript and handwritten sections all fitted together, here in the house. Editor's ms. copy already donated to Northport Public Library. (doublespace ms.)

(3) THE DHARMA BUMS, original typed scroll singlespace, here in house. Also, editor's copy.

(4) THE SUBTERRANEANS, original typed ms. in possession of "Mardou Fox" probably lost by now. But editor's doublespace typed ms. here in house.

(5) MEXICO CITY BLUES
TRISTESSA
DESOLATION ANGELS.....all handwritten, in pocket notebooks, with drawings, all mixed together on fronts and backs of pages, here in house. Flawless, without corrections, some of the drawings in pastels.

(6) DOCTOR SAX, original handwritten ms. in pocket notebooks plus editor's typed doublespace copy, here in house.

---

3. Twardowicz explained that "in some of the letters Jack called me Stashou and signed them Yashou. My close painter friends called me Stashou, a friendly Polish version of Stanley. After hearing it, Jack asked me the Polish version of Jack. I said Yashou."

(7) MAGGIE CASSIDY, orig. handwritten ms. in secretarial notebooks. Editor's copy kept by Avon.

(8) VISIONS OF CODY (Excerpts or complete) in your files, orig. ms. editor's copy. Here in house, orig. handwritten notebook ms.

(9) BOOK OF DREAMS (orig. handwritten ms. here, plus edit's copy.

(10) BIG SUR, orig. singlespace typed scroll ms. here in house.

(11) VISIONS OF GERARD, orig. handwritten ms. in notebooks here in house.

In other words, practically everything intact, including orig. handwritten ms. in notebooks of SOME OF THE DHARMA. (One of my 1948 handwritten diaries that I lost then, has turned up in University of Texas collection called "A Creative Century." They sent me brochure, with photostat of one of pages of diary!)

So Sterling, go right ahead with this plan. Mémère says I'll be a millionaire before I'm fifty, so we'll be needing them thar tax deductions, me and J.P.'s heirs.

P.S. Mémère sending Cindy a package next week, an early gift.

As ever

Jack

P.S. I'm back on my headstands & healing rapidly.[4] J.

TO STERLING LORD

April 16, [19]65
[St. Petersburg, Florida]

Dear Sterling

As long as you can get TIME to agree to the condition that they dont divulge the name of my home city and of course my home address, details

---

4. On March 23, 1965, Kerouac had written Lord about his injuries after a physical attack in a local bar:

Now I have a punctured lung and two broken ribs from a meaningless barroom attack (sneak) on my person. Luckily I got out alive by wrestling the maniac over on his back and then walking out. I broke my own ribs with the off-balance twisting effort. Lung is okay, says the doctor, and ribs are joining and mending. I was alone in a strange bar. I'm through with going out alone and through with hard liquor forever. That's enough of the rough stuff. There was no provocation for these sudden punches into my face: I was just telling my name. Fellow was fast and about 21 and a drifter from the North. (I was stunned and never hit back.) (Again.)

So I'm home, ribs strapped, no Paris trip. I hope I have some luck from "Desolation Angels" to make up for all the bad luck this past 6 months.

of no use whatever in a literary review anyway, tell them to go ahead and have their local photographer or local representative send me a card setting a date for the picture taking at my house, so I'll be here when he comes. Sterling, if it gets out in national print that I live in St. Petersburg, the local people around here are likely to start pestering Mémère's retirement home and ruin everything and all the new peaceful opportunity I've found here to resume my work and studies. Okay? Make sure!! Otherwise I'll sue the bums.

Sterling, Mémère mailed a package to Cindy on March 30th, insured, containing a gift. Did you get it? If not, write and say so, and she'll show your note at the post office and collect the $5 insurance and mail another gift direct to your office. The March 30th gift was mailed to the C.P.W. address.

Enclosed find a letter from the Boston U. Libraries for your file on the Kerouac Archives (ahem).

My recuperation from broken ribs and punctured lung about done, and this summer I'm going to do 30 pushups a day and 9 headstand-toe-touchdowns a day to make up for lost muscle tone (ahem). Havent had hard liquor since March 11 and am all set for an interesting new concept of living without all that dreary repetitious muggleheaded bibulosity.

Till I hear from you.

As ever
Jack

Early in May 1965, after the publication of Desolation Angels, *Kerouac learned that Ellis Amburn had arranged for him to get his share of the payment for a paperback sale to Bantam Books immediately upon signing the contract. Jack wrote Sterling Lord that the money would send him "winging to Paris and Brittany."*

Reviews of Desolation Angels *were generally hostile, but the book got more attention than Kerouac had received in years. The* Saturday Review *understood that "Kerouac seems ... determined to define the sensibility of the members of his own subgeneration in as many ways as he possibly can. We knew them under such guises as the Beat Generation, the Subterraneans, the Dharma Bums; and now we see them as* Desolation Angels, *sadly pursuing their empty futilities....* Desolation Angels *also explains perhaps better than the other Kerouac novels what the place of religion may have been in the Beat mystique." Harper's noted: "There is so much good in this book, and it's all but destroyed by the total egotism of the author."*

Writing in The Atlantic Monthly, *the reviewer Dan Wakefield suggested that the novel be nominated for a Pulitzer Prize as being "the book that is most representative of American life." The critic had revised his earlier negative opinion of Kerouac after reading a passage in the book where Jack evoked Wakefield's sympathy for "the dilemma" Kerouac "found himself in as an unexpected avatar as well as a writer." Wakefield was referring to the end of* Desolation Angels, *where Kerouac had described a party of "hipsters" visiting Burroughs in Tangier:*

> *just like in New York or Frisco or anywhere there they are all hunching around in marijuana smoke, talking, the cool girls with long thin legs in slacks, the men with goatees, all an enormous drag after all and at the time (1957) not even started yet officially with the name of "Beat Generation." To think that I had so much to do with it, too, in fact at that very moment the manuscript of* Road *was being linotyped for imminent publication and I was already sick of the whole subject.... All this was about to sprout out all over America even down to High School level and be attributed in part to my doing! But Irwin [Ginsberg] paid no attention to all that and just wanted to know what they were thinking anyway.*

The New York Review of Books *printed a lengthy essay about* Desolation Angels *accompanied by a David Levine cartoon caricaturing Kerouac as a blowsy vagabond. Flattered at the attention, Jack later gleefully drew a large penis onto the drawing to complete it.*

TO STERLING LORD

May 8, 1965
[St. Petersburg, Florida]

Dear Sterling

Enclosed, find contract signed and royalty sheet. And thanks for sending royalty statement on GERARD, which I hadn't got (nor on SUR). $17.93 due on BIG SUR but Mémêre just asked me to tell you that she knows dozens of people here in St. Petersburg who've all said they can't find my books anywhere so how can they buy em? That goes for DESO ANGELS too. Everybody is looking for the softcover ON THE ROAD but all they can find is CATCHER IN THE RYE. (Who handles *Distribution* business anyway? Do you know?)

Seymour Krim finally wrote and told me Show Mag folded right from under him, and he was going to get $20,000 a year too! He says Nugget not worth writing for (money-wise). Sterling, please send back the ms. of VOYAGE OF THE NOISY GOURMETS so I can run it through on my typewriter again with spontaneous interlacings and make it more sincere. Then we can try Playboy maybe with it. Send it. (It was too heavily studied over, and written on Scotch and beer.)

Thanks for sending Poore's review. I'd love to see the Maloff review, so vitriolic. Could you send that too? And Nelson Algren, if possible? At least this book has been covered in the front leads.

The $1000 will send me winging to Paris and Brittany but I have to leave some for Mémère for emergencies. Sterling, what I'll do is buy a one-way Air France ticket, bring a few hundred in travelers cheques, and correspond with you and when you get further monies (like from Sweden $300 due, from Feltrinelli $200 due, Catalan $100 due, another Sweden $200 due) send me the checks to Europe and I'll cash them via Gallimard or wherever I am. I'll let you know my travel date. I'll see you on the way back thru New York this summer. I want to write SEA part II on the shores of Brittany at midnight in the rain. Also, the new novel. Maybe two of em. I need to travel, to get away from my cozy home, open my mind, work and walk and see things. I think it's ironic I can't travel all I want because of worry about monthly mortgage payments, considering the books I've written and the stir they've made. (Romain Gary's THE SKI BUM bought by Joseph R. Levine for movies: there goes the DHARMA BUMS movie sale.) (Roughly same idea.) And what is THE SANDPIPER? An author on a Big Sur beach in love with a woman who has a small child..... What next? A Japanese version of DOCTOR JAX AND THE GREAT SNAKE OF THE WORLD.

When I get the $900 or whatever from you, I'm going right away. If you can't send me money to Europe to return home on, I'll simply have to walk on water and walkin' on water wasn't built in a day. (But acourse everything'll be alright: and once I know what I want to write, Sterl, I'm going to do the writing in a quiet room in A M S T E R D A M.... how's that sound?)

Excuse prolixity ... I'm feeling talkative on a tranquilizer pill. No booze since March 12. Write soon.

As ever
Jack

TO STERLING LORD FROM GABRIELLE KEROUAC

May 8, 1965
St. Pete, Florida

FROM MÉMÊRE TO STERLING ......(typed up by Jack)

Dear Sterling

I do want to add my lil bit here—I talk to lots of people around the neighborhood and all of them likes Jack's book, and writing, and look around and try Librarys, they want to buy Jack's Books but seems there is none around to be found in any stores around here, even in Orlando at my Lil girl's funeral lots of the women there told me the same story, they love Jack's Books but cant find none. Will you see to this. Jack is losing lots of sales. I'm sure. How can he make money when there is none of his works around. I have yet to hear anyone say anything about Jack's books they didnt like, its sure heart breaking. I've read some of those critics of New

York especially that *Shalom**—and others, how can they say things they dont know about Jack, they never ever talked to him or known him personally. You know something Sterling those critics are so envious and jealous they say anything to hurt Jack, but please look into this matter about Jack's books for Florida, everyone so far I talked to loves Jack and wants to buy his books out here. What's the score. I leave it to you now Honey—

P.S. I hope that Cindy is fine and Bless her heart.... I pray for her so everything will be fine—I love you both

Mémêre

*Her remembrance of the name "Maloff." [J.K.]

TO STERLING LORD

May 26, 1965
[St. Petersburg, Florida]

Dear Sterling:

When you get this, I'll be hurrying down the boulevards of Paris look-ing for a cheapter hotel room. (Right now, as you read this, rather, I'm hur-rying down the etc. . . .) My trip will be divided in 2 parts: (1) Paris and the library, tracing the name Lebris de Kerouac in the book on the officers of the crown, back to the Breton seat, and general eating, sipping, strolling, picturelooking, and a train to Brittany, a quiet week by the sea, where I'll write Part Two of "Sea"—then London I hope via St. Malo ferry to S'Hamp-ton and Michael Sissons and all the London stuff, final checkup on family in records if any on Cornwall, if so, a trip to Cornwall, then (2) Second part of trip, final quiet room on a canal in Amsterdam and brew my own coffee and light candle and stick my huge nose into American literature again, long walks and movies, till I come home midsummer to write further. (Cyrano de Kerouac)

Incidentally, Part Two of "Sea" will be written at midnight on the shore and even in the rain, this will be the real sound of the Finistère roar. I have the clothes for it.

I'll write to you and keep you posted. By the time I've done Paris and Brittany and staggered into London, most of my $500 will be gone or at least, that much of it, that I'll need more via your company representatives (but *not much* because I'll have my return trip ticket on me.) ("Staggered" means weary . . . ain't had a drink since March 12.)

So I'll stock up on some new visions and get on with my work.

I've been very happy lately and I hope you and Cindy are happy also . . . Keep Mémêre posted on the baby, like all ladies she gets vicarious satis-faction from maternal news. Hold the checks in the office till I get there mid-July or so. If you're away on one of your short trips, I'll hang around

NY till you get back. I'll also get to meet Ellis Amburn who is great in his letters.

As ever
Jack

TO LUCIEN CARR

June 2, 1965
Paris

Dear Lucien,

I went into the Bibliothèque Nationale[5] hoping to find Rimbaud drunk & whattaya think I found? In Louys Moveri's *Grand dictionnaire historique?*— "CARR, famille d'Ecoffe, cherchez KERR."

Jack

Two weeks after leaving Florida for Paris, Kerouac was home again, explaining to Sterling Lord that he had to return to the United States after a train trip to Brittany because he'd run out of money and had no friends in France to help him. He blamed the "runaround" of his trip on "that good old cognac," but he was excited enough about what had happened to him that he planned to write a book about his adventure immediately. Later in June 1965, when his elation had worn off, he wrote a letter to Arabelle Porter at the New American Library about the unavailability of the paperback edition of On the Road *(published by Signet/ New American Library). Porter had been Kerouac's editor in 1955, when* New World Writing *had published an early excerpt of the novel, and he felt that she had championed his work. In case she missed the connection between the Beats and the Beatles, who now dominated the record charts and radio stations in the United States and Europe, Jack pointed it out to her.*

TO STERLING LORD

June 11, 1965
[St. Petersburg, Florida]

Dear Sterling:

Now that I'm back from France laden with a thousand new ideas, here's one of em:

5. In the early chapters of *Satori in Paris*, Kerouac complained that he couldn't smoke in the toilet of the Bibliothèque Nationale and revealed that the librarians "smelled the liquor on me and thought I was a nut." Proud of being "the first Lebris de Kerouack ever to go back to France in 210 years to find out" about the origin of his family, he tried to use the library catalogues to research the list of the officers in Montcalm's army who served in Quebec in 1756, when his French ancestor had first come over to Canada.

We take "Visions of Cody" and mark out page 95, top of it, *"Tape recording of Cody Speaking"* and go to page 108, bottom of it, *"report you well and truly"*—and submit that as an excerpt for publication to Playboy for no less than $2,000.

This is because so many people on my trip told me they wanted to see "Visions of Cody" but couldnt find copies of its limited edition anywhere, and would at least like to see a piece of it.

At the same time, as an example of tape-recording transcription, it's of other than literary interest to all the technicians and characters who read PLAYBOY.

Again, as a piece of realistic journalese, of further interest.

All we need is permission from the publisher: plus an extra copy of the book, *marked* (as above) for the use of the linotypist.

At the same time this will stimulate New Directions in the direction of a cheap reprint, which is about time.

If no extra copy of "Excerpts From Visions of Cody" is available from New Directions for $7.50, I'll type up the manuscript myself from my own copy of the book, unless you want to use yours that's in the office, and make them guarantee to send it back to you.

Not such a complicated idea for $2,000.

Jack

Next page for some details
of my trip, Sterling

Dear Sterling

Well I went to Paris primarily to look up my name in the library ... O it's a long story I should really write. But I saw the Bibliotheque Nationale, and the Archives Nationale, the Bibliotheque Mazarine (on Rue de Franc Bourgeois) and visited St. Louis de France (name of Lowell church of my baptism) where I sat in awe listening to redcoated trumpeteers in front of the altar, with my hat up in my hand, and a mother with husband and children laid 20 centimes in it for charity. Visited the Madeleine. At St. Germain de Pres in the company of a luscious teenage Arab (Algerien) girl heard and saw Mozart's Requiem Mass full orchestra and chorus. And all the bars. Had various friends. Tried to see Gallimard, office girls apparently didn't believe I was me. I said "Ah j'm'en vas a L'Angleterre." Even Michel Mohrt wasn't "there." Visited latenight boites of Montparnasse and hooked up with you know what. Fled to Brittany on a train almost broke, everybody knew my name there. Met a Lebris de Kernedec (pretty close but he said Keroack is in Quimper, i.e., those from Cornwall). Had to go straight home, no money, no chance to wash my fingernails since no hotels, no car, no friends to help. Came home. But am reading French fluently all of a sudden in my room here (Voltaire's "Dictionnaire Philosophique") and that in itself was worth the money: because I had a thousand crazy conversations about everything under the sun in rapider and rapider French till I was losing the poor Parisiens and Bretons. Best fellows I met were Jean-Marie Noblet (a mad Breton on train), Mr. Caudal (a mad Breton gynecologist who said he was in that field because he liked women's thighs) and so on into the night. Parisians like Jean Tassart, St. Jeanne d'Arc de la Pucelle (a cabdriver), Mr. G. Didier a bookie in Brest, Mr. Pierre Le Bris a bookdealer in Brest lying there with his genealogical chart on his stomach (recuperating from an operation), Arthur Pobittza an Etruscan, Monsieur Ventejoux an elegant librarian, Madame Oury in the Bibliotheque Mazarine who sympathized with me because they would not bring me the "Rivista Araldica" because it had been bombed out by the Germans, Raymond Baillet, a lovely languid patrone Helene Sampognaro who made an assignation with me which I missed in my excitement so bought her a present, Elie-Charles Flamand who was writing a history of Renaissance art in the library but helped me with the finding of Moreri's Dictionary (which is just a whimsical dictionary and not complete), a Persian, a Senegalese, and others. I was only trying to find the history of Brittany by d'Argentré, Dom Lobineau, and Dom Morice, and l'Histoire genealogique de plusieurs maisons illustres de Bretagne by Pere du Paz, and Histoire des grands officiers de la Couronne by Pere Anselme which was the one they all got excited about saying it was being repaired. In other words, a runaround, really, in the libraries, and in Brest of course no chance to go to any library (just that man in bed) who knows damn well Lebris de Keroack came to Canada (Francois-Xavier I believe) was a Prince. (Les Bretons sont toutes corpulent, I was told, so I'm no longer worried about my shape.) (Excuse French spelling.) "Ca c'est un Kerouac" I heard in the streets, and "c'est un BRETON" I heard behind my back, and finally as my train pulled out back to Paris and I sat alone in the firstclass car in the front seat with my shoes up on the seats reserved for "les mutilees" (not having read the sign) I heard: "Le roi s'amuse."

Voila, Sterling, that good old cognac but that's what happened.

But my big final decision was this: and I'm going to put this at the beginning of my book so don't show this letter around: It doesn't matter how charming cultures and art are, they're useless without sympathy. All the prettiness of tapestries, lands, people:—*worthless* if there is no sympathy— Poets of genius are just decorations on the wall, if without the poetry of kindness and *caritas*—This means that Christ was right & everybody since then (who "thought" and wrote opposing views of their own) (like, say, Freud & his cold depreciation of helpless personalities) was *wrong*—in that, the life of calm and peaceful tiredness, and of honesty, of the hermit or homebody, is minding its own business, which is, Love of Heaven, and Heaven is above us, & witness.

As ever,
Jack

June 22, 1965
[St. Petersburg, Florida]

Chere Arabel [sic] Porter,

If you only knew the enormous demand in this country proper, and not only N.Y.C. & suburbs, for *On the Road,* by people not only who've never read it but people who have read it but lost their copies and want to read it again, why you'd do a flip-flop in front of yr sales chart. Now let us not let jealousy get in the way of this, like Malcolm Cowley whose sudden incomprehensible coldness to my works turned out to be based on the fact that his son wants to be a novelist too (and wanted to be a railroad brakeman when he met me). The same goes for Charlie Van Doren and his father.

It is not true that *On the Road* is an evil influence on the young: it's simply a true story about an ex-cowboy and an ex-football player running around the country looking for pretty girls to love. If this is evil send it back to Eden & Mother Kali. Put out the Signet edition on drugstore & supermarket & bus station and airline terminal bookracks & get it over with. The demand is furious everywhere. I havent once managed to keep my own private copies of *On the Road,* in hard & soft, on my reference shelf. The only copy that's left my mother hides in her bedroom for God's sake.

If you're in business be businesslike. Dont let incompetents tell you *Road* or anything connected with it is "dead." Beatles is spelled Beatles and not Beetles.

Jack

P.S. How are you?

PP.SS. Also look into the matter of reprinting *Lonesome Traveler* thru my agent Sterling Lord, 75 E. 55 St, NY 22 PLaza 1-2533, the plates of which were melted by McGraw Hill but not by London's André Deutsch in hard and Pan Books Ltd. London in soft. Look into the matter of the fact that I've started a whole new avalanche of storytelling by simply being honest in the first place, and that I'm the Classic Originator, in effect, the Classic.

Jack

During seven consecutive nights in mid-July, while drinking cognac in an effort to retrieve the mood of his trip to France, Kerouac hand-lettered in pencil a thirty thousand-word account of his Satori in Paris. On July 21, 1965, he described the process to John Clellon Holmes, who had written him the previous week with an idea for editing an anthology made up of sections from all of Kerouac's books that would give readers the "contours of the [Duluoz] Legend at long last." Jack had figured that his income from his writing, before taxes, came to a meager sixty-five dollars a week, so he also told Sterling Lord he would "keep in mind" his agent's suggestion that he write more conventionally. Lord had sent him a brief review of the Hollywood pianist Oscar Levant's autobiography, The Memoirs of an Amnesiac, *recently published by Putnam. The review read:*

> *The memoirs of show-business people, unless ghosted, frequently read as if they were dashed off in a day, and Levant's is no exception. Whatever popped into his mind apparently was set down forthwith, without regard to organization or even grammar, and when the whole had achieved book length, he sent it along to the publisher with orders to alter not a single line.*

TO JOHN CLELLON HOLMES

[July 21, 1965
St. Petersburg, Florida]

Dear John

Of course your idea is a dilly, just great, I just wonder why someone else didn't think of it a long time ago—For me to initiate such a "Kerouac Reader" (let's say) is a little unseemly—Five years ago when I saw the Viking Portable Steinbeck and the Viking Portable someone-or-other I forget who, I wondered in all honesty, what's wrong with me? Well, the fact that I left Viking after "Dharma Bums," and the fact that Malcolm Cowley disapproved of everything I wrote after "Road," and our subsequent coldness, explains that.

Also, good idea not to call it an "Anthology" since this pepsi generation of twisting illiterates don't even know what the word means. "Reader" I think just fine.

To go over your letter in detail and get everything in:—I'm happy to see you're getting your non-fiction book along. Get mad at me IF YOU WILL, JOHN CLELLON HOLMES, BUT GUESS WHAT I DONE LAST WEEK, FROM ABOUT JULY 10 to JULY 17? I WROTE A WHOLE NEW NOVEL ABOUT MY RECENT TRIP TO PARIS AND BRITTANY. This is only to let you know, I've been working too, God only knows how, but I did it. That makes now John two novels I have, already composed but only to type, and I'm going to take my time and keep them "in the bank" because the money has stopped coming in for me and I'm really getting worried about the future of my economic arrangements to live in a private home with my mother and cats, I'm really beginning to see that hobo life in the future again, only this time I can't leave my mother alone with relatives, they're dead and don't care those that survived, but I'm really going into my savings now just to pay the "rent" mortgage every month and the living expenses. But I refuse to be bandied about like that after 15 major novels and two more to go. There is something rotten in America and I'm gonna find out what it is on my next trip to New York.

Your plan for the "Reader" fits in with my need for making a living and also with my need to be understood, put in essence in one binder for anybody to carry around and read at leisure, and fits in with your own plans to make some money too and be read in the introduction in the context which is the classic context of a couple of the originators of the new literature which Ferlinghetti yelled about recently at the Spoleto festival, telling the European writers they all stunk and were dead, and bravo for him for telling the truth.

I notice you mention "Lonesome Traveler," well, do you know that the plates of that book were melted down in 1962 by McGraw Hill but not by the English publishers, and that I can't even get any American reprint house interested in putting it out for 75 cents? Well, that's another matter.

You go right ahead with the whole plan, write Sterling, or call, and DEPEND ON ME to do anything that's necessary, you be the general and tell me what you want. From the fact that I furiously scribbled a whole novel only last week, you can tell how full my head is with many, many things, but now that my work is done for another year I'll have plenty time to ponder and study with you and correspond and if need be, go visit you and lay off the Scotch.

Now, as I say, I've thought of a "Reader" like this for a long time, and as I say it would've been unseemly for me to broach it meself, but now you have broached it: Coward-McCann may quite well accept this plan: you, YOU my dear boy, go ahead and do this: I really don't know, in fact, how to go about it in all its facets.

And the idea of the uniform pantheon names of the Duluoz Legend is the idea I thought would only be broached in my old age, and really brought a kind of tear to my mind's eye when I read your letter.

You've got my cooperation and good wishes. In fact I think it's time you and I stop taking it on the chin from ignoramuses, and start belting them around for a change, give them some of their own medicine and more. If the publishers throw a stumbling block into this idea with their goddamn and myriad ephemeral rights to something they don't even own, I'll burn the houses down at midnight with an acetylene torch, plastic bombs, fourteen Malayan harpooners, Melville's ghost, seventeen strips of Saul Maloff tied to a TNT box as a fuse, and in court I'll put those publishers in a horseshoe for a horse to wear in the battle of Chickamauga.

Jack

Yes, hot down here, 95 every day from June to September, with no break, but my little house has central airconditioning (one-bathroom two-bedroom cottage), so I'm really cooler than you are in your shorts in Old Saybrook, tho at least you once get an Augustcool hint dontcha from good old New Hampshire on a breezy moony night in the pines?

Reprint sale of Desolation: won't collect anything on that till the *second* royalty statement from C-McCann in 1966, because I'm sure the hardcover

DESO ANGELS didn't sell much, and there was a $6,000 advance there, which enabled me to repay debt to Sterling and settle down here. In other words, nothing in sight. I've noticed lately too, John, this is the most illiterate age, 1960's, I think in the history of the world since Medieval times. Why? Television, frantic dancing, beach parties, endless overlapping hysterical stories in the press: a foolishness the Devil always wanted and got. Where are them old Dostoevsky characters who, with broken shoes, went to see one guy and spent a week studying him in a loft? (I N D I V I D U A L I S M)

My new novel about Paris is about 30,000 words long and I'm going to leave it exactly as I wrote it in pencil. You'll love it someday. I went to France and Brittany to find out why my family never changed its name (Kerouac) in something like 3,000 years, and found out.

Love

to

pretty

Shirley

TO STERLING LORD

Aug. 2, 1965

[St. Petersburg, Florida]

Dear Sterling

Please send back NOTES FROM BRITTANY as I've some new information in letters from Brittany and Canada that make that piece inaccurate (for instance, Finistère and not Morbihan, etc.) Besides, I've this new short novel, SATORI IN PARIS, ready to type up, the full narrative account of the highlights of the trip and the "search" and NOTES is not necessary now.

I hesitate to type up and send you the 2 copies of SATORI IN PARIS because it's so short, and yet it's no shorter than SUBTERRANEANS or TRISTESSA. What do you think? It's a brand new novel, written just now, July 1965, and it slides right along in typical prose but new subject matters. But my hesitation is really based on the fact that I'm discouraged that this year I've not heard from royalties from Viking, Grove, Farrar Straus, Deutsch, Rowohlt Verlag, Italy, or those advances due from Sweden, Catalan and what of the Deutsch deal for ANGELS? My income this year, Sterling, is positively woeful. I wish I hadnt gone to France at all and saved that money to live on & just hang on. Do people really believe all that shite that's written about me lately, and is there not a new sarcasm going around about everybody and his uncle?

As ever,

Jack

August 10, 1965
[St. Petersburg, Florida]

Dear Sterling:

I'm typing up Satori in Paris anyway but my hesitation stemmed from the fact that it *is* a bit short (tho we had no trouble publishing Tristessa a few years ago), that I have to use my real name in the story because the story is about my search for the real family history (not "Duluoz") (tho, again, I *did* use my real name you'll recall in Lonesome Traveler), but finally and worst of all, my "discouragement" stemmed from the fact that there seems to be a general new distaste in the culture since 1960 for works of realistic sentimentality (add Tennessee Williams' new position of disfavor to mine here), a trend towards the Ian Fleming type of sadistic facetiousness and "sickjoke" grisliness about human affairs, a grotesque hatred for the humble and the suffering heart, an admiration for the mechanistic smoothy *killer of sincerity,* a new infernal mockery sniggering down the alleys of the earth (not to mention down the corn-rows outside the Drive-In movies.) I just felt that nobody is going to care any more about my vow to write the truth only as I see it, and with sympathetic intention, "thru the keyhole of my eye," (i.e., autobiographically, in transcriptive detail directly from my own mind, arriving at the universal form the subjective point of view just like Proust and Joyce and Céline rather than from the objective point of view, literally "non-fiction" because you know what I think of fiction and its definition in the dictionary and its tall-told IF), I just felt nobody cared any more whether I or anybody like me lived or died anyway let alone write. But I remember my father's tearful blue eyes and honest Breton face, and I am mindful of what my mother just said: that my way and my philosophy will come back, some great catastrophe is going to make people wake up again, my works and my fellow ham human beings who work in the same spirit, will outlast the sneerers, the uncooperative and unmannerly divisionists, the bloody Godless forever.

So I'll send Satori in Paris soon but also keep in mind what you say about a new tack afterwards: I mean technically, i.e., write slowly and thoughtfully like I've done this letter and the enclosed letter that McGraw-Hill asked me to write, and not so much punning around and not so much mental rave.

As ever

Jack

p.s. But I think you'll find Satori in Paris a bit surprising, I mean, a rare little hunk.

In September 1965, Kerouac told John Clellon Holmes that he had made a buffoon of himself "as usual" with local college students who had just discovered that he lived in St. Petersburg.

TO JOHN CLELLON HOLMES

September 18, 1965
[St. Petersburg, Florida]

Dear John

Now, after a five day binge among the college crowd of Southern Florida U., making a buffoon of myself as usual, I realize in my liverish melancholy hangover it just won't do to go to Brown and make a further fool of myself at the expense of this generation of despisers. You remember the revulsion you felt at Iowa U. I will go see you but I canceled the Brown lecture tonight. It won't alter our own plans and in fact improve them. When I say "generation of despisers" I mean all these kids in their early 20's who are all writers (every single several million of them) and who come pouring in my direction tearing at my sleeves and biting at my heart and laughing at my opinions and finding it funny that I was arrested for sleeping in a car ($25 fine) and milling around me every time I managed to borrow another $10 from the bartender and scooping up my own beer and screaming and breaking bottles in the quiet little street in front of my house and laughing at my mother and in general the "no-respect-for-their-elders" fishy sideglances and laughing at my pot belly (altho I can drink them all under the table, which I did, taking turns from one to the other) and O my, how tired I am of talk, of sociological questions about poetry and literature, of ignorance in campus clothes. . . .

Anyway no sense in going into a big to-do about this, I just canceled the Brown lectures, and I'll accept no more lectures, I'm through with talking to people younger than myself, I want to act my age and associate with people my age, people of my own interests and ability and experience. Why should I exhibit myself any more anyhow. (You don't see Salinger letting himself open to ridicule like that.)

I hope you have a nice stay on Long Island. I'll get to Old Say in a train and let you know in advance, for an October date in any case.

I don't think we need AFTERMATHS in the "Reader," I just realized (in the same realizing mood) it's a lot of shit and this is not a "second-religiousness" generation but the very opposite, granted, maybe, yes, our vision of the hitch-hiking Negro saint WAS but that only lasted till 1949 or so . . . the 1950's began a new sinisterness in America, and now the "Soaring Sixties" is just really a soaring hysteria . . . O we'll talk about it, no need to write it now.

So I write to you around Oct. 7 about my visit. I also want (again) to dig certain other parts of Cape Cod, en route to you, to see if it would be worthwhile to move there. Let's not argue this time. I haven't got much left in the world but a few old friends like you.

Confused, insane, but loving Jack

J.

By October 1965, the students at the University of Southern Florida who had discovered the location of Kerouac's house in St. Petersburg were starting to throw rocks at his door while drunk. Gabrielle learned that her sister was planning to move from Brooklyn to Cape Cod, and she persuaded Jack to put their Tenth Avenue house up for sale after living in it for only a year. As he told Sterling Lord, "We came here just to be near my sister anyway."

This time Mémère said she had always dreamed of living on the Cape, so Jack agreed to go to Hyannis to look for another house. Despite his need for new sources of income to finance the move, Kerouac advised his agent on October 12, 1965, to turn down Allen Ginsberg's proposal to publish his letters along with Ginsberg's and Neal Cassady's in a collection of letters: "I'm refusing any idea of his forever." (In 1963, after Ginsberg returned from Japan, City Lights had published The Yage Letters, *the correspondence between Burroughs and Ginsberg chronicling Burroughs's journey to the Amazon jungle in search of the hallucinogenic drug yage.) About this time Kerouac also wrote Diana List, a secretary in Lord's office, thanking her for not giving his address to Joan Aly or "her" teenage daughter, Jan.*

TO STERLING LORD

Oct. 12, 1965

[St. Petersburg, Florida]

Dear Sterling:

It was the word "penalty" in Cindy's letter (of Aug. 5 1964) that threw me off. I thought it meant that there would have to be a penalty paid by the producers for sitting on the property [*On the Road*] for 2 years. Anyway now, reading the contract myself, I see that if the option was not to be continued, the contract would be terminated 18 months from the screenplay approval. In other words, if I had had a copy of the contract all this time, I would have understood it. I can still tell the "difference between a contract and a Chinese menu" as someone said on TV last night.

In any case, tho, it's sad to read this great masterpiece of a contract and think that the movie was not made. I want to thank you for your prompt, firm, warm, responsible, professional and friendly neighborhood type response to my confusion about the word "penalty," or my confusion about what penalties mean in option contracts.

Also, friendly neighborhood agent, that check for $2,229.00 did not hurt. I see with great delight that it did not include the 300 pound advance due from Deutsch on Desolation Angels, nor the Spanish advance of $400 from Caralt of Barcelona for same book, and so I have further remunerations to look forward to.

I'm putting half of my check right back into savings.

I'm going to move to Cape Cod. I'm going to Cape Cod to look for a suitable house, within a month, and put this one in St. Pete up for sale very soon. It's still 90 degrees every day and the other night some fast getaway car threw two rocks at my door (I dont know why, or who). We came here just to be near my sister anyway. I hope to feel the old tragic joy of New England again somehow. I'll go to Cape Cod then to Old Saybrook see John and work on his "Reader" idea. If you wanta see me en route back, let me know. (I know you're busy.) Mémère is in very bad shape since that rock-throwing but mostly because her poor little cat Pitou ran away. She has her only sister who's going to move to Cape Cod from Brooklyn within a year, might help her.

Keep sending SATORI IN PARIS around. I think they're all sore to find out I'm a descendant of Breton nobles instead of an anonymous bastard product of their own preconceptions. (I really think Amburn was chiefly sore about my saying I was a perfect bed mate, which is pretty cocky, but the whole book is cocky and a "minor key" belongs in any major symphony like Duluoz Legend.) Okay? Grove Press might surprise you. Even Giroux. And how about Sheed & Ward, since I defend the faith?

Long letter this, but, in closing, dont let Ginsberg bother you with his new idea about publishing my letters and Neal Cassady's along with his in a Collection of Letters. I'm refusing any idea of his forever.

As ever
Jack

TO DIANA G. LIST

[n.d.
St. Petersburg, Florida]

Miss Diana G. List
The Sterling Lord Agency
75 East 55 Street
New York 22, NY
Dear Miss List:

Thank you for your circumspection in connection with that call from "Jan." Under no circumstance do I want my address given to Joan Aly and her daughter Jan. I haven't accepted the girl as my daughter. Now I have to take care of my mother who is 71 years old and not well or able enough to take care of a teenager, one, who, by the way, has just come out of Belle-

411

vue psychiatric ward. As long as I keep up my end of the N.Y. State Supreme Court order, that is, mailing in monthly support checks, my responsibility ends there. Besides we are in the process of leaving Florida I hope real soon, so please keep my address from here confidential.

Again, thanks for your sterling assistance.

Sincerely,
Jack Kerouac

In November and December 1965, after another drunken trip to Lowell, Kerouac wrote Tony Sampas and Stella Sampas to tell them how much he had enjoyed visiting them.

TO TONY SAMPAS

Nov. 29 [19]65
[St. Petersburg, Florida]

Dear Tony

Got here fine—Talked with an Army major all the way, and the hostesses—Found [Paul] Bourgeois, he came to my house and my mother threw him out calling him a bum—Saw Mitchell and had few drinks—Cliff came when I was taking captain's nap—I'm going to have to stop seeing all these guys down here and get back to work—

With you had really greatest time of my life—I know you said for me to send only 2 c's but you spent so much money everywhere—Anyway, see if you can get down here this winter—

Bourgeois finally got a job as ice cream dispenser—Yelled in the bar "I'm not a chief I'm a THIEF"—Cops checked up whether he was wanted back in Lowell or not—

I not feeling too good after those twenty days of boozing but coming around—Got two g's from England, which is good, hey?

I hope you tell Stella about what I tell all the girls, and give my love to Ma and to Nicky and Mike, and I'm sending Jarvis that book today—I'll have the publishers send Charley my next book as review copy—Regards Jappy and Ruth Anne—And tell Buffalo Bill my cats smelled him all over my shirt and said "Who dat?"—

I'm worried about signing my name to that article at Albany and will see what happens, they said they would mail it when published—

It was a great experience to know you real well this time and to feel so at home everywhere we went.

My mother sends best. See you, Antoni.

Yours
Jack

Dec. 7 1965
[St. Petersburg, Florida]

Dear Stella

Got your fine letter. Just got back five days ago. Had good time. Tell me in your next note if Tony got his money okay. You might tell Charley S. that there's a big statue of Virgin Mary on front-strip lawn of house where my brother Gerard died, on Beaulieu Street in Centreville, which I saw one Sunday morning while visiting 8 A.M. Mass in St. Louis church. Dont know name of family, or whether family knows book VISIONS OF GERARD or whether just coincidence, but there it is, with two adoring angel statues at Her feet, only house in block with statues on lawn.

Sent Charles Jarvis English book of mine to pay for jacket. Jacket too hot for Florida. But will wear it after my mother cuts off the wool sleevelets and stitches it back neat. She cant take off wool collar. Will have to save jacket for Massachusetts. LOWELL TECH.

Bourgeois followed us here and is trying to bang his way into my mother's house for freeload, my mother's got a friend next door, Mr. B., who has shotguns. Bourgeois better watch out. I let him in for one night. He should go back to Lowell. Mr. B. has wife and kids who watch after my mother when I take trips. Tony got on the phone and got him for me, when I called for Thanksgiving. Lost my address book in Nicky's bar. Anybody find it? Red, small.

Tho I'm crazy I know what I'm doing—as you know, as Tony knows. (Two dogtrack gangsters I think were trying to kidnap me the other night, I sneaked out of bar I asked for, and wound up sneaking down highway, to phone in funeral home, got cab, wound up shooting great pool on Central Avenue.)

Say hello Mike and wife the English girl. I never can remember all the names ... only name I remember, other than some, is Cassandra. Is that the blonde who looks like Mike and Sammy? tall, 11.? [sic] And your sister was Grace? As for Ma Sampas, all the love.

Write soon.

As ever
Jack

Dec. 23 1965
[St. Petersburg, Florida]

Dear Stella

Not much of a card but I just picked one out of my mother's desk, she buys these from girl scouts instead of going to the store to buy fancy ones, anyway who cares about cards, if you wish I can improve on it with one of my inimitable pietas [drawings], as follows:—

Meanwhile, how glad I was to receive my address book from Tony. After we ate in the Parkway that night I remember I ran out (having already lost book on floor, I guess) and ran across the street and lifted up the wreath of fresh flowers laid there for Ladd & Whitney for Memorial Day, wind or hoodlums had knocked it down, and I righted it and leaned it back safe & snug. Only good thing, or deed, I did in Lowell.

Also I appreciate your sending me that clipping about St. Sabbas. That will be Sammy's name in my new book, Sabbas Savakis, or "Sabby" (!) (Good?) A long ways from "Ferdinand Panos" and much better, or that silly "Santos" name I thought was Greek before.... I still dont understand why Charley thinks there are no great writers left in America when there I am sitting in front of him at the house: is he sore because I didnt send him a DESOLATION ANGELS? If you folks dont have a D-A, I'll bring one in Feb., for the whole family. I dare Charley to read that, especially the beginning 60 pages ... Well, anyway, tho I'm vain about my accomplishments, at least I know how much study and work went into my working-out of prose dramas, and they all had to be true-life stories, yet poetic in all the darkness.... The fact of the matter is, I'm not a bestseller because people arent educated enough yet: just wait and see what the Astronauts of the Year 2,000 B.C. [sic] will be reading on Venus and Mars ('t'wont be James Michener).... Can you also tell me if Tony is going to be OK with the proposed putaway of 3 months? or not?... Tony is like "Dean Moriarty," never writes letters.... tell him I'll see him in 2 months. And tell Mike too. My mother just made a French Canadian New Years Port Pie (Tourquère)

Jack   (Write!)

[handwritten on the inside of the Christmas card] To Stella & Family

From Jack

In December 1965, Sterling Lord sold Satori in Paris *to Grove Press for a $2,000 advance. At the end of the year, Kerouac wrote to John Clellon Holmes describing his quick trip to Lowell and inviting his old friend to visit him in St. Petersburg before he moved to Cape Cod.*

TO JOHN CLELLON HOLMES

Dec. 23, 1965
[St. Petersburg, Florida]

Dear John

Who the hell is "Alice"? Or "Eleanor" for that matter? I didn't sing with Eleanor, I only talked to her in the car outside? Is somebody pulling my leg? Very well then, pull my leg, I am large, I contain multitudes. My Maw just bought me a $5 Hohner Marine Band Harmonica on which I can play "Moon River" ANY TAM. . . . . John, if you don't hear from Viking soon, or if they turn it down, try Fred Jordan (tell Sterl) at Grove. That guy is such a conscientious editor I'm even planning on springing COMPLETE VISIONS OF CODY on him (520 pages) followed by another surprise, the 1000-page Pensées-type philosophical-religious tract SOME OF THE DHARMA. *Some*body's got to publish our best works. There are other possibilities. I'll actively see to it that this non-fiction book of yours gets published. Come soon Jan. or Feb. I'm going to Cape Cod, alone, get a motel room, walk around a few days, see what town I like, buy a house, (down payment or binder), get all that done, go to Lowell, see friends about a ride for my Ma and cats from Fla. to Cape, then go down NY-way to see you if you wish, (alone), Sterling, etc. Will make the move. Younly live oncet. Massachusetts is in my heart but I'll go there anyway. Cliff and Patty Mitchell send their felicitations and are even sending a Lowell benefactor a box of cigars for Christmas. They are broke, as usual. I spent $500 on the whole crazy trip, plus another $100 for their return trip alone with my cousin Bourgeois the Indian chief. Said Bourgeois now on a shrimp boat in the Gulf gassing everybody with his wild New England openness. . . . . . So I see you soon, and don't worry, this time we'll get to brass tacks. I mean, also, however, meanwhile, send preliminary list, for the Reader. Don't work on Reader till the non-fiction is sold, which it will be.[6] 'My book, for instance, (SATORI IN PARIS), just accepted by Grove, was rejected by Coward McCann as well as by Little-Brown and it took 3 months too. I was as mad as hell, like you. Wait a second. Miss you today. Skoll.

Never mind my politics, they're really OSS tactics to bring out others' politics ha ha ha. Yours okay. You're passed.

Tell Eleanor-Alice to go out chop some woodum bringum to Chiefum Fireplace make Hot Nog.

As always
Jack
Ti Jean
Louis Lebris de Kéroualles
(descended of the mistress of Charles II England,
Louise de Kéroualle, Dutchess of Portsmouth, altho she
only borrowed the name from old Fambly there, mine)
Indians in Québec couldn't pronounce "L's"–"C's" or "K's" only

---

6. *Nothing More to Declare*, Holmes's nonfiction book, was a "provocative, personal summation of the men and ideas that made his literary generation." It was published by E. P. Dutton in 1967. Holmes never completed his Kerouac Reader project. Between 1957 and 1965, fifteen Kerouac books were issued by nine different publishers, who refused to release material. Years after Holmes's death from cancer in 1988, a single-volume Kerouac Reader became possible. *The Portable Jack Kerouac*, edited by Ann Charters, was published by Viking Penguin in 1995. See preface To the Reader, pp. vii–viii.

1966

During the first months of 1966, Kerouac kept Stella Sampas, John and Shirley Holmes, and Sterling Lord up-to-date on his plans to move from Florida to Cape Cod. With the money from the sale of his house in St. Petersburg he bought a modest three-bedroom tract home at 20 Bristol Avenue in the center of Hyannis, within walking distance of a supermarket and post office. By the first week of April, he and Gabrielle were living in the house, awaiting the arrival of their furniture. The house in Hyannis cost less than the one Jack and his mother sold in Florida, but money was tight. Kerouac's income from his writing in 1964 and 1965 was the lowest since 1957, and he told Holmes he had spent half of his savings in the move.

Satori in Paris *was published in three issues of* Evergreen Review *(February, April, and June 1966), with book publication scheduled for November. Trying to earn more money, Jack wrote an article titled "My Position in the Current Literary Scene," which Lord placed with* Escapade *magazine. As before, his agent continued to negotiate foreign sales of Kerouac's books, sending a stream of contracts and tax forms for Jack to sign throughout the year.*

Lord also arranged for a new Signet reprint of On the Road, *which Kerouac predicted would have "a vitality that's not surprising considering that my fans are broker than most people." He was right. The novel was to sell more than three million copies in the next thirty years. The new paperback edition was published in July 1966, followed by* The Dharma Bums *the next year. Both were mass-market paperbacks sporting similar bright-yellow covers with illustrations that reflected the cultural changes that had occurred since the books were originally published in the previous decade. The reprint of* On the Road, *featuring a cartoon of a hippie couple sharing a hug, was presented as "the riotous odyssey of two American drop-outs, by the drop-out who started it all. . . ." The cover of* The Dharma Bums, *showing the same zany couple playing piggyback, advertised the book as being written "by the man who launched the hippie world, the daddy of the swinging psychedelic generation."*

[Postmarked February 14, 1966
St. Petersburg, Florida]

Stella—
    Be seeing you soon.
    Jack

TO SHIRLEY & JOHN CLELLON HOLMES

Feb. 18, 1966
[St. Petersburg, Florida]

Dear Shirl and John:

Wow, Shirl can write better than both of us! I don't know whether to file that humor-type masterpiece under Holmes or which! I'll just file it in with John's sheaf. You don't know how close I came to driving to Fayetteville on the night of Feb. 11th, with Cliff, when we all got drunk in the Tampa wild-bar student bar. The question of money put a stop to that. If I do go, I'd go alone.

Still trying to sell my little house here so I can go to the Cape. Realtors around here are sorta "furniture vultures" more interested in what you're going to leave. It's like asking John to leave all those fine antiques you have. Here, people leave antiques yes, but here is where all those old re-tired couples die. So I'm sitting here fidgeting like a maniac, not writing, not even thinking, just waiting to leave. The mere thought of S. S. Pierce fishbarrels under gray Atlantic skies puts me in the mind of how I'm going to start next book.

I bet John is already sick and tired of bearded students. Two of them from Univ. of Fla. just knocked on my door as I hid in my mother's bed-room and she told them I was out drinking 20 miles away, to which bar they hurried eagerly. One of them kept nodding and bowing with clasped hands at my mother, she says, saying he was a Zen student. The other was bearded and six foot six. When they knocked I was contemplating how swell it was I couldn't write in my notebook tonight as I had lost it in my coat in a bar or a car among other writers. The writers around here are all working on novels. I've been here 1½ years. Cliff himself started a novel on a scrap of paper 1½ years ago, in front of me, in a bar, and still has it in his wallet. Another one, Fowler, also six-foot-six, was going along swell on his novel when he was arrested for indecent exposure. Another one has abandoned his novel temporarily to train carrier pigeons to carry marijuana in little aluminum tubes from Miami and Atlanta. The bar where they all hang out actually no lie *rocks physically* at times: New Years Eve it was sway-ing. The screaming in here is unbelievable, you can't even hear Pat Mitchell's harmonica, Cliff's guitar, my fiftycent jukebox "Madame Butterfly" turned up loud, several other guitarists, a pianist playing jazz, a chorus of rich girls in the corner singing "What Are You Going to Do with a Drunken Sailor," and the howls of new-arrivers, the banging of beer mugs on oaken tables: and they all wonder why they don't get any "work" done, and they are always there.... God, John can tell you, how he on Lex Ave, and me in Ozone Park, used to spend entire days by rainy windows reading Balzac, brewing coffee, jacking off, tacking on typewriter or scribbling on page, dreaming in chair, walking streets alone for miles for exercise, not seeing anybody t'all for weeks on end. Times have changed so bad. The Lost Twenties, the Depressed Thirties, the Roaring Forties, the Beat Fifties, the Silly Sixties.

Hi there, Alice Mudd, or is it Frank Sinatra? See you somewhere and I hope you and John make it back to Say with loot and go take a nice trip Europe, and all the luck to you in that bedlam ... "The night of the soul" was so much nicer than these orgies called education and Progress.

Jack

Write!

TO STERLING LORD

April 25, 1966
[Hyannis, Massachusetts]

Dear Sterling:

Enclosed, a paper I was asked to fill out by your secretary.

Looking forward now to Coward-McCann's second installment of the $20,000 Bantam reprint money. According to my files that's due any day. Need it, as I just dug into my savings to move to Hyannis, and my last checks from you were for $7, $22, $17, and $19.

Anything in England?

Please call me at Hyannis, 617-775-4869, if anything comes up.

The Lord took care of my mother and the cats and meself on the way up here, the house is all fixed up, it's perfect all around, so I guess he'll take care of my living.

Briefly,
and,
as ever,
Jack

Hope Cindy enjoyed trip

A month after moving to Hyannis, Kerouac answered a letter from Al Gelpi, an instructor in English who had been his host when he had read at Lowell House, Harvard in 1964. Gelpi had written from Cambridge, Massachusetts, to tell him about the birth of his son Christopher Francis, born in April. On January 14, 1966, Kerouac had told Gelpi about his plan to leave Florida:

> *My mind has become dulled in this cracker country and I want to get back to books and scholarship and especially the Atlantic Ocean feeling which I can get out of just looking at an S.S. Pierce barrel of fish—I've had my southern sleep down here—El General is going back to his Union troops.*

On March 8, 1966, Kerouac had sent a poem to his friend, "Something Serious for Al Gelpi," which Gelpi wanted to publish.

> *How trite*
> * the newspapers*
> *   on my chair,*
>
> *The efforts*
> * I make*
> *   to comb my hair.*
>
> *That I believe in God*
> * is only hearsay,*
> *   in me—*
>
> *This suffering*
> * can't be called,*
> *some kind of heresy.*

TO ALBERT J. GELPI

May 18, 66
[20 Bristol Avenue
Hyannis, Massachusetts]

Dear Al

Just got your letter today, glad to hear about Christophe-Francois Gelpi and Mother. You sound like the Indian who gets empathetically sick for his wife during childbirth. All honor to you.

Let me have a copy of my poem in the Harvard publication when you can.[1] I'll ask for the Sheed & Ward book on Karl Rahner, by your brother, when I go to bookstore here. (By the way, is he, or are you, acquainted with THE CLOUD OF UNKNOWING? Great book) ...

---

1. The Lowell House Printers issued another poem, "A Pun for Al Gelpi," in December 1966.

Well, in September I'm being flown to Italy by publishers for lectures, conferences, bashes, all of which I wd. reject in America or England but in Italy how can I care, they dont even understand English too well and I'll just act vaguely something-or-other and go see the bronze doors and maybe Fiorenzi, and re-sign my names on the walls of the catacombs, i.e., the Fish.

So now I'll be at leisure . . . and may drop in on you (with advance warning) if perchance I go to Boston soon to look up Gaelic dictionary on Boylston St. In fact, by the way, they must have good Gaelic and Celtic and Cornish Celtic information in the famous Harvard Library? (I'm not finished at all with the Celtic researches I started in the new novel SATORI IN PARIS, I'm still not completely sure that Ker Ouac means House in the Moor or whether it's Stoneplace by the Sea).

Fixed up my study beautifully. Will start buying more books. Plan to come down before you go to New Orleans or wherever this summer vacation, heh? Completely enclosed backyard for picnics. My mother fine. Now all I have to do is write a new book (gulp).

Jack Gulpi.

In other words, I'm all settled and real lazy and sleeping a lot. Wondering what to do, in fact. I ought to run up to Boston real soon (1-½ hours from here to Boston Common) and go see a track meet or sumptin. Incidentally, Hyannis is terrific for me: very quiet: no snoopy "fan" types who're never "fans" anyway anymore'n my ass: the old Massachusetts feeling even in the Atlantic sky and the trees; and soon I will be slaving like a bearded Leonardo on some new composition that I hope s'll flash silver in the last dawn hours of the page.... Much to talk about when I see you, which oughta be soon now. How's Herman? I mean, Mel. ??

Write soon

Jack

TO NORA AQUILON

June 18, 1966
[Hyannis, Massachusetts]

Dear Nora Aquilon:

Find enclosed the French contracts signed, and the German tax form.

No matter where I move in America I'm so pestered by everyone as soon as they find out where I live, I havent even got time to sign my own contracts let alone write. It will teach you a lesson about "fame without fortune," because otherwise I'd be able to afford to pay someone to take care of thousands of details also such as taxes, fan letters, alumni fund queries, silly piles of stuff from Who's Who in the East etc. etc. and here I am cant even get a silly little advance from my own publishers (McCann) and so once more I'm broke down to the last gloop. I'm telling you this not only to amuse, but to instruct, you: NEVER BE A HEMINGWAY "HERO" WITHOUT A BUSINESS MANAGER.

Please call Sterling on intercom and tell him that the additional material I thought of including in André Deutsch's edition of SATORI is still too short (10 pages) and that I suggest we wait and see what Deutsch thinks later on about just publishing SATORI by itself, or whatever he wants.

Know what would happen right now if I wanted to write? I'd have to sweep a pile of mail off my desk and bend to my stories, but if I did, I'd be arrested for tax "evasion," condemned for not answering soulful communiques from everybody and his uncle, let editors get away with dumb misunderstandings of what I told them on the phone, have the phone cut off, be accused of non-commitment by charlatans who send piles of propaganda for this or that, neglect to study the manuscripts of "writers" who just blandly mail their stuff to me hoping they can accuse me later on of "stealing" their marvelous fresh ideas, be sued for non-support of strangers to my blood, show coldblooded neglect of announcements about art galleries, music recitals. . . . oh enough, you get the point.

Hope you enjoyed my little explanation for the contracts coming in late. Sterling is pestered as I am, in another way, it's a shame.

Peace be with ye

Jack Kerouac

In July 1966, Gabrielle began feeling unwell, experiencing severe pains in her arm. Dreading the prospect of his seventy-one-year-old mother becoming an invalid, Kerouac approached his steadfast Lowell friend Stella Sampas with the idea of marriage. They had known each other for more than thirty years, since Jack's close friendship with her brother Sebastian Sampas. After carefully considering Kerouac's proposal, Stella replied with her characteristic modesty. She addressed the letter to both Jack and his mother, but she directed her statements to Gabrielle.

TO GABRIELLE KEROUAC & JACK KEROUAC FROM STELLA SAMPAS

Thursday July 21 [1966]

[Lowell, Massachusetts]

Dear Mrs. Kerouac & Jack—

I am relieved to know that you are perfectly well and I'm sure that you can handle all problems as they arise. As you know, Jack did come to Lowell and again brought up the subject of he and I getting married.

I don't know how to pursue the subject. You are his mother and know him much better than I could.

This much I can write, I love Jack—have loved him very much for a very long time and have never given the thought of marrying anyone but him.

I look at myself in the mirror, and this is what holds me back. I am no beauty. Probably too old to bear children. Jack deserves much more than I can offer.

This much I can offer—love—devotion and each and every effort to make him happy.

As for his previous marriages, all I can say is that whatever was lacking in these attempts I will try to avoid.

Look to your heart, and give me your blessing to share your son's future life.

Love—
Stella—

P.S. Of course, all this if Jack wants—I am not exactly the ideal woman a man dreams about—If both of you do not think this marriage can come about, please don't answer and I will accept that fact. Please don't send me a letter like the one from Florida the 1st time Jack came to Lowell.

Early in August 1966, one of the first uses Jack made of a new Royal standard typewriter was to reply to a letter that I had sent to Gabrielle Kerouac, in care of the Sterling Lord Agency, asking her to help me compile a bibliography of the works of Jack Kerouac, which I was preparing for the Phoenix Bookshop's series of contemporary authors' bibliographies. I had been told by Robert A. Wilson, owner of the bookshop in Greenwich Village, that visitors to the Kerouac home had stolen most of Jack's copies of his own books, so that he had entrusted his library to his mother for safekeeping. On August 5, 1966, Jack wrote me that he was willing to cooperate with my project and invited me to his home in Hyannis. We agreed that I would visit him on August 16–17, 1966, and in a second letter he sent me directions to his brown-shingled Cape Cod house, located close to the Joseph Kennedy Memorial Skating Rink. He added, "This will be fascinating: I myself am beginning to need a bibliography. And I look forward to meeting a scholar and a gentlewoman." As an afterthought, he penciled a postscript to this second letter: "Throw these instructions away, rather, that is, bring 'em with you—'Beatniks' look like Spooks in my mother's poor door at midnight—You understand."

TO ANN CHARTERS:

Aug. 5, 1966
Box 809
Hyannis, Mass.

Dear Doctor Charters:

I'm willing to go through my collection of editions at my home providing only you don't give my home address to any*one* or any *groups*. I'm trying to work in the privacy of my own thoughts and domicile.

Also, I think my complete bibliography would come to a hundred pages or so. I think I have here, in my study, something like 99.5% information for the entire bibliography: I think the rest I can direct you to. (I've kept the neatest records you ever saw.)

So, if that's not too long, and you keep my address a secret, write and tell me the date you want to come: I'm sure we can get the whole thing done in one afternoon. I'll just pull everything out one by one, hand them to you at the desk, return the things back where they were (innumerable poetry pamphlets, broadsides, sheets from magazine publications, etc.) (and also all the 16 foreign translations of novels are either here or recorded in my pile of contracts and in foreign publishers' announcements)—Anyway, to make a long story short, write, give date, and I'll immediately send you my Hyannis street address and wait for you.

I'm going to Italy (invite of Mondadori publishers) on Sept. 26, so come long before then, please. So come on down.

Sincerely,
Jack Kerouac

During the two days I spent with Jack and Gabrielle Kerouac in Hyannis, they cooperated fully with my work compiling his bibliography. Though I was surprised to see Jack's physical deterioration from the effects of hard drinking, his boast of keeping "the neatest records you ever saw" was justified. Kerouac's archive of books, periodicals, manuscripts, letters, and contracts was so carefully organized in his study that it furnished most of what I needed to complete the project. Throughout both days I spent in the house he drank boilermakers, emptying a fifth and starting a pint of Johnnie Walker Red Label Scotch each day and tossing down the contents of several six-packs of Schlitz malt liquor, but he stayed lucid enough to answer my questions about how he wrote each of his books. I included his comments in the bibliography, and they were of great help to me when I wrote the first biography of him six years later.

During my visit Kerouac told me he looked forward to receiving his copies of the bibliography: "Now I can be like that fellow in Cambridge, Edmund Wilson, always giving a little pamphlet away." The only sour notes were Jack and his mother's openly expressed anti-Semitism directed at me and in their references to Allen Ginsberg, and Kerouac's paranoia about what he called "the Jewish cadre" of fiction writers—Norman Mailer, Philip Roth, Saul Bellow, Bernard Malamud, Joseph Heller, and J. D. Salinger—who he insisted had "tried to suppress" his books. Our days together were productive, yet I was dismayed by Jack's helpless alcoholism. Often the unpredictability of his gestures and speech left me with the feeling that I was in the presence of a blind porcupine.

In her own way Mémère also unsettled me. The first evening she and I finished a large bottle of champagne with the delicious chicken potpie she prepared for dinner in the kitchen. Later back in the living room, she took advantage of one of Jack's frequent trips to the bathroom to lift up a Japanese calendar nailed to the wall across from the framed drawing of Gerard feeding the birds. Gabrielle showed me knife gouges in the plaster, saying, "Jackie did that last week. I was so frightened I didn't go to bed all night." She waited for him to come back into the room before dropping the calendar.

"What things are you telling her?" Kerouac shouted.

His mother taunted him: "Last week he was drunk one night when my friend was here, and he told me I was full of little brown turds. My friend got angry and said, 'You shouldn't speak to your mother that way.' I told her I don't mind. It wasn't true anyway. I took an enema yesterday."

In the ensuing confusion I fled the house to spend the night in the room I had rented in a Hyannis motel. At noon the next day, when I returned to complete my work, Jack and his mother welcomed me back into the house and didn't refer to the incident.

Three weeks after my visit, early in the morning of September 9, 1966, Gabrielle suffered a massive stroke in her bedroom. After more than a week of hospitalization she returned home, bedridden and paralyzed on her left side, totally dependent upon Jack's care. He described his troubled household to John Clellon Holmes on September 22, 1966, saying that his mother blamed a recent encounter with Allen Ginsberg for causing her stroke. Driving with Peter Orlovsky from Boston to New York, Ginsberg had phoned Kerouac and was told to drop by. When he and Peter arrived in Hyannis, Jack never answered the door. Finally Mémêre came out of the house and told them to stay away.

Kerouac had been invited by his Italian publisher, Mondadori, to fly to Milan and Rome to publicize his novels, but he postponed his trip until September 27, when Stella Sampas agreed to come to Hyannis to care for his mother. Jack made it to Italy to collect a substantial fee, but he was so distraught over his mother's stroke that he collapsed in the publisher's office and was barely coherent during his television interview with Nanda Pivano.

TO JOHN CLELLON HOLMES

Sept. 22, 1966
[Hyannis, Massachusetts]

Dear John

Well it's all off, I can't go to Italy and leave my mother alone unvisited daily in the hospital, and the frightened cats who are her little buddies, it's just impossible. I sent the tickets back hoping they could arrange said trip later, like this winter. You can imagine how sad and shook up I am, unstable as I am in any case, alone in a dark house, looking at her poor sewing baskets and things with tears in my eyes. I too, by God, this fall and winter, like you, am going to bury myself in "honest toil" and start writing sincerely like in Town and City days, I'm sick of joking around with linguistics and booze tales. The Dope has given me an idea for a wonderful title. About Allen G., I like him, always have, am a little jealous of everybody else liking him, am a little possessive, and a little jealous that his fame surpasses mine now, but I still think he's a false prophet, sheep's clothing and ravening wolf: I judge this from the fruits, "by their fruits ye shall judge them." My mother claims it was his visit caused her stroke, of course that isn't true altogether, it was booze, or, really, the last 8 years of spooks appearing in the door with bottles when all the time she wanted to enjoy her little home, her TV and her papers, quietly, and so did I: wanting to make my home a refuge for works and meditation. No, outnumbered 5,000-to-1. I'll tell you what, John, what we oughta start doing is charge people for our time: make a living that way if they don't want to buy our books now. Give me your autograph, Okay, said Geo. Bernard Shaw, "make out a check and my endorsement shall be your autograph." Bah, but that's not the main thing, as you know, I'm really bugged about this silly idea that it's abnormal and "wrong" for a man to take care of his old widowed mother: yes, "wrong" to a bunch of libertine cads shaking their hairy asses in the Sodom capitals of the West, waving their arms in the red glow of hell and all howling in one grand insane kibbutssky. Joe Louis took care of his mother and nobody dared call HIM a sissy: so does Tony Bennett, Geo. Hamilton, Liberace, Red Buttons. I suppose I'm wrong and Lucien is right? What has annoyed me more than anything has been this arrogant assumption on the part of the Freudians that to show companion for your parents, compassion that is, parents who are your only link with the horror of birth anyway, who gave you birth in innocence without knowing how bad is birth, that to support them in their old age is some kind of feebleminded mistake instead of what it really is: love on the only unselfish level, Caritas....

Enough,—Say hello to dearly liked Lagniappe Shirley and let's dive into work

Jack

TO STERLING LORD

Oct. 8, 1966
[Hyannis, Massachusetts]

Dear Sterling:

Enclosed find signed contracts for Yugoslavia ROAD.

Now the doctor says my mother is just about going to be permanently paralyzed on the left side.

They cant do any more for her in the hospital. And I am not going to dump her in a nursing home. I'll have to take care of her myself at home, and want to, and besides I couldnt afford a nursing home.

For God's sake try to find me some assignments, or sell a book to the movies or something. It isnt as tho I were an unknown novice in American literature and nothing could be done. Yugoslavia makes the 17th language I'm translated in.

I had to ask Mr. Deutsch for help in London, to find a room and to find a quick plane back. He did everything swiftly and sympathetically. Michael Sissons started the ball rolling. But none of us mentioned publishing matters (as you instructed me).

In Italy I hardly got a word in edgewise on TV and in question-and-answer university seminars: everybody had long prepared statements explaining me even to myself. Advantages of the publicity campaign I have no idea. I lost my luggage but it was just re-found in Boston. Being mailed.

But I did sing in a Roman nightclub all night long, to applause at times, and painted a pieta with Franco Angeli in his studio, and visited the Vatican with bodyguard. And had brilliant fun and banquets in Napoli.

My heart wasnt in it on account of Mémère. The money has not come in yet for my effort (but will).

I dont want to bore you, as you're so busy, but this is the report from your friendly neighborhood gumba, asking, where is that so-called American cultural boom and all them prizes and awards and fellowships and grants. At least, thank God, Medicare is actually taking care of Mémère's hospital and medical bills!

As ever
Jack

On October 12, 1966, Kerouac wrote Stella Sampas, sending her a bus schedule after she offered to make weekly trips from Lowell to Hyannis to help him care for Gabrielle. He thought of Stella as what he called his "sister" in adversity since she was also at home caring for an invalid mother.

TO STELLA SAMPAS

Oct. 12 1966
[Hyannis, Massachusetts]

Dear Stella:

Doing much better than I thought I would—Took Gabe home three days ago in ambulance (Medicare free), rented wheel chair (Medicare free), bought pillows, rubber sheets etc. and am getting extraspecial reclining wheelchair in ten days to rent (I pay $5 a month, Medicare the other $20 per month)—I learned how to pick her up by putting my head under her right armpit and lifting, like wrestler's hold—Bought her a commode (potty) and have it right by bed to sit on, for all purposes—She no longer involuntarily goes in bed but simply rings the bell when she wants to go— The bell is weird: a bunch of Indian elephant holy bells on a rope, tied to a string which has for a weight the medal of Pope John 23rd I just bought in Rome!—(handy because of weight and loop)—Today I wheeled her into livingroom into my big reclining chair—

I give her much better food than hospital, too—No bulk or spices, but delicate chicken pot pie, softboiled eggs with soaked toast, tonight it will be Campbell's frozen oyster stew with fruit, honey, crackers—See? concentrated food to clean her bowels—Hot milk and honey and 2 Bufferins every night on retiring—She says I should have been a doctor—Extended 30 feet of TV aerial into her room, she watching Merv Griffin right now—I got my Italian money finally, paid all my bills and rent, just cashed her SocialSec. check and am solvent and on the beam—

The hospital people would be amazed to see this—They must think Mémère and me are eccentric and irresponsible just because we talk a lot ... The doctor never comes, he doesnt care— Phil Clary only comes to look for free Scotch or food, I go to the store myself when Ma takes naps, hurry and back in 30 minutes—

Your visits would be pleasant to give her a little change, a wash too (by the way), only thing I cant do is wash her body but I clean the potty and everything else, even cat puke as you know—Got kitchen clean and shipshape—But you dont have to break your neck to come here every week, Stella, I am managing everything—Still, she likes you, and I like you like a sister, so come if you want to, if it's convenient—Dont put out your own Mom and family responsibilities—

I'm seriously thinking of maybe moving to Lowell if an old family friend of ours, Laurette Sullivan (born Fournier), who runs a small fine private nursing home somewhere on Andover St. I think, can be found—Only last year she invited my Ma there even for just a vacation—If my Ma is to be like this for 6 months or a year I might put her in Laurette's personal care (she runs nursing home with husband Sullivan) and slowly move to Lowell, first walking all around town to find perfect little house near supermarket and in good area like Bristol St. here—On the other hand, I'm not sure, just an idea now—(Know too many people there? door pounding all day? could I be quiet old exile reading in Lowell Library privatel Y?) etc? Look up this Laurette Sullivan nursing home—Probably we'll have discussed all this on phone before you receive this letter and the enclosed latest Boston-Hyannis ALMEIDA bus schedule, but if Laurette is still available it might be better for me to spend the money on this GOOD PERSONAL nursing home and have free time to write big new novel this Fall winter and Spring, to more than pay for everything, see?

Altho I could write right now here as I am right now—Doing very well—Mrs. Cash washes Ma every two days—She is wonderful—

Okay, sister ... You heard what I said, S I S T E R.... Come on over if you want but remember it's not an emergency situation any more as far as care goes—As for her progress, I dont understand it—Maybe the death of my sister Caroline has taken the gumption out of her, I dont know—She's always been too nervous and scared of nothing—But a lot of strong men who were seamen or lumberjacks all their lives do fall like this suddenly—and recover—All I want is for her to get well enuf to waddle slowly around the house like your own dear Ma. That's all I ask of God ... of Gerard ... of St. Benedict ... of St. Dymphna ... of St. Jude ... of Mary ... of Jesus.

Pitou and Doby (the little grey, and the skinnier orange cat) sleep on her bed all day—The big one has finally changed his sleeping spot, at my instigation, to the hall shelf—Brigitte Bardot calls, and will drop in—She said all the girls at the hospital missed you.

Tell Tony that the Greek who is one of the brothers who runs Charley's store here, Jimmy Atsalis, seems to be hinting all the time he wants to play cards with ME—Saw me with Tony and thinks I'm a cardplayer—Tell Tony to lay off cards, this Atsalis plays at Hot Springs Arkansas—Just to mention local nonsense—Okay.

Jack

After Stella Sampas consented to become his third wife, Kerouac wrote his agent on November 16, 1966, about his plans to move back to Lowell. Sterling Lord was negotiating a contract with Coward-McCann for Vanity of Duluoz, *which Jack proposed to write within the year so that he could afford what he called "a proper home in the country outside Lowell Mass." At the end of November, Jack dropped a note to Allen Ginsberg about his wedding. Allen had written him just before Gabrielle's stroke, saying that he tried to reach Jack by telephone several times but his mother refused to take his phone number: "I think she's carrying things too far, goddamit what's the matter in your house.... Well fuck it—I guess you got enough woes without my added grudgery."*

TO STERLING LORD

Nov. 16, 1966
[Hyannis, Massachusetts]

Dear Sterling:

This missive is addressed to that country gentleman, a symphony in green on an Autumn day in Cape Cod, whose name, in Scottish Celt, means Lord, and whom it would demean to say, that he does not look more than like a lord, nay, like a *laird*. (Samuel Johnson style, now out-of-date.)

I received that surprising check from Grove for the good sale they got on the Zebra edition of THE SUBTERRANEANS I guess because of the coffee-colored back of that honeychild ... (on the cover). (Or maybe because of the brooding beatnik with the Stalin mustache.) In any case it bears out my theory that book covers should be PHOTOGRAPHS, like I wanted Keith Jennison to do with DHARMA BUMS in 1958, instead of "art" work showing two ridiculous surrealistic figures climbing up a sheer cliff wall with *ropes,* of all things, when all you needed was a photograph of me and Japhy Ryder sitting under a tree beside our packs with the High Sierras in the background.

Tell this to Coward-McCann's inestimable Jack Geoaghan (phew, is that it?) [Geoghegan] or to Ellis Amburn in connection with the future dust-jacket of VANITY OF DULUOZ, a novel I will write ("I will, I do"—Prince of Wales, King Henry V, Shakspere) as soon as I have settled my sick mother and my wife-to-be in a proper home in the country outside Lowell Mass. If you can explain to them that I need this new home, even a new standard Royal typewriter that doesnt slide like this one, that this home must be a ranch we can wheel her about in, where I can have a study with a shower and sink of my own and a door of my own to the Druidical trees and the basketball pole, that for this I need an advance of only $10,000, with the rest, another ten, payable as advance on presentation of manuscript for printer, on or before November 16, 1967, I'll be able to go to Lowell with Tony and pick out a decent but simple, rustic, 20-odd thou house without digging into my present savings which are the only thing between me and the dogs of eternity that seek my family before their time.

Voila? (try it)

As ever
Jack

TO ALLEN GINSBERG

[Nov. 28, 1966
Hyannis, Massachusetts]

Allen—

Wedding would be after move to Lowell, maybe January—maybe before New Year's too, with speedy move & settle—I enmeshed in domestic & invalid problems, won't write till house in country (around Lowell) & private study & own door to trees—etc.—but hitting up to new lit'ry season shot.

Jack

On December 18, 1966, Jack and Stella Kerouac both wrote thank-you letters for wedding presents from her sister-in-law Dorothy and her brother Jim Sampas, a career diplomat in the State Department who had just returned from Paris to Washington, D.C., before being posted to Reykjavik. The newly married couple described the new house they were buying in Lowell close to Stella's mother, "Yaya," and reported on Mémère's improving condition. In better spirits than he had been for over a month, Kerouac described himself humorously as "a lumberjack who married a Spartan" and predicted a honeymoon in Iceland in the coming year.

Dec. 18, 1966
[Hyannis, Massachusetts]

Dear Jim and Dorothy:—

Thanx for the beautiful present and the great flowers. And the messages of congratulations.

Stella is a good girl, I'm glad I married her because she is, first and foremost, a real family woman, good buddy, devoted, kind, calm, strong, humane and name it. My playboy life of the past was just like the trip down the lane by the village boy.

We're going to have a lot of fun in our spanking (practically) new house in Lowell. I saw some dreary houses in Chelmsford, with too many trees cut down, or big drafty places made of plywood, or fairly nice ranches in creepy looking "rustic" areas that ain't rustic t'all. In other words, the place I picked out, while in city of Lowell, has a small forest of white birch clumps in the back, where I'll enclose it in stockade fence 6 feet tall, and the feeling there is just as "rustic" as Chelmsford and moreover Stella can go see Yaya even twice a day in car, a 1½ mile run or so, and I can walk to store for incidentals and exercise.

I expect your little boy is getting a lot of worldy experience (worldly) going from Paris to Reykyavik. I also expect you're getting a welcome fresh-air rest from silly Paree. Wait till summer, it gets lovely, only trouble is the sun goes down at midnight in July (I was thereabouts in '42, as I told you.)

My Ma is really slowly getting better. When she can waddle around the house like Yaya, we'll really have a ball all around.

I'm going to Lowell within 5 days and close the deal and see Nicky, Tony, Johnny, et al. I'm driving up there in a sports car with a Negro novelist from Cape Cod, son of a NATO architect. We'll be back in time for Xmas Eve. Hope you all have pretty Christmas in Iceland. Don't let the career diplomatist social abstractionist cruds defer your joy. I'm so glad I'm a lumberjack who married a Spartan and can go around in my hockey muff-cap. Seriously, all joy to you both and see you soon somehow. (Honeymoon in Iceland 1967 later?)

Jack

TO DOROTHY, JIM, & GEORGE LAWRENCE SAMPAS
FROM STELLA KEROUAC

[December 18, 1966
Hyannis, Massachusetts]

Dear Dorothy, Jim & George Lawrence—

As you can see from Jack's note, we'll be moving to Lowell after the 1st of the year—The house is a split-level with kitchen, living, dining and

Mémère's rooms & half-bath on the 1st floor—3 bedrooms, dressing & bathrooms on the 2nd & in the basement the garage-utility & laundry rooms with a big unfinished play-room for Jack—It's quite expensive & Jack likes it & knows he can afford it. Who am I to object?

We decided on this house because it is in the Highland section of Lowell—271 Sanders Avenue off Pine St. near the school. Jim knows the area, he went to school near-by. Being so close to Mother's house helps a lot too. I think it's wonderful, all this & Jackie, too? What more could I want in life?

I have the advantage on most marriages. I do have Mémère to advise me on Jack's likes & dislikes, that way I don't make silly mistakes that most brides do.

She's coming along fine & we do have fun together. As for her health, she is improving in a sense that she's not allowing the illness to discourage her outlook on life.

I've received a lovely night gown of kelly-green sheer nylon & I look beautiful in it for which I am grateful. We married in such a hurry that I hadn't done any trousseau shopping & it's coming in handy. Of course I assumed it came from you. It's from Garfinkel's in Washington & no card was enclosed. Thanks a lot.

I'm enclosing some money for you to buy little George a gift from me. I haven't had a chance to go shopping around here. So there I am. We do wish that you have a Happy Christmas.

Love,
Jack & Stella

1967

In January and February 1967, after less than two months in Lowell, Kerouac began to feel pent-up in his house with "too many women around." He wrote a series of letters to Sterling Lord about royalties and forthcoming editions of his books, including his as-yet unwritten Vanity of Duluoz *for Coward-McCann. On January 20, he added a line telling Lord that despite his mother's access to an excellent stroke therapy center in Cambridge, she "wants to go back to Florida after* Vanity *money comes in." The following week he asked Barney Rosset to send copies of* Satori in Paris *to the shops in Lowell.*

TO STERLING LORD

Jan. 18, 1967
[Lowell, Massachusetts]

Dear Sterling:

Yes, by all means go ahead with Andre Deutsch on *Satori in Paris*, the 150 pound advance on signature and the other 150 on publication and the royalty details. (I knew he'd come around.) When writing him, try to find out where are the ROAD royalties to 6/30/66 and same royalties (6/30/66) for SUR.

Might also find out where's Viking with ROAD royalties to 10/30/66.

Great time of stress, need money to fence-in magnificent part wooded yard (white birch clumps, oaks,), to build wooden steps down into it from my study where I'll be writing VANITY OF DULUOZ in month of March after Greek Orthodox Church wedding in February.

So, and as you see, I have no time for that Canadian Godbout's plans to "make a movie of me,"[1] after all, in fact, you can tell him if I'm to be the star of his movie I ought to receive star's wages, and if he agrees to that,

---

1. Jacques Godbout and a Montreal television crew came to Lowell to make a film about the French-Canadian community in the city.

tell him to wait till I've handed in the completed manuscript of VANITY OF DULUOZ, i.e., early summer.

Meanwhile, Mémère comfortable in warm gas-heated (wholehouse) bedroom and is on waiting list for best therapy training center in America just about, the Holy Ghost Hospital in Cambridge Mass., 3 or 4 weeks now. They promise to make her waddle around, which is all that will be necessary. Ah Sterling, an old home boy like me, supposedly the wild beatster, he just falls apart when his Ma gets sick and helpless. Stella is a rock: her real name is Stavroula: Cross. I'm shying away from Lowell hilarities to unpack house and set it up just right.

I've now added a Greek dictionary to my chairside shelf.

I sip my Scotch before I shave.

I do, I will write VANITY and after watching dull cautious Bob Newhart all week on Tonight Show I'll be smart and write wild and reckless.

As ever,
Jack

TO STERLING LORD

Jan. 20, 1967
[Lowell, Massachusetts]

Dear Sterling:

Use your professional judgment concerning the two manuscripts of Mr. E. Jarvis ... I'm not really obligated to the man at all, in fact just did him a favor by lending him two of my tapes (of me reading prose) for his classes, and of course, by sending in his mss. to you. Just do what you want. (At first I wanted a lecturing job at Lowell Tech, now I see it would be a mess, that of being recognizable by 2,000 extra people on the streets of Stinktown on the Merrimack.)

Besides, reprint sale of VANITY due soon, right?

Here is list of advances that havent come in (my semi annual report for your convenience and checking, really, if necessary):

(1) Second advance on Mondadori reprint ON THE ROAD, $600.
(2) Second advance on Mondadori (Club Degli) DOCTOR SAX $1,440.
(3) Bompiani advance on SATORI IN PARIS $600.
(4) $400. advances *each* on MAGGIE CASSIDY and VISIONS OF GERARD from Spanish Editorial Zig Zag (Chile).
(5) Advance on TRISTESSA from Sugare Editore, Italy, $320.
(6) Royalties on ON THE ROAD from Rowohlt Verlag to 12/31/66 (!)

Not to mention, Sterl, reprint of SATORI by Grove, and reprint of DHARMA BUMS by NAL.

I know it's hard to keep track of all these small items but add them all together if you will.

Let me know now, who's seen movie version of DOCTOR SAX, if anyone at all. I still see it as a great weird, even "psychedelic" vilm.) (Otto Preminger accent). (Why dont you show it to Joe Levine?)

Asian flu all week had me debilitated, thus late answer here. My God how I hate colds. Mémère wants to go back to Florida after Vanity money comes in.

Let me know if you need any specific short pieces for mags at this crucial time, and of pub. date of Vanity.

As ever
Jack

TO BARNEY ROSSET

Jan. 30, 1967
271 Sanders Ave.
Lowell, Mass.

Dear Barney:

Just a note, many people in Lowell Mass. where I just moved, have been trying to place orders for SATORI IN PARIS at the local big bookstores, notably Prince's and Pollard's etc. and cant get them. Must be about 1,000 different relatives and friends and students.

It worked in Hyannis, I told Dick Seaver and he had the copies sent there and one morning Sargent Shriver was seen buying it (presumably for Jackie too, she reads my books according to Reader's Digest.)

My new address here inscribed; no phone as yet.

All best to you, Barney
Jack Kerouac

In the middle of March, after his forty-fifth birthday and his return from a television interview in Montreal conducted in French, Kerouac settled down to begin writing Vanity of Dulouz *on a roll of Teletype paper, a book he subtitled* An Adventurous Education, 1935–46. *The dedication was a word printed in the Greek alphabet, which he explained "means 'from the Cross' in Greek, and is also my wife's first name—Stavroula." Perhaps remembering how he wrote* On the Road *when he was newly married to Joan Haverty as a "letter to his wife" explaining his adventures, Jack began the opening chapter of* Vanity of Dulouz *speaking to Stella: "All right, wifey, maybe I'm a big pain in the you-know-what but after I've given you a recitation of the troubles I had to go through to make good in America between 1935 and more or less now, 1967, and although I also know everybody in the world's had his own troubles, you'll understand that my particular form of anguish came from being too sensitive to all the lunkheads I had to deal with. . . ."*

After the years of alcoholism Kerouac's physical strength had deteriorated so much that he found it an ordeal to sit for many hours at his typewriter, as was his custom, concentrating on his narrative. He unwound in the neighborhood taverns in Lowell, often making long, drunken, early-morning phone calls to his friends. Carolyn Cassady hurt his feelings by hanging up on him during one of these interminable phone calls. Midway into his new book at the end of March, Kerouac apologized to Holmes for sending a silly postcard, and to Lord for calling him "from a mad screaming drunken bar."

TO STERLING LORD

March 30, 1967
[Lowell, Massachusetts]

Dear Sterling:

Please let me apologize for that telephone call. I'd been up all night writing 18,000 words on *Vanity of Duluoz,* had later booze to deaden the nerve-ends of that world's record performance, and was calling you from a mad screaming drunken bar. It's not funny at all, to me, or to you, because of our sweet association through the years.

Enclosd find signed contracts for Gallimard *Satori in Paris.*

May the road rise with you, may the wind be always at your back, and may your tennis get better and better.

As ever,
Jack

p.s. Now at 40,000 words on *Vanity* roll.

TO JOHN CLELLON HOLMES

March 30, 1967
[Lowell, Massachusetts]

Dear John:

Have reached midway point in new novel, full of pep pills and booze I then sat down and wrote you that silly postcard, or letter, for which I sincerely want to apologize. On re-reading your book,[2] I saw that the "three dots" were explained beforehand by you as for avoiding "journalistic repetitiousness."

Meanwhile, when I called Shirley about 3 weeks ago, to talk to you, but you were in N.Y., it was to congratulate you on DECLARE as proving that

2. Holmes's new book, *Nothing More to Declare,* was a collection of essays, including one on his friend Jack Kerouac.

you've found another *métier* besides novel-writing, at which you're going to prove yourself very successful.

But please, for krissakes, if there's a reprint, my eyes are BLUE not brown.

Let me hear from you if you think I warrant forgiveness.

As an example anyway of the hecticness of my mind these days, the other night my "cousin" kicked me in the balls, I shoved him on his ass, nobody in the Moody Street bar even looked up, afterwards we wanted to be blood brothers and tried to slice little bloods out of our arms, later I took him home to talk to my Mother and he was so mad because my new wife wouldn't let him sleep on the sofa he broke a garage window and howled in the night. It's almost as tho the world were trying (was?) to make itself into a madder & madder movie.

"Something will come of it"?

Shelves of ground dust?

"This is the year of the Dharma, 1967," Gary Snyder just wrote me. I did not answer him. Alors.

Yours,
Jack

In May 1967, Kerouac bought a reconditioned standard Smith-Corona typewriter, his favorite model, to facilitate transcribing Vanity of Dulouz *from the Teletype roll to conventional sheets of typing paper. On April 29 he'd invited Sterling Lord to come to Lowell and admire the heft of the first draft of his manuscript: "If you dont believe it, come here and see the big fat roll 83 feet long, which feels heavy and rich, like $83,000 when you hold it in your hand." Then he typed a letter to John Clellon Holmes, responding in detail to his friend's new collection of essays about the writers in their literary generation,* Nothing More to Declare, *including the lesser-known figures Gershon Legman and Jay Landesman, as well as Allen Ginsberg ("The Consciousness Widener") and Jack Kerouac ("The Great Rememberer"). Before closing, he made a mild complaint about Stella's solicitous care, regarding himself as "a victim of a Greek woman's predilection to bring me trays of food which makes me feel even more useless."*

TO JOHN CLELLON HOLMES

May 22, 1967
[Lowell, Massachusetts]

Dear John:

Voila my new typewriter, a re-conditioned Smith-Corona, standard manual, that I bought last week for $125 in my desperation to make a concrete contractual deadline with publishers, Coward-McCann, from whom I borrowed $4,000 last November to pay for this bigger Lowell house. No kidding around. Yes, my novel is finished, all singlespaced and composed on a 93-foot roll, but the typing of it, the name changes, the errors in typing, the smudges, the carbon, and here I am with 18 days to go to bring the manuscript to its 275 pages or so and I'm only at the 54-page mark after 4 days of drunken cursing at the machine but I'm starting to get used to it now. I cant type like I used to, I'm afraid I cant write like I used to neither.

I re-read your DECLARE and found the chapters on Legman and Landesman masterpieces in their genre. You should have submitted each of those chapters separately to *Playboy* or somebody and made yourself 3 grand: the Legman reads like a Balzac section, the Landesman like a Scott Fitz section. The chapter on me makes me sound like Richard Wagner and is blurred by sentimentality but I appreciate your regard for me. Did I ever tell you that the instinctual "fight" we also have for each other may very well stem from the French and Indian wars? When you Redcoats used to throw iron balls at *mon kanowé?* I think I told you that silly joke, just kidding. I'm going thru one of the worst parts of my life: my mother paralyzed is now at Holy Ghost Hospital in Cambridge for rehabilitation, if it's possible, my old buddy cat Timmy is dead of cancer, my little buddy cat Pitou is being beaten up by the other jealous old cat, I drink more than ever, my hands tremble, I cant type, I am become a victim of a Greek woman's predilection to bring me trays of food which makes me feel even more useless as I used to do everything myself for myself, I go out and get drunk like a bum and have silly drunken chats with the mayor, I'm thrown out of all poolhalls except the Negro poolhall where I'm bound to have me head bashed in someday, I hate the springtime because that's when all the idiots come out of the woodwork and toot toot all over the place, I cant keep a telephone because I was spending $150 a month on it on silly longdistance yaks, I havent sold my house in Hyannis where presumably they want to sell it for taxes so I keep paying that rent as well as this one, I cant get ahead of myself sufficiently to build my usual protective fence for outdoor reading i' the sun ... and yet this Sampas family I'm married into is wonderful and helpful and doing their best. If when Mailer wrote *American Dream* he was "doing a Dickens shot," in my writing of this here *Vanity of Dulouz* I actually did a Mozart shot: Mozart sitting in the corner writing a symphony while his wife is having a baby and the creditors are banging on the door and he's coughing his life away. (No my wife's not having a baby, she's too old, thank God.)

Nevertheless I dont feel too bad.

I've been reading MacLuhan (was surprised to hear you and Jay and Anatole knew him personally) and came to the conclusion that he's the biggest "communist conspirator" of them all, i.e., instead of mis-teaching literacy to children in public new-school methods, he simply dismisses the importance of literacy. How can anybody pay their bills and taxes ten years from now if they cant read or write anymore? I feel that those who advocate "anarchy" are people who know very well how to manage their business affairs in a VERY NON-ANARCHISTIC way and only want everybody else to be stupid. Anyway, end of typing practice.

Amigo

Jack

When Kerouac couldn't meet the June 1 deadline for submitting his manuscript of Vanity of Duluoz, *he sent a flurry of letters to Ellis Amburn and Sterling Lord, his panic over the delay prompted by his desperation about how to pay his mother's medical expenses (Medicare didn't cover all the costs of her medication or home nursing). He was so broke that Stella had considered taking a job in one of the mills in Lowell and gave him "the scare of his life" until he convinced her to stay home and continue to care for Mémère. On June 17, Kerouac sent two copies of the completed manuscript special delivery registered mail to his agent, thanking him for helping with the financial crisis by personally advancing him the money that was coming from Coward-McCann upon delivery of the book.*

TO ELLIS AMBURN

June 1, 1967

[Lowell, Massachusetts]

Dear Ellis:

I am showing you a sample of the pages, and the type, I'm using in the preparation of the editor's copy of VANITY OF DULOUZ. As you see the type is small, the margins narrow, and as you see above, I'm on page 124 at this point (in the middle of the 1942 North Atlantic war), and as you can guess, there must be something like 330 words per page and more in some cases. Multiply 330 by 124 and you get 37,920.... and this is exactly the halfway mark of the editor's (or printer's) copy. The original manuscript is 93 feet long of singlespaced typing on my teletype roll. I think it will end up at about 82,000 words.

Now this is no small job, and you're asking me to have it in by today (see, there went the doublespacer of this old used bum typewriter), it is torture. I dont even have any money to pay for my mother's ambulance ride back from the hospital, or for child support in N.Y., or for June state and federal tax estimate, or for a new real typewriter I wanted to buy, or for the next rent on the 15th, or the fence I wanted to have built for outdoor scribbling and reading, or for anything else that may pop up in this most dreadful part of my life. For I always said a writer should live alone, in a room, with his books and pencils, take walks, go see a show, but when he gets up in the morning there's nothing else for him to do but to concentrate on his art. This is all over with for me: I'm trapped in a situation where I cant even get a completed composition typed up on time for my editor and printers. That I wrote the composition itself is well nigh a miracle. You'll love it I'm positive. If you want, Ellis, come on over to my house, pack the editor's copy what there is of it in your briefcase (by that time, probably 180 pages of a projected 280), look at the original roll to assure yourself and your bosses that the composition IS accomplished, and give me till at least the 10th of June. It will only mean that your faith in me was correct, but too swift for my age and condition today.

Jack

TO STERLING LORD

June 17, 1967
[Lowell, Massachusetts]

Dear Sterling:—

Your loan came just in the nick of time, I was actually worried also about this week's groceries—But I think *Vanity of Duluoz,* arriving at your office Tuesday June 20 via Spec. Deliv. Registered, 2 copies of printer's ms. (just wrapped it up tonight, Saturday), will please you & justify your extremely sweet kindness. Have the original messengered to Ellis Amburn, I'm glad I made his June deadline.

Meanwhile, Sterling, find enclosed the Ted Berrigan—(George Plimpton)—Paris Review promissory note. (The interview was accomplished, with Wm. Saroyan's son Aram in attendance.)[3]

Again, *merci avec toute mon coeur.*

As ever,
Jack

In July 1967, Kerouac was in a calmer mood after his editor at Coward-McCann had responded favorably to Vanity of Duluoz *by calling it Jack's "most generous book." Grateful for his support, Jack gave "extra, special thanks to Ellis Amburn for his empathetic brilliance and expertise" on the dedication page of the novel below Stella's name. Early in the month, Jack dropped a postcard to a fan who asked him about his dreams, and ten days later, he sent his agent a new short prose sketch, "A Dream." Kerouac also passed on to Sterling Lord a letter he'd written to Arabelle Porter with the suggestion that Signet reprint* The Dharma Bums *as a companion volume to follow their new mass-market edition of* On the Road.

3. Kerouac's interview with Ted Berrigan and Aram Saroyan was published as "The Art of Fiction XLI" in *Paris Review,* No. 43 (summer 1968).

TO CALVIN HALL

[Postmarked July 11, 1967
Lowell, Massachusetts]

Dear Hall,

Thanks for letter. No longer write down my dreams on waking, too lazy for now, but used to, between 1952 and 1960, all in Book of Dreams. But do make definite practice of mulling them over in detail on waking, nowadays, and am keeping track of strange recurrences and even have a dream novel in mind. So many locations, mixups. Fact, I like to sleep so I can tune in see what's happening in that big show. People say we sleep a third of our lives away, why I'd rather dream than sit around bleakly with bores in "real" life. My dreams (like yours) are fantastically real movies of what's actually going on anyway. Other dream-record keepers include all the poets I know. "Free association" of dreams are really road signs showing you to another location. It's *placey*. People in dreams just wander said landscapes and room places and city ideas. etc.

Jack Kerouac

Dreams must be recorded as they come, spontaneously.

TO STERLING LORD

July 21, 1967
[Lowell, Massachusetts]

Dear Sterling:

Please read enclosed unsealed letter and ms. to Arabel Porter, and then mail it on to her. Keep note of 500-word prose piece, "A DREAM," which I'm submitting to New American Literature Magazine, at her request.

Your $900 carried me over the hump, and now, friendly neighborhood agent, see if you can get those Italians and Germans and English to fork over to pay my next bills, even tho my future is bright, right?

(Glad you and Ellis liked Vanity of Duluoz. He called it "my most generous book.") Why, s h u c k s .

Any little diddly piece of money will be appreciated.

As ever,
Jack

p.s. Mémêre in good mood— Regards Cindy— Stella steady—goodhearted.

[July 1967
Lowell, Massachusetts]

Miss Arabelle Porter
NEW AMERICAN LIBRARY
501 Madison Ave.
New York, N.Y.
Dear Arabelle (Miss Porter):—

If you enjoyed my judgment in asking you, in 1965, to reprint ON THE ROAD, perhaps this inside information would interest you: The "hippies" and the "Now" Generation and the "Love" Generation are all writing me letters that 1967 is to be the "Year of the Dharma."

In that connection, it would be a good idea to reprint "Dharma Bums" this Summer. They can spend 75 cents on three beers, or on a book that will stay in their pocket for a year, and tell them what the "Dharma" is about.

Just a suggestion, as before in 1965, and I think it's a good idea. It has in it all the elements of Hinayana, Mahayana, and Zen thinking in Buddhism, plus tips about rucksack traveling, which they're all trying to do, is readable, brief, etc. and concerns the new interest that the so-called "psychedelic" generation has gleaned from experiences with the insights of Mandala, Mosaic Mesh and Mystic Disaffiliation, as gathered in "visions" gleaned.

I'm sure this is the year of the Dharma. No need, as before, to answer me. But think about it.

Your sincerely,
Jack Kerouac

In November 1967, I sent Kerouac a new English paperback edition of Visions of Gerard *(Mayflower/Dell) I had found in a London bookshop. The cover artwork had originally been used early in 1966 on a U.S. Dell paperback of* Incredible Tales *by Saki. The illustration featured such a bizarre drawing that Jack commented on it, asking me to quote him in future editions of his bibliography, which had just been published. Kerouac was satisfied with my work and was kind enough to annotate the errors in a copy of the bibliography I sent to him, but he disliked the photograph of him I'd used on the cover because the one he wanted had not been available. He was also clearly uninterested in carrying on an exchange of letters with me about his literary method. When I asked him to expand upon a comparison he had made of himself and his work to Marcel Proust, he made short work of his reply.*

Nov. 11, 1967
[Lowell, Masschusetts]

Dear Ann:

Thanks for sending me GERARD English softcover. "The cover depicts a green skinned devil with red eyes and pointed ears and wolfish teeth, the book within is about a little Catholic saint who dies in pain at age of nine, wa?—the art director musta been looking in the mirror at himself." (Quote me).

On page 28 of the biblio., re BIG SUR, you say "JK deleted last line on page 133," naturally, because that whole line is there misplaced by the printer, it really belongs on page 132 on line 5. Please note that down. Subsequent editions all ran that awful error which makes me look like a surrealist. Giroux and myself got confused later and forgot to notify Bantam books reprinting same. It, the error, spoiled one of the SUR's best sentences. (As you see, the misplaced line, apparently a slug of lead, *does* appear in the right place on p. 132, l. 5.)

I forgot to make corrections in your copy of biblio. in the *index*. You can handle that yourself later.

My Proustness? That's just the idea of a whole lifetime, in sections coming as separate books, in personal firstperson depiction and analysis. (No analysis in me? What about Subterraneans, an analysis of the affair with Mardou more than a narration, after all.) What you call my "thoughts" and what you call Proust's "analyses," tho not of same consistency, are of same cornmeal, after all.

And so you see, I'm not going to spend the rest of my life answering questions and "defending" my moves. I just turned down a lecture for that very reason. I'm going to do that most unforgivable faux pas that a contemporary writer can dare to do, simply write and publish. "O my goodness, he doesn't do anything but write! He's not involved, he's not in-depth, he's not *committed*, he doesn't carry placards, he doesn't lecture, he's afraid, he hides, he doesn't do anything but WRITE ... you call that a WRITER?"

Lady Godiva
Jack

When the Phoenix Bookshop told me that copies of the Kerouac bibliography were selling well, we began to plan for a reprint. Jack had objected so strenuously to the cover photograph I took of him in Hyannis (he said it made his face look puffy) that I offered to substitute a drawing of him by Robert LaVigne, and told Jack that if he didn't like that idea, he should send something he liked better. My husband also wrote him, telling him in blunt words not to be so hard on me about the photograph.

[December 1967
Lowell, Massachusetts]

Dear Sam:

Use this picture on the cover of the next (third?) edition of the Kerouac Bibliography. Picture was taken in Lowell Mass. in Nov. 1967, by James Coyne in conjunction with TIME magazine. The cat's name is Tuffy, I mean the kitty-kat in my arms. There are new additions to my biblio that have come in (and some mistakes in the original) but use this picture. I respect you for writing a swearing-Marine prose. I have the corrections of the orig. biblio here.

Jack Kerouac

In December 1967, Kerouac dropped a note to Nick Sampus, thanking him for a loan, and he also wrote John Clellon Holmes and Sterling Lord to catch them up on what he was doing. Aware that he was "running out of long picaresque adventures" after completing Vanity of Dulouz, *he confided to Holmes that he had returned to Thomas Wolfe's novels trying to find a different way to develop a narrative. Jack was also looking forward to seeing the* Paris Review *interview that he had done with Aram Saroyan and Ted Berrigan, and he was corresponding with editors at* The Atlantic Monthly *about new work. On the last day of the year, after shoveling piles of snow out of his driveway, he told his agent not to be surprised if he moved back to Florida "on Mémêre's orders" in 1968.*

12-13-67
[Lowell, Massachusetts]

Dear Nick

I borrowed a ten on one occasion, and then two other tens on another of my visits to your emporium of relaxing booze, fun, frolic etc.—Merry Christmas

Jack Kerouac
JACQUES THE COCK

Dec. 13, 1967
[Lowell, Massachusetts]

Dear John

I had no idea where to write you, in reply of them thar traveling letters of yours, so I figure you'll find this when you get home. And so, when you have time, fill me in on the rest of the trip.

The more I read your letters the more I realize Thomas Wolfe influenced you more than he done me. If you don't believe this, glance at him again. I'm going into Wolfe again now in search of the secret of writing at great length about one short episode: since I'm running out of long picaresque adventures, naturally. Remember that long, long episode about Mr. Jack and the party in Esther Jack's Park Avenue apartment where Piggy Logan enthralled everyone with his puppet show and then a fire broke out? In which fire, the two elevator men, previously dealt with in complete detail, perished? (or one of them did.) I'll be taking an episode out of my life and giving it the full workout next: a la *Tristessa* first part, say.

Meanwhile has there been a complete abandonment of the idea of a Kerouac Reader between you and Amburn's offices? If so, okay, but in casting around for excerpts for magazines lately, I found lots of forgotten prose. What the hell, Mailer's *Cannibals and Christians* is nothing but a Mailer Reader. We could actually put together a "Reader" of absolutely-unpublished-previously stuff . . . and with haikus, outcries, make a "Mosaic" look.

And meanwhile I want to see the *Perfect Fools* book. What, am I the Fire Chief? Do you actually compare Allen as he is at present, to myself as is at present? Per se? Per Se Williams critic and Author?

Winter is upon us, as John Holmes would say, and I can see the hill near Walden Pond from my bedroom window, and there's a lil ole brown wood in my yard, but I drink scotch and soda before the roaring fireplace and watch TV. (Incidentally, this is my new Smith Corona super super 1967 typewriter and it's no better'n shit.) (Shoulda got a Royal.)

Wait till you see Vanity of Duluoz, phew. The part about the football games reads like a good war manual. The part about Lou reads like Dosty. The parts about the sea go real salty and woulda made Melville proud of me. Already Virginia Kirkus has called the whole thing a "faint echo" of something of the "beat style" and made me wish she woulda been with me on the S.S. Dorchester in the submarine waves where she couldnae claimed female inferiority as a right to rap wartime seamen, bloody footballers, jail-birds and the blood of the poet entire. (Try to come and see me with Shirley, you have time, and car. If you want to, I'll send detailed street instructions.)

Jack

WELCOME HOME TO AMERICA

Dec. 31, 1967
[Lowell, Massachusetts]

Dear Sterling:

Will call Dick Schaap for said telephone interview, trust your judgment.

Enclosed find invoice from Coward-McCann for 16 *Vanities* I didn't order and which are being mailed to your office. Are these for yr. own use for publicity reasons, advance readings, or is there a mistake you think? I have to pay this?

Mike Curtis of *Atlantic Monthly:* if he doesn't want the 2 sports stories I sent, send him excerpts from the football sections of *Vanity* (of high school and prep school football) that *Sports Illustrated* didn't even use.

George Plimpton and I involved in warm correspondence and taking care of that package. He will probably be asking you finally for an excerpt from *Vanity* for *Paris Review.*

I'm trim from shoveling 15-inch snow piles, driveway and all, but if *Vanity* sells as we expect don't be surprised if I move back to Florida (on Mémère's orders), later in '68.

Meanwhile, Bonne Nouvelle Année mon cher ami.

As ever
Jack

1968

In January 1968, Kerouac wrote a postcard thanking Stanley Twardowicz for a Christmas gift. He also told Sterling Lord about the sports article he had written for The Atlantic Monthly *while gracefully acknowledging their continuing friendship in the new year.*

TO STANLEY TWARDOWICZ

[Postmarked January 6, 1968
Lowell, Massachusetts]

Dear Stanley:

When your fruitcake arrived as usual, as wd. be expected from a fruitcake, Stella said to me: "Now who is it that remembers you at each Christmastime?" I said: "Gordo?" She said: "Guess again?" I said, "Lucien? Allen? Peter? John the Baptist?" "Awright," I shouted, "Ho?" She said "Stanley." Thank you, will eat, it, and love to "Blondie" too.

Jack

The Bishop orders you not to beat it too much. (Beat the Bishop)

TO STERLING LORD

1-15-68
[Lowell, Massachusetts]

Dear Sterling,

Atlantic Monthly just sent in proofs for IN THE RING—thanx for your New Year's Greeting, your new year is my new year as ever—

Jack

On February 29, 1968, Kerouac wrote his agent to ask about getting paid for the interview he had done the previous summer for Paris Review. *In a postscript he mentioned that he had heard of the death of Jan Kerouac's baby, born prematurely. Jack had met Jan, whom he referred to as his "daughter" (in quotation marks), for the second and last time when she came to his house in Lowell in November 1967 on her way to Mexico with her boyfriend John Lash. Jan got Kerouac's address after randomly calling Doris Kerouac in the Lowell telephone book. She described the brief visit with her father in her memoir,* Baby Driver. *When Stella opened the front door, Gabrielle was in a wheelchair and Jack sat in a rocking chair "about one foot from the TV," watching* The Beverly Hillbillies. *He was "upending a fifth of whiskey and wearing a blue plaid shirt." After the television was turned off, Jan asked to compare hands with him because "My mother says we have the same hands." She found "they were the same, all right, only his were bigger." Apparently confused by the two unexpected young visitors, Gabrielle became upset, and before Stella asked them to leave the house, John Lash explained they were going to Mexico. In Jan's memoir she wrote that to her surprise, Kerouac told her, "Yeah, you go to Mexico an' write a book. You can use my name."*

TO STERLING LORD

Feb. 29, 1968
[Lowell, Massachusetts]

Dear Sterling:

The money came in the nick of time. Thank you so much.

I re-studied my Club Degli Italian contracts for DOCTOR SAX and see what you mean about my over-estimate: the big IF of further printings and price-raisings.

I just mailed in my answers to George Plimpton for the *Paris Review* interview. There's 5,000 words of prose in there, a lot of work, and I wish you'd give him a ring and see about getting money above and beyond the $200 already promissoried for the tape interview of last summer with Ted Berrigan at my house. (FOOTNOTE*)

Let me know what develops with Jack Geoghegan selling VANITY reprint, and with the movie Bob Dylan plan for ROAD.

Was fun to talk to Cindy, and glad to hear Rebecca is fine.

As ever,
Jack

FOOTNOTE*:- Geo. Plimpton, or
Peter Ardery
THE PARIS REVIEW INC.
45-39 171 Place
Flushing, N.Y.
Phone: LE 9-7085

(p.s. My "daughter" had a premature baby that died, in Mexico last month, and my lawyer says that's that: she, the (Janet) "daughter," is now emancipated from my responsibility, inasmuch as her boyfriend is with her. She's now 16. Beware of their visits: the boyfriend is John Lash, a writer-hippie [. . .]. Joan Aly is in Brooklyn. The young couple are now in California. Just to let you know.)

In the spring of 1968, Kerouac put his house in Lowell up for sale so he, Gabrielle, and Stella could move back to Florida, where his mother wanted to live in order to escape the harsh Massachusetts winters. To finance another house in St. Petersburg for his family, Jack offered Ellis Amburn at Coward-McCann three manuscripts, comprising the complete version of Visions of Cody *and two new books as yet unwritten. In his letters to Amburn and Lord, Kerouac described the work he had in mind.*

TO ELLIS AMBURN

April 11, 1968
[Lowell, Massachusetts]
Not mailed

Dear Ellis Amburn:

Maybe my "outline" was too brief, and thin of thought. It could be that I could expand "B– S——" into another picaresque.[1] Whatever, if you can't (cant) extend me a loan on this new projected novel which fits into the shelf of the Duluoz Legend, then maybe I can go out and stitch horseshoes and put you in a Tin Lizzy.

(1) Duluoz, having just written vast notes but in despair staring at the dying ceiling with the crack in't, wonders if he shouldn't take a train to New York and see what's happened to his latest publication, ROAD. He squats in the Orlando Florida sun thinking: "Well I'll just go up there and be lionized as usual." (Forget the part about the Negro with the "hidden pussy.") When my train arrives in Pennsylvania Station I go foraging thru the waste cans to see if there's been a review of "Road" in the N. Y. Times. But seeing that the copy that's in there is covered with a great glob of man spit (or woman spit) I leave the paper there and just trudge up to Madison Avenue. But, nathless my idle feeling of loss, when I walk into the office I am surprised by whoops and outcries saying "Your book is a success."

But all I'm thinking about is how to eat my mandatory and laudatory lunch in peace (without talking) in Schraafts, without a necktie. But now they launch me on publicity campaigns all based on Malcolm Cowley's idea

1. Kerouac called his projected novel *Beat Spotlight.*

of what it is, he says, to be "beat." i.e. poor. The food is tasteless because everyone is purring and pouring his own goblet of Uncle in me ear. (Nuncle.)

Then I shoot right ahead to my lecture at Brandeis University (Hunter College) where I'm roundly booed by a partisan leftwing audience, altho I declined to lecture, but they insisted practically in tears.

Then a few other thematic items, all in-depth, and to the B S television section about Hollywood, and back again, and more.

Under the circumstances of my writing style, it can be done, but if you don't want me to disclose these scandalous wretchifications of my faith to you, in prose, please say so, leave me alone, and I'll get another publisher. Because the time has come (for me) to tell the whole truth as I see it, and nothing but the truth, in my own tongue, which is English.

I know this is just another skimpy outline but trust in me.

And be mindful, that if I were a useless prose writer, or poet in general, I should not have pulled the rug out from everybody; and mindful too, be ye, that envy rules, but fate judges.

With these delectatious words I leave you, to answer me, or not, as wists your wont, or flicks your flack, or whatever.

Ti Jean

TO STERLING LORD

April 20, 1968
[Lowell, Massachusetts]

Dear Sterling:

Here's the ticket, so that you'll have it in writing. I paid $31,000 for this house, in which, as promised, and contracted for, I wrote VANITY OF DU-LUOZ and delivered said sweet manuscript and galleys all straight, with aid of editor Ellis Amburn of Coward-McCann. I see no reason why said novel should be rejected by softcover reprint people because in the book my father called Roosevelt's wife "ugly," and other items. We all have our own forms of ugliness but the ugliest is the formal ugliness, as for instance, the ugliness she displayed in 1944 when she wanted to plant a curfew on the streets of America after dark.

But, as I told you on phone, the people around Lowell here, cheapskates all, as befits Stinktown on the Merrimack, want to buy my house for $25,000, thus depositing me on the sidewalk with paralyzed mother, new wife, and 2 cats, $6,000 short of Equity. The equity I put into this house is close to $10,000, at the drop of an 'onest 'at. The hequity, that is. I'm sticking to my original price. Soon the house will be overrun with snoopers and people who love to look into my bedroom and see me asleep in mid-afternoon naps and say "There he is." (There 'e is.)

So that, by offering Coward-McCann three manuscripts: (1) Complete Visions of Cody, (2) Beat Spotlight (keep that title under your hat), and (3) The Second Coming, at $5,000 apiece, I will be able to afford, say, like a 3 grand loss on sale of this house and get on down to my Florida domicile, already freshly painted by builder and owner Tex O. V. Burrow, and waiting, with $1,000 already paid against the entire $9,000 arrangement (to make said $28,000 house available at $120 a month mortgage payments as against $231 per month mortgage payments here), and where I can write those two books, B.S. and T.S.C., and fulfill my contract like some old composer like Haydn fulfilling his commissions from the Philadelphia-Vienna Company of Burghers in Drang.

The Second Coming is simply a fantasy about the Second Coming: it, or He, comes, as a dark cloud in the sky, "all the windows are darkened," "all the daughters of music are brought low," the earth begins to shake: holes open up in the ground: as the earth shakes more and more and things fall down more and more, great groups of people begin to gather in earnest prayer. People forage, thru supermarkets, carry burdens on their backs, jump crags, cracks, ravines: the earth suddenly begins to shake everybody into the realization of the End and all are AS ONE in prayer. (Gov. John Volpe weeping with de Salvo hand in hand at a wall.) But suddenly the earth stops shaking and everybody slowly begins rebuilding. They rebuild exactly what they had before. Before you know it, everything is the same again, the Governor is the Governor, in his mansion, and the prisoner is the prisoner, in his cell. When all that has been established, and bridges, and fills, made over cracks and abysses, and the status quo of cupiditous and vellelitous conformation to concupiscent soul trash resumed, and blue ribbons are cut, and all's well with the world, Ah, then, the earth starts to shake again,

HARDER...

AS with the prophecy. And at which time Sterling Lord and Jack [incomplete]

After Vanity of Duluoz *was published in February 1968 to tepid reviews, Coward-McCann showed no interest in Kerouac's next book projects, especially after* The New York Times *reviewer said that "A publisher with any real faith in the glow that occasionally generates from a page of any of Kerouac's slapdash novels would not have published this book as it stands." (As a matter of principle, Kerouac had refused to let his editor change anything in the novel.) To raise money to cover his mother's medical expenses, Jack suggested that Sterling Lord sell his letters from Ginsberg, Corso, and Burroughs, filed away carefully in his bedroom archive in Lowell. In June and July 1968, Kerouac corresponded with Ginsberg and Andreas Brown at the Gotham Book Mart about the sale. Ultimately Kerouac's letters from Ginsberg and Cassady were sold to the Harry*

Ransom Humanities Research Center of the University of Texas at Austin, and his letters from Burroughs went to the Rare Book and Manuscript division of the Butler Library at Columbia University.

TO ALLEN GINSBERG

June 4, 1968
271 Sanders Ave.
Lowell, Mass.

Allen:

Coupla urgencies having to do with my personal and family distress—
(1) This Andreas Brown wrote from Gotham Book Mart, saying he saw you, but he says: "Should you wish to dispose of your entire archive (which is what I recommend, for financial reasons), you may stipulate any condition you wish. Universities ..." are more efficient, etc. but "Selling your complete archive en bloc ... has great appeal." For krissakes I have some 2,000,000 words of my own writing, and some one million in wild happy and sad letters, all carefully culled and filed for literary interest, the others were thrown out. All I wanted to do was sell him YOUR letters, and if he wants, Gregory's, Bill's, etc. My complete archive en bloc I'm going to hang on to for my oldage poverty. Also I would want to make SURE he'd Xerox your letters and let me keep at least that. So what do I do? (about selling him the Ginsberg-to-Kerouac correspondence). Let me know when chance. The "complete archive" shot is a laugh, after all, I may be mashuganish but I'm still not yet a schmuck.

(2) And now Coward-McCann has rejected the ms. of COMPLETE VISIONS OF CODY and Sterling and I are sending it to Grove. Can you put in a word there and tell them what it is? Or they know already? Anyway, I suddenly read it the other day (Laughlin's Excerpts) and saw it was completely modern multimedia pop rock peote pot prose (as you know). So why not? It's time. I would like to get back with Grove, secretly, because of literary honesty they have, and Sterling says they're no longer poor, in fact better off than some Madison Avenue chicken firms.

So those 2 things, when you have time. I will be next in *Paris Review* Writers in Progress, interviewed by [Ted] Berrigan and Aram [Saroyan]. I was drunk and yelled against you. So be it. You're lucky Joe McCarthy's family didn't sue you for trompling around the family grave.

Henri Cru is supporting Janet in Frisco, last I hear. Set her up in a menage and sails around the world proudly. Good, because I can't even support this menage any more, 's'why I need money from above sources and for krissakes can you beat this? Nobody wants to do the reprint of VANITY OF DULUOZ. Why? is there a conspiracy against K?

Like the girl in Cheetah magazine says I was on an "anti Zion ride" but likes the book anyway (she'd heard stories, she said, about me being on

such a ride.) VANITY as you know shd. be reprinted. I was thinking of Ferlinghetti for some publishing ventures but he is in can? Well, I was in can
month ago for carrying a bottle of beer (open) in street, in filthy cell in
which I caught strep throat, and there was nothing in the papers about it.
So you and your pals go to jail for disrupting society, and I go to jail for
not disrupting anything at all, so nu, and I get no publicity at all and no
money for the work I've done and want to do. Tell it to Neal and the
Marines. You mentioned creeping statism on phone the other night; you're
only encouraging the bastards with your impossible demands. I never was
arrested in my life till the civil rights movement made the cops jittery and
paranoid of everybody they see on the sidewalk.

How's Pete? (Hunkey? Lucien? Bill? Gregory? etc.?)

Jack

TO ANDREAS BROWN

July 14, 1968
[Lowell, Massachusetts]

Dear Mr. Brown:

I want to go ahead with the disposition of the Ginsberg-to-myself letters but the material is so fabulous and vast, and so well preserved in my
steel file cabinet with moth balls and all since 1962, and number of years
of correspondence involved: from 1944 to now.... I just don't know where
to begin.

And the number of pages? 500.

Number of words? .... some 300,000 words! (app.)

So I would like you to answer these questions:

(1) Should I expect this sale to be in the thousands, since G. said it would
be, and told me not to get in hock with my publishers from whom I've
been trying to get an advance of 5 thou on a newly published book?

(2) And your commission?

(3) Have you contacted my agent Sterling Lord, 75 E. 55 St., NYC 22?

(4) Since I'll be using info. from this vast tome of events, in a future book
about Allen, then I'll be needing a xerox copy, but who is going to pay for
the Xeroxing of 300,000 words and what mailman will be able to carry that
pile?

(5) In case you think I'm being "commercial," I want you to know that this
is the worst financial moment of my life: my mother is paralyzed, I had to
get a wife to help, my books are being turned down by publishers ("Visions of Cody") (the complete one), so I have no money but small savings
left, no prospects, magazines only ask me for Letters-to-the-Editor free
prose, or "my own obituary," my health worsened by ten years in the last
single year, I have to move to a cheaper house in Florida (St. Pete) or get

thrown out on the street here, I'm in debt to a local bank for $1,300, the right is accusing me of "corrupting youth" and the left is accusing me of "do-nothingism," people keep flooding my desk with poems and books and requests so that I can't find my own papers underneath, and in spite of the fact I wrote 17 books some of which are published in 17 languages in 43 different countries I can't pay my rent without hurting on the kitchen. Money requests keep flooding in nevertheless, from poets stranded in Europe, ex-wives, I see no prospect on the horizon but winding up in the madhouse or dead (as I'm sure a lot of my literary rivals would love to see.) (6) I know this is too personal, and silly to burden you like this, since we've never met, but I'm no more money-mad than that Flower Child "daughter" of mine who's trying to get me in court for non support because, as she says, she's "retired" and she won't marry her boyfriend who also is "retired."

I'm really going nuts, and I know it's a pain for you to hear such complaining, but at least you'll know why I'm doing this. Anyway Allen wants his letters to me in a good librarial safety spot; they'll surely be published some day; and there's the reading public, to whom I owe what I got myself to survive on.

So write me a businesslike letter outlining step-by-step how we proceed, even as to how I should mail the pile: registered, whatever.

And as for my own writings, they come to over 2½ million words (from 17 on, the unpublished usual junk some of it good), I'd rather keep them, in fact have to keep them, for consultation. (I've always kept neat files.)

I know this is a confused letter, I feel confused about this, the letters from Allen are so valuable to me, so rich, dammit, it scares me to even mail them. But he says to go ahead and trust your competence implicitly.

You'll be amazed when you see them. They're not just abstract blah blash like Durrell-Miller, they're detailed tales of what he did, with poems everywhere, poems he's forgotten, and great spontaneous prose (better than his poetry, by the way, as I said somewhere.)

"Handle with Care" is all I'm worried about. And so you see why I handled them with care myself. This hurts, but let's go ahead. (I guess, like a miserly Canuck, I'm really worried about not getting my Xerox, but you and he both said that would be taken care of.)

And don't forget to consult my agent, through whom I do all business, at his stern behest.

Best regards,
Jack Kerouac

In late July 1968, Kerouac wrote a postcard to composer David Amram, who had sent him phonograph records and a musical setting of a section of Lonesome Traveler. *A decade earlier Amram had appeared in* Pull My Daisy. *At that time*

Jack had also been the master of ceremonies for a program of jazz and poetry featuring Amram, Howard Hart, and Philip Lamantia at the Circle in the Square nightclub in Greenwich Village.

TO DAVID AMRAM

[Late July 1968
Lowell, Massachusetts]

Dear Dave—

You must have a secretary to be able to turn out so much work and at the same time mail records to people—I just send you this little note to thank you for the beautiful records—I have no picollo but (picolo) I had the nextdoor Lutheran minister play me the Lonesome Traveler piece and of course I found it beautiful—I have just signed your Peters contract [permission to quote the text] and it will be in to you soon, a week or so—That's the main thing—I wish you success with this land of ours oratorio—I'll buy a picolo next year and play the other records too—So, vell, kidsel, see you N.Y. sometime next year.... Excuse postcard but I have so much mail and no time to buy envelopes ugh, fame is a drag to anybody who wants new work done.... as you know already ... stick to guns ... I'll do same

Jack (Kerouac)

In August and September 1968, Kerouac accepted an invitation to be a guest on William Buckley's interview program Firing Line. *It was to be his last appearance on television. During the program he slouched in a chair with a cup of whisky at his side and said that the war in Vietnam was being fought so that both North and South Vietnamese could have access to American jeeps. He also explained, "In the papers they called it 'Beat mutiny' and 'Beat insurrection,' words I never used. Being a Catholic, I believe in order, tenderness, and piety."*

Kerouac continued to write his agent about another book he was planning to write for the Duluoz Legend, to be called Beat Spotlight. *Jack envisioned it as an autobiographical novel organized around his "public appearances on TV," dramatizing what had happened to him after the publication of* On the Road *and showing how the media had falsely represented him. Stella also wrote a letter to Sterling Lord about their financial insecurity.*

TO STERLING LORD

Aug. 24 '68
[Lowell, Massachusetts]

Dear Sterling:—(As Ever):—

Have accepted Bill Buckley programming, On Tues. Sept. 3rd at WOR (where we done June Havoc)—at 7:30 PM—A taping—1481 B'way—

Want to see you there, or at your office, when you avail.

Enclosed find Andreas Brown (GOTHAM BOOKMART) communicados re Ginsberg's letters.

Notice "Top price." [$6,000]

My purpose in going on Buckley program, aside from patriotic reasons, is to publicize the need to reprint VANITY, print COMPLETE VISIONS OF CODY, and advance on BEAT SPOTLIGHT. SEE ABOUT EXPENSE MONIES for New York Trip.

Jack

TO STERLING LORD FROM STELLA KEROUAC

271 Sanders ave.
Lowell, Mass, 01851.
August 27, 1968.

Dear Mr. Lord,

Jack has not been feeling too well lately and is trying to prepare himself for the forthcoming trip to New York, to appear on the Wm. F. Buckley T.V. program.

Therefore, I am taking matters into my own hands and trying to gather whatever available information as to our future financial status.

You must have realized that he has promised Mémêre to take her back to Florida before winter is upon us. The winters here in Lowell are severe and may be injurious to her health.

Jack has been hoping that some arrangements can be made as to a future book and is looking forward to serious concentration.

We also sent you the Allen Ginsberg letters so that you could make arrangements for their sale, to help with the move south. In the meantime we did expect xerox copies of them for future references to be sent us.

Mr. Andreas Brown does claim he has a prospective client and wants to "go on with it".

Jack, of course, wants only you to handle all of his business transactions but winter is coming and Mémêre is getting impatient.

In the meantime we received a letter from Viking Press through your offices dated March 12, 1968, asking Jack to reduce his future royalty expectations from 15% to 10% on special editions of "On the Road".

Surely, you do realize that "On the Road" is his most valuable property, so far, and the publishers would be sure of a return on whatever monies they would invest in its publications.

I do feel that I must bring to your attention the fact that Jack has not received any royalties from any of the American publishers to speak of. All royalties received this past year have been from foreign countries. Apparently, the American people seem to ignore Jack's works and we are wondering if this is really so.

We do realize that you are an extremely busy man and you have many pressing obligations to fulfill, but Jack would feel a great deal better if occasionally you would drop him a friendly note. Being away from New York, he has lost all contact with the book world and you are his only source of what's going on.

Incidently, please forgive whatever offensive remarks were made in the Boston Globe interview. Words were put in both our mouths. Shall I admit to you that I do not know what mescaline is?

Mr. Lord, it is not easy for Jack to see Mémêre bundled up in bed motionless most of the time with neither one of us daring to leave the house with Mémêre in the care of strangers. It is wearing on him.

Please forgive my presumption in writing to you directly. This waiting for something to give, is nervewracking.

I plead for your understanding.

I remain,
Sincerely yours,
Stella Kerouac

[Holograph postscript]
Jack Kerouac
   Your friendly
   neighborhood
   basketball star
(See you Sept. 3 at 4 PM)

TO STERLING LORD

Sept. 27, 1968
[Lowell, Massachusetts]

Dear Sterling,

Here's what I'll do with SPOTLIGHT. I'll use my public appearances on TV and lectures as rungs in the ladder of the narrative. In betwixt, I can throw in more private matters, such as my two physical beatings in bars ("Spotlight" indeed), and other things, but the main tale will be: I'll start with when I'm living on that backporch in Florida with my Maw in 1957, broke, arguing about what to buy for dessert because we have no money for meat, and suddenly *Time* magazine comes in to interview me about the upcoming publication of ON THE ROAD. At which time, also, I have the mumps, caught in the Mexico City earthquake of August 1957. Then I saunter to the railroad station and sit in the warm dry air waiting for my train to New York, figuring I'll go up there and see how this new book makes out. When I arrive in New York City I look in a disposal trash basket in Penn Station to see what my review was like in the *New York Times*. But since someone's spit on the only *Times* in the can, I don't touch it, and only walk up to Viking Press to see what's happened. When I get there they tell me I'm an overnight success. And I'm hungry for food. So we go to Schraaft's across the street and I order my lunch but everybody's yakking so much around me I begin to realize right then and there that "success" is when you can't enjoy your food any more in peace. Ow. Then we go into my first public appearance with John Wingate on his Channel 7 show when the cameraman actually dollied up to my glass of water and spilled it and so Wingate, who was in cahoots with this trick, said "Whatsamatter, drunk?" Then I went on Wingate again later, then on Ben Hecht show, then the lecture at Brandeis University where I was roundly booed for arguing about peace with the editor of the *New York Post*, Wechsler, he saying America was complicated enough with having to have poetry and I telling him he was a son of a you know what, and then details in between. Leading up to the premiere of my movie PULL MY DAISY at the San Francisco film festival, where a lot of other things happened, like a funny meeting with David Niven and his asking me which girl at the party I really thought he should take home, knowing my expertise in such matters (as tho I didn't know his), and then the moving about the country in cars and waiting in trucks, and the beatings I told you about. And then a trip to Montreal, Canada to appear (in French language program 1967), and finally this last appearance on the Wm. F. Buckley, Jr. program (ABC) where Buckley kept kicking my shoes and telling me to shush so the other guests could demonstrate how dull they were, or stupid, and, as I say, all interspersed with the valid details of tale-telling; actually, Sterling, an enormous story and should be okay as local history.

It is the latest chronological part of the Duluoz Legend, and of course I won't go into 1960 BIG SUR experiences or 1965 SATORI IN PARIS, but just mention them in passing. It will complete the "Legend" up to now and may very well be my most exhausting writing experience, since the story is so fraught with eminent peril, men, women, dogs, cats, cornpones, agents, publishers, poolsharks, TV directors calling me a "drunken moron," celebrities, boozers, bookies, phew, wait till you see it.[2] But I can't do it without

2. In 1957, after *On the Road*, made the *New York Times* best-seller list, reporter Jerry Tallmer of *The Village Voice* quoted Kerouac drinking in a West Village bar and talking "about the publicity, the success, the rave reviews, the terrifying half-hour with Wingate on 'Nightbeat'…" Kerouac said: "Some day, if I can write it. If anyone could write it. They have a little girl there, sitting by you, while you wait to go on the TV.… Just to keep you happy. One of those cute little uptown chicks. If I could write it …" (*The Village Voice Reader*, 1962, pages 32–34).

some money to live on, so show this letter to the prospective publisher and let's get at it.

Jack

P.S. I'm using the title SPOTLIGHT because that was the name of my father's old theatrical newspaper in Lowell, when he used to play cards with W. C. Fields, George Arliss and George Burns backstage at the old B. F. Keith's theater (of the Keith's circuit) in Lowell. The title will honor the memory of his own work. I really don't think we have to say BEAT SPOTLIGHT, as I originally proposed, unless the publishers think different, just as long as spotlight is in there. And of course no changes in the prose.

Enclosed find my signature to the Marshall A. Best Viking contract. Your advice suits me, and has suited me, and my wife: *Elle travaille en racuillon,* i.e. backwards, backwards toward the angle and not onward with our friendly neighborhood agent. (I think she oughta mind her own business and wash her dishes.) Give my regards to Cindy and Rebecca.

JK

By mid-November 1968, Jack, Stella, and Mémère were installed in a concrete-block house at 5169 Tenth Avenue North in St. Petersburg, next door to where Kerouac and his mother had lived before moving to Hyannis. They came back to Florida with the help of Joe Chaput and two other friends, who drove them non-stop from Lowell to St. Petersburg in a station wagon. Mémère, Stella, and the cats lay on blankets, pillows, and mattresses in the back of the car while Jack sat beside the driver, playing the harmonica, nursing bottles of Johnny Walker Red Label Scotch and emptying cans from six-packs of malt liquor. After he and his family had settled into their new home, Kerouac wrote to thank his Lowell friend, mentioning that Stella was worried about her mother, whom she had left behind in Lowell.

TO JOE CHAPUT

Nov. 15 '68
[St. Petersburg, Florida]

Dear Joe

Well, just turned my typewriter ribbon over, in spite of the objections built into my Smith-Corona typewriter by the typewriter ribbon people who are in cahoots with the typewriter people, and old printers never quit. The only time an old printer should quit is when he gets itchy eyes and he should go to the bathroom and wash them (of lead). Then he should come back and show the boss printer how to print.

459

I remember when my father was dead in his chair suddenly, I saw all that ink on his fingers.

Anyway, Joe, we made our move real good and you ought to see how nice this house and neighborhood is coming out. It's sleepy time down South, everybody ben sleepin, includin me, since you and Red and Dumphy left.[3] My shinbone I cracked I had to pack ice on it and do extra headstands and I'm okay now. But the doctor, whom we visited remember in that office full of waiting people, he still hasn't shown up: emergency or no. So Mémère is still waiting for her wheelchair and I'm going to get a new doctor somehow and put that latter doctor in the hospital himself? The Mafia, doctors have become. (The nine grand I put on this house here, was spent already on doctors by Tex's wife!)

I hope you found your boy, and that your mother is feeling okay under any circumstances, and as for you, you're my A number One man. I hope you can come down here this winter when you have your next vacation, and relax with a few Scotcheseshes and beer and a swim in the Gulf of Mexico, and grilled outdoor steaks black on the outside and red in the middle.

I've got my office-bedroom all fixed up and tho it's small it's cozy and I'se satisfied. I can step out this very second into the moonlight piney tree night where my cats are already making girls. I got some good money from Italy today and it will pay for my fence and a month's rent. My fence will be five foot tall and way in the back under the banyan tree. It's easy to talk happy like this when you're happy and settled. I don't remember how the hell we ever got down here. I don't think Doucette really screwed me because it would have been worse to wait 10 days for a, say, Mayflower truck at $900, and $700 for a Rent-a-Car, and you with no Red to help you drive. All worked out well ... and your promise to Mémère was fulfilled. I miss you, of course, but I know you'll come to see me once in a while: and I'm coming on annual trips to Lowell anyway, praps on my way to Brittany with you next summer if we can get together on that with Youenn Guernic of Huelgoát, Bretagne (Finistère). See you anyhow: We called Tony collect as he instructed. Stella is all Gaga except she's worried about her mother, who is in good hands however.

I'm now going to undertake getting a good tan and reading Pascal again and getting set for a new book. I only hope you're as satisfied as I am with

3. Red Doherty and Jim Dumphy were Massachusetts friends. See Jack's letter to Tony Sampas, December 5, 1968.

the way St. Christopher treated us and the way St. Joseph continues to treat us, that old Camel hobo.......

Jean-Louis K.

Écrit!

At the end of 1968, desperate to find ways to pay his mounting bills, Kerouac wrote to Keith Jennison, his previous editor at Viking, demanding the return of the original typed manuscript of On the Road. *This consisted of long sheets of architects' drawing paper that Jack had Scotch-taped together and rolled into what he called a "scroll." Kerouac had heard a rumor that Jennison intended to donate it to the Morgan Library, and he insisted rightly that it was his property. The manuscript was returned to Kerouac. It spent many years in the safe in Sterling Lord's office, until Kerouac estate executor John Sampas had it placed on deposit in the Berg Collection at the New York Public Library.*

TO KEITH JENNISON

Dec. 3, 1968
[St. Petersburg, Florida]

Mr. Keith Jennison
Keith Jennison/Franklin Watts Inc.
575 Lexington Ave.
New York, N.Y. 10022
Dear Keith:

I require the return of my original manuscript of ON THE ROAD. We left it in a safe at Viking Press for safekeeping in 1957 and now I want it transferred to Sterling Lord's safe in case I want to donate it or sell it. It is presumptuous to donate a manuscript that is not your personal property.

It's my personal property, also my *concrete* physical property in that it's my paper and my ink and no one's else. I'll be needing this to tide me over middle age in a very surprisingly unlucky literary career, from the financial standpoint, i.e., no movie offers for ROAD, nothing substantial in distribution in book form in spite of the continuing demand over a decade, and the "Route 66" idea-grab and all that.

So tell Morgan Library this and have the manuscript ready for pickup by Mr. Lord, my literary agent.

An other kind of action and I'll just have to submit this information to my attorney.

And don't go around saying I "gave you" the original manuscript. We agreed you'd keep it in safekeeping. Nothing was ever agreed upon, in paper, to the effect that the circumstances were otherwise.

Sterling Lord has been waiting for you to *deliver* this manuscript for years.

Since I'm being black balled by the new "cultural" underground, I am certainly not going to give them the T-shirt off my back too. It's all I've got left. It's mine.

Jack Kerouac
c/o Sterling Lord
660 Madison Ave.
New York, N.Y. 10021

JK:jk

Kerouac's last two surviving letters from 1968 were to Stella's brother Tony Sampas in Lowell, one dictated to Jack by Stella, anxious to hear the news from home.

TO TONY SAMPAS FROM STELLA & JACK KEROUAC

Dec. 5, 1968
[St. Petersburg, Florida]

Dear Tony: [Brackets are JK's]

Stella says, dictating to me now, "What's the matter with you, Tony, dont you know how to write? How's Mother? How often do you see her? Is she comfortable? Is Helen working herself too hard? Nobody bothers to write except for Betty and the kids. I dont get any information that way. I know Johnny's working hard but you could spare a few moments to sit down and concentrate a letter. Everything is coming along here as expected. Jack's gettin' settled. Mémère is comfortable. And above all the weather is as we hoped it would be. It's hard to believe that Christmas is coming, the weather here is like Springtime in the Rockies. I notice people going to the bus to go out to the beach. And to spend the day there. I miss you all very much and I miss your visits, [and so does Jack.] When are you planning to come down so we can see you? The house is absolutely beautiful:—with 3 beautiful baths, cedar closets that take all more than the attic at the house would take, and the ground we're at a corner lot and it's very quiet and peaceful, and we're enjoying it every day very much. It took time but we finally found a competent doctor for Mémère. In fact I would say he was a lot more experienced with Mémère's type of illness, than Doctor Letsou. Right off he told us which medicine were good and which ones to lay off not to give her so much. [Dr. Baker.] [Would you like some pork chops? Yup.] The stores are all so handy it's pathetic. One block down I do all my fresh meat. Six block down is a shopping Plaza Mall and can do every type of every shopping you'd want. I havent gone down town but according to the papers the cars are bumper to bumper and there's plenty of shoplifting going on. Everybody's being picked up. Christmas is sure here. Mink coats and color T V are being picked up like hot cakes. Let me think now, I've gotta think. One thing for sure, this house is worth every cent and more what we paid for it, all those extras that were missing on Sanders are all here. The man built it for his own family and then there was illness, and Jack doesnt know it but he took advantage of the man, unintentionally. [You know the old saying about every Greek can beat a Jew, and every Syrian can beat a Greek, and Jack added every Canuck can beat a Syrian, but the man is not a Syrian.] And Jack scrounged up ten grand to move here but it was all blown on hospital bills, for nothing. So Jack, as usual, is INNOCENT and COMES OUT SMELLING LIKE ROSEWSKI OF THE ROSES. Jack the Polock. I just have to tell you again that the bathrooms are out of this world ... three of them and all tile. And I have my beautiful powder room with mirrors and closets and showers and baths, a large screen porch [you could run the Olympics in,] and in which Mémère can run around her wheelchair when she wants to (in), a beautiful two-car garage, twice as big as the one at Sanders, that Jack can use as an artist's studio, and plenty o room to spare. Next week he's puttin up his fence. For his outdoor library. Sittin in the Sun, to his Heart's Content. Again, how is Mother? That's my cue, Tony, see ya later...." [Signed,]

Stella

TO TONY SAMPAS

Dec. 5, 1968
[St. Petersburg, Florida]

Dear Tony

You should've seen that trip we had gettin down here—We had a driver of the Lincoln Mercury called Red Doherty, plus, of course, old Joe Chaput—The Lincoln Mercury stationwagon belonged to Doucette the Reading Mass. mover—He'd said his own mother had once been paralyzed on the left side and insisted that we should rent his own car and get Mémère down here soft and fast and easy—With the mattress in the back, and Stella on pillows, and the cats in their two cages with pre-tranquillized catfood, we zoomed suddenly through New York City with Red Doherty at the wheel—He knows a trick (Geo. Washington Bridge)—to Jersey—and onto the N.J. turnpike, and suddenly we were going around Washington and boom, in the South—At this point Red took a big snoring nap alongside Mémère on the mattress and Joe drove ... Both Joe and Red went 90 most of the way—We made Lowell to St. Petersburg in less than 24 hours, 1600 miles or so—We were stopped for speeding in South Carolina but when the cop saw Mémère and the cats and Stella in the back he just told us to pull over to a station and have our rear red warning lights refurbished—(hit by a truck at the moving warehouse in Reading)—I stayed awake all the way, drinking and yelling and playing harmonica and watching that old road, as usual, and I insisted on riding shotgun near the window because I told Joe he was skinnier than I am, and Red was skinny—We piled right in—I was amazed when I thought of it a week later—Of course it cost money but we got here safe and fast like a long, soft river—Meanwhile the one-truck-load was right behind us and when we arrived here we figured we'd have to wait a few days for said truck, driven by a big German kid called Jim Dumphy (of Somerville). All the time, unbeknownst to us, he was only some 8 hours behind us in arriving in St. Pete but lost his way and had to park his truck downtown and sleep in a motel ... Meanwhile I got motel suite for Joe and Red, two nights in a row, while we tried to find Dumphy—Joe even swam in the swimmingpool and did a couple of swan dives off the board—We went out and played pool and drank by the Gulf of Mexico waves at the Red Barn club, Red Doherty played partners all night with a cute young woman detective (!) but me and Joe won most of the games—And there was southern singing live on the bandstand—I jumped in the air, doing my Russian ballet entrechat, and kicked myself right on the nerve that runs along the shin, and had to have my foot up in packs of ice and aluminum acetate (Burow's solution) for 2 weeks.... Doctor said I should at once go see him but I cured myself my own way, completely, and saved a hundred or so for booze. Rent down here is only 120 instead of 243 in Lowell and we'll have our heads out of the water now. So come on down, Antoni, and have a ball, when you're ready. I got my library card yesterday, magnificent additions in the shelves there from retirees from all over U.S. (in all languages too) and my friend Phil Whalen in Frisco is mailing me my carton of 1949 dusty-shop books that I thought he'd lost— Jacky WRITE!

And just as we were going to call the police to locate the Reading Massachusetts moving truck, Jim Dumphy pulled up in front of the door and the furniture was all piled in. Since that time Stella and I have been decorating and fixing it up nice and everything came out okay just like Mémère said it would. That pain-in-the-ass Stella Sarris keeps coming here and clacking up and down the house in her high heels as tho she owned it: made Stella do a hundred bucks worth of dress and coat work, and brought a few Greek breads and citruses. (Pooey) ... Zaggo

1969

On January 16, 1969, after selling his Ginsberg letters, Kerouac suggested to Philip Whalen that he also sell off his manuscripts and letters before moving back to Kyoto. Jack assured his friend that Allen had told him, "We're all living off our original mss. and letters."

TO PHILIP WHALEN

Jan. 16, 1969
[St. Petersburg, Florida]

Dear Phil:

Delay in answering deplorable, indefensible—due to foolish illnesses self administered,[1] and Christmas, etc. But was I amazed to see my beautiful books again! And how 'bout them footnotes (stupid brat footnotes most)— But it reminded me of how much reading I've done, like you, fantastic eclectic rundown of practically everything in "English" letters & literature from first to last—(And s'why they call my prose "pretentious")—Vy not?— Who can escape or forget the "purple kirtles" of Caedmon?

So I want to thank you for the trouble you took preserving the books, since 1957 yet, and then wrapping them and trudging down to the post office. Here is a check for ten and please accept it with my gratitude.

(Blake's Jerusalem alone is worth a fartune.) For instance, too, I told Allen Ginsberg on the phone I was thinking of borrowing money from my publishers on a projected book. He said "Dont get in hock with the publishers, just sell my letters that I wrote to you, to Andreas Brown, Gotham Book Mart, 41 West 47 Street, N.Y.C., and he will sell them to Univ. of Texas. We're all living off our original mss. and letters, Gregory, even Peter." So I did, and got $6,000 for Allen's big pile of letters, minus Brown's 10% commission. So now, you, Phil, write to him and tell him you have the

---

1. In Kerouac's journal he recorded that he took LSD at this time.

letters of Allen, Gary and others I may not know about (ME) like, say, Duncan or whatever, because the Univ. of Texas is really going all out with "federally granted educational (creative?) funds" to amass the history of our literary movement on that one campus, in that one library, where things are kept under "maximum librarial conditions" and they even have the courtesy to Xerox what you send them and send you the Xerox copies on nice thick paper and you dont lose the words, just the original (fragrance I guess?) (original hand-scribble). Think of it. Write to Andreas Brown and tell him who you are, what I said, and what you have. He would go gaga over my Blake Jerusalem because it's also inscribed to James Agee. I'm not making any money to speak of anymore, and apparently I'm going to have to dribble off my magnificent collection of letters (yours, Gary's, Burroughs', my own letters to Neal in my possession now, etc.) I'm more published and read in England than in USA, not to mention Italy and France and now Germany

Yes, go to Kyoto till that "creepy New Left" blows over. You believe in American Revolution 1776 because in a previous lifetime you were Benjamin Franklin trudging the Bradford road in the mud and rain with letters for log cabins. As for the Westerner not being fit for Oriental Zen or Chan or Buddhism, it was Burroughs told me that in a letter 1954 and got me pissed off. Just saw him, he just sits on the edge of hotel beds pursing his lips. And I think a Kafkaesque imaginary Europe novel by you would be fine. Myself, what to write next, I dont know, but everything is unpacked and ready to go and house fixed and Mémère paralyzed on left side nevertheless looks the same and eats and sings French and Indian songs anyway, and my wife a rock of devotion.

Jack

The last day of February 1969, Kerouac wrote to John Clellon Holmes mentioning a short trip he had taken the previous spring to Lisbon, Madrid, Geneva, Munich, and Stuttgart with Stella's brothers Tony and Nick, when Jack had squandered $2,000 in less than two weeks on prostitutes and liquor. The same day he also wrote Tony Sampas, describing a recent trip to New York City. Shortly after Jack's forty-seventh birthday in March, he learned that the former owner of his house hadn't paid property taxes, so Kerouac had to come up with $1,600 to keep his home. Once more Jack turned to Sterling Lord and Stella's family for a loan. Kerouac's royalty statements were meager, but his agent advanced some money and Stella borrowed the rest from one of her brothers. She worked as a seamstress at home to repay it while Jack set to work revising a story he had begun in 1951 as a new short novel called Pic. *It was a departure from his usual autobiographical approach. A fictional narrative told in Southern dialect from the point of view of an African-American boy, it began, "Ain't never nobody loved me like I love myself, cept my mother and she's dead." In the first week of April 1969, he sent the manuscript of his new book by registered mail to Sterling Lord.*

February 28, 1969
[St. Petersburg, Florida]

Dear John,

Just make the effort, as Tolstoi says, and all gets done. Lyov Tolstoi. My father's name was Leon, so was Neal's. Up your twitty twatt poop doopy gloopy doodah.

Took a trip myself about a year ago, from Boston to Lisbon (rhymes), got there, my Greek buddies were standing under a streetlamp on the corner countin cruzos and so I went to a cat with a moustache and said "A donde es les muchachas" (and everybody in France, Spain or Portugal understands that) and he took me to a bar where I met Linda and all that, and my Greek buddies (two brothers in law, one cousin in law, and another who calls everybody "Poosti" (Cocksucker))—They got mad as hell cause they couldn't find me. Then we went to Madrid. I tell you John I didn't see anything at all, no bridges, no churches, nada, just joints, but I guess bridges and churches are built with joints, or jointed thereunto like my old relatives who put up a Griffin on the Gothic spire ... Give my very best to your lovely wife Shirley. Your sister I haven't seen since she was a pale young oyster of 12 in my dreams. Your mother divine. Really.

What else? You said you haven't heard from me. Went to Stuttgart too. Got home by hook or crook, alone. I see by the New York Times that "Phillip Roth has discerned that modern literature is a form of confessional monologue." Ain't he tho? I can't even get vanity of duluoz reprinted meanwhile. Giroux sent me a telegram saying "Sorry no Vanity at Noonday, (signed) Farrarcomp." Some poor bastard around here thought I'd got a letter from a Syrian or a Finn or maybe mightly like a Whale. Cheers old boy, call me up on phone, 343-1541 ... Dick Gregory made a speech here t'other night saying "Who has the right to call me a boy, I'm 45 years old." Good luck, old boy John. (They call me white boy.) But he also made a good statement. I wasn't there. Read in the paper. But in NYC Lucien took me to hear Ginsberg lecture and Allen didn't show up. So Lucien took me and the gang to Allen's door in Lower East Side and was trying to kick the door down when I told him it was gainst the law. What a mess of events. It IS a Dostoyevskyan world. Leroi Jones was sposed to talk down here but didn't show up. Take a lion by the tail, I say, and give it a twist. My mother knows of a 13 year old girl in Nashua N.H. in 1909 who took the boss's cock when he showed it to her in the office of the shoe factory, and twisted it broke.

Jack

[February 28, 1969
St. Petersburg, Florida]

Dear Tony

Last night I went to a pool hall bar called Dew Drop Inn and was beating everybody including colonels retired from the Army and one young gyrene but suddenly a crazy Polock gyrene came in and beat the shit out of all of us. I almost got him at one point. (pool) It was a very gay happy scene. Before that I'd done the work I was supposed to do, downtown, to get the widow's exemption and homestead exemption papers filed in county and took my copies with me stuffed deep in my bottomless pockets and took off for drink and pool. Place very much nice. Because here I've been missing your bar. But later on in the night, when the two gyrenes started to fight over one of the gyrene's blondes (wife) I said "Beg off Jack and go someplace else, no business of mine" and I went to a rock joint to find my 300 pound Syrian buddy—He was playing and singing on the stand but I had no more money, so he ordered drinks for me, but the waitress (who, with her mother, is s'posed to be thieving cash) tried to take the drinks away, and the Syrian knocked them off the bar before she could touch them, and said to me today: "If they're going to deny, we'll do the denying first," a point of honor with him, and me too. Then he took me out to his car to wait for a cab so that no cops would see me loitering about (the manager of the bar had called the cops.) So this Yellow Cab or Independent red cab pulled up and I got in and got home. This Syrian says I am so neutral and so interested in observing events and talk so much that everybody thinks I'm something else. So I'm not having as much fun as in Lowell. My mother is still lying in bed looking at TV only difference is the view is different out the window. But Stella really likes it here, the joint is much better built than the one in Lowell, which is going a long way. Come on down, as Rodney Magee said. I miss you. I know you probably can't get off from work but when you can, come on down. I flew to N.Y.C. 7 days ago, caught a cold, got a love tap punch on the jaw from Lucien, was threatened to be killed by a Breton, went to Harlem, saw my Swiss buddy, and snuck back on an airplane full of soldiers and sailors and marines, and I heard two Cubans say in sorta French Spanish "Ah this damn ship is full of militaries." We went from Newark to Atlanta to Jacksonville and Tampa. I was sitting next to a rookie pitcher for the Kansas City Royals, name of John Warden, and I'm going to buy a baseball magazine and check up on the rosters for this year.

I could hear gyrenes behind me saying "Oh, he's English" and "Oh he's French Canadian" and "Oh he's a Breton" because they all thought at first I was Cuban. But no Cuban could talk about baseball like me and Warden was doing. And then when we landed in Tampa, safe, everybody home, I saw this Sgt. of the army wake up from a long nap, and he said his name was Sgt. Ortega. He was watching everything. The airlines are probably hiring Cubans to check on Cubans. It's not that to be Cuban is bad, but the Hijacking shot is too much (it means spending extra money in Havana). (Right?) But on this ship there were 60 militaries and incidentally, I had a firstclass ticket but they told me to take any seat I could find. They're all coming home, thank God. Traveling is getting to be too much: too many people are traveling: it's tough. I ask you to come see me and Stella but you'll have a hell of a time getting here. But it always turns out to be worth it depending on where you're going. In Lisbon we could have been trapped in an earthquake, in Spain by the blondes (instead of which we heard Flamenco with Tony Z.), and in Stuttgart I could have been incinerated in a garbage can as Big John said, for being what I am, which aint Jew.

Well they all learned their lessons from those who make a distinction between "aggression" and "reprisal" (or *"riposte"*) (French word used in swordfencing, meaning counterthrust). This is a Swiss typewriter and hard to master. Good thing I didnt come from Basle or Doubt, near Lake Geneva. Be happy, Tony, make every day a holiday whichever way. Regards to Jap, Ruthie, and Joey Decay the Portuguese Decoy Cop.

[Holographic postscript] Jack

Regards to Johnny S.

TO STERLING LORD

[March 3, 1969
St. Petersburg, Florida]

Dear Sterling

Heard a wonderful story last night. God came to man and said "I will give you 20 years of normal productive sex life, since you are Man." So be it. So God next goes to the monkey and says "I will give you 20 years of normal productive sex life." The monkey says "But I'm only a monkey and I'm an inferior to man, give me 10 years and give the other 10 to man." So be it. Then God goes to the parrot and says "I'll give you 20 years of n.p.sex life." The parrot says give man the other ten years, I'm inferior to Man. Then the lion is visited, same proposition (we cant got into endless typewritten repetitions) and lion says same thing, I'll take ten years, give the other ten to man. And then God goes to the poor sweet pretty little gray donkey and the same thing happens. So that the net result of it all is that mankind goes through 60 years of normal productive sex life monkeying around, talking about it, lyin' about it, and making an ass of himself.

This is to be definitely copyrighted under the name of Ron Lowe.

By the by, dearie, if you don't send me some money soon I wont be able to pay my taxes OR rent.

If I annoyed your working hours in the office, and brought that painter's stuff, it still has nothing to do with literature as based 'pon shelves as long as civilization (or English) last.

As ever,
Jack

TO TONY SAMPAS

March 18 1969
[St. Petersburg, Florida]

Dear Tony

I want you to hand this letter personally to Marina Sampas, Charley Sampas' daughter, if you can. It only concerns the fate of what happened to the 12 foreign editions of my books I gave her to give the Head Librarian of Lowell Tech. I don't want her mother to open her mail: because Pertinax wanted them for "Charles G. Sampas' Library": I just wanted foreign students studying technology at LTI to get a kick out of reading about the neighborhood surrounding their own campus, but in their own language.

If you can find her present Youth Corps address, the stamp is on her envelope, and just write in DO NOT FORWARD.

Write to me when you can, or call.

I've been studying the baseball situation a little, and I might say to keep your eye on a 100–1 shot, Kansas City Royals (American League). Rico, Kirkpatrick, Warden, Gelnar, all new great boys.

I take North Carolina over Purdue in the NAACP basketball (college) finals, *(semi)* and N.C. might even take UCLA in the finals.

Nobody'll beat the Super-Lakers of L.A. in the pro basketball scene: they've got Elgin Baylor, Chamberlain AND Jerry West.

Stella wants you to come
down here eat some
pork chops
with us.
Signed,
Jack

p.s. And I also dont want those 12 foreign editions of my books to wind up in the Charles J. Jarvis Library.

pp.ss. Stella insists you come, you nut, she says. Now is the best time to come, she says.

April 7, 1969
[St. Petersburg, Florida]

Dear Sterling:

Haven't heard from you about receiving my new manuscript PIC. Notify me. It was registered, mailed about a week ago today. Be sure to have it copyrighted. Is also a good movie prospect. Is in Huck Finn tradition. Hope the dialect not too tough for you-all. Learned it from little country boys in North Carolina.

As ever,
Jack

TO NICK SAMPAS

Monday May 18 1969
[St. Petersburg, Florida]

Dear Nicky:

Thanks a 500 for lending me that 500 exactly when me and Stella needed it. Now I think I'm about to make a hit on three shots: (1) My new novel, PIC, all about a little 10-year-old Negro boy in North Carolina in 1949 who escapes from the tenant farmer fields to New York with his big hipster saxophone brother Slim Jackson carrying him on his back, a kind of "Huckleberry Finn" of today.

Second, I'm selling William Seward Burroughs' letters to the University of Texas for 6 grand at least. I'll take no price below that. His letters to me.

Third, I'm selling my house in Hyannis, in which there's almost 5 G in equity.

So I'll make a hit and send you back the 500 pronto, Ole 66 Inc. But there might be dealys. Delays. But take care of your sister and your poor long suffering brother-in-law.

Well, that's Stella and me I'm talking about, not the others, for a while.

Field Marshell Montgomery steps out of a jeep in the driving, sleeting rain, carrying his military baton. All the Commandos are standing at attention naked in the rain. Monty hits the first guy on the chest and demands "That 'urt?" "No sir!" "Why not?!" "Commando, sir!" Monty hits another guy on the stomach with his military crop: "That hurt?" "No sir!" "Why not?" "Commando, sir." Then he hits a guy on the hard-on. "*That* hurt?" "No sir." "Why not?" "Man b'hind me, sir."

Jacky
Jean-Louis Lebris de Kerouac'h
of Meslan, Cornouiailes
Finistere, Bretagne
Hereditary Count, or King,
of Cornwall

"Black Prince" Phhhtt—NAMO AMITHABA BUDDHA
Regards to Walter, Ingrid and Marianne

On July 7, 1969, Kerouac dropped a postcard to Lawrence Ferlinghetti in response to an offer to write an introduction to Neal Cassady's autobiography, The First Third, *which City Lights would publish in 1971. Cassady had died of exposure on the railroad tracks in San Miguel de Allende, Mexico, on February 4, 1968, after mixing liquor and barbiturates. Jack had refused to accept the news of his friend's death when Carolyn had telephoned him in Lowell about it. Jokingly he told Ferlinghetti that he hoped "Neal is really wearing a beard with changed name in Spain."*

TO LAWRENCE FERLINGHETTI

July 7, 1969
[St. Petersburg, Florida]

Cher Lawrence—

I can write intro for FIRST THIRD if I'm made cognizant of what's in it, like, any lost-and-found letters included? Let me know scene-set of first chapter and of last chapter. Better yet, try to come see me as you say in July, wd. be wonderful see you again. If you don't make it Fla., be sure send me sorta synopsis and source-materials of FIRST THIRD. Then, after that, mebbe you could print COMPLEAT VISIONS OF CODY, 500 p. ms. & have the N.C. Legend *etablis* solid & beauteous way he deserves. ("Tom Wolfe" ass). ("Kool Aid Acid Test") junk makes mediocre Kesey more important than holy bold noble Neal. Let time tell with his First Third. Hope Neal is really wearing a beard with changed name in Spain & Carolyn comfortable collectin' r.r. retirement, pensions etc.

Copain Jean-Louis

TO STERLING LORD

Aug. 27, 1969
[St. Petersburg, Florida]

Dear Sterling:

Well, to become garrulous again. I'm going to en-de-a-vour to type up the conclusion of PIC for you only on condition that you write right quick (or when possible, which is I s'pose quick as quick as quick can) and tell me who's seen the manuscript so far, where it is now, and what you think the prospects of having it published, are. (Great sentence.) What I wrote, those extry pages you wanted, simply take the boys out to the Coast, where they re-unite with Sheila, which is the point. Only trouble is, who do you

472

think rides them there all the way from Pennsylvania: Jack the Louse and Neal Cassaday (Pomeray)? However there is some dialog, some scenes, some interest, so I'll send it on anyway.

(2) Still waiting for Transatlantic Review on "First Night of the Tapes," proofs of which I proof-read.[2]

(3) There's such a lack of communication today amongst slowpokes like you and me, nothing gets done any more. Remember the old days? We used to get things done in two shakes of a lamb's tail. Why? Women in the way? Hiding files in the wrong place? Why when I met you, you were in great shape, alone doing your own typing in an office, and bing bang, here, bing bang, there, and now we've instead of a Secret Storm become a Public Gale.

As ever,
Jack

On September 4, 1969, Kerouac went to his lawyer to sign a will that named Gabrielle as the beneficiary of his entire estate. The night before, Jack was beaten up in the Cactus Bar in St. Petersburg. Apparently Kerouac had tried to help a disabled Air Force veteran who had been attacked by a band manager. When Jack protested that the veteran wasn't "queer," the manager replied, "So you want it too?" He cracked Jack's ribs and then called the police, who put Kerouac in jail.

Stella bailed him out and became his typist at the end of the month, when his taped ribs and a hernia hurt so much that he couldn't type anymore. Before his wife took over as his typist, Jack wrote to Andreas Brown on September 7, 1969, explaining why he refused to have anything to do with a book of photographs of the Beat writers I was compiling from Allen Ginsberg's collection of snapshots on deposit at Butler Library at Columbia University. The book was titled Scenes Along the Road, *to be published by our small press, Portents, in Brooklyn Heights. Despite his many boasts of being "the classic originator" of the Beat Generation, Kerouac insisted, "I'm on my own and always was on my own."*

Kerouac was still angry at me for taking what he considered a "Bowery Bum photo" of him. In his letter he told Andreas Brown that I had been "fishing around" in his papers and took a photograph of him without permission after he woke up and came into the room while I was working. Actually, as my proof sheet shows, Jack had consented to pose for me sitting beside the window of his bedroom, and he went on to let me take another photograph of him with his mother in the living room after we had finished our second day together compiling his bibliography.

2. "First Night of the Tapes," an excerpt from *Visions of Cody*, was published in the winter 1969/spring 1970 issue of *Transatlantic Review*.

Sept. 7, 1969
[St. Petersburg, Florida]

Dear Andreas:

Enclosed is a letter from Ann and Samuel Charters, PORTENTS, which you can throw away after you've read, or not, but don't send it back. I'll be only too glad to give you the three most important literary influences on my *childhood* on provision that I BE NOT INCLUDED IN ANY UNDER-GROUND SCENE PUBLISHING SHOT. I'm on my own and always was on my own. No photos. And I see no connection between your 50th Anniversary celebration which has Bowles, Auden, Durrell, Isherwood, Saroyan, Tate, Porter, Updike, Welty, Aiken, Buck, Fowles, Inge, Wilbur, Dos Passos, Boyle and this bullshit she sends about wanting photos of me and Ferlinghetto [sic] et cetera Ginsberg, Corso. Just thought you might want to see Ann's letter.

On provision that you see I don't get into any such Underground horse-shit publication (and that you also proviso me that if you meet Ann Charters, or write, that the picture of me on the back cover of VANITY OF DULUOZ in profile with a smile holding up a butt in a chair was taken three or four months after she took that awful Bowery Bum photo of me when I got up with a hangover and without combing, shaving or washing just walked into my own study to see how she was fishing around thru my papers and she immediately snapped me like that with her camera), I'll certainly send you the name of the three literary influences of my childhood since you said *please* so heartily, and I say to you now, *please,* heartily also, do you now want Corso's letters for the Archives and *please* get a good price. (I think you've been a good man to deal with) (sic) (grammar sic) and let's get on with our own affairs and let portents portend as portent portends.

P.S. I'm selling you my valuable letters from Ginsberg, Burroughs, Corso, et al (later Whalen and Snyder and others if you want) only because I have to clear my files for my own writings (can't get to find my own shit for the shit of all others I had to keep neatly filed with mothballs to keep them Shakespearean worms away from the kindly old millennial paper they were written on) (sic again grammar).... However, Andreas, make said proviso concerning the association of me with any kind of "underground" in America, I am open and above board and always have been, like my father and grandfather, and that's the way them Kerouacs want it.

Write soon.

Yrs
Jack Kerouac

On September 8, 1969, Kerouac wrote to his first wife, Edith Parker (nicknamed Frankie), to tell her about the beating he had taken in the Cactus Bar and invite her to visit him in Florida.

TO EDITH PARKER KEROUAC

Sept. 8, 1969
[St. Petersburg, Florida]

Dear Frankie,

This is Johnnie. Three hours after I talked to you on the phone I was stupid enough to take a 100% disabled retired Air Force Lieutenant to a Negro bar in St. Pete here, where he put his arm affectionately around the Negro band manager while the band was rehearsing. The manager, 22, slugged him. I jumped up and said, "He's not a queer." "So you want it too!?" said the ex-boxer. I said "He's a lieutenant in the Air Force. Band manager said "So what, I'm a lieutenant too." (Lieutenant in what? I thought.) He came over. Another Negro came up behind me. The other five musicians got up. 25 other Negroes were watching in the door. I realized I'd have to accept a beating of some kind or wind up me and the Swede (the Lt.) stabbed, shot or killed. So he mauled me. I held him off best as I could. Cops came and arrested *Me* and the Swede for drunk. Four minutes getting stitches in the hospital and a shot of taetnus [sic], then four hours in jail. My wife Stella Sampas Kerouac, only phone call I made, came at 8 PM bailed me out $25. Affair all closed and not mentioned in papers at all. Don't know who my assaulters were or what happened to them. Nothing, I think. I no more go to Negro bars. so I am too sick to go to Detroit, all black eyes and blue arms and stitches over eye (4) and twisted knee. So if you want to see me (and my mother and I both want to see you) get a roundtrip ticket to here and come have pleasant quiet visit. By bus if necessary. Expect no money from me on any scale, I'm not rich like you think. But the house is a beaut, the yard has a fenced in grass, shrub, tree and jungled area: there's a screened porch. Walk to store. Hurricane proof Spanish modern C A S T L E, which explains where all my money went. Come on down, therefore, and we'll hash out whatever future there is. Stella is from Lowell, she's the sister of that young Greek soldier Sebastian who died at Anzio beach head in 1943. She won't like it but come on down anyway. No moochy moochy. For some reason my Ma (paralyzed in bed but still funny) wants to have you visit. And I don't mind at all because I'd like to talk over things and all old times with you. Relax and be calm. Tell your DuPonts lend you fare, for krissakes.

Jack

p.s. And dont you dare bring anyone else or any dogs or cats or any animals. I've got 3 quiet happy cats, beauts, and plenty peaceful area (svelte).

On September 20, 1969, Kerouac sent an impulsive telegram to his first wife of-
fering to pay her airfare to Florida, but the next day he canceled the invitation.
Two days later he told Andreas Brown that he had no photographs to send him
for a brochure celebrating the fiftieth anniversary of the Gotham Book Mart.

TO EDITH PARKER KEROUAC

Sept. 21, 1969
[St. Petersburg, Florida]

Dear Edith,

My mother, my wife, and I, myself have decided you should not come
here at all.

You would not enjoy it here anyway, with a paralytic patient under 24
hour care. There is no room to put you in, and I am so busted (hernia) that
I can't see straight, or walk straight, or think logically.

Cancel the message in the telegram and try to go see your friend, Mil-
ner in California.

Bad time for both of us.

Jack

You'll be Okay

TO ANDREAS BROWN

Sept. 22, 1969
[St. Petersburg, Florida]

Dear Andreas:

My mother in a fit of pique in 1960 tore up all the snapshots of me covering the period which you mentioned. I thereupon fished out the torn
snapshots from the garbage can and scotch taped them together again, but
they disappeared again. So that's that.

My earliest childhood readings were Catechism in French, the Bible in
French, and the LITTLE SHEPHERD OF KINGDOM COME.... plus the
Bobbsey Twins and REBECCA OF SUNNYBROOK FARMS ... and ROLL
RIVER, by James Boyd, and then the later slavering over Shadow Maga-
zine, Phantom Detective Magazine, and Street & Smith's Star Western
Magazine............

Okay?

Dictating to Stella at the typewriter on September 29, 1969, Kerouac wrote a
postcard to Dan De Sole, a sympathetic psychiatrist he'd met four years before
who had been a college friend of Tony Sampas and was now teaching at Oak-

land University in Rochester, Michigan. Dr. De Sole had recognized that Jack needed professional help to stop drinking and had given him prescriptions for Benadryl and Dexedrine. Jack threw away the Benadryl but relied on the Dexedrine to help him write Satori in Paris, Vanity of Duluoz, *and* Pic, *which he dedicated to De Sole. The drug intensified Kerouac's paranoia, especially after he experimented with LSD for the last time that autumn.*

TO DAN DE SOLE

Sept. 29, 1969
[St. Petersburg, Florida]

Dear Danny,

I have no money to go traipsing up to Michigan, and I am not interested in specialized seminars, because I've got a seminar of my own right here in this rocking chair. And I have got to watch my health and write another book. The book that I dedicate to you also has to be finished.

Beware of bums of the anti-American variety, I'm only Buffalo Bill. Stella says Hawaii. Stella appropriated the medal of Pope John 23 that I bought for you at the Vatican but you had already complained that it might be too heavy. (Stella typing, I've been beat up by Negro soul-brothers.)

As ever,
Jack Kerouac

In late September and early October 1969, Jack and Stella collaborated on two postcards inviting her brother Nick and his wife, Ingrid, to visit them in Florida.

TO INGRID & NICK SAMPAS

Sept. 30 1969
[St. Petersburg, Florida]

Dear Ingrid and Nick,

Let us know about Nicky's supposed pneumonia. Jack wants to know how is your Weltanschauung. Tell your father to keep up his painting, tell your mother to keep laughing, tell Nicky to relax, tell yourself [illeg.], Jack saying all this, and come on down and visit us. Jack has a hernia and now we are going to watch old time actor William Powell on TV. We are planning to move back to Lowell area next year, nothing but con men and snobs around here, whom we could buy in a second, and keep your eye open for a house safe for kitty-cats and recalcitrant mothers.

Best ever,
Jack Kerouac

Oct. 9 1969
[St. Petersburg, Florida]

Dear Nicky:

Why don't you come down with Ingrid and see me and Stella. Stella has a double bed and says she'll sleep in the sofa in the parlor. I'll charcoal broil a three-inch thick sirloin steak in the night fenced-in yard under the stars, make cheese sauce for the asparagus, make an apple salad with slightly hot dressing, garlic toast, and strawberry ice cream mixed with heavy cream for dessert.

(Stella now typing:) "Stop gallivantin all over Europe and New York and come and lay down in the sun and relax. We miss you very much."

Stella & Jack

In mid-October 1969, Kerouac wrote his last words to Sterling Lord about the conclusion of Pic *and sent off a postcard to Andreas Brown about the sale of his letters from Gregory Corso.*

TO STERLING LORD

Oct. 12, 1969
[St. Petersburg, Florida]

Dear Sterling:

Here is the conclusion of PIC.

And please let me hear from my royalties in Europe before I go broke again, and also any news about reprinting VANITY OF DULUOZ.

I'm not giving anyone your new address in New England.

For God's sake man, I've got to live too, that is, pay my rent.

As ever,
Jack

TO STERLING LORD

Oct. 14, 1969
[St. Petersburg, Florida]

Dear Sterling:

Now that I've sent you the only possible conclusion of PIC, see if you might not try Andre Deutsch before the American publishers set to make up their mind.

And I want you to do this annotation on the dedication page:

DEDICATED TO DR. DANNY DE SOLE, LULU OF BIG EASON-
BURG WOODS NORTH CAROLINA, CLARENCE HAWKINS OF
KEY WEST, AND KENNY SHELTON.

Okay? Tell me what you think of my final decision on the ending.

As ever, Jack

(But tell Deutsch that the package includes a British printing of DOCTOR
SAX)

TO ANDREAS BROWN

Oct. 14, '69
[St. Petersburg, Florida]

Dear Andreas—
Let me know if you want the Corso letters now, I finally fished them out
of my attic. You seem to be too busy with "openings"—openings of what?

Jack Kerouac

CORSO IS GREAT POET

*On October 17, 1969, Kerouac became upset when a large Georgia pine was cut
down in front of a neighbor's house, complaining to Stella that he could no longer
hear the wind speaking to him in the branches of the tree. Two nights later, when
he couldn't sleep, he lay outside to watch the stars in his backyard on a cot Stella
had gotten for him by saving S & H green stamps.*

*Apparently in the early hours of the morning of October 20, Kerouac returned
to his work in progress,* The Beat Spotlight, *rereading old family letters by his
father, Leo, and others to refresh his memory. Tony Sampas remembers that Jack
phoned him in Lowell to talk about the old days and complain about Stella. After listening for a few minutes, Tony hung up the phone. Rebuffed by Stella's
brother, Jack sat down at his typewriter to compose a blustering letter to his
twenty-one-year-old nephew, Little Paul, who had moved to Alaska with his father after Nin's death. Kerouac ended the letter by conveying a message from
Mémère to her grandson, which Jack translated from her patois into English. The
postmarked envelope to this letter has never been found.*

*Around 12:00 noon, Jack began to vomit blood in the bathroom, the result of
hemorrhaging esophageal varices. Stella heard him and called an ambulance to
take him to the hospital. Twenty-six blood transfusions couldn't save Ti Jean, Jean
Louis Lebris de Kerouac, known to readers around the world as Jack, who passed
away at 5:30 A.M. on October 21, 1969.*

Oct. 20, 1969
[St. Petersburg, Florida]

Dear Little Paul,

This is Uncle Jack. I've turned over my entire estate, real, personal, and mixed, to Mémère, and if she dies before me, it is then turned to you, and if I die thereafter, it all goes to you. The will is locked in a bank vault of the Citizens National Bank of St. Petersburg. I have a copy of the new will in the house just for reference. My St. Pete attorney who did this for me is Fred Bryson. I just wanted to leave my "estate" (which is what it really is) to someone directly connected with the last remaining drop of my direct blood line, which is, me sister Carolyn [sic], your Mom, and not to leave a dingblasted fucking goddamn thing to my wife's one hundred Greek relatives. I also plan to divorce, or have her marriage to me, annulled. Just telling you the facts of how it is. My home here at 5169-10th Ave. North, St. Pete, is right next door to the little house you last saw me in, on the corner, where, remember, you met that girl Cheryl. Corner of 52nd St. and 10th Avenue North. Now Mémère wants to speak to you, but before she recites her portion of this letter to me to type for you (reciting in French so the Greek wife won't understand) I want you to know that if you're a crazy nut you can do anything you want with my property, if I kick the bucket, because we're of the same blood, and also were good buddies and have had an association that went back to when you were one year old (if you recall). Don't let Big Paul, your Pop think that he can get anything out of this as he owes me $5,500 but doesn't have to pay it, but it's for you, just for the blood line of it. Now Mémère dictating to me her words, in French, which I put in English on this yar typewriter:

Mémère is saying: "The last letter I wrote you I asked you for a reply and you still haven't replied. I'm very proud of you, my little blond boy, because you work for your country. If you are making progress in the airplanes, let me know, and be very careful not to get hurt. Do you go out with girls? do you have a steady? Send me a picture of you posing in an Eskimo suit. I want a picture of it. I want you to write and tell me what's going on with you in Alaska. If you want to take a vacation to come and warm yourself up in the sun, come on down, and if you have a car with you we have a two-car garage that's empty. I love you, and I'm lonely. I'd like to see you because it makes me renew the instincts I had with your Ma."

Jack (& Mémère)

A year after Kerouac's funeral in Lowell, Stella erected a gray marble headstone engraved HE HONORED LIFE *over Jack's grave. On March 8, 1971, she wrote her mother and brother John, asking to move with paralyzed Gabrielle back to the Sampas family home in Lowell:*

Dear Mother & Johnny,

Mémère and I have thought it over, our moving to Lowell and it seems that if it's ok with both of you the best thing for us to do is move in with you for a while.

I don't want to move into any house if it means that we have to quibble over rents, expenses & etc. After all, the important thing will be for me to be with Mémère and Mother during the day-time when others are out doing their work. If we pool our resources we should be able to manage.

This, of course, will mean that we will have to store some of our furniture in the garage for a while. Perhaps, we can put Jack's desk in the upstairs room where you used to sleep John & the piano in the front hall—Mémère and I can sleep downstairs—If you wish you can set up the hospital-bed up in the den for Mémère & I can have the front couch or something. The refrigerator we can use or store in the garage whatever you think is advisable.

I don't want to rent or buy from Mike or have any business considering the circumstances—I've never been an imposition to him or any body & don't intend to be now. All I have is a paralyzed Mémère & the kittens & surely we can make a comfortable life in such a large house—

If things work out maybe next year you won't have to take in boarders.

In this way, we can be close to everybody & comfortable too.

Please, please—let this come true. I've wanted it so much and now that Mémère thinks it's a good idea, don't disappoint me. Even she thinks it's a grand idea.

It would be a great releaf to me that we are going somewhere we are wanted.

Take care of yourselves & God bless you.

Love,

Stella & Mémère

Finally Stella decided it would be more convenient to continue to nurse Mémère in the house she and Jack had bought in St. Petersburg. Gabrielle Kerouac died there in October 1973. Stella Kerouac continued to live in the house until her death in February 1990. She is buried with her husband at the Edson Cemetery in Lowell.

NOTES

Key to abbreviations: AL = autograph letter; ALS = autograph letter, signed; APCS = autograph postcard, signed; TL = typed letter; TLS = typed letter, signed; TPC = typed postcard.

MAIN SOURCES

John Sampas
Stella and Jack Kerouac Estate
Lowell, Massachusetts

Henry W. and Albert A. Berg Collection
The New York Public Library
Astor, Lenox, and Tilden Foundations
Forty-second Street and Fifth Avenue
New York, New York

Allen Ginsberg Papers
Rare Book and Manuscript Room
Butler Library
Columbia University
New York, New York

Lawrence Ferlinghetti Papers
City Lights Records
The Bancroft Library
University of California
Berkeley, California

Gary Snyder Papers
Department of Special Collections
University of California Library
Davis, California

Philip Whalen Collection
Special Collections Library
Eric V. Hauser Memorial Library
Reed College
Portland, Oregon

Donald M. Allen Papers
Mandeville Department of Special Collections
University of California
San Diego, California

Malcolm Cowley Papers
The Newberry Library
Chicago, Illinois

Punctuation in the letters mostly conforms to Kerouac's style, including the dots and dashes he used when composing them. Additions or omissions that the editor has made in the text are indicated by bracketed words or by [....]. Spelling has been regularized when Kerouac did not intend wordplay in his letters, as in "Huncke" (not "Hunkey"), "hassle" (not "hassel"), or "Tangier" (not "Tangiers").

1957

January 1.	To Sterling Lord.	TPCS. Sterling Lord.
January 5.	To Sterling Lord.	TLS. Sterling Lord.
January 5.	To Helen Weaver.	TPCS. Helen Weaver.
January 5.	To Donald Allen.	TPCS. University of California, San Diego.
January 10.	To John Clellon Holmes.	ALS. John Clellon Holmes.
January 28.	To Edith Parker Kerouac.	TLS. Edith Parker.
February 4.	To Malcolm Cowley.	TLS. Newberry Library.
Undated [1957].	To Joyce Glassman.	ALS. Joyce Johnson.
March 4.	To Sterling Lord.	TLS. Sterling Lord.
March 8.	To Malcolm Cowley.	TLS. Newberry Library.
March 19.	To Donald Allen.	TLS. University of California, San Diego.
March 25.	To Sterling Lord.	TLS. Sterling Lord.
March 25.	To Neal Cassady.	TLS. University of Texas.
April 3.	To Sterling Lord.	TLS. Sterling Lord.
April 3.	To Gary Snyder.	TLS. University of California, Davis.
April 10.	To Philip Whalen.	ALS. Reed College.
April 20.	To Sterling Lord.	TLS. Sterling Lord.
April 28.	To Ed White.	TLS. *Missouri Review.*
Early May.	To Allen Ginsberg & William S. Burroughs.	TL. Columbia University.
May 15.	To Sterling Lord.	APCS. Sterling Lord.
May 17.	To Allen Ginsberg.	ALS. Columbia University.
May 25.	To Gary Snyder.	TLS. University of California, Davis.
Late May.	To Sterling Lord.	TLS. Sterling Lord.
June 7.	To Allen Ginsberg, Peter Orlovsky, William S. Burroughs, & Alan Ansen.	TLS. Columbia University.
June 24.	To Gary Snyder.	TLS. University of California, Davis.
June 26.	To Sterling Lord.	TLS. Sterling Lord.
July 4.	To Malcolm Cowley.	TLS. Viking Press.

July 5.	To Sterling Lord.	TPCS. Sterling Lord.
July 12.	To Philip Whalen.	TPCS. Reed College.
July 19.	To Patricia MacManus.	TLS. Viking Press.
July 21.	To Malcolm Cowley.	TLS. Viking Press.
July 21.	To Allen Ginsberg, Peter Orlovsky, & Alan Ansen.	ALS. Columbia University.
July 22.	To Joyce Glassman.	ALS. Joyce Johnson.
July 29.	To Philip Whalen from Gabrielle Kerouac.	ALS. Reed College.
August 9.	To Allen Ginsberg.	ALS. Columbia University.
Mid August.	To Philip Whalen.	TL. Reed College.
August 18.	To Joyce Glassman.	ALS. Joyce Johnson.
Mid-August.	To Malcolm Cowley.	TLS. Viking Press.
August 23.	To Joyce Glassman.	TLS. Joyce Johnson.
September 15.	To Jack Kerouac from Stella Sampas.	ALS. Kerouac Estate.
October 1.	To Allen Ginsberg.	TL. Columbia University.
October 12.	To Charles Olson.	APCS. University of Connecticut.
October 15.	To Pat MacManus.	TPCS. Viking Press.
October 18.	To Allen Ginsberg.	TLS. Columbia University.
Late October.	To Neal Cassady.	TLS. Carolyn Cassady.
October 22.	To Helen Weaver.	TLS. Helen Weaver.
October 22.	To Lucien and Cessa Carr.	TLS. Columbia University.
October 25.	To Stella Sampas.	TLS. Kerouac Estate.
November 8.	To John Clellon Holmes.	TLS. John Clellon Holmes.
November 11.	To Donald Allen.	TLS. University of California, San Diego.
November 11.	To Hiram Haydn.	TLS. Sterling Lord.
November 23.	To Sterling Lord.	TLS. Sterling Lord.
November 30.	To Allen Ginsberg.	TLS. Columbia University.
December 10.	To Allen Ginsberg, Peter Orlovsky, & Gregory Corso.	TL. Columbia University.
December 10.	To Sterling Lord.	TLS. Sterling Lord.
December 12.	To Patricia MacManus.	TPCS. Viking Press.
December 14.	To Lucien Carr.	TPCS. Columbia University.
December 28.	To Elbert Lenrow.	TLS. Elbert Lenrow.
December 28.	To Allen Ginsberg.	TLS. Columbia University.

1958

January 7.	To Philip Whalen.	TLS. Reed College.
Before January 8.	To Lawrence Ferlinghetti.	TLS. University of California, Berkeley.
January 8.	To Allen Ginsberg.	TL. Columbia University.
January 13.	To Elbert Lenrow.	TLS. Elbert Lenrow.
January 13.	To Joyce Glassman.	TLS. Joyce Johnson.
January 15.	To Gary Snyder.	TLS. University of California, Davis.
January 16.	To Lucien Carr.	TPCS. Columbia University.

January 29.	To Sterling Lord.	TLS. Sterling Lord.
February 4.	To Joyce Glassman.	TLS. Joyce Johnson.
February 11.	To Robert Creeley.	TPCS. Stanford University.
February 11.	To Donald Allen.	TLS. University of California, San Diego.
February.	To William S. Burroughs.	TLS. Columbia University.
March 4.	To Philip Whalen.	TPCS. Reed College.
Undated [1958].	To Keith Jennison.	TLS. Viking Press.
April 13.	To John Clellon Holmes.	TLS. John Clellon Holmes.
Undated [1958].	To Philip Whalen.	TLS. Reed College.
Undated [1958].	To Philip Whalen.	TLS. Reed College.
Early June.	To Joyce Glassman.	TLS. Joyce Johnson.
Before June 12.	To Philip Whalen.	ALS. Reed College.
June 12.	To Philip Whalen.	TL. Reed College.
June 18.	To Helen Taylor.	TLS. Viking Press.
June 19.	To Gary Snyder.	TLS. University of California, Davis.
Early July.	To Philip Whalen.	TL. Reed College.
Early July.	To Tom Guinzburg.	TLS. Viking Press.
July 14.	To Gary Snyder.	TLS. University of California, Davis.
July 21.	To John Clellon Holmes.	TLS. John Clellon Holmes.
July (24?).	To Allen Ginsberg.	TL. Columbia University.
July 30.	To Donald Allen.	TLS. University of California, San Diego.
August 4.	To Philip Whalen.	TLS. Reed College.
August 28.	To Allen Ginsberg.	TLS. Columbia University.
September 8.	To Allen Ginsberg.	TLS. Columbia University.
September 16.	To Donald Allen.	TLS. University of California, San Diego.
September 23.	To Patricia MacManus.	TPCS. Viking Press.
October 5.	To Allen Ginsberg.	ALS. Columbia University.
October 12.	To Jack Kerouac from Gary Snyder.	TLS. University of California, Davis.
October 13.	To Gregory Corso.	TLS. Sterling Lord.
October 15.	To Allen Ginsberg.	TPCS. Columbia University.
October 28.	To Allen Ginsberg.	TLS. Columbia University.
After November 6.	To John Montgomery.	TL. John Montgomery.
Early November.	To Philip Whalen.	TLS. Reed College.
November 12.	To Philip Whalen.	TLS. Reed College.
November 12.	To Stan Isaacs.	TPCS. Berg Collection.
November 28.	To Stan Isaacs.	TPCS. Berg Collection.
December 1.	To Gary Snyder.	TLS. University of California, Davis.
December 12.	To Tom Guinzburg.	TLS. Viking Press.
December 16.	To Allen Ginsberg.	TLS. Columbia University.

1959

January 8.	To Sterling Lord.	TLS. Sterling Lord.
January 10.	To Philip Whalen.	TLS. Reed College.
January 29.	To Caroline Kerouac Blake.	TLS. Berg Collection.

February 3.	To Sterling Lord.	TLS. Sterling Lord.
February 5.	To Jeanne Unger.	TLS. Syracuse University.
February 13.	To Stella Sampas.	TLS. Kerouac Estate.
February 21.	To John Clellon Holmes.	TLS. John Clellon Holmes.
February 23.	To Gary Snyder.	TLS. University of California, Davis.
Before March.	To Caroline Kerouac Blake.	TLS. Berg Collection.
March 15.	To Philip Whalen.	TLS. Reed College.
March 24.	To Allen Ginsberg, Gregory Corso, & Peter Orlovsky.	TL. Columbia University.
April 5.	To Lawrence Ferlinghetti.	TLS. University of California, Berkeley.
April 17.	To Carolyn Cassady.	TLS. Carolyn Cassady.
April 18.	To Allen Ginsberg.	TLS. Columbia University.
April 19.	To Philip Whalen.	TPCS. Reed College.
April 23.	To Allen Ginsberg.	TLS. Columbia University.
April 23.	To Philip Whalen.	TLS. Columbia University.
May 8.	To Barney Rosset.	TLS. Syracuse University.
May 19.	To Allen Ginsberg.	TLS. Columbia University.
May 23.	To Stella Sampas.	TPCS. Kerouac Estate.
Late May.	To Caroline Kerouac Blake.	TLS. Berg Collection.
June 4.	To Lawrence Ferlinghetti.	TPCS. University of California, Berkeley.
June 10.	To Philip Whalen.	TLS. Reed College.
June 18.	To Allen Ginsberg.	TLS. Columbia University.
June 18.	To Caroline Kerouac Blake.	TLS. Berg Collection.
June 30.	To Donald Allen.	ALS. University of California, San Diego.
June 30.	To Donald Allen.	TPCS. University of California, San Diego.
July 28.	To Dick [Grove Press].	TLS. University of California, San Diego.
August 19.	To Allen Ginsberg & Peter Orlovsky.	TPCS. Columbia University.
September 22.	To Lawrence Ferlinghetti.	TPCS. University of California, Berkeley.
September.	To Stella Sampas.	TLS. Kerouac Estate.
October 1.	To Donald Allen.	TLS. University of California, San Diego.
Fall [1959].	To Donald Allen.	TLS. University of California, San Diego.
October 6.	To Allen Ginsberg.	TLS. Columbia University.
October 19.	To Allen Ginsberg.	TLS. Columbia University.
November 2.	To Allen Ginsberg.	TLS. Columbia University.
November 6.	To Allen Ginsberg.	TLS. Columbia University.
Undated [1959].	To Gary Snyder.	TPCS. University of California, Davis.
November 8.	To John Clellon Holmes.	TPCS. John Clellon Holmes.
December 6.	To Gary Snyder.	TLS. University of California, Davis.

December 6.	To Philip Whalen.	ALS. Reed College.
December 6.	To Barney Rosset.	TPCS. Syracuse University.
December 6.	To Caroline Kerouac Blake.	TLS. Berg Collection.
December 7.	To Lawrence Ferlinghetti.	TLS. University of California, Berkeley.
Early December.	To Gary Snyder.	TLS. University of California, Davis.
December 21.	To Henri Cru.	TLS. Private collection.
December 24.	To Roberto Muggiati.	TPCS. Roberto Muggiati.
December 24.	To Allen Ginsberg.	TLS. Columbia University.
December (30?).	To Donald Allen.	TLS. University of California, San Diego.

1960

January 4.	To Allen Ginsberg.	TLS. Columbia University.
January 14.	To Sterling Lord.	TLS. Sterling Lord.
January 18.	To Philip Whalen.	TLS. Reed College.
January 19.	To Lois Sorrells.	TLS. Lois Beckwith.
February 20.	To Allen Ginsberg.	TPCS. Columbia University.
ca. February.	To Lawrence Ferlinghetti.	TLS. University of California, Berkeley.
March 12.	To Caroline & Paul Blake.	TLS. Berg Collection.
April 12.	To Philip Whalen.	TLS. Reed College.
April 20.	To Carolyn Cassady.	TLS. Carolyn Cassady.
April 28.	To Lawrence Ferlinghetti.	TLS. University of California, Berkeley.
May 4.	To Lawrence Ferlinghetti.	TPCS. University of California, Berkeley.
May 20.	To Lawrence Ferlinghetti.	TLS. University of California, Berkeley.
June 3.	To Lawrence Ferlinghetti.	TPCS. University of California, Berkeley.
June 20.	To Allen Ginsberg.	TLS. Columbia University.
July 8.	To Lawrence Ferlinghetti.	TLS. University of California, Berkeley.
July 21.	To Lawrence Ferlinghetti.	APCS. University of California, Berkeley.
July 21.	To Allen Ginsberg.	APCS. Columbia University.
September 14.	To Lawrence Ferlinghetti.	TLS. University of California, Berkeley.
Mid-September.	To Philip Whalen & Lew Welch.	TL. Reed College.
September 22.	To Allen Ginsberg.	TLS. Columbia University.
September.	To Neal Cassady.	TLS. Carolyn Cassady.
September.	To Lawrence Ferlinghetti.	TLS. University of California, Berkeley.
September 24.	To Lawrence Ferlinghetti.	TPCS. University of California, Berkeley.
Before October 18.	To Lawrence Ferlinghetti.	TLS. University of California, Berkeley.

October 18.	To Lawrence Ferlinghetti.	TPCS. University of California, Berkeley.
November 22.	To Granville H. Jones.	TLS. Private collection.
November 26.	To Caroline Kerouac Blake.	TLS. Berg Collection.
December 16.	To Philip Whalen.	APCS. Reed College.

1961

February 2.	To Philip Whalen.	TLS. Reed College.
February.	To Jack Kerouac from Philip Whalen.	TLS. Reed College.
February 15.	To Bill Michell.	TPCS. Bill Michell.
April 14.	To Allen Ginsberg.	TPCS. Columbia University.
May 5.	To Sterling Lord.	TLS. Sterling Lord.
May 9.	To John Montgomery.	TLS. John Montgomery.
May 9.	To Carroll Brown.	TLS. Carroll Brown.
May 25.	To Lawrence Ferlinghetti.	TLS. University of California, Berkeley.
May 31.	To Lois Sorrells.	TLS. Lois Beckwith.
June 10.	To Donald Allen.	TLS. University of California, San Diego.
June 15.	To Bernice Lemire.	TLS. Private collection.
August 11.	To Bernice Lemire.	TLS. Private collection.
October 9.	To Sterling Lord.	TLS. Sterling Lord.
October 17.	To Philip Whalen.	TLS. Reed College.
October 17.	To Carolyn Cassady.	TLS. Carolyn Cassady.
October 19.	To Tom Guinzburg.	TLS. University of Oregon.
October 22.	To Jack Kerouac from Carolyn Cassady.	TLS. Carolyn Cassady.
October 23.	To Lawrence Ferlinghetti.	TLS. University of California, Berkeley.
November.	To Lawrence Ferlinghetti.	TLS. University of California, Berkeley.
Early December.	To Gary Snyder.	TPCS. University of California, Davis.
December 28.	To Allen Ginsberg & Peter Orlovsky.	TLS. Columbia University.
Late December.	To Jacqueline Stephens.	TLS. Sterling Lord.

1962

January 7.	To Carolyn Cassady.	TLS. Carolyn Cassady.
January 15.	To Robert Giroux.	TLS. Berg Collection.
January 17.	To Tom Guinzburg.	TLS. Sterling Lord.
February 9.	To Stella Sampas.	TLS. Kerouac Estate.
February 16.	To Robert Creeley.	TLS. Kerouac Estate.
March 28.	To Sterling Lord.	TLS. Sterling Lord.
March 31.	To Robert Giroux.	TLS. Berg Collection.
April 4.	To Donald Allen.	TLS. University of California, San Diego.
April 12.	To Robert Giroux.	TLS. Berg Collection.

April.	To Hugo Weber.	ALS. Berg Collection.
April 17.	To John Clellon Holmes.	TLS. John Clellon Holmes.
June 2.	To Sterling Lord.	TLS. Sterling Lord.
June 8.	To John Clellon Holmes.	TLS. John Clellon Holmes.
June 15.	To Lawrence Ferlinghetti.	TPCS. University of California, Berkeley.
August 8.	To Lois Sorrells.	TLS. Lois Beckwith.
August 17.	To Lois Sorrells.	TLS. Lois Beckwith.
September 3.	To Robert Giroux.	TLS. Berg Collection.
September 15.	To *Time* magazine from Lawrence Ferlinghetti.	TLS. University of California, Berkeley.
October 2.	To Tony Sampas & Stella Sampas.	ALS. Kerouac Estate.
October 9.	To John Clellon Holmes.	TLS. John Clellon Holmes.
November 13.	To Robert Giroux.	TLS. Berg Collection.
November 17.	To Stella Sampas.	TLS. Kerouac Estate.
December 13.	To Philip Whalen.	TLS. Reed College.
Late December.	To Philip Whalen from Gabrielle Kerouac.	ALS. Reed College.

1963

January 14.	To Philip Whalen.	TLS. Reed College.
February 19.	To Robert Giroux.	TLS. Berg Collection.
March 9.	To Sterling Lord.	TLS. Sterling Lord.
March 25.	To Caroline Kerouac Blake.	TLS. Berg Collection.
April 18.	To Robert Giroux.	TLS. Berg Collection.
May 7.	To Barney Rosset.	TLS. Syracuse University.
May 23.	To Gary Snyder.	TLS. University of California, Davis.
June 29.	To Allen Ginsberg.	TLS. Columbia University.
July 29.	To Robert Giroux.	TLS. Berg Collection.
August 16.	To Carolyn Cassady.	ALS. Carolyn Cassady.
October 5.	To John Clellon Holmes.	TLS. John Clellon Holmes.
November 18.	To Philip Whalen.	TLS. Reed College.
December 11.	To John Clellon Holmes.	TLS. John Clellon Holmes.

1964

Early 1964.	To Fernanda Pivano.	TLS. Sterling Lord.
April 22.	To Stella Sampas.	TLS. Kerouac Estate.
May 21.	To Tony Sampas.	ALS. Kerouac Estate.
September 9.	To Sterling Lord.	TLS. Sterling Lord.
September 19.	To Stanley & Anne Twardowicz from Gabrielle Kerouac.	ALS. Stanley Twardowicz.
October 16.	To John Clellon Holmes.	TLS. John Clellon Holmes.
November 11.	To Sterling Lord.	TLS. Sterling Lord.
December 8.	To John Clellon Holmes.	TLS. John Clellon Holmes.

1965

January 9.	To Ellis Amburn.	TLS. Sterling Lord.
January 10.	To Philip Whalen.	TLS. Reed College.
February 11.	To Ellis Amburn.	TLS. Sterling Lord.
March 2.	To John Clellon Holmes.	TPCS. John Clellon Holmes.
March 22.	To Stanley & Anne Twardowicz.	ALS. Stanley Twardowicz.
March 27.	To Sterling Lord.	TLS. Sterling Lord.
April 16.	To Sterling Lord.	TLS. Sterling Lord.
May 8.	To Sterling Lord.	TLS. Sterling Lord.
May 8.	To Sterling Lord from Gabrielle Kerouac.	TLS. Sterling Lord.
May 26.	To Sterling Lord.	TLS. Sterling Lord.
June 2.	To Lucien Carr.	APCS. Columbia University.
June 11.	To Sterling Lord.	TLS. Sterling Lord.
June 22.	To Arabelle Porter.	TLS. Sterling Lord.
July 21.	To John Clellon Holmes.	TLS. John Clellon Holmes.
August 2.	To Sterling Lord.	TLS. Sterling Lord.
August 10.	To Sterling Lord.	TLS. Sterling Lord.
September 18.	To John Clellon Holmes.	TLS. John Clellon Holmes.
October 12.	To Sterling Lord.	TLS. Sterling Lord.
Undated [1965].	To Diana G. List.	TLS. Sterling Lord.
November 29.	To Tony Sampas.	TLS. Kerouac Estate.
December 7.	To Stella Sampas.	TLS. Kerouac Estate.
December 23.	To Stella Sampas.	TLS. Kerouac Estate.
December 23.	To John Clellon Holmes.	TLS. John Clellon Holmes.

1966

February 14.	To Stella Sampas.	APCS. Kerouac Estate.
February 18.	To Shirley & John Clellon Holmes.	TLS. John Clellon Holmes.
April 25.	To Sterling Lord.	TLS. Sterling Lord.
May 18.	To Albert J. Gelpi.	TLS. Albert J. Gelpi.
June 18.	To Nora Aquilon.	TLS. Sterling Lord.
July 21.	To Gabrielle Kerouac & Jack Kerouac from Stella Sampas.	ALS. Kerouac Estate.
August 5.	To Ann Charters.	TLS. Berg Collection.
September 22.	To John Clellon Holmes.	TLS. John Clellon Holmes.
October 8.	To Sterling Lord.	TLS. Sterling Lord.
October 12.	To Stella Sampas.	TLS. Kerouac Estate.
November 16.	To Sterling Lord.	TLS. Sterling Lord.
November 28.	To Allen Ginsberg.	APCS. Columbia University.
December 18.	To Jim & Dorothy Sampas.	TLS. Kerouac Estate.
December 18.	To Dorothy, Jim, & George Lawrence Sampas from Stella Kerouac.	ALS. Kerouac Estate.

1967

January 18.	To Sterling Lord.	TLS. Sterling Lord.
January 29.	To Sterling Lord.	TLS. Sterling Lord.
January 30.	To Barney Rosset.	TLS. Sterling Lord.
March 30.	To Sterling Lord.	TLS. Sterling Lord.
March 30.	To John Clellon Holmes.	TLS. John Clellon Holmes.
May 22.	To John Clellon Holmes.	TLS. John Clellon Holmes.
June 1.	To Ellis Amburn.	TLS. Sterling Lord.
June 17.	To Sterling Lord.	ALS. Sterling Lord.
July 11.	To Calvin Hall.	TPCS. Private collection.
July 21.	To Sterling Lord.	TLS. Sterling Lord.
July.	To Arabelle Porter.	TLS. Sterling Lord.
November 11.	To Ann Charters.	TLS. Berg Collection.
December.	To Samuel Charters.	TPCS. Berg Collection.
December 13.	To Nick Sampas.	ALS. Kerouac Estate.
December 13.	To John Clellon Holmes.	TLS. John Clellon Holmes.
December 31.	To Sterling Lord.	TLS. Sterling Lord.

1968

January 6.	To Stanley Twardowicz.	TPCS. Stanley Twardowicz.
January 15.	To Sterling Lord.	APCS. Sterling Lord.
February 29.	To Sterling Lord.	TLS. Sterling Lord.
April 11.	To Ellis Amburn.	TLS. Sterling Lord.
April 20.	To Sterling Lord.	TL. Sterling Lord.
June 4.	To Allen Ginsberg.	TLS. Columbia University.
July 14.	To Andreas Brown.	TLS. University of Texas.
Late July.	To David Amram.	TPCS. David Amram.
August 24.	To Sterling Lord.	ALS. Sterling Lord.
August 27.	To Sterling Lord from Stella Kerouac.	TLS. Sterling Lord.
September 27.	To Sterling Lord.	TLS. Sterling Lord.
November 15.	To Joe Chaput.	TLS. Private collection.
December 3.	To Keith Jennison.	TLS. Sterling Lord.
December 5.	To Tony Sampas from Stella & Jack Kerouac.	TLS. Kerouac Estate.
December 5.	To Tony Sampas.	TLS. Kerouac Estate.

1969

January 16.	To Philip Whalen.	TLS. Reed College.
February 28.	To John Clellon Holmes.	TLS. John Clellon Holmes.
February 28.	To Tony Sampas.	TLS. Kerouac Estate.
March 3.	To Sterling Lord.	TLS. Sterling Lord.
March 18.	To Tony Sampas.	TLS. Kerouac Estate.
April 7.	To Sterling Lord.	TLS. Sterling Lord.
May 18.	To Nick Sampas.	TLS. Kerouac Estate.
July 7.	To Lawrence Ferlinghetti.	TPCS. University of California, Berkeley.
August 27.	To Sterling Lord.	TLS. Sterling Lord.
September 7.	To Andreas Brown.	TLS. University of Texas.

September 8.	To Edith Parker Kerouac.	TLS. Kerouac Estate.
September 21.	To Edith Parker Kerouac.	TLS. Kerouac Estate.
September 22.	To Andreas Brown.	TLS. University of Texas.
September 29.	To Dan De Sole.	TPCS. Private collection.
September 30.	To Ingrid & Nick Sampas.	TPCS. Kerouac Estate.
October 9.	To Nick Sampas.	TPCS. Kerouac Estate.
October 12.	To Sterling Lord.	TLS. Sterling Lord.
October 14.	To Sterling Lord.	TPCS. Sterling Lord.
October 14.	To Andreas Brown.	APCS. University of Texas.
October 20.	To Paul Blake, Jr.	TLS. Berg Collection.

INDEX

Cudworth, Jim, 296
Curtis, Mike, 446

Dastou, George, Jr., 297, 299
Davis, Miles, 86, 185
Dean, James, 109, 120*n*, 170*n*, 202
Decline of the West (Spengler), 57
de Kooning, Willem, 158
Dell, Gabriel, 236
Demarest, Donald, 58
Dempsey, David, 119, 206
Desolation Angels (Kerouac) 4, 8, 286
  Big Sur as sequel to, 301
  Cowley's rejection of, 10, 12*n*–13*n*,
    17*n*, 23, 47, 68, 326, 327
  critical responses to, 390, 397–98
  introduction to, 385–86, 390, 392–93
  models for fictional characters in, 63*n*,
    152, 153, 159*n*, 301, 391
  original manuscript of, 395
  publication of, 103, 144, 242, 327, 333,
    367, 371–72, 381, 384, 385, 386,
    389–90, 396*n*, 397, 411
  sales of, 393, 398, 406–7
  subject matter of, 2*n*, 5*n*, 9, 12, 19*n*, 34,
    37*n*, 44*n*, 46*n*, 49, 152, 159*n*, 173,
    252, 358, 391
  writing process of, xxiv, xxvii, xxviii, 1,
    2, 45*n*, 48, 54, 55, 239, 242, 355,
    395, 414
"Desolation Blues" (Kerouac), 290
De Sole, Dan, 476–77, 479
Deutsch, André, 22, 25, 27, 404, 407, 411,
  422, 427, 478, 479
Dharma Bums, The (Kerouac), 102, 238*n*,
  319*n*
  Buddhist themes in, 97, 111, 118,
    137–38, 185, 186, 442
  copyediting on, 125–26, 128, 130–31,
    132, 326
  critical responses to, 119, 154, 157,
    163, 171–72, 173, 183, 189, 226,
    234
  Desolation Angels as sequel to, 152, 286
  dust jacket of, 137–38, 429–30
  excerpts published from, 111, 135*n*
  film rights to, 399
  foreign editions of, 180, 234
  JK's assessments of, 104, 119, 186,
    189, 300, 303, 316

models for fictional characters in, xxiv,
    13*n*, 23, 24, 38–39, 86, 87, 106, 128,
    132, 137, 138, 149, 185, 186, 188,
    271, 272*n*, 301, 391
  original manuscript of, 395
  paperback editions of, 417, 440, 442
  prose style of, 132, 270
  publication of, 118, 128, 153, 169, 170,
    180, 294, 326, 405, 417, 434, 440,
    442
  sales of, 158, 279
  writing process of, xxvii, 38–39, 82, 85,
    86, 87, 95, 148, 295, 395
Dial Press, 264
Diamant, Ruth Witt, 294, 301
Dickens, Charles, 386, 438
Dickinson, Emily, 36, 71*n*, 99, 184, 296,
  340, 378, 386
Doctor Sax (Kerouac), xxvii, 9, 13, 47, 48,
  49*n*, 54, 285, 300, 346
  critical responses to, 68, 69*n*, 102,
    171*n*, 199–200, 201, 203, 228, 326
  excerpts published from, 111, 152
  film version of, 435
  foreign editions of, 353, 434, 448, 479
  JK's boyhood in, 152, 182–83
  JK's drawing for, 193
  libel concerns and, 144
  original manuscript of, 395
  prose style of, 97, 150, 152, 301
  pseudonyms in, 152, 182, 296, 297, 299
  publication of, 122, 139, 144, 152, 158,
    159, 161, 168, 174, 179, 181–82,
    189, 199, 208, 324
  sequel to, 205, 207
  title of, 181
  writing of, 51, 53, 58, 60, 62, 87, 181,
    355, 395
Doherty, Red, 463, 464, 460
Donlin, Bob, 35, 36, 66, 73, 110–11, 132,
  218
Dorn, Ed, 113, 114, 218, 329
Dostoevsky, Fyodor, 66, 67, 88–89, 120,
  217, 225, 283, 284, 287, 303, 364,
  373, 386, 407, 467
Douglas, Jack, 128–29
"Dream, A" (Kerouac), 440, 441
Dream Already Ended, A (Kerouac), 7*n*
Dufresne, Roland, 297
Dufy, Raoul, 178

financial concerns of, 439, 455, 456–57, 463, 466, 471

Gabrielle Kerouac tended by, 425, 439, 481

in household move, 463–64, 468

JK's dependence on, xxv, 434

JK's letters to, vii, 76–78, 182–83, 203–4, 215, 327–28, 347, 351–52, 379–80, 413–14, 427–29

JK's marriage to, xxviii, 422–23, 429, 430–32, 435, 437, 438, 441, 457, 479, 480

JK's writing and, 64–65, 435, 440, 456–57, 473, 476, 477

Kesey, Ken, 303, 305, 309–10, 326, 381, 472

Kierkegaard, Søren, 9, 10, 198

King, Alexander, 302

Kingsland, John, 151

Kirkus, Virginia, 445

Knowles, John, 80, 140, 339

Koch, Kenneth, 114

Konitz, Lee, 16, 100

Krim, Seymour, 264n, 386, 390, 392–93, 394, 398

Kubrick, Stanley, 120

Kulchur, 219, 304

Kyger, Joanne, *see* Snyder, Joanne Kyger

Lamantia, Philip, 35, 58, 59, 60, 94, 99, 114, 142–43, 257, 294, 329, 455

"Lamb, No Lion" (Kerouac), 81n

Landesman, Jay, 202–3, 437, 438

Lash, John, 448, 449

Laughlin, James, 17n, 81, 83, 84, 86, 93, 160, 189, 203, 209, 228, 452

Laughton, Charles, 287, 341

Lavigne, Robert, 42, 55, 178, 443

Lax, Robert, 115, 148, 175, 280, 281

Lea, George, 80

Leary, Timothy, 277n, 279–80, 317, 381

Le Bris, Pierre, 403

Lee, Alene, 14n, 58

Legman, Gershon, 437, 438

Lemire, Bernice, 295–300

Lenrow, Elbert, 100
  JK's letters to, 91–93, 101–3

Leonard, Herbert, 302

Lerner, Max, 148, 149, 151

Leslie, Alfred, 72n, 100, 175, 177, 179, 232

Leslie, Hubert, 40

Levant, Oscar, 405

Levertov, Denise, 58, 68n, 372

Levine, David, 398

Levine, Joseph R., 399, 435

Liberace, 426

Life, 51, 71n, 122n, 124, 229, 230n, 231n, 266

Li Po, 250, 304, 353, 364

Lippincott, Bruce, 32n

Lippman, Jill, 157

Lipton, Lawrence, 202, 377

List, Diana G., 411–12

Liston, Melba, 80

Loewinsohn, Ron, 35, 41, 197

Lonesome Traveler (Kerouac), xxviii, 195, 236n, 250, 251, 257, 271, 273, 275, 277, 279, 300, 332, 371, 404, 406, 408, 454, 455

Lord, Cindy, 302, 332, 382, 385, 396, 397, 400, 410, 419, 441, 448, 457

Lord, Rebecca, 448, 457

Lord, Sterling, 14, 25, 37–38, 42, 57, 68, 69, 125, 147, 171, 172, 246, 294, 295, 332, 381, 384, 404, 414, 422, 452, 461, 462

in film rights negotiations, 72n, 83, 84, 410

JK's finances and, 31, 53, 95, 99, 109–10, 158, 159, 176, 180, 219, 238, 330, 382, 392, 399–400, 417, 437, 439, 456–57, 466

JK's letters to, xxiv, 1, 2–3, 5n, 11–12, 13n, 17–19, 21–23, 26–27, 34, 38–39, 43, 46–47, 49–50, 84, 90, 108, 109–10, 169–70, 175–76, 180–81, 241, 242–43, 285–86, 300–303, 330–31, 338–39, 359, 378, 382, 385, 395–403, 407–8, 410–11, 419, 426–27, 429–30, 433–36, 440, 441, 446, 447–49, 450–51, 455–59, 469–70, 471, 472–73, 478–79

on JK's prose style, 404–5, 408

other clients of, 67, 151, 175–76, 208, 337

on publicity efforts, 91, 110, 199

Viking relations with, 325, 326, 327

Louis, Joe, 426

Lowell, Mass., 183, 295–99, 327, 349, 433n
Lowell, Robert, 344, 345
Lowell House Printers, 420n
Lowry, Robert, 158
Lucien Midnight (Kerouac), *see Old Angel Midnight*
Lustig, Joe, 66, 68, 70, 111
Lyndon, Roger, 340

MacArthur, Barney, 297
McCarthy, Mary, 116, 316
MacClaine, Chris, 197, 202
McClure, Michael, 16n, 32n, 54, 81, 98, 106, 133, 144, 150n, 210, 267, 268, 305, 306
　fictional portrayals of, 294, 301, 303, 308
　on JK's work, 95n–96n, 219n
　writing by, 114, 133, 197, 202, 251, 304, 366
McCorkle, Locke, 24, 36, 132, 139, 140, 145, 169
McCorkle, Sean, 36
McCorkle, Valerie, 306
McDarrah, Fred, 175, 184n, 225, 254, 255
McDarrah, Gloria S., 225, 255n
MacDonald, Dwight, 202n
MacDonald, Ian, 296
McDowall, Roddy, 259
McFadden, Dave, 242
McGovern, Don, 79
McGraw-Hill, 250, 251, 257, 271n, 332, 404, 406, 408
MacLachlan, Colin, 246
MacLeish, Archibald, 100, 102
McLuhan, Marshall, 438–39
MacManus, Patricia, 50–52, 53, 57, 63, 68, 76, 78, 153–54, 158
　JK's letters to, 69, 91
Mademoiselle, 5
Maggie Cassidy (Kerouac), xxvii, 300, 355, 384, 386
　critical responses to, 171n, 206
　models for characters in, 296, 297, 299, 349
　publication of, 170, 175, 181, 184, 205, 207, 326, 434
　subject matter of, 183, 184, 205

writing of, xxvii, 285, 396
Mailer, Norman, 67, 82n, 110n, 148, 160, 196, 202, 306, 365, 368, 371, 373, 394, 424, 438, 445
Malamud, Bernard, 345, 394, 424
Maloff, Saul, 398, 400, 406
Mann, Thomas, 342
Manocchio, Tony, 340
Mark, Gospel According to, 49
Marshall, Edward, 112, 114, 147, 184n
Meadows, Jayne, 129
Measure, 68, 81n
Mekas, Jonas, 202n
Melody, Little Jack, 66, 72
Melville, Herman, 183, 210, 357, 368
Memory Babe (Kerouac), 68, 69n, 82, 122, 124, 127, 131, 133, 135, 144, 145, 153, 158, 285
Merims, Bob, 74, 75
Mew, Charles, 70, 72, 74
"Mexican Girl, The" (Kerouac), 12n
Mexico City Blues (Kerouac), xxvii, 41, 81n, 98, 99, 144, 149, 189, 192n, 199, 200, 216, 228, 232–33, 241, 286, 300, 333, 395
　poetic form of, 293, 294, 295
MGM, 38, 126, 127, 133, 136, 145, 147, 168, 180, 189, 204, 259
Micheline, Jack, 256, 258
Michell, Bill, 283
Michener, James, 345, 414
Milarepa, 195, 196
Miles, Barry, 85n
Miles, Josephine, 16n, 32n
Miller, Bob, 306
Miller, Henry, 16n, 33, 58, 133n, 157, 158, 171, 172, 173, 177, 198n, 200n, 290, 303, 362, 377, 454
Mills, Charley, 256
Millstein, Gilbert, 64, 80
Milton, John, 238, 369
Minor Characters (Johnson), 5, 56n, 60, 63n, 158
Mitchell, Cliff, 412, 415, 418
Mitchell, John, 284
Mitchell, Patty, 415, 418
Mohrt, Michel, 402
Monk, Thelonious, 80, 373
Montagu, Ashley, 162
Montgomery, John, 24, 26, 36, 44, 96,

Putterman, Zev, 99, 105, 151
Pynchon, Thomas, xxv

Rabelais, François, 88, 353
Rahner, Karl, 420
Randall, Bill, 109, 110
Random House, 82, 84n, 114
Redd, Freddie, 373, 374
Redl, Harry, 16n
Reich, Wilhelm, 116
Rembrandt van Rijn, 28–29, 46, 386
Rexroth, Kenneth, 16, 24, 41, 44
    fictional portrayal of, 132, 272n
    JK's dissociation from, 111, 121, 127
    literary criticism by, 32, 43, 55, 64,
        93–94, 96, 97, 100–101, 119, 120,
        121, 232, 233, 254
    poetry of, 32, 133, 233
Reynolds, Kelly, 79–80, 100
"Rimbaud" (Kerouac), 231n, 253, 254,
    300
Rimbaud, Arthur, 92, 119, 217, 299
Rivers, Larry, 72n, 114, 158, 168, 177,
    179, 271n
"Roaming Beatniks, The (New York
    Scenes)" (Kerouac, Ginsberg,
    Orlovsky and Corso), 195
Roberge, Skippy, 299
Rollins, Sonny, 120–21
Rondeau, Bobby, 297, 299
"Ronnie on the Mound" (Kerouac), 78,
    123n
Rosenberg, Anton, 114
Rosenthal, Irving, 149, 157, 159, 172, 173,
    201
Ross, Nancy Wilson, 97, 106, 157
Rosset, Barney, 3, 4n, 11, 114, 122, 152,
    200n, 240, 294, 335, 338, 373, 433
    JK's letters to, 199–200, 228–29,
        361–62, 435
Roth, Philip, 345, 372, 394, 424, 467
Rothman, Adolf, 366
Route 66, 301–2, 326, 461
Rowohlt Verlag Publishers, 71, 81, 434
Rumaker, Michael, 16n, 334
Russell, Vicki, 299
Rynne, Xavier, 369

Sahl, Mort, 136, 147
Saijo, Albert, 225, 226, 227, 228, 232,
    233, 234, 238, 239, 243, 244, 255,
    287, 306
Salinger, J. D., 345, 394, 409, 424
Salvas, Roland, 296, 298
Sampas, Anthony, 65, 352, 379, 413, 414,
    429, 466, 476, 479
    JK's letters to, 347, 380–81, 412,
        462–64, 468–69, 470
Sampas, Charles, 76, 182, 327, 379n, 380,
    412, 414, 470
Sampas, Claire, 379n
Sampas, Dorothy, 430, 431–32
Sampas, George Lawrence, 431–32
Sampas, Helen, 379n
Sampas, Ingrid, 477
Sampas, James, 65, 379n, 380, 430,
    431–32
Sampas, John (Yanni), 355n, 379, 461,
    481
Sampas, Marina, 470
Sampas, Michael, 65, 379n, 413, 414
Sampas, Nicholas, 65, 379n, 380, 444,
    466, 471–72, 477–78
Sampas, Sebastian (Sammy), 65, 182,
    203, 296, 327, 349, 352, 379n, 380,
    413, 414, 422, 475
Sampas, Stella, *see* Kerouac, Stella Sampas
Sampognaro, Helene, 403
Sandburg, Carl, 52
Sanders, Ed, 364
"San Francisco Blues" (Kerouac), xxvii,
    41, 81n, 216, 293–94, 295, 334
Saroyan, Aram, 440, 444, 452
Sarris, Stella, 464
Sasaki, Ruth, 163, 167, 186
Satori in Paris (Kerouac), 435
    foreign editions of, 422, 433, 434, 436
    publication of, 411, 414, 415, 417, 422,
        434
    subject matter of, 401n, 405, 407, 408,
        458
    writing of, xxiv, xxviii, 404, 405, 407,
        408, 477
Saturday Review, 61, 170n
Savage, William J., Jr., xxiv
Schaap, Dick, 446
Schmitt, Harley, 48n
Scripture of the Golden Eternity, The
    (Kerouac), 7n, 212, 213n, 257, 300,
    353

511